ツングース語研究

Researches
on
the Tungus Language

by

Jirô IKEGAMI

Tokyo

Kyûko Shoin

2001

ツングース語研究

池上　二良

東　京
汲　古　書　院

平成13年

はしがき

ツングース（トゥングース）語（Tungus）は，ツングース人の固有の言語であるが，いくつかの方言に分かれている。しかし，これらの方言は互にかなり異なるので，今日それぞれが一つの言語であるとみなされている。したがってこれらを合せてツングース諸語ともいう。ツングース諸語は，互に親縁関係をもつ，すなわち，同一祖語にさかのぼるとみられる。

そのツングース諸語のおのおのはつぎの通りである。

1）エウェンキ(ー)語（Evenki）

2）エウェン語（Even）〔＝ラムート語（Lamut)〕

3）ソロン語（Solon）

4）ネギダル語（Negidal）

5）ウデヘ語（Udehe）

6）オロチ語（Orochi）

7）ナーナイ語（Nanai）〔＝ゴルディ語（Goldi)〕

8）オルチャ語（Olcha）〔＝ウルチャ語（Ulcha)〕

9）ウイルタ語（Uilta）〔＝オロッコ語（Orok)〕

10）満洲語（Manchu）

ただし，このうち満洲語は他の上記の言語と著しく異なる点があるので，満洲語を除いて他の上記言語だけをツングース(諸)語ともよび，また両方合せて全部をツングース・満洲(諸)語とよぶ。本書の書名での「ツングース語」はこの意味で使ったものである。

しかし，またツングース語の名称は，さらに狭義に使うこともあり，もっとも狭くはエウェンキー語だけをツングース語とよぶ。

ツングース諸語の分布地域は，エウェンキー語がロシアのシベリアのエニセイ川以東，オホーツク海西岸・サハリンまでと中国東北部北辺，エウェン語はレナ川以東，カムチャツカ，さらに東のアナディルまで，ソロン語は中国東北部北辺，ネギダル語はアムール川下流地方，オロチ語・ウデヘ語は沿海地方，ナーナイ語・オルチャ語はアムール川下流地方，ウイルタ語はサハリン，満洲語は中国東北部と新疆ウイグル自治区の一部でおこなわれる。精しい分布は拙文「ツングース諸語」（亀井孝・河野六郎・千野栄一『言語学大辞典』第2巻［三省堂 1989年］所載）を参照されたい。

ツングース語は，人口の非常に少ないツングース諸民族の言語であるが，その話し手の数はさらに少ない。ツングース諸語のうち，話し手の数が多い方の例にエウェンキー語，少ない方の例にウデヘ語を挙げると，1989年のソ連人口調査では，総人口が，エウェンキー族は3万，ウデヘ族は2千である。さらに，その民族の言語を自分の母語と考える人の数は，その民族の総人口のうち，前者で30.4%，後者では26.3%にすぎない。なお，1994年のロシアの国の人口の5%についての人口小調査では，それぞれの民族の総数のうち，自分の民族の言語を母語と考える人はエウェンキー族でも，ウデヘ族でもさらに少ない。これらの人口統計は必ずしも正確とはみられないが，ツングース語の話し手は，ロシア語や中国語，その他近隣有力言語を使うようになり，ツングース語の話し手数が減少の道をたどって来ていることは確かである。過去の減少過程は，拙文「東北アジアの土着言語」（三上次男・神田信夫編『東北アジアの民族と歴史』［山川出版社 1989年］所収）を参照されたい。

本書は，著者がツングース・満洲語の研究において特にツングース語について記した拙文をまとめたものであるが，本書に載せるに当っては，一部を補訂し，あるいは末尾に補記，追記，Addenda を加え，またいくつかの論文はその文章を書き直した。さらに，ある論文は記述方法を変更し，本書の他論文との整合をはかった。

以下に，拙文の各編を，目次においてつける番号で示しつつ，多少の説明を加えたい。

1から20までは，著者がなが年調査研究をおこなってきたツングース語の一つ，ウイルタ語（おもに南部の方言）に関するものである。このウイルタ語は，筆者のツングース語についての共時論上および通時論上の考察の基盤となった。この言語の旧称はオロッコ語であるが，今日はその話し手の自称によってウイルタ語とよぶ。

そのうち1から7は文法の特に形態論に関するものである。8は音韻に関するもの。ウイルタ語の音韻と発音については下に記す『ウイルタ語辞典』xii－xxi ページを見られたい。9から12は，従来文字がなかったウイルタ語の文字制定のためにロシア・サハリン州行政府の北方民族担当官から依頼されてつくった文字案に関するもの。13から16は，ウイルタ語について文化人類学にまたがるような問題を扱ったもの。13は，また意味論の問題を考える上で好材料を提供している。17から20は，ウイルタ語の言語地理学のようないわゆる外的言語学の問題などに関するものである。

21から24は，ウイルタ語以外のツングース諸語に関するもの。21はわが国江戸時代に記録されたサンタン語彙の多くの語はオルチャ語であることを例証したもの。

25から29は，ツングース語全体に関するもので，比較研究の成果やツングース諸語の分類など。29はこうした研究によって今日あきらかになったことの要略。

30，31，32は書評。これら書評は，ツングース語の比較研究などにふれる。

なお，筆者の集めたツングース語の語彙・原文など資料的なものは，別にツングース・満洲諸語の資料集として一本にまとめたいと思う。ウイルタ語語彙は筆者編『ウイルタ語辞典』（北海道大学図書刊行会 1997年）として，満洲語研究に関する拙文はまとめて『満洲語研究』（汲古書院　1999年）として刊行した。

本書上梓に当っても，河野六郎先生の御生前のお心配りを想起し，改めて感謝の念を捧げる。

出版に関して，汲古書院坂本健彦氏に感謝するとともに、校正に携わった同書店の雨宮明子氏やそのほかの方々にも謝意を表す。また，英文の添削について Mr. Steven J. Searle にお礼を述べたい。なお，原稿整理には妻みちも当ったことを書き留めたい。

本書の刊行には，平成12年度日本学術振興会科学研究費補助金「研究成果公開促進費」の交付を受けた。

平成十二年十一月

池上　二良

目　次

Contents

ツングース語研究

The Substantive Inflection of Orok

1. In Orok (Orokko), a dialect of Tungus,[1)] substantives are inflected through the addition of various endings (substantive endings and the other endings given below) to substantive stems. This occurs with or without the alternation of the final phoneme of the stems. Also, a kind of stem-alternation can occur in place of the addition of these endings. The substantive stem, moreover, can appear as a word without the addition of any ending. Most of these endings also have alternants.

2. Most substantives can be grouped into Classes 1. and 2. given below, according to the different ways in which they are inflected. For the inflection of the substantives in these two classes, we take the simple nominative form (see below) as the basic form or the basic stem. The last phoneme or phonemes of the basic stems of these substantives are peculiar to the class to which they belong. Accordingly, the inflections of these substantives are automatically determined by the last phoneme or phonemes of their basic stems.

However, a number of substantives are inflected in different ways from the above-mentioned substantives in spite of the coincidence of the last phoneme or phonemes in the simple nominative forms. Many of these substantives can be also grouped into Classes 0.1, 0.2 and 0.3 according to their inflections. In addition to these, there are such substantives, as *amma* 'father', *ənnə* 'mother', *əgə* 'elder sister', which alternate with the stems *amin-*, *ənin-*, *əigə-*, respectively, and *ulaa* 'domesticated reindeer', which is not accompanied by *-wa*, *-wi* or *-wari*, but by *-ba*, *-bi* or *-bari* (the simple accusative and reflexive accusative-nominative case-endings), cf. Class 1.21 given below.

3. The *substantive endings* are as follows.

-ba 'an object which is subjected to action'

-la 'a place with some extension in space or a period of time in which an action occurs or a state exists'

-ndoo 'a co-agent'

-ddoo '"as (something) designated for someone"'

-du 'a position where action occurs or a state exists'

-zi 'something complementary with which action occurs or a state exists' and 'unequalness in comparison to another'

-duu 'a starting-point from which action or a state begins'

-tai 'something at which action is aimed'

-kki 'a position through or along which action occurs or a state exists'

We call these endings *simple case-endings* and give traditional case-names to them, respectively: *accusative, locative, comitative, designative, dative, instrumental, ablative, allative,* and *prolative.* The *simple nominative form* refers to a stem that appears as a word without being accompanied by any ending and without having any of the meanings of the above-mentioned case-endings. The substantives of Class 2.22 have a variant of the simple nominative form that ends in n and appears before *ǰii-* 'being about the size of '. We take this as the basic stem for the inflection of each substantive of this class.

4. There is yet another group of substantive endings. We call them *singular* and *plural reflexive case-endings.* The sing. reflexive case-endings are *-bi* (acc. -nom.), *-lli* (1oc.), *-ǰǰi* (dat. -instr. -design.), *-dukki* (abl.), *-takki* (all.), and *-kki* (prol.). The pl. reflexive case-endings are *-bari* (acc. -nom.), *-lari* (loc.), *-ddoori* (dat. -design.), *-ǰǰeeri* (instr.), *-dukkoori* (abl.), *-takkeeri* (all.) and *-kkeeri* (prol.).[2] We apply to these the case-names given in parentheses. The reflexive case-endings have the same meanings as the above simple case-endings and simple nominative form, with the additional

meaning 'one's own', that is, 'my, our, your, his, her or their own.'

5. Each of the simple and reflexive case-endings is added to a basic stem, with or without the alternation of the final phoneme of the basic stem. Most of these endings also alternate between basic and other forms according to the basic stems of different classes. The above-mentioned forms are the basic forms of these endings. The other alternants of these endings are shown in Tables I, II, and III. Two alternants of the simple prolative case-ending *-kkee* and *-kee* appear when they are followed by any of the personal endings (given below). The simple designative case-ending is always followed by one of the personal endings. However, in the case of the substantives of Classes 1.1 and 0.1, a kind of stem-alternation takes the place of the addition of the simple accusative case-ending or the reflexive accusative-nominative case-ending to a stem. We call the alternate stems the *simple accusative stem* and the *reflexive accusative-nominative stem.*[2] The details of substantive inflection are shown in Tables I, II, and III.[3]

Example of simple case-endings and the simple accusative stem, etc.:

Accusative: *čaa səəmbə təttu* 'Put on that overcoat', *suŋdattaa waarini* 'He catches fish'.

Locative: *utələ baaxani* 'He found [it] on the doorway', *nəələ waaxani* 'He caught [it] in the river'.

Comitative: *čaa puttəndəə ŋənnəu* 'Go with that child'.

Designative: *tari əəktə puttə mərkəddəəni gaččini* 'That woman bought [it] (so that it may serve) as a comb for the child'.

Dative: *təəndu ačikta biini* 'There are metal-ornaments on the skirt', *utədu osu* 'Be on the doorway'.

Instrumental: *xupikkuǰi xuppini* 'He plays with a toy', *tuksaǰi daaǰi* 'It is bigger than a hare'.

Ablative: *čiktə mərkəduu tukkini* 'A louse falls from the comb' , *səulduu sabǰeeni* 'It drips from the rudder'.

Allative: *məəktəi uurini* 'He embarks toward the prow', *seettaini simmөөččini* 'He whispers in her ear'.

Prolative: *utəkki iixəni* 'He entered through the doorway', *bəgǰikkeeni moiččalaxani* 'He shot through its leg with a gun'.

The simple nominative form: *tuksa pukcixəni* 'The hare ran', *boo xosiktani* 'The stars of the sky'.

The reflexive accusative-nominative case-ending: *dərəlbi silcini* 'He washes his own face', *puttəbi seembani siiweesini* 'He cleans the ear of his [own] child'.

6. Further, the endings which we call *personal endings,* can be added after simple case-endings or simple accusative stems, or immediately to the basic stems of substantives, with or without the alternation of the final phoneme of the basic stems, when none of the above-mentioned case-endings or accusative stems appears. The personal endings are the first-person sing. *-bi,* the first-person pl. *-pu,* the second-person sing. *-si,* the second-person pl. *-su,* the third-person *-ni,* and the third-person pl. *-či.* Many of these endings also alternate between basic and other forms. The details are given in Table IV. (3)

These endings usually mean 'belonging to the first, second, or third person': *-bi* 'my', *-pu* 'our', *-si* 'your (sing.)', *-su* 'your (pl.)', *-ni* 'belonging to the third-person', *-či* 'their'. When included in the predicate, they often mean 'the person (I, II or III) of the subject.' For instance, *bii əəktəbi* 'I am a woman', *sii əəktəsi* 'You are a woman'.

7. Furthermore, the *interrogative endings -i, -ka,* etc., the *vocative ending -kaa,* and others can be added after the above-mentioned endings, or directly to stems, when none of the above-mentioned endings appears. Also, stem-alternations can take the place of the addition of these endings. E. g., *əri xaǰai* 'Is this a pair of scissors ?', *ŋui aapuniga* 'Whose cap is it ?', *purilkəə* 'Children!'. A detailed description of these endings and stem-alter-

nations is omitted here.

8. For the inflection of the substantives of Class 0.1 we set up two basic stems, —V and *–VkV (=*–C*a*k*a*, *(–)Cuk*a*, etc.) (a non-existent theoretical basic stem). The latter basic stem alternates with the simple accusative stem –VkkVV (= –C*a*kk*aa*, (–)Cukk*aa*, etc.), the sing. reflexive accusative-nominative stem –Vkki, and the pl. reflexive accusative-nominative stem –VkkVVri (= –Vkk*aa*ri, etc.). These alternations occur instead of the addition of the simple accusative case-ending and the sing. and pl. reflexive accusative-nominative case-endings.[4)] The details are given below in Table V. As is the case with the basic stem —V of Class 1., the former basic stem —V (= –C*aa*, –Cuw*a*, etc.) appears as the simple nominative form, and is accompanied by the same endings as those which are added to the basic stem —V of Class l. The sing. reflexive accusative-nominative ending *-bi* can be added to the alternate stem —V in another kind of sing. reflexive accusative-nominative inflection.

9. Class 0.21 contains the substantives that are different from the substantives of Class 1. only in that the basic stem —V is accompanied by another set of alternant forms of the simple accusative case-ending and the reflexive accusative-nominative case-ending, viz., the simple accusative *-pa*, the sing. reflexive accusative-nominative *-pi* and the pl. reflexive accusative-nominative *-pari*. The inflection of these substantives is not automatically determined by the above-mentioned basic stem —V because this is also the basic stem of Class 1. For these substantives, however, it is possible to set up a non-existent theoretical basic stem which ends in *p* (*t* or *s*). As for the meaning of these substantives, a large number of them have meanings referring to 'some relative position in space or time'. For instance, *dullee* 'the front, previousness', *sollee* 'the upper part of a river', but *xusənnee* 'man (male)'.

10. Class 0.31 contains a small number of substantives. For each of

them we can set up the theoretical basic stem —k. Except for the simple nominative forms, the inflection of these substantives is automatically determined by their basic stem. However, the simple nominative forms of these substantives appear as —x*a* or other forms, such as given below.

Simple Nominative Form		Basic Stem
paaxa	'liver'	*paak-*
məəxə	'prow'	*məək-*
burixə	'bow (for hunting)'	*burik-*
duxu	'house'	*duk-*
pərə	'bottom'	*pərək-*
axa	'elder brother'	*aak-*

However, these substantives also are sometimes inflected in the same way as those of Class 1.

Addition to Section 5. Substantive inflection in a narrow sense refers to the inflection mentioned in this paragraph.

Addition to Section 8. The stem –Vkki of Class 0.1 also appears as *the first-person sing. nominative stem.* E.g. *mini oksokki čadu biini* 'My sledge is there'. However, the first-person sing. *-bi* can also be added to the alternate stem —V of Class 0.1.

Table II. Sing. Reflexive Case-Endings and Accusative-Nominative Stem

Class \ Basic form of case-ending	Accusative - Nominative -bi		Locative -lli		Dative- Instrumental- Designative -ǰǰi		Ablative -dukki		Allative -takki		Prolative -kki	
1.1	—CV-											
1.2	(—)VV-wi											
0.1	—Vkki and —V-		—V-lli		—V-ǰǰi		—V-		—*V*- or —*o*=		—V-kki	
	(On 0.1 see Table V.)	-bi										
0.21	—*V*- pi							-dukki		-t*a*kki or =t*o*kki		
2.11	—l-		—l-		—l-		—l-		—*V*l-		—l-	
2.2	—m-		—n-	-dulli	—n-	-ǰi	—n-		—*V*t- or —*o*t=		—k-	-ki
0.31	—g-		—g-		—g-		—g-		—*V*k-			

Table I. Simple Nominative Forms, Basic Forms,

Basic form of case-ending / Class	Simple Nominative Form (I)	(Simple Nominative Form II)	Basic Stem	Accusative -ba	Locative -la
1.111	(–)VC*a*		Each simple nom. form is taken as basic stem.	(–)VCC*aa*	
1.112	(–)VC*o*			(–)VCC*oo*	
1.113	(–)VCu				
1.114	(–)VCi		= –CV	(–)VCCee	
1.121	–CC*a*			–CC*aa*	
1.122	–CC*o*		=—V (—*V* or —*o*)	–CC*oo*	—*V*-l*a* or —*o*-l*o*
1.123	–CCu				
1.124	–CCi			–CCee	
1.21	–V*V*		=(–)VV	–V*V*-w*a*	
1.22	(–)V*o*			(–)V*o*-w*o*	
0.1	—V= —*V* or —*o*		*–VkV and —V(*V* or *o*) (On 0.1 see Table V.)	–VkkVV	
0.21	—*V*		—*V* or * —*V*p	—*V*-p*a*	
2.11	–*V*l		Each simple nom. form (for 2.22 s.n.f.II) is taken as basic stem. = —l	–*V*l- –*o*l=	—l-
2.12	–*o*l			-b*a* or =b*o*	-dul*a*
2.211	(C)V*V*n				
2.212	CV*o*n		= —n (–*V*n or –*o*n)	=–Vm- or –*o*m=	—n-
2.221	–C(V) *V*	–C(V) *V*n			
2.222	–C(V) *o*	–C(V) *o*n			
0.31	—x*a* or other forms		–*V*k = —k	–*V*g-	—g-

Simple Case-Endings and Simple Accusative Stems

Comitative -ndoo	Designative -ddoo	Dative -du	Instrumental -ǰi	Ablative -duu	Allative -tai	Prolative -kki
—V -nd*oo*	—V -dd*oo*	—V - -du	—V - -ǰi	—V - -duu	—*V*- or —*o*= -t*a*i or =t*o*i	—V-kki (or —V-kkee)
—l- -d*oo*	—l- -d*oo*	—l- -du	—l- -ǰi	—l- -duu	—*V*l- —*o*l= -t*a*i or =t*o*i	—l- -ki (or -kee)
—n- -d*oo*	—n- -d*oo*	—n- -du	—n- -ǰi	—n- -duu	—*V*t- or —ot= -t*a*i or =t*o*i	—k- -ki (or -kee)
—g- -d*oo*	—g- -d*oo*	—g- -du	—g- -ǰi	—g- -duu	—*V*k- -t*a*i or =t*o*i	

Table III. Pl. Reflexive Case-Endings

Class \ Basic form of case-ending	Accusative-Nominative -bari	Locative -lari	Dative-Designative -ddoori
1.111	(–)VCC*aa*ri		
1.112			
1.113	(–)VCC*oo*ri		
1.114	(–)VCCeeri		
1.121	–CC*aa*ri		
1.122			
1.123	–CC*oo*ri	—*V*-l*a*ri or —*o*-l*o*ri	—V-dd*oo*ri
1.124	–CCeeri		
1.21	–V*V*-w*a*ri		
1.22	(–)V*o*-w*o*ri		
0.1	–VkkVVri		
(On 0.1 see Table V.)			
0.21	—*V*-p*a*ri		
2.11	–*V*l-	—l-	—l-
2.2	–*V*m- or –*o*m= ; -b*a*ri or =b*o*ri	—n- ; -dul*a*ri	—n- ; -d*oo*ri
0.31	–*V*g-	—g-	—g-

and Accusative-Nominative Stems

Instrumental -ǰǰeeri		Ablative -dukkoori		Allative -takkeeri		Prolative -kkeeri	
—V-ǰǰeeri		—V-	-dukk*oo*ri	—*V*- or —*o*=	-t*a*kkeeri or =t*o*kkeeri	—V-kkeeri	
—l-	-ǰeeri	—l-		—*V*l-		—l-	-keeri
—n-		—n-		—*V*t- or —*o*t=		—k-	
—g-		—g-		—*V*k-			

Table IV. Personal Endings

	Basic form of personal ending / Class	The 1. Person Sing. -bi		The 1. Person Pl. -pu		The 2. Person Sing. -si		The 2. Person Pl. -su		The 3. Person -ni		The 3. Person Pl. -či	
Added to basic stems.	1.1	–CV-											
	1.2	(–)VV-wi											
	0.1	—V-	-bi	—V-		—V-si		—V-su		—V-		—V-	
	0.21	—*V*- pi			-pu						-ni		-či
	2.11	—l-		—l-		—l-		—l-		—l-li and —l-		—l-	
	2.2	—m-		—p-		—č-	-či	—č-	-ču	— -		—č-	
	0.31	—g-		—k-		—k-		—k-		—ŋ-		—k-	
Added to simple case-endings and accusative stems.		-wwee		-pp*oo*		-si		-su		-ni		-či	

Table V. Simple Nominative Forms, Basic Forms and Simple Accusative Stems etc. of Class 0·1

Stem / Class	Simple Nominative Form		Basic Stem		Simple Accusative Stem		Sing. Reflexive Accusative-Nominative Stem and Ending	Pl. Reflexive Accusative-Nominative Stem	
0.111	–C*aa*		*–C*ak*a*						
0.112	(–)Cuw*a*		*(–)Cuk*a*		–Vkk*aa*			–Vkk*aa*ri	
0.113	–Cig*a*		*–Cik*a*						
0.114	–VVg*a*		*–VVk*a*						
0.121	–CV*o*	=—V	*–CVk*o*	=*–VkV		=–VkkVV	–Vkki and —V-bi		=–VkkVVri
0.131	–CVu		*–CVku		–Vkk*oo*			–Vkk*oo*ri	
0.132	–VVwu		*–VVku						
0.141	–CVi		*–CVki		–Vkkee			–Vkkeeri	
0.142	–VVji		*–VVki						

Example for Table I. [5]

	Simple Nominative Form (I)	(Simple Nominative Form II)	Basic Stem	Accusative	Locative
1.111	utə 'doorway', patala 'girl'		utə	uttəə	utələ
1.112	keede 'bellows'		keede	keeddee	keedele
1.113	sinu 'tongue'		sinu	sinnee	sinulə
1.114	keččeeli 'bucket', dooktori 'doctor (physician)'		keččeeli	keččeellee	keččeelilə
1.121	mərkə 'fine-toothed comb', puttə 'child'		mərkə	mərkəə	mərkələ
1.122	xekte 'a kind of coat', jokko 'Yakut'		xekte	xektee	xektele
1.123	xupikku 'toy', maŋbu 'Olcha'		xupikku	xupikkee	xupikkulə
1.124	bəǧǰi 'foot, leg', takkuramǰi 'servant'		bəǧǰi	bəǧǰee	bəǧǰilə
1.21	bee 'place in a dwelling, where men sit or lie down', saldaa 'soldier'		bee	beewa	beela
1.22	ee 'eruption (rash)'		ee	eewe	eele
0.1	əmuwə 'cradle for day-use', giləə 'Gilyak'		əmuwə,*əmukə	əmukkəə	əmuwələ
0.21	dəunǰee 'left', xusənnee 'man (male)'		dəunǰee or *dəunǰeep	dəunǰeepə	dəunǰeelə
2.11	səul 'rudder', puril 'children'		səul	səulbə	səuldulə
2.12	bejel 'undomesticated mammals'		bejel	bejelbe	bejeldulə
2.211	təən 'skirt (edge)'		təən	təəmbə	təəndulə
2.212	seen 'fur overcoat'		seen	seembe	seendulə
2.221	tuŋə 'chest', kiilləə 'Kilin (Tungus)'	tuŋən	tuŋən	tuŋəmbə	tuŋəndulə
2.222	pere 'thumb'	peren	peren	perembe	perendulə
0.31	burixə 'bow', axa 'elder brother'		burik	burigbə	burigdulə

Continued from the preceding page.

Dative	Instrumental	Ablative	Allative	Prolative	Designative	Comitative
utədu	utəǰi	utəduu	utətəi	utəkkee	utəddɵɵ	patalandoo
kɵɵdɵdu	kɵɵdɵǰi	kɵɵdɵduu	kɵɵdɵtɵi	kɵɵdɵkkee	kɵɵdɵddɵɵ	
sinudu	sinuǰi	sinuduu	sinutəi	sinukkee	sinuddɵɵ	
kəččɵɵlidu	kəččɵɵliǰi	kəččɵɵliduu	kəččɵɵlitəi	kəččɵɵlikkee	kəččɵɵliddɵɵ	dooktorindoo
mərkədu	mərkəǰi	mərkəduu	mərkətəi	mərkəkkee	mərkəddɵɵ	puttəndɵɵ
xɵktɵdu	xɵktɵǰi	xɵktɵduu	xɵktɵtɵi	xɵktɵkkee	xɵktɵddɵɵ	jokkondoo
xupikkudu	xupikkuǰi	xupikkuduu	xupikkutəi	xupikkukkee	xupikkuddɵɵ	maŋbundoo
bəgǰidu	bəgǰiǰi	bəgǰiduu	bəgǰitəi	bəgǰikkee	bəgǰiddɵɵ	takkuramǰindoo
beedu	beeǰi	beeduu	beetai	beekkee	beeddoo	saldaandoo
ɵɵdu	ɵɵǰi	ɵɵduu	ɵɵtɵi	ɵɵkkee		
əmuwədu	əmuwəǰi	əmuwəduu	əmuwətəi	əmuwəkkee	əmuwəddɵɵ	giləəndɵɵ
dəunǰeedu	dəunǰeeǰi	dəunǰeeduu	dəunǰeetəi	dəunǰeekkee	dəunǰeeddɵɵ	xusənneendɵɵ
səuldu	səulǰi	səulduu	səultəi	səulkee	səuldɵɵ	purildɵɵ
bɵjɵldu	bɵjɵlǰi		bɵjɵltɵi	bɵjɵlkee		
təəndu	təənǰi	təənduu	təəttəi	təəkkee	təəndɵɵ	
sɵɵndu	sɵɵnǰi	sɵɵnduu	sɵɵttɵi	sɵɵkkee	sɵɵndɵɵ	
tuŋəndu	tuŋənǰi	tuŋənduu	tuŋəttəi	tuŋəkkee	tuŋəndɵɵ	kiilləəndɵɵ
pɵrɵndu	pɵrɵnǰi	pɵrɵnduu	pɵrɵttɵi	pɵrɵkkee	pɵrɵndɵɵ	
burigdu	burigǰi	burigduu	buriktəi	burikkee	burigdɵɵ	aagdoo

Examples for Table II.

	Accusative-Nominative	Locative	Dative-Designative-Instrumental	Ablative	Allative	Prolative
1.1	utəbi	utəlli	utəǰǰi	utədukki	utətəkki	utəkki
1.2	beewi	beelli	beeǰǰi	beedukki	beetakki	beekki
0.1	əmuwəbi	əmuwəlli	əmuwəǰǰi	əmuwədukki	əmuwətəkki	əmuwəkki
	əmukki					
0.21	dəunǰeepi	dəunǰeelli	dəunǰeeǰǰi	dəunǰeedukki	dəunǰeetəkki	dəunǰeekki
2.11	səulbi	səuldulli	səulǰi	səuldukki	səultəkki	səulki
2.2	tuŋəmbi	tuŋəndulli	tuŋənǰi	tuŋəndukki	tuŋəttəkki	tuŋəkki
	səəmbi	səəndulli	səənǰi	səəndukki	səəttəkki	səəkki
0.31	burigbi	burigdulli	burigǰi	burigdukki	buriktəkki	burikki

Examples for Table III.

	Accusative-Nominative	Locative	Dative-Designative	Instrumental	Ablative	Allative	Prolative
1.111	uttəəri	utələri	utəddɵɵri	utəǰǰeeri	utədukkɵɵri	utətəkkeeri	utəkkeeri
1.112	kɵɵddɵɵri	kɵɵdələri	kɵɵdəddɵɵri	kɵɵdəǰǰeeri	kɵɵdədukkɵɵri	kɵɵdətəkkeeri	kɵɵdəkkeeri
1.113	sinnɵɵri	sinuləri	sinuddɵɵri	sinuǰǰeeri	sinudukkɵɵri	sinutəkkeeri	sinukkeeri
1.114	kəččɵɵlleeri	kəččɵɵliləri	kəččɵɵliddɵɵri	kəččɵɵliǰǰeeri	kəččɵɵlidukkɵɵri	kəččɵɵlitəkkeeri	kəččɵɵlikkeeri
1.121	mərkəəri	mərkələri	mərkəddɵɵri	mərkəǰǰeeri	mərkədukkɵɵri	mərkətəkkeeri	mərkəkkeeri
1.122	xəktɵɵri	xəktələri	xəktəddɵɵri	xəktəǰǰeeri	xəktədukkɵɵri	xəktətəkkeeri	xəktəkkeeri
1.123	xupikkɵɵri	xupikkuləri	xupikkuddɵɵri	xupikkuǰǰeeri	xupikkudukkɵɵri	xupikkutəkkeeri	xupikkukkeeri
1.124	bəǰeeri	bəǰiləri	bəǰiddɵɵri	bəǰiǰǰeeri	bəǰidukkɵɵri	bəǰitəkkeeri	bəǰikkeeri
1.21	beewari	beelari	beeddoori	beeǰǰeeri	beedukkoori	beetakkeeri	beekkeeri
1.22	ɵɵwɵri	ɵɵləri	ɵɵddɵɵri	ɵɵǰǰeeri	ɵɵdukkɵɵri	ɵɵtəkkeeri	ɵɵkkeeri
0.1	əmukkəəri	əmuwələri	əmuwəddɵɵri	əmuwəǰǰeeri	əmuwədukkɵɵri	əmuwətəkkeeri	əmuwəkkeeri
0.21	dəunǰeepəri	dəunǰeeləri	dəunǰeeddɵɵri	dəunǰeeǰǰeeri	dəunǰeedukkɵɵri	dəunǰeetəkkeeri	dəunǰeekkeeri
2.11	səulbəri	səulduləri	səuldɵɵri	səulǰeeri	səuldukkɵɵri	səultəkkeeri	səulkeeri
2.2	{tuŋəmbəri	tuŋənduləri	tuŋəndɵɵri	tuŋənǰeeri	tuŋəndukkɵɵri	tuŋəttəkkeeri	tuŋəkkeeri
	{sɵɵmbəri	sɵɵnduləri	sɵɵndɵɵri	sɵɵnǰeeri	sɵɵndukkɵɵri	sɵɵttəkkeeri	sɵɵkkeeri
0.31	burigbəri	burigduləri	burigdɵɵri	burigǰeeri	burigdukkɵɵri	buriktəkkeeri	burikkeeri

Examples for Table IV.

		The First Person Sing.	The First Person Pl.	The Second Person Sing.	The Second Person Pl.	The Third Person	The Third Person Pl.
Added to basic stems.	1.1	utəbi	utəpu	utəsi	utəsu	utəni	utəči
	1.2	beewi	beepu	beesi	beesu	beeni	beeči
	0.1	əmuwəbi	əmuwəpu	əmuwəsi	əmuwəsu	əmuwəni	əmuwəči
	0.21	dəunǰeepi	dəunǰeepu	dəunǰeesi	dəunǰeesu	dəunǰeeni	dəunǰeeči
	2.11	səulbi	səulpu	səulči	səulču	səulli səulni	səulči
	2.2	tuŋəmbi	tuŋəppu	tuŋəčči	tuŋəčču	tuŋəni	tuŋəčči
	0.31	burigbi	burikpu	burikči	burikču	buriŋni	burikči
Added to simple case-endings and accusative stems.	Accusative	uttəəwwee	uttəəppɵɵ	uttəəsi	uttəəsu	uttəəni	uttəəči
	Locative	utələwwee	utələppɵɵ	utələsi	utələsu	utələni	utələči
	Designative	utəddɵɵwwee	utəddɵɵppɵɵ	utəddɵɵsi	utəddɵɵsu	utəddɵɵni	utəddɵɵči
	Dative	utəduwwee	utəduppɵɵ	utədusi	utədusu	utəduni	utəduči
	Instrumental	utəǰiwwee	utəǰippɵɵ	utəǰisi	utəǰisu	utəǰini	utəǰiči
	Ablative	utəduuwwee	utəduuppɵɵ	utəduusi	utəduusu	utəduuni	utəduuči
	Allative	utətəiwwee	utətəippɵɵ	utətəisi	utətəisu	utətəini	utətəiči
	Prolative	utəkkeewwee	utəkkeeppɵɵ	utəkkeesi	utəkkeesu	utəkkeeni	utəkkeeči

Examples for Table V.

	Simple Nominative Form	Basic Stem	Simple Accusative Stem	Sing. Refl. Acc. -Nom. Stem and Ending	Pl. Refl. Acc. -Nom. Stem
0.111	kaltaa ‘a half’	kaltaa, *kaltaka	kaltakkaa	kaltaabi, kaltakki	kaltakkaari
0.112	əmuwə ‘cradle for day-use’	əmuwə, *əmukə	əmukkəə	əmuwəbi, əmukki	əmukkəəri
0.113	olǯiga ‘hooked iron-stick for hanging a pan, etc. over a fire’	olǯiga, *olǯika	olǯikkaa	olǯigabi, olǯikki	olǯikkaari
0.114	xəəgə ‘improvisation’	xəəgə, *xəəkə	xəəkkəə		
0.121	oksoo ‘sledge for a reindeer’	oksoo, *oksoko	oksokkoo	oksoobi, oksokki	oksokkoori
0.131	pəruu ‘drawers (underclothing)’	pəruu, *pəruku	pərukkɵɵ	pəruubi, pərukki	pərukkɵɵri
0.132	taldaawu ‘the middle finger’	taldaawu, *taldaaku	taldaakkoo	taldaawubi, taldaakki	taldaakkoori
0.141	apai ‘the back of the head’	apai, *apaki	apakkee	apaibi, apakki	apakkeeri
0.142	čuuji ‘upper thigh’	čuuji, *čuuki	čuukkee	čuujibi, čuukki	čuukkeeri

Illustrations of arabic numerals, abbreviations and symbols

Arabic numerals indicate classes.

1. indicates the class with the basic stem ending in V.
2. indicates the class with the basic stem ending in C.

These classes are subdivided as follows:

1.1 indicates the class with the basic stem ending in CV.

1.2 indicates the class with the basic stem VV and the basic stem ending in VV.

2.1 indicates the class with the basic stem ending in l.

2.2 indicates the class with the basic stem ending in n.

These classes are further subdivided as follows:

1.11 indicates the class with both the basic stem VCV and the basic stem ending in VCV.

1.12 indicates the class with the basic stem ending in CCV.

2.21 indicates the class with the basic stem(C)VVn.

2.22 indicates the class with the basic stem ending in C(V)Vn.

Further subdivisions indicate subclasses with basic stems that have different final or next-to-last vowel phonemes.

0. indicates the class of substantives that are inflected in different ways from those of Classes 1. and 2. in spite of the coincidence of the last phoneme or phonemes in the simple nominative forms. This class is also divided into subclasses.

V stands for a vowel phoneme and C for a consonant phoneme. *V* stands for any vowel phoneme other than/o, ɵ/. *a* stands for/a/or/ə/, *o* for/o/or/ɵ/. The two C's in the simple accusative stem and the pl. reflexive accusative-nominative stem of Class 1. 11 are identical.

The marks —, –or – indicate the former part of a stem. The same mark used in each class indicates the same part of a stem.

Parentheses ( ) indicate a part that the stems of some substantives do not have.

Hyphens - and ₌ divide a stem from an ending, or one ending from another. In the same column the - after a stem is connected to the - before an ending, and the ₌ after a stem with the ₌ before an ending.

The sign of equal = indicates a different formulation of the same stem.

Notes

1) The material for this paper was acquired from my informant, Napka, an Orok woman approximately 47 years of age. She lived in southern Sakhalin from her birth until 1947, at which time she emigrated to Hokkaidô.

Orok has the vowel phonemes/ ə, a, o, ɵ, u, i, e/ and the consonant phonemes /p, t, č, k, b, d, ǰ, g, m, n, ɲ, ŋ, l, r, s, x, w, j/. I no longer admit the distinction between / u / and / ʊ /, between / i / and / ɪ /, and between /e/ and /ɛ/, which I had previously set up as a hypothesis. In Orok, as in Tungus in general, there is vowel harmony. Thus the phonemes/a, o/do not usually co-exist in the same word with the phonemes /ə, ɵ/. Also, /o/ may not succeed /a, u/ as the next vowel phoneme in a word. /ɵ/ may not succeed /ə, u/ as the next vowel phoneme in a word. However, /oo/ may succeed /a, u/, and /θθ/ may succeed /ə,u/.

2) Genetically, we believe the simple accusative stems and the reflexive case-endings result from the following changes : *(–)VC*a*-b*a*→ (–)VCC*aa* ; *(–)VC*o*-b*o*, *(–)VCu- b*a*→ (–)VCC*oo* ; *(–)VCi-b*a*→ (–)VCCee ; *–CC*a*-b*a*→ –CC*aa* ; *–CC*o*-b*o*, *–CCu-b*a*→ –CC*oo* ; *–CCi-b*a*→ –CCee and similarly **-la-bi*→ *-lli* ; **-du-bi*, **-ǰi-bi*→ *-ǰǰi* ; **-duku-bi*→ *-dukki* ; **-taki-bi*→ *-takki* ; **-kki-bi*→ *-kki* ; **-du-bari* → *-ddoori* ; **-ǰi-bari*→ *-ǰǰeeri* ; **-duku-bari*→ *-dukkoori* ; **-taki-bari*→ *-takkeeri* ; **-kki-bari*→ *-kkeeri*. The reflexive accusative-nominative stems also result from similar changes. However, as for the pl. reflexive locative case-ending, the following change occurred: **-la-bari*→ *-lari*. In addition, the following changes occurred: a designative case-ending plus *-bi*→ *-ǰǰi* and a designative case-ending plus *-bari*→ *-ddoori*.

3) Except for the alternants of the simple prolative case-ending *-kkee* and *-kee* and the simple designative case-ending *-ddoo*, the forms that end in one of these endings can appear as words. Also, simple accusative stems and reflexive sing. and pl. accusative-nominative stems can appear as words without being accompanied by any ending.

4) Genetically, in many of these words, we believe, a single *k* between the last two vowel phonemes was dropped or changed to *g*, *w* or *j* , whereas double *k* (*kk*) in the simple accusative stems and the reflexive accusative-nominative stems is preserved. For instance, words such as *kaltaa* and *əmuwə* were formerly **kaltaka* and **əmukə*. Similarly, we believe the following changes occurred in the simple ablative and allative case-endings: **-duku*→ *-duu*, **-taki*→ *-tai*.

5) Lexically, in the case of stems that have meanings referring to kinship, the simple case-endings and the simple accusative stems are usually followed by personal endings. Also, in the case of stems that mean 'a part of the body', the simple case-endings and the simple accusative stems usually seem to be followed by personal endings.

（昭和29年度文部省科学研究費補助金を受けた研究の一部）

This article is a revised version of my previous paper with the same title, which was published in *Gengo Kenkyu, Journal of the Linguistic Society of Japan*, No. 30 (September, 1956), pp. 77–96.

The Verb Inflection of Orok

1. In Orok, a dialect of Tungus,[1] verbs are inflected through the addition of various endings (verb endings and the other endings given below) to verb stems. This occurs with or without the alternation of the final phoneme of the stems. Also, a kind of stem-alternation can occur in place of the addition of these endings. Most of these endings also have alternants.[2]

2. A large number of verbs can be grouped into Classes 1. and 2. given below, according to the different ways in which they are inflected. For the inflection of each of these verbs, we take the stem accompanied by the ending *-raa*, etc., as the basic form or the basic stem. The last phoneme or phonemes of the basic stems of these verbs are peculiar to that class to which they belong. Accordingly, the inflections of these verbs are automatically determined by the last phoneme or phonemes of their basic stems.

Other verbs are inflected in different ways from the above-mentioned verbs in spite of the coincidence of the last phoneme or phonemes in the stems accompanied by the ending *-raa*, etc. Most of these verbs can be grouped into Classes 0.1, 0.2 and 0.3, according to their inflections. The remainder are a few irregular verbs.

3. The basic forms and alternants of the verb stems of Classes 1. and 2. are shown in Table I.[3] The basic stems of Class 1.1 alternate with other stems instead of the addition of the verb endings *-ra*, *-ri*, *-ru* and the constituents of verb endings *-ra-*, *-ri-*.[4]

For the inflection of each verb in Class 0.11, a subclass of Class 0.1, we set up two basic stems, —V- and *–VkV- (a non-existent basic stem). The latter stem alternates with the stems —VkkV(V), instead of the addition of the endings *-ra, -ri, -ru* and the constituents of endings *-ra-*, *-ri-*. The details are given in Table II.

For the inflection of each verb in Class 0. 12, a subclass of Class 0.1 we set up two basic stems, (C)Vi- and *(C)Vji-. The latter basic stem alternates with the stems (C)Vjjee, (C)Vjji and (C)Vjju, instead of the addition of the endings *-ra, -ri, -ru* and the constituents of endings *-ra-*, *-ri-*. In addition to these, yet another alternant C(V)ju- occurs. The details are given in Table II.

For the inflection of each verb in Class 0.2, we set up the basic stem—V-. However, the inflection of these verbs is not automatically determined by this basic stem—V-, because this stem coincides with the basic stem of Class 1. For each of them we might also be able to set up a basic stem —C-, which ends in *s, t* or a voiceless consonant phoneme. As to its meaning, a number of verbs that belong to this class have a common element of meaning, such as 'quality' or 'state'. The details of the verb stems of this class are shown in Table I.

For the inflection of each verb in Class 0.3, we set up the basic stem –p-. This basic stem alternates with the form –ptu-, which we regard as a stem consisting of –p- plus -tu-, an element that functions exclusively to form a verb stem. The details are given in Table I.

In addition to these verbs, there are a few irregular verbs such as *bi-* 'to be (to exist), to be (copula)', *o-*^{1} 'to do', *o-*^{2} 'to become, to move [to a place]', *to-* 'to do, to copulate', *ə-* (a negative verb), *bul-* 'to die' and *ga-* 'to buy, to take to wife'. The details of the inflections of these irregular verbs are given below (on page 53 ff. in this book). The inflection of *to-* seems to be parallel to that of *o-*^{1}. See Section **9** for the irregular inflection of the verb stems ending in the suffix *-bu-*.

4. The various endings that are added to verb stems are classified as

(1) *verb endings* (*primary verb-endings*) — (1a) *simple verb-endings,* (1b) *reflexive verb-endings,* (1c) *personal verb-endings,* and (1d) other verb endings, (2) the *plural ending,* (3) *personal endings,* (4) *secondary verb-endings,* and (5) other endings that appear not only in verbs but also in other words. A verb stem is always accompanied by a verb ending or by a combination of a verb ending plus one or more of the other endings. These endings occupy the following places in the combinations of endings that are added to verb stems:

Verb endings	Plural ending	Personal endings	Secondary verb-endings	Plural ending	Other endings
a simp. v. e.	+the pl. e.				accompanied
a simp. v. e.	+the pl. e.	+a per. e.			by
a simp. v. e.		+a per. e.			no other
a simp. v. e.		+a per. e.	+a sec. v. e.		ending
a simp. v. e.	+the pl. e.		+a sec. v. e.		or
a simp. v. e.			+a sec. v. e.		one or more
a simp. v. e.			+a sec. v. e.	+the pl. e.	of
a per. v. e.			+a sec. v. e.		the other
a per. v. e.	+the pl. e.				endings.
a simp. v. e.					+one of
a refl. v. e.					the other
a per. v. e.					endings.

The alternate stems that take the place of a stem plus the verb ending -*ra*, -*ri* or -*ru*, appear alone or are accompanied by an ending or a combination of endings that can be added after -*ra*, -*ri* or -*ru*. In addition, certain substantive endings can be added after certain verb endings (the verbal-noun-forming endings -*ra*^{2} and -*ri*^{1}) or immediately to the alternate stems that appear in place of a verb stem plus -*ra*^{2} or -*ri*^{1}.

5. Simple verb-endings They are classified as (a) and (b), those making up the verb forms that can serve as the predicate of a complete sentence; and (c), those making up the verb forms that cannot appear as the predicate of a complete sentence. The former are classified again as: (a), those making up the verb forms that neither can appear as the subject of a sentence or the modifier to a substantive, nor can take a substantive ending; and (b), those making up the verb forms that can appear as the subject of a sentence or the modifier to a substantive, or take a substantive ending. We respectively call (a), (b) and (c) *finite-verb-forming endings*, *verbal-noun-forming endings*, and *converb-forming endings.*

(a) FINITE-VERB-FORMING ENDINGS

-ru 'a command that is expressed concisely'[5)]

-ja 'a command that is expressed politely or affectionately'

-ttaari, -ssaari 'a command to perform an action later on'[6)]

-ra^{1}*-* 'the occurrence of an action at the present time'[7)]

-ta- 'the occurrence of an action in the past'

-ŋa- 'the occurrence of an action in the future'

-raŋa- (always accompanied by a personal ending plus *-i*) This ending with the ending *-i* appearing after a personal ending has the following meanings : 'the occurrence of an action in the distant future, the occurrence of an action in the future that the speaker thinks possible, or the occurrence of an action in the future that the doer is compelled to perform'

-rila- 'the occurrence of an action in the near future, the occurrence of an action in the future of which the speaker is sure, or the occurrence of a spontaneous action of the doer in the future' (This ending is always accompanied by a personal ending.)

(b) VERBAL-NOUN-FORMING ENDINGS

-ra^{2} 'an unfinished action, the doer(s) or the undergoer(s) of an unfinished action, or a place in space or a period in time where an

unfinished action occurs' This ending occurs in a verb that is placed after any inflected form of the negative verb *ə-* or the adverb *əččeeli* 'not yet' in a negative construction.

-ri[1] 'an unfinished action, the doer(s) or the undergoer(s) of an unfinished action, or a place in space or a period in time where an unfinished action occurs' [8)]

-xan 'a finished action, the doer(s) or the undergoer (s) of a finihed action, or a place in space or a period of time where a finished action occurs'

-rilaxam- 'an action that was about to occur in the past, or that the speaker, reconsidering it, wishes had actually taken place'

-bilaxam 'an action of the speaker that was about to occur in the past, or that the speaker, reconsidering it, wishes had actually taken place'

(c) CONVERB-FORMING ENDINGS

-mi[1] 'an unfinished action that occurs simultaneously with another action, or an unfinished action that is the condition for the occurrence of another action' (This ending is always added after the verb-stem-forming suffix *-bu-* and has no alternant.)

-ŋassee[1]*-* 'an action in the past that occurs while another action by a different doer takes place' (This ending is always accompanied by a personal ending.)[9)]

-kuta- 'a finished action, after which an action by a different doer occurs; or a finished action that is the condition for the occurrence of an action by a different doer' (This ending is always accompanied by a personal ending.)

-rai- 'an unfinished action that is the condition or the reason for the occurrence of an action by a different doer' (This ending is always accompanied by a personal ending.)

-mǰee 'a long-continued or repeated action after which another action occurs'

-mǰikəə 'a continued action before the completion of which another action occurs' (This ending can also be added to verb stems containing/a, o/, in which case vowel harmony is lost.)

-dalaa 'an action until the occurrence of which another action continues'

The basic forms and alternants of these verb endings are given in Table III.

Examples of simple verb-endings:

(a)

-ru: *otokoo ŋənnəu* 'Go later on', *pakčiraǰǰillaa, bala bala ŋənnəu* 'It will be dark soon ; go quickly'.

-ja: *ŋənəjə* 'Please go'.

-ttaari: *taraŋači uttəəri* 'Say [a message] that way'.

-ssaari: *ajakaanǰi bissəəri* 'Farewell!' (These are the parting words of a person who sets out on a journey.)

For *-ra*[1]*-* see the examples of *-*ka, -see* and *-ijuu* in **12** and **13**.

For *-ta-* see the examples of *-*ka, -see, -soo* and *-ijuu* in **12** and **13**.

For *-ŋa-* see the examples of *-tta, -see* and *-ijuu* in **12** and **13**.

-raŋa-: *suu doolǰipissaa inəsiŋəsui* 'If you hear [it], you will laugh', *buu ŋənnəəŋəpui* 'We are obliged to go'.

-rila-: *mini dulleekkeewwee buǰiləsi* 'You will die before I', *apaaččilami* 'I will lie down'.

(b)

-ra[2]: *əǰǰeeŋənnəə* 'Do not go', *əččeeli ŋənnəə ŋuigə* ('Who is the person who has not yet gone?' *sii əččeel siltoosi biinii* 'Are there things which you have not yet washed?'

-ri[1]: *ŋənni nari biini* 'There is a man who will go back', *ŋənnee ŋuigə*

'Who is the person who is going?' *sii dəpčisi xaiga* 'What is the thing that you are eating?'

-*xan*: *ŋənuxə nari bɵɵxɵni* 'The man who went home had given [it to me]', *somixa ŋuigə* 'Who is the person who shut [it]?' *sii waaxasi əri* 'The game you caught is this'.

-*rilaxam*-: *nooni dugdu beejini ŋənneeləxəmbi biččì* 'If he had been at home, I would rather have gone [there]', *bujalǰilaxambani ətəxuxəmbi* 'He almost broke [it], but I took [it from him]'.

-*bilaxam*: *nooni dugdu beejini ŋənəwiləxə biččì* 'If he had been at home, I would rather have gone [there]', *umbiləxəmbə oŋboxombi* 'I was going to say [something], but I forgot what I was going to say]'.

(c)

-*mi*[1]: *ŋənnəumi bɵɵxɵni* 'The moment [I] went [there], she gave [it to him]', *sommumi tagdaaŋŋai* 'If [the door] is shut, she will become angry'.

-*ŋassee*[1]- : *čeennee sini auŋasseesi ŋənəxəmbi* 'Yesterday I went while you were sleeping'.

-*kuta*- : *unitai tuuwutənnee itəxəni* 'After she had fallen into the river, he saw [her]', *bɵɵwutənnee gaduttaari* 'If he has given [it to you], bring it'.

-*rai*-: *uuraini uuwoonǰiwi* 'If he gets on, I shall allow him to ride', *tugdəəjini əččimbi ŋənnəə* 'As it rained, I did not go'.

-*mǰee*: *čadu bimǰee isuxambi* 'I had been there for a long time and then came back'.

-*mǰikəə*: *uumǰikəə tuuxəni* 'When he was riding, he fell'.

-*dalaa*: *bujaldalaa takkuraxani* 'He used [it]until he broke [it]'.

6. Reflexive verb-endings These endings contain a common element of meaning, that is, 'the subject of the verb taking this ending is the same as the subject of the verb that it modifies'. If the classification given in

Section 5 is applied here, these endings can all be grouped as converb-forming endings. They are as follows:

*-mi*² 'an unfinished action that occurs simultaneously with another action by the same doer(s), or an unfinished action that is the condition or the reason for the occurrence of another action by the same doer(s)'

-kačči 'a finished action after which another action by the same doer(s) occurs, or a finished action that is the reason for the occurrence of another action by the same doer(s)'

*-ŋassee*² 'an action in the past that occurs while another action by the same doer(s) takes place'

-pee 'a finished action that is the condition for the occurrence of another action by the same doer(s), or a finished action after which another action by the same doer(s) occurs'

-rraa 'an action immediately after which another action by the same doer(s) occurs'[10)]

In addition to these endings there are the following reflexive verb-endings:

-mari

-kaččeeri

-ŋasseeri

-pissaa

-mari has meanings identical with those of *-mi*², *-kaččeeri* has meanings identical with those of *-kačči*, *-ŋasseeri* has a meaning identical with that of *-ŋassee*², and *-pissaa* has meanings identical with those of *-pee*, but to each of these meanings the meaning 'the subject is plural in number' is added.[11)]

The basic forms and the other alternants of these verb endings are given in Table III.

Examples of reflexive verb-endings :

-mi[2]: *ŋənəmi baaxani* 'While going along he found[it]', *itəmi saariwi* 'If I see [it], I will know[what it is]'.

-kačči: *ɵlɵgɵčči dəpɵɵččini* 'She boiled[it] and made [him] eat[it]'.

-ŋassee[2]: *čadu biŋəssee gaččimbi* 'While I was there, I bought[it]'.

-pee: *xɵɵlpee irajjini* 'If he has emptied[it], he will carry [it] back'. *bujalpee saaxani* 'After he had broken [it], he knew[that he had done so]'.

-rraa: *dəpturrəə ŋənuxəni* 'As soon as he ate, he went back'.

7. Personal verb-endings There is a group of endings which also convey an indicaton as to the person of the subject, in addition to meanings identical with those of some of the above-mentioned verb endings. We call them *personal verb-endings*. If the classification given in Section 5 is applied here, they are all grouped as finite-verb-forming endings. They are the following:

-ri[2]- (This ending is always accompanied by the ending *-tta*.)

-ŋi-

-raŋŋi- (This ending is always accompanied by the ending *-i*.)

-raŋŋa-

-rillaa

-ri[2]- has a meaning identical with that of *-ra*[1]-, *-ŋi-* has a meaning identical with that of *-ŋa-*, and *-raŋŋi-* (with *-i*) has meanings identical with those of *-raŋa-* (with *-i*), but to each of these meanings a meaning identical with that of the first-person singular ending *-bi* is added. *-ri*[2]- serves as the alternant of *-ra*[1]*-mi-*. *-ŋi-* and *-ŋŋi-* take the place of **-ŋa-mi* (or **-ŋa-bi*).[12)]

-raŋŋa- (with or without *-i*) has meanings identical with those of *-raŋa-* (with *-i*), and *-rillaa* has meanings identical with those of *-rila-*, but to each of these meanings the meaning 'the subject=the third-

person' is added. *-raŋŋa-* may be considered to replace the *-raŋa-*, which is accompanied by no personal ending. *-rillaa* may be considered to take the place of the *-rila-* accompanied by no personal ending.

The basic forms and alternants of these verb endings are given in Table III.

8. Some of the above-mentioned verb endings may be divided into constituents.[13] *-raŋa-*, *-raŋŋi*, *-raŋŋa-*, *-rila-*, *-rillaa*, *-rilaxam-*, *-bilaxam* and *-rai-* are respectively divided into the following constituents:

ra+ŋa, ra+ŋŋi, ra+ŋŋa, ri+la, ri+llaa, ri+la+xam, bi+la+xam, ra+i

The constituents *-ra-*, *-ri-*, *-ŋa-* and *-xam* included in these verb endings may be regarded as identical with the above-mentioned endings *-ra²*, *-ri¹*, *-ŋa-* and *-xan* respectively. The other constituents included in these verb endings may be considered to be as follows:[14]

-ŋŋi-, which has a meaning identical with the meaning of *-ŋa-* plus the meaning of the first-person singular ending *-bi*

-ŋŋa-, which has a meaning identical with that of *-ŋa-* plus the meaning 'the subject=the third-person'

-la- 'the occurrence of an action in the future'

-llaa, which has a meaning identical with that of *-la-* plus the meaning 'the subject=the third-person'

-bi- 'an unfinished action by the speaker'

-i- 'the condition under which an action occurs'

The constituents of these verb endings combine with each other in the following order:

1		2		3
bi	+	la	+	xam
ri	+	la	+	xam

ri	+	la
ri	+	llaa
ra	+	ŋa
ra	+	ŋŋi
ra	+	ŋŋa
ra	+	i

9. As mentioned above, an alternate stem appears in place of the basic stems of Classes 1.1 and 0.1 plus one of the verb endings *-ra*, *-ri*, *-ru* (and the constituents of verb endings *-ra-*, *-ri-*). Similarly, the alternate stem *bee* appears in place of the irregular verb stem *bi-* plus *-ra*. The alternate stems that replace a stem plus the verbal-noun-forming ending *-ra*^{2} or *-ri* are called *verbal noun stems* here.

The verbal-noun-forming endings *-ra*^{2} and *-xan* may not be added after the verb-stem-forming suffix *-bu-*. However, in place of **-bu-ra*^{2}, the form -**bboo* (the non-existent basic stem of *-wwoo* ~ *-boo* ~ *-ppoo*) appears, and in place of **-bu-xan*, the form *-pula* appears. -**bboo* has meanings identical with those of *-ra*^{2} except for the meaning 'the doer(s) of an unfinished action', and *-pula* has meanings identical with those of *-xan* except for the meaning 'the doer(s) of a finished action'. To each of these meanings, however, a meaning identical with that of the verb-stem-forming suffix *-bu-* 'the subject of the verb containing this suffix is not referred to' is added.[15] Some examples are: *əpulə dəptuwwɵɵ dəppi biini* 'There is food that has not been eaten', *əččeeli anduppoo biini* 'There is a thing that is not yet made', *ŋənupulə pokto biini* 'There are the footprints that [somebody] left returning', *andupula biini* 'There is a thing that has been made'.

10. Plural ending The plural formational element *-l* appears as the plural ending in verb inflection and means 'the subject is plural'. See Table IV for the endings followed by the plural ending *-l*. After *-ja-l-* the second-person plural ending always appears, thus *-ja-l-tu*. *-soo-l* has the same meaning as the ending *-soo* given below. The plural formational element *-l* added after the verbal-noun-forming ending when it means the doers of an action may be regarded as a substantive-stem-forming suffix.

11. Personal endings The personal endings are the first-person sing. *-bi*, the first-person pl. *-pu*, the second-person sing. *-si*, the second-person pl. *-su*, the third-person (sing. and pl.) *-ni* and the third-person pl. *-či*. The first four mean, as to the subject that is a person, persons, or something personified, 'I (the first-person sing.)', 'we (the first-person pl.)', 'you (the second-person sing.)', and 'you (the second-person pl.)', respectively. The third-person *-ni* means 'the subject=the third-person (animate or inanimate)'. The third-person pl. *-či* means 'the subject=the third-person pl. (persons or mammals, especially domesticated reindeer)'.

The basic forms and alternants of the personal endings and the verb endings followed by them are given in Table V.

The combination of endings *-ŋa-p-* is always followed by the ending *-tta*, thus *-ŋa-p-ta*; each of the combinations *-ta-mi-*, *-ta-pu-*, *-ta-si-*, *-ta-su-* is always followed by the secondary verb-ending *-*ka*, thus *-ta-mi-ga*, *-ta-pu-wa*, *-ta-si-ga*, and *-ta-su-wa*; and each of the combinations *-ra-ŋa-pu-*, *-ra-ŋa-si-*, *-ra-ŋa-su-* is always followed by the ending *-i*, thus *-ra-ŋa-pu-i*, *-ra-ŋa-si-i*, and *-ra-ŋa-su-i*.

There is a set of four personal endings: *-mi*, *-pu*, *-si*, *-su*. These personal endings are added to the finite-verb-forming endings *-ta-* and *-ri-la-*, and to the verbal-noun-forming ending *-ra* (or the verbal noun stem replacing a verb stem plus *-ra*) in an inflected form that is employed as the predicate of a complete sentence. They are used only in verb inflection.[16)]

After *-ta-* and *-ŋa-*, and after *-ra²* (or the alternate stem replacing a verb stem plus *-ra²*) in such an inflected form as mentioned above, the absence of any ending indicating the person of the subject implies that the subject is the third-person.

Further, there are three sets of six personal endings each :-*bi*, -*pu*, -*si*, -*su*, -*ni*, -*či* added to the verbal-noun-forming ending -*xan*; -*wi*, -*pu*, -*si*, -*su*, -*ni*, -*či* added to the verbal-noun-forming ending -*ri* (or the verbal noun stem replacing a verb stem plus -*ri*); and -*wwee*, -*ppoo*, -*si*, -*su*, -*ni*, -*či* added to the converb-forming endings -*ŋassee*[1]- and -*ra-i*-. They are identical in shape with the three sets of personal endings added to the basic stems of the substantives of Class 2.2, to the basic stems of the substantives of Class 1.2 and to the simple case-endings and accusative stems in the substantive inflection.

There is still another set of six personal endings: -*wwee*, -*ppoo*, -*ssee*, -*ssoo*, -*nnee*, -*ččee*. These are added only after the converb-forming ending -*kuta*- in verb inflection.[17)]

The combination of the verb ending -*ri*[1] plus the second-person plural ending -*su* has in some cases the meaning 'the speaker's (or the speaker and somebody else's) inducing the person or persons spoken to to perform an action immediately together with the speaker (or the speaker and somebody else)', as in *bala bala ŋənneesu* 'Let us go quickly'.

In addition to a set of combinations of a personal ending plus the secondary ending -**ka*: -*mi-ga*, -*pu-wa*, -*si-ga*, -*su-wa* added to the verb ending -*ra*, there is a set of alternate personal endings: -*mee*, -*poo*, -*see*, -*soo*. These are added to the same ending -*ra* and are identical in meaning with -*mi-ga*, -*pu-wa*, -*si-ga* and -*su-wa* respectively.

12. Secondary verb-endings These are as follows:

-*tta* 'the intention of the speaker to cause an action'

-**ka* 'the speaker's having experience of (or the speaker's witnessing) the occurrence of an action'[18)]

-*see* 'the subject of the verb taking this ending is a person other than the speaker, and the speaker asks either with modesty or in soliloquy for an answer to the question expressed by the interrogative word in the sentence that contains the verb taking this ending'[19)]

-soo This ending has a meaning identical with that of *-see*, except for 'the subject=plural'.[19)]

-i The meaning is as yet unknown. (Cf. pp. 27, 32 in this book.)

The basic forms and alternants of these endings and the endings followed by these endings are given in Tables VI-IX. After *-ta-kka-* the plural ending *-l* always appears, thus *-ta-kka-l*.

The combinations of one or two of the above-mentioned endings and *-tta* have the following meanings:

-ri^2*-tta* 'the speaker's intention to perform an action immediately'

-ŋi-tta 'the speaker's intention to perform an action later on'

-ŋa-p-ta 'the intention of the speaker and somebody else to perform an action later on, or the speaker's (or the speaker and somebody else's) inducing the person or persons spoken to to perform an action later on together with the speaker (or the speaker and somebody else)'

-ŋa-tta 'the speaker's permission or command to perform an action for somebody other than the speaker and the person(s) spoken to (through the person(s) spoken to)'

-ŋa-l-ta and *-ŋa-tta-l* Both of these combinations have a meaning identical with the meaning of *-ŋa-tta* plus the meaning of *-l*.

For the indications as to the person of the subject that are contained in the meanings of these combinations see Sections **7** and **11**.

Examples of these endings:

-ri-tta: *bii ŋənneettə* 'I will go'. (This is used in a case where the speaker volunteers to go.)

-ŋi-tta: *otokoo ŋənuŋittə* 'I will go home later on'. (This is used in a case where, for instance, the speaker's son has come for him because a visitor called at his own house.)

-ŋa-p-ta: *buu dөөnnee ŋənəŋəptə, sii bakkaa ŋənneesii* 'We two will go; will you go, too?' *dөөnnee otokoo ŋənəŋəptə* 'Let us two go later on'.

-ŋa-tta: *soŋoŋotto* 'Leave him cry' (This is used in a case where the speaker has been informed that his child is crying.), *tari nari ŋənəŋəttə* 'He may go', *tari puttə mooloŋotto* 'Make the child go to gather firewood'.

-ŋa-tta-l: *məənə ŋənəŋəttəl* 'They may go themselves'.

-ŋa-l-ta: *məənə ŋənəŋəltə* 'same as the above'.

*-*ka*: *tari nari məənə moollookko* 'He is going to gather firewood himself'. (This is used in a case where the speaker sees him go.), *məənə moolotoo* 'He went to gather firewood himself' (This is used in a case where the speaker has seen him go.).

-see: *əsi xaiwa ŋənnəəsee* 'I wonder where he is going along [through] now', *tari nari xawasai ŋənətəsee* 'I wonder where he went', *xaali mooloŋosee* 'I wonder when he will go to gather firewood'.

-soo: *xawasai ŋənətəsөө* 'I wonder where they went'.

For *-i* see the examples of *-ra-ŋa-* given above.

13. There are other endings that appear not only in verbs but also in other words: the interrogative ending *-i* (~*-ji*) 'asking for an affirmative or negative answer to an interrogative sentence that contains the word taking this ending', the interrogative ending *-ka* (~*-kə*~*-ko*~*-kө*~*-ga*~*-gə*~*-go*~*-gө*~*-wa*~*-wə*~*-wo*~*-wө*) 'asking for an answer to the question expressed by the interrogative word in the sentence that contains the word taking this ending', the interrogative ending *-ijuu* (~*-jjuu*~*-luu*) used when asking a question modestly or in soliloquy, the exclamatory ending *-kaa* (~*-kəə*~*-koo*~*-kөө*) expressing exclamation or emphasis or used when crying out to a hearer or hearers at a distance from the speaker, and so forth. Some examples are: *sii ŋənneesii* 'Will you go ?' *sii xaali ŋənneesigə* 'When will you go ?' *tari nari xawasai ŋənneenijjuu* 'I wonder where he is going', *tari nari ŋənətəijuu* 'I wonder whether he went', *tari puttə mooloŋoijuu* 'I wonder whether the child will go to gather firewood', *tari narisal xaiwaa ŋənnəəlluu* 'I wonder through what place they are going', *bii xooni ŋənəŋijjuu* 'However shall I go? (I want to go somehow or other.)' *əjjeekəə* 'You must not !' A detailed description of these endings is omitted here.

14. In addition, there is a group of endings, each of which has a meaning identical with that of the combination of a verb ending or a personal ending plus the interrogative ending *-ka.* Except for the final vowel difference, each ending in this group is identical in shape with the preceding ending in the corresponding combination. The final vowel phonemes of each ending in this group are *aa* or *əə*, when the preceding ending in the corresponding combination ends in *a* or *ə*; *oo* or *ɵɵ*, when it ends in *o, ɵ* or *u*; and *ee*, when it ends in *i.* The form-alternation of each ending in this group is parallel to that of the preceding ending in the corresponding combination. The alternants of each ending in this group follow the same alternants of stems or endings that those of the preceding ending in the corresponding combination follow. An example is: *sii xaali ŋənneesee* 'When will you go ?'

Further, there is a group of endings, each of which has a meaning identical with that of one of the verb endings or the personal endings but expresses exclamation or emphasis, or is used when calling out to a hearer or hearers at a distance from the speaker. Each ending in this group appears in place of a combination of one of the verb endings or the personal endings plus the exclamatory ending *-kaa.* Except for the final vowel difference, each ending in this group is identical in shape with the preceding ending in the corresponding combination. The final vowel phonemes of these endings are *aa* or *əə*, when the preceding ending in the corresponding combination ends in *a* or *ə*; *oo* or *ɵɵ*, when it ends in *o, ɵ* or *u*; and *ee*, when it ends in *i*. The form-alternations of most of these endings are parallel to those of the preceding ending in the corresponding combinations. The alternants of each ending in this group follow the same alternants of stems or endings that those of the preceding ending in the corresponding combinations follow. An example is: *ŋənəxənee* ‘He has gone !’

The endings *-raa* and *-roo*, which we call *exclamatory verb-endings*, appear in place of the combinations of **-ra*^{2}*-kaa* and **-ru-kaa*, respectively. However, the form-alternations of *-raa* and *-roo* are not parallel to those of *-ra*^{2} and *-ru*. The alternants of *-raa* and *-roo* do not always follow the same alternants of verb stems that the alternants of *-ra*^{2} and *-ru* follow. The basic forms and alternants of these exclamatory verb-endings are given in Table III. Some examples are *əǰǰee ŋənərəə* ‘Don’t go!’ *daparoo* ‘Catch [it] !’[20)]

15. Some of the substantive endings can be added after the verbal-noun-forming endings, or immediately to the verbal noun stems. That is, the *verbal nouns* can take some of the substantive endings.

After *-ra*^{2}, *-ri*^{1}, *-xan* and the verbal noun stems, the simple case-endings *-ba, -la, -du, -ǰi, -tai, -kki*, and the sing. and pl. reflexive case-endings *-bi, -bari*, etc., can be added. In case inflection, the verbal nouns consisting of a verb stem plus *-ra*^{2} or *-ri*^{1}, or only a verbal noun stem are inflected in the manner of the substantives of Class 1. However, *-wi* or *-mi* appears as the alternant of the sing. reflexive accusative ending added after *-ra*^{2}, and the form *-rree* appears as the alternant of *-ri*^{1}*-wa* added after the verb-stem-forming suffix *-bu-*. The verbal nouns consisting of a verb stem plus *-xan* are inflected in the manner of the substantives of Class 2.22. After a combination of a verb stem plus *-ra*^{2}, *-ri*^{1} or *-xan* plus a simple case-ending, one of the personal endings *-wwee, -ppoo, -si, -su, -ni, -či* can be added in the same manner as after a combination of a substantive stem plus a simple case-ending.

After -**bboo* and *-pula* the simple dative ending *-du* can be added. In place of -**bboo* or *-pula* plus the simple accusative ending *-ba,* the accusative form -**bboo* or *-pullaa* appears.

After *-ri-la-xam* the simple accusative ending *-ba,* the sing. reflexive accusative ending *-bi,* or the pl. reflexive accusative ending *-bari* can be added. *-ri-la-xam-ba* is always accompanied by one of the personal endings *-wwee, -ppoo, -si, -su, -ni, -či.* After *-bi-la-xam* the simple accusative ending *-ba* can be added.

The details of further inflections of verbal nouns are not given here.[21)]

Table I. Basic and Alternant Forms of

Set / Class	I			Basic Stems	II	
1.111	(–)VC*a*-				(–)VCC*aa*(-)	
1.112	(–)VC*o*-				(–)VCC*oo*(=)	
1.113	(–)VCu-				(–)VCC*oo*(-)	
1.114	(–)VCi-				(–)VCCee(-)	
1.121	– CC*a*-	= –CV-			– CC*aa*(-)	
1.122	– CC*o*-				– CC*oo*(=)	
1.123	– CCu-				– CC*oo*(-)	
1.124	– CCi-		= —V-		– CCee(-)	
1.2	(–) VV- = (–)V*V*- or –V*o*=		= —*V*- or —*o*= = —*V*· —u·· or —*o*=	Each stem of Set I is taken as basic stem, except Class 0.3 where the stem in Set II is taken as basic stem.		
0.211	–C*a*-					
0.212	–C*o*-					
0.213	–Cu-	= –CV-				—V-
0.214	–Ci-					
0.22	(–)VV- = (–)V*V*- or –V*o*=					
0.3	–ptu- = –CV-				–p-	
2.1	—l- = –*V* l- or –*o*l=				—l-	
2.2	—g- = –*V*g- or –*o*g=				—g-	
2.3	—n- = –*V*n- or –*o*n=				—n-	
0.1	For 0.1 see Table II.					
Verb Ending to Accompany Each Set of Verb Stems	-roo -raa -rraa -dalaa				-ra[1]- -ra[2] -ra-ŋa- -ra-ŋŋi- -ra-ŋŋa- -ra-i-	

Verb Stems and Following Verb Endings

III	IV	V	VI
(–)V*C*Cee	(–)V*C*C*a*u (–)V*C*C*o*u	—V-	—V-
(–)V*C*Ci	(–)V*C*Cu		
– CCee	– CC*a*u – CC*o*u		
– CCi	– CCu		
—V-	—V-		
–p-	–p-		
—l-	—l-	—l-	—l-
—g-	—g-	—g-	—g-
—n-	—n-	—m-	— -
-ri[1] -ri[2]- -ri-la- -ri-llaa- -ri-la-xam-	-ru	-bi-la-xam	-ja

VII	VIII	IX	X
—V-	—V-	—V-	—V-
—1-	—1-	—1-	—1-
—ŋ-	— -	—k-	—k-
— -		—p- = —*C*-	—t- = —*C*-

-mi²- -mari -mǰee -mǰikəə	-ŋa- -ŋi- -ŋassee¹- -ŋassee² -ŋasseeri	-pee -pissaa	-ttaari -ta-

XI	XII	XIII	XIV		Set / Class
			–C*a*-		1.111
			–C*o*-		1.112
			–Cu-	= –CV-	1.113
					1.114
					1.121
					1.122
					1.123
					1.124
—V-	—V-	—V-	(–)VV-		1.2
					0.211
					0.212
					0.213
					0.214
					0.22
			–ptu-		0.3
—l-	—l-	—l-	—l-		2.1
—k-	—k-	—k- = —*C*-	—k- = —*C*-		2.2
—s- = —*C*-	—č- = —*C*-				2.3
					0.1
-ssaari	-xan	-kačči -kaččeeri	-kuta-		Verb Ending to Accompany Each Set of Verb Stems

Table II. Basic Forms and Other Alternants of Verb Stems of Class 0.1

Set / Class	I	Basic Stems			II	III	IV	V—XIII	XIV
0.1111	C*aa*-		*C*a*k*a*-		–Vkk*aa*(-)	–Vkkee	–Vkk*a*u	—V-	–VV=
0.1112	(–)Cuw*a*- –Cig*a*- –VVg*a*-		*(–)Cuk*a*- * –Cik*a*- * –VVk*a*-	=*–VkV-					–C*a*- =–CV-
0.112	(–)CV*o*-	—V- =–VV-	*(–)CVk*o*-		–Vkk*oo*(=)		–Vkk*o*u		
0.113	(–)CVu-	or–CV- =—*V*-	*(–)CVku-		–Vkk*oo*(-)	–Vkki	–Vkku		
0.114	(–)CVi-	or—*o*= =—*V*·	*(–)CVki-		–Vkkee(-)				
0.12	(C)Vi-	—u·· or—*o*=	*(C)Vji-		(C)Vjjee(-)	(C)Vjji	(C)Vjju		(C)Vju-

Table III. Basic Forms and Other Alternants of Verb Endings

<table>
<tr><th rowspan="2">Set of Stems / Basic Form of Verb Ending / Class of Stems</th><th colspan="3">I</th><th colspan="5">II</th><th colspan="3">III</th></tr>
<tr><th>-dalaa</th><th>① -raa
② -rraa</th><th>-roo</th><th>-ra^{1,2}</th><th colspan="2">① -ra-ŋa-
② -ra-ŋŋi-
③ -ra-ŋŋa-</th><th colspan="2">-ra-i-</th><th>-ri^{1,2}</th><th colspan="2">① -ri-la-
② -ri-llaa
③ -ri-la–xam-</th></tr>
<tr><td>1.1,
0.1</td><td rowspan="6">-dalaa,
⸗doloo</td><td rowspan="3">① -raa, ⸗roo
② -rraa, ⸗rroo</td><td rowspan="3">-roo</td><td></td><td></td><td rowspan="6">① -ŋa-, ⸗ŋo-
② -ŋŋi-
③ -ŋŋa-, ⸗ŋŋo-</td><td></td><td>-ji-</td><td></td><td></td><td rowspan="6">① -la-
② -llaa
③ -la-xa-$_1$,
-la-xam-$_3$</td></tr>
<tr><td>1.2</td><td>-ra,
⸗ro</td><td>-ra-,
⸗ro⸗</td><td>-ra-,
⸗ro-</td><td rowspan="5">–i–</td><td>-ri</td><td>-ri-</td></tr>
<tr><td>0.3</td><td>-ta</td><td>-ta-</td><td>-ta-</td><td>-či-</td><td>-či-</td></tr>
<tr><td>2.1,
2.2</td><td rowspan="2">① -daa, ⸗doo
② -daa, ⸗doo</td><td>-doo</td><td rowspan="2">-da,
⸗do</td><td rowspan="2">-da-,
⸗do⸗</td><td rowspan="2">-da-,
⸗do-</td><td rowspan="2">-ǰi</td><td rowspan="2">-ǰi-</td></tr>
<tr><td>2.3</td><td>-oo</td></tr>
<tr><td>0.2</td><td>① -see
② -ssii</td><td>-soo</td><td>-si</td><td>-si-</td><td>-si-</td><td>-si-</td><td>-si-</td></tr>
</table>

Set of Stems / Basic Form of Verb Ending / Class of Stems	IV	V		VI	VII	VIII	IX
	-ru	-bi-la-xam		-ja	① -mi[2] ② -mari ③ -mǰee ④ -mǰikəə	① -ŋa- ② -ŋi- ③ -ŋassee[1,2] ④ -ŋasseeri	① -pee ② -pissaa
1.1, 0.1		-wi-	-l*a*-x*a*, -l*a*-x*a* m-$_3$	-j*a*, ≠j*o*	① -mi ② -m*a*ri, ≠m*o*ri ③ -mǰee ④ -mǰikəə	① -ŋ*a*-, ≠ŋo≠ ② -ŋi- ③ -ŋ*a*ssee, ≠ŋ*o*ssee ④ -ŋ*a*sseeri, ≠ŋ*o*sseeri	① -pee ② -piss*aa*
1.2	-ru						
0.3	-tu						
2.1, 2.2	-du	-bi-					
2.3	-u						
0.2	-su	-ppi-					

Set of Stems / Basic Form of Verb Ending / Class of Stems	X		XI	XII	XIII	XIV
	-ta-	-ttaari	-ssaari	-xan	① -kačči ② -kaččeeri	-kuta-
1.1, 0.1	-t*a*-, =t*o*=	-tt*aa*ri, =tt*oo*ri	-ss*aa*ri, =ss*oo*ri	-x*a*($-_1$) =x*o*($=_1$) -x*a*n$-_2$ =x*o*n$=_2$ -x*a*m$-_3$ =x*o*m$=_3$ -x*a*t$-_4$ =x*o*t$=_4$ -x*a*k$-_5$ =x*o*k$=_5$	①·g*a*čči, ··w*a*čči, =w*o*čči ②·g*a*ččeeri, ··w*a*ččeeri, =w*o*ččeeri	-ut*a*-, =wut*a*-
1.2						
0.3						
2.1, 2.2		-t*aa*ri, =t*oo*ri	-s*aa*ri, =s*oo*ri	-či($-_1$) -čin$-_2$ -čim$-_3$ -čit$-_4$ -čik$-_5$	①-k*a*čči, =k*o*čči ②-k*a*ččeeri, =k*o*ččeeri	-kut*a*-
2.3						
0.2						

Table IV. Plural Ending

<table>
<tr><th colspan="2">Basic Form / Preceding Ending</th><th>-l</th><th>Following Ending</th></tr>
<tr><td colspan="2">-ja</td><td rowspan="5">-l-</td><td>-su</td></tr>
<tr><td colspan="2" rowspan="2">-ŋa</td><td>-tta</td></tr>
<tr><td rowspan="3">-ijuu</td></tr>
<tr><td colspan="2">-ta</td></tr>
<tr><td colspan="2">-ra^{1}</td></tr>
<tr><td colspan="2">-ra^{2}</td><td rowspan="9">-l</td><td rowspan="9"></td></tr>
<tr><td colspan="2">-ra-ŋŋa</td></tr>
<tr><td colspan="2">-ri-llaa</td></tr>
<tr><td>-ŋa</td><td>-tta</td></tr>
<tr><td>-ta</td><td rowspan="2">-kka</td></tr>
<tr><td>-ra^{1}</td></tr>
<tr><td>-ŋa</td><td rowspan="3">-soo</td></tr>
<tr><td>-ta</td></tr>
<tr><td>-ra^{1}</td></tr>
</table>

Table V. Basic Forms and Other Alternants of Personal Endings

<table>
<tr><th>Basic Form / Preceding Ending</th><th>-bi</th><th>-pu</th><th>-si</th><th>-su</th><th>-ni</th><th>-či</th><th>Following Ending</th></tr>
<tr><td>-ja-l</td><td rowspan="4" colspan="3"></td><td>-tu</td><td rowspan="4" colspan="2"></td><td rowspan="4"></td></tr>
<tr><td>-ru</td><td rowspan="3">-su</td></tr>
<tr><td>-ttaari</td></tr>
<tr><td>-ssaari</td></tr>
<tr><td rowspan="2">-ŋa</td><td>[-ŋi-tta]</td><td>-p-</td><td colspan="2"></td><td>[-ŋa-tta]</td><td>[-ŋa-l-ta, -ŋa-tta-l]</td><td>-tta</td></tr>
<tr><td>[-ŋi-jjuu]</td><td rowspan="4">-pu-</td><td rowspan="4">-si-</td><td rowspan="4">-su-</td><td>[-ŋa-ijuu]</td><td>[-ŋa-l-luu]</td><td>-ijuu</td></tr>
<tr><td>-ra-ŋa</td><td>[-ra-ŋŋi-i]</td><td>[-ra-ŋŋa-i]</td><td>[-ra-ŋŋa-l]</td><td>-i</td></tr>
<tr><td>-ta</td><td rowspan="2">-mi-</td><td>[-ta-a]</td><td>[-ta-kka-l]</td><td rowspan="2">-*ka</td></tr>
<tr><td>-ra^1</td><td>[-ra-kka]</td><td>[-ra-kka-l]</td></tr>
<tr><td>-ra^2</td><td rowspan="2">-mi</td><td rowspan="2">-pu</td><td rowspan="2">-si</td><td rowspan="2">-su</td><td>[-ra]</td><td>[-ra-l]</td><td rowspan="8"></td></tr>
<tr><td>-ri-la</td><td>[-ri-llaa]</td><td>[-ri-llaa-l]</td></tr>
<tr><td>-xan</td><td rowspan="2">$_3$-bi</td><td rowspan="2">$_1$-pu</td><td rowspan="2">$_1$-si</td><td rowspan="2">$_1$-su</td><td rowspan="2">$_1$-ni</td><td rowspan="2">$_1$-či</td></tr>
<tr><td>-ri-la-xam</td></tr>
<tr><td>-ri^1</td><td>-wi</td><td>-pu</td><td rowspan="3">-si</td><td rowspan="3">-su</td><td rowspan="3">-ni</td><td rowspan="3">-či</td></tr>
<tr><td>-ŋassee^1</td><td rowspan="3">-wwee</td><td rowspan="3">-ppoo</td></tr>
<tr><td>-ra-i</td></tr>
<tr><td>-kuta</td><td>-ssee</td><td>-ssoo</td><td>-nnee</td><td>-ččee</td></tr>
</table>

Table VI–IX. Basic Forms and Other Alternants of Secondary Verb-endings

VI.

Preceding Ending \ Basic Form		-tta
-ŋa	-p	-t*a*, =t*o*
	-l	
-ŋa		=tt*a*, =tt*o*
-ŋi		-tt*a*
-ri[2]		

VII.

Preceding Ending \ Basic Form		-*ka
-ta	-mi· -pu·· -si· -su··	·g*a*, ··w*a*
-ra[1]		
-ta		-*a*, =*o*
		-kk*a*-, =kk*o*-
-ra[1]		-kk*a*, =kk*o*

VIII.

Preceding Ending \ Basic Form	-see	-soo
-ŋa	-see	-s*oo*
-ta		
-ra[1]		

IX.

Preceding Ending \ Basic Form		-i
-ra-ŋa	-pu -si -su	-i
-ra-ŋŋi		
-ra-ŋŋa		

Examples for Tables I–III and Inflections of Irregular Verbs

Set of Stems	I		
Verb Ending / Class of Stems	-dalaa	-raa	-rraa
1.111	ŋənədələə	ŋənərəə	ŋənərrəə
1.112	moolodoloo	mooloroo	moolorroo
1.113	ŋənudələə	ŋənurəə	ŋənurrəə
1.114	somidalaa	somiraa	somirraa
1.121	aundadalaa	aundaraa	aundarraa
1.122	tokpodoloo	tokporoo	tokporroo
1.123	siltudalaa	silturaa	silturraa
1.124	bargidalaa	bargiraa	bargirraa
0.1111	baadalaa	baaraa	baarraa
0.1112	paluwadalaa	paluwaraa	paluwarraa
	sapčigadallaa	sapčigaraa	sapčigarraa
	xəəgədələə	xəəgərəə	xəəgərrəə
0.112	loodoloo	looroo	loorroo
0.113	gajaudalaa	gajauraa	gajaurraa
0.114	bəliidələə	bəliirəə	bəliirrəə
0.12	gəidələə	gəirəə	gəirrəə
1.2	uudalaa	uuraa	uurraa
	bɵɵdɵlɵɵ	bɵɵrɵɵ	bɵɵrrɵɵ
0.211	gatadalaa	gatasee	gatassii
0.212	ɵlɵdɵlɵɵ	ɵlɵsee	ɵlɵssii
0.213	andudalaa	andusee	andussii
0.214	moolidalaa	moolisee	moolissii
0.22	allaudalaa	allausee	allaussii
0.3	dəptudələə	dəpturəə	dəpturrəə
2.1	bujaldalaa	bujaldaa	bujaldaa
	xɵɵldɵlɵɵ	xɵɵldɵɵ	xɵɵldɵɵ
2.2	xaagdalaa	xaagdaa	xaagdaa
	orogdoloo	orogdoo	orogdoo
2.3	undələə	undəə	undəə
	kɵjɵɵndɵlɵɵ	kɵjɵɵndɵɵ	kɵjɵɵndɵɵ
Irregular Verbs		birəə	birrəə
	odoloo	oroo	orroo
	odoloo	osee	ossii
	budələə	budəə	buddəə
	gadalaa	gadaa	gaddaa

Basic Stems
ŋənə- 'to go'
moolo- 'to go to gather firewood', soŋo- 'to weep, to cry'
ŋənu- 'to go back'
somi- 'to shut [the door]', niməri- 'to visit'
aunda- 'to lodge for the night', əldə- 'to lead [a child, a dog etc.]'
tokpo- 'to twist [a rope]'
siltu- 'to wash'
bargi- 'to prepare'
baa-, *baka- 'to find, to see [a person], to get [a child]'
paluwa-, *paluka- 'to hammer'
sapčiga-, *sapčika- 'to whip'
xəəgə-, *xəəkə- 'to improvise (in song)'
loo-, *loko- 'to hang', *čolmoko- 'to leap up and down'
gajau-, *gajaku- 'to put a riddle'
bəlii-, *bəliki- 'to get ready', *čoki- 'to peck'
gəi-, *gəji- 'to compete'
uu- 'to ride, to take [a boat]'
bɵɵ- 'to give', soo- 'to scoop [water]'
gata- 'to pick fruits (berries)'
ɵlɵ- 'to boil (to cook)', eero- 'to look at, to read, to examine'
andu- 'to make'
mooli- 'to gather firewood'
allau- 'to teach'
dəp- 'to eat'
bujal- 'to break'
xɵɵl- 'to spill, to empty'
xaag- 'to come to land (a boat)'
orog- 'to carry'
un- 'to say'
kɵjɵɵn- 'to whistle', dotolon- 'to listen'
bi- 'to be (to exist), to be (copula)'
o-[1] 'to do'
o-[2] 'to become, to move [to a place]'
ə- 'not to.....(negative)'
bul- 'to die'
ga- 'to buy, to take to wife'

| \multicolumn{4}{c}{II} |
-ra¹- plus -*ka	-ra²	-ra-ŋŋa- plus -i	-ra-i- plus -ni
ŋənnəəkkə	ŋənnəə	ŋənnəəŋŋəi	ŋənnəəjini
moollookko	moolloo	moollooŋŋoi	moolloojini
ŋənnөөkkə	ŋənnөө	ŋənnөөŋŋəi	ŋənnөөjini
sommeekka	sommee	sommeeŋŋai	sommeejini
aundaakka	aundaa	aundaaŋŋai	aundaajini
tokpookko	tokpoo	tokpooŋŋoi	tokpoojini
siltookka	siltoo	siltooŋŋai	siltoojini
bargeekka	bargee	bargeeŋŋai	bargeejini
bakkaakka	bakkaa	bakkaaŋŋai	bakkaajini
palukkaakka	palukkaa	palukkaaŋŋai	palukkaajini
sapčikkaakka	sapčikkaa	sapčikkaaŋŋai	sapčikkaajini
xəəkkəəkkə	xəəkkəə	xəəkkəəŋŋəi	xəəkkəəjini
lokkookko	lokkoo	lokkooŋŋoi	lokkoojini
gajakkookka	gajakkoo	gajakkooŋŋai	gajakkoojini
bəlikkeekkə	bəlikkee	bəlikkeeŋŋəi	bəlikkeejini
gəjjeekkə	gəjjee	gəjjeeŋŋəi	gəjjeejini
uurakka	uura	uuraŋŋai	uuraini
bөөrөkkө	bөөrө	bөөrөŋŋөi	bөөrөini
gatasikka	gatasi	gatasiŋŋai	gatasiini
өləsikkə	өləsi	өləsiŋŋəi	өləsiini
andusikka	andusi	andusiŋŋai	andusiini
moolisikka	moolisi	moolisiŋŋai	moolisiini
allausikka	allausi	allausiŋŋai	allausiini
dəptəkkə	dəptə	dəptəŋŋəi	dəptəini
bujaldakka	bujalda	bujaldaŋŋai	bujaldaini
xөөldөkkө	xөөldө	xөөldөŋŋөi	xөөldөini
xaagdakka	xaagda	xaagdaŋŋai	xaagdaini
orogdokko	orogdo	orogdoŋŋoi	orogdoini
undəkkə	undə	undəŋŋəi	undəini
kөjөөndөkkө	kөjөөndө	kөjөөndөŋŋөi	kөjөөndөini
beekkə	bee	beeŋŋəi	beejini
ookko	oo	ooŋŋoi	oojini
osikka	osi	osiŋŋai	osiini
			əsiini
budəkkə	budə	budəŋŋəi	budəini
gadakka	gada	gadaŋŋai	gadaini

III				IV
-ri[1]	-ri[2]- plus -tta	-ri-llaa	-ri-la-xam- plus -ba plus -ni	-ru
ŋənnee	ŋənneettə	ŋənneelləə	ŋənneeləxəmbəni	ŋənnəu
moollee	moolleetta	moolleellaa	moolleelaxambani	moollou
ŋənni	ŋənnittə	ŋənnilləə	ŋənniləxəxəmbəni	ŋənnu
sommi	sommitta	sommillaa	sommilaxambani	sommu
aunǰee	aunǰeetta	aunǰeellaa	aunǰeelaxambani	aundau
tokpee	tokpeetta	tokpeellaa	tokpeelaxambani	tokpou
silči	silčitta	silčillaa	silčilaxambani	siltu
bargi	bargitta	bargillaa	bargilaxambani	bargu
bakkee	bakkeetta	bakkeellaa	bakkeelaxambani	bakkau
palukkee	palukkeetta	palukkeellaa	palukkeelaxambani	palukkau
sapčikkee	sapčikkeetta	sapčikkeellaa	sapčikkeelaxambani	sapčikkau
xəəkkee	xəəkkeettə	xəəkkeelləə	xəəkkeeləxəmbəni	xəəkkəu
lokkee	lokkeetta	lokkeellaa	lokkeelaxambani	lokkou
gajakki	gajakkitta	gajakkillaa	gajakkilaxambani	gajakku
bəlikki	bəlikkittə	bəlikkilləə	bəlikkiləxəmbəni	bəlikku
gəǰǰi	gəǰǰittə	gəǰǰilləə	gəǰǰiləxəmbəni	gəǰǰu
uuri	uuritta	uurillaa	uurilaxambani	uuru
bɵɵri	bɵɵrittə	bɵɵrilləə	bɵɵriləxəmbəni	bɵɵru
gatasi	gatasitta	gatasillaa	gatasilaxambani	gatasu
ɵlɵsi	ɵlɵsittə	ɵlɵsilləə	ɵlɵsiləxəmbəni	ɵlɵsu
andusi	andusitta	andusillaa	andusilaxambani	andusu
moolisi	moolisitta	moolisillaa	moolisilaxambani	moolisu
allausi	allausitta	allausillaa	allausilaxambani	allausu
dəpči	dəpčittə	dəpčilləə	dəpčiləxəmbəni	dəptu
bujalǰi	bujalǰitta	bujalǰillaa	bujalǰilaxambani	bujaldu
xɵɵlǰi	xɵɵlǰittə	xɵɵlǰilləə	xɵɵlǰiləxəmbəni	xɵɵldu
xaagǰi	xaagǰitta	xaagǰillaa	xaagǰilaxambani	xaagdu
orogǰi	orogǰitta	orogǰillaa	orogǰilaxambani	orogdu
unǰi	unǰittə	unǰilləə	unǰiləxəmbəni	unu
kɵjɵɵnǰi	kɵjɵɵnǰittə	kɵjɵɵnǰilləə	kɵjɵɵnǰiləxəmbəni	kɵjɵɵnu
bii	biittə	biilləə	biiləxəmbəni	buu
oi	oitta	oillaa	oilaxambani	ou
osi	ositta	osillaa	osilaxambani	osu
əsi			əsiləxəmbəni	əǰǰee
buǰi	buǰittə	buǰilləə	buǰiləxəmbəni	budu
gaǰi	gaǰitta	gaǰillaa	gaǰilaxambani	gadu

V	VI	VII		
-bi-la-xam plus -ba	-ja	-mi[2]	-mǰee	-mǰikəə
ŋənəwiləxəmbə	ŋənəjə	ŋənəmi	ŋənəmǰee	ŋənəmǰikəə
moolowilaxamba	moolojo	moolomi	soŋomǰee	moolomǰikəə
ŋənuwiləxəmbə	ŋənujə	ŋənumi	ŋənumǰee	ŋənumǰikəə
somiwilaxamba	somijaa	somimi	nimərimǰee	somimǰikəə
aundawilaxamba	aundaja	aundami	əldəmǰee	əldəmǰikəə
tokpowilaxamba	tokpojo	tokpomi	tokpomǰee	tokpomǰikəə
siltuwilaxamba	siltuja	siltumi	siltumǰee	siltumǰikəə
bargiwilaxamba	bargija	bargimi	bargimǰee	bargimǰikəə
baawilaxamba	baaja	baami	baamǰee	baamǰikəə
paluwawilaxamba	paluwaja	paluwami	paluwamǰee	paluwamǰikəə
sapčigawilaxamba	sapčigaja	sapčigami	sapčigamǰee	sapčigamǰikəə
xəəgəwiləxəmbə	xəəgəjə	xəəgəmi	xəəgəmǰee	xəəgəmǰikəə
loowilaxamba	loojo	loomi	čolmoomǰee	loomǰikəə
gajauwilaxamba	gajauja	gajaumi	gajaumǰee	gajaumǰikəə
bəliiwiləxəmbə	bəliijə	bəliimi	čoimǰee	bəliimǰikəə
gəiwiləxəmbə	gəijə	gəimi	gəimǰee	gəimǰikəə
uuwilaxamba	uuja	uumi	uumǰee	uumǰikəə
bɵɵwiləxəmbə	bɵɵjɵ	bɵɵmi	soomǰee	bɵɵmǰikəə
gatappilaxamba	gataja	gatami	gatamǰee	gatamǰikəə
ɵlɵppiləxəmbə	ɵlɵjɵ	ɵlɵmi	eeromǰee	ɵlɵmǰikəə
anduppilaxamba	anduja	andumi	andumǰee	andumǰikəə
moolippilaxamba	moolija	moolimi	moolimǰee	moolimǰikəə
allauppilaxamba	allauja	allaumi	allaumǰee	allaumǰikəə
dəptuwiləxəmbə	dəptujə	dəptumi	dəptumǰee	dəptumǰikəə
bujalbilaxamba	bujalja	bujalmi		bujalmǰikəə
xɵɵlbiləxəmbə	xɵɵljɵ	xɵɵlmi		xɵɵlmǰikəə
xaagbilaxamba	xaagja	xaaŋmi	xaaŋmǰee	xaaŋmǰikəə
orogbilaxamba	orogjo	oroŋmi	oroŋmǰee	oroŋmǰikəə
umbiləxəmbə	ujə	umi	umǰee	umǰikəə
kəjɵɵmbiləxəmbə	kəjɵɵjɵ	kəjɵɵmi	dotolomǰee	kəjɵɵmǰikəə
biwwiləxəmbə	bijə	bimi	bimǰee	bimǰikəə
owwilaxamba	ojo	omi	omǰee	omǰikəə
oppilaxamba	ojo	omi		omǰikəə
		əmi		
bulbiləxəmbə		bulmi	bulmǰee	bulmǰikəə
gawwilaxamba	gaja	gami	gamǰee	gamǰikəə

VIII			IX	X
-ŋa- plus -pu plus -tta	-ŋi- plus -tta	-ŋassee[2]	-pee	-ta- plus -*ka
ŋənəŋəptə	ŋənəŋittə	ŋənəŋəssee	ŋənəpee	ŋənətəə
mooloŋopto	mooloŋitta	mooloŋossee	moolopee	moolotoo
ŋənuŋəptə	ŋənuŋittə	ŋənuŋəssee	ŋənupee	ŋənutəə
somiŋapta	somiŋitta	somiŋassee	somipee	somitaa
aundaŋapta	aundaŋittaa	aundaŋassee	aundapee	aundataa
tokpoŋopto	tokpoŋitta	tokpoŋossee	tokpopee	tokpotoo
siltuŋapta	siltuŋitta	siltuŋassee	siltupee	siltutaa
bargiŋapta	bargiŋitta	bargiŋassee	bargipee	bargitaa
baaŋapta	baaŋitta	baaŋassee	baapee	baataa
paluwaŋapta	paluwaŋitta	paluwaŋassee	paluwapee	paluwataa
sapčigaŋapta	sapčigaŋitta	sapčigaŋassee	sapčigapee	sapčigataa
xəəgəŋəptə	xəəgəŋittə	xəəgəŋəssee	xəəgəpee	xəəgətəə
looŋopto	looŋitta	looŋossee	loopee	lootoo
gajauŋapta	gajauŋitta	gajauŋassee	gajaupee	gajautaa
bəliiŋəptə	bəliiŋittə	bəliiŋəssee	bəliipee	bəliitəə
gəiŋəptə	gəiŋittə	gəiŋəssee	gəipee	gəitəə
uuŋapta	uuŋitta	uuŋassee	uupee	uutaa
bɵɵŋɵptɵ	bɵɵŋittə	bɵɵŋɵssee	bɵɵpee	bɵɵtɵɵ
gataŋapta	gataŋitta	gataŋassee	gatapee	gatataa
ɵlɵŋɵptɵ	ɵlɵŋittə	ɵlɵŋɵssee	ɵlɵpee	ɵlɵtɵɵ
anduŋapta	anduŋitta	anduŋassee	andupee	andutaa
mooliŋapta	mooliŋitta	mooliŋassee	moolipee	moolitaa
allauŋapta	allauŋitta	allauŋassee	allaupee	allautaa
dəptuŋəptə	dəptuŋittə	dəptuŋəssee	dəptupee	dəptutəə
bujalŋapta	bujalŋitta	bujalŋassee	bujalpee	bujaltaa
xɵɵlŋɵptɵ	xɵɵlŋittə	xɵɵlŋɵssee	xɵɵlpee	xɵɵltɵɵ
xaaŋapta	xaaŋitta	xaaŋassee	xaakpee	xaaktaa
oroŋopto	oroŋitta	oroŋossee	orokpee	oroktoo
uŋəptə	uŋittə	uŋəssee	uppee	uttəə
kɵjɵɵŋɵptɵ	kɵjɵɵŋittə	kɵjɵɵŋɵssee	kɵjɵɵppee	kɵjɵɵttɵɵ
biŋəptə	biŋittə	biŋəssee	bipee	bitəə
oŋopto	oŋitta	oŋossee	opee	otoo
oŋopto	oŋitta	oŋossee	opee	otoo
			əpee	
bulŋəptə	bulŋittə	bulŋəssee	bulpee	buttəə
gaŋapta	gaŋitta	gaŋassee	gapee	gattaa

X	XI	XII	XIII	XIV
-ttaari-	-ssaari-	-xan	-kačči	-kuta- plus -ni
ŋənəttəəri	ŋənəssəəri	ŋənəxə	ŋənəgəčči	ŋənəutənnee
moolottoori	moolossoori	mooloxo	moolowočči	mooloutannee
ŋənuttəəri	ŋənussəəri	ŋənuxə	ŋənuwəčči	ŋənuutənnee
somittaari	somissaari	somixa	somigačči	somuutannee
aundattaari	aundassaari	aundaxa	aundagačči	aundautannee
tokpottoori	tokpossoori	tokpoxo	tokpowočči	tokpoutannee
siltuttaari	siltussaari	siltuxa	siltuwačči	siltuutannee
bargittaari	bargissaari	bargixa	bargigačči	barguutannee
baattaari	baassaari	baaxa	baagačči	baawutannee
paluwattaari	paluwassaari	paluwaxa	paluwagačči	paluwautannee
sapčigattaari	sapčigassaari	sapčigaxa	sapčigagačči	sapčigautannee
xəəgəttəəri	xəəgəssəəri	xəəgəxə	xəəgəgəčči	xəəgəutənnee
loottoori	loossoori	looxo	loowočči	loowutannee
gajauttaari	gajaussaari	gajauxa	gajauwačči	gajauwutannee
bəliittəəri	bəliissəəri	bəliixə	bəliigəčči	bəliiwutənnee
gəittəəri	gəissəəri	gəixə	gəigəčči	gəjuutənnee
uuttaari	uussaari	uuxa	uuwačči	uuwutannee
bɵɵttɵɵri	bɵɵssɵɵri	bɵɵxɵ	bɵɵwɵčči	bɵɵwutənnee
gatattaari	gatassaari	gatači	gatagačči	gatautannee
ɵlɵttɵɵri	ɵlɵssɵɵri	ɵlɵči	ɵlɵwɵčči	ɵlɵutənnee
anduttaari	andussaari	anduči	anduwačči	anduutannee
moolittaari	moolissaari	mooliči	mooligačči	mooluutannee
allauttaari	allaussaari	allauči	allauwačči	allauwutannee
dəptuttəəri	dəptussəəri	dəptuxə	dəptuwəčči	dəptuutənnee
bujaltaari	bujalsaari	bujalči	bujalkačči	bujalkutannee
xɵɵltɵɵri	xɵɵlsɵɵri	xɵɵlči	xɵɵlkɵčči	xɵɵlkutənnee
xaaktaari	xaaksaari	xaakči	xaakkačči	xaakkutannee
oroktoori	oroksoori	orokči	orokkočči	orokkutannee
uttəəri	ussəəri	učči	ukkəčči	ukkutənnee
kɵjɵɵttɵɵri	kɵjɵɵssɵɵri	kɵjɵɵčči	kɵjɵɵkkɵčči	kɵjɵɵkkutənnee
bittəəri	bissəəri	bičči	bigəčči	biwutənnee
ottoori	ossoori	očči	owočči	outannee
ottoori	ossoori	očči	owočči	outannee
		əčči	əgəčči	əutənnee
buttəəri	bussəəri	bučči	bulkəčči	bulkutənnee
gattaari	gassaari	gačči	gagačči	gautannee

Examples for Table IV.

Stem	Preceding Ending	-l	Following Ending
ŋənə-	-ja	ŋənəjəltu	-su
	-ŋa	ŋənəŋəltə	-tta
		ŋənəŋəlluu	
	-ta	ŋənətəlluu	-ijuu
	-ra¹	ŋənnəəlluu	
	-ra²	ŋənnəəl	
	-ra-ŋŋa	ŋənnəəŋŋəl	
	-ri-llaa	ŋənneelləəl	
	-ŋa-tta	ŋənəŋəttəl	
	-ta ⎫ -kka -ra¹ ⎭	ŋənətəkkəl ŋənnəəkkəl	
	-ŋa ⎫ -ta ⎬ -soo -ra¹ ⎭	ŋənəŋəsøøl ŋənətəsøøl ŋənnəəsøøl	

Examples for Table V.

Stem	Preceding Ending	-bi	-pu	-si	-su	-ni	-či	Following Ending
	-ja-l				ŋənəjəltu			
	-ru				ŋənnəusu			
	-ttaari				ŋənəttəərisu			
	-ssaari				ŋənəssəərisu			
	-ŋa	[ŋənəŋittə]	ŋənəŋəptə			[ŋənəŋəttə]	[ŋənəŋəltə, ŋənəŋəttəl]	-tta
		[ŋənəŋijjuu]	ŋənəŋəpuijuu	ŋənəŋəsijjuu	ŋənəŋəsuijuu	[ŋənəŋəijuu]	[ŋənəŋəlluu]	-ijuu
	-ra-ŋa	[ŋənnəəŋŋii]	ŋənnəəŋəpui	ŋənnəəŋəsii	ŋənnəəŋəsui	[ŋənnəəŋŋəi]	[ŋənnəəŋŋəl]	-i
ŋənə-	-ta	ŋənətəmigə	ŋənətəpuwə	ŋənətəsigə	ŋənətəsuwə	[ŋənətəə]	[ŋənətəkkəl]	-*ka
dəp-	-ra[1]	dəptəmigə	dəptəpuwə	dəptəsigə	dəptəsuwə	[dəptəkkə]	[dəptəkkəl]	
bul-	-ra[2]	dəptəmi	dəptəpu	dəptəsi	dəptəsu	[dəptə]	[dəptəl]	
	-ri-la	ŋənneeləmi	ŋənneeləpu	bujiləsi	bujiləsu	[ŋənneelləə]	[ŋənneelləəl]	
	-xan	ŋənəxəmbi	ŋənəxəpu	ŋənəxəsi	ŋənəxəsu	ŋənəxəni	ŋənəxəči	
	-ri-la-xam	ŋənneeləxəmbi	ŋənneeləxəpu	ŋənneeləxəsi	ŋənneeləxəsu	ŋənneeləxəni	ŋənneeləxəči	
	-ri[1]	ŋənneewi	ŋənneepu	ŋənneesi	ŋənneesu	ŋənneeni	ŋənneeči	
	-ŋassee[1]	ŋənəŋəsseewwee	ŋənəŋəsseeppɵɵ	ŋənəŋəsseesi	ŋənəŋəsseesu	ŋənəŋəsseeni	ŋənəŋəsseeči	
	-ra-i	ŋənnəəjiwwee	ŋənnəəjippɵɵ	ŋənnəəjisi	ŋənnəəjisu	ŋənnəəjini	ŋənnəəjiči	
	-kuta	ŋənəutəwwee	ŋənəutəppɵɵ	ŋənəutəssee	ŋənəutəssɵɵ	ŋənəutənnee	ŋənəutəččee	

Examples for Tables VI.–IX.

VI.

Stem	Preceding Ending	-tta
ŋənə-	-ŋa -p	ŋənəŋəptə
	-ŋa -l	ŋənəŋəltə
	-ŋa	ŋənəŋəttə
	-ŋi	ŋənəŋittə
	-ri	ŋənneettə

VII.

Stem	Preceding Ending	-*ka	Following Ending
ŋənə- / dəp-	-ta -mi	ŋənətəmigə	
	-ta -pu	ŋənətəpuwə	
	-ta -si	ŋənətəsigə	
	-ta -su	ŋənətəsuwə	
	-ra[1] -mi	dəptəmigə	
	-ra[1] -pu	dəptəpuwə	
	-ra[1] -si	dəptəsigə	
	-ra[1] -su	dəptəsuwə	
	-ta	ŋənətəə	
	-ta	ŋənətəkkə	-l
	-ra[1]	dəptəkkə	-l

VIII.

Stem	Preceding Ending	-see	-soo
ŋənə-	-ŋa	ŋənəŋəsee	ŋənəŋəsɵɵ
	-ta	ŋənətəsee	ŋənətəsɵɵ
	-ra[1]	ŋənnəəsee	ŋənnəəsɵɵ

IX.

Stem	Preceding Ending	-i
ŋənə-	-ra-ŋa -pu	ŋənnəəŋəpui
	-ra-ŋa -si	ŋənnəəŋəsii
	-ra-ŋa -su	ŋənnəəŋəsui
	-ra-ŋŋi	ŋənnəəŋŋii
	-ra-ŋŋa	ŋənnəəŋŋəi

Illustrations of numerals, abbreviations and symbols

Arabic numerals indicate classes.

1. indicates the class with the basic stem ending in V.
2. indicates the class with the basic stem ending in C.

These classes are subdivided as follows:

1.1 indicates the class with the basic stem ending in CV.

1.2 indicates the class with the basic stem VV and the basic stem ending in VV.

2.1 indicates the class with the basic stem ending in l.

2.2 indicates the class with the basic stem ending in g.

2.3 indicates the class with the basic stem ending in n.

These classes are further subdivided as follows:

1.11 indicates the class with the basic stem VCV and the basic stem ending in VCV.

1.12 indicates the class with the basic stem ending in CCV.

Further subdivisions indicate subclasses with basic stems which have different final vowel phonemes.

0. indicates the class of verbs that are inflected in different ways from those of Classes 1. and 2. in spite of the coincidence of the last phoneme or phonemes in the stems accompanied by the verb ending *-raa*, etc. This class is also divided into subclasses.

Each Roman numeral indicates a set of alternants of the verb stems of each class accompanied by the same ending. V stands for a vowel phoneme and C for a consonant phoneme. *V* stands for any vowel phoneme other than /o/or/ɵ/. *V* stands for any vowel phoneme other than /o,ɵ,u/. *a* stands for /a/or/ə/, *o* for /o/or/ɵ/. *C* stands for the consonant phoneme identical with the following one.

The marks —, – or – indicate the first part of a stem. The same mark used in each class indicates the same part of a stem.

Parentheses ( ) indicate a part that the stems of some verbs do not have.

Hyphens -, ˊ, ˶, ˋ, ˵, ·, ·· separate morphological units. Hyphens ˊ, ˶, ˋ, ˵, ·, ·· and small numerals (before or after hyphens) indicate mutual correlations. The presence of a hyphen after a stem, an ending or a combination of endings that is referred to separately indicates that they are always followed by some ending. A hyphen with or without a small numeral is also used to indicate the alternants of the endings that are occasionally added to a stem, an ending, or a combination of endings. However, in such cases a hyphen and a small numeral are put into small parentheses.

Notes

1) The material for this paper was acquired from an Orok woman, Napka. This informant was born about 1910 in southern Sakhalin and emigrated to Hokkaidô in 1947.

Orok has the vowel phonemes /ə, a, o, ɵ, u, i, e /and the consonant phonemes /p, t, č, k, b,d, ǰ, g, m, n, ɲ, ŋ, l, r, s, x, w, j/. In Orok, as in Tungus in general, there is vowel harmony. Thus the phonemes /a/ and /o/ do not usually co-exist in the same word with the phonemes /ə/ and /ɵ/. Also, /o/ may not succeed /a, u/ as the next vowel phoneme in a word. /ɵ/ may not succeed /ə, u/ as the next vowel phoneme in a word. However, /oo/ may succeed /a, u/, and /ɵɵ/ may succeed /ə, u/.

2) Here, as well as in the preceding article, "The Substantive Inflection of Orok," although a form is a combination of two elements, this form is not divided into its two constituents in the following cases: (1) when the doubling of the next-to-last consonant of the first element compensates for the loss of the initial consonant of the second element, and/or (2) when there is the reciprocal assimilation or the contraction of the neighbouring vowels of the two elements. In addition to this, if a form is a combination of a vowel-final element plus a vowel-initial element that is also the latter element of such an undivided form as mentioned above (or the alternant of the latter element of such an undivided form), we never divide the form into two constituents.

3) Orok does not tolerate the phoneme combinations /*ti, *di, *te, *de/. The next-to-last consonant *t* in the basic stems of the verbs of Class 1.1 alternates with *č* before *i* or *e* in the alternate stems, and similarly *d* with *ǰ*.

4) Genetically, the alternate stems of Classes 1.1 and 0.1 are, excluding the cases in which they are later analogic new-formations, derived from the combination of stems identical with the basic stems plus one of the verb endings **-ra*, **-ri* and **-ru*. However, such changes as the above did not take place in the combination of the stems of Classes 1.1 and 0.1 plus the exclamatory verb-ending **-roo* or **-raa*, which is derived from the combination of the verb ending **-ru* or **-ra* plus the exclamatory ending **-a*.

5) Genetically, the verb ending *-ru* (~-*su*) might result from the contraction of **-ra* (~**-si*) and the imperative ending **-u* (or **-Cu* with the loss of the initial consonant).

6) Genetically, *-ttaari* and *-ssaari* seem to be derived from combinations of endings.

7) It is still open to question whether the form *-si* added to the stems of Class 0.2 has genetically the same origin as the forms *-ra*, *-da*, *-ta* added to the stems of the other classes.

8) The verb endings *-ra*^{1}- and *-ra*^{2} may be regarded as the alternants of the same ending, and the occurrence of each of these is grammatically conditioned. Genetically, however, *-ri*^{1} might result from the contraction of **-ra* and an unidentified element **-i* (or **-Ci* with the loss of the initial consonant).

9) Genetically, *-ŋassee*^{1}- seems to be derived from a combination of endings.

10) The verb ending *-rraa*, such as in *uttəə niirrəə somirraa oini* 'He is opening and shutting the door', is regarded as the juxtapositional form of the verb ending *-ra*.

11) Genetically, we believe *-mi*^{2}, *-mari*, *-kačči*, *-kaččeeri*, *-ŋassee*^{2} and *-ŋasseeri* result from the following changes: **-m(i)* plus the singular reflexive ending **-bi*→*-mi*^{2}; **-m(i)* plus the plural reflexive ending **-bari*→*-mari*; some ending plus the sing. reflexive ending **-bi*→*-kačči*; the same ending as above plus the pl. reflexive ending **-bari*→*-kaččeeri*; **-ŋassee* plus the sing. reflexive ending **-bi*→*-ŋassee*^{2}; **-ŋassee* plus the pl. reflexive ending **-bari*→*-ŋasseeri*.

12) Genetically, we believe *-ri*²- and *-ŋi-* result from the following changes: **-ra* plus **-mi* or **-bi*→*-ri*²-; **-ŋa* plus **-mi* or **-bi*→*-ŋi-*.

13) *-mǰee* and *-mǰikəə* seem to consist of the following constituents: *-m-ǰee* and *-m-ǰi-kəə*. However, the details are not given here.

14) Genetically, the combinations of endings *-ŋŋi-i*, *-ŋŋa-i* and *-ŋŋa-l* seem to result from the following changes: **-ŋa*+**-mi* or **-bi*+ **-i*→*-ŋŋi-i*, or **-ŋa*+**-mi* or **-bi*+**-Ci*→**-ŋi-Ci*→*-ŋŋii*; **-ŋa*+**-Ca*+**-i*→**-ŋŋa* or **-ŋŋaa*+**-i*→*-ŋŋa-i*, or **-ŋa-Ci*→*-ŋŋai*; **-ŋa*+ **-Ca*+ **-l*→*-ŋŋa-l*, **-ŋa*+ **-Ca*+ **-i*+ **-l*→**-ŋŋa* or **-ŋŋaa*+**-i*+**-l*→**-ŋŋa-i-l*→*-ŋŋa-l*, or **-ŋa-Ci-l*→**-ŋŋai-l*→*-ŋŋa-l*. *-llaa* seems to be derived from **-la-Ca*. The **-Ca* here is an unidentified ending. The **-Ci* here is what the older form of **-i* might possibly have been in former times. *-bi-* in *-bi-la-xam* may possibly be derived from the verb-stem-forming suffix **-bu* (cf. Section **9**) plus **-ri* identical with *-ri-* in *-ri-la-xam-*.

15) Genetically, the alternants of -**bboo* are derived from the verb-stem-forming suffix **-bu* plus **-ra*. *-pula* corresponds to Negidal *-pla* as in *wāpla* 'killed (slain)', etc. (according to K. M. Myl'nikova and V. I. Cincius, Materialy po issledovaniju negidal'skogo jazyka, Tungusskij sbornik I, p. 174), Lamut *-tla*, *-tlə* as in *xūnātla* 'sawdust', etc. (according to V. I. Cincius and L. D. Rises, Russko-ėvenskij slovar', p. 719), and Udehe *-ptilə* as in *xūptilə* 'sawdust', etc. (according to E. R. Šnejder, Kratkij udėjsko-russkij slovar', p. 82).

16) There is another set of four personal endings: *-bi*, *-pu*, *-si*, *-su*. Substantives, adjectives and the verbal noun *bičči* 'was, were (copula)' end with these when they are used as the predicate of a complete sentence.

17) Genetically, *-wwee*, *-ppoo*, *-ssee*, *-ssoo*, *-nnee* and *-ččee*, excluding the cases in which they are analogic new-formations, seem to be derived from **-wi*, **-pu*, **-si*, **-su*, **-ni* or **-či* plus an unidentified ending **-Ca*. This ending may possibly be the simple accusative ending **-ba* or **-pa*.

18) Genetically, *-kka*, an alternant of **-ka* might possibly be derived from **-ka* plus an unidentified ending **-Ca* (perhaps the same as given in note 14 ?).

19) Genetically, *-see* and *-soo* seem to be derived from the second-person endings **-si* and **-su* plus the interrogative ending **-ka*.

20) Genetically, each of the endings mentioned in Section **14** is derived from an ending plus the interrogative ending **-ka* or the exclamatory ending **-a*.

21) For the inflection of substantives see my article referred to in note 2.

Supplementary Notes

A note to Table IV. In the word-final position, this plural ending has free alternation between *-l* and *-li*.

A note to Table V. Each form in brackets [ ] is the ending or the combination of endings complementary as to person to the combinations of the preceding ending(s) plus a personal ending (plus the following ending given at right). The occurrences of the alternants of each personal ending *-mi* ~*-wi* ~*-wwee*, *-pu* ~ *-ppoo*, *-si* ~*-ssee*, *-su* ~*-ssoo*, *-ni* ~*-nnee*, *-či* ~*-ččee* are determined grammatically by the preceding verb endings.

A note to Table VII. The occurrences of the alternants *-kka*, *-kka-* and *=kko*, *=kko-*

are grammatically conditioned: they occur after the verb endings *-ta-* and *-ra*[1]-, but in the former case always accompanied by *-l*.

（本研究は昭和33年度文部省科学研究費補助金を受けた）

This article is a revised version of my previous paper with the same title, which was published in *Kokugo Kenkyu* No. 9 (Kokugakuin Daigaku Kokugokenkyukai, Tokyo,December, 1959), pp. 34–73.

Addenda

1. On the verb ending *-si* mentioned in Note 7 see pp. 353 ff. in this book.

2. For a closer view of the *-ri* mentioned in Note 8 see p. 382 in this book.

3. On the combination of the verb ending *-ra* plus the first-person sing. ending *-mi* mentioned in Sections **5**(b) and **11** and Table V. The verb accompanied by the verb ending *-ra* and the personal ending *-mi* appears as the predicate of the negative complete sentence composed of the adverb *əččeeli* 'not yet' and a verb with the above-mentioned endings *-ra -mi*, thus *əččeeli saarami* 'I do not yet know' (the verb stem *saa-* means 'to know')'.

In one view, it may be considered that the above-mentioned *-ra* is the finite-verb-forming ending *-ra*[1] in distinction from the verbal-noun-forming ending *-ra*[2] in the negative sentence, such as *əsiwi saara* 'I do not know' (the *ə-* is the stem of the negative verb and the *saa-* is the same stem as given above).

4. For a new view of the *-kka* mentioned in Note 18 see pp. 378, 384 in this book.

5. The morpho-phonological fusion that is mentioned as genetical or diachronical facts in the above notes may also be dealt with in static or synchronical descriptions.

6. On the verb ending *-ŋa-* mentioned in Sections **5**(a), **12**,**13**. I add the following examples of the negative sentence that consists of the negating verb *ə-* accompanied by the verb ending *-ŋə* (and the personal ending) and the (negated) verb accompanied by the verb ending *-ra*^{2}. The verb *əŋə* (plus the personal ending) is the finite verb of the complete sentence. The personal endings that are added to *əŋə* are the first-person sing. *-bi*, the first-person pl. *-pu*, the second-person sing. *-si* and the second-person pl. *-su*. In the case of the third-person no personal ending but the plural ending *-l* appears.

Examples are: *bii əŋəbi ŋənnəə* 'I shall not go', *buu əŋəpu ŋənnəə* 'We shall not go', *sii əŋəsi ŋənnəə* 'You (sing.) shall not go', *suu əŋəsu ŋənnəə* 'You (pl.) shall not go', *tari nari əŋə ŋənnəə* 'He will not go', *tari narisal əŋəl ŋənnəə* or *tari narisal əŋə ŋənnəəl* 'They will not go'.

7. I referred to the verb form *ŋənəŋijjuu* in Section **13** of this article. However, in 1962 I obtained *ŋənəŋŋijjuu* rather than the preceding form from the same informant. If this was due to mishearing on my part, then *ŋənəŋijjuu* is incorrect, and the form *ŋənəŋŋijjuu* is correct. If that is the case, then it would be necessary to replace *ŋənəŋijjuu* in Section **13** with *ŋənəŋŋijjuu*; to change [*-ŋi-jjuu*] in Table V with [*-ŋŋi -jjuu*]; to insert *-ŋŋi-* in a new line between *-ŋi-* in the preceding line and *-raŋŋi-* in the following line in Section **7** ; and to place *-ŋŋi-* after *-ŋi-* (in two places) in Note 12.

8. For details on the combination of the verb ending *-ra*^{1}-, *-ta-*, or *-ŋa-* (plus the personal ending or the plural formational element *-l*) with the ending *-ijuu*, cf. Sections **5**, **7**, **13**. No personal ending appears for this kind of the third person form.

The verb ending *-ra*^{1}- (plus the plural formational element *-l*) plus the ending *-ijuu* (in the third-person form) indicate 'a present action one cannot confirm'.

The verb ending *-ta-* (plus the plural formational element *-l*) plus the ending *-ijuu* (in the third-person form) indicate 'a past action one cannot confirm'.

The verb ending *-ŋa-* (plus the personal ending or the plural formational element *-l*) plus the ending *-ijuu* indicate 'a future action one will not be able to confirm'. As to the personal ending that is inserted, the first-person pl. *-pu*, the second-person sing. *-si* and the second-person pl. *-su* are used. The first-person sing. verb form includes the personal verb ending *-ŋi-* (*-ŋŋi-* ?), which is a result of the fusion of the verb ending *-ŋa-* and the first-person sing. ending *-bi*.

Examples :

-ra^{1}*-* plus *-ijuu* *tari nari xaiwaa ŋənnəəjjuu* 'I wonder (or I wish to know) through which place he is going', *tari narisal xaiwaa ŋənnəəlluu* 'I wonder (or I wish to know) through which place they are going'.

-ta- plus *-ijuu* *tari nari ŋənətəijuu* 'I wonder (or I wish to know) whether he went', *tari narisal ələ ŋənətəlluu* 'I wonder (or I wish to know) whether they went yet'.

-ŋa- plus *-ijuu* *bii xooni ŋənəŋi(ŋŋi?) jjuu* 'However shall I go? (I want to go somehow or other)', *buu xooni ŋənəŋəpuijuu* 'However shall we go? (We want to go somehow or other)', *sii xooni ŋənəŋəsijjuu* 'How will you (sing.) go?' *suu xooni ŋənəŋəsuijuu* 'How will you (pl.) go?' *tari nari xoon xətuŋəijuu* 'I wonder how he will cut [it]', *tari narisal xoon xətuŋəlluu* 'I wonder how they will cut [it]'.

I did not obtain from the informant Napka the first/second-person (sing./pl.) present and past forms parallel to the third-person (sing./pl.) present and past finite verb forms *ŋənnəəjjuu* and *ŋənətəijuu*. She had doubts about the actual use of such first/second person (sing./pl.) past forms.

9. The combination of the verb ending *-ŋa-* plus *-iǰi-* (or *-iǰǰi*, *-iǰǰeeri*)

(plus a personal ending after the *-iǰi-*) signifies 'for fear that one should (may) ·····'. Semantically the *-ŋaiǰi-*, *-ŋaiǰǰi-* and *-ŋaiǰǰeeri-* are in contrast with the *-buddoo-*, *-buǰǰi* and *-buddoori* given below. The personal endings that are added to the *-iǰi-* are as follows : the first-person sing. *-wi*, pl. *-ppoo*, the second-person sing. *-si*, pl. *-su*, the third-person *-ni*, and the third person pl. *-či* (according to the informant Ǝəktəŋgu). The *-iǰǰi* is the reflexive sing. alternant of the *-iǰi-* and the *-iǰǰeeri* is the reflexive pl. alternant of the *-iǰi-*. The above *-ǰi-*, *-ǰǰi* and *-ǰǰeeri* seem to be substantive endings. Assumably the *-ǰi-* is the instrumental case-ending and the *-ǰǰi* and *-ǰǰeeri* are the sing. or pl. reflexive instrumental case-ending. Accordingly I consider the *-i-* to be a verbal-noun-forming suffix. This combination of endings is added to the verb-stem forms of Set VII (see Table I and Examples for Addenda).

Some examples are: *dəptuŋəiǰini dapaǰǰini* 'For fear the baby should eat[it], he takes[it]away', *uuŋaiǰini xərəssini* 'For fear he should take a boat, she prevents [him]'.

10. In the combination of the verb ending *-ri-* plus the ending *-li-* plus the personal or reflexive ending, the ending *-li-* appears. This ending seems to be a verbal-noun-forming ending meaning 'likelihood'. This combination of endings is added to the verb-stem forms of Set III (see Table I and Examples for Addenda). The personal or reflexive endings that are added are as follows : the first-person sing. *-wi*, the first-person pl. *-pu*, the second-person sing. *-si*, the second-person pl. *-su*, the third-person *-ni*, the third-person pl. *-či*, the reflexive sing. *-wi*, and the reflexive pl. *-wari*.

Some examples are: *dabǰilini* 'It is likely that he will win', *məənə moolleelini* 'He is likely to go to gather firewood by himself', *simanneelini* 'It is likely to snow', *xaali ŋənneelinee* 'When is it likely that he will go?' *bɵɵrilini taani* or *bɵɵriltaani* (syncope) 'It is likely that he will give [it]', *xaaliddaa bujiliwiddəə əsiwi saara* 'I do not know when I shall die', *čimanaa karumasilisi* 'You are likely to receive [your] wages tomorrow'.

Further in the northern dialects of Uilta the verb form that is composed of the stem, the ending *-li-* and a personal ending is found. It conveys a different shade of meaning.

11. We find the verb ending *-bukki* in the northern dialects of Uilta. This ending indicates 'customary action'. The personal endings are not added to the *-bukki*. The plural formational element *-l* is added to the *-bukki* and indicates 'the doers (plural) of the action.' The verb form ending in *-bukki* is accompanied by *bičči* (the verbal noun of the verb *-bi* 'to be') and represents 'customary action in the past'. The ending *-bukki* may be analyzed into the verbal-noun-forming suffix *-bu-*[3] and the verb ending *-kki*. The *-bu-*[3] alternates in the following way: *-bu-*~*-pu-*~*-wu-*. The *-wu-* appears after the basic-stem-final VV- of the verbs of Class 1.2. The *-bu-* appears after the stem-final *m* of the verbs of Class 2.3 and the *-pu-* appears after the basic-stem-final vowel of the verbs of Class 0.2. The basic-stem-final CV of the verbs of Class 1.1 and *-bu-*[3] are fused. The basic-stem-final *-p-tu-* of the verbs of Class 0.3 and *-bu-*[3] are also fused.

Some examples are: *waawukki* (*waa-* 'to kill, to catch (beast, fish)' of Class 1.2), *iwambukki* (*iwan-* 'to make or feed a fire' of Class 2.3), *pulipukki* (*puli-* 'to go, to wander' of Class 0.2), *ŋənnəukki* (*ŋənə-* 'go' of Class 1.1), *dəptukki* (*dəp-tu-* 'to eat' of Class 0.3).

12. The endings *-buddoo-*, *-bujji*, *-buddoori* may be appended to the group of converb-forming endings. As to their origin, there is a possibility that these endings are composed of the verbal-noun-forming suffix *-bu-*[4] and a designative case ending of substantive inflection, i. e., *-ddoo-*, *-jji* or *-ddoori*.

The ending *-buddoo-* is a simple verb ending meaning 'in order that one other than the subject of the main sentence may do... (purpose)'. This ending is always accompanied by one of the following personal endings: the first person sing. -*wwee* and pl. -*ppoo*; the second person sing. -*si* and pl. -*su*; and the third person -*ni* and the third person pl. -*či*. Some example sentences are: *somibuddooni puttəə xəwəčču* 'Call[my] boy in order that he shuts[the door]', *dəppee bargibuddooni səsuččini* 'He asks [his wife] to prepare a meal'.

The second ending -*bujji* is a singular reflexive verb ending; and the third ending -*buddoori* is a plural reflexive verb ending. These two endings resulted from the fusion of the above-mentioned -*buddoo*- and a reflexive ending -*bi* (sing.) or -*bari* (pl.). They mean 'in order that the subject (sing. or pl.) of the main sentence may do ··· (purpose)'.

These three endings are added without any alternation to the verb-stem forms of Set V (see Table I and Examples for Addenda).

Examples for Addenda 9, 10 and 12

	-ri-li-ni	-ŋa-i-ǰi-ni	-bu-ddoo-ni
1.111	ŋənneelini	ŋənəŋəiǰini	ŋənəbuddooni
1.112	moolleelini	mooloŋoiǰini	moolobuddooni
1.113	ŋənnilini	ŋənuŋəiǰini	ŋənubuddɵɵni
1.114	sommilini	somiŋaiǰini	somibuddooni
1.121	aunǰeelini	aundaŋaiǰini	aundabuddooni
1.122	tokpeelini	tokpoŋoiǰini	tokpobuddooni
1.123	silčilini	siltuŋaiǰini	siltubuddooni
1.124	bargilini	bargiŋaiǰini	bargibuddooni
0.1111	bakkeelini	baaŋaiǰini	baabuddooni
0.1112	palukkeelini	paluwaŋaiǰini	paluwabuddooni
	sapčikkeelini	sapčigaŋaiǰini	sapčigabuddooni
	xəəkkeelini	xəəgəŋəiǰini	xəəgəbuddɵɵni
0.112	lookkeelini	looŋoiǰini	loobuddooni
0.113	gajakkilini	gajauŋaiǰini	gajaubuddooni
0.114	bəlikkilini	bəliiŋəiǰini	bəliibuddɵɵni
0.12	gəǰǰilini	gəiŋəiǰini	gəibuddɵɵni
1.2	uurilini	uuŋaiǰini	uubuddooni
	bɵɵrilini	bɵɵŋɵiǰini	bɵɵbuddɵɵni
0.211	gatasilini	gataŋaiǰini	gatabuddooni
	ɵlɵsilini	ɵlɵŋɵiǰini	ɵlɵbuddɵɵni
	andusilini	anduŋaiǰini	andubuddooni
0.212	moolosilini	mooliŋaiǰini	moolibuddooni
0.22	allausilini	allauŋaiǰini	allaubuddooni
0.3	dəpčilini	dəptuŋəiǰini	dəptubuddɵɵni
2.1	bujalǰilini	bujalŋaiǰini	bujalbuddooni
	xɵɵlǰilini	xɵɵlŋɵiǰini	xɵɵlbuddɵɵni
2.2	xaagǰilini	xaaŋŋaiǰini	xaagbuddooni
	orogǰilini	oroŋŋoiǰini	orogbuddooni
2.3	unǰilini	uŋəiǰini	umbuddɵɵni
	kɵjɵɵnǰilini	kɵjɵɵŋɵiǰini	kɵjɵɵmbuddɵɵni
Irregular Verbs	biilini	biŋəiǰini	bibuddɵɵni
	oilini	oŋoiǰini	obuddooni
	osilini	oŋoiǰini	obuddooni
	əsilini	əŋəiǰini	əbuddɵɵni
	buǰilini	bulŋəiǰini	bulbuddɵɵni
	gaǰilini	gaŋaiǰini	gabuddooni

Orok Verb-Stem-Formative Suffixes

In Orok, a dialect of Tungus,[1] verbs are inflected mainly by adding various endings (verb endings and other endings) to verb stems. Verb stems are grouped into several classes according to differences of inflection.[2] (See Table I.[3])

Verb stems are also divided into primary stems and secondary stems. A primary stem is not divisible into a stem and a suffix; a secondary stem is divided into a stem and a suffix. This stem, in turn, is either a primary stem that is not divisible, or a secondary stem that is divided into a stem and a suffix. However, this stem, in turn, will be analysed in the same way as above. Accordingly, a secondary stem contains one or more suffixes. A verb-stem-formative suffix is one which can be the final suffix in a secondary stem functioning as a verb stem. In the description below we call this suffix a verb suffix. A verb suffix follows a stem that functions alone without a suffix as a verb stem or as a substantive, adjective or adverb stem, or follows a stem which does not appear without a suffix. A large number of adjective stems also function as substantive stems.

We shall deal with a number of verb suffixes below. A form in thick type is the basic form of a suffix. Some verb suffixes have variants occurring after different stems. Some verb or substantive stems have the basic form and one or more variants. Such a stem appears as a variant when accompanied by a certain suffix. The other stems, however, have only the basic form, i. e., they appear always as one and the same form.

-boon- (~ *-bɵɵn-* ~ *-poon-* ~ *-pɵɵn-* ~ *-woon-* ~ *-wɵɵn-* ~ *-oon-* ~ *-ɵɵn-*).

This is a causative-passive suffix. It appears after a verb stem. Verb stems with this suffix belong to Class 2.3. *-boon-* and *-bɵɵn-* appear after —*l*-, —*g*- or —*n* (→*m*)- ; *-poon-* and *-pɵɵn-* after —V- belonging to Class 0.2; *-woon-* and *-wɵɵn-* after –VV- belonging to Class 1.2; and *-oon-* and *-ɵɵn-* after –p-. In verbs belonging to Classes 1.111, 1.112, 1.121, 1.122, 0.1111, 0.1112 and 0.112 the stem and the suffix *-*bun-* (a non-existent form)are fused. In verbs belonging to Classes 1.113, 1.114, 1.123, 1.124, and 0.12 the stem and the suffix *-boon-* are fused. The details are given in Table I. After some irregular verb stems CV-, *-wwoon-* or *-wwɵɵn-* appears. After *o-*[2], *-poon-* appears. E. g., *ŋənnəun-* 'to make go' (: *ŋənə-* 'to go'), *waa-woon-* 'to make kill, to be killed' (: *waa-* 'to kill'). Further examples are given in Table I below.

-bu-[1] (~ *-wú-* ~ *-u-*). A transitive suffix. This suffix appears after a verb stem. Verb stems with this suffix belong to Class 1.113, 1.123 or 1.2. Some examples are:

(After —*l*-, —*g*- or —*n* (→*m*)-, *-bu-*) *meel-bu-* 'to wake [somebody]' (: *meel-* 'to wake'), *xaag-bu-* 'to discharge [a load], to take [a pot] off the fire' (: *xaag-* '(of a boat) to come to land'), *miirəm-bu-* 'to bring a woman for marriage' (: *miirən-* 'to go to a man for marriage').

(After –VV-, *-wu-*) *ii-wu-* 'to allow in, to bring in' (: *ii-* 'to enter').

(After –*p*-, *-u-*) *dalup-u-* 'to fill [something] up' (: *dalup-* 'to be filled up').

In verbs belonging to Class 1.1 or 0.1 the stem and the suffix -bu-[1] are fused. Some examples are : *pulləu-* 'to leave (to allow to remain)' (: *pulə-* 'to be left (to remain)'), *təttuu-* 'to clothe' (: *tətu-* 'to put on (to wear)'), *tattuu-* 'to teach' (: *tači-* 'to get into the habit of, to learn'), *tuksau-* 'to make run' (: *tuksa-* 'to run'), *baljuu-* 'to make multiply' (: *balji-* 'to be born, to live').

-bu-[2] (~ *-pu-* ~ *-wu-* ~ *-u-*). This suffix indicates that the doer of the action expressed by a verb with this suffix is not referred to. It appears after a verb stem. The suffix concerned is ordinarily accompanied by the verb ending *-ri*[1] or *-mi*[1].[4)] For example, *ŋənnəu-ri* 'going' (: *ŋənə-* 'to go'). *-bu-* appears after —*l-*, —*g-* or —*n* (→*m*)- ; *–pu-* after —V- belonging to Class 0.2 and *o-*[2]; *-wu-* after –VV- belonging to Class 1.2 ; and *-u-* after *–p-*. In verbs belonging to Class 1.1 or 0.1 the stem and the suffix *-bu-*[2] are fused. The details are given in Table I. Further, after some irregular verb stems CV-, *-wwu-* appears. Examples of this suffix are given in Table I below.

-či-. A durative-iterative suffix. This suffix follows (1) a verb stem, (2) a substantive stem, or (3) a stem which does not appear without a suffix as a verb or substantive stem. We find instances of this suffix added to the basic stem ending in V, *l* or *n*. Verb stems with this suffix belong to Class 1.114. The stem-final *l* and *n* are dropped. Some examples are :

(1) *itə-či-* 'to keep on seeing' (: *itə-* 'to see'), *silo-či-* 'to keep on roasting fish on skewers' (: *silo-* 'to roast fish on skewers'), *somi-či-* 'to shut [the door] many times' (: *somi-* 'to shut [the door]'), *aunda-či-* 'to stop for several nights (away from home)' (: *aunda-* 'to lodge for the night'), *tugbu-či-* 'to haggle over a price' (: *tugbu-* 'to drop, to lower, to lay [an egg]', *dəgǰi-či-* 'to continue to burn [something]' (: *dəgǰi-* 'to burn [something]'), *bɵɵ-či-* 'to give many times' (: *bɵɵ-* 'to give'), *loo-či-* 'to hang up many times' (: *loo-* 'to hang up'), *ui-či-* 'to tie many times' (: *ui-* 'to tie'), *buja-či* 'to continue to break [something]' (: *bujal-* 'to break [something]'), *xətu-či-* 'to snap many [strings]' (:*xətun-* 'to snap [a string]').

(2) *moičča-či-* 'to fire shots with a gun' (: *moičča-la-* 'to fire a shot with a gun,' *moiččan-* 'a gun').

(3) *gida-či-* 'to put in many times' (: *gida-la-* 'to put in once, to put [a ring] on a finger'), *tørøŋø-či-* 'to trample' (: *tørøŋø-lø-* 'to stamp on'), *ŋooxi-či-* 'to smell [something] continuously' (: *ŋooxi-la-* 'to smell [something] once'), *suukpi-či-* 'to flip with the point of something repeatedly' (: *suukpi-lə-* 'to flip with the point of something once').

This suffix contrasts semantically with the suffix *-la-* after stems (2) and (3).

-da-[1] (~ *-də-* ~ *-do-* ~ *-dø-*). An intransitive suffix. This suffix follows (1) a verb stem, or (2) a stem which does not appear without a suffix as a verb stem. We find instances of this suffix added to the basic stem ending in V, *l* or *n*. Verb stems with this suffix belong to Class 1.111 or 1.112. The stem-final *l* and *n* are dropped. This writer has found no instance of *-do-* yet. Some examples are :

(1) *buja-da-* 'to break' (: *bujal-* 'to break [something]'), *gudə-də-* '(of cloth) to tear' (: *gudən-* 'to tear [something]').

(2) *čiga-da-* 'to be cut, to be broken off' (: *čiga-li-* 'to cut [something] once'), *gurə-də-* '(of something rolled up in a ball) to spread out, (of thread) to become loose' (: *gurə-li-* 'to spread out [something], to make loose'), *løpø-dø-* 'to be lost' (: *løpø-li-* 'to lose'), *xəkpə-də-* '(of earth) to break loose, (of ice) to crack' (: *xəkpə-li-* 'to break [a lump of soil] loose once'), *uŋdu-da-* 'to get a bruise' (: *uŋdu-li-* 'to bruise [some part of one's body]'), *mokči-da-* 'to curve, to turn' (: *mokči-li-* 'to bend [something]').

This suffix contrasts semantically with no suffix (zero) after stem (1), and with the suffix *-li-* after stem (2).

-da-[2] (~ *-də-* ~ *-do-* ~ *-dø-*). This suffix appears after a substantive stem. We find instances of *-da-* added to the basic stem ending in V or *n*. Although no instances have yet been found by this writer, it is probable that the variants *-də-*, *-do-* and *-dө-* of this suffix will be found. Some examples are:

pana-da- 'to slap' (: *pana* 'the palm'), *aun-da-* 'to lodge for the night' (: *aun* 'a whole day and night').

-du-[1] (~ *-tu-*).[5)] This suffix expresses 'to return to a former place or state.' It appears after a verb stem. Verb stems with this suffix belong to Class 1.113. Examples :

(After —V- belonging to Class 1. or 0.1, —*l*-, —*g*-, —*n*- or—*p* (+*tu*)-, *-du-*) *geuli-du-* 'to row back' (: *geuli-*'to row'), *nuri-du-* 'to rewrite' (: *nuri-* 'to write'), *itəndə-du-* 'to go back to see' (: *itəndə-* 'to go to see'), *likpi-du-* 'to stop up again, to reclose [the door] firmly' (: *likpi-* 'to stop up, to close [the door] firmly'), *ii-du-* 'to return into one's own house' (: *ii-* 'to enter'), *tuu-du-* '(of something thrown up) to fall back, (of the sun or moon) to set '(: *tuu-* 'to fall, to tumble'), *bujal-du-* 'to break [something] and put [it] back in such a state as before it was made' (: *bujal-* 'to break [something]'), *xaag-du-* 'to come back to land' (: *xaag-* '(of a boat)to come to land'), *agbin-du-* 'to reappear' (: *agbin-* 'to appear'), *aaptu-du-* 'to reach one's own place again' (: *aap-* 'to reach').

(After —V- belonging to Class 0.2, *-tu-*) *andu-tu-* 'to mend' (: *andu-* 'to make'), *gata-tu-* 'to pick berries and come back' (: *gata-* 'to pick berries'), *ǰeela-tu-* 'to ask [somebody] to go back together with oneself' (: *ǰeela-* 'to ask [somebody] to go together with oneself'). We have also *o-tu-* 'to recover [from illness etc.]' (: *o-*[2] 'to become').

-du-[2]. This suffix expresses 'coming of a season of the year or a certain time of the day.' It appears after an adverb stem. We find instances of this suffix added to the basic stem ending in V. Verb stems with this suffix belong to Class 1.113. Some examples are :

tuwə-du- 'winter comes.' (: *tuwə* 'in winter'), *bolo-du-* 'autumn comes.' (: *bolo* 'in autumn'), *səksə-du-* 'evening sets in.' (: *səksə* 'in the evening'), *dolbo-du-* 'night falls.' (: *dolbo* 'at night').

-i- (~ *-ji-*). A transitive suffix. This suffix appears after a verb stem. We find instances of this suffix added to the basic stem ending in V. Verb stems with this suffix belong to Class 1.114 or 1.124. Stems ending in CV receive modifications. Some examples are :

(After –CV-, *-i-*) *xur-i-* 'to rescue' (: *xura-* 'to be rescued'), *dəgǰ-i-* 'to burn [something]' (: *dəgdə-* 'to be burnt'), *xolǰ-i-* 'to[make]dry' (: *xoldo-* 'to [become] dry').

(After –VV-, *-ji-*) *naa-ji-* 'to let rot' (: *naa-* 'to rot').

These intransitive verb stems in the parentheses can be assumed to refer to involuntary actions which are not under human control and are beyond human power.

-kaači- (~ *-kəəči-* ~ *-kooči-* ~ *-kөөči-*). A caressive suffix. This suffix appears after a verb stem. We find instances of this suffix added to the basic stem ending in V or *n*. Verb stems with this suffix belong to Class 1.114. The stem-final *n* is dropped. This writer has found no instances of *-kooči-* and *-kөөči-* yet. Some examples are :

siri-kaači- 'to play hide-and-seek' (: *siri-* 'to hide oneself'), *dəri-kəəči-* 'to romp' (: *dərin-* 'to leap').

-kita- (~ *-kitə-* ~ *-ita-* ~ *-itə-* ~ *-jita-* ~ *-jitə-*). This suffix expresses 'intention or wish to perform an action' or 'being about to perform an action.' It appears after a verb stem. Verb stems with this suffix belong to Class 1.111. *-kita-* and *-kitə* appear after —*l-*, —*g* (→*k*)- or —*n* (→*k*)-; *-ita-*

and *-itə-* after –CV- or *–p* (+*tu*)-; *-jita-* and *-jitə-* after (–)VV-. Some examples are: *ələitə-* 'to intend to cook [something]' (: *ələ-* 'to cook [something]'), *orok-kita-* 'to wish to carry' (: *orog-* 'to carry'), *bul-kitə-* 'to be about to die' (: *bul-* 'to die'). Further examples are given in Table I below.

-kta- (~ *-ktə-* ~ *-kto-* ~ *-ktə-*). An iterative suffix. This suffix appears after a verb stem. We find an instance of this suffix added to the basic stem ending in *a* ; thus, *xasa-kta-* 'repeatedly to go after one's love or lover' (: *xasa-* 'to chase' This verb stem belongs to Class 0. 21.). Although no instances have yet been found by this writer, it is probable that the variants *-ktə-*, *-kto-* and *-ktə-* of this suffix will be found.

-la- (~ *-lə-* ~ *-lo-* ~ *-lə-* ~ *-a-* ~ *-ə-* ~ *-o-* ~ *-ə-*). This suffix follows: (1) a substantive stem, (2) a verb stem, or (3) a stem which does not appear alone without a suffix as a substantive or verb stem. We find instances of this suffix added to the basic stem ending in V, *l* or *n*. This suffix expresses: (a) 'to utilize (or make use of) something,' 'to establish a personal relationship (e. g., to make friends or to take a wife),' or 'to go to get something or to call for somebody' after stem (1); and (b) 'to perform an action once or for a short time' after stems (2) and (3) and some substantive stems. After these substantive stems the suffix concerned expresses both (a) and (b). Verb stems with this suffix belong to Class 1.111, 1.112 or (in some cases, e. g., *ǰee-la-*) 0. 2. The stem-final *n* is dropped. This writer has yet to find instances of the variants *-ə-*, *-o-* and *-ə-* of this suffix. Some examples are :

(After —V- or —*n* (→zero), *-la-*, *-lə-*, *-lo-* or *-lə-*) (1) *jooso-lo-* 'to lock once' (: *jooso* 'a lock,' *jooso-lo-či-* 'to lock many times'), *maatu-la-* 'to lasso once' (: *maatu* 'a lasso,' *maatu-či-* 'to lasso many times'), *asi-la-* 'to take a wife' (: *asi* 'a wife'), *pɵkkɵ-lɵ-* 'to cover one's cheeks with a handkerchief' (: *pɵkkɵ* 'a handkerchief'), *moo-lo-* 'to go to get firewood' (: *moo* 'firewood'), *ǰee-la-* 'to ask [somebody] to go together with oneself' (: *ǰee* 'a companion'), *olǰiga-la-* 'to hook' (: *olǰiga* 'a hooked iron-rod for hanging a pan, etc. over a fire'), *moiččca-la-* 'to fire a shot with a gun' (: *moiččan-* 'a gun,' *moiččca-či-* 'to fire shots with a gun'), *aapu-la-* 'to put on a cap' (: *aapun-* 'a cap'), (2) *bagba-la-* 'to poke once' (: *bagba-* 'to poke repeatedly'), (3) *gida-la-* 'to put in once, to put [a ring] on a finger' (: *gida-či-* 'to put in many times'), *ŋooxi-la-* 'to smell [something] once' (: *ŋooxi-či-* 'to smell [something] continuously'), *suukpi-lə-* 'to flip with the point of something once' (: *suukpi-či-* 'to flip with the point of something repeatedly').

(After —*l-*, *-a-*, *-ə-*, *-o-* or *-ɵ-*) (1) *umul-a-* 'to tie a girdle' (: *umul* 'a girdle').

This suffix expressing (b) contrasts semantically with the suffix *-či-* after stem (3). After some substantive stems, this suffix expresses (a), but also (b) contrasting semantically with *-či-* immediately after a substantive stem, such as in *maatu-či-* given above. However, *-či-* follows *-lo-* in *jooso-lo-či-*, also above. This *-lo-* seems to express (a).

-li-. A transitive suffix. This suffix also functions as a suffix expressing 'to perform an action once or for a short time.' It follows (1) a verb stem, or (2) a stem which does not appear without a suffix as a verb stem. This writer has found one instance of this suffix added to a verb stem ending in *ə*. Verb stems with this suffix belong to Class 1.114. Some examples are:

(1) *sinə-li-* 'to strip off a piece of bark' (: *sinə-* 'to strip off pieces of bark'), (2) *čiga-li-* 'to cut [something] once' (: *čiga-da-* 'to be cut', *čiga-su-* 'to cut [something] continuously'), *lɵpɵ-li-* 'to lose' (: *lɵpɵ-dɵ-* 'to be lost'), *xəkpə-li-* 'to break [a lump of soil] loose once' (: *xəkpə-də-*

'(of earth) to break loose, (of ice) to crack,' *xəkpə-su-* 'to continue cracking [ice]'), *uktu-li-* 'to bump against [something] once' (: *uktu-su-*. 'to bump against [something] again and again'), *mokči-li-* 'to bend [something]' (: *mokči-da-* 'to curve, to turn').

This suffix contrasts semantically with the suffix *-da-*[1] and / or *-su-* after stem (2).

-lu-. This is an inchoative suffix, i. e., it expresses 'to begin an action'. It appears after a verb stem. We find instances of this suffix added to the basic stem ending in V, *p* or *n*. Verb stems with this suffix belong to Class 1.113. The stem-final *n* is dropped, and *tu* is added to the stem-final *p*. Some examples are:

simana-lu- 'to begin to snow' (: *simana-* 'to snow'), *tugdə-lu-* 'to begin to rain' (: *tugdə-* 'to rain'), *tugbu-lu-* 'to begin to drop [something]' (: *tugbu-* 'to drop [something]'), *təə-lu-* 'to begin to sit' (: *təə-* 'to sit'), *ɵlɵ-lu-* 'to begin to cook [something]' (: *ɵlɵ-* 'to cook [something]'), *kəə-lu-* 'to begin to speak' (: *kəən-* 'to speak'), *dəptu-lu-* 'to begin to eat' (: *dəp-* 'to eat'), *bi-lu-* 'to begin to be [somewhere]' (: *bi-* 'to be').

-mači- (~ *-məči-* ~ *-moči-* ~ *-mɵči-*). This is a reciprocal suffix, i. e., it expresses 'to perform an action to each other'. It appears after (1) a verb stem, or (2) a substantive stem. We find instances of this suffix added to the basic stem ending in V. Verb stems with this suffix belong to Class 1.114. This writer has no instances of *-moči-* and *-mɵči-*. Some examples are :

(1) *sori-mači-* 'to quarrel with each other' (: *sori-* 'to quarrel'), *mində-məči-* 'to beat each other' (: *mində-* 'to beat'), *toktou-mači-* 'to make an agreement with each other' (: *toktou-* 'to decide'),

gaajuu-mači- 'to dally with each other' (: *gaajuu-* 'to dally with [somebody]').

(2) *jili-mači-* 'to push or thrust at each other with their heads' (: *jili* 'the head').

-mu-. An optative suffix. This suffix appears after a verb stem. Verb stems with this suffix belong to Class 0.21. The stem-final *g* becomes *ŋ*, the stem-final *n* is dropped, and *-tu-* is added to the stem-final *p*. An example is : *ŋənə-mu-* 'to wish to go' (:*ŋənə-* 'to go'). Further examples of this suffix are given in Table I below.

-na- (~ *-nə-* ~ *-no-* ~ *-nɵ-* ~ *-i-*). An iterative suffix. This suffix appears after a verb stem. We find instances of this suffix added to the basic stem ending in V or *n*. Verb stems with this suffix belong to Class 0.21. Some examples are :

(After —V-, *-na-*, *-nə-*, *-no-* or *-nɵ-*) *xəkpədə-nə-* '(of earth) to break loose again and again, (of ice) to crack again and again' (: *xəkpədə-* '(of earth) to break loose, (of ice) to crack'), *olo-no-* 'to be startled again and again' (*olo-* 'to be startled'), *ali-na-* 'to stop blows again and again' (: *ali-* 'to accept, to stop a blow'), *sumu-na-* '(of fish) to splash repeatedly' (: *sumu-* '(of fish) to splash'), *garpa-na-* 'to shoot many arrows [with a bow]' (: *garpa-* 'to shoot an arrow'), *pɵččɵ-nɵ-* 'to jump repeatedly' (: *pɵččɵ-* 'to jump'), *mii-nə-* 'to cut repeatedly' (: *mii-* 'to cut'), *tuu-nə-* 'to tumble again and again' (: *tuu-* 'to fall, to tumble').

(After —*n*-, *-i-*) *dawwaan-i-* 'to yawn again and again' (: *dawwaan-* 'to yawn').

-ŋda- (~ *-ŋdə-* ~ *-ŋdo-* ~ *-ŋdɵ-* ~ *-nda-* ~ *-ndə-* ~ *-ndo-* ~ *-ndɵ-* ~ *-ni-* ~ *-i-*). This suffix expresses 'to go to perform an action.' It appears after a verb stem. Verb stems with this suffix belong to Class 1.121, 1.122, 1.114 or 1.124. *-ŋda-*, *-ŋdə-*, *-ŋdo-* and *-ŋdɵ-* appear after –VV- belonging to Class 1.2 or 0.1; *-nda-*, *-ndə-*, *-ndo-* and *-ndɵ-* after –CV- belonging to Class 1.1 or 0.1; *-ni-* after —V- belonging to Class 0.2, —*l*-, —g (→*ŋ*)- or some irregular verb stems, and *-i-* after —*n*-. The stem *dəp-* 'to eat' ending in *p* and the suffix *-ni-* are fused into *dəŋmi-* meaning 'to go to eat'. For example, *itə-ndə-* 'to go to see' (: *itə-* 'to see'), *moolo-ndo-* 'to go to another's house (to ask him) to go gathering firewood (together)' (: *moolo-* 'to go to gather firewood'). Further examples of this suffix are given in Table I below.

-p-. A potential- reflexive-passive suffix. This suffix appears after a verb stem. Verb stems with this suffix belong to Class 0.3. The stem-final *g* becomes *k*, the stem-final *n* is dropped, and to the stem-final *p*, the connective *-tu-* is added. For example, *itə-p-* 'to be seen' (: *itə-* 'to see'), *ŋənə-p-* 'it is possible to go [somewhere]' (: *ŋənə-* 'to go'), *somi-p-* '(of a door) to shut of itself' (: *somi-* 'to shut [the door]'), *bujal-p-* 'to be able to be broken' (: *bujal-* 'to break [something]'), *dəptu-p-* 'to be edible, to be able to be eaten' (: *dəp-* 'to eat'). Further examples of this suffix are given in Table I below.

-pači- (~ *-pəči-* ~ *-poči-* ~ *-pɵči-*). This suffix expresses 'to repeat an action in time or space.' It appears after a verb stem. We find instances of this suffix added to the basic stem ending in V, *l*, *g* or *n*. Verb stems with this suffix belong to Class 1.114. The stem-final *g* becomes *k*, and the stem-final *n* becomes *p*. This writer has found no instance of *-pɵči-* yet. Some examples are:

itə-pəči- 'to see repeatedly' (: *itə-* 'to see'), *mukta-pači-* 'to climb a tree or trees repeatedly' (: *mukta-* 'to climb a tree'), *nulǰi-pəči-* 'to remove from one place to another' (: *nulǰi-* 'to remove'), *nəə-pəči-* 'to go in and out repeatedly' (: *nəə-* 'to go out'), *puli-pəči-* 'to travel from place to place' (: *puli-* 'to travel'), *orok-poči-* to carry about' (: *orog-* 'to carry'), *paap-pəči-* 'to become out of breath again and again' (: *paan-* 'to become out of breath'), *bul-pəči-* 'to become giddy' (: *bul-* 'to die').

-pila- (~ *-pilə-*). This is probably a passive suffix. We have found two instances of this suffix added to the basic stem ending in *ə* or *n*. In these instances this suffix seems to express 'to be moved by a natural phenomenon, such as wind or the flowing of water.' It appears after a verb stem (or a substantive stem ?). Verb stems with this suffix belong to Class 1.111. The stem-final *n* is dropped. This writer has yet to find an instance of *-pila-*. Some examples are:

xəjə-pilə- 'to be carried down stream, (of spilt water)to run down [a board]' (: *xəjə-* 'to flow,' *xəjə* 'a rapid stream, a swift current in the sea'), *xədu-pilə-* 'to be carried away by the wind' (: *xədun-* '(of a wind) to blow,' *xədun-* 'a wind').

-pin-. This is a diminutive suffix, and expresses 'to perform an action to a slight degree or for a short time.' It follows: (1) a verb stem, or (2) a stem that does not appear alone without a suffix as a verb stem. We find instances of this suffix added to the basic stem ending in V or *n*. Verb stems with this suffix belong to Class 2.3. The stem-final *n* is dropped. Some examples are:

(1) *geuli-pin-* 'to row gently' (: *geuli-* 'to row'), *siru-pin-* 'to tear a little' (: *siru-* 'to tear'), *siltu-pin-* 'to wash but not thoroughly' (: *siltu-* 'to wash'), *inə-pin-* 'to laugh momentarily' (: *inə-* 'to laugh').

(2) *toroo-pin-* 'to turn over onto one's back' (: *toroo-či-* 'to lie on one's back'), *waa-pin-* 'to put [something] on one's shoulder' (: *waan-* 'to carry [something] on a stick over one's shoulder').

-si-. This suffix expresses 'to regard …… as …….' It appears after an adjective stem. We find instances of this suffix added to the basic stem ending in V or *n*. Verb stems with this suffix belong to Class 1.114. The stem-final *n* is dropped. Some examples are:

tədə-si- 'to accept [something] as true, to believe' (: *tədə* 'true'), *ǰaa-si-* 'to regard [somebody or something] as weak or cheap' (: *ǰaa* 'weak, cheap'), *orki-si-* 'to think ill of [somebody]' (: *orkin-* 'bad').

-su-. An iterative-durative suffix. This suffix follows a stem not appearing without a suffix as a verb stem. We find instances of this suffix added to the basic stem ending in V. Verb stems with this suffix belong to Class 1.113. Some examples are:

čiga-su- 'to continue to cut [something]' (: *čiga-li-* 'to cut [something] once'), *xəkpə-su-* 'to continue cracking [ice]' (: *xəkpə-li-* 'to break [a lump of soil] loose once'), *uktu-su-* 'to bump against [something] again and again' (: *uktu-li-* 'to bump against [something] once'). This suffix contrasts semantically with the suffix *-li-* after stems not appearing without a suffix as a verb stem.

-ta- (~ *-tə-* ~ *-to-* ~ *-tɵ-*). This suffix expresses 'to maintain an action or state caused by, or following, another action.' It appears after a verb stem. We find instances of this suffix added to the basic stem ending in V, *g*, *n* or *p*. Verb stems with this suffix belong to Class 1.111, 1.112, 1.121 or 1.122. The stem-final *g* becomes *k*, the stem-final *n* becomes *t*, and *tu* is added to the stem-final *p*. Some examples are:

tura-ta- 'to open [something] and leave [it] opened' (: *tura-* 'to open [something]'), *mɵɵlɵ-tɵ-* 'to go to get water and come back' (: *mɵɵlɵ-* 'to go to get water'), *tətu-tə-* 'to have [clothes] on' (: *tətu-* 'to put on [clothes]'), *somi-ta-* 'to shut [the door] and keep [it] shut' (: *somi-* 'to shut [the door]'), *mukta-ta-* 'to climb to a higher place and remain there' (: *mukta-* 'to climb a tree'), *sokto-to-* 'to be drunk' (: *sokto-* 'to get drunk'), *tugbu-tə-* 'to take [something] down to a place and keep [it] there' (: *tugbu-* 'to drop [something], to lower [something]'), *likpi-tə-* 'to stop up and keep stopped up' (: *likpi-* 'to stop up'), *doo-to-* '(of a bird or an insect) to settle on the ground, etc., and remain there' (: *doo-* '(of a bird) to alight'), *loo-to-* 'to hang up and keep hung up' (: *loo-* 'to hang up'), *dai-ta-* 'to hide [something] and keep [it] hidden' (: *dai-* 'to hide [something]'), *puli-tə-* 'to go out and come back'(: *puli-* 'to walk to and fro, to travel from place to place'), *xaak-ta-* 'to come back to land for a short time and then put out to sea' (: *xaag-* '(of a boat) to come to land'), *iktəmət-tə-* 'to bite into [something] and hold [it] in the mouth' (: *iktəmən-* 'to bite'), *xuriptu-tə-* 'to remain colored' (: *xurip-* 'to be colored').

The formation of verb stems by means of some productive verb suffixes is shown in the Table I below.

In forming verb stems, we take the forms (–) VV-, –CV-, –ptu- (= —V-) and —l-, —g-, —n- (= —C-) as the basic forms of the verb stems. These forms are identical to the verb stems accompanied by the verb ending *-raa* or *-dalaa.* (See Table I in "The Verb Inflection of Orok".)

However, when we form a verb stem using a verb stem of Class 0.1111, 0.1112, 0.112 or 0.12 plus the suffix **-bun-* (a non-existent form) or *-bu-*[2], we set up additional basic forms of the verb stem : *–VkV- (a non-existent form) for Classes 0.1111, 0.1112 and 0.112 and *(C)Vji- for Class 0.12. The suffixes **-bun-* and *-bu-*[2] do not accompany the basic stems of Classes 1.1 and 0.1. Rather these basic stems and suffixes are fused into another form that functions as an alternate stem.

The basic stem –ptu- of Class 0.3 can be further divided into the stem –p- and the connective -tu-.

Table I. Basic stems of verbs grouped into classes and Examples of verb stems with the suffix -*boon*-, -*bu*-^{2}, -*ŋda*-, -*kita*-, -*mu*- or -*p*-.

Class	Basic Stems				
1.111	(–)VC*a*-				
1.112	(–)VC*o*-				
1.113	(–)VCu-				
1.114	(–)VC i-				
1.121	–CC*a*-	= –CV-			
1.122	–CC*o*-				
1.123	–CCu-				
1.124	–CC i-				
1.2	(–)VV-		= —V-		
0.1111	C*aa*-			*C*a*k*a*-	
0.1112	–VVg*a*-	–CV-		*–VVk*a*-	= * –VkV-
0.112	(–)CV*o*-	= or		*(–)CVk*o*-	
0.12	(C)Vi-	–VV-		*(C)Vji-	
0.211	–CV-				
0.22	(–)VV-				
0.3	–p-tu-	= –CV-			
2.1	—l-				
2.2	—g-		= —C-		
2.3	—n-				

Class	I -boon-	II -bu-[2]	III -ŋda-	IV -kita-
1.111	(–)V*C*C*a*un-	(–)V*C*C*a*u-		
1.112	(–)V*C*C*o*un-	(–)V*C*C*o*u-		
1.113	(–)V*C*C*oo*n-	(–)V*C*Cu-		
1.114				
1.121	–CC*a*un-	–CC*a*u-		
1.122	–CC*o*un-	–CC*o*u-		
1.123	–CC*oo*n-	–CCu-	–CV-nd*a*-	–CV-it*a*-
1.124			or	or
1.2	(–)VV-w*oo*n-	(–)VV-wu-	(–)VV-ŋd*a*-	(–)VV-jit*a*-
0.1111	–V*k* k*a*un-	–V*k* k*a*u-		
0.1112	–VV*k* k*a*un-	–VV*k* k*a*u-		
0.112	–V*k* k*o*un-	–V*k* k*o*u-		
0.12	(C) Vjj*oo*n-	(C) Vjju-		
0.211	–CV- -p*oo*n-	–CV- -pu-	—V- -ni-	
0.22	(–)VV-	(–)VV-		
0.3	–p-*oo*n-	–p-u-	–ŋ-mi-	
2.1	—l- -b*oo*n-	—l- -bu-	—l-	—l- -kit*a*-
2.2	—g-	—g-	—ŋ-	—k-
2.3	—m-	—m-	—n-i-	

Class	V -mu-		VI -p-	
1.111				
1.112				
1.113				
1.114				
1.121				
1.122				
1.123				
1.124				
1.2	—V-		—V-	
0.1111		-mu-		-p-
0.1112				
0.112				
0.12				
0.211				
0.22				
0.3				
2.1	—l-		—l-	
2.2	—ŋ-		—k-	
2.3	— -		— -	

Examples

Class	Basic Stem	-boon-	-bu-[2]
1.111	ŋənə- 'to go,' itə- 'to see'	ŋənnəun-	ŋənnəu-
1.112	moolo- 'to go to gather firewood'	moolloun-	moollou-
1.113	ŋənu- 'to go back,' atu- 'to undo, to untie'	ŋənnɵɵn-	ŋənnu-
1.114	somi- 'to shut [the door]'	sommoon-	sommu-
1.121	aunda- 'to lodge for the night'	aundaun-	aundau-
1.122	tokpo- 'to twist [a rope]'	tokpoun-	tokpou-
1.123	siltu- 'to wash'	siltoon-	siltu-
1.124	bargi- 'to prepare'	bargoon-	bargu-
1.2	uu- 'to ride, to take [a boat]'	uuwoon-	uuwu-
	bɵɵ- 'to give' ⌈to get [a child]	bɵɵwɵɵn-	bɵɵwu-
0.1111	baa-, *baka- 'to find, to see [a person],	bakkaun-	bakkau-
0.1112	xəəgə-, *xəəkə- 'to improvise (in song)'	xəəkkəun-	xəəkkəu-
0.112	loo-, *loko- 'to hang up'	lokkoun-	lokkou-
0.12	gəi-, *gəji- 'to compete'	gəjjɵɵn-	gəjju-
0.211	andu- 'to make'	andupoon-	andupu-
	ɵlɵ- 'to boil (to cook) [something]'	ɵlɵpɵɵn-	ɵlɵpu-
0.22	allau- 'to teach'	allaupoon-	allaupu-
0.3	dəp- 'to eat'	dəpɵɵn-	dəpu-
2.1	bujal- 'to break [something]'	bujalboon-	bujalbu-
2.2	xaag- '(of a boat) to come to land'	xaagboon-	xaagbu-
2.3	un- 'to say'	umbɵɵn-	umbu-
Irregular Verbs	bi- 'to be'	biwwɵɵn-	biwwu-
	o-[1] 'to do'	owwoon-	owwu-
	o-[2] 'to become, to move [to a place]'	opoon-	opu-
	bul- 'to die'	bulbɵɵn-	bulbu-
	ga- 'to buy, to take to wife'	gawwoon-	gawwu-

Class	-kita-	-mu-	-ŋda-	-p-
1.111	ŋənəitə-	ŋənəmu-	itəndə-	ŋənəp-
1.112	mooloita-	moolomu-	moolondo-	moolop-
1.113	ŋənuitə-	ŋənumu-	atunda-	ŋənup-
1.114	somiita-	somimu-	sominda-	somip-
1.121	aundaita-	aundamu-	aundanda-	aundap-
1.122	tokpoita-	tokpomu-	tokpondo-	tokpop-
1.123	siltuita-	siltumu-	siltunda-	siltup-
1.124	bargiita-	bargimu-	barginda-	bargip-
1.2	uujita-	uumu-	uuŋda-	uup-
	bɵɵjitə-	bɵɵmu-	bɵɵŋdɵ-	bɵɵp-
0.1111	baajita-	baamu-	baaŋda-	baap-
0.1112	xəəgəitə-	xəəgəmu-	xəəgəndə-	xəəgəp-
0.112	loojita-	loomu-	looŋdo-	loop-
0.12	gəijitə-	gəimu-	gəiŋdə-	gəip-
0.211	anduita-	andumu-	anduni-	andup-
	ɵlɵitə-	ɵlɵmu	ɵlɵni-	ɵlɵp-
0.22	allaujita-	allaumu-	allauni-	allaup-
0.3	dəptuitə-	dəptumu-	dəŋmi-	dəptup-
2.1	bujalkita-	bujalmu-	bujalni-	bujalp-
2.2	xaakkita-	xaaŋmu-	xaaŋni-	xaakp-
2.3	ukkitə-	umu-	uni-	up-
Irregular Verbs	biitə-	bimu-	bini-	bip-
	oita-	omu-	oni-[6]	op-
	oita-	omu-	oni-[6]	op-
	bulkitə-	bulmu-	buni-	bulp-
	gaita-	gamu-	gani-	gap-

Notes

1) The material for this paper was acquired from an Orok woman, Napka. She was born about 1910 in southern Sakhalin and emigrated to Hokkaido in 1947. I wish to express my cordial thanks to her. I am also indebted to Hisaharu MAGATA's grammatical description of Orok (unpublished), which brought certain suffixes to my notice.

2) For details of the inflection of verbs see The Verb Inflection of Orok. Substantives are also inflected in a similar way to verbs; for the inflection of substantives, see The Substantive Inflection of Orok.

3) A key to abbreviations and symbols in this article is found in the note at the end of the paper, The Verb Inflection of Orok.

4) Cf. -**bboo* (←* -*bu*^{2}-*ra*), which is found in "The Verb Inflection of Orok" Section **9**.

5) The verb stem —C-*du*- has a parallel form —C-*du-du*- without a clear difference of meaning, e. g., *bujal-du-du-*, *xaag-du-du-*. The imperfect verbal noun of —C-*du*- is —C-*ǯi*-, which is homonymous with that of the verb stem —C-. We assume that the verb stem —C-*du-du*- originates from the imperfect verbal noun —C-*du-ǯǯi*-, which was formed instead of the imperfect verbal noun —C-*ǯi*- of the verb stem —C-*du*- in order to avoid homonymity.

6) We find also another form *oninda*- (= *o-ni-nda*-).

Additional Note

As the basic form of a stem included in a secondary stem in the above examples , we take the form (the one before the first hyphen when two or more hyphens are used) given in the parentheses following the secondary stem concerned. However, the basic form of the stem in *moičča-la* (or *či*)- is *moiččan*-.

This article was rewritten from a previous paper I wrote that appeared with the same title in *Hoppo Bunka Kenkyu, Bulletin of the Institute for the Study of North Eurasian Cultures Hokkaido University*, 7(March 1973), pp. 1–17. I changed the method of description in this article to make it agree with the method of description used in the preceding two articles.

Addendum

The above verb-stem-forming suffix -*boon*- in causative-passive verb-forms (see pp. 73–74) seems to be derived from the combination of the suffix -*bu*-^{2} plus another verb-stem-forming suffix, such as -**ka*(*a*)*n*-. The causative-passive forms composed of a verb stem of Class 1.111, 1.112,

1.121, 1.122, 0.1111, 0.1112 or 0.112 and the suffix -**bun*- seem to have resulted from the dropping of the *wa* (*a*) in the sequence of the stem-final vowel -*a* or -*o* plus -*u*-(← -*bu*-[2]) plus -**wa* (*a*) *n*- (← -**ka*(*a*)*n*-) with the doubling of the preceding consonant in compensation for the dropping of the *b* in -*bu*-[2] (in verb forms of Classes 1.111, 1.112, 0.1111, 0.1112 and 0.112) or without (in verb forms of Classes 1.121 and 1.122). The causative-passive forms composed of a verb stem of Class 1.113, 1.114, 1.123, 1.124 or 0.12 and the suffix -**boon*- seem to have resulted from the dropping of the stem-final vowel *u* or *i* and the *b* of the suffix -**boon*- with the doubling of the preceding consonant in compensation for the dropping of the *b* in -*boon*- (in verb forms of Classes 1.113, 1.114 and 0.12) or without (in verb forms of Classes 1.123 and 1.124).

樺太のウイルタ語の感嘆・疑問その他の語尾について

Exclamatory, Interrogative and Other Word Endings in Uilta

1

ウイルタ語（旧称　オロッコ語）は，樺太の少数民族の一つウイルタ族の話す言語で，ツングース・満州諸語の一つである。

ウイルタ語の単語は，語幹一つだけからなるか，一つの語幹にさらにそのあとに語尾が一つまたは一つ以上接着（膠着）してできている。別に，語幹二つからなる複合語もある。なお，語幹には，単一の語幹のほかに，また，語幹にさらに接尾辞がついてできているものがある。動詞は，動詞語幹が語尾をともなわずにそれだけで動詞となることがなく，つねに動詞語尾（活用語尾）が接着している。名詞は，語幹だけで主格形としてあらわれることもあるが，また名詞語尾（格語尾または曲用語尾ともよぶ）が接着して斜格形としてあらわれる（池上1956，1959参照。）

このほかに，さらに，人称語尾および反照語尾（再帰語尾）がある。人称語尾には，動詞につく述語人称語尾と名詞につく所属人称語尾の二種がある。これらの語尾は，動詞では，動詞語尾のあとに接着し，名詞では，語幹に接尾するが，名詞語尾をともなっていると，そのあとに接着する。なお，名詞述語文では，名詞に述語人称語尾がつくことがある。（池上1956，1959，1994参照。）

ウイルタ語の単語には，さらにそのほかいくつかの語尾が用いられることがあり，これらの語尾は，動詞，名詞ばかりでなく，代名詞，形容詞，副詞にもつく。

また，ウイルタ語には，上述のように語幹に一つまたは一つ以上の語尾が単に接着している接着形ではないが意味・用法上で接着形に相当する語形をもつ語がある。この語形は，語幹と語尾，あるいは語尾と語尾が，融合しているとみられ，融合形とよぶことにする。

ウイルタ語では，上述の語は自立語であり，このあとにさらに付属語が連続してあらわれることがある。付属語（小詞）（例，goči，taani）は，自立語と異なり，つねに他の語につづけて付加的に用いられる。まえの語とは母音調和をしない。

2

この拙文は，動詞語尾，名詞語尾，人称語尾，反照語尾以外の上にふれた語尾とこの語尾が接尾した語形に相当する融合形について述べるものである。拙文がもとづくウイルタ語資料は，故佐藤チヨ（Napka）さんから採取したものである。

これらの語尾を以下に列記する。

1．-kaa（～ -kəə～ -koo～ -kɵɵ）　感嘆語尾。　感動，感嘆を表わし，また，遠くへの呼びかけやさけびに使われる。末尾がCVである語および末尾がＶＶである語のあるもの（第Ⅱ図参照）および末尾がCVlである語には，この語尾が接着する語形のほかに，これに相当する融合形があって使われる。

末尾がCVlである語の感嘆融合形については，pureel（こどもらよー）やほかにたとえばmapareel（じいさんらよー）は，puril（子ら）やmaparil（じいさんら）の本来のｉがeeとなっており，一つのある要素が加わって融合しているとみられるが，ただし，その要素が末尾のlのまえでその語形の内部に組みこまれていることが注意される。並列融合形についても同様のことがあり，のちにふれる。しかし，一方，puriil（こどもらよー），umuul（帯だよー）は，語の最後の母音が長く発音され，同一母音音素の連続となっているとみて，融合形とは異なる語形とみなすべきかもしれない。（toxoの感嘆形のtoxoo［ボタンだよー］とpuriilの音形の形成の相違は，日本語のハナコ，オカアサンの呼びかけの形のハナコオとオカアサアンの音形の形成のちがいを参照。）tarisaal

（その人らよー），bɵjɵɵl（けだものらよー）は，pureelの類の語形とも，puriilの類の語形ともとれる。なお，末尾がVVlである語には，感嘆融合形はないとみられる。

また，末尾がCVである語が，あとに付属語gočì（日本語口語間投助詞「ね」のような意味を表わす）をともなうと，この融合形と同じ語形をとる。例，naree gočì.（人［nari］だね。）

用例　（名詞）［主格形］əri purilkəə. このこどもらだよー。／əri kaltaakaa（またはkaltagaaまたはkaltagəə).　　これ半分に割れてるよー。／［人称形］mini xuldabee.　ぼくの箱だよー。　（代名詞）biikəə.　おれだよー。（形容詞）jəkki gurəikəə（またはgurəjee).　ここが広いよー。　（動詞）tari nari ŋənəxənee.　その人行ったよー。／soottooree. あとで（水を）くんでおけよー。／čadu beekkəə. それはそこにあるよー（čadu biinii.［それはそこにあるか。］に答えて）。

2．-ka（～ -kə ～ -ko ～ -kɵ ～ -wa ～ -wə ～ -wo ～ -wɵ ～ -ga ～ -gə）疑問語尾。　疑問詞をつかう質問文で使われるが，また疑問詞を欠くがそれを略したとみられる質問文においても使われて疑問を表わす。末尾がＣＶである語には，この語尾のついた接着形のほかに，また，上記の感嘆を表わす融合形と同形の疑問融合形が使用される。この融合形も上記の疑問語尾が接着した語形と同じ意味・用法をもつ。

この語尾のついた語を文末にもつ文は，文音調の末尾が下降するが，疑問詞を欠くと平らであり，その融合形を文末にもつ文の文音調の末尾も平らである。

用例　（名詞）［主格形］xamačiga xuldaa. どんな箱か。／əri paduwa. このたばこ入れは（だれのか）。／［対格］xamačee toxxoowo. どんなボタンをか。／［人称形］əri ŋui xuldaniga. これはだれの箱か。／sini xuldasiga. おまえの箱は（どれか）。　（形容詞）ŋui tənəə bajakka. だれが一番裕福か。　（副詞）xaaliga. いつですか。　（動詞）xawasai ŋənneesigə. どちらへあんたは行くか。

3．-i（～ -ji）疑問語尾。　質問に対する肯定的または否定的返答（yes or no）をもとめる質問を表わす。この語尾がついた語を文末にもつ文は，文音調の末尾が上昇する。

末尾が子音音素である語には，この語尾はつかわれない。この意味の質問文の末尾にこの語がおかれると，語尾をとらず，ただ文音調の末尾が上昇する。

用例　（名詞）［位置格］čadu dugdui. その家にか。／［人称形］əri mini aapumbii. これはおれの帽子か。　（形容詞）tari taagdai. それは白いか。（副詞）gočii. またか。／boloi. 秋にか。　（動詞）ŋənneesii. きみは行くか。

4．-ijuu（～ -jjuu ～ -juu）　疑問語尾。　疑念をあらわす。ひかえめの質問，ひとりごとの質問につかう。「……かしら」の意。この語尾のついた語を文末にもつ文は，文音調の末尾が平らである。

用例　（名詞）［主格形］umuljuu.　帯だべか。帯かしら。／xamačee xuldaijuu.　どんな箱かしら。／taatari narijjuu. 遠くのあれ人かしら。（形容詞）xaawu maŋgaijuu pərgeeni. どちら（の人）が強いだろうか，かれはためす。（動詞）xaali ŋənəxənijjuu. いつかれは行ったかしら。／xaiwa xaixanijjuu.　əsiwi saara. かれは何をしたかしら，わたしは知らない。／［被動完了動名詞］xai sələǰini andupulaijuu.　どんな金属でつくられたものだろうか。

なお，この疑問語尾がついた語を連続・並列させ，二者のうちのどちらかをたずねる用法がある。例（代名詞）［主格形］biijjuu siijjuu.　おれか，おまえか。／（動詞）bii ŋənneewijjuu sii ŋənneesiijjuu.　おれが行くか，おまえが行くか。

5．-nda（～ -ndə ～ -ndo ～ -ndɵ ～ -da ～ -də ～ -do ～ -dɵ）伝聞を表わす語尾。「……だそうだ」「……だと（いう話だ）」の意。また，口頭文芸には -ndamaa（……だとさ）という伝聞の語尾の感嘆融合形があらわれる。例　čii biččinindəməə.（ながくずーっとかれはいたんだとさ。）

用例　（名詞）［対格］toxxoondo.　ボタンをとのことだ。／［方向格］utətəində. 戸口へだそうだ。／［人称形］tari nari xuldaninda. その人の箱だそうだ。（動詞）isuxaninda. かれが帰って来たんだと。

6．-dda(a)（～ -ddə(ə) ～ -ddo(o) ～ -ddɵ(ɵ) ～ -da(a) ～ -də(ə)

～ -do(o) ～ -dɵ(ɵ)）日本語の助詞「も」に似た意味をもち，逆接条件(「行っても，行けども」）も表わす。

用例　（名詞）［主格］toxoddo anaa. ボタンもない。／［対格］toxxooddo (o) paddoodda(a) əččimbi ittəə. ボタンもたばこ入れもぼくは見なかった。／［人称形］munu xuldapuddaa daaji. ぼくらの箱も大きい。（動詞）undəiniddə(ə) əsini dooljee. かの女が言ってもかれは聞かない。

7. -gdaa（～ -gdəə ～ -gdoo ～ -gdɵɵ）　他と区別して限定する意味を表わす。「……なら」の意。末尾が子音音素である語に，この語は使われないとみられ，語例は採取されていない。

用例　（名詞）［主格］durigdaa biini. 夜間のゆりかごならある（duriか，əmuwə［昼間用のゆりかご］があるかと借りに来たのに答えて）。／［対格］toxxoogdoo buisini. ボタンならかの女がしまってもっている。／［位置格］čaa padudugdaa biini. そのたばこ入れにならそれはある。（副詞）bologdoo biiwi. 秋ならおれはいる。（動詞）ŋənnəəjinigdəə ǰeelaččiwi. かれが行くならばおれは仲間にして連れて行く。

8. -lakka（～ -ləkkə ～ -lokko ～ -lɵkkɵ）　他と区別して限定する意味を表わす。「……は」「……なら」の意。

用例　（名詞）［主格］utələkkə biini. 戸口ならある（bujaa duxu［壊れた家］について言っている）／［方向格］duritailakka əǰǰee məətəlləə. 幼児かごへは投げるな。／［場所格］laxalalakka ŋənneewi. 近いところならばぼくは行く。（動詞）xaidu xənumi oččini umi saarilakka.「どこで軽くなった」と言ってわからばこそ。(北川五郎［Gɵrgɵlɵ］氏口述昔話「カルジャメ」）／ŋənnəəjiniləkkə gaǰǰiwi. かれが行くならばぼくは連れて行く。

9. -mali（～ -məli ～ -moli ～ -mɵli）　これだけに制限することを意味する。「……だけ」の意。

なお，この語尾は，「……だらけの」の意味の接尾辞 -mali とは区別される。

用例　（名詞）［主格形］durimali biini. 幼児かごだけある。／［対格］paddoomali itəxəmbi. たばこ入れだけをおれは見た。／［位置格］duridumali biini. 幼児かごにだけそれはある。／［人称形］sini xuldasimali biini. おまえの箱だけある。　（副詞）əsiməli gujjeeləsini. いまだけかれはかわいがる。　（動詞）əmiddəə uilləə pulisinimәli. かれは働かないであるいているだけ。

10. -kkəə（～ -kkuu ～ -kəə ～ -kuu）　並列語尾。　連続する２語がそれぞれ並列語尾をとり，「……と……（と)」という並列の意味を表わす。

この語尾は，末尾がＶＶまたはＶＣである語に接尾する。一方，末尾がＶまたはCVlである語（第Ｉ図の１．２類の ee に終る語と0.01類の語は除く）には，その語形に一つのある要素が代償重音化をともなって融合している語形もある。ただし，naa（土地)，moo（たきぎ)，ɵɵ（発疹）のような（Ｃ)VVだけからなり，かつVVが同一音素の連続である語は，この融合形を有しない。なお，末尾がCVlである語においては，感嘆融合形におけると同様に，末尾のlのまえでその語形の内部にその要素がくみ入れられて融合しているといえる。以上に記した融合形は，上記の並列語尾が接着した語形と等しい意味・用法をもつ。

用例　（名詞）[主格形] naakkəə bookkuu　地と天（と）／seekkəə issəəl　耳と目（と）／sagjii puriggəə　年寄りと若い者（と）／məwwuu jaajjəə　踊りと歌（と）／seəktuu xuigiikkəə aldaakkeeni　敷香（シスカ）と保恵（ホエ）との間（ともに地名）／［位置格］paduddu itaŋgidduu biini. たばこ入れとわんとにそれはある。／［人称形］munu paduppuu sunu itanŋgissuu　われわれのたばこ入れときみらの神事用のわん（と）　（代名詞）siikkəə biikkəə　ŋənneepu. きみとぼくが行く。／ərrii tarrii. たれもかれも。　（副詞）bolluu nəŋnəə　秋と春（と）に

3

以上の各語尾の交替形とその接続については，第Ｉ，第IIの図に記す。また，語例として，ほかの語尾がついていない名詞主格形（一部は対格形）をあげて二つの表に示す。第Ｉ表は第Ｉ図の語例，第II表は第II図の語例である。

図における *a* は，その語のなかで，まえにａまたはｏがあると，ａであり，

ə または ɵ があると，ə となる。a，o，ə，ɵ がないと，語により，a か，または ə となる。

また，図の *o* は，すぐまえの *o* が，o であると，o であり，ɵ であると，ɵ となる。

第Ⅱ図のなかの1.2類・2類の語の感歎語尾 -kaa 接着形および1.2類の語の感歎融合形における *əə* は，その語のなかで，まえに ə か ɵ があると，əə であり，まえに a か o があると，aa とも，əə ともなり，この両形がある。また，語のなかで，まえに a，o，ə，ɵ がないと，語により，əə となるか，または aa，əə のどちらともなり，この両形がある。

同じく上記二形における *ɵɵ* は，その語のなかで，まえに ə か ɵ があると，ɵɵ であり，まえに a か o があると，oo とも，ɵɵ ともなり，この両形がある。また，語のなかで，まえに a，o，ə，ɵ がないと，語により，ɵɵ となるか，または oo，ɵɵ のどちらともなり，この両形をもつ。

名詞の0.1類（kaltaa［半分］，pəruu［パンツ］，oksoo［そり］，apai［後頭部］など），0.2類（daajinnee［おとな］，aanǰee［右］など）の各単語は，その主格形によって第Ⅰ，第Ⅱの両図の1.2類に入る。名詞0.3類の語は，1.2類の語と同様の語形をとるほかに特殊な語形をとる。例，məəxə（舟のへさき）の語には，məəxəijuu とともに məəgjuu，また məəxəgdəə とともに məəgdəə の語形もあり，それぞれ両形は同義である（前二者は「へさきかしら」，後二者は「へさきなら」）。名詞2.22類の語については，たとえば，illau（木幣）は第Ⅰ，Ⅱ図の1.2類の並列および感嘆の語尾接着形と融合形をとり，形容詞でまた名詞ともなる baja（裕福な，裕福な人）は同図の2.2類の疑問語尾接着形をとっている。なお，umul（帯）に -mali が接尾した形は，採取したままに umul-məli と記入してある。

名詞1.1類の対格の感嘆形としては，名詞1.1類の単純主格形に対格語尾 -wa（～ -wə ～ -wo ～ -wɵ）が接着した形（－CV）の第Ⅱ図1.1類感嘆融合形が用いられる。anduma を例にとると，andumawaa（アンドマ「食物容器」をよー）。また，名詞の0.1類の対格の感嘆形も，単純主格形に対格語尾 -wa または -wə が接着した形（－CV）の第Ⅱ図1.1類感嘆融合形が使われる。例　əmuwəwəə（ゆりかごをよー）。（名詞1.1類については池上 1956 参照。）

また，名詞1.1類の対格の並列形にも，名詞1.1類の単純主格形に対格語尾 -wa またはその交替形が接着した形（－CV）の第Ⅱ図1.1類並列融合形が用いられる。例，paduwwəə itaŋgiwwəə（たばこ入れとわんとを）。

なおまた，動詞1.1類の命令形の感嘆形として，動詞1.1類の基礎語幹に命令形語尾 -ru が接着した形（－CV）の第Ⅱ図1.1類感嘆融合形が用いられる。動詞 ira-（とどける）を例にとると，iraroo（とどけろよー［遠くへ言う］）。（動詞1.1類については池上 1959 参照。）

4

上記の語尾を，おおまかに分類すると，つぎの2類となる。

第一類　(1) -kaa　(2) -ka　(3) -i　(4) -ijuu　(5) -nda

第二類　(6) -dda(a)　(7) -gdaa　(8) -lakka　(9) -mali

(10) -kəə は，並列語尾として別に分類しておく。

第一類の語尾は，文に感嘆の感情を加えたり，文が話し相手への呼びかけであることを特に表出したり，あるいは，その文が相手への質問であること，または，話し手以外からの伝聞であることを表わし，この語尾は，話し手と聞き手の間のことがらや文全体に関することがらにかかわる。この類の語尾は，語の一番末尾に立つ。しかし，伝聞語尾 -nda のついた語形や疑問語尾 -ka のついた語形は，さらに感嘆融合形となることがある。例，…… uččinindəə.（……とかれが言ったとよー。）第一類の語尾は，文を終結するはたらきを有するようにみえ，この類の語尾をもつ語は，文の末尾に立つが，しかし，そのあとにさらにその文の補足を加えることもある。

第二類の語尾は，文中のこの語尾のついた語に限定などの意味を付加し，語の末尾に立つ。しかし，第一類の語尾とともに接尾することもあるが，たとえば，第一類の -nda と第二類の -mali が接尾すると，-mali が -nda のまえに来る。例，kəəkku xuldamalinda.（からの箱だけだそうだ。）第二類の語尾をもつ語は，文のいずれの位置にも立ち，この類の語尾には，文を終結するはたらきはないようにみえる。

また，並列融合形は，同一の語のなかに第一類の -nda または第二類の -mali があると，そのまえに来る。例，mookkuu mɵɵkkuundə.（たきぎと水だそうだ。）／seeltəə punəktəəməli.（炭と灰ばかり。）

付記

第Ｉ，Ⅱ図および本文における略号・記号等についての説明。

ローマ数字による類名は，拙文において扱う語尾が接尾する各単語のなかのその語尾よりまえの部分を，その音形，特に末尾の音形により分類したそれぞれの類を示す。1.類は末尾が母音音素であるものの類，2.類は末尾が子音音素であるものの類である。小数点以下の数字をもつ類は，その下位類である。

Ｖは母音音素を，Ｃは子音音素を示す。

a は／ａ／または／ə／であることを，*o* は／ｏ／または／ɵ／であることを示す。*əə* は，ある語では／əə／であり，ある語では／aa／と／əə／の両形があることを示す。*ɵɵ* は，ある語では／ɵɵ／であり，ある語では／oo／と／ɵɵ／の両形があることを示す。

V は，／ｏ，ɵ／以外の母音音素を示す。

C は，つぎに続くＣと同じ子音音素を示す。

括弧（　）は，そのなかの部分があったり，なかったりすることを示す。

斜線／は「または」を表わす。Ｖ／Ｃは「ＶまたはＣ」を示す。

同じ欄において，ハイフン - が末尾についている形式には，同じく - をかしらにもつ形式が接尾し，ハイフン = が末尾についている形式には，同じく = をかしらにもつ形式が接尾する。

図のなかで，斜線を引いた空欄は，そこに相当する語例が採取できなかった箇所であり，体系的空白とみられる部分である。全くの空欄は，そこの語例も採れなかったが，それが体系的空白であることによるのか不明である箇所か，または，そこの語例がたまたま採取もれで図式化してない箇所である。

第Ｉ図

類	単語における接尾する下記の語尾より前の部分				並列融合形	10. 並列語尾 -kkəə　接着形
1.111	(−)VC*a*	=—CV (1.111–1.124)	=——V (1.111–0.01)		(−)V*C*Cəə	
1.112	(−)VC*o*				(−)V*C*Cuu マタハ (−)V*C*Cəə (1.112–1.113)	
1.113	(−)VCu					
1.114	(−)VCi				(−)V*C*Cii	
1.121	− CC*a*				− CCəə	
1.122	− CC*o*				−CCuuマタハ −CCəə	
1.123	− CCu					
1.124	− CCi				−CCii	
1.2	— ee	=—V*V* (ee, *aa*, Vi, Vu)	=—VV (ee–*oo*)			—V*V*-kkəə (ee, *aa*, Vi)
	— *aa*				—*agg*əə	
	— Vi				—Vjjii	
	— Vu				—Vwwuu (Vu, *oo*)	
	(—)*oo*	(—)*oo* ((—)*oo*, 0.01)				(—)*oo*-kkuu（マタハ-kkəə）
0.01	— *oo*（uトaノ同化）					
2.1	(−)VC*al*	=—Vl (2.1)	= {—*V*l, —*ol*}	=——C (2.1–2.2); = {——l, ——n}	−V*C*Cəəl	—*V*l- マタハ —*ol*= (2.1) ; -kəə =kuu マタハ =kəə (2.1–2.2)
	− VCil				−V*C*Ciil	
	(−)VCul				−V*C*Cuul (VCul, VC*o*l)	
	− VC*o*l					
	− CC*al*				−CCəəl	
	− V*V*l					
2.2	CV*V*n　=— *V*n	=—Vn (2.2)				—*V*k-
	CVon　=— *on*					— ok=

第Ⅱ図

類	単語における接尾する下記の語尾より前の部分	1. 感嘆語尾 -kaa 接着形	感嘆融合形	疑問融合形	2. 疑問語尾 -ka 接着形
1.111	—C*a* (=—CV; =—V)		—C*aa*		—C*a*- (-g*a*)
1.121	〃		〃		〃
1.112	—C*o* (=—CV; =—V)		—C*oo*		—C*o*= (-w*a* =w*o*; -g*a*)
1.122	〃		〃		〃
1.113	—Cu (=—CV; =—V)		—C*oo*		—Cu- (-w*a* =w*o*; -g*a*)
1.123	〃		〃		〃
1.114	—Ci (=—CV; =—V)		—Cee		—Ci- (-w*a* =w*o*; -g*a*)
1.124	〃		〃		〃
1.2	—ee (=—V*V*; =—VV; =—V; =—*V*)	—V*V*-kəə			—ee- (-w*a* =w*o*; -g*a*)
1.2	—*aa* (=—V*V*; =—VV; =—V; =—*V*)	—V*V*-kəə	—*ag*əə		—*aa*- (-w*a* =w*o*; -g*a*)
1.2	—Vi (=—V*V*; =—VV; =—V; =—*V*)	—V*V*-kəə	—Vjee		—Vi- (-w*a* =w*o*; -g*a*)
1.2	—Vu (=—V*V*; =—VV; =—V; =—*V*)	—V*V*-kəə	—Vwɵɵ		—Vu- (-w*a* =w*o*; -g*a*)
1.2	(—)*oo* (=—oo; =—VV; =—V; =—*o*)	(—)*oo*-kɵɵ	—*o*wɵɵ		(—)*oo*= (-w*a* =w*o*; -g*a*)
0.01	—*oo*(u ト *a* ノ同化ニヨル) (=—oo; =—VV; =—V; =—*o*)				— *oo*- (-g*a*)
2.1	—*V*l (=—Vl = {(—) V/c CVl, —VVl}; =—C)	—*V*l- (-kəə =kɵɵ)	(—) V/c CVVl (—VVl ハ融合形ナシ)		—*V*l- (-k*a* =k*o*)
2.1	—*o*l (=—Vl = {(—) V/c CVl, —VVl}; =—C)	—*o*l= (-kəə =kɵɵ)	〃		〃
2.2	—*V*n (=—Vn; =—C)	—*V*n- (-kəə =kɵɵ)			—*V*n- (-k*a* =k*o*)
2.2	—*o*n (=—Vn; =—C)	—*o*n= (-kəə =kɵɵ)			—*o*n= (-k*a* =k*o*)

第II図の続き

<table>
<tr><th>類</th><th>3. 疑問語尾
-i 接着形</th><th colspan="2">4. 疑問語尾 -ijuu
接着形</th><th colspan="2">5. 伝聞語尾
-nda接着形</th><th colspan="2">6. 語尾 -dda(a)
接着形</th><th>7. 語尾 -gdaa
接着形</th><th colspan="2">8. 語尾 -lakka
接着形</th><th colspan="2">9. 語尾 -mali
接着形</th></tr>
<tr><td>1.111</td><td rowspan="8">—CV-i</td><td rowspan="2">—Ca-</td><td rowspan="6">-ijuu</td><td rowspan="9" colspan="2">—V-nda
—o-ndo</td><td rowspan="9" colspan="2">—V-dda(a)
—o-ddo(o)</td><td rowspan="9">—V-gdaa
—o-gdoo</td><td rowspan="9">—V-
—o=</td><td rowspan="14">-lakka
=lokko</td><td rowspan="9">—V-
—o=</td><td rowspan="14">-mali
=moli</td></tr>
<tr><td>1.121</td></tr>
<tr><td>1.112</td><td rowspan="2">—Co-</td></tr>
<tr><td>1.122</td></tr>
<tr><td>1.113</td><td rowspan="2">—Cu-</td></tr>
<tr><td>1.123</td></tr>
<tr><td>1.114</td><td rowspan="2">—Ci-</td><td rowspan="4">-jjuu</td></tr>
<tr><td>1.124</td></tr>
<tr><td>1.2</td><td rowspan="2">—VV-ji</td><td rowspan="2">—VV-</td></tr>
<tr><td>0.01</td><td colspan="2">—oo-nda</td><td colspan="2">—oo-dda(a)</td><td>—oo-gdaa</td><td>—oo-</td><td>—oo-</td></tr>
<tr><td rowspan="2">2.1</td><td rowspan="4"></td><td>—Vl-</td><td rowspan="4">-juu</td><td>—Vl-</td><td rowspan="4">-da
=do</td><td>—Vl-</td><td rowspan="4">-da(a)
=do(o)</td><td rowspan="4"></td><td>—Vl-</td><td>—Vl-</td></tr>
<tr><td>—ol-</td><td>—ol=</td><td></td><td>—ol=</td><td>—ol=</td></tr>
<tr><td rowspan="2">2.2</td><td>—Vn-</td><td>—Vn-</td><td>—Vn-</td><td>—Vn-</td><td>—Vm-</td></tr>
<tr><td></td><td>—on=</td><td>—on=</td><td>—on=</td><td>—om=</td></tr>
</table>

第I表（第I図の語例）

類	単語における接尾する下記の語尾より前の部分（例は名詞主格形，ただし0.01類の例は対格形）	並列融合形	10. 並列語尾 -kkəə 接着形
1.111	anduma（食物容器），utə（戸口）	uttəə	
1.112	toxo（ボタン）	toxxuu	
1.113	padu（たばこ入れの袋）	padduu	
1.114	duri（夜間幼児を入れるかご）	durrii	
1.121	xulda（箱）	xuldəə	
1.122	kombo（ひしゃくに使う器）	kombuu	
1.123	təəkku（ざぶとん，こしかけ）		
1.124	itaŋgi（神事の器［わん］）	itaŋgii	
1.2	bee（月），daajinnee（おとな）		daajinneekkəə
	saldaa（兵隊），naa（土地）	saldaggəə	saldaakkəə，naakkəə
	sipsii（虫の一種），kəŋədəi（かも［鳥］の一種）	sipsijjii	sipsiikkəə
	pau（大砲），illau（木幣，イナウ）	illawwuu, pawwuu	illaukkəə
	moo（たきぎ），bootoo（木の実），oksoo（そり）	bootowwuu	bootookkəə；mookkuu，mookkəə
0.01	paddoo（たばこ入れを［padu の対格形］）		
2.1	isal（目），tarisal（その人ら）	issəəl	isalkəə
	puril（子ら）	purriil	purilkəə
	umul（帯）	ummuul	umulkəə
	bəjəl（けだものら）	bəjjuul	bəjəlkuu，bəjəlkəə
	suŋdattal（さかなら［魚］）	suŋdattəəl	
	piil（うおのめ［いぼ］）		piilkəə
2.2	saan（魚干しの掛け木）		saakkəə
	səən（がいとう［オーバー］），ǰoon（＋）		səəkkuu，səəkkəə

第Ⅱ表（第Ⅱ図の語例）

類	1．感嘆語尾 -kaa接着形	感嘆融合形	疑問融合形	2．疑問語尾 -ka 接着形	3．疑問語尾 -i 接着形
1.111		utəə	utəə	andumaga, utəgə	andumai
1.121		xuldaa	xuldaa	xuldaga	xuldai
1.112		toxoo	toxoo	toxowo	toxoi
1.122		komboo	komboo	kombowo	komboi
1.113		padoo	padoo	paduwa	padui
1.123		təəkkɵɵ	təəkkɵɵ	təəkkuwə	təəkkui
1.114		duree	duree	duriga	durii
1.124		itaŋgee	itaŋgee	itaŋgiga	itaŋgii
1.2	beekaa, beekəə			beega	beeji
	saldaakaa, saldaakəə	saldagaa, saldagəə			
	sipsiikaa, sipsiikəə	sipsijee, kəŋədəjee			
	illaukaa, illaukəə	illawoo, illawɵɵ			
	bootookoo, bootookɵɵ, oksookoo	oksowoo, oksowɵɵ		moowo	mooji
0.01				paddooga	paddooji
2.1	umulkaa, umulkəə, purilkəə	tarisaal, umuul, puriil,		umulka	
	bɵjəlkɵɵ	bɵjɵɵl └pureel			
2.2	saankaa, saankəə			saakka	
	ǰoonkoo, ǰoonkɵɵ, sɵɵnkɵɵ			sɵɵkkɵ	

類	4．疑問語尾 -ijuu接着形	5．伝聞語尾 -nda接着形	6．語尾-dda(a) 接着形	7．語尾-gdaa 接着形	8．語尾-lakka 接着形	9．語尾-mali 接着形
1.111	andumaijuu	andumanda	andumadda(a)	andumagdaa	andumalakka	andumamali
1.121	xuldaijuu	xuldanda	xuldadda(a)	xuldagdaa	xuldalakka	xuldamali
1.112	toxoijuu	toxondo	toxoddo(o)	toxogdoo	toxolokko	toxomoli
1.122	komboijuu	kombondo	komboddo(o)	kombogdoo	kombolokko	kombomoli
1.113	paduijuu	padunda	padudda(a)	padugdaa	padulakka	padumali
1.123	təəkkuijuu	təəkkundə	təəkkuddə(ə)	təəkkugdəə	təəkkuləkkə	təəkkuməli
1.114	durijjuu	durinda	duridda(a)	durigdaa	durilakka	durimali
1.124	itaŋgijjuu	itaŋginda	itaŋgidda(a)	itaŋgigdaa	itaŋgilakka	itaŋgimali
1.2	beejjuu	beenda	beedda(a)	beegdaa	beelakka	beemali
	moojjuu	moondo	mooddo(o)	moogdoo	moolokko	moomoli
0.01	paddoojjuu	paddoonda	paddoodda(a)	paddoogdaa	paddoolakka	paddoomali
2.1	umuljuu	umulda	umulda(a)		umullakka	umulməli
	bɵjəljuu	bɵjəldɵ			bɵjəllɵkkɵ	bɵjəlməli
2.2	saanjuu	saanda	saanda(a)		saanlakka	saammali
		sɵɵndɵ	sɵɵndɵ(ɵ)		sɵɵnlɵɵkkɵ	sɵɵmməli

引用文献

池上二良，1956.「オロッコ語の名詞変化」（英文）『言語研究』30号　日本言語学会。
———，1959.「オロッコ語の動詞変化」（英文）『国語研究』 9 号　國學院大学国語研究会。
———，1994.「ウイルタ語の南方言と北方言の相違点」『北海道立北方民族博物館研究紀要』 3 号。

初出　『北海道方言研究会20周年記念論文集　ことばの世界』［北海道方言研究会　札幌　平成 6 年（1994年）12月15日］158－167ページ。

追記

感嘆語尾 -kaa 接着形および感嘆融合形についての採集用例は第Ⅱ表に挙げたが，調査例がなお不十分で，第Ⅱ図の該当欄に記したその一般化した語形はまだ確定的なものでない。

感嘆語尾については，ほかに，xəpəə boowoo.（ずぶぬれだ，ひどい天気だなあ。）の例があり，VVにおわる語について接着形をつくる感嘆語尾として -woo がみられる。

また，疑問語尾として -(k)kaa（ ～ -(k)kəə ～ -koo）が，つぎのような例にある。（名詞）(kaltaa) bee(k)kaa.（半）月か。／əəktənnee(k)kəə. 女の人か。（数詞）ǰookkoo. 十か。（代名詞）bii(k)kəə. おれかい。（上記の əəktənneekkəə，biikkəə は北川五郎氏からも採取。）末尾が VV または VC である語について接着形をつくり，語末の Vn は Vk となる。

なお，疑問語尾 -ijuu と同義で遠くへ言う場合に使う語尾として -ijoo，-ijɵɵ がつかわれる。　例 naaǰǰeesuijoo. あんたら入用だろか。／naaǰǰeesuijɵɵ. 前文と同義。

なおまた，ほかに1.1類の語には感歎・疑問融合形と同形の並列融合形がある。bəjəni daajjee ǰiktoo nari（体が大きく太い人）の例では，daaji（大きい）とǰiktu（太い）が連続してdaajjee ǰiktoo の語形をとり，大きくて太いという並列の意をもつとみられる。

名詞語幹のあとに接尾する -ijaa（～ -ijəə ～ -(j)jaa ～ -(j)jəə）という付属部分があり，「およびそのほか（etc.)」を意味し，そのあとに格語尾（たとえば対格語尾は -pa）や人称語尾または反照語尾（単数 -pi，複数 -pari）が接尾することもある。これは接尾辞であり，一種の複数接尾辞とみることができよう。例 ammaijaa sinǰeeči. とうさんたちが（andaxa（客）がまじっていても言う）来る。／ami(j)-jaapani かれの父たちを／ami(j)jaapi 自分の父たちを／ami(j)jaapari 自分らの父たちを／ammaijaa annəijəə とうさんたちやかあさんたち（とうさんかあさんたち）。

しかし，この接尾辞をふくむ語は二つ連続すると，「――と――」という並列の意味も生じ，特に，この接尾辞は，他の語尾があとに伴わない名詞主格形につく場合，並列語尾のようにさえみえるが，この接尾辞のついた語は一つだけ単独でも使われ，本文で扱っている並列語尾と同類とみなすことはできないだろう。

引用文献として挙げた拙文はすべて本書に載る。

ウイルタ語の場所などを表す語の構成について

Uilta Word Formation for Terms Indicating ‘Place etc.’

1

ツングース・満洲諸語の一つであるサハリンのウイルタ語には，名詞・代名詞語幹に接尾辞 -(ǰ)ǰee，-kkee，-wwee，-in または -wu が接尾した形，あるいはその語幹と接尾辞が融合した形をもち，場所・位置・方向・方面の意味を表す語（名詞・代名詞）がある。本文は，これらの語の構成などについて述べるものである。

2

まず，ウイルタ語のこれらの語（主格形 nominativus）とその斜格形を，構成の相違によって1.，2.，3.，4.の４類に大別し，さらにこれを1.1，1.2，2.1，2.2，2.3，2.4，3.1，3.2，3.3，4.1，4.2の小類に細分して掲げる。対格（目的格）(accusativus)，位置格（与格）(dativus)，場所格（locativus)，起点格（奪格）(ablativus)，指向格（allativus)，縦走格（沿格，由格）(prolativus)，道具格（造格）(instrumentalis) はそれぞれ acc.，dat.，loc.，abl.，all.，prol.，instr. と略記する。なお，本文のウイルタ語資料は，故佐藤チヨ（ウイルタ名 Napka）さん（1910年ごろ生，1985年没）から採集したものであるが，ただし，故北川五郎（ウイルタ名 Gərgələ）さん（1899年ごろ生，1978年没）や故中川和四郎（ウイルタ名 Jəuriŋənu）さん（1914年生，1988年没）から採集した語も補足的に挙げる。これらの語にはそれぞれ G，J と記してある。ウイルタ語のここに扱う語には，これ以外の語や各語の斜格形がさらに補足されることがありうる。特に，1.類の語の接尾辞 -(ǰ)ǰee は生産的であり，これをもつ語は多いだろう。

1．この類のうち，1.1類では語幹に接尾辞 -ǰǰee が，1.2類では語幹に接尾辞 -ǰee が接着している。

1.1 buniǰǰee（よみのくにの方，西），acc. buniǰǰeepə.
nimǝǰǰee（近所，となり）。

1.2 aanǰee（右），acc. aanǰeepa.
dəunǰee（左），acc. dəunǰeepə.
əəŋinǰee（よみのくにの方，西）（西Ｇ，西，北Ｊ）.
minǰee（わたくしの方）.
sinǰee（あなたの方），acc. sinǰeepə.
suunǰee（南Ｊ，東），acc. suunǰeepə.
dugǰee（家のあるところ），acc. dugǰeepa，loc. dugǰeela，abl. dugǰeeduu，instr. dugǰeekki.

2.，3．これらの類のうち，2.1類では語幹に接尾辞 -kkee が，2.2類では語幹に接尾辞 -wwee が接着している。2.3類，2.4類では語幹と接尾辞が前者で接尾辞 -kkee と，後者で接尾辞 -wwee と融合している。3.1類では語幹に接尾辞 -in が接着しており，3.2類では両者が融合している。3.類の語は，主格形が見いだされず，また，パラダイムのなかで2.3類，2.4類の語とともに，同じ格形として併存する例もあるが，一方，相補的にひとつのパラダイムを組み立てているとみられることがある。こうした点から，3.類の語は2.3類，2.4類の語と合せて挙げるが，3.であることを記してある。

2.1 bookkee（屋外），acc. bookkeepa, loc. bookkeela, prol. bookkeekki, instr. bookkeeǰi.
dookkee（内がわ），acc. dookkeepa, loc. dookkeela, abl. dookkeeduu, prol. dookkeekki.

2.2，3.1

duwwee（海・川から遠い，やまに近いところ），acc. duwweepə，（3.1）ǰiippə，dat.（3.1）ǰiinu，loc.（3.1）ǰiilə，all. duwweeduu，all.（3.1）ǰiisəi，prol. duwweekki，（3.1）ǰiikki.

ŋowwee（海・川に近いところ），acc. ŋowweepa，（3.1）ŋoippa，dat.（3.1）ŋoinu，loc.（3.1）ŋoila，abl. ŋowweeduu，all.（3.1）ŋoisai，prol. ŋowweekki，（3.1）ŋoikki.

uwwee（上の方），acc. uwweepə，（3.1）uippə，dat.（3.1）uinu，loc. uwweelə，（3.1）uilə，abl. uwweeduu，（3.1）uiččuu，all.（3.1）uisəi，prol.（3.1）uikki.

2.3，3.2

baǰǰee（向こう側，対岸），acc. baǰǰeepa，loc. baǰǰeela，abl. baǰǰeeduu，all.（3.2）baisai，prol. baǰǰeekki，instr. baǰǰeeǰi.

dullee（前方［空間，時間］），acc. dulleepə，loc. dulleelə，abl. dulleeduu，prol. dulleekki.

ojjee（おもてがわ），acc. ojjeepa.

pəǰǰee（下の方），acc. pəǰǰeepə，（3.2）pəǰippə，dat.（3.2）pəǰinu，loc. pəǰǰeelə，（3.2）pəǰilə，abl. pəǰǰeeduu，all.（3.2）pəisəi，prol.（3.2）pəǰikki，instr. pəǰǰeeǰi.

sollee（川上），acc. solleepa，（3.2）solippa，dat.（3.2）solinu，loc. solleela，abl. solleeduu，all.（類外）soloi，prol. solleekki，（3.2）solikki，instr. solleeǰi.

tullee（そと），acc. tulleepə，loc. tulleelə，abl. tulleeduu，prol. tulleekki.

xamarree（後方［空間，時間］），acc. xamarreepa，loc. xamarreela，abl. xamarreeduu，prol. xamarreekki.

xaŋŋee（わきにそれた方），acc. xaŋŋeepa，（3.2）xaŋippa，dat.（3.2）xaŋinu，loc. xaŋŋeela，（3.2）xaŋila，abl. xaŋŋeeduu，all. xaŋŋeetai，（3.2）xaŋisai，prol. xaŋŋeekki，（3.2）xaŋikki.

xəǰǰee（川下），acc. xəǰǰeepə，（3.2）xəǰippə，dat.（3.2）xəǰinu，

loc. xəǰǰeelə, abl. xəǰǰeeduu, all.（類外）xəjəi, prol. xəǰǰeekki,（3.2）xəǰikki, instr. xəǰǰeeǰi.

2.4, 3.3

talǰee（沖）, acc. talǰeepa,（3.3）talǰippa, dat.（3.3）talǰinu, loc. talǰeela,（3.3）talǰila, abl. talǰeeduu, all. talǰeetai,（3.3）taisai, prol. talǰeekki,（3.3）talǰikki, instr. talǰeeǰi.

xaagǰee G, xaaǰǰee（おか，陸の方）, acc. xaaǰǰeepa, dat. xaaǰǰeedu, loc. xaaǰǰeela,（類外）xaagǰila G,（類外）G xaaǰila, abl. xaaǰǰeeduu, all. xaaǰǰeetai, prol. xaaǰǰeekki, instr. xaaǰǰeeǰi.

əwwee（こちら）, acc. əwweepə, loc. əwweelə, abl. əwweeduu, prol. əwweekki, instr. əwweeǰi.

tawwee（そちら）, acc. tawweepa, abl. tawweeduu, prol. tawweekki, instr. tawweeǰi.

xawwee（どちら）, acc. xawweepa, loc. xawweela, abl. xawweeduu, prol. xawweekki, instr. xawweeǰi.

taatawwee（ずっと遠いあちら）, acc. taatawweepa.

tootowwee（すこし遠いあちら）, acc. tootowweepa.

4．この類のうち，4.1類の語は語幹に接尾辞 -wu が接着し，4.2類の語では両者が融合しているとみられる。

4.1 boowu（屋外）.

čauwu（そちら）.

doowu（内）, acc. dookkoo.

duuwu（山に近いあたり）.

əuwu（こちら）.

ŋoowu（海・川に近いあたり）.

uuwu（上）, acc. uukkөө.

xauwu, xaawu（どちら）, acc. xaakkoo.

4.2 baduu（向こう側・敵）.

duluu（前）.

ojuu（おもて）.

pəduu（下）, acc. pədukkɵɵ.

soluu（川上）.

xamaruu（後）.

xəduu（川下）.

3

各類の語は，それぞれつぎのように構成されている。なお，Vは母音音素，Cは子音音素を表す。*C*はつぎに来るCと等しい子音音素を表す。ハイフン - は語形中の語幹と接尾辞の境を示す。ダッシュの－は語形のはじめの部分を表す。括弧（　）内はないこともある。

1.1　－V-ǰǰee

1.2　－C-ǰee

2.1　CVV-kkee

2.2　(C)V-wwee

2.3　(－)V*C*Cee

2.4　－VCCee

3.1　(C)V-in

3.2　－VCin

3.3　－VCCin

4.1　(C)VV-wu

4.2　－VCuu

1.1類，1.2類の語の接尾辞 -(ǰ)ǰee と2.1類，2.2類の -kkee，-wwee はどちらも母音音素に終る語幹に接着して分布が部分的に重なる点から，-(ǰ)ǰee は -kkee，-wwee と異なる接尾辞とみる。2.1類の -kkee と2.2類の -wwee は，同一接尾辞の結合的変体とみて扱う。しかし，これら三つの接尾辞の異同は，なお必ずしも明らかでない。

1.類，2.1類，2.2類，3.1類，4.1類の語は，語幹に接尾辞が接着して構成されている。一方，2.3類，2.4類，3.2類，3.3類，4.2類の語は，やはり語幹と接尾辞から成っていると考えられるが，語形をその両者に分離しようとしても境を定め難い様相を呈しており，このような事情にあることを融合とよぶことにしている。これはつぎのことによるとみられる。

すなわち，2.3類，3.2類，4.2類の語形には名詞語幹（－)VCV-が，2.4類，3.3類の語形には名詞語幹－VCCV- がふくまれており，そのあとに接尾辞として2.3類，2.4類の語では -wwee（あるいは -kkee)，3.2類，3.3類の語では -in，4.2類の語では -wu（あるいは *-ku）がやはりふくまれているとみられる。しかし，2.3類，2.4類の語では語幹（－)VCV-，－VCCV- のそれぞれの末尾のVが脱落し，また接尾辞 -wwee（または -kkee）のかしらの ww（または kk）も消失し，さらに2.3類の語では，接尾辞の ww（またはkk）の脱落の代りに語幹の末尾から一つ前のCが重複され，そのCと等しい*C*が加えられて*CC*となっていると考えられる。4.2類の語では，語幹（－)VCV- の末尾の母音音素が逆行同化によってuとなり，接尾辞 wu- の w が消失したとみられる。1.類，2.類の上述の接尾辞をさらに分析することは，今後にゆずりたい。

融合形のなかにふくまれている個々の語幹がそれぞれどんな末尾母音音素をもつ形かについては，ojjee（2.3)(おもてがわ)，dullee（2.3)，duluu（4.2)(前)，xamarree（2.3)，xamaruu（4.2)(後）は，別に ojo（おもて)，duləsəi（前へ)，xamarakkeeni（それの後を通って）の語があることから，それぞれの語幹は ojo-，dulə-，xamara- とみられる。sollee（2.3)，solin-(3.2)，soluu（4.2)(川上）については，動詞語幹 solo-(川上へのぼる）があることからみて，同形の名詞語幹（川上）もあって，それらはこの語幹をふくむものだろう。その他の tullee（2.3)(そと)，xaŋŋee（2.3)，xaŋin-（4.2)(わき)，talǰee（2.4)，talǰin-（3.3)(沖）や baǰǰee（2.3)，baduu（4.2)(向こう側)，pəǰǰee (2.3)，pəǰin-（3.2)，pəduu（4.2)(下)，xəǰǰee（2.3)，xəǰin-（3.2)，xəduu（4.2)(川下）の語幹，特にその後半部については，その形を設定する根拠となるほかの語がウイルタ語内にいまだ見出せないので，ここではふれない。

3.類の語には，主格形がみられず，斜格形だけが採取されている。これらの語には，斜格語尾が，一般には接着的（膠着的）に接尾している。この類の接尾辞は，dat. 格形中にみられる -in の形をその基本形として扱うが，こうすると dat. の語尾は -du の d が消失して -u となっていることになる。一方，この基本形の末尾の n は，acc. 語尾 -pa～ -pə のまえで p，prol. 語尾 -ki のまえで k となり，loc. 語尾 -la～ -lə，all. 語尾 -sai～ -səi のまえで消失する。abl. 語尾のまえでは，これが -čču̇u であるならば，末尾の n は消失し，-čuu ならば，č となっていることになる（čč の発音は［ttʃ］）。また，all. の baisai（向こう側へ），pəisəi（下へ）(3.2)，taisai（沖へ）(3.3) では語中で i のまえの ǰ または lǰ が消失している。

xaagǰee G（おかの方は）は，上陸するを意味する動詞語幹としてあるような xaag- に1.2類の接尾辞 -ǰee が接着しているのでなく，動名詞 xaagǰi（上陸する）に1.1類の接尾辞 -ǰǰee が接着したものに重音消失（haplology）がおきたものとみる。（動名詞に -ǰǰee が接尾した例には suun agbinǰiǰǰeeni（日が現れる方，東），suun tuuǰǰiǰǰeeni（日のおちる方，西）がある。agbinǰi（現れる），tuuǰǰi（おちる）が動名詞。xaaǰǰee（おかの方）は，さらに g が ǰ に逆行同化したものとみる。しかし，loc. 格形に xaagǰila G，xaaǰila G の形もあるのは，talǰee（沖）などの loc. talǰila (3.3)のような形からの類推形成と考えることができよう。

əwwee（こちらは），tawwee（そちら），xawwee（どちら）は，2.2類の語のように，ə-，ta-，xa- という語幹に接尾辞 -wwee が接尾しているものともみられるが，むしろこの語形は əwə-，tawa-，xawa- という語幹と上記の -wwee をふくみ，それが融合している2.3類の語ではないかとみられる。əwə-，tawa-，xawa- の語幹は，əwəsəi（ここへ），tawasai（そこへ），xawasai（どこへ）の語にもふくまれている。

taatawwee（ずっと遠いあちら），tootowwee（すこし遠いあちら）の語も，上記の三語と同様に2.3類に入る語とみられる。なお，これらの語の taa-，too- は，本来，語幹の ta-，to- のまえに重複的におかれた強調的な音とみられよう。

上にみてきた語幹については，同じ語幹が相異なる形を二つまたは二つ以上

もつものがある。すなわち，

u-～uu-（上），ŋo-～ŋoo-（海・川に近いあたり），du-～duu-～（-inのまえで）ǰi-（やまに近いあたり）．また，ə- かまたは əwə-～əu-（これ），ta-かまたは tawa-～tau-，čau-（それ），xa- かまたは xawa-～xaa-～xau-（どれ）．

du-～duu-～ǰi- の語幹交替については，四の意のウイルタ語の ǰiin とナーナイ語 duin の同一語の語形を参照。代名詞語幹 əu-，tau-（または čau-），xau-の語幹は，əudumə（これの方），čauduma（それの方），xauduma（どの方），əukki（こっちを通って），taukki（そっちを通って）の語にもみられる。ə-，əwə-，ta-，tawa-，xa-，xawa- は上を参照。これらの語幹の分析は今後にゆずる。

2.2類，2.3類，2.4類の各語のパラダイムは，すでにみたように，部分的には3.1類，3.2類，3.3類の斜格形によって補充されているが，さらに語によっては，これらの類の語幹とは一応異なる語幹による格形か，2.類や3.類の接尾辞をふくまない語形がパラダイムの一部をなしているようである。すなわち，əwwee（こちら），tawwee（そちら），xawwee（どちら）の語のパラダイムには，all. 格形に既述の əwəsəi，tawasai，xawasai が使われ，abl. 格形には əwweeduu，xawweeduu とともに əməččuu，tamaččuu，xamaččuuの形がある。taatawwee（ずっと遠いあちら），tootowwee（すこし遠いあちら）にも all. 格形に taatawasai，tootowosoi が使われる。これらの all. 格形の語幹は əwə-，tawa-，xawa-，taatawa-，tootowo- であり，abl. 格形の語幹は，語尾 -ččuu か -čuu のまえで əmə(č)-，tama(č)-，xama(č)- の形をもっている。同様の語幹は，əməčigə（こんな），tamačiga（そんな），xamačiga（どんな）にみられる。2.3類の dullee（前），xamarree（後）の all. 格形には duləsəi，xamasai が使われるが，これらは2.類・3.類の接尾辞をふくまず，語幹の dulə-，xama- に直接に接尾辞が接着している。2.3類の sollee（川上），xeǰǰee（川下）の all. 格形には soloi，xəjəi が使われるが，これらは2.類，3.類の接尾辞をふくまず，前者は語幹 solo- と -i という要素からできており，後者は名詞語幹 xəjə（急流），動詞語幹 xəjə-（流れる）と同形の語幹と上と同じ-iという要素から成り立っている。なおまた，2.1類のbookkee（屋外），dookkee（内がわ）のパラダイムは，この類の接尾辞をもたないboo（そと），doo（内部）の語の斜格形（たとえばall. 格形bootoi，dootoi）によって補われているようである。

4

本文に扱ってきた語は，すでに触れたように，場所（空間，時間における），位置，方面，方向などをその語義とするが，これらの語は，二つの語が意味上互に反意語の関係に立って対をなすものが多い。2.類の語を例に引くと，

uwwee（上の方）(2.2):pəǰǰee（下の方）(2.3)/dullee(前方)(2.3):xamarree（後方）(2.3)/aanǰee（右）(1.2):dəunǰee(左)(1.2)/dookkee（うちがわ）(2.1):ojjee（おもてがわ）(2.3)/sollee（川上）(2.3):xəǰǰee（川下）(2.3)/ŋowwee（海・川に近い方）(2.2):duwwee（海・川から遠い方）(2.2)/talǰee(沖)(2.4):xaagǰee G，xaaǰǰee（陸の方）(2)/əwwee（こちら）(2.2):tawwee（そちら）(2.2).

これらの語の語義のなかには，語義とするある場所等がこれに対比される場所等との対立的な関係にあるものであるということもふくまれているとみるべきだろう。そして，この意味はその語の使用される場面によっては強くあらわれるといえよう。たとえば，uwwee，下に対する上，すなわち，上の方。

本文で扱ってきた語の用法について若干記すと，1.類，2.類，4.類の語は，その語のまえに名詞，代名詞または動名詞（動詞連体形）が下記の例におけるような名詞的修飾語として立つ構造では，人称語尾や反照語尾が接尾される。例，duxu duwweeni（家の裏).

また，1.類，2.類，4.類の語が下記の例におけるような形容詞的修飾語として名詞のまえに立つ構造では，この名詞は人称語尾をとらない。例，tawwee nari（そちらの人).

1.類，2.類，4.類の語の主格形は，副詞的に動詞に対する修飾語としても使われる。例，əwwee təəru.（こっちへすわれ。）

2.類，3.類の語には，まえに指示形容詞などがおかれることがある。例，jəə talǰinu（この沖に）.

用例

1.類，2.類の語の主格形

uwwee pəmu 上唇／ pəǰǰee pəmu 下唇／ aanǰee xoldo 右わき／ dəunǰee xoldo 左わき／ jəə duwwee この奥（裏）／ uni baǰǰeeni 川の向こう岸／ tari tawweeni その向こう／ mini xaŋŋeepi təəru. おれのわきにすわれ。／ xawwee biinigə. かれはどちらにいるか。／ tawwee biini. かれはあちらにいる。／ sinǰee biini. それはきみの方にある。／ sollee suŋdatta sumunasini. 川上で魚が跳ねている。

1.類，2.類，3.類の語の斜格形

acc. tawweepa oossu. そっちをかたづけろ。／ sinǰeepə kəənǰini. かれはきみの方のことを話す。／ pəǰippə səgǰeeni.（鳥が）地をすれすれに飛ぶ。／ solippa əərə gooǰǰini. 川上で鱒がぶなけとなる。／ xəǰippə suŋdatta biini. 川下に魚がいる。／ jəə ǰiippə pulisini. この奥のやまをかれは歩いている。

dat. uinu biini. それは上にある。

loc. jəə talǰeela moičča uisini. この沖で鉄砲の音がしている。／ jəə talǰila moičča uisini. 同上。／ xamarreela kəəŋittə. ぼくはあとで話そう。

abl. solleeduu əurini. かれは川上からくだる。／ pəǰǰeeduu kaappeeni. かれは川下からのぼる。／ duwweeduu əurini. かれはやまの方からおりる。／ ŋowweeduu kaappeeni. かれは川の方からあがる。／ uiččuu tuuxəni. それは上から落ちた。

all. xaŋisai ŋənnəu. わきの方へ行け。

prol. xawweekki ŋənnəuree. どっちから行くか。／ jəə ǰiikki biini. それはこのうらてにある。／ ŋənneewi dulleekkeeni dəpčiwi. ぼくは自分が行くまえに食事する。

instr. tawweeǰi goro. そっちより遠い。／ jəə talǰeeǰi sukta. こ

の沖より深い。

4.類の語

xaawu toŋdowo. どちらが正しいか。/ soluu duxu 川上の家/ xəduu duxu 川下の家/ ŋoowu duxu 川に近い家/ duuwu duxu 川から離れている家/ ŋoowu nari 人が集っている中で一番前の人/ duuwu nari 人の集っている中で一番奥の人/ doowu gəlbu 本名/ ojuu gəlbu 俗称/ xamaruu oksoo うしろのとなかい橇/ ɵtuu pəduu təwəskə 一番下の雲/ tootori duxu baduuduni biini. それはあの家の向かいにある。/ uukkɵɵ dappeeni. かれは上のをとる。

初出 **알타이학보** (*Journal of the Altaic Society of Korea*) 5号 (1995年12月), 21−28頁。なお, 同誌6号 (1996年12月), 206ページに訂正表を付してある。

追記

ツングース語と比較してみると, ウイルタ語の上掲の接尾辞 -ǰǰee は, エウェンキー語の下記の接尾辞と本来同じものであろう。-gidā(-gidə) (prostranstvo, storona を表す) [G. M. Vasilevič, Ėvenkijsko-russkij slovar'(Moskva, 1958), str. 751], -gida (意味 — nazvanija storon predmeta) [O. A. Konstantinova, Ėvenkijskij jazyk (Moskva-Leningrad, 1964), str. 91].

ウイルタ語代名詞とその格変化

Uilta Pronouns and Their Inflections

ウイルタ語は，サハリン（カラフト）の少数民族の一つであるウイルタ族の言語である[1]。ウイルタ語には，代名詞として，人代名詞，反照（反射）代名詞（これはまた再帰代名詞ともよぶ），指示代名詞があるほか，疑問代名詞，不定代名詞とみることもできるものがある。ただし，疑問代名詞は，その語幹に名詞語幹形成接尾辞と等しい接尾辞が接尾して形成されている語もあり，名詞の一種ともみられるものである。

代名詞の格変化は，名詞（実詞）の格変化[2]に類するものであり，その一種とも言え，代名詞の語幹に格語尾が接尾しておこなわれるが，これらの代名詞の格変化には特異な点もある。

代名詞にはつぎの格がある。

主格（nominativus）	起点格（奪格）（ablativus）
属格（所有格）（genitivus）	指向格（allativus）
対格（目的格）（accusativus）	縦走格（沿格・由格）（prolativus）
位置格（与格）（dativus）	道具格（造格）（instrumentalis）
場所格（locativus）	共同格（comitativus）

代名詞の格形は，名詞の相応の格形と同様の意味[2]を表わすとみられる。属格形は，この語がさす人にものや人が所属することを意味する。

なお，代名詞の種類によって，これらの格のあるものは欠けている。

1　人代名詞

第１人称・第２人称および第３人称の単数・複数の人代名詞がある。

	第１人称単数	第１人称複数
主格	bii	buu
属格	mini	munu
対格	mimbee	mumbeepə
位置格	mindu	mundu
場所格	mindulə	mundulə
起点格	minduu	munduu
指向格	mittəi	muttəi
縦走格	mikki	mukki
道具格	minǰi	munǰi
共同格	mindɵɵ	mundɵɵ

	第２人称単数	第２人称複数
主格	sii	suu
属格	sini	sunu
対格	simbee	sumbeepə
位置格	sindu	sundu
場所格	sindulə	sundulə
起点格	sinduu	sunduu
指向格	sittəi	suttəi
縦走格	sikki	sukki
道具格	sinǰi	sunǰi
共同格	sindɵɵ	sundɵɵ

	第3人称単数	第3人称複数
主格	nooni	noos̆i
対格	noomboni	noombos̆i
位置格	noonduni	noondus̆i
場所格	noondulani	noondulas̆i
起点格	noonduuni	noonduus̆i
指向格	noottoini	noottois̆i
縦走格	nookkeeni	nookkees̆i
道具格	noonǰini	noonǰis̆i
共同格	noondooni	noondoos̆i

用例

mini aŋmabi　ぼくの口／　mimbee gaǰǰini.　ぼくをかれはつれて行く。／　mindu biini.　ぼくのところにある。／　mindulə gaduxani.　ぼくからかれはもって行った。／　munduu ŋənneeni. ぼくらのうちからかれは行く。／　mittəi bəəru. ぼくにくれ。／　mikki uktulixani. ぼくにかれはぶつかった。／　sunǰi daaji.　きみたちより大きい。／　sindəə ŋənneeči.　きみとかれらは行く。きみとだれかひとりが行く。

第1，第2人称人代名詞は，主格と斜格の語幹の形が異なり，また，名詞と異なり，属格がある。

第3人称人代名詞は第1，第2人称人代名詞と語の構成が異なる。第3人称人代名詞としては，指示代名詞単数形のəri（これ），tari（それ），複数形のəril，ərisəl（この人たち），taril，tarisal（その人たち）もその役をするが，ほかにnooni，noočiがある。この二語の語幹は，noon-である。noon-は，2.222類の名詞(2)と同様の格変化をし，語幹末尾のnが，脱落したり，m，tまたはkと交替したりする。語末には第3人称語尾-ni，-čiが必ずつく。すなわち，その付加は義務的である。nooni，noočiは，人間を指す名詞が文脈上他の人間を指す名詞に対比される場合に，その一方の名詞の代用の語となり，それを他方の名詞から区別するとみられる(3)。この2語は，名詞と同様に，属格がなく，主格がその役を兼ねる（例，nooni ŋaalani　かれの手）。

また，所有物を意味する人代名詞のつぎの語形がある。miniŋŋi（わたしのもの），munuŋŋi（わたしたちのもの），siniŋŋi（きみのもの），sunuŋŋi（きみたちのもの），nooŋini（かれのもの），nooŋŋini（対格 nooŋŋeeni）（同上），nooniŋini（同上），nooŋiči（かれらのもの），nooŋŋiči（対格 nooŋŋeeči）（同上），noočiŋiči（同上），nooniŋiči（同上）.

2　反照代名詞

単数形と複数形がある。主格形はない。

	自分自身	自分たち自身
属格	məənə	məənə
対格	məəpi	məəpəri
位置格	məənǰi	məəndəəri
場所格	məəndulli	məənduləri
起点格	məəndukki	məəndukkəəri
指向格	məəttəkki	məəttəkkeeri
縦走格	məəkki	məəkkeeri
道具格	məənǰi	məənǰeeri

用例

məənə uttabi　自分のくつを／ məəndəəri buisiči.　自分たちのところにかれらは置いている。／ məənduləri gaduxači.　自分たちのうちからかれらはもって行った。／ məəndukki bəəxəni. 自分のもっているものからかれはくれた。／ məəttəəkkeeri gaduxači.　自分たちのところへかれらはもって行った。／ məəkki uixəni. 自分にかれはつないだ。

反照代名詞には，主格がないが，一方，人代名詞と同様に属格がある。属格以外は，語幹 məən- ＋ 格語尾のあとに反照接尾辞 -pi（自分の）または -pəri（自分たちの）が，接尾するか，または格語尾と融合している。語幹末尾の n

は，脱落したり，あるいはｔ，ｋとなることがある。

また，所有物を意味する反照代名詞のつぎの語形がある。məəniŋŋi（自分のものを），məəniŋŋeeri（自分たちのものを）。

3　指示代名詞

指示代名詞には，近称əri（これ）と遠称tari（それ）の対立がある。さらにこのほかに，遠いものの指示について，少し遠いあれを指示するtootoriとずっと遠いあれを指示するtaatariの対立がある。

	これ	それ
主格	əri	tari
対格	jəwə	čawa
位置格	jədu	čadu
場所格	jələ	čala
起点格	əməččuu	tamaččuu
指向格	əwəsəi	tawasai
縦走格	jəkki	čakki
道具格	jəǰi	čaǰi

	少し遠いあれ	ずっと遠いあれ
主格	tootori	taatari
対格	tootowo	taatawa
位置格	tootodu	taatadu
場所格	tootolo	taatala
起点格	tootomoččuu	taatamaččuu
指向格	tootowosoi	taatawasai
縦走格	tootokki	taatakki
道具格	tootoǰi	taataǰi

用例

čala ŋənneewi. そこへぼくは行く。／ čala bəəru. それにやれ（与えよ）。／ čakki dappau. そこからとれ。

これらの指示代名詞は，場所をさして，それぞれ，ここ，そこ，すこし遠くのあそこ，ずっと遠くのあそこの意味ともなる。起点格，指向格の語形は，補充法によるものである。əri，tari の斜格の語幹はそれぞれ je-， ča- であり，主格の語幹と異なる。əri，tari に対しては，それぞれの複数形として，əril および ərisəl（この人たち），taril および tarisal（その人たち）の語がある。

əri，tari，tootori，taatari は，また指示形容詞として，それぞれ，この，その，すこし遠くのあの，ずっと遠くのあのの意味をもつ。ただし，əri，tari が斜格の名詞を修飾する場合は，それぞれ jəə，čaa の形をとる。

このほか，指示代名詞として，əwwee（この方面）（対格 əwweepə），tawwee（その方面）（対格 tawweepa），əuwu（こちら），čauwu（そちら），əməčigə（このような（もの）），tamačiga（そのような（もの））（対格 tamačikkaa）があり，あとの 2 語は指示形容詞ともなる。

なお，指示副詞として，ərəŋəči（このように），taraŋači（そのように）がある。また təəli（そのときに）の語もある。

4　疑問代名詞

	なに
主格	xai
対格	xaiwa
位置格	xaidu
場所格	xaila
起点格	xamaččuu
指向格	xaitai，xawasai
縦走格	xaikki

道具格	xaiǰi	
	だれ	だれたち
主格	ŋui	ŋuijjəə
対格	ŋuiwə	ŋuijjəəpə
位置格	ŋuidu，ŋuindu	ŋuijjəədu
場所格	ŋuilə，ŋuindulə	ŋuijjəələ
起点格	ŋuiduu	ŋuijjəəduu
指向格	ŋuitəi	ŋuijjəətəi
縦走格	ŋuikki	ŋuijjəəkki
道具格	ŋuiǰi，ŋuinǰi	ŋuijjəəǰi
共同格	ŋuindɵɵ	ŋuijjəəndɵɵ

用例

xaidu əksəuree. どこに置くか。／ xaila ŋənneesee. どこまでおまえは行くか。／ xaitai əksəuree. どこへ置くか。／ xaikki ŋənnəuree. どこから行くか。／ xaiǰi andupuree. 何でつくるか。

ŋuidu（または ŋuindu）biinee. だれのところにそれはあるか。／ ŋuilə（または ŋuindulə）saaxasee. だれからきみはきいて知ったか。／ ŋuiduu sindaxanee. だれからそれは来たか（ものが送られて来た場合などにいう）。／ ŋuitəi bɵɵrisee. だれにきみはあげるか。／ ŋuikki saaxasee. だれからきみはきいて知ったか。／ ŋuiǰi（または ŋuinǰi）daajiga. だれより大きいか。／ ŋuindɵɵ ŋənneesee. だれときみは行くか。

xai（何）は，1.21類の名詞(3)と同様の格変化をする。ŋui（誰）は1.21類の名詞と同様の格変化をするが，またある格形では，2.211類の名詞と同様の格変化もする。ŋui（誰）の複数形 ŋuijjəə は，語幹 ŋui に名詞の複数を表わす接尾辞 -ijaa ～ -jjaa ～ -ijəə ～ -jjəə が接尾してできている。この接尾辞は，語幹が表わす人間とそれを代表とする他の人間とを合せて表わす。例，ammaijaa（お父さんたち）（amma はお父さんの意）。

xai（何）の語幹 xai- には，名詞や形容詞に接尾する接尾辞も接尾する。例，xaiska（何というけだものの皮，何皮）（疑問名詞），xaima（何でつくった）（疑問形容詞），xaiskami（何の皮でつくった）（疑問形容詞）。

また，疑問動詞語幹として xai-（何をするか）があり，これを語幹とする xairi-ni（かれは何をするか）の疑問動詞がある。これは0.22類の動詞[4]である。さらにこの動詞の未完了連用形 xaimi は，どうして，なぜという意味で使われる。

このほか，疑問代名詞として xawwee（どっちの方面）（対格 xawweepa），xaawu，xauwu（どちら）（対格 xaakkoo），xamačiga（どんな（もの））があり，最後の語は疑問形容詞ともなる。また，sari（どちら）（場所格 sala（どこへ，どこまで））があり，疑問形容詞としてどのの意味ともなる。なおまた，saaga はどれか（質問）を意味する。

また，疑問数詞には，疑問基数詞として xasu（いくつ）（対格 xasumba），疑問序数詞として xassee（何番め）がある。また，xasu と -nnee（人）が合成した xasunnee（なん人，いく人）のような語もある。

なお，疑問副詞には，xooni（どのように），xoottoi（どっちへ），xaali（いつ）がある。さらに，xaali を語幹として，名詞，形容詞，副詞の語幹につく接尾辞 -pči がそれに接尾した形容詞 xaalipči（いつの）の語もある。また，疑問回数副詞として xasulta（何回）がある。この語は，数詞に接尾して回数副詞をつくる接尾辞 -lta が xasu についてできている。

また，疑問動詞語幹として xai-（何をするか）があり，これにさらに動詞語幹形成接尾辞 -ŋda（あることをしに行く）がついた xaŋda- を語幹とする xaŋǰee-ni（かれは何をしに行くか）の疑問動詞がある。この動詞は，1.121類の動詞である。

5　不定代名詞

疑問代名詞に語尾 -dda(a) ～ -ddə(ə)（も）がついた xaidda(a)（なにか，なんでも），ŋuiddə(ə)（だれか，だれでも）が不定代名詞としての役をする。

なお，疑問副詞 xaali や疑問回数副詞 xasulta に -dda(a)（も）が接尾した xaalidda（いつか），xasultadda（なん回も）の語があり，これらはそれぞれ不定副詞，不定回数副詞ともいえよう。

このほかにも，代名詞ともいえる anu（えーといま思い出せないがあれ）という語がある。anu は，文法的機能，特に話線上の文法的機能（統語論的機能）をもつが，言わば意味のわくだけを示して実際の意味内容は有しない。不明の語の代用語ともいえよう。話し手が，文脈上その箇所で使おうと意図する名詞をそのとき想起できず，従って実際に発音して使用できず，やむをえずかわりにとにかくそれに代る語をおき，表現上，話線上の前後の語に対して少くとも統語論的機能をとりつくろい，文法的には全体の文をつくり上げるものである。anu を使ったあと，使うことのできなかった語を思い出し，補うようにその語を話線上あとにおくこともある。anu は，格変化をおこなって斜格形も有し，名詞の1.113類のように対格は annoo であり，文脈中，対格を使うべき箇所では annoo を使う。人称語尾・反照語尾も付く。mini anubi（おれのえーとあれ），məənə anubi（自分のえーとあれを）．また，動詞語幹として anu-（えーと言いたいそのことばがいま口に出て来ないがあれであるまたはあれをする）があり，これを語幹とする代動詞 anni-ni（かれはえーと言いたいそのことばがいま思い出せないがあれであるまたはあれをする）があり，これは動詞の1.113類に属す。

注

(1) 本稿では，ウイルタ語ポロナイ方言（ポロナイスク（敷香）を中心とする南の地方，すなわち旧日本領地方，かつての敷香支庁の地方の方言）を扱う。戦後サハリンから北海道へ移住したウイルタの人びとのウイルタ語もこの方言である。これに対するワール方言（今日ワールを中心とする北の地方の方言）とは異なる点がある。資料は，故佐藤チヨ（Napka）さんから得たものである。

(2) Ikegami, J., The Substantive Inflection of Orok.『言語研究』30，日本言語学会，1956. 以下，名詞の類はこの文献を参照されたい。

(3) Ikegami, J., The Orok Third Person Pronoun nooni. *Ural-Altaische*

Jahrbücher, Band 40, Heft 1-2, Otto Harrassowitz, Wiesbaden, 1968参照。

(4) Ikegami, J., The Verb Inflection of Orok.『国語研究』9, 国学院大学国語研究会, 1959. 以下, 動詞の類はこの文献を参照されたい。

初出　札幌大学女子短期大学部創立25周年記念論文集［平成5年（1993年）3月］363－371ページ。

The Orok Third Person Pronoun *nooni*[1)]

The Orok language (one of the Tungus languages which is spoken in Sakhalin) has, as the first person sing. and pl. pronouns, *bii* and *buu* and, as the second person sing. and pl. pronouns, *sii* and *suu*, and further *nooni* and *nooči*, which, with the proviso mentioned below, we may call the third person sing. and pl. pronouns.

The inflection of these pronouns is as follows:

case/person	1. sing.	1. pl.	2. sing.
nominative	bii	buu	sii
accusative	mimbee	mumbeepə	simbee
genitive	mini	munu	sini
locative	mindulə	mundulə	sindulə
comitative	mindɵɵ	mundɵɵ	sindɵɵ
dative	mindu	mundu	sindu
instrumental	minǰi	munǰi	sinǰi
ablative	minduu	munduu	sinduu
allative	mittəi	muttəi	sittəi
prolative	mikki	mukki	sikki

case/person	2. pl.	3. sing.	3. pl.
nominative	suu	nooni	nooči
accusative	sumbeepə	noomboni	noomboči
genitive	sunu		
locative	sundulə	noondulani	noondulači

comitative	sundөө	noondooni	noondooči
dative	sundu	noonduni	noonduči
instrumental	sunǰi	noonǰini	noonǰiči
ablative	sunduu	noonduuni	noonduuči
allative	suttəi	noottoini	noottoiči
prolative	sukki	nookkeeni	nookkeeči

The third person pronouns have, as the basic stem, *noon-*. These third person pronouns are different from the first and second person pronouns in that those contain a personal ending i.e. the third person ending *-ni* or the third person plural ending *-či*, whereas these contain no personal ending.

The third person pronouns have a peculiarity in their usage, which we shall deal with here. In Orok the demonstrative pronouns *əri* 'this', *tari* 'that', *əril* 'these', *taril* 'those' etc. refer also to the third person(s). But the usage of *nooni* and *nooči* is restricted in comparison with that of *tari* etc. I assume *nooni* is used as a substitute for any of the class of substantives designating a personal object, provided that a personal object designated by the substantive contrasts with another personal object[2] in the context. The class also contains substantive phrases designating a personal object, such as *purigə nari* 'a young man'. In personification *nooni* is also used as a substitute for any substantive designating an animal or a devil. *nooči* is the plural form of this substitute.

I cite some typical instances of *nooni* from the Orok folk tale texts which I have published[3].

1. *ənəj nari gugdani nari n o o m b o n i waapikkat orogǰini.*
   'Oh my! An extremely tall man is carrying h i m on his shoulder'.
   [OM p. 632, 1.9]
2. *n o o n*ǰiinii əəktə puttə geeda puttə biinindəə.*

'There was a girl of about the same age as s h e'. [OK p. 160, 1.64]

3. *suŋdattaa čii waarin n o o n** *ɵmɵɵkɵ.*

   'He alone catches fish all the time without fail'. [OK p. 171, 1.64]

   * = *noon i* The final *i* is apocopated.

I obtained a helpful information on the usage of *nooni* from Napka, one of my informants. I had given her two story beginnings (A and B) of my own invention in order to put questions on two different situations, one with only one character and another with two characters distinguished from each other.

A. 1. *geeda mapaačča suŋdattaa waaŋdami unnee soloxoni.* 2. *suŋdattaa mastaa baramba waaxani.* 3. *dolboduxani.* 4. *tari mapaačča uni kiraduni aundaxani.* — 1. An old man went fishing upstream. 2. He caught a large number of fish. 3. Night fell. 4. The old man passed the night by the side of the river.

B. 1. *geeda mapaačča suŋdattaa waaŋdami unnee soloxoni puriga narree oroŋmi.* 2. *suŋdattaa mastaa baramba waaxači.* 3. *dolboduxani.* 4. *tari mapaačča puriga naritai uččini.* 5. *uni kiraduni aunǰeesu.* — 1. An old man went fishing upstream with a young man. 2. They caught a large number of fish. 3. Night fell. 4. The old man said to the young man. 5. ≪Shall we pass the night by the side of the river ?≫

Then I questioned her, as to which of the following expressions she would use for part 4. of each of the two stories, if she were the teller.

A. a. *tari mapaačča uni kiraduni aundaxani.* 'The old man passed the night by the side of the river'.

   b. *n o o n i uni kiraduni aundaxani.* 'H e passed the night by the side of the river'.

B. a. *tari mapaačča puriga naritai uččini.* 'The old man said to the young man'.

b. *nooni purigə naritai uččini.* 'He said to the young man'.

c. *tari mapaačča noottoini uččini.* 'The old man said to him'.

In answer to my question she said that in A she would use the first expression (a) and not the second one (b), but that in B all three expressions (a, b, c) would be possible. I believe her answer confirms the above-mentioned usage of *nooni.*

Napka also reported that in conversation a young married man or woman refers to his wife or her husband as *nooni,* which suggests, I think, that young married people make a clear distinction between their life partners and all others.

We find that the usage of *nooni* in Orok has a feature in common with the usage of the obviative forms of nouns in Algonquian, where they refer to one of the two animate objects (the third person) appearing in a context[4)]. In Algonquian, however, they are the inflected forms of nouns, whereas the Orok obviative *nooni* is a pronoun.

The Orok *nooni* and *nooči* have their correspondents in other Tungus languages: Evenki *nungan* and *nungartyn,* Negidal *nuŋan* and *nuŋatil,* Even *nongan* and *nongartan,* Udehe *nua* and *nuati,* Orochi *nuan* ~ *nungan* and *nuati,* Goldi *njoani* and *njoanči,* Olcha *nān* and *nāti*[5)]. Hitherto these words have simply been described as third person pronouns used generally for one (personal) object or more and not, so far as I know, as third person pronouns in such a restricted use as given above. A similar usage, however, may possibly be discovered also in other Tungus languages besides Orok. It seems to me to be older than the usage of these words as general pronouns for the third person(s). The stem *noon-* is probably derived from a substantive stem. But the etymology is yet open to question, although some opinions have been advanced[6)]. It is possible that the usage of Orok *nooni* may help us trace this word to its origin.

Notes

1) The following is a revised version of a paper with the same title that I read at the XXVIIth International Congress of Orientalists in Ann Arbor, on 17 August, 1967. The summary of the original paper appeared in the *Proceedings of the Twenty-seventh International Congress of Orientalists, Ann Arbor, Michigan 1967* (Otto Harrassowitz, Wiesbaden 1971), pp. 607–608.

2) or personal objects.

3) J. IKEGAMI: Orokko-zoku no minwa to uta sûrei (Some specimens of the folk tales and songs of the Oroks), *Minzokugaku-Kenkyu* (*The Japanese Journal of Ethnology*) 27, 1963 (abbrev. to OM) — J. IKEGAMI: Orokko-zoku no kôtô-bungei (The oral literature of the Oroks), *Eurasia Bunka Kenkyu* (*Bulletin of the Institute of Eurasian Cultural Studies Hokkaido University*) 1, 1965 (abbrev. to OK). On p. 171, l. 64, *waari*, read *waarin.*

4) L. BLOOMFIELD: *Language*, 1933, p. 193, etc. — H. HOIJER and others: *Linguistic Structures of Native America*, 1946, p. 94, etc.

5) G. M. VASILEVIČ: *Ėvenkijsko-russkij slovar'*, 1958, pp. 697, 698. — K. M. MYL'NIKOVA and V. I. CINCIUS: Materialy po issledovaniju negidal'skogo jazyka, *Tungusskij sbornik* I, 1931, pp. 146, 147. — V. I. CINCIUS and L. D. RIŠES: *Russko-ėvenskij slovar'*, 1952, pp. 725, 726. — E. R. ŠNEJDER: *Kratkij udėjsko-russkij slovar'*, 1936, pp. 105, 106. — V. I. CINCIUS: Očerk morfologii oročskogo jazyka, *Učenye zapiski LGU*, 98, Serija vostokovedčeskich nauk, 1, 1949, pp. 139–141. — V. A. AVRORIN: *Grammatika nanajskogo jazyka*, 1, 1959, pp. 246–252. — T. I. PETROVA: *Ul'čskij dialekt nanajskogo jazyka*, 1936, pp. 30, 31.

6) G. J. RAMSTEDT: *Studies in Korean Etymology*, 1949, p. 170, *Einführung in die altaische Sprachwissenschaft*, II, 1952, pp. 56, 76. — J. BENZING: *Die tungusischen Sprachen, Versuch einer vergleichenden Grammatik*, 1956, pp. 108, 109. — G. M. VASILEVIČ: op. cit., p. 697. — V. A. AVRORIN: op. cit., pp. 153, 249.

This article was published in *Ural-Altaische Jahrbücher*, Band 40, Heft 1–2 (1968), pp. 82–84.

ツングース語オロッコ方言の母音音素 ö について

On the Vowel Phoneme ö in the Orokko Dialect of Tungus

1. ツングース語オロッコ方言には筆者の調査によれば十の母音音素/i, ɪ, ə, a, o, ɵ（＝ö）, ᴜ, u, e, ε/が認められる。ただし/ i /と/ ɪ /の差異, / u /と/ᴜ/の差異, / e /と/ ε /の差異はなお問題であるが，その点についてはここには触れない。そのうち/ɵ/の母音音素は従来明確に認められていなかったので，それについてここに述べたいと思う。母音音素に隣接しない/ɵ/は短母音［ȯ］に該当し，連続する二つの/ɵɵ/には長母音［ȯː］が該当する。ただし澗潟久治氏に昭和26年３月にお会いした折この母音があることをお話ししたが，同氏も以前にオロッコ方言の［ȯːrȯ］（鱒）の発音においてこの母音を認められた由である。

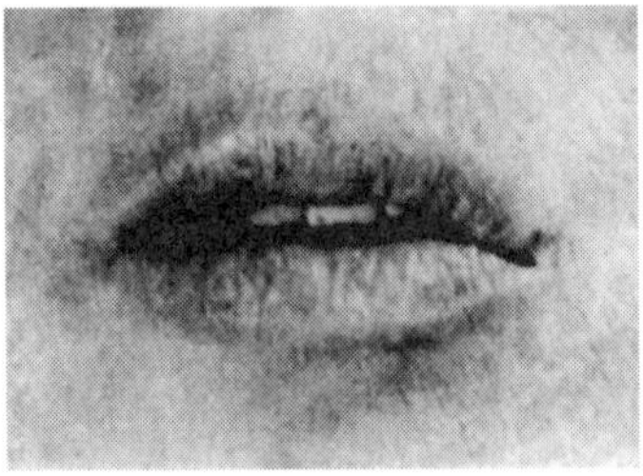

［ȯː］（被調査者の一人カヨさんの /ɵɵ/［ȯː］（できもの）の発音）

2. 短母音［ȯ］はややせまい前寄りの後舌円唇母音である。［ȯː］はその長母音である。［ȯːrȯ］（鱒）の発音における［ȯː］を観察したところではその母音の唇のまるめはせばめが著しくなく，唇の突出しもほとんど認められない。

3. オロッコ方言にも母音調和の現象があり，/ɵ/は所謂女性母音音素として，通常一つの語形（これに該当する音声には前後にとぎれがあることがあるが，通常中間にとぎれがない）のなかで/ə, u, i, e/とは共存しうるが，そのほかの母音音素とは共存しえない。また一つの語形のなかの母音音素の配列に関する制限もあり，母音音素に隣接しない/ɵ/は/ə, u /のあとには続きえない。しかし連続する二つの/ɵɵ/は/ə, u /のあとにも続くことができる。たとえばsəpteө（さびを），tugbөө（əsini tugbөө（彼がおとさない））。

なお接尾辞や語尾においては，それが接尾する語幹の母音音素に応じて或一組の母音音素が交替してあらわれる。その点については接尾辞や語尾に含まれる/ө/は/a/～/o/～/ə/～/ө/の交替をする。ただし連続する二つの/өө/は/oo/とだけ交替することもある。例 tamna-ska（霧のけむり），xoldo-sko（棺），səəpə-skə（貂の皮），bөjө-skө（熊の皮），dapa-xa（つかんだ），soŋo-xo（泣いた），ŋənu-xə（帰った），tөjө-xө（御馳走した），aag-doo（兄と），puril-dөө（こどもたちと）。

4. 連続する二つのөөについてみると，かわうそを意味する語形には［mȯ:dȯ:］に該当するmөөdөөのほかに［mȯ:duɣ̈ə］に該当する別の語形もある。また蠅を意味する語形には［dʒi:lȯ:］に該当するǰiilөөのほかに［dʒi:luɣ̈ə］に該当する別の語形もある。mөөdөө，ǰiilөөはそれぞれその別の語形から変化したものとみられる。

またたとえばtugbөө（əsini tugbөө（彼がおとさない））はtugbu-（おとす）に動詞語尾-rəが接尾した形から変化したとみられ，səptөө（さびを）はsəptu（さび）に名詞語尾-bə～-wəが接尾した形から変化したとみられる。

これらの例からみて或単語における連続する二つのөөはu＋子音の或もの＋əに該当する音素連続から変化して来たとみられる。

5. つぎに挙げるような語においてオロッコ方言の母音音素に隣接しないө及び連続する二つのөөは満洲語文語の母音字uに対応している。

	オロッコ方言		満洲語文語	
例	xөlө	木鼠	ulhu	銀鼠，灰鼠の総称
	mөlөxi	倉庫の棟木	mulu	棟木
	čirөlө-	枕にする	ciru-	枕にする
	bөө-	与える	bu-	与える
ただし				
	pөrө	おやゆび	ferhe	おやゆび
	sirө	野生となかい	iren	草原に住むとなかい

なお mɵɵ（水）は満洲語文語の muke（水）に対応し，この mɵɵ は *[mukə] に該当する語形から変化したのではないかとみられる。

dɵɵ（二）は満洲語文語の juwe（二）（諺文文献におけるその uwe の転写諺文は u'ue）に対応する。この ɵɵ はさきに挙げた ǰiilɵɵ のような例からも考えて *[uɣ̫ə] に該当する音素連続から変化した蓋然性があり注意される。

6. ツングース語のそのほかの方言についてみると，ソロン方言のポッペの採集資料（Н. Н. Поппе: Материалы по солонскому языку. Ленинград, 1931.）には ʊ̈（high-mixed-wide-round と mid-mixed-narrow-round の中間の音）及び ɔ̈（low-front-wide-round と low-mixed-wide-round の中間の音）の母音がある。ソロン方言のその資料から三例を挙げる。

dʊ̈nɔ̈̄ʊ̈（четырехлетнее животное).（蒙古語文語 dönen 参照）

ʊ̈lɔ̈̄-（варить).（なお *e̤lɔ̈̄-*（варить), *ɯlɔ̈̄-*（сварить）もある。）

tʊ̈rʊ̈（косяк двери).

あとの二語はそれぞれオロッコ方言の ɵlɵsini（彼が炊く），tɵrɵ（戸口のつく柱）に対応する。

またワシレーヴィッチは o̤ 及び ō̤（中開き中舌円唇母音）がエヴェンキ方言の東部方言の或下位方言やカトンガ民族区やエヴェンキ管区のイリンペヤ区にひろがっている北部方言の若干の下位方言にあることを記している。しかし同氏はこの o̤，ō̤ を э，э̄ の変種とみており，精しいことは明らかでない（Г. М. Василевич: Очерк грамматики эвенкийского (тунгусского) языка. Ленинград, 1940. стр. 14.）。

ウルルガ及びマニコヴァのツングース方言のカストレンの採集資料（M. Alexander Castrén's Grundzüge einer Tungusischen Sprachlehre nebst kurzem Wörterverzeichniss. St. Petersburg, 1856.）にはかかる母音は表記されていない。

バルグジン・ツングース方言のポッペの採集資料（Н. Н. Поппе: Материалы для исследования тунгусского языка. Ленинград, 1927.）にもかかる母音は特に表記されてはいない。しかしその記述によるとたとえば第二人称単数現在の命令形の語尾 -кал（-кєл，-кол，-кул）があるが，語

尾においてせまい母音が a，є，o と交替することはツングース語において通例みられないし，また -кул のつく語例

кōру-кул（гнать）[ポッペは（蒙 köge- гнать 比較）と記している].

кудōлу-кул（высаживаться на берег）[ポッペは кудō суша < 蒙 ködege степьと記している].

суру-кул（уходить).

уру-кул（радоваться).

буᵖгу-кул（жиреть).

умку-кул（влить).

のうちあとの二語はそれぞれオロッコ方言 bɵdɵ-（肥える），ソロン方言 *üŋkɯ-*（проливать）に対応する。（なおたとえば муду-кєл（рвать зубами）はオロッコ方言の mudu-（歯でかじってさく）に対応する。）これらの点から上にあげた語の y は中舌的な中開き円唇母音ではないかとも考えられ，この方言にもかかる母音がある蓋然性が大きい。

母音音素/ɵ/に該当すべき中舌的な中開き円唇母音がオロッコ方言以外にも少なくとも一部の方言にはあるとみておそらく誤りでないであろう。しかし従来の記述はこの点必ずしも正確とはみられない。もしツングース語において/ɵ/に該当すべきかかる母音とほかの母音との差異を無視するならばそれはあだかも蒙古語において/ö/に該当する［ö］とほかの母音との差異を無視するのに等しく，言語の記述上の誤りとなるばかりでなくツングース語方言の比較研究，さらにアルタイ諸言語との比較研究にとっても重大な欠陥となる。ここにツングース語のかかる母音差異を記述することがツングース語研究にとって重要であることを強調したい。

Summary

Orokko Dialect has /ö/ as one of vowel phonemes. It corresponds to the half-close outer-back rounded vowel [ȯ]. The photograph shows the pronunciation of [ȯː]. At least some dialects of Tungus have probably a vowel corresponding to /ö/, like Orokko Dialect. The author emphasizes that, in the study of Tungus, it is important to describe the difference between such a vowel and other vowels.

本稿は昭和27年（1952年）10月11日の日本人類学会，日本民族学協会第7回連合大会における同じ題名の研究発表を補訂したものであり，昭和27年度文部省科学研究費補助金の交付を受けた研究の一部である。

初出　『言語研究』22・23号［昭和28年（1953年）3月］75－78，135ページ。

なお，その口頭発表の要旨は『日本人類学会日本民族学協会連合大会第7回紀事　昭和27年10月　松本』［昭和29年（1954年）3月5日］122－123ページに載る。

追記

1. について。　ウイルタ語の/ɵ/の母音には，ややせまい前寄りの後舌円唇母音［ȯ］のほかに，またややせまい後舌円唇母音［o］の発音があることを，その後知った。旧稿では，添付した母音口形写真に写る被調査者の/ɵɵ/の発音を［ȯː］としたが，これは［oː］とするのが正しかったろう。
6. について。　ポッペ採録のバルグジン・ツングース方言の -кул の у の母音について筆者が推測したことは，その後筆者自身がゼーヤ川地方の方言についておこなった調査の結果からみて，当っていなかった。その母音が *ɵに由来することは考えられるが，今日ではせまい円唇母音である例があることを知った。なお，推測したように，/ɵ/の母音音素をもつツングース語方言はほかにもあることがその後知られるようになってきている。拙文「エウェンキー語方言語彙　付記」3.22，3.23（『北方文化研究』10　北海道大学　1976年）参照。

北方諸言語の文字
――ロシヤ字がいいか，ローマ字がいいか

On the Suitability of Scripts for the Languagesof the Northern Regions : Russian script versus Latin script

ここにいう北方諸言語とは，旧ソ連領内のシベリア少数民族の言語のことである。これらの言語の大部分は，いまだ文字をもっていないか，または，今世紀にソ連邦治下ではじめて文字をもった言語である。ただし，そのうちヤクート語ではすでに前世紀に文字で書く試みがあったし，1910年代には，ヤクート人 S. A. Novgorodov のローマ字表記法ができた。また，ブリヤート語は古くは蒙古字を使っていた。

文字を新たにもった言語は，1930年代に，はじめローマ字（ラテン字）で，その後ロシヤ字で書かれるようになった。また，同じ時期に，ブリヤート語でもローマ字の採用とロシヤ字への変更がおこなわれ，ヤクート語もロシヤ字を使うことになった。なお，チュクチャ語では，1920年代にチュクチャ人の牧者が独特の表意字を考案したが，普及しなかったという。北方諸言語のうちツングース諸語についてみると，十近い言語のうち，文字をもったのは，そのなかで有力なエウェンキー語，エウェン語，ナーナイ語である。このほかにウデヘ語も同年代に文字をもつようになったが，その後は口頭で話すだけで，その文字で書くことがなくなってしまった。

ここでは，ツングース諸語の文語の文字について，筆者の年来考えていることを述べてみたい。

ところで，一つの言語の文字の組織は，原則として，異なる音素は異なる文字で表わし，同じ音素はつねに同じ文字で表わすような組織がよいと考えられる。ここでも，この原則に立つのが文字表記の良い方策と考えたい。

ロシヤ字は，ローマ字と同じくギリシヤ字に由来するが，ローマ字とは異なる改変の過程をへてきた文字である。ロシヤ語を表記する文字であるロシヤ字は，ロシヤ語に存する硬音と軟音の二類のちがいを表わし，ロシヤ語に適した文字となっている。

しかし，ここにエウェンキー語文語のロシヤ字表記（Г. М. Василевич, Эвенкийско-русский словарь, Москва, 1958）を例にとってみると，そのロシヤ字使用には，いくつかの問題点がある。

⑴ 母音音素 u（および ʊ），o，a，ə は，一般に，ロシヤ字ではそれぞれ y，o，a，э で表記され，子音音素 t，d，n のつぎでも同様の母音字で記される。すなわち，

tu（および tʊ）	to	ta	tə
ту	то	та	тэ
du（および dʊ）	do	da	də
ду	до	да	дэ
nu（および nʊ）	no	na	nə
ну	но	на	нэ

またほかの種々の子音音素のつぎでも同様に表記されるが，ただし，子音音素 ǰ，ɲ のつぎではそれぞれ軟音字 ю，ё，я，e で表記される。すなわち，

ču（および čʊ）	čo	ča	čə
чу	чо	ча	чэ
ǰu（および ǰʊ）	ǰo	ǰa	ǰə
дю	дё	дя	де
ɲu（および ɲʊ）	ɲo	ɲa	ɲə
ню	нё	ня	не

このように，（イ）ǰ，ɲ のつぎでは，上の場合と異なり，同じ母音音素が軟音字で表わされる。しかし，（ロ）この場合，これらの軟音字は，また，まえに立つ子音が硬口蓋音であることも表わしている。すなわち，硬口蓋子音音素 ǰ を表わすのに，d を表わすのと同じ子音字 д を使い，つぎの硬音字・軟音字で d と ǰ を区別して表わしている。かなり便宜的な表記といえよう。したがっ

て t:č=d:ǰ の関係にある t，č と d，ǰ の表記は，ǰ の表記の仕組みが異なるので，表記に平行性を欠く。n，ɲ の表記にもそれと同様のことがみられる。

(2) 子音音素 j は，つぎにくる母音音素とともに軟音字一字で表記されている。すなわち，

ju（および jʊ） jo ja jə
ю ё я е

この場合，同じ子音音素 j が，つぎにくる母音音素によって相異なる軟音字で表わされている。なお，ロシヤ字 е は，一方また，別の母音音素 ē を表わすのにも用いられる。

(3) 母音音素 i は，一般には，軟音字 и で表記している。しかし ti, di はそれぞれ ты，ды と表記し，この場合 i が硬音字 ы で表わされる。このように i は相異なる二つの文字で表記される。なお，母音音素 ɪ も同様に и と ы で表記される。

エウェンキー語のロシヤ字表記には，上記の原則に反するこのようないくつかの点がある。こうした点は，ロシヤ語のような硬音と軟音の対立をもたず，ロシヤ語とは異なる音韻体系をもつ言語に，ロシヤ字を，その文字体系に立ったまま使用することによるものといえよう。

上に，エウェンキー語文語についてみてきたが，エウェン語，ナーナイ語の文語についても，これらの点は大体同様である。ただし，ナーナイ語には ti，di の子音・母音結合が通常ないので，そのロシヤ字表記もない。

ロシヤ字に対してローマ字はどうだろうか。

エウェンキー語の子音音素 ŋ は，ロシヤ字表記では，ロシヤ字の нг の二字で表記されるが，ng も同じ нг で表わされる。нг がそのどちらを表わすかは，その表記だけからでは不明である。一方，ローマ字も ŋ を表わす単一の文字はないから，ローマ字を使用しても同様であろう。

しかし，ローマ字は硬音・軟音の区別がなく，また j を表わすのにも単一の文字 j または y を使うことができ，これを使えば，上述の難点も生じない。こうした点からツングース諸語の文語の表記には，かつて使用したことのあるローマ字の方が適当であるといえよう。ただし，ローマ字表記でも，若干の補

助記号や変形文字は必要である。

ところが，これらの言語の話し手の今日の状況に目を向けると，かれらは現実においてロシヤ語を併用し，ロシヤ人の文化のなかでその強い影響下にある。したがって，かれらは自分の固有言語の文字としてもロシヤ字を使用する方が便利と考えるだろう。また，ロシヤ字のほかにさらにローマ字を学ぶことは，特に文字をはじめて学ぶこどもにとっては負担となろう。ローマ字の採用はなかなか容易でないと思われる。

これまで通りにロシヤ字を使うとすれば，ロシヤ字の使い方を考えなおすことが必要だろう。ロシヤ字の硬音・軟音の文字上の区別を利用せず，ǰ，ɲ，j の表記にも軟音字を当てずに，たとえば，д'，н'，й の文字で表わすなどして，上述の原則に立った使い方をすれば，上にふれた難点は解消されるだろう。このような表記法は，すでにソ連の何人ものツングース語研究者が自身の著書中のツングース語表記に使っている。また，ツングース諸語以外の北方諸言語には，その字母制定にこのような方法をとる試みがある（Опыт создания адфавитов для ранее бесписьменных народностей Севера [Палео-азиатские языки, Издательство НАУКА, Ленинград, 1986]）。

付記　この文の内容は，昨年（1991年）5月25日札幌で開催された北海道ローマ字研究会のシンポジウム「ローマ字の過去・現在・未来」において述べたものである。

初出　『月刊言語』21巻2号（通巻242号）[平成4年（1992年）2月1日] 77－79ページ。

追記

なお，さらにその後ウデヘ語ではロシヤ字で書くことが復活した。

Проект письменности уйльтинского языка

1. Введение

Уйльтинский язык является одним из тунгусо-маньчжурских языков, который употребляется на Сахалине. Носители этого языка известны под названиями ороки, орочёны, ульты и уйльты. На своем родном языке они называют себя **улта** или **уилта**. Ниже для их названия употребляется термин уйльты, потому что этот термин звучит яснее, чем термин ульты, для отличия от названия соседней народности ульчей.

Уйльтинский язык — бесписьменный, но письменность и литературный язык необходимы для чтения и письма на уйльтинском языке. При создании письменности следует создать алфавит и установить орфографию.

2. Наречие как основа письменного языка

Уйльтинский язык делится на два наречия: южное наречие, распространенное в Поронайске и др., и северное наречие, распространенное на Валу и др. Между этими наречиями существуют некоторые различия в фонематической системе, лексике и грамматике. Так, например, юж. *aŋma* (*-ŋm-*) "рот," сев. *aŋma, amŋa* (*-ŋm-, -mŋ-*); юж. *ǰakpu* (*-kp-*) "восемь," сев. *ǰakpu, ǰapku* (*-kp-, -pk-*); юж. orokto "трава," сев. *pəiktə*; юж. *kəənǰini* "говорит," сев. *ləədənǰini*; юж. *mini ŋaalabi* "моя рука," сев. *bii* *ŋaalabi*. Южное наречие отражает ранний этап уйльтинского языка. Между тем, в нем, как в северном наречии, старая система уйльтинского языка, по-видимому, претерпевает новые изменения. Уйльтинский письменный язык должен опираться главным образом на южное наречие, чтобы поддерживать систему, свойственную уйльтинскому языку. Впрочем, необходимо позволить носителям северного наречия отразить особенности их наречия в письменном языке. Поэтому о различиях между этими наречиями следует упомянуть в учебниках и словарях. Однако не требуется составлять отдельные учебники и словари для двух наречий.

3. Конспект фонематики уйльтинского языка

В обоих наречиях уйльтинского языка имеются гласные фонемы *a*, *ə*, *o*, *ɵ*, *u*, *i*, *e*, которые произносятся как [*a* (или a), ə, ɔ, ɵ, u, i, e] и согласные фонемы *p*, *b*, *t*, *k*, *g*, *m*, *n*, *ɲ*, *ŋ*, *l*, *r*, *w*, *s*, *j*, *x*, *č*, *ǰ*, которые произносятся как [p, b, t, d, k (или q), ɡ (или ɢ), m, n, ɲ, ŋ, l, r (=ɾ или ɹ), w, s, j, x, (или χ), tʃ, dʒ]. [w] и [j] — полугласные звуки. Шумы фрикативных [x] и [χ] слабы. Далее будут подробно рассмотрены фонемы *g*, *w*, *j*, *s*, *n*. В квадратных скобках обозначается произношение с помощью знаков Международного фонетического алфавита.

Фонема *g* произносится в начале слова как [ɡ, ɢ], но в положении между гласными в середине слова как [γ, ʁ]. В положении между *i* и *a* (или *ə*) эти фонемы произносятся часто слабо, и потому трудно различимы.

Причем в положениях между *u* (последующей за согласной) и *a* (или *ə*), а также между какой-то гласной и *u* (или *o*) в ряде слов стоит фонема, произносящаяся как лабиовелярный [γ̫] или лабиоувулярный [ʁ̫]. Но возможно принять эту фонему за фонему *w*. Эти звуки [γ̫, ʁ̫] часто слабы и не отчетливы. Примеры: *duwa* "летом," *tuwə* "зимой," *xauwu, xaawu* “который.”

Фонема *j* произносится обыкновенно как [j], но в положении перед *i* ее звучание часто не отчетливо, и этот звук трудно расслышать ясно.

Фонема *s* произносится, то как [s], то как палатализованный [s'] или [ʃ].

Фонема *n,* стоящая в положении перед *i* или *e,* произносится как палатализованный [n'] или [ɲ]. В этом положении фонема *ɲ* не встречается.

Повторение одной и той же гласной фонемы ГГ произносится обычно как долгий гласный звук. Так, *aa, əə, oo, ɵɵ, uu, ii* и *ee* произносятся как [*a*ː (или aː), əː, ɔː, ɵː, uː, iː, eː (или ɛː)]. Но такие ГГ в конце слова часто произносятся кратко. Однако различие между краткими и долгими гласными звуками в уйльтинском языке является фонологически важным. Сочетания различных гласных фонем ГГ произносятся как дифтонги. Так, *ai, əi, oi, ɵi, ui, au, əu, ou, ɵu* и *eu* произносятся как [aĭ, əĭ, ɔĭ, ɵĭ, uĭ, *a*ŭ, əŭ, ɔŭ, ɵŭ, eŭ, (или ɛŭ)]. Следовательно, комбинации фонем ГГ в ряде слов произносятся как долгие гласные звуки, а в ряде слов — как дифтонги. Но ГГ в положении перед сочетанием одинаковых согласных фонем СС произносятся часто как сочетание кратких гласных звуков.

Повторение одной и той же согласной фонемы СС произносится как двойной согласный звук после краткого гласного звука первого слога в слове. Это типичное произношение сочетания одинаковых согласных фонем, но оно часто произносится как простой согласный звук с предшествующим напряжением гортани после сочетания гласных фонем ГГ. Причем *čč* и *ǰǰ* произносятся как [ttʃ, ddʒ].

Примечание: Г = гласная фонема. С = согласная фонема.

4. Обозначение на письме фонем уйльтинского языка

Обозначение на письме фонем базируется на следующем принципе.

Разные фонемы обозначаются разными буквами. Одна фонема постоянно обозначается одной и той буквой.

При создании уйльтинской письменности первый шаг — выбор графики, на основе которой уйльтинский алфавит создается, т.е. русской или латинской графики.

Русский алфавит пригоден для выражения противопоставления твердых и мягких звуков, которое играет важную роль в русской языковой системе. Однако тунгусо-маньчжурские языки, в том числе и уйльтинский, отличаются от русского языка отсутствием такого противопоставления твердых и мягких звуков, как в русском языке.

Эвенкийский, эвенский и нанайский языки, включаемые в тунгусо-маньчжурские языки, ныне имеют письменность на основе русской графики. При обозначении на письме фонем этих языков, фонема *j* в сочетании с последующей гласной фонемой *a*, *ə*, *o* или *u* передается различными русскими буквами **я, е, ё, ю**. Буквы **д** и **н** в сочетании с последующими гласными буквами **а, э, о, у, ы** или **я, е, ё, ю, и** обозначают различные фонемы *d*, *n* или *ǰ*, *ɲ*.

В правописании этих языков соответствие между фонемами и буквами очень сложное. В этом отношении обозначение на латинском письме проще, так как возможно употребить латинскую букву *j* или *y* для обозначения фонемы *j*.

Впрочем, русское письмо необходимо для жизни уйльтинского народа в настоящее время. Автор этих строк боится, что овладение русским алфавитом и в то же время латинским алфавитом дается тяжело учащимся. Распространение грамоты на уйльтинском языке — первоочередная задача. Поэтому принятие русской графики в практическое письмо является вынужденным. Однако при обозначении русским алфавитом уйльтинских слов не следует употреблять мягкие буквы **я, е, ё, ю** для сочетания фонем *ja,jə,jo, ju* и буквы **д** и **н** в сочетании с мягкими буквами **я, е, ё, ю** (**дя, де, дё, дю** и **ня, не, нё, ню**) для сочетаний фонем *ǰa, ǰə, ǰo, ǰu* и *ɲa, ɲe, ɲo, ɲu*, потому что такое употребление букв не согласуется с вышеупомянутым принципом.

Следовательно латинский алфавит более пригоден для уйльтинского языка. Автор настоящих строк надеется на принятие латинского алфавита на следующем этапе после распространения грамоты на уйльтинском языке.

5. Письменности на основе латинской и русской график

Разработаны два плана письменности уйльтинского языка (I и II). Первый план (I) основывается на латинской графике, второй план (II) — на русской графике.

Гласные фомемы *a, ə, o, u, i, e*, кроме фонемы *ɵ*, обозначаются латинскими буквами *a, ə, o, u, i, e* (I) и русскими *а, э, о, у, и, е* (II). Буква *ə* — латинская буква **e** перевернутая. Фонема *ɵ* обозначается в обоих планах (I, II) буквой *ɵ*. Начертание этой буквы тождественно начертанию буквы фиты раньше употреблявшейся в русском письме.

Согласные фонемы *p, b, t, d, k, g, m, n, l, r, w, s, j, x*, кроме фонем *ɲ, ŋ, č, ǰ*, обозначаются теми же самыми латинскими буквами *p, b, t, d, k, g, m, n, l, r, w, s, j* (или *y*), *x*. Фонемы *ɲ* и *ŋ* обозначаются специальными буквами *ɲ* и *ŋ*, или фонема *ɲ* обозначается буквой с подстрочной запятой *ņ*. Фонемы *č* и *ǰ* обозначаются буквами с диакритическим знаком *č* и *ǰ*. (I)

Вышеупомянутые согласные фонемы *p, b, t, d, k, g, m, n, l, r, w, s, x, č*, кроме *ɲ, ŋ, j, ǰ*, обозначаются русскими буквами **п, б, т, д, к, г, м, н, л, р, в, с, х, ч**. Фонемы *ɲ, ŋ, j, ǰ* обозначаются особыми буквами или русскими буквами с дополнительным начертанием **ӈ** (или **ӊ**), **ŋ, j, ʒ**. (II) Буквы **н'** и **д'** с последующим знаком ' не рекомендуются для обозначения фонем *ɲ* и *ǰ*, потому что эти буквы заставляют ошибочно думать, что они обозначают не самостоятельные фонемы, а варианты фонем, обозначаемых буквами **н** и **д**.

Примеры: *pɵrɵ* (**пɵрɵ**) "большой палец," *goro* (**горо**) "далекий," *əgə* (**эгэ**) "старшая сестра," *gugda* (**гугда**) "высокий," *waarini* (**ваарини**) "убивает," *tawa* (**тава**) "огонь," *jokko* (**jокко**) "якут," *aja* (**аjа**) "хороший," *daaji* (**дааjи**) "большой," *ɲoogdo* (**ӈоогдо**) "зеленый, желтый," *ŋinda* (**ŋинда**) "собака," *tuŋə* (**туŋэ**) "грудь," *toŋdo* (**тоŋдо**) "прямой," *čai* (**чаи**) "чай," *ŋənəxəči* (**ŋэнэхэчи**) "шли," *tamaččuu* (**тамаччуу**) или *tamatčuu* (**таматчуу**) "оттуда," *ǰolo* (**ʒоло**) "камень," *mooǰi* (**мооʒи**) "с палкой," *əǰǰee* (**эʒʒее**) или *ədǰee* (**эдʒее**) "не надо!"

В письменности уйльтинского языка необходимо обозначать различие между гласной фонемой и сочетанием гласных фонем. Сочетание двух различных гласных фонем (произносимых как дифтонг) обозначается двумя буквами ГГ. Повторение одной и той же гласной фонемы (произносимых как долгий гласный звук) обозначается также двумя буквами ГГ или одной гласной буквой с надстрочной чертой Г̄. (I, II) Однако кажется, что обозначение ГГ удобнее, чем обозначение Г̄, для понимания и описания фонематической и морфологической систем уйльтинского языка. Так, имена существительные и глаголы изменяются различно в зависимости от наличия одной гласной фонемы или двух гласных фонем в конце основы, т.е. Г (произносится как краткий гласный звук) или ГГ (произносятся как долгий гласный звук или дифтонг):

а)

Основа имени существительного | Дательный падеж | Винительный падеж

Основа, кончающаяся на Г		
gasa (**гаса**) "птица"	*gasadu* (**гасаду**)	*gassaa* (**гассаа**)
nari (**нари**) "человек"	*naridu* (**нариду**)	*narree* (**наррее**)
namu (**наму**) "море"	*namudu* (**намуду**)	*nammoo* (**наммоо**)
Основа, кончающаяся на ГГ		
naa (**наа**) "земля"	*naadu* (**нааду**)	*naawa* (**наава**)
bee (**бее**) "луна, месяц"	*beedu* (**бееду**)	*beewa* (**беева**)
čai (**чаи**) "чай"	*čaidu* (**чаиду**)	*čaiwa* (**чаива**)
dau (**дау**) "содержимое"	*daudu* (**дауду**)	*dauwa* (**даува**)

б)

Основа глагола	Причастие прошедшего времени	Причастие настоящего времени
Основа, кончающаяся на Г		
ana- (**ана-**) "толкать"	*anaxa* (**анаха**)	*annee* (**аннее**)
dapa- (**дапа-**) "схватить"	*dapaxa* (**дапаха**)	*dappee* (**даппее**)
soso- (**сосо-**) "страдать поносом"	*sosoxo* (**сосохо**)	*sossee* (**соссее**)
Основа, кончающаяся на ГГ		
saa- (**саа-**) "знать"	*saaxa* (**сааха**)	*saari* (**саари**)
xau- (**хау-**) "вытирать"	*xauxa* (**хауха**)	*xauri* (**хаури**)

В словах, оканчивающихся на сочетание гласных фонем (произносимое как долгий гласный звук), хотя это сочетание произносится часто кратко, рекомендуется принять в письменный язык формы, оканчивающиеся на ГГ как формы этих слов.

Примеры: *moo* (**моо**) "дерево, палка," *ŋənnee* (**ŋэннее**) "идущий," *jaajjeeni* (**jaajjeeни**) "поет," *aisi* (**аиси**) "золото," dausu (**даусу**) "соль."

Повторение одной и той же согласной фонемы СС обозначается

двумя теми же самыми согласными буквами CC (I, II). Но можно обозначать сочетания согласных фонем *čč* и *ǰǰ* буквами *tč* (**тч**) и *dǰ* (**дʒ**) вместо букв *čč* (**чч**) и *ǰǰ* (**ʒʒ**).

Примеры: *puttə* (**путтэ**) “ребенок,” *soŋŋeeni* (**соӈӈеени**) “плачет,” *suŋdatta*(**суӈдатта**) “рыба,” *ŋəəlleeni* (**ӈээллеени**) “боится,” *iččeeni* (**иччеени**) или *itčeeni* (**итчеени**) “смотрит.”

Примечание: Г = гласная буква. C = согласная буква.

Приложение

Обозначение латинской и русской графиками фонем уйльтинского языка

Фонема	Буква на основе латинской графики	Буква на основе русской графики
Гласная фонема		
a	a	а
ə	ə	э
o	o	о
ɵ	ɵ	ө
u	u	у
i	i	и
e	e	е
Согласная фонема		
p	p	п
b	b	б
t	t	т
d	d	д
k	k	к
g	g	г

m	m	м
n	n	н
ɲ	ɲ (или ņ)	ӈ (или ӊ)
ŋ	ŋ	ӈ
l	l	л
r	r	р
w	w	в
s	s	с
j	j (или y)	j
x	x	х
č	č	ч
ǰ	ǰ	з

In this paper I present my personal project aimed at founding the Uilta written language. The project was fulfilled as requested by Mrs. N. A. Laigun, the Sakhalin Region Administration Peoples of the North Department Head, and later submitted to the RF (Russian Federation) National Language Relations (национально-языковые отношения) Section of the Russian Academy of Sciences (РАН) National Language Relations Scientific Research Center. A special meeting on consideration of my project presided by Prof. M. Isaev, chief of the relevant section, was held at the Russian Academy of Sciences Institute of Linguistics in Moscow on July 8, 1993. As a result, for the Uilta language the Russian script was adopted.

In Section 3, some of the phonetic descriptions of the paper submitted there were revised and supplemented in this paper.

This article was published in *Acta Slavica Iaponica*, Tomus XII (The Slavic Research Center, Hokkaido University, Sapporo, 1994), pp. 253-258.

Письменная практика на уйльтинском языке — Дополнение к Проекту письменности уйльтинского языка

1.

В "Проекте письменности уйльтинского языка" (далее "Проект")[1] уйльтинский алфавит на основе русской графики состоит из 21 русской буквы: **а э о ө у и е п б т д к г м н л р в с х ч** и 4 специальных букв **ӈ** (или **ӊ**) **ӈ j ӡ**. Каждая из этих специальных букв введена в уйльтинский алфавит по причине отсутствия соответствующей русской буквы. Фонетическое описание уйльтинского языка в третьем разделе "Проекта" основано на южном наречии.

2.

В уйльтинском языке, в отличие от русского, существует фонологическое противопоставление кратких и долгих гласных. Для поддержания этой особенности уйльтинского языка необходимо обозначать последовательно различие кратких и долгих гласных в уйльтинских

---

1 См. выше, с. 145-153.

словах. Для обозначения долгого гласного в уйльтинском языке повторение одной и той же гласной буквы кажется удобнее, чем написание одной гласной буквы с надстрочной чертой, потому что первое обозначение согласуется с языковой структурой уйльтинского языка (см. "Проект", раздел 5.). Повторение одной и той же гласной буквы используется также для обозначения долгого гласного в орфографиях якутского, бурятского и калмыцкого языков, которые имеют фонологическое противопоставление кратких и долгих гласных. См. образец I.

Для уйльтинского языка также необходимо точно обозначить различие между одной согласной фонемой и сочетанием двух одинаковых согласных фонем, например: **пута** "петля" и **путтэ** "ребенок" (именительные формы).

Для обозначения уйльтинских фонем рационально употреблять последовательно отдельную букву для каждой фонемы, в особенности буквы **ч, ʒ, ɲ** (**ņ**) или **j** для каждой из среднеязычных фонем. Тунгусовед из Новосибирска, М.М. Хасанова (сообщение 1994 года) также предложила использовать буквы **ч, ʒ, н'**, и **ŋ** для обозначения среднеязычных фонем и заднеязычной носовой фонемы в проекте орфографии негидальского языка, одного из тунгусских языков.

3.

В плане употребления предложенного в "Проекте" алфавита, автор настоящих строк надеется, что носители уйльтинского языка попробуют писать слова и предложения на своем языке с помощью этого алфавита. Автору этих строк хотелось бы узнать их мнение об этом алфавите в целом и об обозначении каждой отдельной фонемы, в особенности о следующих обозначениях гласных фонем.

Как было упомянуто в “Проекте”, гласная фонема *ə* обозначается русской буквой **э**, а повторение этой фонемы *əə* — сочетанием одинаковых букв **ээ**; фонема *e* — русской буквой **е**, а повторение этой фонемы *ee* — сочетанием одинаковых знаков **ее**. Автор настоящих строк беспокоится о том, что русская буква **е** не годится для обозначения фонемы *e* и особенно для обозначения повторения этой фонемы *ee*. У автора этих строк есть другой план, по которому гласная фонема *ə* обозначается буквенным знаком **ə**, а повторение этой фонемы *əə* — сочетанием одинаковых знаков **əə**; фонема *e* обозначается русской буквой **э**, а повторение этой фонемы *ee* — сочетанием одинаковых букв **ээ**. Примеры: **ŋэннееви** или **ŋəннээви** “иду” и **ееккутчеени** или **ээккутчээни** “правит рулевым веслом”. См. образец II.

4.

Если некоторые из букв, употребляемых для обозначения уйльтинских звуков в “Проекте”, непригодны для этих звуков, необходимо внести исправления.

Для обозначения уйльтинского долгого гласного, как упомянуто выше, повторение одной и той же гласной буквы кажется более удобним, чем написание одной гласной буквы с надстрочной чертой. Но второе обозначение отчетливее первого, если согласные фонемы *j* и *w*, звучащие слабо в середине слова перед определенными гласными (см. “Проект”, раздел 3.), исчезают в положении перед ГГ или после ГГ (Г = гласная фонема), например, в словах **дааjи** или **дājи** “большой”, **ууву** или **ӯву** “верхняя часть чего-либо” и **уувоонʒини** или **ӯвōнʒини** “заставить сесть в лодку или нарту” → **дааи, ууу, ууонӡини** или **дāи, ӯу** или **ӯōнӡини**. Впрочем, в первом обозначении можно поставить знак ’ (или дефис -) между двумя гласными для указания на границу слога, например, **даа’и, уу’у** и **уу’оонӡини**. Нужно выбрать одно из этих двух обозначений. См. образец III.

Приложение

Образец I.

1) Асимуна нари пурэттэи ӈэнэхэчи. Ваајитамари битчичи. Хаивадда мастаа барамба ваахачи. Тари нари андаилли нари нимэрими синдахани. Андаилби синдахандуни геeда ваӈгаива ваахни. Андахатаи төөјөбуӡди баргихани. Баргими хоӡихани. Андахатаи дэппее төјөхөни. Тари андаха утчини. Миттэи дуллээ эдӡее бөөрө. Таватакки дуллээ бөөру. Тари дуӈнееени нарини. Тавaтаи эсиви бөөрө. Муналисиви. Дэпчичи. Дэптумэри хоӡихачи. Тари андаха акпаккатчи долбо толчичихани. Тава нарини унӡивэни толчитчини. Мини дугби нарини хаивадда ваапеедда миттэи эсини бөөрө . Хуманами элээ буӡиви.

2) Горопчиннее аундау доодуни битчичиндэ. Геeда пооду. Дууннее геeд геeда мамаӈулу дуу ээктэ. Човотчеери ноомбочи гои нарисал гаттагатчи аундаккоори вээдэгэтчи мэгдэмбэ мээтэлэгэтчи ӈэнэгэтчеери ӈэнухэчи. Мапаӈучи исухачи дуктаккеери. Мамаӈучи анаа. Улаалчиддаа анаа. Хаичидда ојоскомбочи чипал гадухачи. Човотчеери хамараккеечи ӈэнэхэчи. Поктоккеечи ӈэнэхэчи. Ӈэнэгэтчеери аaптухачи. Геeда ээктэ муулуутутэкки муулэхэни. Хаӈдамари синдахасоо. Сумбеепэ ваариллаал суддээкки амбасал унӡини. Эси хуригатчичи унӡини. Бујуӈӈөөри ваагатчеери хуригатчичинда.

Образец II.

1) Асимуна нари пурэттэи ŋэнэхэчи. Ваајитамари битчичи. Хаивадда мастаа барамба ваахачи. Тари нари андаилли нари нимэрими синдахани. Андаилби синдахандуни гээда ваŋгаива ваахани. Андахатаи төјөбудʒи баргихани. Баргими хоʒихани. Андахатаи дэппээ төјөхөни. Тари андаха утчини. Миттэи дуллээ эдʒээ бөөрө. Таватакки дуллээ бөөру. Тари дуŋнээни нарини. Таватаи эсиви бөөрө. Муналисиви. Дэпчичи. Дэптумэри хоʒихани. Тари андаха акпаккатчи долбо толчичихани. Тава нарини унʒивэни толчитчини. Мини дугби нарини хаивадда ваапээдда миттэи эсини бөөрө. Хуманами элээ буʒиви.

2) Горопчиннээ аундау доодуни битчичиндэ. Гээда пооду. Дууннээ геед гээда мамаŋулу дуу ээктэ. Човотчээри ноомбочи гои нарисал гаттагатчи аундаккоори вээдэгэтчи мэгдэмбэ мээтэлэгэтчи ŋэнэгэтчээри ŋэнухэчи. Мапаŋучи исухачи дуктаккээри. Мамаŋучи анаа. Улаалчиддаа анаа. Хаичидда ојоскомбочи чипал гадухачи. Човотчээри хамараккээчи ŋэнэхэчи. Поктоккээчи ŋэнэхэчи. Ŋэнэгэтчээри ааптухачи. Гээда ээктэ муулуутутэкки мууләхэни. Хаŋдамари синдахасоо. Сумбээпэ ваариллаал судДэкки амбасал унʒини. Эси хуригатчичи унʒини. Бујуŋŋөөри ваагатчээри хуригатчичинда.

Образец III.

1) Асимуна нари пурэттэи ŋэнэхэчи. Ва̄јитамари битчичи. Хаивадда маста̄ барамба ва̄хачи. Тари нари андаилли нари нимэрими синдахани. Андаилби синдахандуни гēда ваŋгаива ва̄хани. Андахатаи төјөбудʒи баргихани. Баргими хоʒихани. Андахатаи дэппē төјөхөни. Тари андаха утчини. Миттэи дуллэ̄ эдʒē бө̄рө. Таватакки дуллэ̄ бө̄ру. Тари дуŋнēни нарини. Таватаи эсиви бө̄рө. Муналисиви. Дэпчичи. Дэптумэри

хоӡихачи. Тари андаха акпаккатчи долбо толчичихани. Тава нарини унӡивэни толчитчини. Мини дугби нарини хаивадда ва̄пе̄дда миттэи эсини бө̄рө. Хуманами элэ̄ буӡиви.

2) Горопчинне̄ аундау до̄дуни битчичиндэ. Ге̄да по̄ду. Дӯнне̄ ге̄д ге̄да мамаӈулу дӯ э̄ктэ. Човотче̄ри но̄мбочи гои нарисал га̄ттагатчи аундакко̄ри вэ̄дэгэтчи мэгдэмбэ мэ̄тэлэгэтчи ӈэнэгэтче̄ри ӈэнухэчи. Мапаӈучи исухачи дуктакке̄ри. Мамаӈучи ана̄. Ула̄лчидда̄ ана̄. Хаичидда ојоскомбочи чипал гадухачи. Човотче̄ри хамаракке̄чи ӈэнэхэчи. Поктокке̄чи ӈэнэхэчи. Ӈэнэгэтче̄ри а̄птухачи. Ге̄да э̄ктэ мӯлӯтутэкки мӯлэхэни. Хаӈдамари синдахасо̄. Сумбе̄пэ ва̄рилла̄л суддэ̄кки амбасал унӡини. Эси хуригатчичи унӡини. Бујуӈӈө̄ри ва̄гатче̄ри хуригатчичинда.

This paper was originally presented in Yuzhno-Sakhalinsk on 4 October 1995 at a meeting devoted to the founding of the Uilta written language. The meeting was organized by Mrs. N. R. Laigun, the chief of the Peoples of the North Department of the Sakhalin Region Administration.

This article was published in *Acta Slavica Iaponica*, Tomus XIV (The Slavic Research Center, Hokkaido University, Sapporo, 1996), pp. 120-123.

Письменная практика на уйльтинском языке[1] — Продолжение

1.

С точки зрения диалектологии, существуют различия не только между южным и северным наречиями уйльтинского языка, но и между их местными говорами.

Исторически уйльтинский язык находится сейчас в процессе значительных изменений. Вследствие этого, в современном уйльтинском языке употребляются старые и новые (измененные) формы.

Кстати, в настоящее время уйльта — двуязычны. В повседневной жизни они говорят на русском языке. В результате языкового контакта возникла интерференция, и старая система уйльтинского языка разрушается под влиянием русского.

При этом уйльтинский язык находится под угрозой исчезновения в связи с уменьшением носителей этого языка.

В сложившейся ситуации распространение и изучение нового уйльтинского алфавита является безотлагательной задачей.

Первый шаг в этом направлении — обозначение носителями языка каждого произнесенного ими слова с помощью уйльтинского алфавита.

---

1 См. выше, с. 154-159.

Для обучения уйльтинскому языку и алфавиту нужен букварь на этом языке. Орфографическое обозначение звуковой формы каждого слова и создание общего уйльтинского языка для его носителей — также важная задача. Но эта задача может рассматриваться только после того, когда будут освоены основы уйльтинской письменности.

2.

В уйльтинском письменном языке, использующем латинскую графику, рекомендуется обозначать повторение одной и той же гласной фонемы двумя буквами ГГ (см. “Проект”[2], раздел 5). Это обозначение, в особенности, пригодно для языка пожилых людей.

В уйльтинском языке на основе русской графики употребление гласной буквы **е** встречает затруднения. Как изложено выше, уйльта употребляют, кроме уйльтинского языка, русский язык и русский алфавит. В русском языке буква **е** обозначает [je]. Однако в уйльтинском письменном языке на основе русской графики буква **е** обозначает /e/ (произношение — [e]).

Уйльтинская письменность использует русский алфавит. Но уйльтинский язык отличается от русского языка по своему звуковому строю и произношению, основанному на этом звуковом строе. Поэтому следует обратить внимание на то, что одна и та же буква обозначает разные звуки в русской и уйльтинской письменностях.

Употребление буквы **е** после среднеязычных и смягчающихся переднеязычных согласных в уйльтинском языке вполне допустимо. Однако в уйльтинском языке нужно употреблять букву **е** также в положе-

2 См. выше, с. 149-152.

нии после заднеязычных и губных согласных.

Кстати, в русском языке обычно отсутствует обозначение гласного [e] буквой **e**, но в некоторых заимствованных словах буква **e** обозначает [e].

Кроме того, как мне кажется, людям, употребляющим русский алфавит, трудно обозначать гласный [e] буквой **e** в начале слова. Тем не менее, надеюсь, что они привыкнут к обозначению фонемы /e/ [e] буквой **e**, так же, как в графике на латинской основе. Если очень трудно употреблять букву **e** в начале слова, употребляющие русский алфавит пока вынуждены использовать другой знак, например ɛ, вместо буквы **e**, чтобы обозначить /e/ [e] в начале слов. Однако эти меры — паллиативные и не рекомендуются.

Далее, употребляющим русский алфавит очень трудно обозначать удвоение фонемы /e/, т.е. /ee/ (произношение — [e:]), буквами **ee**. Но зато /ee/ может обозначаться буквой **e** с надстрочной чертой, т.е. **ē** (см. “Проект”, раздел 5).

Параллельно обозначению **ē** на основе русской графики, удвоение каждой гласной фонемы должно обозначаться не двумя гласными буквами ГГ, а одной гласной буквой с надстрочной чертой Г̄.

3.

В орфографии современного уйльтинского языка существует еще проблема обозначения фонем произносящихся как среднеязычный и смягчающийся переднеязычный согласный перед /i/ и /e/. См. следующую таблицу.

переднеязычные согласные					среднеязычные согласные						
					ji	je	jу	jө	jо	jэ	ja
та	тэ	то	тө	ту	×ти	×те					
					чи	че	чу	чө	чо	чэ	ча
да	дэ	до	дө	ду	×ди	×де					
					ӡи	ӡе	ӡу	ӡө	ӡо	ӡэ	ӡа
на	нэ	но	нө	ну	ни	не					
					×ԩи	×ԩе	ԩу	ԩө	ԩо	ԩэ	ԩа

× обозначает непринятую форму.

В положении перед /i/ и /e/ среднеязычные аффрикаты [tʃ, dʒ] и смягченные переднеязычные [t´, d´] произносятся.

Последние звуки [t´, d´], вероятно, результат влияния русского произношения. Различия между [tʃ] и [t´] и между [dʒ] и [d´] не соответствуют фонематическому различию. Первые звуки [tʃ] и [t´] соответствуют одной фонеме /č/, а последние [dʒ] и [d´] — другой фонеме /ǰ/. В “Проекте” фонема /č/ обозначается не буквой **т**, а буквой **ч**, и фонема /ǰ/ — не буквой **д**, а буквой **ӡ**, по причине палатальности в произношении этих фонем.

Перед /i/ и /e/ произносятся также носовой среднеязычный [ɲ] и носовой смягченный переднеязычный [n´]. Различие между этими носовыми перед /i/ и /e/ не соответствует фонематическому противоположению. В “Проекте” соответствующая этим носовым фонема перед /i/ и /e/ обозначается не буквой **ԩ**, а буквой **н**, потому что частота буквы **н** гораздо выше чем частота буквы **ԩ**.

4.

Каждая буква в уйльтинском алфавите обозначает фонему, а не

различие между ее фонетическими вариантами. В случае, если нужно обозначать щелевой вариант фонемы /g/, он обозначается буквой γ. Но эта буква — не буква уйльтинского алфавита, а фонетический знак.

5.

Буквы **у** и **и** обычно обозначают после другой гласной буквы второй компонент дифтонга [ŭ] (фонему /u/) или [ĭ] (фонему /i/). Примеры: **хаусал** “бумага” и **муирэ** “плечо”.

Но в случае, если согласный звук [w] (фонема /w/) или [j] (фонема /j/) или согласный, близкий к [w] или [j], произносятся вместо вышеупомянутых гласных, буква **в** или **j** употребляется вместо **у** или **и** для того, чтобы выразить такие согласные. Примеры: **хавсали** “бумага” и **муjрэ** “плечо”.

This article was published in *Acta Slavica Iaponica*, Tomus XVI (The Slavic Research Center, Hokkaido University, Sapporo, 1998), pp. 181-183.

Orok Kinship Terminology[1)]

0. INTRODUCTION. An attempt to make a semantic analysis of the kinship terms of the Oroks in Sakhalin and to describe the system of Orok kinship terminology is made here.

The main materials for this paper were acquired in 1953, 1957 and in following years by interviewing Napka, a woman born about 1910, in her own language. Some materials were also acquired from Gɵrgulu, a man born about 1897 and Ɜəktəŋgu, his daughter born in 1919. These informants are Oroks who emigrated from Sakhalin to Hokkaido and who speak both Orok and Japanese.

I should think that inductions from inquiries into a large number of actual instances of kinship relations of individuals would be preferable, but I was compelled to adopt a different method because of the very small number of informants. In interviews, I inquired about various typical instances of kinship of nonspecified persons. For instance, I obtained an example of the term *irgəni* in answer to my question: *əǯini aaŋni xusə puttəni asini xaiga*; the translation of this is "What do you call the wife of the son of the elder brother of her husband?"

When I dealt with terms of reference, I usually did not use the first person but an unspecified third person as the person central to a kinship system. From the informant we can obtain an answer, such as, in the former case, "my …", but in the latter case, "his or her …". We may say that we used is or ea instead of ego. It was perplexing and difficult for my informants to give answers about kinship relations different from their own, pretending that they wẹre their own. This may also be true of other peoples.

In this way I obtained from informants examples of kinship terms for the following relatives: a male's or female's patrilineal consanguineal relatives and their spouses, a male's consanguineal relative's, spouse's consanguineal relatives, a male's or female's matrilineal consanguineal relatives, a male's or female's lineal descendants, their spouses and consanguineal relatives of the spouses, the spouse and his or her consanguineal relatives, and the wives of male consanguineal relatives of the husband.

I would like to dwell briefly on the social organization of the Oroks and their rules of marriage. Orok society is composed of sibs (*xala*), which are each a consanguineal kin group of common descent in the paternal line, but not a unilocal kin group.[2] The characteristic of the sibs is exogamy. In connection with this, the Oroks have some regulations of marriage. The parallel cousin marriage and a type of cross-cousin marriage, i.e., mating with FaSiDa are taboo (*ənnəuri*). But another type of cross-cousin marriage, i.e., mating with MoBrDa is preferred. In secondary marriages the junior levirate and the junior sororate are practised.

1.0. TERMS OF REFERENCE. We deal with the terms of reference listed below with their denotations, but not with combinations of these terms, for example, *aaŋni asini* 'his (or her) elder brother's wife' or *puttəni puttəni* 'his (or her) child's child [=grandchild]'. We may say that the terms listed form the essential part of the Orok kinship terminology.

1.1. A list of terms of reference with examples of the relatives denoted by them is as follows.[3]

Denotation

(1) *daaji amini* $FaFa^{N}$, $FaelBr^{N}$, FaFaelBr, FaFayoBr (o), FaFaelBrSo (o), FaFayoBrSo (o), MoFa.

(2) *daaji ənini* $FaMo^{N}$, $FaelBrWi^{N}$, FaFaelBrWi, FaFayoBrWi (o), FaFaelBrSoWi (o), FaFayoBrSoWi (o), MoMo, MoelSi.

(3) *nuuči amini* FayoBr, FaFayoBr (y), FaFaelBrSo (y), FaFayoBrSo (y).

(4) *nuuči ənini* FayoBrWi^{N}, FaFayoBrWi (y), FaFaelBrSoWi (y), FaFayoBrSoWi (y).

(5) *amini* Fa.

(6) *ənini* Mo.

(7) *puttəni* So, Da, SoSo, SoDa.

(8) *aaŋni* elBr. For a male: FayoBr.

(9) *əigəni* elSi. For a female: elBrWi, HuelSi.

(10) *nəuni* yoBr, yoSi.

(11) *sagǰimǰini* For a male: FaelBrSo, FayoBrSo (o).

(12) *purigəmǰini* For a male: FayoBrSo (y), FaelBrSoSo, FayoBrSoSo, elBrSo, yoBrSo, elBrSoSo, yoBrSoSo. For a female: HuFaelBrSoSo, HuFayoBrSoSo, HuelBrSo, HuyoBrSo, HuelBrSoSo, HuyoBrSoSo.

(13) *naadaktani* For a female: FayoBr^{N}, FaelBrSo, FayoBrSo, FaelBrSoSo, FayoBrSoSo, elBr^{N}, yoBr^{N}, elBrSo, yoBrSo, elBrSoSo, yoBrSoSo.

(14) *pundaduni* For a male : FaelSi^{N}, FayoSi^{N}, FaFaelSi, FaFayoSi, FaelBrDa, FayoBrDa, FaelBrSoDa, FayoBrSoDa, elSi^{N}, yoSi^{N}, elBrDa, yoBrDa, elBrSoDa, yoBrSoDa. For a female : HuFaelSi^{N}, HuFayoSi^{N}, HuFaFaelSi, HuFaFayoSi, HuFaelBrDa, HuFayoBrDa, HuFaelBrSoDa, HuFayoBrSoDa, HuelSi^{NƎ}, HuyoSi^{NƎ}, HuelBrDa, HuyoBrDa, HuelBrSoDa, HuyoBrSoDa.

(15) *taajini* For a female : FaelSi^{NƎ}, FayoSi^{NƎ}, FaFaelSi, FaFayoSi, FaelBrDa, FayoBrDa, FaelBrSoDa, FayoBrSoDa, elSi^{NƎ}, yoSi^{NƎ}, elBrDa, yoBrDa, elBrSoDa, yoBrSoDa.

(16) *gamasuni* DaSo, DaDa. For a male : FaelSiSo, FaelSiDa, FayoSiSo, FayoSiDa, FaFaelSiSo, FaFaelSiDa, FaFayoSiSo, FaFayoSiDa. elSiSo^{NƎ}, elSiDa^{NƎ}, yoSiSo^{NƎ}, yoSiDa^{NƎ}.

(17) *gusini* MoFaelBr, MoFaelBrSo, MoelBr (MoelBr^{Ǝ} for a male),

MoyoBr, MoelBrSo, MoyoBrSo, MoelBrSoSo, MoyoBrSoSo, MoelBrSoSoSo.

(18) *tuwəni* MoelSiSo[NƎ], MoelSiDa[NƎ], MoyoSiSo[NƎ], MoyoSiDa[NƎ].

(19) *əǰini* For a female: Hu.

(20) *asini* For a male: Wi.

(21) *əpini* For a male: WiFa[NƎ]. For a female: HuFa[NƎ], HuFaFa, HuFaelBr[NƎ], HuFayoBr (o), HuFaelBrSo (o), HuFaFaelBr, HuFaFayoBr, HuelBr.

(22) *ačini* For a male: WiMo[NƎ], WiFaelSi, WiFayoSi (o), WiFaelBrDa (o), WielSi[NƎ]. For a female: HuMo[NƎ], HuFaMo, HuFaelBrWi[NƎ], HuFayoBrWi (o), HuFaelBrSoWi (o), HuFaFaelBrWi, HuFa-FayoBrWi, HuelBrWi[Ǝ] (o)[N].

(23) *irgəni* SoWi, SoSoWi, DaHu, SoDaHu. For a male: yoBrWi[NƎ], elBrSoWi, yoBrSoWi, FayoBrWi[Ǝ], FayoBrSoWi (y). For a female: yoSiHu[NƎ], elBrDaHu (y), yoBrDaHu, FayoSiHu (y); HuyoBrWi[Ǝ] (y)[N], HuyoBrSoWi, HuyoBrSoSoWi, HuFayoBrWi[Ǝ]; yoBrWi[Ǝ].

(24) *inani* For a female: elSiHu[NƎ], elBrDaHu (o), FayoSiHu (o); HuyoBr[NƎ], HuelBrSo, HuFayoBr(y)[NƎ], HuFaelBrSo(y), HuFayoBrSo, HuFaelBrSoSo.

(25) *əəwəni* For a male: elBrWi[NƎ], FayoBrWi, FaelBrSoWi, FayoBrSoWi (o); WiyoSi[NƎ], WielBrDa, WiFayoSi (y), WiFaelBrDa (y), WiFayoBrDa.

(26) *andani* For a female: HuelSi, HuyoSi, HuelBrDa, HuFayoSi, HuFaelSiDa, HuFayoSiDa; elBrWi, yoBrWi, elBrSoWi, FayoBrWi, FaelBrSoWi, FayoBrSoWi.

(27) *poojoini* For a female: HuelBrWi (y), HuyoBrWi (o), HuFayo-BrWi (y), HuFaelBrSoWi (y), HuFayoBrSoWi, HuelBrSoWi.

(28) *səŋgini* SoWiFa, SoWiMo, SoWiFaFa, SoWiFaMo, SoWiFaelBr, SoWiFayoBr, SoWiFaelBrSo, SoWielBr, SoWiyoBr, SoSoWiFa,

SoSoWiMo, SoSoWiFaelBr, SoSoWielBr, SoSoWiyoBr, SoDaHuFa, SoDaHuMo, SoDaHuelBr, SoDaHuyoBr, DaHuFa, DaHuMo, DaHuelBr, DaHuyoBr. For a male: WiFaelBr, WiFayoBr, WiFaelBrSo, WiFayoBrSo, WielBr[NƎ], WiyoBr[NƎ], WielBrSo, WiyoBrSo; FaelSiHu, FayoSiHu, FaFaelSiHu, FaFayoSiHu, elSiHu[NƎ], yoSiHu[NƎ], elBrDaHu, yoBrDaHu; FaelBrWiFa, FaelBrWiMo, FaelBrWielBr, FaelBrWiyoBr, FaelBrSoWiFa, FaelBrSoWielBr, FaelSiHuFa, FaelSiHuMo, FaelSiHuelBr, FaelSiHuyoBr, FayoBrWiFa, FayoBrWiMo, FayoBrWielBr, FayoBrWiyoBr, FayoSiHuFa, FayoSiHuMo, FayoSiHuelBr, FayoSiHuyoBr, elBrWiFa, elBrWiMo, elBrWielBr, elBrWiyoBr, elBrWiFaelBr, elBrWiFaelBrSo, elSiHuFa, elSiHuMo, elSiHuelBr, elSiHuyoBr, yoBrWiFa, yoBrWiMo, yoBrWielBr, yoBrWiyoBr, yoSiHuFa, yoSiHuMo, yoSiHuelBr, yoSiHuyoBr.

(29) *puttərəni* DaSo[Ǝ], DaDa[Ǝ].

1.2. Further, we find some specific terms with the suffix *-ŋasa*~ *-ŋəsə* or with the suffix *-ran*~ *-rən* :

amiŋasani	deceased father
əniŋəsəni	deceased mother
puttəŋəsəni	deceased child
aaŋasani	deceased elder brother
əigəŋəsəni	deceased elder sister
nəuŋəsəni	deceased younger brother or sister
əǰiŋəsəni	deceased husband
asiŋasani	deceased wife
amirani	stepfather
ənirəni	stepmother
puttərəni	stepchild cf.(29).

1.3. The above terms each contain only one substantival stem except for *daaji amini, daaji ənini, nuuči amini* and *nuuči ənini.* These differ grammatically from the other terms in that they contain two stems: an adjectival stem *daaji* 'grand' or *nuuči* 'little' and a substantival one *amin-* 'father' or *ənin-* 'mother'. We regard them, therefore, as phrases containing an adjective and a substantive, or as a compound word. On the other hand, lexically, these terms alone have the semantic elements A and *A* mentioned below. We may say that these terms stand grammatically and lexically on a level different from the other terms in the system of the Orok kinship terminology.

1.4. The final *-ni* in the terms listed above is the third person ending 'his' or 'her'. Terms of reference normally contain a personal or reflexive ending. But we have some exceptions, such as *amma* 'papa', *ənnə* 'mamma', *axa* or *aka* 'elder brother', *əgə* 'elder sister', which have no personal or reflexive ending. These are informal familiar forms of *amin-* 'father', *ənin-* 'mother', *aak-* 'elder brother' and **əikə-* 'elder sister'. The forms *amma* and *ənnə* are also included in *daa(ji) amma, daamma* 'grandpapa, old uncle', *daa(ji) ənnə, daannə* 'grandmamma, old aunt', *nuuči amma* 'young uncle', *nuuči ənnə* 'young aunt', *mapaačča amma* 'old uncle', *mam ənnə* 'old aunt', *kadar(a) amma* 'rather old uncle', *kadar(a) ənnə* 'rather old aunt'. We have also the informal familiar forms *ammaŋasa, ənnəŋəsə, axaŋasa, əgəŋəsə* of *amiŋasa-, əniŋəsə-, aaŋasa-* and *əigəŋəsə-* 'deceased father, mother, elder brother or elder sister'.

For Gɵrgulu, *nuuči amma* means 'papa', and *nuuči ənnə* 'mamma' as distinguished from *daa amma* 'grandpapa' and *daa ənnə* 'grandmamma'. Similarly *nuuči amimbi* containing the singular reflexive ending *-bi* means 'one's own father'and *nuuči ənimbi* containing the same ending 'one's own mother' for him.

1.5. On the other hand, *puttə* can be used without any personal or reflexive ending as a word designating 'a child', regardless of whether a kinship relation exists or not. The accusative form of *puttə* in this case is *puttəə* or *puttəwə*. *anda* can also be used independently of kinship relations to designate 'a companion of the same sex and of about the same age'.

1.6. It is noteworthy that denotations of some terms are likely to vary according to different personal and reflexive endings to be contained in them, which refer to the central person. In comparison to *aaŋni*, *əigəni* and *nəuni* given above, *aagbi*, *əigəbi*, and *nəuwi* containing the first person singular ending seem to have wider denotations, which are similar to denotations of the corresponding terms of address, *axaa*, *əgəə* and *nunee*. Those denotations would be respectively indicated by $S^{m}Mc^{1}L^{c}A^{1}$, $S^{f}Mc^{1}L^{c}A^{1}$ or $Mc^{1}L^{c}A^{-1}$ in our notation given below.

1.7. Besides the above terms, we find some terms different from these in that the suffix *-ŋu* is added before a personal or reflexive ending: *nariŋubi* 'my husband'=*əǰibi*, *əəktəŋubi* 'my daughter-in-law' used by an old man or woman=*irgəmbi*, *mapaaččaŋubi* 'my husband' used by an old woman= *əǰibi*, *mamaŋubi* 'my wife' used by an old man= *asibi*, *mapaaččaŋupu* 'my father-in-law'= *əpimbi and mamaŋupu* 'my mother-in-1aw'=*ačibi*.[3)]

2.1. We distinguish the following semantic elements of Orok kinship terms, various values of which make the distinctive features of the meaning of each term.

1. Sex of the person referred to, S, with the values *m* male and *f* female.
2. Sex of a person central to the kinship system in question, s, with the values *m* male and *f* female.
3. Sex of the central person, relative to the sex of the person referred to, *s*, with the values *s*, the same sex, and *o*, opposite.
4. Mode of kinship between the central person and the person referred

to, M, with the values c consanguineal, m marital, and a affinal.

Permutational differences of successions of male and female consanguineal relatives connecting the central person and the person referred to, produce additional values to c, such as c^1, c^2, c^3, c^4. Each of these denotes the following kind of successions of intervening relatives, *1, 2, 3* or *4* respectively.

1. male relatives, a male relative or none —*m*'s, *m* or zero.

2. one or more male relatives and a female relative, or a female relative alone —*m* (or *m*'s) *f*, or *f*.

3. a female relative and one or more male relatives —*fm* (or *m*'s).

4. a female relative, a male relative and a female relative —*fmf*.

Permutational defferences of successions of blood-tie (through c^1) and marital bond intervening between the central person and the person referred to, produce various values additional to a, such as a^1, a^2, a^3 and a^4. Each of a^1, a^2, a^3 and a^4 denotes the following *1, 2, 3* or *4* respectively.

1. marital-consanguineal connection —The person referred to is a consanguineal relative of the spouse of the central person.

2. consanguineal-marital connection —The person referred to is the spouse of a consanguineal relative of the central person.

3. marital-consanguineal-marital connection —The person referred to is the spouse of a consanguineal relative of the spouse of the central person.

4. consanguineal-marital-consanguineal connection —The person referred to is a consanguineal relative of the spouse of a consanguineal relative of the central person.

5. Lineality, L, *L* or *L*', with the values *l* or l lineal and *c* non-lineal or collateral. For *c* we can differentiate between 2 colineal and 3 ablineal. Lineals are direct ancestors and descendants of the central person. Colineals are connected to a direct ancestor without any intervening rel-

ative. Ablineals are connected indirectly to a lineal relative through one or more linking relatives.[5]

6. Generation, G, *G* or *G'*, with the values *l* (lower generations), 0 (the same generation), and *h* (higher generations). *l* comprises: 1 (one generation lower), 2 (two generations lower) and so on. *h* comprises: –1 (one generation higher), –2 (two generations higher) and so on.

7. Relative age, A, *A* or *A'*, with the values *o* older and *y* younger. For *o* we can differentiate between 1 (a little older) and 2 (much older). For *y* we can differentiate between –1 (a little younger) and –2 (much younger). In the 2 and –2 the disparity in age between two persons is greater than that of siblings, but in the 1 and –1 it is not greater than that of siblings and so small as to make marriage possible if no restrictions exist.

The L, G and A are combined with Mc and concerned with the person referred to as against the central person, but the *L*, *G* and *A* are combined with Ma. In combination with Ma^1, they are concerned with the person referred to as against the spouse of the central person. In combination with Ma^2, they are concerned with the spouse of the person referred to as against the central person. In combination with Ma^3, they are concerned with the spouse of the person referred to as against the spouse of the central person. In combination with Ma^4, they are concerned with a consanguineal relative of the central person (i.e., the spouse of a consanguineal relative of the person referred to) as against the central person. The *L'*, *G'* and *A'* are combined with Ma^4 and concerned with the person referred to as against the person's consanguineal relative who is the spouse of a consanguineal relative of the central person.

8. Age relative to the age of the father of the centeal person, A or *A* with the values *o* older and *y* younger. A is combined with Mc and concerned with the person referred to. But in connection with Mc^3 A indicates the age relative to that of the mother of the central person. *A* in combination

with Ma^2 is concerned with the spouse of the person referred to.

2.2. When the consanguineal relation between two persons is traced, we have some rules of reckoning. The consanguineal relation between two persons is traced only through immediate connections between a father (or mother) and his (or her) son (or daughter) successively. When we pass from the lineal line to a collateral line in order to measure the position of a collateral relative in the Orok patrilineal kinship system, the last lineal linking relative is always a male. In parallel relations between the same two persons, a male relative takes precedence over a female relative; e.g., the brother of a man is not the son of his mother, but the son of his father. Consanguineal relation takes precedence over the marital bond; e. g., the son of a man is not the son of his wife, but his son.

Higher and lower generations dealt with here are limited to 1, 2 and –1, –2.

Criteria as to whose age a person's age is compared with are set up here on the basis of suggestions by informants. But I could obtain no information on explicit criteria for such relative age comparisons.

2.3. We have another semantic element of kinship terms, i.e., the extension of consanguineal connections, E, with the values 1 and 2. The extension E^1 is so large that in reality the consanguineal connection cannot always be traced genealogically; consequently the term is applied for the whole sib. The extension E^2 is small, rendering the consanguineal connection easily traceable, and consequently the use of the term is restricted to close relatives. The terms with L^1 and *sagǰimǰini, purigəmǰini, naadaktani, pundaduni, taajini* have E^1. *gamasuni, gusini, tuwəni, əpini, ačini* and *irgəni* seem to have E^2. *inani, əəwəni, andani, poojoini* and *səŋgini* are obscure in regard to the value of this element. This element is important for the so-called 'classificatory terms' denoting collaterals, but its value in a kinship term is not always obvious. This semantic element seems to be on a level different from the semantic elements given above. A detailed description of this element will not be given here. We believe there are also emotional elements in the meaning of kinship terms, which, however, will also not be dealt with here.

3.1. We define terms of reference (1)–(28) by means of the distinctive features. The terms are defined on the basis of material obtained from Napka. The definitions of these terms of reference are here formularized by combinations of a symbol for a semantic element and a value sign given above.[6)] The symbol for an element, together with a sign for its value, is dropped when the term does not specify a particular value of the element but ranges over all the values.

(1) *daaji amini* $\mathrm{S}^{m}(\mathrm{Mc}^{1+2}\mathrm{L}^{1}\mathrm{G}^{-2}+\mathrm{Mc}^{1}\mathrm{L}^{c}\mathrm{G}^{h}\mathrm{A}^{o})$

(2) *daaji ənini* $\mathrm{S}^{f}(\mathrm{Mc}^{1+2}\mathrm{L}^{1}\mathrm{G}^{-2}+\mathrm{Ma}^{2}L^{c}G^{h}A^{o})$

(3) *nuuči amini* $\mathrm{S}^{m}\mathrm{Mc}^{1}\mathrm{L}^{c}\mathrm{G}^{h}\mathrm{A}^{y}$

(4) *nuuči ənini* $\mathrm{S}^{f}\mathrm{Ma}^{2}L^{c}G^{h}A^{y}$

(5) *amini* $\mathrm{S}^{m}\mathrm{Mc}^{1}\mathrm{L}^{1}\mathrm{G}^{-1}$

(6) *ənini* $\mathrm{S}^{f}\mathrm{Mc}^{1}\mathrm{L}^{1}\mathrm{G}^{-1}$

(7) *puttəni* $\mathrm{Mc}^{1}\mathrm{L}^{1}\mathrm{G}^{l}$

(8) *aaŋni* $\mathrm{S}^{m}\mathrm{Mc}^{1}\mathrm{L}^{2}\mathrm{G}^{0}\mathrm{A}^{o}$

(9) *əigəni* $\mathrm{S}^{f}\mathrm{Mc}^{1}\mathrm{L}^{2}\mathrm{G}^{0}\mathrm{A}^{o}$

(10) *nəuni* $\mathrm{Mc}^{1}\mathrm{L}^{2}\mathrm{G}^{0}\mathrm{A}^{y}$

(11) *sagǰimǰini* $\mathrm{S}^{m}s^{s}\mathrm{Mc}^{1}\mathrm{L}^{3}\mathrm{G}^{0+l}\mathrm{A}^{o}$

(12) *purigəmǰini* $\mathrm{S}^{m}(s^{s}\mathrm{Mc}^{1}\mathrm{L}^{3}\mathrm{G}^{0+l}\mathrm{A}^{y}+s^{o}\mathrm{Ma}^{1}L^{3}G^{0+l}A^{y})$

(13) *naadaktani* $\mathrm{S}^{m}s^{o}\mathrm{Mc}^{1}\mathrm{L}^{c}\mathrm{A}^{1+y}$

(14) *pundaduni* $\mathrm{S}^{f}(s^{o}\mathrm{Mc}^{1}\mathrm{L}^{c}+s^{s}\,\mathrm{Ma}^{1}L^{c})$

(15) *taajini* $\mathrm{S}^{f}s^{s}\mathrm{Mc}^{1}\mathrm{L}^{c}$

(16) *gamasuni* $\mathrm{Mc}^{2}\,(\mathrm{L}^{l}\mathrm{G}^{2}+\mathrm{s}^{m}\mathrm{L}^{c})$

(17) *gusini* $\mathrm{S}^{m}\mathrm{Mc}^{3}\mathrm{L}^{c}$

(18) *tuwəni* $\mathrm{Mc}^{4}\mathrm{L}^{c}\mathrm{G}^{0}$

(19) *əǰini* $\mathrm{S}^{m}s^{o}\mathrm{Mm}$
(20) *asini* $\mathrm{S}^{f}s^{o}\mathrm{Mm}$
(21) *əpini* $\mathrm{S}^{m}\mathrm{Ma}^{1}\ (L^{l}G^{h}+s^{o}L^{c}A^{o})$
(22) *ačini* $\mathrm{S}^{f}\{\mathrm{Ma}^{1}\ (L^{l}G^{h}+s^{o}L^{c}A^{o})+s^{s}\mathrm{Ma}^{3}L^{c}\mathrm{A}^{2}\}$
(23) *irgəni* $\mathrm{Ma}^{2}\ (L^{l}G^{l}+s^{o}L^{c}A^{y})+\mathrm{S}^{f}\ s^{s}\mathrm{Ma}^{3}L^{c}\mathrm{A}^{-2}$
(24) *inani* $\mathrm{S}^{m}s^{o}(\mathrm{Ma}^{1}L^{c}A^{-1}+\mathrm{Ma}^{2}L^{c}A^{o})$
(25) *əəwəni* $\mathrm{S}^{f}s^{o}(\mathrm{Ma}^{1}L^{c}A^{y}+\mathrm{Ma}^{2}L^{c}A^{1})$
(26) *andani* $\mathrm{S}^{f}s^{s}(\mathrm{Ma}^{1}L^{c}+\mathrm{Ma}^{2}L^{c})\mathrm{A}^{-1+1}$
(27) *poojoini* $\mathrm{S}^{f}s^{s}\mathrm{Ma}^{3}L^{c}\mathrm{A}^{-1+1}$
(28) *səŋgini* $\mathrm{S}^{m}s^{s}(\mathrm{Ma}^{1}L^{c}+\mathrm{Ma}^{2}L^{c})+\mathrm{Ma}^{4}\{\mathrm{s}^{m}L^{c}(L'^{l}G'^{h}+\mathrm{S}^{m}L'^{c})$
$+L^{l}G^{l}\ (L'^{l}G'^{h}+\mathrm{S}^{m}L'^{c})\}$

3.2. Information obtained from Ǝəktəŋgu differs from that gained from Napka in the following points. The terms *sagǰimǰini, purigəmǰini, poojoini* and *andani* were not obtained from Ǝəktəŋgu. Some terms have a wider denotation. *daaji ənini* covers even MoelSi, and so includes $\mathrm{S}^{f}\mathrm{Mc}^{2}\mathrm{L}^{c}\mathrm{G}^{-1}\mathrm{A}^{o}$. *aaŋni* covers FayoBr and *əigəni* elBrWi and HuelSi, so that they range to G^{-1} or Ma^{1}, Ma^{2}. It is worth noting that *irgəni* covers yoBrWi ($\mathrm{S}^{f}s^{s}\mathrm{Ma}^{2}L^{2}G^{0}\mathrm{A}^{y}$), taking the place of *andani.* As a term for DaSo and DaDa ($\mathrm{Mc}^{2}\mathrm{L}^{l}\mathrm{G}^{2}$), whereas Napka has *gamasuni* which denotes also a male's elSiSo, etc. ($\mathrm{s}^{m}\mathrm{Mc}^{2}\mathrm{L}^{c}$), Ǝəktəŋgu has *puttərəni* which, for Napka, means 'stepchild'.

4. We will show the semantic interrelationships of terms of reference by mapping them in Figures 1–14.[7)]

5.1. Reciprocals. We find reciprocal pairs of kinship terms where two terms are in reverse relation to each other with regard to the central person and the person referred to. In some cases, instead of a term, a set of terms forms one counterpart in a pair. We give below the reciprocal pairs of terms of reference. The sign ↔ between two terms indicates that they are reciprocals to each other.

Term	Formula	Reciprocal	Group term
amini	$S^{m}Mc^{1}L^{1}G^{-1}$	$\leftrightarrow Mc^{1}L^{1}G^{l}$ *puttəni*	
ənini	$S^{f}Mc^{1}L^{1}G^{-1}$		
daaji amini	$S^{m}Mc^{1}L^{1}G^{-2}$		
daaji ənini	$S^{f}Mc^{1}L^{1}G^{-2}$		
aaŋni	$S^{m}Mc^{1}L^{2}G^{0}A^{o}$	$\leftrightarrow Mc^{1}L^{2}G^{0}A^{y}$ *nəuni*	
əigəni	$S^{f}Mc^{1}L^{2}G^{0}A^{o}$		
sagǰimǰini	$S^{m}s^{s}Mc^{1}L^{3}G^{0}A^{o}$	$\leftrightarrow S^{m}s^{s}Mc^{1}L^{3}G^{0}A^{y}$ *purigəmǰini*	
daaji amini	$S^{m}Mc^{2}L^{1}G^{-2}$	$\leftrightarrow Mc^{2}L^{1}G^{2}$	*gamasuni*
daaji ənini	$S^{f}Mc^{2}L^{1}G^{-2}$		
gusini	$S^{m}Mc^{3}L^{c} \leftrightarrow s^{m}Mc^{2}L^{c}$		
əǰini	$S^{m}s^{o}Mm \leftrightarrow S^{f}s^{o}Mm$ *asini*		
əpini	$S^{m}Ma^{1}L^{1}G^{h}$	$\leftrightarrow Ma^{2}L^{1}G^{l}$	*irgəni*
ačini	$S^{f}Ma^{1}L^{1}G^{h}$		
əpini	$S^{m}s^{o}Ma^{1}L^{c}A^{o}$	$\leftrightarrow s^{o}Ma^{2}L^{c}A^{y}$	
ačini	$S^{f}s^{o}Ma^{1}L^{c}A^{o}$		
ačini	$S^{f}s^{s}Ma^{3}L^{c}A^{2} \leftrightarrow S^{f}s^{s}Ma^{3}L^{c}A^{-2}$		
inani	$S^{m}s^{o}Ma^{1}L^{c}A^{-1} \leftrightarrow S^{f}s^{o}Ma^{2}L^{c}A^{l}$		*əəwəni*
	$S^{m}s^{o}Ma^{2}L^{c}A^{o} \leftrightarrow S^{f}s^{o}Ma^{1}L^{c}A^{y}$		

However, *purigəmǰini* $S^{m}s^{o}Ma^{1}L^{3}G^{0+l}A^{y}$ or *pundaduni* $S^{f}s^{s}Ma^{1}L^{c}$ does not function completely but only partially as a reciprocal to *daaji ənini* $S^{f}Ma^{2}L^{c}G^{h}A^{o}$ and *nuuči ənini* $S^{f}Ma^{2}L^{c}G^{h}A^{y}$; similarly *sagǰimǰini* $S^{m}s^{s}Mc^{1}L^{3}G^{l}A^{o}$ and *purigəmǰini* $S^{m}s^{s}Mc^{1}L^{3}G^{l}A^{y}$ to *daaji amini* $S^{m}Mc^{1}L^{c}G^{h}A^{o}$ and *nuuči amini* $S^{m}Mc^{1}L^{c}G^{h}A^{y}$; *pundaduni* $S^{f}s^{o}Mc^{1}L^{c}$ to the same *daaji amini* $S^{m}Mc^{1}L^{c}G^{h}A^{o}$ and *nuuči amini* $S^{m}Mc^{1}L^{c}G^{h}A^{y}$ or to *naadaktani* $S^{m}s^{o}Mc^{1}L^{c}A^{1+y}$.[8)]

Some other terms do not form a reciprocal pair with any term, but feature reciprocal relation in themselves, i.e., they are self-reciprocal: *taajini* $S^{f}s^{s}Mc^{1}L^{c}$, *tuwəni* $Mc^{4}L^{c}G^{0}$, *andani* $S^{f}s^{s}Ma^{1}L^{c}A^{-1+1} \leftrightarrow S^{f}s^{s}Ma^{2}L^{c}A^{-1+1}$, *poojoini* $S^{f}s^{s}Ma^{3}L^{c}A^{-1+1}$, *səŋgini*[1] $S^{m}s^{s}Ma^{1}L^{c} \leftrightarrow S^{m}s^{s}Ma^{2}L^{c}$, *səŋgini*[2] $s^{m}Ma^{4}L^{c}L'^{l}G'^{h} \leftrightarrow S^{m}Ma^{4}L^{l}G^{l}L'^{c}$, *səŋgini*[3] $S^{m}s^{s}Ma^{4}L^{c}L'^{c}$, *səŋgini*[4] $Ma^{4}L^{l}$

$G'^{l}L'^{l}G'^{h}$.

5.2. In a similar way, each of the above-mentioned semantic elements with a value other than A^{o},A^{y},A^{o} and A^{y} is a reciprocal to the same semantic element with another value or another semantic element with a value, or is self-reciprocal as follows:

	(1) Forming a reciprocal pair	(2) Self-reciprocal
S, s, *s*	$\mathrm{S}^{m} \leftrightarrow \mathrm{s}^{m}$	
	$\mathrm{S}^{f} \leftrightarrow \mathrm{s}^{f}$	s^{s}, s^{o}
	$\mathrm{S}^{m} s^{o} \leftrightarrow \mathrm{S}^{f} s^{o}$	$\mathrm{S}^{m} s^{s}$, $\mathrm{S}^{f} s^{s}$
M		Mc^{1}
	$\mathrm{Mc}^{2} \leftrightarrow \mathrm{Mc}^{3}$, where there are two or more linking relatives.	Mc^{2}, where there is one linking relative.
		Mc^{4}
		Mm
	$\mathrm{Ma}^{1} \leftrightarrow \mathrm{Ma}^{2}$	Ma^{3}, Ma^{4}
L		L^{1} ($=\mathrm{L}^{l}$), L^{2}, L^{3}, L^{c}
G	$\mathrm{G}^{l} \leftrightarrow \mathrm{G}^{h}$	G^{0}
	$\mathrm{G}^{1} \leftrightarrow \mathrm{G}^{-1}$	
	$\mathrm{G}^{2} \leftrightarrow \mathrm{G}^{-2}$	
A	$\mathrm{A}^{o} \leftrightarrow \mathrm{A}^{y}$	
	$\mathrm{A}^{1} \leftrightarrow \mathrm{A}^{-1}$	A^{-1+1}
	$\mathrm{A}^{2} \leftrightarrow \mathrm{A}^{-2}$	

S with *m* or *f* is a reciprocal to s with *m* or *f*. Each of the other semantic elements with a value is a reciprocal to the same element with another value or is self-reciprocal. But S and *s* in combination function as a unit to bear a reciprocal relation. *L*, *L'*, *G*, *G'* or *A*, *A'* with a value bears the same reciprocal relation as L, G, or A with an equal value. In the case of forming a reciprocal pair, however, *L'*, *G'* or *A'* forms a pair with *L*, *G* or *A*.

A^o,A^y,A^o or A^y is not self-reciprocal and also has no reciprocal in the system of Orok kinship terminology.

A reciprocal pair of kinship terms contains at least one reciprocal pair of semantic elements, besides one or more semantic elements with a certain value which are self-reciprocal. In a self-reciprocal kinship term each semantic element with a certain value is self-reciprocal, if we take only the above-mentioned semantic elements into consideration.

5.3. *puttəni, gamasuni, nəuni* and *irgəni* with the element G^l (or G^1, G^2) or A^y (or A^y) commonly do not distinguish male and female sexes. This stands in marked contrast to their reciprocals with G^h (or G^{-1}, G^{-2}) or A^o (or A^o): *amini* and *ənini, daaji amini* and *daaji ənini, aaŋni* and *əigəni*, or *əpini* and *ačini.*

6.1. Substantival inflection of terms of reference and their plural forms.[9)] We give here three inflected forms of terms of reference which are classified as substantives, viz., the nominative form, the accusative form, the singular reflexive accusative-nominative form, and their basic stems. Besides these, we will give the plural forms of these terms.[10)] In Orok the inflection of a substantive is predicted by the basic stem or by the nominative and accusative forms of the substantive. An asterisk indicates an artificial basic stem. The inflected forms and plural forms given below contain the third person ending *-ni* or *-li* 'his or her' or the singular reflexive ending *-bi* or *-wi* 'one's own'. But in the word *poojokki* the singular reflexive ending is fused with the stem of the word.

Nominative	Accusative	Basic Stem	Singular Reflexive Nom.-Acc.	Plural
aaŋni	*aagbani*	*aak-*	*aagbi*	*aajilni*[G], *aajilli*
aaŋasani	*aaŋassaani*	*aaŋasa-*	*aaŋasabi*	*aaŋasalli*

ačini	*aččeeni*	*ači-*	*ačibi*	*ačinilni*[G], *ačinilli*
amini	*amimbani*	*amin-*	*amimbi*	*aminilni*[G]
amiŋasani	*amiŋassaani*	*amiŋasa-*	*amiŋasabi*	
amirani	*amirambani*	*amiran-*	*amirambi*	
andani	*andaani*	*anda-*	*andabi*	*andailli*
asini	*asseeni*	*asi-*	*asibi*	
asiŋasani	*asiŋassaani*	*asiŋasa-*	*asiŋasabi*	
əəwəni	*əəwəmbəni*	*əəwən-*	*əəwəmbi*	*əəwəilni*[G], *əəwəilli*
əigəni	*əikkəəni*	**əikə-*	*əigəbi*	*əigəilni*[G], *əigəilli*
əigəŋəsəni	*əigəŋəssəni*	*əigəŋəsə-*	*əigəŋəsəbi*	*əigəŋəsəlli*
əǰini	*əǰǰeeni*	*əǰi-*	*əǰibi*	
əǰiŋəsəni	*əǰiŋəssəəni*	*əǰiŋəsə-*	*əǰiŋəsəbi*	
ənini	*ənimbəni*	*ənin-*	*ənimbi*	*əninilni*[G]
əniŋəsəni	*əniŋəssəəni*	*əniŋəsə-*	*əniŋəsəbi*	
ənirəni	*ənirəmbəni*	*ənirən-*	*ənirəmbi*	
əpini	*əpimbəni*	*əpin-*	*əpimbi*	*əpinilni*[G], *əpinilli*
inani	*inambani*	*inan-*	*inambi*	*inailni*[G], *inailli*
irgəni	*irgəmbəni*	*irgən-*	*irgəmbi*	*irgəilni*[G], *irgəilli*
gamasuni	*gamasumbani*	*gamasun-*	*gamasumbi*	*gamasuilni*[G], *gamasuilli*
gusini	*gusimbani*	*gusin-*	*gusimbi*	*gusinilni*[G], *gusinilli*
naadaktani	*naadaktaani*	*naadakta-*	*naadaktabi*	*naadailni*[G],

				naadailli
nəuni	*nəuwəni*	*nəu-*	*nəuwi*	*nənilni* [G], *nənilli*
nəuŋəsəni	*nəuŋəssəəni*	*nəuŋəsə-*	*nəuŋəsəbi*	*nəuŋəsəlli*
poojoini	*poojokkeeni*	**poojoki-*	*poojokki*	*poojoilli*
pundaduni	*pundaddooni*	*pundadu-*	*pundadubi*	*punǰiilni* [G], *punǰiilli*
purigəmǰini	*purigəmǰeeni*	*purigəmǰi-*	*purigəmǰibi*	*purigəmǰilni* [G], *purigəilli*
puttəni	*puttəəni*, *puttəbəni*	*puttə-*	*puttəbi*	*purilni* [G], *purilli*
puttəŋəsəni	*puttəŋəssəəni*	*puttəŋəsə-*	*puttəŋəsəbi*	*puttəŋəsəlli*
puttərəni	*puttərəmbəni*	*puttərən-*	*puttərəmbi*	*puttərəlli*
sagǰimǰini	*sagǰimǰeeni*	*sagǰimǰi-*	*sagǰimǰibi*	*sagǰimǰilni* [G]
səŋgini	*səŋgeeni*	*səŋgi-*	*səŋgibi*	*səŋgisilni* [G], *səŋgisilli*
taajini	*taakkeeni*	**taaki-*	*taajibi*	*taajilni* [G], *taajinilli*
tuwəni	*tuwəmbəni*	*tuwən-*	*tuwəmbi*	*tuwəilni* [G], *tuwəilli*

6.2. The plural form *aminilni* 'his (or her) fathers' includes 'father-in-law' in its meaning, and *əninilni* 'his (or her) mothers' includes 'mother-in-low'.

In the terms *daaji amini, daaji ənini, nuuči amini, nuuči ənini,* the first part *daaji* 'grand ' or *nuuči* 'little' is not inflected, but only the second, in the same way as single *amini* or *ənini.*

7.0. TERMS OF ADDRESS.

7.1. A list of terms of address with examples of relatives denoted by them.[11)]

	Denotation
daa (ji) ammaa	daaji amimbi[NG], gusimbi.
daa (ji) ənnəə	daaji ənimbi[NG], pundadubi, taajibi.
nuuči ammaa	nuuči amimbi[N] (=amimbi)[G], gusimbi.
nuuči ənnəə	nuuči ənimbi, pundadubi, taajibi.
mapaačča ammaa	daaji amimbi.
mam ənnəə	daaji ənimbi.
ammaa	amimbi[NG].
ənnəə	ənimbi[NG].
axaa (or *akaa* used by children)	aagbi[NG], naadaktabi[NG].
əgəə, əxəə (or *əkəə* used by children)	əigəbi[NG], pundadubi[NG], taajibi[NG].
nunee	nəuwi[NG], naadaktabi[NG], pundadubi[NG], taajibi[NG].
purigəmǰee	purigəmǰibi[G].
gamasoo	gamasumbi[NG].
gusee	gusimbi.
tuwəə, tuwəkəə	tuwəmbi[NG].
irgəə	irgəmbi.
andaa	andabi.
səŋgee	səŋgibi[NG].

7.2. It is worth noting that the father frequently calls his child using the word *ammaa*, and that the mother calls her child using the word *ənnəə*. Terms of address are morphologically vocative forms of substantive-stems with no personal ending. However, some of them are vocatives of informal forms. The terms of address given above correspond to some terms of reference. Other terms of reference have no corresponding term of address; therefore, some terms of address have a wider denotation than the corresponding terms of reference.

Expressions which do not belong to kinship terminology are also used in addressing a relative as well as a non-relative: *mapaaččaa, mamaa, nөgөnee.* These are the vocative forms of *mapaačča* 'old man', *mama* 'old woman' and *nөgөni* ' baby, infant' respectively. *mapaaččaa* applies to *sagǯimǯibi, əǯibi*^{NG}, *əpimbi*^{NG}, when the addressee is an old man; *mamaa* to *pundadubi, taajibi, asibi* ^{NG}, *ačibi* ^{NG}, when the addressee is an old woman; *nөgөnee* to *nəuwi*$^{\cdot NG}$, *puttəbi*$^{\cdot NG}$, *naadaktabi*$^{\cdot NG}$, *pundadubi*$^{\cdot NG}$, *taajibi*^{NG}, when the addressee is a baby or a young child. These words differ from kinship terms in that the addressee's own present age is relevant to the usage of them.

Such phrases as a little child's name X plus *aminee* (or *əninee*) 'X's father (or mother)!' (teknonymy), *nөgөni* plus *aminee* (or *əninee*)'the baby's father (or mother) !' are used to call a relative who is the father or mother of a child. They are also used to call a non-relative. The speaker's own wife or an unmarried relative younger than the speaker is called by the personal name.

Instead of using a kinship term the husband frequently calls his wife *əəji*, 'hey, dear!' (an interjection), and vice versa.

8. We find some marked correspondences between some kinship terms and the social organization or regulations of marriage, though we must not draw the too hasty conclusion that the distinction between these kinship terms is derived from the present social structure or rules of marriage. The first two instances refer to terminological gaps in the system of the Orok kinship terms.

There is no single term for $S^{m}s^{s}Mc^{1}L^{c}A^{1+y}$ which by itself is in contrast to *naadaktani* $S^{m}s^{o}Mc^{1}L^{c}A^{1+y}$ in the same way as *taajini* $S^{f}s^{s}Mc^{1}L^{c}$ is in contrast to *pundaduni* $S^{f}s^{o}Mc^{1}L^{c}$. The presence of the sole term *naadaktani* for a male, in opposition to the pair of terms *taajini* and *pundaduni* for a female, corresponds to the behaviour of a male toward the exogamous sib different from that of a female toward it, for a male continues to be a member of the same sib after marriage, whereas a female is married into a different sib.

Concerning cousins of the opposite sex, we find terms denoting parallel cousins and cross-cousins of a type with whom mating is taboo: *naadaktani, pundaduni* or *tuwəni* for the former, and *gusini* or *gamasuni* for the latter. For the reciprocal relation of these terms see Sections 5.1.–5.3. In contrast to them, no single term is found to denote cross-cousins of another type with whom mating is preferred.

The distinction between *inani* $\mathrm{S}^{m}s^{o}\mathrm{Ma}^{1}L^{c}A^{-1}$ and *əpini* $\mathrm{S}^{m}s^{o}\mathrm{Ma}^{1}$ $(L^{l}G^{h}+L^{c}A^{o})$ or the distinction between their reciprocals *əəwəni* $\mathrm{S}^{f}s^{o}\mathrm{Ma}^{2}L^{c}A^{1}$ and *irgəni* $\mathrm{S}^{f}s^{o}\mathrm{Ma}^{2}$ $(L^{l}G^{l}+L^{c}A^{y})$ coincides with the difference between potential spouses and other affinal relatives of the opposite sex in regard to the junior levirate. Similarly the destinction between *əəwəni* $\mathrm{S}^{f}s^{o}\mathrm{Ma}^{1}L^{c}A^{y}$ and *ačini* $\mathrm{S}^{f}s^{o}\mathrm{Ma}^{1}$ $(L^{l}G^{h}+L^{c}A^{o})$ or the distinction between their reciprocals *inani* $\mathrm{S}^{m}s^{o}\mathrm{Ma}^{2}L^{c}A^{o}$ and *irgəni* $\mathrm{S}^{m}s^{o}\mathrm{Ma}^{2}$ $(L^{l}G^{l}+L^{c}A^{y})$ coincides with the difference between potential spouses and other affinal relatives of the opposite sex in regard to the junior sororate.

Addition to Section 5.3. We may suppose that, whether there is a distinction between S^{m} and S^{f} or not is connected with the difference between A^{o} (or A^{o}) and A^{y} (or A^{y}) or G^{l} (or G^{1}, G^{2}) and G^{h} (or G^{-1}, G^{-2}).

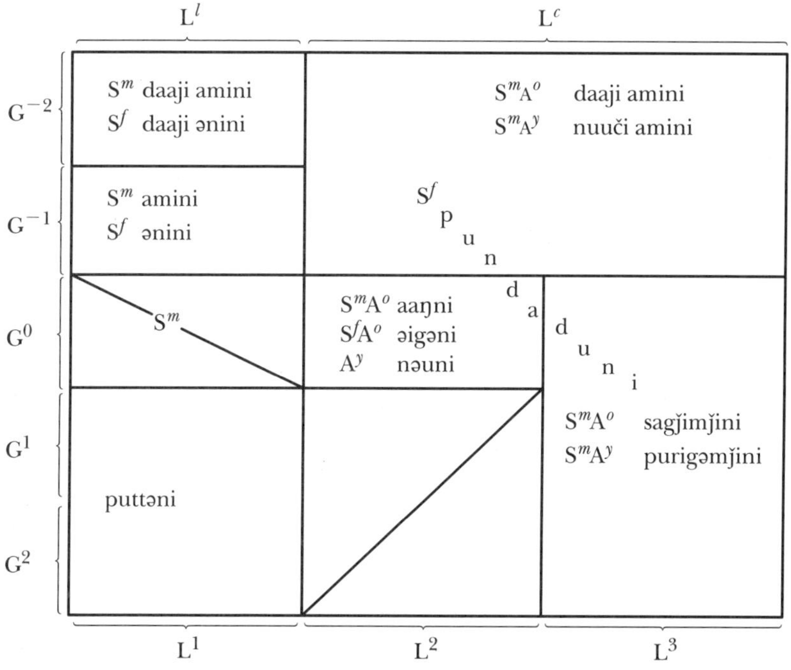
L^l
L^c
G^-2
G^-1
G^0
G^1
G^2
S^m daaji amini
S^f daaji ənini
S^m amini
S^f ənini
S^mA^o daaji amini
S^mA^y nuuči amini
S^f
pundadun
S^m
S^mA^o aaŋni
S^fA^o əigəni
A^y nəuni
duni
S^mA^o sagǰimǰini
S^mA^y purigəmǰini
puttəni
L^1
L^2
L^3

Fig. 1. $s^m Mc^1$

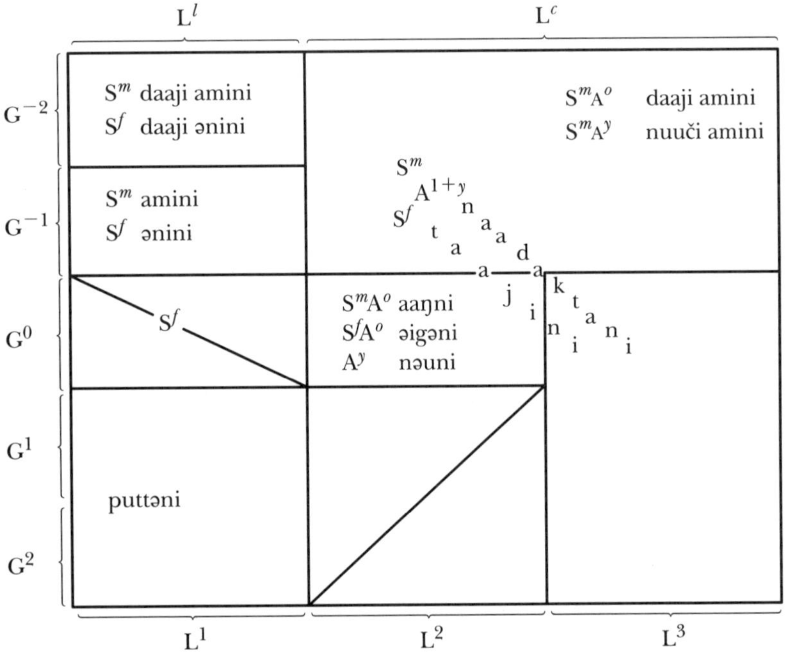

L^l
L^c
G^-2
G^-1
G^0
G^1
G^2
S^m daaji amini
S^f daaji ənini
S^m amini
S^f ənini
S^f
puttəni
S^m A^o daaji amini
S^m A^y nuuči amini
S^m
A^1+y
S^f
n
t
a
a
a
d
a
a
j
i
k
t
a
n
i
n
i
S^m A^o aaŋni
S^f A^o əigəni
A^y nəuni
L^1
L^2
L^3

Fig. 2. $s^f Mc^1$

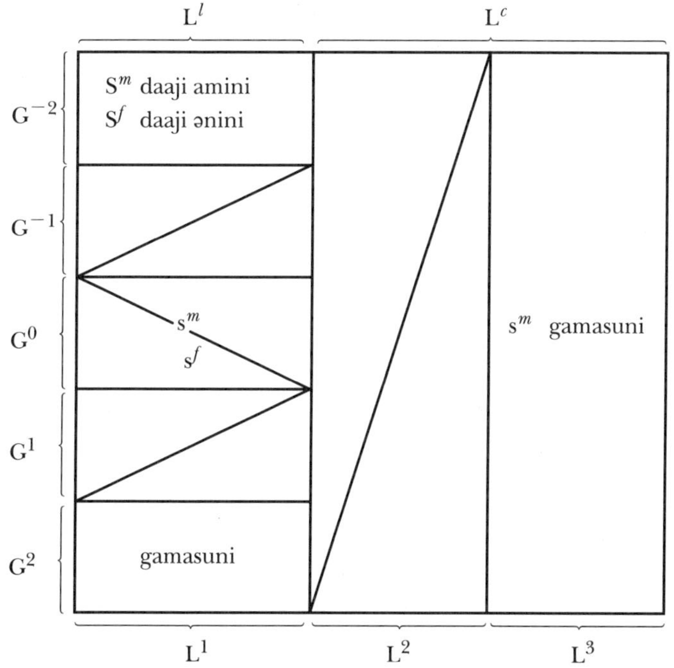
L^l
L^c
G^−2
G^−1
G^0
G^1
G^2
S^m daaji amini
S^f daaji ənini
s^m
s^f
gamasuni
s^m gamasuni
L^1
L^2
L^3

Fig. 3. Mc^2

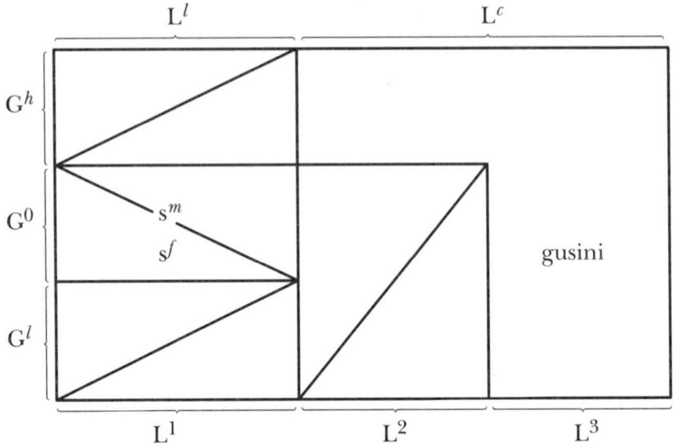

Fig. 4. $S^m Mc^3$

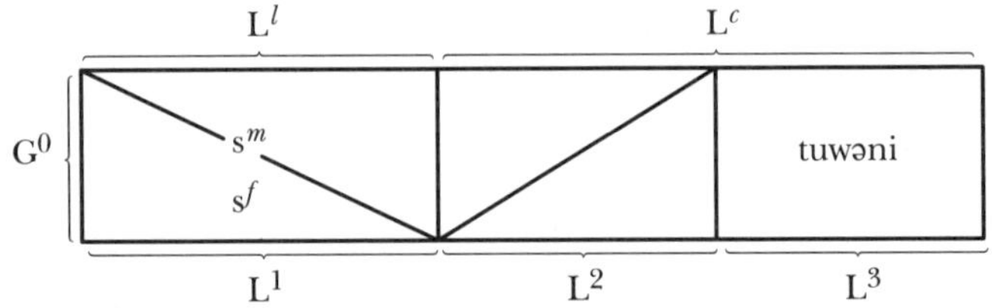

Fig. 5. Mc^4

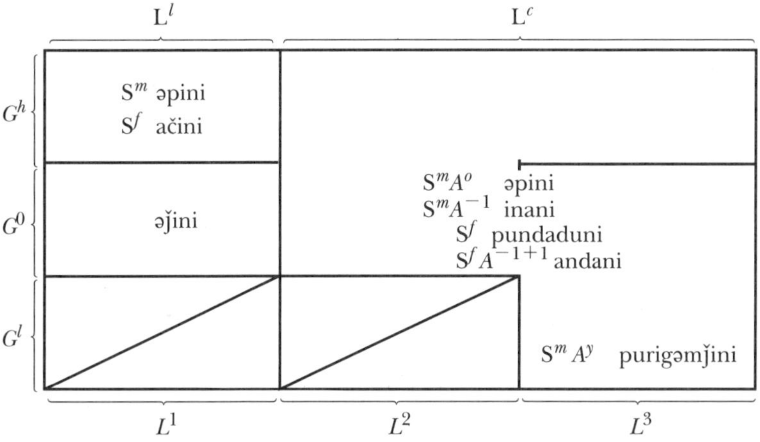

Fig. 6. $s^f(Mm+Ma^1)$

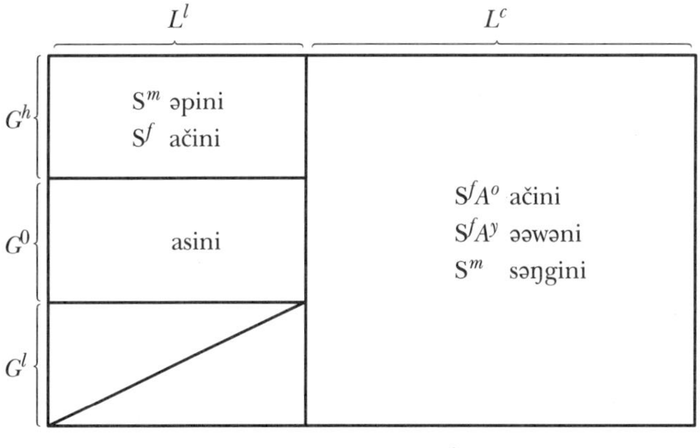

Fig. 7. $s^m(Mm+Ma^1)$

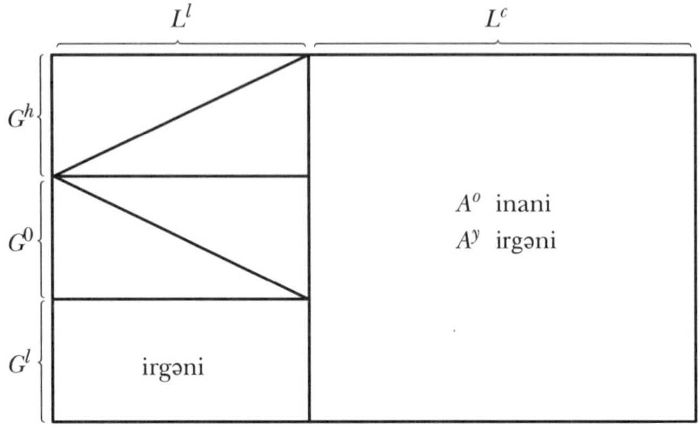

Fig. 8. $S^m s^o Ma^2$

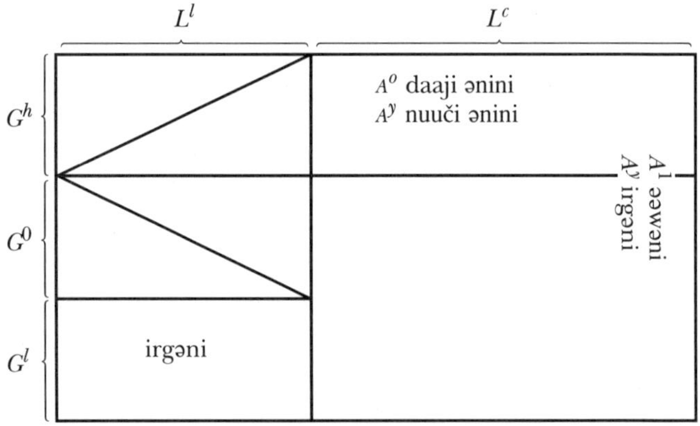

Fig. 9. $S^f s^o Ma^2$

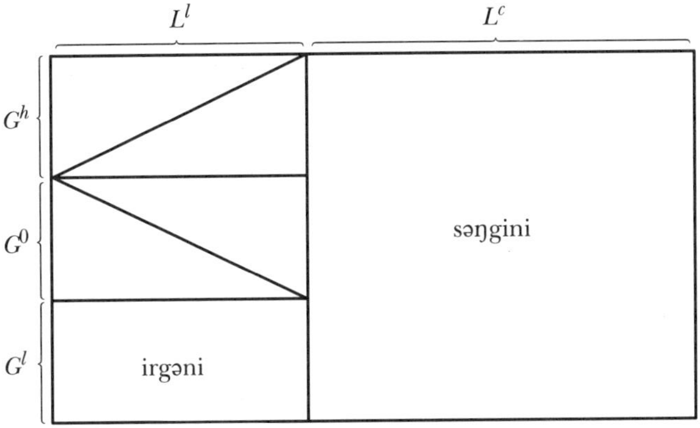

Fig. 10. $S^m s^s Ma^2$

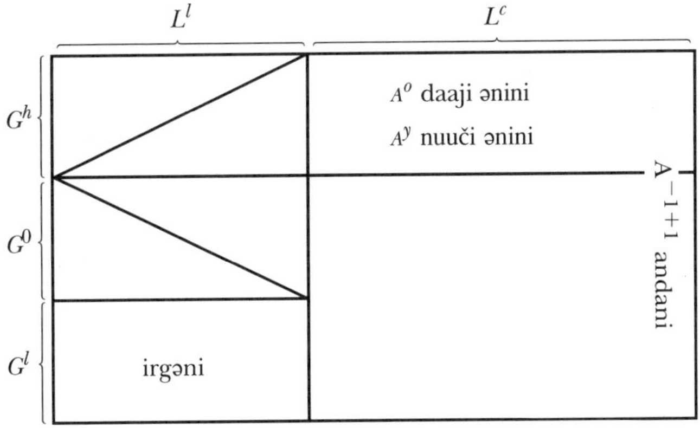

Fig. 11. $S^f s^s$ Ma^2

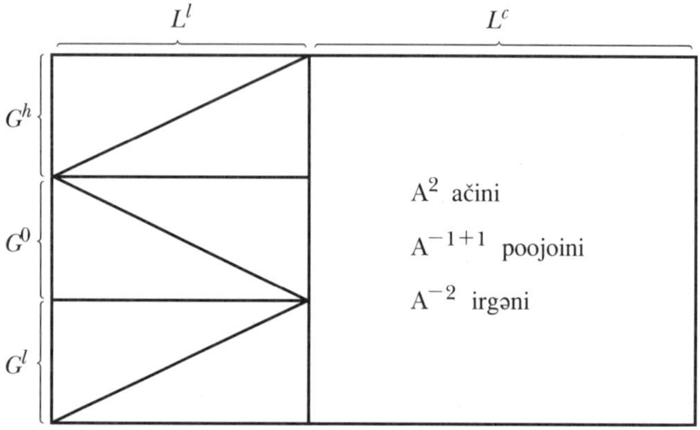

Fig. 12. S^f s^s Ma^3

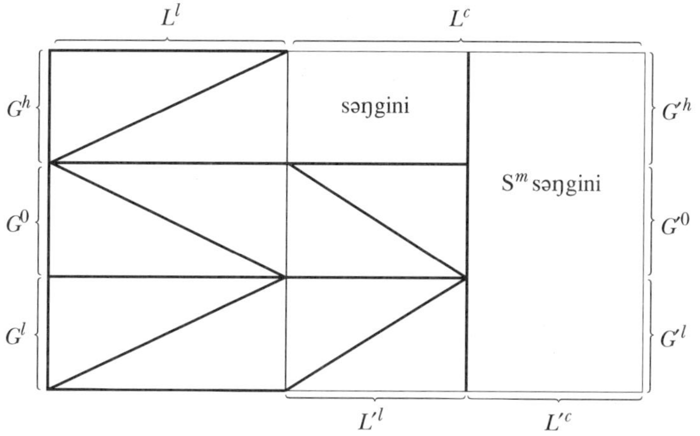

Fig. 13. $s^m Ma^4 L^c$

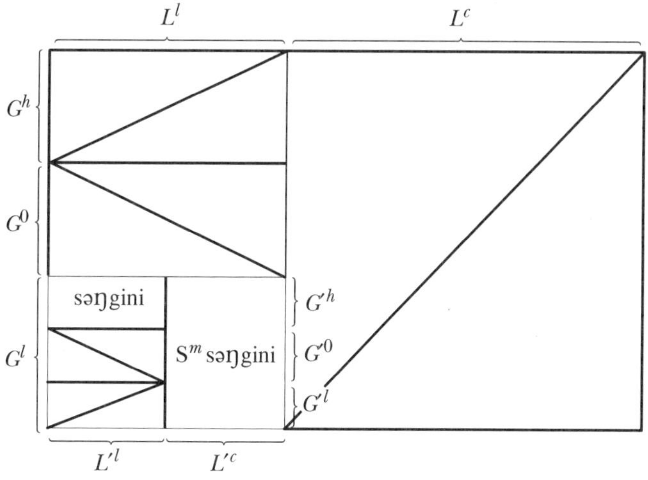

Fig. 14. $Ma^4 L^l G^l$

Notes

1) This work on the Orok kinship terminology was supported by the Grant-in-Aid for Scientific Research from the Japanese Ministry of Education. I am indebted to Takeshi Hattori and the late Eiichirô Ishida for their helpful suggestions. I have also benefited from the studies made by F. G. Lounsbury, A Semantic Analysis of the Pawnee Kinship Usage, *Language* 32 (1956), W. H. Goodenough, Componential Analysis and the Study of Meaning, *Language* 32 (1956), A. F. C. Wallace, J. Atkins, The Meaning of Kinship Terms, *American Anthropologist* 62 (1960) and E. A. Nida, *Toward a Science of Translating* (Leiden, 1964). In addition, I consulted G. P. Murdock, *Social Structure* (New York, 1949).

2) In southern Sakhalin we find the following sibs: *muigəttə, sɵɵktɵ, torisa, waaleetta, daaxinneeni, naiputunneeni.* The sib *sɵɵktɵ* is divided into two subgroups, *daaǰi sɵɵktɵ* (or *warabainneeni*) and *nuuči sɵɵktɵ,* which do not contract marriage with each other.

3) Abbreviations : Fa for father, Mo for mother, Br for brother, Si for sister, So for son, Da for daughter, Hu for husband, Wi for wife, el for elder, and yo for younger. We use combinations of these abbreviated words, such as, for instance, MoelBrSo, which is to be read as 'his (or her) mother's elder brother's son.'

o in parentheses indicates 'older' and y in parentheses 'younger'. We use these marks only in the case that two terms are provided for a position in a genealogical chart.

The denotations marked with Ǝ were obtained from Ǝəktəŋgu, those marked with NƎ from Napka and Ǝəktəŋgu, and those with no mark from Napka alone.

4) From the viewpoint of semantic change, the words *mapaačča,* 'an old man', *mama* 'an old woman', *nari* 'a man', *əəktə* 'a woman' seem to have come to denote a relative. The *-pu* in the last two of those terms is the first person plural ending designating 'our'. They mean originally 'our old man'or 'our old woman', in which case 'our'includes 'my, my husband's, his brothers' and sisters' and our children's'.

5) A division of collaterality into such degrees as defined here was already given in Hisashi Nakajima, Ainu-go no shinzoku meishô ni tsuite (=On Ainu kinship terms) (B.A. thesis at the Hokkaido University, 1968).

6) In our notation, XY indicates 'X and Y', $X+Y$ 'X or Y' and $XY+XZ$ '(X and Y) or (X and Z)', where each of X, Y and Z stands for a combination of a symbol for a semantic element and a sign (or a numeral) for a value of it. The mark $+$ is also used in the same sense as above between value signs (or numerals). X and Y, which are juxtaposed or connected with the mark $+$, are commutative, i.e., $XY=YX$, $X+Y=Y+X$. Further, we have another rule: $XY+XZ=X(Y+Z)$.

7) A space with the diagonal / is a theoretical gap. A space with the diagonal \ is one occupied by the central person or a corresponding one.

8) From the viewpoint of semantic change, it seems that in *purigəmǰini* $S^m s^o Ma^1 L^3 G^{0+l} A^y$ and *pundaduni* $S^f s^s Ma^1 L^c$ the central person was transferred from the husband to the wife. Cf. *purigəmǰini* $S^m s^s Mc^1 L^3 G^{0+l} A^y$ and *pundaduni* $S^f s^o Mc^1 L^c$.

9) For the details of the substantival inflection see Jirô Ikegami, The substantive inflection of Orok, *Gengo Kenkyu,* 30 (1956).

10) Plural forms marked with G were obtained from Gɵrgulu, other plural

forms from Napka.

11) Denotations marked with G were obtained from Gərgulu, those marked with NG from Napka and Gərgulu, and those without any mark only from Napka. The forms *akaa* and *əkəə* were obtained from Gərgulu, and the form *tuwəkəə* from Napka. As to the four terms of address *gamasoo, gusee, tuwəə* and *tuwəkəə,* Napka told me afterwards she had doubts about the actual use of these terms.

This article is the second revised and expanded version of my paper "Orok Kinship Terms" that I read at the VIIIth International Congress of Anthropological and Ethnological Sciences in Tokyo in 1968. The original paper was published in the *Proceedings, VIIIth International Congress of Anthropological and Ethnological Sciences, 1968, Tokyo and Kyooto* (Science Council of Japan, Tokyo, 1969), Vol.II, pp. 407–410.

The first revised and expanded version of my paper appeared with the same title "Orok Kinship Terminology" in *Hoppo Bunka Kenkyu, Bulletin of the Institute for the Study of North Eurasian Cultures Hokkaido University,* 4 (March, 1970), pp. 133–156.

オロッコ族の歌謡

Orok Songs

まえがき

カラフトのオロッコ族の歌謡の録音を資料として，池上二良が歌詞の韻律的性質について，谷本一之氏が歌謡の音楽上の性質について研究をおこなった。両者は密接に結びついており，専門を異にするふたりが分析の過程において互に知識と意見を交換したことは有益であった。本稿はその研究結果であり，第1章「オロッコ語歌詞の韻律論的分析」は池上が執筆し，第2章「オロッコ歌謡の音楽的分析」は谷本氏が執筆した。

オロッコ語歌詞の韻律論的分析

The Metrical Analysis of Orok Song-Texts

カラフトのオロッコ族の口頭文芸には，歌謡として，ハーガ xəəgə というジャンルがある。これは元来即興歌であろうが，以下に扱う歌詞は，それが固定化したと思われるものである。ほかに，童謡というジャンルを立てることができる。これは童謡とよんでおくが，子もり歌やこどもをあやしながらうたう歌である。(1) 以下にハーガの1篇をかかげ，(2) さらに筆者の旧稿からハーガ2篇（その1篇はふたりの歌い手のものをそれぞれ記す）と童謡を再録する。(3) ただし，歌詞は，ふしをつけてうたうとき音を長くのばしたりして本来の語形をゆがめることがあるので，本稿では通常のはなしことばでの発音によって表記し

た。(4)

ハーガ（**xəəgə**）Ⅰ.（譜例 23a）　逐語訳

gənnəŋgəkkə	gəənənnəə	ガンナンガッカ	ガーナナ
nootono	ajjaannii	四歳のおすとなかいの	いいのを
patala＋kaa	ajjaannii	むすめの	いいのが
itəxəni	maaŋijjoo	見た	のよねー
gənnəŋgəkkə	gəənənnəə	ガンナンガッカ	ガーナナ
attanǰeeduuni	ittəummii	背の方から	見れば
ananauli	maaŋijjoo	すきな	のよねー
gənnəŋgəkkə	gəənənnəə	ガンナンガッカ	ガーナナ
ataptai	ittəummii	むかって	見れば
gosipsuuli	maaŋijjoo	にくにくしい	のよねー
dərəlbəni	ittəummii	かおを	見れば
duuruuli	maaŋijjoo	すかない	のよねー
gənnəŋgəkkə	gəənənnəə	ガンナンガッカ	ガーナナ

ハーガ（**xəəgə**）Ⅱ.（譜例 23b）　逐語訳

gənnəŋgəkkə	gəənənnə*ə*	ガンナンガッカ	ガーナナ
undiləkkə	goirumbani	わたしが言いましょう	(普通のうたと)ちがったのを
umburi	biŋəijəə	言っていいでしょう	
gənnəŋgəkkə	gəənənnə*ə*	ガンナンガッカ	ガーナナ
oxoliŋa	nootonno*o*	〔語義不明〕	四歳のおすとなかいよ
motoliŋa	porokkeen*i*	まるい	いただきへ
xaralu＋kaa	lautamba	ひものついた	刀を
waannauduutawweela*kka*		わたしがまたつるしてからは	
əŋəsi＋kəə	dəlbirə*ə*	あんたがぬらすことはさせません	
gənnəŋgəkkə	gəənənnə*ə*	ガンナンガッカ	ガーナナ
sitəri＋kəə	iiŋuwəttəi	あたらしい	わか木へ
siisulləuri	mərəmbə	ひかれて行く	きもちを

əsiwi＋kəə	mərəčirəə	わたしはもちません	
gənnəŋgəkkə	gəənənnəə	ガンナンガッカ	ガーナナ
undiləkkə	goirumbani	わたしが言いましょう	(普通のうたと)ちがったのを
uppulə	biŋəijəə	言ったっていいでしょう	
gənnəŋgəkkə	gəənənnəə	ガンナンガッカ	ガーナナ

ハーガ（**xəəgə**）Ⅲa.（譜例 23c）　逐語訳

gənnəŋgəkkə	gəənənnəə	ガンナンガッカ	ガーナナ
xeedargaa	nootonnoo	ヘーダルガよ	四歳のおすとなかいよ
nootono	ajjaannii	四歳のおすとなかいの	いいのを（見た）
gənnəŋgəkkə	gəənənnəə	ガンナンガッカ	ガーナナ
dosobuwaǰi	xujəlləə	火になべをかける棒の	つのをもち
muxumaiǰi	pəəjəlləə	ほっき貝の	ひたいをもち
itaŋgiǰi	isalləə	椀の	目をして
kulaučiǰi	sinulləə	さら貝の	舌をもつ
gənnəŋgəkkə	gəənənnəə	ガンナンガッカ	ガーナナ
nəmdəukə	xumanakkoo	ほそくて	やせていて
xudəənǰi	daramalloo	縫ったものをのす板の	腰をして
siruktəǰi	xəŋgəjəlləə	蟻の	胴まわりをもつ
gənnəŋgəkkə	gəənənnəə	ガンナンガッカ	ガーナナ
silopunǰi	bəgǰilləə	焼きぐしの	足をして
sipsii＋kaa	joonopunnii	きりぎりすの	そりのかじ棒だ
gənnəŋgəkkə	gəənənnəə	ガンナンガッカ	ガーナナ

ハーガ（**xəəgə**）Ⅲb.（譜例 25）　逐語訳

gənnəŋgəkkə	gəənənnəə	ガンナンガッカ	ガーナナ
dosobuwaǰi	xujəlləə	火になべをかける棒の	つのがあり
muxumaiǰi	pəəjəlləə	ほっき貝の	ひたいがあり
itaŋgiǰi	isalloo	椀の	目があり

kulaučiǰi	sinulleө	さら貝の	舌があり
siruktəǰi	xəŋgəjəlleө	蟻の	胴まわりをもち
silopunǰi	bəgǰilleө	焼きぐしの	足がある
gənnəŋgəkkə	gəənənnəə	ガンナンガッカ	ガーナナ

童謡Ⅰ.（子もり歌，譜例４）　逐語訳

bəəbə	bəəbə	ねんねんよ	ねんねんよ
nөgөni	bəəbə	ぼうやは	ねんねんよ
bəəbə	bəəbə	ねんねんよ	ねんねんよ
gaakki	sinǰeellaa	からすが	くるよ
bəəbə	bəəbə	ねんねんよ	ねんねんよ
əǰǰee	soŋoroo	泣いてはだめよ	
bəəbə	bəəbə	ねんねんよ	ねんねんよ

bəəbə	bəəbə	ねんねんよ	ねんねんよ
nөgөni	bəəbə	ぼうやは	ねんねんよ
bəəbə	bəəbə	ねんねんよ	ねんねんよ
ŋanakatai	gəikəmi	いぬのこと	競争しながら
bəəbə	bəəbə	ねんねんよ	ねんねんよ
nəəčikətəi	gəikəmi	ことりと	競争しながら
bəəbə	bəəbə	ねんねんよ	ねんねんよ
gaakkitai	gəikəmi	からすと	競争しながら
bəəbə	bəəbə	ねんねんよ	ねんねんよ
xaiǰǰi	gələmee	なにを自分に	ほしくて
soŋŋeesiga		おまえは泣くの	
bəəbə	bəəbə	ねんねんよ	ねんねんよ

童謡Ⅱ.（あそび歌，譜例１）　逐語訳

gaakee	mammajoo	からすよ	たべなさい

nəəčikəə mammajoo	ことりよ たべなさい
ŋinakaa mammajoo	いぬのこよ たべなさい
gaakiŋun*i* oonii gaak gaak gaak	その子のからすに なって ガーク ガーク ガーク
nəəčikəŋun*i* oonii čiin čiin čii*n*	その子のことりに なって チーン チーン チーン
ŋinakaŋun*i* oonii wau wau wau	その子のいぬのこに なって ワウ ワウ ワウ
tək aa pək aa	タック アー パック アー

この資料に立って，ハーガやその他の歌詞に詩（韻文）としての形式があれば，それはどんなものかについてみてみたい。

しかしこれらの歌詞はつねに音楽的旋律をもってうたわれるものであり，音楽をはなれた詩としてあるのではない。すなわち音楽とは不可欠の関係にある。このため，音楽に属することか，詩の韻律に属することかを分析することがむずかしいことがあり，歌詞が詩として韻律的な形をそなえているかどうかをみることは必ずしも容易でない。しかし，まずハーガの歌詞についてみると，それは詩の行（line）のような韻律的単位からなっているようにみえる。gənnəŋ-gəkkə gəənənə（実際にはgəənənnə(ə) となっている。注4参照）という冒頭，中間あるいは末尾にあらわれる折返し句（refrain）はその基本的１行をなしているとみられる。そしてこの折返し句の行は７音節からなる[5]。他の各行をなすそれぞれの句の音節数については，多少の増減がある句も少くないが，かなりの数の句はやはり折返し句に等しい音節数をもっているところからみて，ハーガの１行は基本的には７音節というきまった音節数をもっているといえるようである。

一面，曲として，Ⅰ，Ⅱ，Ⅲa では各行が，概略的に音楽上の同じ旋律の１節に対応する。ただし，Ⅲｂでは連続する各２行が音楽上の同じ旋律の１節に対応する。この音楽上の一定の旋律の節に対応することが，行というものをいわばうら打ちしているといえよう。

このように，歌詞を組み立てる韻律の単位とみられる行の存在は，上述のように基本的には一定の音節数をもつ一方，１行または２行が音楽上の１節にあたるということに強いよりどころをもっている。行は音楽と不分離の関係でできている。むしろ，一定の音楽上の１節があって，それによって歌詞の行という形式が成り立っているとも言える[6]。

１篇の歌詞（詩）はこうした行からできている。ただし，１篇の歌詞の行数は一定していない。なお歌詞の中間にはさまる折返し句によって区切られる節にさらにわけることもできよう。

行についてさらにみると，７音節からなる多くの行の各音節は，それらの行が対応する同じ旋律における７つの部分に，若干の場合を除いて，通常それぞれ対応している。すなわちそれらの各行内の同じ配列順位の音節は，旋律のなかの同じ部分に対する位置をとっていることが知られる。このことは，基本的には，音節を単位とする音の連続が音楽上のリズムと対応することを示すものとみられよう。

ところで，行をなす句は，折返し句は別として，大抵２語からなっている。ただし１例では１語だけからなっている。折返し句は意味が不明であるが，その gənnəŋgəkkə と gəənənə は，音楽上の旋律の１節に対応する位置が他の行の２語に等しいので，それぞれ１語に相当するとみる。前者は４音節，後者が３音節である。

なおまた折返し句を除いて，１行をなす句が２語からなるときの語の音節数をみると，７音節からなる多くの行においては，その２語の音節数は折返し句のふたつの部分に等しく，それぞれ４音節，３音節である。また音節数に増減のある行でも，その２語は折返し句のふたつの部分の４音節，３音節に近似する音節数をもっていると言えよう。

以下に，各歌詞の行数，１行の各語の音節数を示すとともに，第１行に当る谷本氏採譜[7]によって各音節と音楽上の旋律の１節の各部分との対応関係を示す。なお通常の対応から著しくはみ出る箇所を→または←の記号で示す。

ハーガ　I.

1	^{1}gən	^{2}nəŋ	^{1}gək	^{4}kə	^{1}gəə	^{2}nən	^{3}nəə
2		^{1}noo	^{2}to	^{3}no	^{1}aj	^{2}jaan	^{3}nii

3	1 pa	1 ta	3 la	4 kaa		1 aj	2 jaan	3 nii
4	1 i	2 tə	3 xə	4 ni		1 maa	2 ŋij	3 joo
5	1 gən	2 nəŋ	3 gək	4 kə		1 gəə	2 nən	3 nəə
6	1 at	2 tan	3 ǰee	4 duu	5 ni	1 it	2 təum	3 mii
7	1 a	2 na	3 nau	4 li		1 maa	2 ŋij	3 joo
8	1 gən	2 nəŋ	3 gək	4 kə		1 gəə	2 nən	3 nəə
9	1 a	2 tap	3 tai			1 it	2 təum	3 mii
10	1 go	2 sip	3 suu	4 li		1 maa	2 ŋij	3 joo
11	1 də	2 rəl	3 bə	4 ni		1 it	2 təum	3 mii
12		1 duu	2 ruu	3 li		1 maa	2 ŋij	3 joo
13	1 gən	2 nəŋ	3 gək	4 kə		1 gəə	2 nən	3 nəə

ハーガ II.

1	1 gən	2 nəŋ	3 gək	4 kə	1 gəə	2 nən	3 nə	
2	1 un	2 di	3 lək	4 kə	1 goi	2 rum	3 ba	4 ni
3		1 um	2 bu	3 ri	1 bi	2 ŋəi	3 jɵ	
4	1 gən	2 nəŋ	3 gək	4 kə	1 gəə	2 nən	3 nə	
5	1 o	2 xo	3 li	4 ŋa	1 noo	2 ton	3 no	
6	1 mo	2 to	3 li	4 ŋa	1 po	2 rok	3 keen	
7	1 xa	2 ra	3 lu	4 kaa	1 lau	2 tam	3 ba	
8		1 waan ← 2 nau			3 duu	4 taw 5 wee 6 la		
9	1 ə	2 ŋə	3 si	4 kəə	1 dəl	2 bi	3 rə	
10	1 gən	2 nəŋ	3 gək	4 kə	1 gəə	2 nən	3 nə	
11	1 si	2 tə	3 ri	4 kəə	1 ii	2 ŋu 3 wət	4 təi	
12	1 sii →	2 sul ←	3 ləu	4 ri	1 mɵ	2 rɵm	3 bɵ	
13	1 ə	2 si	3 wi	4 kəə	1 mɵ	2 rɵ 3 či	4 rə	
14	1 gən	2 nəŋ	3 gək	4 kə	1 gəə	2 nən	3 nə	
15	1 un	2 di	3 lək	4 kə	1 goi	2 rum	3 ba	4 ni

16		^{1}up	^{2}pu	^{3}lə	^{1}bi	^{2}ŋəi	^{3}jə
17	^{1}gən	^{2}nəŋ	^{3}gək	^{4}kə	^{1}gəə	^{2}nən	^{3}nə

ハーガ　IIIa.

1	^{1}gən	^{2}nəŋ	^{3}gək	^{4}kə	^{1}gəə	^{2}nən	^{3}nəə
2		^{1}xee	^{2}dar	^{3}gaa	^{1}noo	^{2}ton	^{3}noo
3		^{1}noo	^{2}to	^{3}no	^{1}aj	^{2}jaan	^{3}nii
4	^{1}gən	^{2}nəŋ	^{3}gək	^{4}kə	^{1}gəə	^{2}nən	^{3}nəə
5	^{1}do	^{2}so ^{3}bu ^{4}wa		^{5}ǰi	^{1}xu	^{2}jəl	^{3}lɵɵ
6	^{1}mu	^{2}xu	^{3}mai	^{4}ǰi	^{1}pəə	^{2}jəl	^{3}lɵɵ
7	^{1}i	^{2}taŋ	^{3}gi	^{4}ǰi	^{1}i	^{2}sal	^{3}loo
8	^{1}ku	^{2}lau	^{3}či	^{4}ǰi	^{1}si	^{2}nul	^{3}lɵɵ
9	^{1}gən	^{2}nəŋ	^{3}gək	^{4}kə	^{1}gəə	^{2}nən	^{3}nəə
10		^{1}nəm	^{2}dəu	^{3}kə	^{1}xu	^{2}ma ^{3}nak	^{4}koo
11	^{1}xu	^{2}dəən		^{3}ǰi	^{1}da	^{2}ra ^{3}mal	^{4}loo
12	^{1}si	^{2}ruk	^{3}tə	^{4}ǰi	^{1}xəŋ	^{2}gə ^{3}jəl	^{4}lɵɵ
13	^{1}gən	^{2}nəŋ	^{3}gək	^{4}kə	^{1}gəə	^{2}nən	^{3}nəə
14	^{1}si	^{2}lo	^{3}pun	^{4}ǰi	^{1}bəg→	^{2}ǰil	^{3}lɵɵ
15	^{1}sip	^{2}sii		^{3}kaa	^{1}joo	^{2}no ^{3}pun	^{4}ni
16	^{1}gən	^{2}nəŋ	^{3}gək	^{4}kə	^{1}gəə	^{2}nən	^{3}nəə

行はすでにふれたように，大抵２語からなる。その２語はそれぞれ音楽上の旋律のある点をさかいとして旋律のはじめの部分とあとの部分に対応する。旋律のそのさかいめに相当するところに韻律的にもさかいめがある，それによって行はふたつの部分にわかれるとみたい。その各部分をかりに小節とよんでおく。小節の音節数は，基本的に，はじめの小節が４音節，あとの小節が３音節であるとみて，基本的行にくらべ音節数に増減のある行についても小節にわけてみて行くと，説明上有利であると言えよう。

小節の音節数が基本的音節数より少く，たりない場合[8]，小節のかしらにおいて，旋律との最初の対応部分をなくすか（楽譜参照。ただし谷本氏の記述によれば，実際にはこの音節数のたりない分を小節の全体にのばして補っている(9)），またはかしら以外の位置でひとつの音節をのばして旋律の上記部分ふたつに対応させている。さらにあるいはkaa（またはkəə）という意味のない単なる音節を語末に加えて音節数を補う。上掲の歌詞では第1小節における例しか見出されないが，そこでは，このkaa（またはkəə）が，短母音開音節3つからなる単語の末尾にあらわれるか，または閉音節と長母音音節との2音節からなる単語の末尾にあらわれる。第1小節において，長母音（または二重母音）音節または閉音節をふくむ3音節からなる単語にはkaa（またはkəə）がつかず，上記のようにのばして発音されている。

なおひとつの音節をのばす場合の発音は，音節主音の短母音あるいは長母音をのばすか，本来は尻さがりである二重母音の副音や閉音節末の有声継続音（たとえば鼻音mや側面音l）を長く発音している(10)。

小節の音節数が，小節の基本的音節数より多くて，いわば字あまりと言える場合は，連続するふたつの音節をはやく発音して旋律の上記各部分ひとつに対応させているとみられよう。語末では，長母音が短く発音されることもある。

以上のように音をゆっくりのばしたり，あるいははやく発音して長さをあわせているというのは，小節を単位としてこのなかで行われているとみる

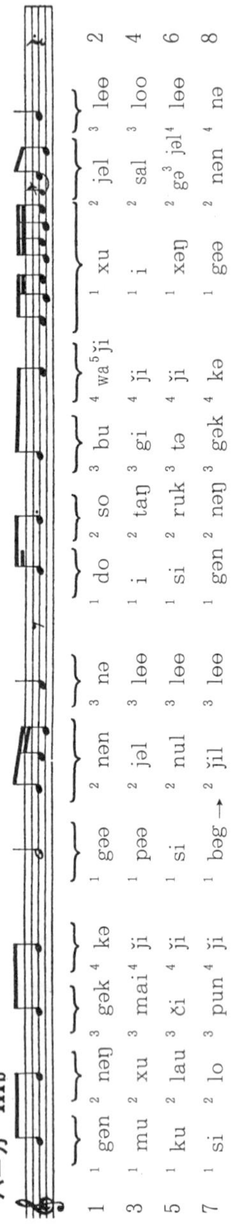

ことができる。1語がふたつの小節にわたる1例においても，小節のさかいにまたがってひとつの音節がのばされてはいない。これらのことは，その箇所に小節とよんだものを区切る韻律的さかいがあるとみることをつよめることになろう。

またⅢa の10，11行は，音節数が基本的行と同様，7音節であるが，第1小節が3音節，第2小節が4音節であり，基本的第1，2小節がそれぞれ4音節，3音節であるのと異なる。その2行では，基本的行と異なり，第1小節では基本的第1小節の4音節にたりない分を音節をのばして補い，第2小節でははやく発音して基本的第2小節の3音節分にあてているといいうる。基本的行と音節数が同じ行でも，うたうときの発音がこのように異なるのは，行における小節という単位の存在を示すものであろう。

なおまた，上述のように，3音節に kaa という1音節を補って4音節としている点は，はじめの小節を基本的には4音節とする見方を補強すると言えよう。

ふたつの小節からなるとみた行がさらにある韻律的構造をもっているかどうかが残る問題であるが，ハーガの歌い手の少くともひとりは長さの長短のリズムを上述の音楽的1節の各部分にのせてうたっているとみられることは重要である。すなわちハーガ Ⅰ，Ⅱ，Ⅲa の歌い手ははじめの小節を短長短長，あとの小節を長長短というリズムでうたっているとみられる。このことは，旧稿でテキストの上にも多少とも反映するように表記しておいた[(11)]。さらに，このことは谷本氏によって音楽の上からハーガの旋律に関して指摘されている[(12)]。なお7音節からなる基本的行では各音節に長短のいずれかをあてている。この点から，さきに1行の基本的音節数を7としたことは妥当であると言えよう。しかしその長短のリズムは音楽上のことであって，歌詞の韻律的性質に属することではないようである。もし韻律的性質に属するならば，短にあたる部分にはたとえば短母音開音節，長にあたる部分には長母音音節，二重母音音節あるいはさらに閉音節が対応するとか，またはそのような傾向があると認められるべきであろうが，そのような言語の音韻とのなんらかの一定の対応も，またそのような傾向もあるとは言えないようである。したがって，長短による韻律があるとは言えなかろう。むしろ，歌詞をそのような音楽上の長短のリズムでうたっているのである。すなわち音楽上の1節の7つの長短に歌詞の音をわりふってうたうのである。7音節からなる基本的な行ではそれぞれに1音節をあて，基本的にはこのように音節単位にあてると考えられるが，その他の行では発音を時間的にのばしたり，ちぢめたりしてあてるのである。歌詞は音楽からその長短リズムが与えられ，音楽上の長短リズムがいわば韻律の代役を果している。こうした点には，歌詞が音楽と一体となって融合していることがうかがえる。そしてここにオロッコ族の歌詞の特質があると言えよう[(13)]。

つぎに，子もり歌についても，韻律的に行というものが認められるようであり，折返し句の bəəbə　bəəbə は基本的な行をなしているとみられる。この折返し句の行は4音節を含むが，ただし他の行はほとんど音節数がこれより多く，7音節と音節数がかなり多い例もある。したがって行の基本的音節数をいうことは簡単でない。しかし折返し句の行が非常に頻繁にあらわれる（行の総数の半分またはそれを上廻る）点から，基本的音節数を4音節とみておく。4音節を基本的音節数とすると，音節数がそれより多い他の行では音節をはやく発音して4音節分の長さにあてているとみられる。

一方，これらの行は，ハーガにおけると同様，ある同じ旋律の1節に相当する。音節数が一定しているということより，むしろこのことが，詩として子もり歌における行の存在をうらづけているように思われる。

子もり歌1篇の行の総数は，不定のようである。このことは子もり歌がうたわれる目的，情況とも関係していよう。上掲の子もり歌は2篇の連続とみられよう。

なお，子もり歌の行は，1行1語である1例を除いて2語からなる句でできている。子もり歌の折返し句においてもふたつの bəəbə が各々1語にあたると言えよう[(14)]。2語の間に韻律的なさかいをみとめ，まえとあとのふたつの小節にわけることもできるかもしれない。

以下に，子もり歌の行数，1行の各語の音節数を示すとともに，第1行に当る谷本氏採譜[(15)]によって各音節と音楽上の旋律の1節の各部分との対応関係を示す。

童　謡　I.（子もり歌）

1	^{1} bəə	^{2} bə	^{1} bəə	^{1} bə
2	^{1} nɵ ^{2} gɵ	^{3} ni	^{1} bəə	^{2} bə
3	^{1} bəə	^{2} bə	^{1} bəə	^{2} bə
4	^{1} gaak	^{2} ki	^{1} sin	^{2} ǰəl ^{3} laa
5	^{1} bəə	^{2} bə	^{1} bəə	^{1} bə
6	^{1} əǰ	^{2} ǰee	^{1} so ^{2} ŋo	^{3} roo
7	^{1} bəə	^{2} bə	^{1} bəə	^{2} bə

1	^{1} bəə	^{2} bə	^{1} bəə	^{2} bə
2	^{1} nɵ ^{2} gɵ	^{3} ni	^{1} bəə	^{2} bə
3	^{1} bəə	^{2} bə	^{1} bəə	^{2} bə
4	^{1} ŋa ^{2} na	^{3} ka ^{1} tai	^{1} gəi	^{2} kə ^{3} mi
5	^{1} bəə	^{2} bə	^{1} bəə	^{2} bə
6	^{1} nəə ^{2} či	^{3} kə ^{4} təi	^{1} gəi	^{2} kə ^{3} mi
7	^{1} bəə	^{2} bə	^{1} bəə	^{2} bə
8	^{1} gaak	^{2} ki ^{3} tai	^{1} gəi	^{2} kə ^{3} mi
9	^{1} bəə	^{2} bə	^{1} bəə	^{2} bə
10	^{1} xaiǰ	^{2} ǰi	^{1} gə ^{2} lə	^{3} mee
11	^{1} soŋ	^{2} ŋee	^{3} si	^{4} ga
12	^{1} bəə	^{2} bə	^{1} bəə	^{2} bə

子もり歌の各行は短長短長のリズムでうたわれているようである。このことは谷本氏によって音楽上から指摘されている[16]。なお4音節からなる基本的行には各音節に長短のいずれかをあてている。この点から1行の基本的な音節数を4とみることは妥当であろう。

こどもをあやしてうたうもう1篇の童謡には，同じ表現がくり返しあらわれるが，上にみて来たような折返し句はみられない。しかしこの歌詞にも詩の行がみとめられる。なおこの歌詞ははじめの３行となかの３行とあとの残りの３部分にわけられ，なかの３行は同じひとつの旋律の１節の対応し，はじめの３行もとなえごと風の同じ旋律の１節に対応している。あとの残りの部分は幼児がはじめて立って歩くさまを表現するものであるというから[17]，象徴音からなっているとみられるが，全体が１行とみなされるべきではないだろうか。

ハーガと童謡を通して歌詞は，同じ語尾（または接尾辞）が行の末尾にくり返しあらわれる場合を除いて，一般には脚韻（end rhyme）をもっていない。しかしハーガには頭韻（alliteration）がみとめられることがある。例，Ⅱの２，３行の undiləkkə と umburi，11，12行の sitəri＋kəə と siisulləuri，Ⅰの６，７行の attanǰeeduuni と ananauli，11，12行の dərəlbəni と duuruuli の各頭音。

修辞的には，同型の表現がくり返されることがある。すなわちハーガⅠの６，７行と９，10行と11，12行，Ⅲa の５，６，７，８，11，12，14行，Ⅲbの２，３，４，５，６，７行，童謡のⅠの第２部分の４，６，８行，Ⅱの１，２，３行，４，５，６行。

またハーガには比喩（隠喩）がしばしばみられる。たとえば，一般にハーガでは nootono（４歳のおすとなかい）は若い男の意につかう。Ⅱの11行では sitəri iiŋuwə（新しい若木）は若い男の意。Ⅲの多くの行にも比喩の例がみられる。

上掲のハーガは，女がうたったものであり，その歌詞は女が男を揶揄する意味をふくんでいる。しかしハーガには男がうたったものもあるようである[18]。

音韻的には，オロッコ語の音韻構造において通常みられない di のような結合がハーガⅡの undiləkkə にあらわれている。

また語彙的には，ハーガには日常語にない語（例，Ⅱの undiləkkə goirumbani）や古語とみられるもの（Ⅱの oxoliŋa（意味不明））などがふくまれている。童謡には幼児語が用いられている。例，nəəčikə（小鳥）など。

注

(1) 池上二良「オロッコ族の口頭文芸」(ユーラシア文化研究1 1965) 138ページ参照。

(2) 佐藤チヨさんから昭和34年に採録した。若い女が若い男のかお，すがたをからかってうたったものである。3行めの「が」の訳は佐藤さんによる。

(3) 池上二良「オロッコ族の民話とうた数例」(民族学研究27巻4号 1963) 5，6，31-32 ページと「オロッコ族の口頭文芸」(上掲) 3，4，5，148-151ページ。なお歌詞の意味については旧稿のそのページの脚注も参照されたい。ハーガⅠ，Ⅱ，Ⅲa，童謡Ⅰは佐藤チヨさんがうたうのを，ハーガⅢb，童謡Ⅱは中川（高橋）カヨさんがうたうのを録音，採取したものである。

(4) ただしハーガ（特にⅠ，Ⅲ）で行の最後の子音や母音がそれぞれ重複してあらわれるのは，形態論的にそのような形をなしているのか，歌の調子によるものかまだあきらかでないが，そのまま表記した。発音されなかった語末の音もイタリック体で補っておく。なおうたうとき語末に加えられる意味のない kaa（または kəə）の音節は＋の記号を前に入れて表記しておく。

(5) オロッコ語の音韻構造では，一つの音節は (C)V(V)(C) という構造をもつ。Vは母音音素，Cは子音音素を表し，(　) はこの部分がないことがあることを示す。

(6) おなじようなことがギリヤーク語の歌について R. アウステルリッツ氏によって述べられている。R. Austerlitz, Two Gilyak song-texts, *To Honor Roman Jakobson, Essays on the Occasion of His Seventieth Birthday*, Vol. 1 (The Hague-Paris, 1967), p. 104参照。

(7) 谷本一之氏執筆の第2章の楽譜参照。

(8) 正確に言えば，第1小節についてである。第2小節では3音節以下の例がないので，その場合については不明である。

(9) 谷本氏執筆の第2章の楽譜と17ページ参照。

(10) 尻さがり二重母音の副音や音節末の流音が，音節主音と同様に長く発音されることがあるのは，日本語の俳句，和歌の字数にみられるような韻律的単位が生じうるきざしを示していると言えないだろうか。

(11) 旧稿では，語中で普通の発音よりながくのばされている部分を［　］に入れた。

なおⅡの11行の sitəərikəə は sitə[ə]rikəə と記すべきであった。Ⅲa の10行の xu[u]manaakkoo も xu[u]mana[a]kkoo とすべきではないかと思う。行末では，注4に記したように，形態論的にある形式なのか，うたうときゆがめられた形なのか，なおあきらかでない点もあり，[　] を一般につけなかった。

(12) 谷本氏執筆の第2章17ページ参照。なおもうひとりの歌い手は，Ⅲbを短長短短，長短短とうたっているようにも筆者には思われるが，谷本氏によれば音楽的にはそのように認められない。

(13) ただしあるいはこうしたことが発達段階としては長短の韻律をもつ詩の形式の発生の前段階なのであろうか。

(14) bəəbə は əmuwə（ひるま用のゆりかご）の幼児語でもある。

(15) 谷本氏執筆の第2章の楽譜参照。

(16) 谷本氏執筆の第2章17ページ参照。

(17) 佐藤チヨさんによる。

(18) 北川五郎さんによる。

Summary

I shall deal with the problem of what kind of metrical structure is to be found in Orok song-texts, if any. For the corpus by two singers, Napka (A) and Kayo (B), see p. 197－p. 200.

These Orok texts are always accompanied by musical melody. For this reason, it is not easy to distinguish metrical elements from musical elements to see whether Orok songs have any metrical structure. But we may assume that the improvisation, a kind of Orok oral literature, (which is called *xəəgə*) is composed of lines forming a poem. In the improvisation appears a refrain, *gənnəŋgəkkə gəənənə*. This may be regarded as the basic line. The refrain line, and many other lines, contains seven syllables. That is to say, the basic line seems to have seven syllables.

From the musical viewpoint, one line in songs by Singer A, or two successive lines in the song by Singer B, correspond to an almost fixed melodical period. Cf. p. 201–p. 204. The existence of lines is supported by the correspondence with the melodical period. Each syllable in a seven-syllable line ordinarily corresponds to the same part of the melodic period as does the corresponding syllable in the other seven-syllable lines in the same text. This fact seems to mean that the succession of syllables corresponds to musical rhythm.

If we assume that a line is divided into two sections, and that the first section normally contains four syllables and the second section three syllables, it seems easy to explain not only the basic line but other lines. When a section of a line contains less than the normal number of syllables, we find the following cases. In the case of the first section of a line being composed of three syllables including a closed syllable or a non-short vowel, no syllable corresponds to the first part of the melodical period (or the three syllables extend over the whole of the first four parts of the melodical period [see the second chapter by Kazuyuki Tanimoto, p. 17]), or one of the non-initial syllables corresponds to two of the above-mentioned parts of the melodical period. In the case of the first section of a line being composed either of only two syllables, or of three open syllables each with a short vowel, a meaningless syllable *-kaa* (or *-kəə*) is added as the final syllable. When a section of a line contains more than the normal number of syllables, two of these syllables are pronounced quickly, corresponding to one part of the melodical period.

The next problem is whether each section of a line has metrical structure. Singer A sings each line with a kind of rhythm consisting of short (⏑) and long (–) time divisions, such as ⏑–⏑ | ––⏑. Cf the second chapter by K. Tanimoto, p. 17. In the basic seven-syllable line, each syllable is sung with short or long duration. This kind of rhythm belongs to music and not to metrics, because it is not the case that short and long time divisions in this kind of rhythm normally correspond to linguistically different durations of sound, such as, for instance, of short and long vowels. We can say that musical rhythm operates as a substitute for metrical rhythm. This substitution is characteristic of Orok improvisations.

Two nursery songs also seem to consist of lines.

The lullaby (nursery song I) has the refrain *bəəbə bəəbə* which is a line with four syllables. The refrain line may be regarded as the basic line in the lullaby. This basic line and all the other lines correspond to about the same musical period. Cf. p. 207. The lullaby is also sung with a kind of musical rhythm composed of short (◡) and long (—) time divisions, such as ◡—◡—. Cf. the second chapter by K. Tanimoto, p. 17. In the basic line each syllable is sung with short or long duration.

In another nursery song (Ⅱ), the first three lines correspond to one melodical period, the second three lines to another, different, melodical period. The last line seems to contain onomatopoeic expressions.

In the Orok song-texts we do not find end rhyme, whereas alliteration is found in some lines.

初出　北方文化研究８号［発行年月は表紙によると昭和49年（1974年），奥付によると昭和50年（1975年）３月］１－12ページ。谷本一之氏執筆の第２章（13－27ページ）がこのあとにつづけて掲載されている。

追記　次章の谷本一之氏執筆「オロッコ歌謡の音楽的分析」（Kazuyuki Tanimoto, The Musical Analysis of Orok Songs）は、本書には掲載せず割愛することを御了承願う。In this book the second chapter by K. Tanimoto is omitted. A page number of three figures in the summary signifies a page number of this book.

カラフトのウイルタ族の英雄物語とその伝来

The Heroic Stories of the Sakhalin Uiltas and the Uiltas' Own Introduction to Them

広義のツングース族の一派であるカラフトのウイルタ族（オロッコ族）の口頭文芸のジャンルの一つに，ニグマー（niŋmaa）というものがある。これは，一種の語り物で，内容の上からひとことで言えば，英雄物語である。

ある民族の口頭文芸の分類は，かれら自身が名づける分類名称があれば，まずそれにもとづいてなされるべきであろう。ツングース諸族の口頭文芸の分類についても，同じことが言えよう。ウイルタ族の口頭文芸のうち，テールグ（təəluŋu）というのは，昔話，伝説の類で，かれら自身はこれを実話と考えている。またサフリ（saxuri）というのは，おとぎ話の類で，ウイルタ人はこれをつくり話，フィクションと考えている。これに対してハーガ（xəəgə）は即興歌で，ある旋律をもってうたわれ，この点で上の二つと異なる。ウイルタの歌謡の旋律・韻律については池上・谷本（1974）を参照されたい。このほかガヤウ（gajau），すなわち，なぞなぞがあり，これも発音があるリズムをもつとみることができよう。一方，ニグマーは，語りの部分以外はふしをつけてうたわれるが，上記の歌と異なり，叙事的である。

ニグマーでは，語りの部分とうたう部分が交互に連続し，語りの部分はウイルタ語で語られるが，うたう部分は，おなじツングース語に属するキーリン語（エウェンキー語）でうたわれる。後者の部分では，物語の登場人物が第一人称で述べ，各登場人物に特有の折返し句（refrain）がこの部分の前後につく。ニグマーの聞き手は，きれめきれめにgəəという合いの手を入れる（そうすることをdari-［動詞語幹］（合いづちを打つ）ということばで表す）。内容的にみると，筆者がきくことのできたニグマーの篇では，主人公が親子２代（dəə dala）にわたり，これは二段物とよべようが，さらに代を重ねるものもあるという。ニグマーは，一篇の長さもかなり長く，見方によってはウイルタ口頭文芸中最たるものと言えよう。

筆者は，ウイルタ族出身で北海道に住んでおられる佐藤チヨ（Napka）さんの語るのをきくことができた。佐藤さんはウイルタの口頭文芸のすぐれた保持者で，上述のテールグやサフリなどを何篇もおぼえていてきかせてもらったが，さらにニグマーも演ずることができ，シーグーニ（Siiŋuuni）を主人公とするものとアグジナーシ・オモシナイ（Agǰinaasi Θməsinəi）を主人公とするものの二篇をきくことができた。佐藤さんの口述した口頭文芸の諸篇は，ほかの口述者のものとともに，池上［採録・訳注］(1984）におさめられている。ニグマーは昭和32年に録音した「シーグーニ物語」のはじめの部分がのっている。

ウイルタの人々のなかには，ニグマーを演ずる人は何人もいて，その語り方には上手へたがあり，そのうたう声（əəwurə）にはよいわるいがあったという。Paasa は非常に上手，Suudəri Miitəri も上手，Wassuuka も直接きいたことはなかったが上手といわれていたという。Otopči もニグマーを語ったがあまり上手ではなかったという。女の Nəəksinnə も，声がよく，上手で，女だけにきかせたという。なお，女がニグマーを語ると不幸になるともいうようである。

佐藤さんは，ニグマーの箇所箇所が折りにふれてよく頭に浮ぶようであり，ウイルタとしてのかの女にとっては，ニグマーが文芸的な素養となっていると言えるように思われる。佐藤さんは，幼くしてすでに才女であったようで，十代前半のころにニグマーに強く魅せられ，冬の間，近所に住む Loǰiŋgeenu という老人のところに夜通っては，ニグマーを語ってもらい，それをおぼえたという。家人の寝しずまったかれの円錐形小屋（aundau）の暗いなかで，たき火のあかりは，そのはたで演ずるおじいさんのニグマーをひとことも聞きもらさじと聞き入っている幼い少女の顔を映し出していたことであろう。かの女は，おじいさんに気をくばって，わが家から祖母の刻みたばこをこっそりもち出してはあげたという。うちでは，おばあさんのたばこがなくなるのが不思議でならなかったようであるが，あとでわかって家族の笑いの種となったという。

筆者が佐藤さんからニグマーをきかせてもらって最初に書きとったのは昭和26年ごろであったと思う。以来すべてウイルタ語で話してもらって書きとったり，またニグマーの本来の語り方によってウイルタ語とエウェンキー語で書きとることもおこなったが，いずれもはじめの部分だけでおわった。その後，磁気録音器が市販されて利用できるようになり，わたくしもウイルタ語調査に使うようになった。これまで佐藤さんが語るのを直接書きとったテールグ，サフリなどを改めてまた語ってもらって録音し，その録音から新しくテキストを書きとった。ニグマーも録音をはじめた。昭和32年には，亡くなった中川カヨさんに聞き手になって合いの手を入れてもらい，２回おこなったが，２回とも30分か１時間ほどであいにく録音器が故障し，残念ながら中止した。「シーグーニ物語」と「アグジナーシ・オモシナイ物語」の全曲を録音できたのは，ずっとのちになって昭和52年の文部省科学研究費補助金を受けた調査においてであった。この録音の際には，録音器操作などに津曲敏郎君も協力してくれた。二篇の物語のうち，前者の方が長く，そのときの録音では約４時間40分，後者は３時間10分である。

元来，ウイルタのニグマーは，キーリン人すなわちエウェンキー人から伝わったものであることは想像にかたくない。上に述べたように，その語りの部分はウイルタ語であるが，うたいの部分はエウェンキー語である。ウイルタ人にとっては，ニグマーは，いわば上方方言による義太夫節を坂東方言を話す人が習って語るようなものと言えよう。

エウェンキー人の間には英雄物語が広く伝承されている。英雄物語をふくめ，エウェンキー人の口頭文芸については，豊富な資料を提供したワシレーヴィチがくわしい解説を与えている（Василевич 1936, 1966, Романова, Мыреева, 1971)。ヴォスコボイニコフ（Воскобойников, 1960）の著書も有益である。ワシレーヴィチによれば，スタノヴォイ地方のアルダン川，ウチュル川のエウェンキー人の英雄物語とウチュル川上流，アムール川，サハリン（カラフト）のエウェンキー人のものとは，語り方が異なり，また前者はヤクート語とその英雄叙事詩オロンホの強い影響をうけた点で後者と異なるという（Романова,

Мыреева, 1971, стр. 4. なお99ページ以下の英雄物語は精細に採録している)。

それでは，ウイルタのニグマーにくらべて，エウェンキー人の英雄物語はどんなものであろうか，それを自分の耳できいてみたいものと筆者はかねがね思っていたが，1979年第14回太平洋学術会議が開催されたハバーロフスクに行ったおりに，思いがけなくもそれをきく機会にめぐまれたのである。学会開催中のある晩，アムール川流域少数民族の音楽舞踊会が催され，会場でわたくしの近くの席についたものしずかな老婦人を，ウラジオストーク遠東科学センターでギリヤク語を研究するギリヤク婦人オタイナ（Галина Александровна Отаина）さんから紹介された。その老婦人は，アムール川河口の近いマゴの学校でのオタイナさんの恩師のアファナーシエヴァ（Антонина Васильевна Афанасьева）さんという方で，サハリンのエウェンキー人とのことであった。数日したある晩，アファナーシエヴァさんが食事に招いて下さり，オタイナさんに案内され，市の中央から遠くない団地のアパートのお宅を訪問した。かの女は，いつもは，結婚した娘さんがいる北サハリンのオハで暮すが，夏の間だけはハバーロフスクですごされるよしだった。エウェンキー人のなぞなぞを聞かせてもらったあと，もしやと思いながらエウェンキーの英雄物語もできるかどうかおたずねすると，できるとのこと，早速ウムスニンジャ（Умуснинде）を主人公とする一篇のはじめの部分を演じて下さり，手帖にも書いてくれた。かの女の演ずるものは，勿論すべてエウェンキー語であるが，ウイルタのニグマーと同様にやはり語りの部分とうたう部分からなり，ウイルタのニグマーのうたい方はまさにこの英雄物語のものである。さらに，うたう部分できかれるウムスニンジャの折返し句 niki niki mō は，ウイルタの「シーグーニ物語」に登場するシーグーニの弟のギーワーニ（ŋiiwəəni）の折返し句としてあらわれるものと同じと言えよう。また Умуснинде の人名は，ウイルタの「アグジナーシ・オモシナイ物語」の主人公のその名前 Θməsinəi と語幹が本来同じものではないだろうか。

ウイルタのニグマーは，このエウェンキー人の英雄物語をとり入れ，そのうたう部分は，エウェンキー語をそのままとし，語りの部分をウイルタ語にかえたものであることは論をまたないだろう。しかし内容はもとのままか，あるいは改変，新増の箇所があるかは今後調べてみなければならない。

なお，ワシレーヴィチのエウェンキー・フォークロア資料集（Василевич, 1936, стр. 115-117）にも Ụmụsŋinḍạ の物語の原文とロシヤ語訳がのっている。しかし，これをよんだだけでは，エウェンキー人の英雄物語がどんな風に演ぜられるか，またウイルタのニグマーとくらべてどうかを想像することはむずかしかった。同氏は大体，各英雄物語の概略の原文を提示しているようである。帰国して見直して驚いたことだが，このテキストの提供者は Sahalin の A. Afanasjewa とある。ハバーロフスクのアファナーシエヴァさんからは，ワシレーヴィチのことは聞かなかったが，同一人であったのだろうか。

アファナーシエヴァさんは，実はブレーヤ川岸（上ブレーヤ区 Чекунда 町）で1914年に生れ，翌1915年にサハリン北部（ルイブノフスク区）に移ったのだという。このことを聞いてわたくしは，シロコゴーロフの著書「北方ツングースの社会構成」(Shirokogoroff, 1933, p.81, 川久保・田中訳, 1941, 148ページ）に，近年ブレーヤ川のツングース人（エウェンキー人）がサハリンへ移ったことが簡単に記されていたのを思い出し，このことを口にすると，かの女はシロコゴーロフを知っているという。かの女の姉がウラジオストークのシロコゴーロフのところで手伝いをしていたので，かの女も小さいときに会ったということのようであった。その晩は，この思いがけない話にさらに話がはずんだのであった。

さて，ウイルタのニグマーは，どこのエウェンキー人から入ったか，そして直接か，あるいは他のツングース人を経由してか，また，いつごろウイルタに伝来したものか。これらの点については，アムール川・シホタアリン地方のツングース諸族にも英雄物語の伝承があれば，その発生・伝播についてくわしく調べたあとでないと正確なことは言えないが，ウイルタのニグマーがカラフトのエウェンキー人から伝わったことも十分に考えられるところである。アムール川下流のオルチャ族にも，スモリャーク（Смоляк, 1966, стр, 134）によれば，その口頭文芸に нингма とよぶものがあるが，これは鳥やけものの話で，英雄物語ではないようである。

上の問題は，エウェンキー人がいつカラフトへ移住したかの問題ともかかわる。

日本の江戸時代の間宮林蔵は，文化５年（1808年）のカラフト調査に関する報告書の「キーレン人物大概の様子」の条に，「キーレンと申す人物はサハリン川辺又はマンゴー川の東北余程奥山に住居候者」と述べてキーリンは大陸にいるとし，先年カラフトに渡来したものは西海岸に一・二年いたが，殺されて当時はひとりもいなかったと記している（高倉，1982，153-154ページにも載る）。1854年から1856年にかけてアムール地方・カラフトを調査したロシヤのシュレンク（Schrenck，1881，S.34，35，および民族分布付図）の記述でも，キーリンの居住分布はカラフトにおよんでいない。

パトカーノフ（Патканов，1912，стр. 88）によれば，カラフトへは，エウェンキー人が1860年代に当時の沿海州ウダ管区すなわちカラフトに近接する大陸部から，天然痘の流行を避けて，移住したという。そして1897年に143人をかぞえた。今世紀10年代にエウェンキー人を調査したシロコゴーロフも，カラフトにエウェンキー人が分布することを著書のなかの分布図に記している。シロコゴーロフは，古くから今日までのエウェンキー人の南方への移動のうち，カラフトへのエウェンキー人の移動をもっとも新しい第４波に属すとしている。(Shirokogoroff，1933，p.164，川久保・田中訳，1941，317ページ。)

このように，カラフトへのエウェンキー人の移動は，ほぼ1860年代以後くらいのことのようである。すると，ウイルタ人のニグマーも，カラフトのエウェンキー人から入ったものであれば，それ以後の比較的新しいもので，それがウイルタ人の間に流行したのであろうか。

それでは，さらにウイルタのニグマーとなったエウェンキーの英雄物語は，元来どこのエウェンキー人のものだったろうか。それにはニグマーのエウェンキー語がどこの方言であるかを調べることも重要なかぎとなるだろう。たとえば，ニグマーのエウェンキー語の10代の数詞は，数詞10が「から」の意味の格語尾 -duk をともない，そのあとにひとけたの数詞が来る構造をもち，13はǰānduk ilān，19はǰānduk jəgin である（ǰān が10，ilān が３，jəgin が９である）。数詞のこの構造は，ワシレーヴィチの辞典（Василевич，1958， стр. 693）をみると，イリンペア方言やウチュル・ゼーヤ方言にある。

また，もしウイルタのニグマーがカラフトのエウェンキー人から入ったものであれば，その問題は，カラフトのエウェンキー人がどんな経路をたどってどこから来たかの問題と関連する。パトカーノフによれば，上述のように，かつてのウダ管区から来たというが，そのどこから来たかは不明である。一部はブレーヤ川地方から来たことは，アファナーシエヴァさんの例（および上述のシロコゴーロフの記述）から知られる。

カルゲルの調査報告（Каргер，1929，富田訳，1944）には，ブレーヤ川のエウェンキー人がアムグン川を下って移動したが，先発のものがアムグン川の途中で上陸したのに，後続の舟は連絡が間違ってアムール川を下り，リャングル島に至ったことが記されている。アムール川下流地方の左岸支流のウルミ川などやその西のブレーヤ川地方，あるいはひょっとするとさらに西方ないし西北方のエウェンキー人がアムール川やアムグン川を経て，海峡を渡ってカラフトまで移動したことはありえよう。

上に述べてきたように，エウェンキー人の英雄物語は，東方のカラフトまで伝えられ，さらにウイルタのニグマーとなったが，それを伝承する佐藤チヨさんはさらに北海道に移り，現在，釧路に住んでおられる。ウイルタ人のニグマーがサハリンで記録されているか不明であり，佐藤さんの伝承保存するニグマーは重要な価値をもつ。

佐藤さんからくりかえしくりかえし聞きながらテキストをつくる作業をおこなって，夕刻，札幌へ帰る特急にのると，ニグマーの故地から南に遠い北海道の地でそれを聞くという感慨が，あらためてわいてくる。海岸線が列車に近づいては遠のき，近づいては遠のいて行くたそがれの車窓を眺めながら，佐藤さんもすでに70代なかば，それにわたくしも60歳をいくつかこえ，佐藤さんの伝承を記録保存するためにも，このさきニグマーのテキスト作製の作業をすすめられるだけすすめなければと思うのである。

引用文献

池上二良［採録・訳注］，1984.『ウイルタ口頭文芸原文集』札幌・北海道教育委員会（『ウイルタ民俗文化財緊急調査報告書６』），網走・網走市立中央公民館内・網走市北方民俗文化保存協会。

池上二良・谷本一之，1974.「オロッコ族の歌謡」［１．オロッコ語歌詞の韻律論的分析（池上執筆）（本書所収）２．オロッコ歌謡の音楽的分析（谷本執筆）］，『北方文化研究』８，札幌・北大文学部附属北方文化研究施設。

高倉新一郎，1982.『犀川会資料』札幌・北海道出版企画センター。

間宮林蔵，1808.「カラフト島見分仕候趣申上候書付」『松田間宮両人カラフト見分申上書』北海道庁蔵。

Schrenck, L. v., 1881. *Reisen und Forschungen im Amur-lande*, Band Ⅲ, Erste Lieferung. St. Petersburg.

Shirokogoroff, S. M., 1933. *Social Organization of the Northern Tungus*. Shanghai. 川久保悌郎・田中克己訳，1941.『シロコゴロフ 北方ツングースの社会構成』東京・岩波書店。

Василевич, Г. М., 1936. Материалы по эвенкийскому (тунгусскому) фольклору, вып. 1, Сборник материалов по эвенкийскому (тунгусскому) фольклору. Ленинград.

———, 1958. Эвенкийско-русский словарь. Москва.

———, 1966. Исторический фольклор эвенков, Сказания и предания. Москва-Ленинград.

Воскобойников, М. Г., 1960. Эвенкийский фольклор, Учебное пособие для педагогических училищ. Ленинград.

Каргер, Н. Г., 1929. Отчет об исследовании родового состава населения бассейна р. Гарина, Гарино-амгунская экспедиция 1926 года. Ленинград. エヌ・ゲ・カルゲル，富田良作訳，1944.「サマーギル族に就いて——ガリン河流域の住民の氏族構成に関する調査報告——」，『書香』16巻１，２号　大連・満鉄大連図書館。

Паткановъ, С., 1912. Статистическiя данныя, показывающiя племенной составь населенія Сибири, языкъ и роды инородцевъ, Томъ1. С.-Петербургъ.

Романова, А. В., Мыреева, А. Н., 1971. Фольклор эвенков Якутии. Ленинград.

Смоляк, А. В., 1966. Ульчи, хозяйство культура и быт в прошлом и настоящем. Москва.

初出　アジア・アフリカ言語文化研究所通信　52号［東京外国語大学　昭和59年（1984年）11月25日］1－4ページ。

ウイルタ語・オルチャ語研究における B.ピウスツキ

B. Pilsudski in Uilta and Olcha Studies

アイヌ語・ギリヤク語研究に対するB.ピウスツキ（B. PIŁSUDSKI）の貢献については，すでにひろく知られているが，かれはまたツングース系二言語，ウイルタ語（オロッコ語）とオルチャ語についても業績を残しているのである。ウイルタ語・オルチャ語についてのかれの業績は，ポーランドの学者コトヴィチ（W. KOTWICZ）によってロシヤの民族学の雑誌のなかの論文［Котвичъ 1909:6］において言及されたことがあるが，その業績は刊行されておらず，われわれがそれに接することはできなかった。しかし，最近，ピウスツキの原稿は，クラクフのポーランド科学アカデミーの図書館のなかの古文書庫において，マイエヴィチ（A.F. MAJEWICZ）と井上紘一の両氏によってふたたび発見され，われわれはこれに接することができるようになった。この原稿は，1）ポーランド語で書かれたオロッコ語の文法略説，オロッコ語テキスト，オロッコ・ポーランド語彙，オロッコ語固有名詞の表，およびロシヤ語によるオロッコ語音とオロッコ語単語についての略記，オロッコ語文法素描とオロッコ語テキスト（W.コトヴィチの解説文とピウスツキの書簡文が付いている），ならびに2）オルチャ・ポーランド語彙，固有名詞の表，テキストをおさめるポーランド語で書かれたオルチャ族言語資料（はじめにかれ自身の序言が付してある）をふくんでいる。かれは，ウイルタ語資料を1904年にカラフトのタライカ湾のポロナイ川河口付近で採集し，またオルチャ語資料を同年カラフトのその地方で，翌年アムール川地方であつめた（ウイルタ語資料中のコトヴィチの解説とオルチャ語資料の序言による）。カラフトにおけるかれの研究作業のあとすでに約

80年がたっている。ここで，ピウスツキのウイルタ語・オルチャ語の記録およびそれについてのかれの記述を言語学とフォークロアの研究の立場から再検討し，そしてかれの業績をウイルタ語・オルチャ語の研究史ならびにこれらの言語の歴史において展望することをおこないたい。

ウイルタ語研究史の上で，B.ピウスツキ以前には松浦武四郎が19世紀なかばカラフトを旅行し，そこでウイルタ語単語を書きとめた［松浦　1860；高倉　1978；池上　1971,1979および谷沢　1978参照］。ピウスツキ以後は，中目覚が1912年とその翌年にカラフトをたずね，かれのウイルタ語の著作のための資料を採集した［中目1917 a,b；NAKANOME 1928］。また，1912年に金田一京助がウイルタ語単語を採集した。それは刊行された語彙にふくまれている［金田一　1912］。

オルチャ語の研究史の早期においては，18世紀末から19世紀ながばにかけてカラフトで日本人渡航者が書留め，これを当時日本人がサンタンことばとよんだオルチャ語単語がある［池上　1967参照］。マキシモーヴィチ（К. И. Максимович）は19世紀の後半にオルチャ語単語を採集した。これはグルーベ（W. GRUBE）のゴルジ・ドイツ語辞典のなかで刊行された［GRUBE　1900］。ピウスツキのすぐあと，1908年にシュミット（P. SCHMIDT）はアムール川下流地方のオルチャ族をふくむ諸民族の実地調査をおこない，採集したオルチャ語単語と若干のテキストを1923年に刊行した［SCHMIDT　1923］。

年代的には，われわれの知る限り，ピウスツキはウイルタ語・オルチャ語の今世紀最初の研究者であった。かれは，ウイルタ語の最初の文法記述とウイルタ語テキスト，ウイルタ語語彙および若干のテキストのついたオルチャ語の語彙を作成した。しかし，これらの言語に関するかれの原稿は，少なくともそのあるものがソ連の一部の研究者にはすでに利用できたが，今日まで一般の人々の目からは遠ざけられていた。もし，かれの原稿がもっとはやくに日の目をみていたならば，ウイルタ語・オルチャ語研究やアムール川・カラフト地方の研究の進歩にもっと大きな寄与をなしていたことであろう。

ピウスツキによって記録された約180の人名を含む固有名詞の表には，川村秀弥がおそらく1940年代に記録した人名のあるものと同定できる約6人の男性人名がある［川村　1983 : 72-76］。さらに，これらの人名および表中の他の3名ほどの人名は，1910年ごろに生まれたウイルタの老婦人佐藤チヨさんの記憶のなかにいまもなおのこっている。それらの6名と3名の名前は Boksiiri, Čimuleenu, Čoroldoonu, J̌əwweenu, Mačipari, Tuŋgəkkə と Čeexara, Loǰiŋgeenu, Naaksauna である。川村秀弥の記録によれば，同定された人々のうち，最年長者は1817年生まれであり，最年少者は1880年生まれである。したがって，これらの名前の人々は佐藤さんより一世代から三世代上であることがわかる。これらの人々の年齢は，ウイルタ語史におけるピウスツキのウイルタ語資料の相対的年代を見出すのに手助けとなろう。1876年生まれで，ピウスツキにこのあとふれるおとぎばなしを口述したキシュンギン（Kiśungin）は，わたくしがいま上にのべたことを証する一つの実際の事例を供する。

ピウスツキの著述はこれらの言語の研究の早期の段階になされたものであるので，かれのテキストや記述のある箇所は誤っているか，または疑わしいとみられることは避けられない。それにもかかわらず，かれの著述の多くの部分は独特の価値を有している。

わたくしは，ウイルタ語とオルチャ語のかれの文法素描と語彙における注目すべき若干の点に言及したい。

ウイルタ語に関するピウスツキの資料のなかのいくつかの単語には，今日のウイルタ語の対応単語に現れない母音間の h がみられる。ピウスツキの資料のなかのそれらの単語の少なくともあるものは，*k または他のある軟口蓋音を h として保存するとみられる。今日のウイルタ語では，母音間の単独の *k は，幼児語における場合を除いては，消滅したと考えられる。たとえば，ný̆muhu「脂肪（溶けていないもの）」（今日のウイルタ語 nəmuu「獣脂」），エウェン語 nəmə̆k「脂肪」参照。この h は有声摩擦音を表わすものかもしれない。松浦武四郎が書きとめたウイルタ語単語のうち，今日のウイルタ語の dəsii「そりの荷台に敷きならべた棒」に対応するテシキニのような語については池上［1979 : 74］を参照。

つぎに，ウイルタ語の完了の反照連用形は，母音に終る動詞語幹の場合には，池上採集資料ならびにペトローヴァ採集資料にみられるように，語幹に動詞語

尾 -gačči（単数形）または -gaččeeri（複数形）を付加して形成される。しかし，ウイルタ語のある話し手たちはまた動詞語尾 -xačči（単数形）または -xaččeeri（複数形）がともなう反照連用形を使用する［池上　1984:10,11その他]。ピウスツキもまた iśuxatciri（＝isuxaččeeri)「帰って来てから」のような連用形をあげているのは注意すべきである。-xačči という形の存在は，連用形語尾 -gačči が *-xačči の段階を経て完了動名詞の形成素 *-xan プラスおそらく道具格語尾の一種である *-či(？) プラス反照単数語尾 *-bi の結合へさかのぼることを暗示するように思われる。それは，ツングース語の一つ，オロチ語における完了の反照連用形語尾 -xanǰij［Цинциус　1949：156］が完了動名詞の形成素 *-xan プラス道具格語尾 *-ji プラス反照単数語尾 *bi の結合にさかのぼるのと同様と思われる。

これらの点で，ピウスツキのウイルタ語資料はウイルタ語の早期の段階のいくつかの特色を有している。また，かれのウイルタ語語彙のなかのある数の単語は今日では同定できない。

オルチャ語語彙では，たとえば，オルチャ語 ǰa‖ウイルタ語 da およびオルチャ語 di‖ウイルタ語 ǰi のようなオルチャ語と他のツングース語との音韻対応に符合しないいくつかの語形が，これらの音韻対応に符合する形にまじっているのがみられる。例，bilʒ́á と bildá 両者とも「のど」，sagdí と sagʒí 両者とも「年とった」。音韻対応に符合しない語は，ウイルタ語単語であり，これが誤ってオルチャ語単語にまじったとみられる。なぜなら，ピウスツキは，オルチャ語資料の大部分を，カラフトのウイルタ人の住む地方へ来てそこに滞在していたオルチャ人から採集したのである（かれのオルチャ語資料の序言による)。ゴルツェフスカヤ（B. A. Горцевская）は，ピウスツキがオルチャ語とオロッコ語を同一言語と確信してオルチャ語単語とオロッコ語単語を区別しなかったとのべたが［Горцевская 1959：21]，これは正しくないとみられる。

つぎに，ピウスツキが採集したテキストを扱いたい。かれのウイルタ語テキストには，おとぎばなしが一つある。このおとぎばなしのもう一種は，上に言及したウイルタ老婦人佐藤チヨさんによってわたくしに口述された。ピウスツキは，この話をサフリのジャンルに入れた。サフリは，ウイルタ口頭文芸のジャンルの一つであり，架空物語である。一方，わたくしは，提供者の佐藤さんがその話をサフリの例とみないので，それをサフリのジャンルに入れなかった。しかし，この話をサフリに入れることは，それの内容に適切であるように思われる。

この話の梗概を記すと，ねずみの母親とかえるの母親が，一緒に舟をこいで川上へ木になる漿菓をとりに行った。かえるの母親は，木にのぼることができず，木の実をとれなかった。ねずみの母親は，たくさんの木の実をとったが，かえるの母親へひとつもやらなかった。ねずみのこどもたちは喜んだが，かえるのこどもたちは悲しがった。うちへ帰ってから，かえるの母親は大じかをとり，たくさんの肉をえた。ねずみの母親は夜その肉をぬすみに行ったが，ぬすみに失敗し，かえるの母親にひどくぶたれた。ねずみの母親は，けがをして，からすのシャマンとわたりがらすのシャマンと小鳥のシャマンを呼びにやった。けれども，小鳥のシャマンはかの女の本当のことを暴露してかの女に追いかえされた。

若干の箇所では，両人のこの話はたがいに異なる。たとえば，佐藤チヨさん口述のテキストでは，からすのシャマンとわたりがらすのシャマンは本当のことを暴露してかの女をあざけったが，小鳥のシャマンは，ねずみの母親を満足させて報酬をうるために，うその陳述をした。一方，ある数の句は両人の話に共通している。これらの句のあるものは，すでに意味が不明である。たとえば，waaŋaa waaxani という句が両方に出るが，waaxani は，「そこにけがをした」の意味であるが，waaŋaa は意味がはっきりしない。ある共通の句は擬音語である。たとえば，tomboo bok bok は，櫂を水へ入れる音と水があわ立つ音を表わす。ある表現は，物語のなかで永続的に固定してしまい，その結果として，その表現が両人の話のどちらにも特に保存されたと考えられる。

この話は，当時26歳のウイルタの男性のキシュンギンがピウスツキに口述したものである。佐藤チヨさんには，この話はかの女の母によって語られた。佐藤さんの母とキシュンギンは，ほぼ同時代の人であったといえよう。

この話の相異なる二種の比較は，口承において内容と表現の両面でなにがもとのまま残るかを知るかぎを与える。

つぎに，ピウスツキのウイルタ語資料は16のなぞなぞをふくんでいる。そのうちの七つは池上のウイルタ語資料中佐藤チヨさんが口述したなぞなぞと一致し［池上　1984 : 82-84］，六つはペトローヴァのテキスト中のなぞなぞと一致するが［Петрова 1967］，七つはどちらのテキストにもみられないものである。

ウイルタのなぞなぞは，gaŋ gaŋ gajawoo という導入句ではじまり，つぎになぞかけの内容が言い表わされ，それから，「(それ) なあに，(あててごらん)」の意味の (tari) xaigəək (toksiik unuu) のような正しい解答の要請でとじられる (括弧内の部分は省略されることもある)。こたえの最後の母音は長くのばして発音され，通常 (並列的単語の場合を除いて) k 音が末尾につけ加えられる。

なぞなぞ問答のこの修辞的形式は，佐藤さんがわたくしに口述したなぞなぞにみられるが，ペトローヴァのなぞなぞのテキストにはみられない。ピウスツキのなぞなぞはまたなぞなぞ問答のこの修辞的形式の存在の証左を供する。

ほかに，かれのテキストには，歌 (xəəgə 即興歌３篇と子守り歌１篇) と言い伝えと文例がある。言い伝えとして，ウイルタの起源についての短い話，偶像 (お守り) 約６点の説明，血の病の治療法などのほかに，火への祈禱のことばがある。この祈禱のことばは貴重であろう。

かれはつねにテキストをそれが語られるそのままに書きとめる努力をしたと，わたくしには思われる。ピウスツキが記録したウイルタ語テキストをみていると，話し手が語ったさまが，ありありと感じとれるように思われることがある。かれはよき野外研究家であったと，わたくしは思う。

かれのテキストは，蓄音器の円筒にも，磁気録音テープにも保存されたものでなく，かれ自身の手で書きとめられたものである。それにもかかわらず，かれのテキストはもとの口述に忠実であるとみられ，今日なおウイルタ語・オルチャ語研究に役立つ。かれの業績は，アイヌ語研究におけると同様に，ウイルタ語・オルチャ語研究においても決して忘れられることはないだろう。

付記

なおまたピウスツキの研究分野について言えば，それは言語学と民族学にわたっている。ここでは民族学という用語の意味を，民族誌や民俗学もふくめて非常に広くとっていただきたい。言語学と民族学という二つの学問分野が，ピウスツキというひとりの研究者において分化せず一体をなしている。このことは，ピウスツキだけでなく，当時のロシヤの V.G.ボゴラース や L.Ya.シュテルンベルグも，またアメリカの F.ボアズもそうであったろう。その後，研究が進むにつれ，これらの学問は専門化して分化した。これは，両者の専門研究が非常に進歩したことによる。言語学においては，その固有分野といえる音韻や文法の研究が著しく進み，精密になった。それは，ピウスツキの時代の比ではないと言えよう。しかし，そのように進歩してきた今日の段階において，両学問はあらためてそれぞれの研究成果を相互にとり入れ，再び連携し，総合化して行くことが必要ではないかと思う。

言語学の側についてみると，たとえば言語の意味の記述，語義の記述を的確におこなうためには，民族学の成果として得られた知識をとり入れることが必要であろう。基礎語彙も，少なくとも一面では，その言語の話し手たちの生活，文化に立って考えるべきものであろう。また基礎語彙に関して，人間言語の基礎語彙における普遍性をさぐるようなとき，まず個別言語の基礎語彙をあきらかにすることが前提であり，これの正確な記述は，各言語について民族学的知識に基いておこなうことが必須であろう。その普遍性の探索も，こうして記述された諸言語の基礎語彙を通してなされるべきであろう。

一方，民族学の側を考えると，一民族の文化を理解し，把握するためには，その民族の言語によらざるをえない面が大きい。口碑，神話，宗教，宇宙観については言うまでもない。物質文化についても，一民族の物質文化を体系的に理解，把握するためには，その民族の言語によることも必要であろう。folk taxonomy がわからなければ，一民族の物質文化も十分には理解できないだろう。そのためにも，各文化要素についてその本来の言語における正確な名称を知ることが必要である。ものごとの異同は，その言語における名称の異同によってみることが重要であろう。具体的には，博物館の民具の分類，展示にも関係するだろう。展示物には，その言語による正確な名称も記載することが望ましいと思う。

実は，筆者は北海道教育委員会から依頼されてウイルタ民俗文化財緊急調査を８年ほどおこなってきて，このことを感じたのである。このことはアイヌ文化研究においても同様であろう。

ピウスツキを主題においた今回の機会に，こうしたことを改めて考えることは有意義であり，重要であると思う。実際におこなわれる研究において，両学問の研究がたがいの成果をとり入れ合い，連携し結合して行くことが大切であり，研究が今後このような方向に向って行くことを望んでやまない。

本稿は1985年９月北海道大学で開催されたピウスツキに関する国際シンポジウムでの英和両文による口頭発表の和文を補訂したものである。なお付記は1986年２月28日国立民族学博物館におけるピウスツキ研究会での研究発表につけ加えて述べたものである。

謝辞　A. F. MAJEWICZ 博士と R. KASZA 氏に，ピウスツキの原稿中のポーランド語の記述および語義注解の英訳を用意下さったことに対して深く感謝の意を表す。

引用文献

池上二良，1967.「サンタンことば集」『北方文化研究』2号　27-87。

―――，1971.「19世紀なかごろのオロッコ語集」『北方文化研究』5号　79-184。

―――［編・解説］，1979.『ウイルタ古画集録』札幌　北海道教育委員会・北海道文化財保護協会。

―――［採録・訳注］，1984.『ウイルタ口頭文芸原文集』札幌　北海道教育委員会，網走　網走市北方民俗文化保存協会。

川村秀弥（池上二良編），1983.『川村秀弥採録カラフト諸民族の言語と民俗』札幌　北海道教育委員会，網走　網走市北方民俗文化保存協会。

金田一京助編，1912.『日本国内諸人種の言語』東京　東京人類学会。

松浦武四郎，1860.『北蝦夷餘誌』江戸。

中目覺，1917a.『樺太の話』東京　三省堂。

———，1917b.『オロッコ文典』東京　三省堂。

高倉新一郎［解説］，1978.『竹四郎廻浦日記　下』札幌　北海道出版企画センター。

谷澤尚一，1978.「安政三年採録のニクブン語彙を繞って」『北方文化研究』13号　135-161.

GRUBE, W., 1900. *Goldisch-deutsches Wörterverzeichniss, Dr. Leop. v. Schrenck's Reisen und Forschungen im Amur-Lande*. Anhang zum III. Bande. St. Petersburg.

NAKANOME, A., 1928. *Grammatik der Orokko-Sprache*. Osaka.

SCHMIDT, P., 1923. The Language of the Olchas. *Acta Universitatis Latviensis* VIII.

Горцевская, В. А., 1959. Очерк истории изучения тунгуско-маньчжурских языков. Учпедгиз, Ленинград.

Котвичъ, Вл., 1909. Матеріалы для изученія тунгусскихъ нарѣчій. Живая Старина, вып. II-III, 1909 г. С.-Петербургъ.

Петрова, Т. И., 1967. Язык ороков (ульта). НАУКА, Ленинград.

Цинциус, В. И., 1949. Очерк морфологии орочского языка. Ученые записки ЛГУ, No. 98, Серия востоковедческих наук, вып. 1.

This article is a revised Japanese version of my paper "B. Pilsudski in Uilta and Olcha Studies", which I presented in English and Japanese at the International Symposium on B. Piłsudski's Phonographic Records and the Ainu Culture held in Hokkaido University, Sapporo on 16-20 September, 1985. An English version of the paper was published in the *Proceedings of the International Symposium on B. Piłsudski's Phonographic Records and the Ainu Culture* (edited by the Executive

Committee of the International Symposium Hokkaido University, Sapporo, 1985) pp.168-172.

和文初出　『国立民族学博物館研究報告別冊』5号［昭和62年（1987年）3月］275－282ページ。

ツングース語オロッコ方言のその近隣方言間における位置

The Position of Orokko among the Neighboring Tungus Dialects

ツングース語オロッコ方言とはオロッコ族の話す言語である。オロッコ族は樺太の幌内川下流からタライカ湖にかけての地域及びツイミ川河口を中心とする地域に住むツングース人の一種族である。その人口は少なく，旧日本領の南樺太においては258人（昭和16年）[1]，北樺太では157人（1925）[2]である。このオロッコ族の由来及び分類上の位置については，つとにシュレンク（L. v. Schrenck）が述べていて，同氏は言語の点などからオロッコ族（die Oroken）にとってオルチャ族が最も近い親族であり，オロッコ族は恐らく少し前に大陸から渡って来たオルチャ族の一派にすぎないだろうとし，さらにオロッコ族自身もまたオルチャ族に属していることを意識しているのがシュミット（Fr. Schmidt），グレーン（P.v.Glehn），ブルイルキン（A.D.Brylkin）らによって認められた由がシュレンクの記述にみえる。さらにシュレンクは黒龍江流域のツングース人の諸種族を言語の点から分類しているがその際オルチャ族とオロッコ族とを「黒龍江沿岸のオルチャ族及び樺太のオルチャ族（オロク族）」として両者を一つにして扱っている[3]。オロッコ族とオルチャ族とのこの関係はそれ以来定説となっていたとみてよいだろう。ところがその後シロコゴロフ（S.M.Shirokogoroff）はこれと異なった説を立てたのである。すなわちオロッコ族（Oroki）は恐らくオロチ族と同じ起源のものであって，オロチ族にその領域を譲って沿海州から樺太に移ったものであると述べ，さらにこれら種族はともにその体質上の特徴，民族誌的複合及び言語の点で北方ツングース要素を多分に保持して来たと述べている[4]。また同氏はこれよりさきツングース語の方言を分類してこれを北方派と南方派とに大別しているがオロッコ方言，オロチ方言はともに北方派に入れ，なおオルチャ方言は南方派に入れている。(5)

すなわち上にみたようにシュレンクの説に対してシロコゴロフの説は異なっている。そしてシュレンクの説がオロッコ方言に関して拠るところは同氏がオロッコ人とかわした会話であることが述べられていて，(6) そこには具体的な根拠は明確に示されていない。シロコゴロフの説もオロッコ方言に関する根拠が具体的に示されていない。それゆえいまここにオロッコ方言が，従来問題とされて来たこれら近隣方言の間にあって分類上どんな位置にあるかについて充分ではないが少々再検討してみたい。なおオロッコ方言がツングース語方言中に占める分類上の位置について述べることは他日ツングース語諸方言を総括して分類する際にゆずりたい。

本稿ではオロッコ方言については，

中目覺　オロッコ文典　東京　大正６年　A. Nakanome : Grammatik der Orokko-Sprache Osaka 1928 (übersetzt von W. Othmer).

服部健　オロッコ語「北風と太陽」［音声学協会会報第72・73号　東京　昭和18年］

に拠るが，オロッコ方言の語形は中目氏のドイツ語訳本から，語義は中目氏の原本から引用する。服部氏の資料は貴重であるが分量が少なく，中目氏のそれは言語学的に不正確な点があるとみられる。そのためそれに基く考察も残念ながら制限されざるをえない。同方言の資料としてはこれよりさき金田一京助先生が編まれた「日本国内諸人種の言語」（東京人類学会　大正元年）に載るものがある。また服部氏にほかに未発表のものがあり，またやはり未発表の澗潟(泻)久治氏採集の資料がある。(7) ロシヤにおいては1909年ごろまででは ぺ．オ．ピリスドスキー採集の資料があることが記されている。(8)

そのほかの方言についてはオロチ方言は，P. Schmidt(Šmits): The language of the Oroches (Rīgā 1927) に拠る。

ウデヘ方言は，シュミットの上掲書に載るウデヘ方言の資料とその下位方言の一つであるホル方言に基くE. R. Šnejder: Kratkij udėjsko-russkij slovar' s priloženiem grammatičeskogo očerka (Moskva-Leningrad 1936) とに拠る

が，この方言の語の引用は後者からする。

オルチャ方言は，P. Schmidt(Šmits) : The language of the Olchas (Rīgā 1923) に拠るが，主としてシュミット採集の資料から引用し，時によりクラスチン（P. Krastin）採集の資料によって補う。略称 K. はこれをさす。

ゴリド方言は上に挙げたシュミットの二書においてオルチャ方言，オロチ方言の語に比較して挙げられたこの方言の語形に拠る。

まず語彙についてみる。オロッコ方言には日本語，ロシヤ語及びそのほかの系統の異なる言語からの借用語，外来語が含まれているがこれについてここには触れない。いまオロッコ方言の語彙を近隣方言のそれに比べると，オロッコ方言の多くの語は近隣方言のそれに一致する。例えば，

ウデヘ inəŋi（dnem）‖オロチ inöŋi（a day）‖ゴリド ini‖オルチャ inöŋi（a day）‖オロッコ inuṅi（日，天気）

ウデヘ namu（more, okean）‖オロチ namu（a sea）‖ゴリド namu‖オルチャ namu（a sea）‖オロッコ namû（海）

ウデヘ nā（zemlja）‖オロチ na（the earth）‖ゴリド na‖オルチャ na（the earth）‖オロッコ na（陸，野，国）

ウデヘ ʒaŋge（načal'nik, čelovek, obladajuščij darom reči, orator）‖オロチ dzjaŋge（a superior, an officer）‖ゴリド dzjaŋgin‖オルチャ džaŋgi（a superior, an officer）‖オロッコ jange（役人，紳士）

オロッコ方言の或語はいうまでもなくこれらの近隣方言ばかりでなくツングース語のすべての方言乃至かなり多くの方言の語とも一致するが，またオロッコ方言の或語の形に一致するものはほとんど黒龍江下流地方及び沿海州のそれらの方言及び満洲語にしか見出されない。「地」を意味する語形はその例である。また満洲語からの借用語とみられる語が見出されるのはこれら近隣方言とともにオロッコ方言も満洲語の影響のもとにあったことを物語っている。jange はその一例である。しかしオロッコ方言の語彙をくわしく近隣方言のそれに比べると或語の形は或方言の語形には一致するがほかの方言の語形には一致しない。特にオロチ方言，オルチャ方言をとってこれと比べてみると，オルチャ方言の語形と異なり，オロチ方言の語形に一致するものがある。

ウデヘ saŋa (dyra, otverstie) ‖ オロチ saŋa (a hole, a split) ‖ ゴリド saŋgar ‖ オルチャ saŋali (a hole, a split, a fissure) ‖ オロッコ saṅa (穴)

ウデヘ kusigə (nož) ‖ オロチ kučigö (a knife) ‖ ゴリド kuče ‖ オルチャ kuče (a knife) ‖ オロッコ kutigû (小刀)

しかしオロチ方言の語形と異なり，むしろオルチャ方言の語形に一致するものもある。

オロチ čālba (a birch), čaba (a birch, a birchbark) ‖ ゴリド pja ‖ オルチャ pja (a birch) ‖ オロッコ pyê (白樺)(9)

ウデヘ ʒugu (vydra) ‖ オロチ dzjuku, džoku (an otter) ‖ ゴリド muödu, mudu ‖ オルチャ muödu, mōdo (an otter) ‖ オロッコ mödö (かはうそ)(10)

ウデヘ xəjə (lob) ‖ オロチ guluka, giluka (the forehead) ‖ ゴリド pöjö ‖ オルチャ pöjö (a forehead) ‖ オロッコ pöyö (額)

ウデヘ s'ai (sol') ‖ オロチ daksu (the salt) ‖ ゴリド dausun ‖ オルチャ dausu (the salt) ‖ オロッコ daoso (塩)

はじめの三語のようにオロッコ方言，オルチャ方言の語形がオロチ方言の語形と全く異なるものもある。しかも一番目，二番目の二語のオロチ方言の語形はこれら近隣方言以外のツングース語の多くの方言の語形に一致するものである。なおまたオロッコ方言の語形がこれら近隣方言のいずれとも異なるものがある。例えば，

ウデヘ in'ai (sobaka) ‖ オロチ inaki (a dog) ‖ ゴリド inda ‖ オルチャ inda (a dog) ‖ オロッコ ṅenda (犬)(11)

しかしオロッコ方言の語彙は，概括的に言ってオロチ方言の語彙よりもオルチャ方言のそれに一層ちかいように思われる。

つぎに音韻についてみると，オロッコ方言と近隣方言との間に語頭においてまず下の対応を示す語がある。

ウデヘ x, (iの前) s ‖ オロチ x, h ‖ ゴリド p, f ‖ オルチャ p ‖ オロッコ p

例

ウデヘ xaṇa (odna iz duš čeloveka 下略) ‖ オロチ xaṇa (a shadow, a soul, the manes) ‖ ゴリド paṇa ‖ オルチャ paṇa (the manes, the shades of the departed, the souls) ‖ オロッコ pâna (影，魂)

ウデヘ xaluga (molotok) ‖ オロチ xaluka, xaluha, xaluva (a hammer) ‖ ゴリド paloa ‖ オルチャ paloa (a hammer) ‖ オロッコ paloa (槌)

ウデヘ xəigi (štany, brjuki) ‖ オロチ xeigi, xörki, xöiki (the trousers) ‖ ゴリド pöru ‖ オルチャ pöru (the trousers) ‖ オロッコ pölö (股引)(12)

ウデヘ xəmu (guby) ‖ オロチ xömu (the lips) ‖ ゴリド fömun, pömun ‖ オルチャ pömu (a lip) ‖ オロッコ pômö (口，唇)(13)

ウデヘ sitə (ditja, rebenok, syn, doč', detenyš, ptenec) ‖ オロチ hitö (a child) ‖ ゴリド piktö ‖ オルチャ piktö (a child) ‖ オロッコ pöttô (子供)(14)

しかしその例外としてつぎのような語がある。

ウデヘ xokto (doroga, tropa, tropinka, sled, 下略) ‖ オロチ xokto (a way, a trace) ‖ ゴリド pokto ‖ オルチャ pokto (a way, a trace, a footstep) ‖ オロッコ pokto (足跡，道), hokto (足跡)

ウデヘ xəkuhi (gorjačij, -o, žarkij, -o) ‖ オロチ xöku (hot), hökusi (warm) ‖ ゴリド pöku, pökuli ‖ オルチャ pöku (hot) ‖ オロッコ hökkô (暑い)

オロチ xuŋda (an alder, alnus incana) ‖ ゴリド puŋda ‖ オルチャ puŋda (an alder) ‖ オロッコ huṅda (榛の木)

つぎにやはり語頭において下の対応を示す語がある。

ウデへ零 ‖ オロチ零 ‖ ゴリド x, (iの前) s ‖ オルチャ x, (iの前) s ‖ オロッコ h, (iの前) s

例

ウデヘ agdu (berloga, nora) ‖ オロチ agdu (a house) ‖ ゴリド xagdu ‖ オルチャ xagdu (a house) ‖ オロッコ hâgdu (穴小屋)

ウデヘ wad-īni (prekraščat', perestavat', končat') ‖ オロチ odi (to finish) ‖ ゴリド xodži ‖ オルチャ xodi (to finish) ‖ オロッコ hodihömbi (終る)

ウデヘ waji, uai (dvadcat') ‖ オロチ oi (twenty) ‖ ゴリド xorin ‖ オルチャ xori (twenty) ‖ オロッコ hôre (二十)

ウデヘ iŋi (jazyk (organ)) ‖ オロチ iṇṇi, iŋi (a tongue) ‖ ゴリド sigmu, simu ‖ オルチャ siṇu (a tongue) ‖ オロッコ シヌー (舌) (この語は金田一京助博士の上掲書に拠る), オロッコ sinô (言語, 国語)[(15)]

しかしその例外としてつぎのような語がある。

ウデヘ waikta, wahikta (nogot', zvezda) ‖ オロチ hosikta, xosikta, ohekta (a star, a nail) ‖ ゴリド xosixta ‖ オルチャ xosta, xosita K. (a star, a nail) ‖ オロッコ hosyekta (星)[(16)]

ウデヘ waikta, wahikta (nogot', zvezda) ‖ オロチ hosikta, xosikta, ohekta (a star, a nail) ‖ ゴリド xosixta ‖ オルチャ xosta, xosita K. (a star, a nail) ‖ オロッコ hotikta (蹄爪), wasekta (爪)

つぎに語中において下の対応を示す語がある。

ウデヘ零, j ‖ オロチ零, j ‖ ゴリド r ‖ オルチャ r ‖ オロッコ r

例

ウデヘ gō (dolgij, -o, dalekij, -o) ‖ オロチ gō (far) ‖ ゴリド goro ‖ オルチャ goro (far) ‖ オロッコ goro (遠い, 昔の)

ウデヘ ʙəi (luk (dlja strel'by)) ‖ オロチ böji (a bow) ‖ ゴリド buri, bure ‖ オルチャ buri (a bow) ‖ オロッコ burihô (弓)

ウデヘ geæmaha (kost', skelet, 下略) ‖ オロチ gijamsa (a bone) ‖ ゴリド giramsa, girmasa, girmaxsa, germaxsa ‖ オルチャ giramsa (a bone) ‖ オロッコ gerapsa (骨)

ウデヘ waji, uai (dvadcat') ‖ オロチ oi (twenty) ‖ ゴリド xorin ‖ オルチャ xori (twenty) ‖ オロッコ hôre (二十)

オロチ方言のかかる語においては母音間の *r がつぎのような変化をなしたと考えられる。同種の母音の間では消失してその母音は長くなった。i とそのほかの母音との間ではjとして残るかまたは消失した。なおまた子音のまえで*rが消失したと考えうる語がある。またウデヘ方言でもそれに類する変化がおきたと考えられ，そのホル方言においては今日rは一般には借用語，外来語及び間投詞にしか現れないようである。(17)

なおつぎのような語もある。

ウデヘ muji, mui (lošad', 下略) ‖ オロチ muri, mori (a horse) ‖ ゴリド morin ‖ オルチャ muri (a horse) ‖ オロッコ mûri (馬)

ウデヘ n̦ūktə (volosy) ‖ オロチ n̦uktö, nuktö (the hair) ‖ ゴリド n̦uktö, nuktö ‖ オルチャ nuktö (the hair) ‖ オロッコ niröttö (頭髪)

語中においてまたつぎの対応を示す語がある。

ウデヘ (dの前) g ‖ オロチ (dの前) g ‖ ゴリド l ‖ オルチャ l ‖ オロッコ l

例

ウデヘ ʙagd-īni (žit', rodit'sja, 下略) ‖ オロチ bagdixa (was born) ‖ ゴリド baldixa ‖ オルチャ baldixa (was born, lived) ‖ オロッコ baljêwi (生れる)

ウデヘ dogd-īni (slyšat') ‖ オロチ dogdixa (heard) ‖ ゴリド doldixa, doldžixa ‖ オルチャ dōldixa (heard) ‖ オロッコ doljîwi (聞く)

オロチ ogdokso (a coffin) ‖ ゴリド xoldokso (a board, a plank), xoldoxso ‖ オルチャ xoldokso K. (a board, a plank) ‖ オロッコ holdosko (棺)(18)

オロチ方言のかかる語においてはdのまえの*lがgに変化したと考えられる。なおほかの子音のまえの*lが或変化をなしたと考えうる語もある。ウデヘ方言にもこれに類似した変化がおきたと考えられる。

つぎに音節の頭において下の対応を示す語がある。

ウデヘ c, (母音間) s ‖ オロチ č ‖ ゴリド č (cj) c ‖ オルチャ č ‖ オロッコ t

ウデヘ ʒ ‖ オロチ dzj ‖ ゴリド dž ‖ オルチャ dž ‖ オロッコ d

例

ウデヘ caligi（belyj）‖オロチ čāgdzja（white）‖ゴリド čāgdžan, cāgdzan（sagdza の語もあるが，これは老いたの意の別の語）‖オルチャ čāgdža, čādža（white）‖オロッコ tâgda（白い）

ウデヘ вugasa（ostrov）‖オロチ buača（an island）‖ゴリド boacja ‖オルチャ boača（an island）‖オロッコ buata（島）[19]

ウデヘ ʒəp-tə-ini（est', kušat'）‖オロチ dzjöptömi（to eat）‖ゴリド džöpčiuri‖オルチャ džöpti（to eat）‖オロッコ döptyêwi（食べる）

ウデヘ ʒugdi（dom, žilišče）‖オロチ dzju（a house）（dža の語もあるが，これは漢語の家の借用語）‖ゴリド džō, džog‖オルチャ džug（a house）‖オロッコ duhû（家）

なおほかにつぎのような語もある。

ウデヘ ʒolo（kamen'）‖オロチ dzjolo（a stone）‖ゴリド džolo‖オルチャ džolo（a stone）‖オロッコ jolo（岩，砂利）

ウデヘ ʒā（desjat', 下略）‖オロチ dzja（ten）‖ゴリド džuan‖オルチャ džua（ten）‖オロッコ jon（十）

上に大体五つの著しい音韻対応をみたが，ここで拠った資料では種々の音韻対応を精密にたしかめることは望めない。母音に関しては特にそうである。しかし上にのべた音韻対応のうち少なくともはじめの二つはツングース語諸方言間において重要なものであり，ほかに種々の対応が見出されてもやはりその重要性には変りないものであると思う。これらはじめの四つの対応においてオロッコ方言はオルチャ方言，ゴリド方言に一致して，オロチ方言，ウデヘ方言とは異なっている。ただし一番しまいの対応でオロッコ方言はそれらすべての近隣方言と異なっている。

文法についてみることは筆者が現在みうる近隣方言の文法の資料が僅少のため差控えたい。方言の分類は音韻，語彙，文法の分野にわたって精しく考察したものでなければ，勿論妥当なものではなく，従って以上のような結果だけに基いてオロッコ方言の分類上の位置を決定することはできない。本稿ではただ音韻，語彙については上述の点からみるとオロッコ方言がオロチ方言よりはむしろオルチャ方言にちかいと考えられることを記すにとどめる。

23.5.18.　　23.7.13.

注

(1) 石田英一郎「邦領南樺太オロッコの氏族に就て（一）」［民族学年報第3巻東京昭和16年］346ページ。

(2) Malaja sovetskaja enciklopedija. Moskva 1929－1931.

(3) L. v. Schrenck. Reisen und Forschungen im Amur-Lande in den Jahren 1854－1856. St. Petersburg 1858－1900. Bd. III S. 20, 134 －135, 278－279, 284.

なおその分類はつぎのようなものである。

1 ダウール族及びソロン族——蒙古人と強度の混淆をなしたツングース種族

2 満洲族，ゴリド族，オロチ族

3 オロチョン族，マネギル族，ビラル族，クル河沿岸のキレ族

4 黒龍江沿岸のオルチャ族及び樺太のオルチャ族（オロク族），ネグダ族，サマギル族

(4) S. M. Shirokogoroff. Social organization of the Northern Tungus. Shanghai 1933 pp. 157. なお pp. 349－352 参照。川久保悌郎・田中克己訳「シロコゴロフ 北方ツングースの社会構成」［東京　昭和16年］307ページ。なお 667－672 ページ参照。

この点を積極的に述べているのではないがなおS. M. Shirokogoroff : Northern Tungus migrations in the Far East (Goldi and their ethnical affinities) [Journal of the North China Branch of the Royal Asiatic Society, vol. LVII. Shanghai 1926] p. 161 註 82, p. 168及び附図を参照。

(5) S. M. Shirokogoroff. Study of the Tungus languages [Journal of the North-China Branch of the Royal Asiatic Society, vol. LV. Shanghai 1924] p. 263.

この論文は声音教育　八ノ二［東京　昭和16年］に野村正良氏によって紹介され

ている。

なおその分類はつぎのようなものである。

北方派

イェニセイ河，ヤクーツク州及びアムール州の諸方言

外バイカルの諸方言

興安嶺ツングース方言

ソロン方言

ビラル方言（クマル方言もともに）

オロキ方言

オロチ方言

ネギダル方言

樺太の馴鹿ツングース方言

その他

南方派

恐らく或南満洲方言に起源した満洲語文語

松花江，ウスリ河及び黒龍江のゴリド方言

オルチャ方言

ウデヘ方言

恐らく他に或未調査の諸方言

オロッコ族の由来についてのシュレンク，シロコゴロフの説は注1に挙げた石田氏の論文 348ページにも紹介されている。

(6) シュレンクの上掲書の第三巻 276ページ。

(7) 昭和20年10月附の私信によればその資料は戦災を無事まぬがれた由である。

(8) ヴエ・コトヴィチ　原田道治訳「ツングース諸方言の研究のための資料」［書香 15巻6号　大連　昭和18年］24ページ。

(9) W. Grube. Goldisch-deutsches Wörterverzeichniss mit vergleichender Berücksichtigung der übrigen tungusischen Dialekte (L. von Schrenck's Reisen und Forschungen im Amur-Lande, Anhang zum III. Bande. St. Petersburg 1900) によればオロチ方言のプロトジャコノフ採集の資料には ṕa,

ṕä の語形があり，上掲のシュミットの「オルチャ人の言語」の pja（a birch）の項にはオロチ方言の語形も同じであるとしてあるが，プロトジャコノフ採集資料をも吟味し，「オルチャ人の言語」よりはあとで発表された同氏の上掲「オロチ人の言語」にはこれらの語形は載っていない点からみて一応オロチ方言にはないとみられよう。なおプロトジャコノフ採集の資料の価値についてはシネイデルの上掲書の4，5ページ参照。またグルーベの上掲書に載る松花江河口のゴリド方言のマキシモヴィチ採集の資料に cállba の語形が見出されるがこの方言はいまゴリド方言から除いて考えることにする。

(10) グルーベの上掲書によればオロチ方言のプトロジャコノフ採集の資料にはmudu の語形があるが注9に述べたと同じことがこれについても言える。

(11) ただしシュレンクの上掲書（Bd.1 S.87）には犬を意味する語はマングン人（ここではオルチャ族を意味するとみられる），ゴリド族，サマギル族，海岸のオロチ族及び樺太のオロッコ族では，enda，inda であると記されている。

(12) オロチ方言のマルガリトフの資料（V.P.Margaritov. Ob oročach imperatorskoj gavani. Sanktpeterburg 1888）に gejky（štany）とあるが，シュミットの「オロチ人の言語」では xöiki に改められている点からみてその語形は考慮に入れない。

(13) グルーベの上掲書に載るゴリン河のサマギル族のゴリド方言のマキシモヴィチ採集の資料には ximma の語形があるが，ゴリン河サマギル族の方言はいまゴリド方言から除いて考えることにする。

(14) シュミットの「オロチ人の言語」に載るウデヘ方言の資料には hitömi（a daughter）という語形があり，ウデヘ方言にはかかる方言差を示す下位方言もあるとみられる。また上掲のオロチ方言のマルガリトフの資料に gitto（rebenok）とあるが，シュミットの「オロチ人の言語」では hitö に改められている点からみてその語形は考慮に入れない。

(15) グルーベの上掲書に載るマキシモヴィチ採集の資料には，ゴリド方言にximmu，オルチャ方言に xénó の語形がみられる。

(16) グルーベの上掲書に載るマキシモヴィチ採集の資料には，ゴリド方言にośkta，ośxa（Stern），オルチャ方言に ośkta（Stern）の語形もみられる。

(17)　シネイデルの上掲書の90ページ。

(18)　シュミットの「オロチ人の言語」に載るウデヘ方言の資料には ogdoho, ogdo, ordo（a coffin）という語がある。従ってウデヘ方言には ordo のような語形をもつ下位方言もあるとみられる。

(19)　シュミットの「オロチ人の言語」に載るウデヘ方言の資料には buača（an island）という語形があり，ウデヘ方言にはかかる方言差を示す下位方言もあるとみられる。

本稿は島村孝三郎先生の御厚意により東亜考古学会を通して文部省科学研究費補助金を受けた研究。

その後筆者は昭和24年9月北海道においてオロッコ人についてオロッコ方言を少しく調査することができたので，その資料のうちからここに使用した語の若干をここに附記する。ただしその形については音韻論的形を完全にうるまでにまだ至っていない。

inəŋi	ひるま，日（一日，二日の）	pʊŋd*a*	榛の木
n*a*mʊ	海	horɪ	二十
n*a*ː	地	goro	遠い
s*a*ŋ*a*	穴	nuriktə	髪
ŋɪnd*a*	犬	holdosko	棺
p*a*n*a*	たましい	t*a*ːgd*a*	白い
pəruː	ももひき	dʒolo	石
puttə	子供	dʒoːn	十
pokto	道		

なお ind*a*（犬）という形やここに述べた対応の例外をなすような hokto（道），hʊŋd*a*（榛の木）という形は得られなかった。　24.10.14.

Summary

Schrenck classified the Orokko as an Olcha tribe in Sakhalin on the basis of his observations of their speech. Afterwards Shirokogoroff included the Orokko dialect together with the Orochi dialect in the Northern Branch of Tungus and the Olcha dialect in the Southern Branch. However, neither of them has submitted the linguistic evidence for these views. The present author investigates the position of the Orokko dialect anew. Its vocabulary seems to be more similar to that of the Olcha dialect than to that of the Orochi dialect. In the four sound correspondences (p- ‖ h-, h- ‖ zero, -r- ‖ zero, -l- ‖ -g-) the Orokko dialect coincides with the Olcha dialect, and not with the Orochi dialect. Although the materials available are scanty, the Orokko dialect seems to be nearer to the Olcha than to the Orochi dialect, so far as the present investigation is concerned.

初出　民族学研究　14巻2号［昭和24年（1949年）12月］54－58ページ。

補記

文法，特に文法的要素の形態については，その後みることのできたペトローワ（Petrova, 1936）のオルチャ語の記述やツィンツィウス（Cincius, 1949）のオロチ語の記述をオロッコ語（池上　1956，1959）とくらべてみると，名詞の格語尾のうち，まず起点格（奪格）語尾はオロチ語 -duj，オルチャ語 -ǰiǰiであり，両者は異なっているが，オロッコ語は -duu（基本形は*-duki）であり，これはオロチ語と本来同じものであろう。（ツィ，136ページ，ペ，28ページ。）

一方，名詞縦走格語尾は，オロチ語 -li（～ -duli），オルチャ語 -ki に対して，オロッコ語は -ki であり，オルチャ語と同じものである。（ツィ，ペ，同上。）

また，「だれだれの……にするために」を意味する指定格の語尾は，オロチ語 -ja（～ -a），オルチャ語 -ǰū（～ -ǰʊ̄）であるが，オロッコ語は -doo（～ -ddoo ～ -dɵɵ ～ -ddɵɵ）であり，これはオロチ語のものとは異なり，オルチャ語と本来同じものであろう。(ツィ，144ページ，ペ，29ページ。)

人称代名詞第1人称複数形には，オロチ語では除外形 bu（きみ［たち］を除いてのわれわれ）と包括形 biti（きみ［たち］をふくめてのわれわれ）の二種があって両者が区別される。これに対して，オルチャ語には būə（または bū）（われわれ）だけがあり，除外形と包括形の区別がないが，ウイルタ語も buu（われわれ）だけで，その区別がないことはオルチャ語と同様である。(ツィ，139－141ページ。ペ，30，31，114ページ。)

動詞直説法の未来の語尾として，オルチャ語には -rila があるが，オロチ語にはみえない。しかし，オロッコ語には -ri-la があり，オルチャ語と一致する。(ペ，56，61ページ。)

オロチ語の動詞第2人称命令形は動詞語幹に語尾 -ɣa（またはその交替形）が接尾している。これに対して，オルチャ語の第2人称現在命令形は語尾 -ru（またはその交替形）が接尾している。オロッコ語の（第2人称現在）命令形の語尾はやはり -ru（基本形）であり，オルチャ語と一致する。(ツィ，153，154ページ。ペ，57，62ページ。)

動詞語幹に接尾して「なになにするために」の意味を表わすのに，オロチ語は -laa という語尾をつかうが，オルチャ語にはそのような語尾はみられず，-bda（～ -bdə）がつかわれる。(ツィ，156ページ。ペ，58，63ページ。) オロッコ語でも，オルチャ語と同様，オロチ語のような語尾はみられず，-bu-ddoo（～ -bu-ddɵɵ）がつかわれる。-bu はオロッコ語動詞のV類の語幹に接尾する名詞語幹形成接尾辞であり，-ddoo は上述の名詞指定格語尾である。オルチャ語とオロッコ語は，オロチ語の上記のような語尾をつかわない点で一致するが，さらに，オルチャ語のその語尾の少くともその b はオロッコ語のその -bu と同じものであろう。

しかし，「……したあいだに」を意味する動詞語尾として，オロチ語には -ŋasa があるが，オルチャ語の上記の記述にはこのような語尾はみられない。しかし，オロッコ語には -ŋassee があり，これはオロチ語の上述の語尾と同じものをふくむものであろう。(ツィ，156ページ。)

上にみたように，オロッコ語は，オロチ語と一致し，オルチャ語と異なる点もあるが，オロチ語よりむしろオルチャ語に一致する点がいくつもみられる。

他方，オロッコ語には，条件を表す動詞語尾 -i（本来は*-ki）があるが，オロチ語，オルチャ語にはともにこれがみられず，オロッコ語と異なる。

引用書

Petrova, T. I., 1936. Ul'čskij dialekt nanajskogo jazyka, Moskva-Leningrad. Cincius, V. I., 1949. Očerk morfologii oročskogo jazyka, Učenye Zapiski LGU, t. 98, Serija vostokovedčeskikh nauk, vyp. 1.

池上二良，1956，1959. The substantive inflection of Orok,『言語研究』30, The verb inflection of Orok,『国語研究』（国学院大学国語研究会）9.（本書収載）

追記

233ページに引用したペ・オ・ピリスドスキーとある人名は，ぺはべの誤植で，ポーランドのブロニスワフ・O・ピウスツキ（Bronislav O. Pilsudki）のことである。本書所収「ウイルタ語・オイチャ語研究におけるB.ピウスツキ」参照。

235ページにおけるオロッコ kutigû（小刀）と他方言の単語との比較は，ウイルタ方言には kučee（小刀）の語も認められるので，そこに挙げた意味が失われる。

ウイルタ語の南方言と北方言の相違点

Differences between the Southern and Northern Dialects of Uilta

1　まえがき

ウイルタ語は，サハリン（カラフト）の少数民族・ウイルタ族の言語である。この言語は，ツングース・満洲諸語の一つであるが，これらの言語は，同じ一つの言語から分かれたものとみられる。

ウイルタ人は，第二次大戦時まで，日本領の南カラフトでは敷香（ポロナイスク）の近郊のオタスのほか，タライカ湾沿岸，タライカ湖，ポロナイ川およびこれらに入る川の沿岸などに居住していた。なお，終戦後この地方のウイルタの成年男子の多くが，日本軍に加担したとして逮捕され，服役のためシベリアに送られ，その地で死亡した者が少なくない。このことは，この少数民族の存続に重大な影響を与える事件となった。また，戦後，ウイルタの一部（少なくとも20名）の人びとは北海道（の網走その他）へ移住した。今日では，ウイルタの多くがポロナイスクの市街地やユジヌイ島（もとの佐知）およびポロナイスクに近接する地域に居住する。ポロナイスク区のウイルタの人口は1990年173人である。かれらはロシア語も話し，その多くはすでにロシア語だけを話す。かれらが話すウイルタ語は，かつて地方により方言差もあったようである。（たとえば，後述の2.4の項，4の最後の条，池上1989a，81を参照）。しかし，総括して南方言とよぶことにする。

一方，戦前からすでにロシア領であった北カラフトでは，ウイルタ人はかつて南のナビリ入江，ノグリキからダーギ，ワール，ガラマイなど，さらに北のピリトゥン入江までの地方に居住し，あるいはその地域を移動した。今日では，その多くはワールに居住している。ワールのウイルタの人口は127人ないし144人である。しかし，また一部はノグリキの市街地や北のオハ地方にも居住する。これらのウイルタ人の話すウイルタ語も地方により方言に分かれていたであろうが，全体を北方言とよぶことにする。

南・北方言の話し手たちはそれぞれ，他方の方言で話されるのを理解できるようであり，両方言の差異は異なる言語間におけるほどの大きな差異ではない。しかし，両方言は異なる点もあり，本稿ではこの二つの方言の相違点についてみたい。本稿が基づくウイルタ語資料は，北海道に移住したウイルタについての筆者のこれまでの南方言調査において，および1990年から3年間おこなわれた文部省科学研究費補助金の交付をうけた「サハリンにおける少数民族の言語に関する調査研究」（代表　村崎恭子教授）における北方言調査において，下記の被調査者からえたものである。

南方言

故佐藤チヨ（Napka）さん　1910年ごろ留久玉（ルクタマ）に生まれ，のち多蘭（タラン）に移り，1947年北海道に移住した。1985年死去された。以下でNと略す。

故中川和四郎（Jəuriŋənu）さん　1914年佐知（サチ）に生まれ，オタスに居住した。1955年北海道に移住し，1988年死去された。以下でJと略す。

北方言

セミョーノワ・オリガ・ニコラーエヴナ（Семенова Ольга Николаевна）さん　1910年ガラマイ川沿岸の地に生まれ，今はワールに住む。以下でOと略す。

故ミヘーエワ・マリーヤ・ステパーノヴナ（Михеева Мария Степановна）さん　1912年ノグリキ近くのティミ川河口の地に生まれ，のちワールに移った。1993年死去された。以下でMと略す。

故セミョーノワ・アンナ・ワシーリエヴナ（Семенова Анна Васильевна）さん　1919年ナビリに生まれた。のちネクラソフカに住んだ。1992年死去された。以下でAと略す。

被調査者は，上記のようにともに1910年代の生まれで，同世代と言えよう。なお，補足的に，やはりウイルタのイ・ヤ・フェジャーエワ（Федяева Ирина Яковлевна）さん（1940年ワール生まれ），エ・ア・ビービコワ（Бибикова Елена Алексеевна）さん（1940年ダーギの近くに生まれた）の教示によった。以下でそれぞれF，Bと略す。ただし，上記の老年の被調査者にくらべて，これらの年層の人びとは，ロシア語の影響も強いだろうし，その継承するウイルタ語に種種の点で変化があったろう。

調査の際大変お世話になったこれらの被調査者に深く感謝の意を表すとともに，亡くなられたかたがたの御冥福を祈りたい。

今日のウイルタ語は，上に記したように，ポロナイスクを中心とする地方の南方言とワールを中心とする地方の北方言の二つの方言に分けられる。しかし，かつては旧日本領の地方から北の地方へ，ウイルタ語の小地域ごとの方言がいくつも分布していたこともありうる。そうした方言の状態において，南の地方の方言と北の地方の方言の顕著な境界がどこかにあったか，あったならばどのあたりにあったかなどの問題は，あきらかになっていない。

2 音　　韻

両方言は，ともに，母音音素a, ə, o, ɵ, u, i, e, 子音音素p, b, t, d, k, g, m, n, ɲ, ŋ, l, r, w, s, j, x, č, ǰという同じ音素目録をもつとみられるが，音韻体系の細部においては異なる点もある。

1．母音音素間における唇音と軟口蓋音の子音音素の連続について，南方言では通常，軟口蓋音・唇音の順の連続であり，これがこの方言の一般的な型である。ただし，まれには人名のNapkaのような逆の順の例もある。これに対して，北方言では，軟口蓋音・唇音の順のこともあるが，逆の順序の連続が広くみられる。例，

南　ǰakpu‘8’ ‖ 北　ǰakpu O, ǰapku M‘同’

南　siikpisi-ni‘かれが咳をする’ ‖ 北　siipkisi-ni O‘同’

南　tokpo‘いと，ひも’ ‖ 北　tokpo OM, topko F‘同’

南　tukpə‘くぎ’‖北　tupkə O‘同’

南　pəgbirə‘スキーのつえ’‖北　pəbgirə MA‘同’

南　sugbu‘さかなの皮’‖北　subgu O‘同’

南　oŋbee-ni‘かれが忘れる’‖北　oŋbee-ni OM, omgee-ni O‘同’

南　aŋma‘口’‖北　aŋma M, amŋa MO‘同’

ただし，これは調音点に関する子音音素の順序についてのことであり，oŋbee-ni‖omgee-ni の例にもみられるように，調音の仕方に関しての鼻音・閉鎖音の順序は両方言間で等しい。

2. いくつかの語例においては，南方言の母音音素間の x に，北方言で k（発音は［kx］）が対応する。北方言の k を有する形の方が一般に古いだろう。

南　duxu‘家’‖北　duku OM‘同’

南　laxa‘近い’‖北　laka OM‘同’

南　burixə‘弓’‖北　burikə M（ただし burikkə O）‘同’

3. 北方言の母音音素間の g が，南方言で Ø（ゼロ）に対応する語例がある。北方言の g を有する形が古いとみられる。

南　kotoo‘ゆび’‖北　kotogo O, kotoo OM‘同’

南　əərə‘ます(魚)’‖北　əgərə O‘同’

南　saari‘黒い’‖北　sagari OM‘同’

なお，muigi‘へび’の語では，南・北方言ともに g を保っている。

4. 南方言には，iga, igə N に ee J が対応する語例があるが，この違いは南方言のなかの方言差であろう。iga, igə が古い形である。北方言には，語により，やはり ee が対応する例もあるが，このほかに iga に対して aa が，igə に対して əə が現れて南方言の上記の形と異なる形をもつ語例がある。

南　koliga N‘虫’‖北　koliga M, kolee O‘同’

南　kučigə N‘小刀’‖北　kučəə M‘同’

南　unigəri N, uneeri J‘星’‖北　uŋəəri OM‘同’

南　xuriga NJ, xuree J‘鼻’‖北　xuriga M, xuraa O‘同’

なお，əigə-ni‘かれの姉’の語では，南・北方言ともに g を保っている。

3 文　法

北方言が南方言と文法上異なるいくつかの点を挙げる。

1. 南方言では，末尾に母音音素を一つだけもつ動詞語幹に，不完了動名詞語尾 -ri がつく場合，両者が融合（代償重音化）をおこして合体した形となるが，北方言では，このような融合形も使われるが，このほかに，その動詞語幹に上記の動名詞語尾が接着しただけで両者が融合していない語形も使われる。このような語形は，南方言には通常みられない。例，南方言　ŋənnee-ni‘かれが行く’，北方言　ŋənnee-ni, ŋənəri-ni（ŋənə-‘行く’が動詞語幹，-ri は不完了動名詞語尾，ŋənnee は ŋənə- と -ri の融合形，-ni は第３人称語尾‘かれが’/南方言　sinǰee-ni‘かれが来る’，北方言　sinǰee-ni, sindari-ni（sinda-‘来る’が動詞語幹，sinǰee は sinda- と -ri の融合形）。しかし，北方言において，この融合形と接着形は，意味がやや異なるようであり，イ・ヤ・フェジャーエワは，前者は確定的，後者は不確定的であると言い，エ・ア・ビービコワは，前者は現在形，後者は未来形であるとする。例　ŋənnee-ni‘かれが行く’，ŋənəri-ni‘かれが行くだろう’，sinǰee-ni‘かれが来る’，sindari-ni‘かれが来るだろう’。

2. 北方言には，-bukki という動詞語尾がある（Петрова 1967　参照。ただしペトローワは -buki と表記する）。この語尾のはじめの子音音素は，n のような有声子音音素におわる動詞語幹につく場合は b であるが，動名詞不完了形となるとき -si という語尾が接尾するような動詞語幹につく場合は p となり，末尾に母音音素を二つもつ動詞語幹につく場合は w となる。末尾に母音音素をひとつだけもつ動詞語幹のあとにこの動詞語尾がくる場合には，両者の間に代償重音化がおき，二つは融合している。例，

iwambukkil M（動詞語幹は iwan-‘（火を）たく’。b のまえで n が m となる。）［池上　1993a, 75］

pulipukki F（動詞語幹は puli-‘あるいて行く’。この動詞語幹には -si がつく。）

waawukki B（動詞語幹は waa-‘（さかなを）とる’，uuwokki F（動詞語幹

は uu-‘乗る’。o の母音についてはなお検討を要する。)

ŋənnəukki B F (動詞語幹は ŋənə-‘行く’。融合形。)

xupiddukki biččiči M (動詞語幹は xupidu-‘くままつりで遊戯する’。融合形。) [池上　1993a, 75]

wəədəptukki A (動詞語幹は wəədəp-‘いなくなる’。p におわる動詞語幹には-tu という音節がつく。融合形。) [池上　1993a, 79]

この動詞語尾-bukki には，動作主体が複数であることを表す-l が接尾することもある。-bukki のついた動詞形は，多くの場合，ある行動が習慣的にくりかえしおこることを表し，また文を終結するはたらきをもつ。また，あとに bičči (あった) をともなうことによって，その行動が過去におきたことを表す。

この動詞語尾は，南方言には普通みられないようである。

3. 南方言における (何なにだ，何なにだったのような) 名詞を述語とする構文について，筆者が被調査者 N から採取した例文を示す。なお，ここにいう名詞の意味には実詞と形容詞を合わせてふくめている。実詞の語幹の類については Ikegami (1956) (本書にも収載) 参照。

(1) 語幹が 1. 類に属する (母音音素に終る) 実詞

bii lučabi.	ぼくはロシア人だ。	buu lučapu.	ぼくらはロシア人だ。
sii lučasi.	きみはロシア人だ。	suu lučasu.	きみらはロシア人だ。
tari nari luča.	その人はロシア人だ。	tari narisal lučal.	その人らはロシア人だ。

(2) 語幹が 0.1 類に属する実詞

bii giləəbi. bii giləkki.	ぼくはニブフ人だ。	buu giləəpu.	ぼくらはニブフ人だ。
sii giləəsi.	きみはニブフ人だ。	suu giləəsu.	きみらはニブフ人だ。
tari nari giləə.	その人はニブフ人だ。	tari narisal giləəl.	その人らはニブフ人だ。

(3) 語幹が 0.2 類に属する実詞

bii xusənneepi.　　　buu xusənneepu.

ぼくは男子だ。　ぼくらは男子だ。

sii xusənneesi.　きみは男子だ。　suu xusənneesu.　きみらは男子だ。

tari nari xusənnee.　その人は男子だ。　tari narisal xusənneel.　その人らは男子だ。

(4) 語幹が2.2類に属する（子音音素nに終る）実詞

bii samambi.　わたしは巫者だ。　buu samappu.　わしらは巫者だ。

sii samačči.　あなたは巫者だ。　suu samačču.　あなたらは巫者だ。

tari nari sama.　その人は巫者だ。　tari narisal samal.　その人らは巫者だ。

(5)

bii saldaa biččimbi.　おれは軍人だった。　bii saldaa(l) biččipu.　おれたちは軍人だった。

sii saldaa biččisi.　きみは軍人だった。　suu saldaa(l) biččisu.　きみらは軍人だった。

tari nari saldaa bičči.　その人は軍人だった。　tari narisal saldaa(l) biččil.　その人らは軍人だった。

tari narisal saldaal bičči.　同上

(6) 語幹が実詞に用いられると1.類に属する（母音音素に終る）形容詞

bii ərkəbi.　おれはおそい。　buu ərkəpu.　おれたちはおそい。

sii ərkəsi.　おまえはおそい。　suu ərkəsu.　おまえらはおそい。

tari nari ərkə.　その人はおそい。　tari narisal ərkəl.　その人らはおそい。

(7) 語幹が実詞に用いられると0.1類に属する形容詞

bii ugdəəbi. bii ugdəkki.　わたしは弱い。　buu ugdəəpu.　わたしらは弱い。

sii ugdəəsi.　おまえは弱い。　suu ugdəəsu.　おまえらは弱い。

tari nari ugdəə.　その人は弱い。　tari narisal ugdəə(l).　その人らは弱い。

(8) 語幹が実詞に用いられると2.1類に属する（子音音素1に終る）形容詞

bii mastaa kusalbi.
ぼくは大変はやい。

buu mastaa kusalpu.
ぼくらは大変はやい。

sii mastaa kusalči.
きみは大変はやい。

suu mastaa kusalču.
きみらは大変はやい。

tari nari mastaa kusal.
その人は大変はやい。

tari narisal mastaa kusal.
その人らは大変はやい。

(9)

bii kusuttu biččimbi.
ぼくは力があった。

buu kusuttu biččipu.
ぼくらは力があった。

sii kusuttu biččisi.
きみは力があった。

suu kusuttu biččisu.
きみらは力があった。

tari nari kusuttu bičči.
その人は力があった。

tari narisal kusuttu(1) bičči.
その人らは力があった。

(10)

bii uilta. ぼくはウイルタ人だ。

bii purigə. おれは若い。

buu saldaa bičči. われわれは軍人だった。

(11)

bii saldaa əsiwi bee.
ぼくは軍人でない。

buu saldaa əsipu bee.
ぼくらは軍人でない。

sii saldaa əsisi bee.
きみは軍人でない。

suu saldaa əsisu bee.
きみらは軍人でない。

tari nari saldaa əsi bee.
その人は軍人でない。

tari naril saldaal əsi bee (1).
その人らは軍人でない。

(12)

bii saldaa əččimbi bee.
ぼくは軍人でなかった。

buu saldaa əččipu bee.
ぼくらは軍人でなかった。

sii saldaa əččisi bee.
きみは軍人でなかった。

suu saldaa əččisu bee.
きみらは軍人でなかった。

tari nari saldaa əčči bee.　　tari narisal saldaal əčči beel.

その人は軍人でなかった。　　その人らは軍人でなかった。

tari nari saldaa əččini bee.　同上　　tari narisal saldaal əččiči bee.　同上

(13)

bii (または buu, sii, suu, tari nari, tari narisal) saldaa əsi bee.

ぼく(または，ぼくら，きみ，きみら，その人，その人ら)は軍人でない。

(5)（11）―（13）には実詞主格形があらわれる。(9) には形容詞のそれぞれの語形があらわれる。(10) には実詞主格形または形容詞の語形があらわれる。

上掲の例文からみると，南方言において名詞を述語とする構文は，現在の事実を表すもの（1－4，6－8）と過去の事実を表すもの（5，9）が異なる構造をもつ。まず，後者では，連辞（copula）の役割をするものとしてその名詞のあとに，動詞語幹 bi-‘ある’の動名詞完了形 bičči(n-)‘あった’がおかれるが，前者では，名詞のあとに連辞の役割をするものを欠く。換言すれば，その位置にØ（ゼロ）が立つ。さらに，どちらの構造においても，主語が（これは省略されることもあるが），第1，2人称単，複数のいずれかであると，文の末尾に人称語尾をおく。すなわち，人称語尾が，過去の事実を表す構造では，名詞のあとの bičči に接尾し，現在の事実を表す構造では，名詞に直接，接尾する。この人称語尾は，述語人称語尾であり，所属人称語尾ではない。しかし，第3人称では，人称語尾を欠く。ただし，第3人称複数では普通，複数接尾辞 -l が接尾する。

その人称語尾は，第1人称単数 -bi ～ -pi，複数 -pu，第2人称単数 -si ～ -či，複数 -su ～ -ču である。第1人称単数の -pi は，0.2 類の名詞語幹に接尾する形（例3参照）。-bi はその他の名詞語幹および bičči(n-)に接尾する形。また 0.1 類の名詞語幹は，これに -bi がついた形のほかに，語幹が人称語尾と融合して全体が -Vkki（V は母音音素）という形をとることもある（例2，7参照）。bičči (n-)は，-bi が接尾すると biččim- となり，全体は biččimbi となる（例5，9参照）。第2人称の -či，-ču は 2.類名詞語幹に接尾する形（例4，8参照），-si，-su はその他の名詞語幹および bičči に接尾する形。なお，2.2 類の名詞語幹は，その基本形の末尾の n がそのあとに人称語尾 -bi がつくと m となり，人称語尾 -pu がつくと p となり，人称語尾 -či，-ču がつくと č となる（例 4 参照）。(以上に類名を数字で示した名詞語幹の各類については Ikegami 1956 を参照。)

ただし，このほかに，人称語尾をつけない構文もある（10）。

上述の構文は肯定文であるが，否定文は，否定動詞（語幹は ə-）と動詞語幹 bi- の動名詞不完了形 bee とから成る否定構造をもつ。人称語尾は，現在の事実を表す構造（11）では，その否定動詞が動名詞不完了形 əsi となり，これが人称語尾として第 1 人称の単数の -wi，複数の -pu，第 2 人称の単数の -si，複数の -su をとるが，第 3 人称語尾を欠く。過去の事実を表す構造（12）には，2 種あるとみられ，第 1 の構造では，否定動詞が動名詞完了形 əčči(n-) となり，これが人称語尾として第 1 人称の単数の -bi，複数の -pu，第 2 人称の単数の -si，複数の -su をとり，第 3 人称語尾は欠く。第 2 の構造では，その否定動詞の同じ形に第 1，2 人称では第 1 構造と同じ人称語尾がつき，さらに第 3 人称でも単数の -ni，複数の -či が接尾する。なお，これらの構造のなかの否定動詞の動名詞完了形の əčči(n-) は，第 1 人称単数の -bi が接尾すると əččim- となり，他の人称語尾が接尾すると əčči- となる。なお，否定文にも，このほかに，人称語尾をつけない構文もある（13）。

過去の事実を表す第 2 構造の否定文を除く上述の名詞述語構文の人称語尾について，第 3 人称で語尾を欠く点は，（動名詞の機能を兼有しない）定動詞における人称語尾の接尾と軌を一にし，その接尾法は，動名詞の人称語尾の接尾法と異なり，そのような定動詞の人称語尾の接尾法と同類とみなされよう［Ikegami 1959, 37f., 45f.; 1985, 88 Uilta, Class II（本書にも収載）］。この点が，南方言の名詞述語構文の注意すべき点である。ただし，過去の事実を表す第 2 構造の否定文の名詞述語構文における否定動詞の動名詞完了形は，第 3 人称語尾も接尾し，通常の動名詞の人称語尾の接尾法である。

一方，北方言のテキスト資料［池上 1993a］のなかから名詞述語構文の例を引用する。

bii bakkaa suu əččisu nari bii. A わしもあんたらと同じ人間だ。(79 ページ)

ėto pervyj mamaŋuni bičči. O（はじめの2語はロシア語）

これは最初にめとったかれのつれあいであった。（86ページ）

amičči ənini lilak mama biččini. O かれらの父の母がリラクばあさんであった。（90ページ）

tari oŋdo biččini. A それは魔ものであった。（78ページ）

北方言の名詞述語構文（肯定文）のこれらの例文をみると，連辞の役割をする動詞語幹 bi-の動名詞完了形 bičči が第3人称の主語に対して第3人称語尾を欠いている例のほかに，第3人称語尾-ni をとって biččini となっている例がある点が注意される。また，動詞 bi-の動名詞不完了形 bii が連辞の役割をつとめ，しかも第1人称単数の主語に対して第1人称単数の人称語尾をとっていない例がある。

4. 第1・2人称単・複数人代名詞をふくみ，これが所有者を表す所有構造について，たとえば「わたくしの手」の意味を南方言では mini ŋaalabi と言うのに対して，北方言では bii ŋaalabi と言う。南方言では，こうは言わないようである。mini（末尾の i はときに脱落する）は，南方言における第1人称単数人代名詞の属格（所有格）である（これをロシアの研究者はロシア語文法にならって物主代名詞とよんでいる）。bii はウイルタ語の第1人称単数人代名詞の主格であるが，北方言で所有構造において所有者を表すのにもつかわれている。ŋaala は手を意味し，-bi はこの ŋaala（手）がわたくしに所属することを表す第1人称単数所属語尾である。上述のように人代名詞が所有者を表す所有構造において，その人代名詞が，南方言では属格形，北方言では主格形であり，両方言はこの点に違いがある。ただし，両方言の所有構造で，mini や bii のような人代名詞は省かれることも多い。しかし，所属人称語尾（または自分のを表す反照語尾）は義務的に接尾し，さらにこの語尾のまえに譲渡可能性の接尾辞が文脈に応じて義務的に入る。所属人称語尾は，これが接尾する名詞語幹に応じて交替形がつかわれ，またその名詞語幹の末尾の子音音素も交替する。以下に例を示す。

南方言（N）

(1) 語幹が1.1類に属する（子音音素＋母音音素に終る）実詞

mini ŋaalabi	ぼくの手	munu ŋaalapu	ぼくらの手
sini ŋaalasi	きみの手	sunu ŋaalasu	きみらの手
tari nari ŋaalani	その人の手	tari narisal ŋaalači	その人らの手

(2) 語幹が1.2類に属する（母音音素＋母音音素に終る）実詞

mini nəuwi	ぼくの弟（妹）	munu nəupu	ぼくらの弟（妹）
sini nəusi	きみの弟（妹）	sunu nəusu	きみらの弟（妹）
tari nari nəuni	その人の弟（妹）	tari narisal nəuči	その人らの弟（妹）

(3) 語幹が0.2類に属する実詞

mini aanǰeepi	ぼくの右	munu aanǰeepu	ぼくらの右
sini aanǰeesi	きみの右	sunu aanǰeesu	きみらの右
tari nari aanǰeeni	その人の右	tari narisal aanǰeeči	その人らの右

(4) 語幹が2.1類に属する（子音音素1に終る）実詞

mini isalbi	ぼくの目	munu isalpu	ぼくの目
sini isalči	きみの目	sunu isalču	きみの目
tari nari isalli（または isalni）その人の目		tari narisal isalči	その人らの目

(5) 語幹が2.2　類に属する（子音音素nに終る）実詞

mini aapumbi	ぼくの帽子	munu aapuppu	ぼくらの帽子
sini aapučči	きみの帽子	sunu aapučču	きみらの帽子
tari nari aapuni	その人の帽子	tari narisal aapučči	その人らの帽子

(6) 語幹が0.3類に属する実詞

mini aagbi	ぼくの兄	munu aakpu	ぼくらの兄
sini aakči	きみの兄	sunu aakču	きみらの兄
tari nari aaŋni	その人の兄	tari narisal aakči	その人らの兄

北方言（M）

(1) 語幹が子音音素＋母音音素に終る実詞

bii ŋaalabi	ぼくの手	buu ŋaalapu	ぼくらの手
sii ŋaalasi	きみの手	suu ŋaalasu	きみらの手
tari ŋaalani	それ（その人）の手	tari narisal ŋaalači	その人らの手

(2) 語幹が子音音素 l に終る実詞

bii aapumbi	ぼくの帽子	buu aapuppu	ぼくらの帽子
sii aapučči	きみの帽子	suu aapusu	きみらの帽子
tari aapuni	それ(その人)の帽子	tari narisal aapučči	その人らの帽子

なお，ウイルタ語においては，第3人称単数・複数人代名詞の役を，tari‘それ’などの指示代名詞がするか，またはそれが指示形容詞として前置されたnari‘人’などの名詞，すなわちtari nari‘その人’のような名詞句がするか，またはnoo-ni，noo-čiのような，この役にしかつかわれないが語構造が名詞的な語がつとめている。ウイルタ語の名詞は属格形がないが，指示代名詞やnooni，noočiも属格がなく，この点，第1・2人称人代名詞と異なる。したがって，それらの語・句が所有者を表す所有構造においては，一般の名詞が所有者を表す所有構造におけると同様に，南・北両方言ともに，所有者を表す語が格語尾のつかない形，つまり主格形をとる。そこで，このような所有構造には，上述の南・北方言の相違は生じないのである。

4 語　　彙

南・北方言について，基礎的な単語，260語あまりについて以下にみる。これらの単語は，『アジア・アフリカ言語調査票　上・下』(東京外国語大学アジア・アフリカ言語文化研究所　1966，1967) の第1表 (A・B) の調査項目によって調査したものである。南方言についての調査は佐藤チヨさん (N) によったが，その調査資料は，池上 (1980) にすでに収載されているので，主としてこれによる。北方言についての調査は，おもにO.N.セミョーノワさん (O) とM.S.ミヘーエワさん (M) によった。

北方言の被調査者への各調査項目の質問はロシア語による。そのロシア語は，上記の言語調査票の下巻に載るロシア語の各単語を使用するが，いくつかの項目については別のロシア語単語をつかい，これは〔　〕に入れてある。

両方言の単語を，質問に使った日本語とロシア語の単語とともに，以下の表に掲げる。動詞については動名詞不完了形をあげ，動名詞完了形を (　) に入れて示す。動詞形についている-niは第3人称語尾である。

各項目には通し番号をふる。なお，（　）内の番号は上記の調査票における番号である。

	日本語	佐藤チヨ（Napka）	ロシア語	М.С.Михеева	О.Н.Семенова
1(1)	あたま(頭)	ǰili	голова	ǰili	ǰili
2(2)	かみのけ(髪の毛)	niruktə, K nuriktə	волос	niruktə	nuriktə
3(3)	ひたい(額)	pəəjə	лоб		pəəjə
4(4)	まゆげ(眉毛)	xoppokto	бровь		xoppokto
5(5)	め(目)	isal	глаз	isal	isal
6(6)	なみだ(涙)	indumuska	слеза		indumaska, isal mɵɵni
7(7)	みみ(耳)	seen	ухо	seen	seen
8(8)	はな(鼻)	xuriga	нос	xuriga	xuraa
9(9)	くち(口)	aŋma	рот	aŋma, amŋa	amŋa
10(10)	くちびる(唇)	pəmu	губа		pəmu
11(11)	した(舌)	sinu	язык		sinu
12(12)	つば(唾)	tupi	слюна		tupi
13(13)	は(歯)	kərəktɵ	зуб	iktə	iktə
14(14)	あご(顎)	geega	подбородок		geega
15(15)	ほお(頬)	pulči	щека		dərə
16(16)	ひげ	gudakta	усы		gudakta
17(17)	かお(顔)	dərəl	лицо		dərəl
18(18)	くび(頸)	moŋo	шея		koǰi
19(19)	のど(喉)〔喉頭〕	xoombo	горло		xoombo
20(19)	のど〔咽頭〕	bilda	〔глотка〕		bilda
21(20)	かた(肩)	muirə	плечо		muirə
22(21)	せなか(背中)	atta	спина		atta

23(22) こし(腰)〔上部〕	darama	поясница		darama
24(22)　〔下部〕	dəwə			dəwə
25(23) しり(尻)	ura	зад		ura
26(24) むね(胸)	tuŋə	грудь		tuŋə
27(25) ちぶさ(乳房)	kɵɵ	грудь		kɵɵgɵ
28(26) おなか，はら	bokko	живот		bokko
29(27) へそ	xunu	пут		xunu
30(30) て(手) (28) うで(腕)	ŋaala, ŋaali	рука	ŋaala	ŋaala
31(29) ひじ(肱)	uitə	локоть		uitə
32(31) ゆび(指)	kotoo	палец	kotoo	kotoo, kotogo
33(32) つめ(人の爪・動物の爪)	xosikta	ноготь		xosikta
34(33) あし(足，脚)	bəgǰi	нога	bəgǰi	bəgǰi
35(35) かんぞう(肝臓)	paaxa	печень		paaxa
36(36) しんぞう(心臓)	meewa	сердце		meewa
37(38) ひふ(皮膚)	xərəktə	кожа	xərəktə	xərəktə
38(39) あせ(汗)	ǰilata	пот		ǰilata
39(40) あか(垢)	naŋisa	грязь	naŋisa	naŋisa
40(42) け(毛，人間の体毛)	sinakta	волосы	sinakta	sinakta
41(44) ち(血)	səəksə	кровь	səəksə	səəksə
42(45) ほね(骨)	girapsa	кость	girapsa	girapsa
43(46) にく(肉)	ulisə	мясо	ulisə	ulisə
(60)	(人体の肉，食料としての肉)		(人体の肉，食料としての肉)	
44(47) からだ(体)	bəjə	тело		bəjə
45(48) びょうき(病気)	ənuu	болезнь	ənuu	ənuu
46(49) きず(傷)	pujə	рана		pujə
47(50) くすり(薬)	okto	лекарство	okto	okto

48(51) こめ(米)	buda	рис		buda
49(52) こな(粉)	upa	порошок		upa
50(53) しお(塩)	dausu	соль	dausu	dausu
51(54) あぶら(油)	ilda	масло	ilda	ilda
52(55) さけ(酒)	arakki	〔водка〕	arakki	arakki
53(56) タバコ	saŋna	табак	saŋna	saŋna
54(58) におい(匂)	puun	запах		puun
55(59) たべもの(食物)	dəppi	пища	dəppi	dəppi
56(61) たまご(卵)	ŋojokko(鳥の卵)	яйцо	ŋojokko	ŋojokko
57(63) とり(鳥)	gasa	птица	gasa	gasa
58(64) つばさ(翼)	xasa	крыло		xasa
59 はね(羽)〔一本一本の〕	dəktəktə	перо		dəktəktə
60(66) す(巣)	omo	гнездо	omo	
61(68) つの(角)	xujə	рог	xujə	
62(69) うし(牛)	ixa	корова	ixa	
63(70) こがたな(小刀)	kučigə	нож, ножик	kučəə	
64(71) かたな(刀)	lauta	меч	lauta	lauta
65(72) は(刃)	dəjə	лезвие	dəjə MB	
66(73) ぼう(棒)	moo	палка		moo
67(74) ゆみ(弓)	burixə	лук	burikə	burikkə
68(75) や(矢)	ləkkə	стрела		ləkkə
69(76) やり(槍)	gida	копье		gida
70(77) いと(糸)	kupə, tokpo	нитка	kupə, tokpo	kupə, tokpo
71(78) はり(針)	kitaa	игла		kitaa
72(79) きもの(着物), いふく(衣服)	tətuwə	одежда	tətuwə	bagduxi
73(80) かみ(紙)	xausal(i)	бумага	xausali	xausali
74(81) もの(物)	ojosko	вещь	ojosko	ojosko
75(82) へび(蛇)	muigi	змея		muigi

76(83) むし(虫)	koliga	червяк	koliga	kolee
77(84) はえ(蝿)	ǰiiluwə, ǰiiləə	муха		ǰiiləə
78(85) か(蚊)	nalmakta	комар		nalmakta
79(86) のみ(蚤)	sura	блоха		pəččəxi
80(87) しらみ(虱)	čiktə	вошь		čiktə
81(88) あり(蟻)	siruktə	муравей		siruktə
82(89) さかな(魚)	suŋdatta	рыба	sundatta	sundatta
83(90) かい(貝)	kəjuwə	раковина	kəjuwə	
84(93) あみ(網)	aduli	сеть		aduli
85(94) いぬ(犬)	ŋinda	собака	ŋinda	ŋinda
86(95) つな(綱)	madurukku	канат		madurukku
87(98) うま(馬)	muri	лошадь		muri
88(100) しっぽ(尻尾), お(尾)	xudu(けものの尾)	хвост		xudu(牛などの)
89(103) ふくろ(袋)	puutaa	мешок		puutaa
90(105) かま(釜)	ənuwə	котел	ənuwə	ənugə
91(110) まど(窓)	paawa	окно		paawa
92(111) とびら(扉)	utə	дверь	utə	utə
93(112) いえ(家), じゅうきょ(住居)	duxu	дом	duku	duku
94(114) ふね(船)	ugda(丸木舟)	〔лодка〕	ugda	ugda
95(115) いど(井戸)	məəluutu	колодец		muuluutu
96(117) かね(金), きんせん(金銭)	gumas(ik)ka	деньги	gumaaska	gumaaska
97(118) き(木)	moo	дерево	moo	moo
98(121) くさ(草)	orokto	трава	pəiktə	pəiktə
99(124) は(葉)	xamdatta	лист	xamdatta	xamdatta
100(125) はな(花)	sillaa	цветок	sillaa	
101(126) み(実)	bootoo(木の実) bookto(はい松の実)	орех	bookto	bookto

102(132)みち(道)	pokto	путь, дорога	pokto	pokto
103(135)かわ(川)	uni	река	uni	uni
104(136)やま(山)	xurigə	гора	xurigə	xurigə
105(143)みず(水)	məə	вода	muu	muu
106(144)こおり(氷)	duwə	лед	duwə	
107(145)いし(石)	ǰolo	камень	ǰolo	ǰolo
108(146)つち(土)	naa	почва	naa	naa
109(151)ひ(火)	tawa	огонь	tawa	tawa
110(152)かぜ(風)	xədu	ветер	xədu	xədu
111(153)くも(雲)	təwəskə	облако	təwəskə	təwəskə
112(155)あめ(雨)	tugdə	дождь	tugdə	tugdə
113(157)そら(空)	boo	небо		naŋna
114(159)たいよう(太陽)	suun	солнце	suunə	suun, suunə
115(160) (166) つき(月)	bee(天体の月, (年月の月)	луна месяц	bee	bee
116(162)ほし(星)	unigəri, xosikta	звезда	uɲəəri	uɲəəri
117(163)ひ(日) (169)ひるま(昼間)	inəŋi	день	inəŋi	inəŋi
118(167)とし(年), ねん(年)	anani	год	anani	anani
119(168)あさ(朝)	čimai, čimani	утро	čimai	čimai
120(170)ゆうがた(夕方)	səksə, səksəni	вечер	səksə	səksə
121(171)よる(夜)	dolbo, dolboni	ночь	dolbo	dolbo
122(172)きのう(昨日)	čeennee	вчера	čeennee	čeennee
123(173)あす(明日)	čimanaa	завтра	čimanaa	čimanaa
124(174)きょう(今日)	əsinəŋi	сегодня	əsinəŋi	əsinəŋi
125(175)いま(今)	əsi	сейчас	əsi	əsi
126(176)いつ(何時)	xaali	когда	xaali	xaali
127(179)いち(一)	geeda	один	geeda	geeda

128(180)に(二)	dəə	два	duu	duu
129(181)さん(三)	ilaa	три	ilaa	ilaa
130(182)し(四)	ǰiin	четыре	ǰiin	ǰiin
131(183)ご(五)	tunda	пять	tunda	tunda
132(184)ろく(六)	nuŋu	шесть	nuŋu	nuŋu
133(185)しち(七)	nada	семь	nada	nada
134(186)はち(八)	ǰakpu	восемь	ǰapku	ǰapku
135(187)く，きゅう(九)	xuju	девять	xuju	xuju
136(188)じゅう(十)	ǰoon	десять	ǰoon	ǰoon
137(189)にじゅう(二十)	xori	двадцать	xori	xori
138(190)ひゃく(百)	taŋgu	сто	taŋgu	taŋgu
139(191)いくら (192)いくつ	xasu	сколько	xasu	xasu
140(193)はんぶん(半分)	kaltaa	половина		kaltaa
141(194)ぜんぶ(全部)，すべて	gəəm, čipal	все	čipaali	čipaali
142(199)おっと(夫)	əǰi	муж	əǰi-ni	əǰi
143(200)つま(妻)	asi	жена	asi-ni	asi
144(201)けっこん(結婚)	miirənǰi-ni (とつぐ)	брак		miirənǰi-ni
145(202)ちち(父)	ami-ni, amma	отец	ami-ni, amaka	ami-ni, amaka
146(203)はは(母)	əni-ni, ənnə	мать	əni-ni, ənəkə	əni-ni, ənəkə
147(206)むすこ	xusə puttə-ni	сын	puttə	puttə
148(207)むすめ	əəktə puttə-ni	дочь	əəktə puttə	əəktə puttə
149(208)こ(人間の子)，こども(子供)	puttə	ребенок		puttə
150(211)あに(兄)	aaŋ-ni, axa	старший брат	aaŋ-ni	aag-bi
151(212)あね(姉)	əigə-ni, əgə	старшая сестра	əigə-ni	əigə-bi
152(213)おとうと(弟)	nəu, xusə nəu-ni	младший брат	nəu-ni	nəu-bi
153(214)いもうと(妹)	nəu, əəktə nəu-ni	младшая сестра		nəu-bi

154(218)ともだち(友達)	andail, ǰee	друг	ǰee-ni	ǰee-ni
155(224)おとこ(男)	nari, xusə	мужчина	xusə	xusə
156(225)おんな(女)	əəktə	женщина	əəktə	əəktə
157(226)ひと(人)	nari	человек	nari	nari
158(227)わたし(私)	bii	я	bii	bii
159(228)あなた	sii	ты, вы	sii	sii
160(229)かれ(彼)	tarinnee, noo-ni	он	tari, əri	noo-ni
161(230)かのじょ(彼女)	tari əəktə, tari əəktənnee, noo-ni	она	noo-ni	noo-ni
162(231)わたしたち(私達)	buu	мы	buu	buu
163(232)あなたたち	suu	вы	suu	suu
164(235)じぶん(自分)	məənə	себя	məənə	məənə
165(236)ほかの(他の)	goi	другой	goi	goi
166(237)だれ(誰)	ŋui	кто	ŋui	ŋui
167(238)な(姓名の名) (239)なまえ(名前)	gəlbu	имя	gəlbu	gəlbu
168(241)こえ(声)	ǰilda	голос	ǰilda	
169(243)ことば(言葉)	kəsə	речь	kəsə	kəsə
170(249)これ	əri	это	əri	əri
171(250)それ	tari	это	tari	tari
172(251)あれ	tari, tootori taatari	то	tari, tootori taatari	tari, taatari
173(252)どれ	xaawu	который, какой	xau, xamačiga	xauduma, xamačiga
174(253)なに(何)	xai	что	xai	xai
175(254)なぜ(何故)	xaimi	почему	xaimi	xaimi
176(257)ここ(此処)	jədu	здесь	jədu	jədu
177(258)そこ(其処) (259)あそこ	čadu	там	čadu, taatadu	čadu

178(260)どこ	xaidu	где	xaidu	xaidu, sadu
179(266)ひだり(左)	dəunǰee	левый	dəunǰee	dəunǰee
180(267)みぎ(右)	aanǰee	правый	aanǰee	aanǰee
181(268)まえ(前)(場所), ぜんぽう(前方)	dullee	перёд	dullee	dullee
182(269)うしろ(後)	xamarree	зад	xamarree	xamaree
183(270)うち(内), ないぶ(内部)	doo	внутренность	doo	doo
184(271)そと(外), がいぶ(外部)	bookkee	наружность		boo
185(273)うえ(上)	uwwee	верхний	uwwee	uwwee, uinu
186(274)した(下)	pəʝʝee	нижний	pəʝʝee	pəʝʝee, pəduu
187(275)みる(見)	iččee-ni (itəxə-ni)	посмотреть	iččee-ni (itəxə-ni)	iččee-ni (itəxə-ni)
188(277)きく(聞)	doolǰi-ni (doolǰixa-ni)	слушать	doolǰi-ni (doolǰixa-ni)	doolǰi-ni (doolǰixa-ni)
189(278)かぐ(嗅)	ŋooxičči-ni (ŋooxičixa-ni)	нюхатъ		ŋoosičči-ni
190(279)こきゅうする(呼吸), いきをする(息)	əərisi-ni (əəriči-ni)	дышать		əərisi-ni
191(280)いう(言)	unǰi-ni (učči-ni)	сказать	unǰi-ni (učči-ni)	unǰi-ni (učči-ni)
192(283)うたう(歌)	jaaʝʝee-ni (jaajaxa-ni)	петь	jaaʝʝee-ni (jaajaxa-ni)	jaaʝʝee-ni (jaajaxa-ni)
193(284)おどる(踊)	məuri-ni (məuxə-ni)	танцевать		məuri-ni
194(285)はなす(話)	kəənǰi-ni (kəəčči-ni)	говорить	ləədənǰi-ni (ləədəčči-ni)	ləədənǰi-ni (ləədəčči-ni)
195(291)わらう(笑)	inəsi-ni	смеяться	inəsi-ni	inəsi-ni

	(inəči-ni)		(inəči-ni)	(inəči-ni)
196(292)なく(泣)	soŋŋee-ni	плакать	soŋŋee-ni	soŋŋee-ni
	(soŋoxo-ni)		(soŋoxo-ni)	(soŋoxo-ni)
197(296)おこる(怒)	tagǰee-ni	сердиться	tagǰee-ni	tagǰee-ni
	(tagdaxa-ni)		(tagdaxa-ni)	(tagdaxa-ni)
198(297)おどろく(驚)	ollee-ni	[испугаться]		ollee-ni
	(oloxo-ni)			(oloxo-ni)
199(297)	pəskee-ni(めずらしさに)	удивляться	pəskee-ni	pəskee-ni
	(pəskəxə-ni)		(pəskəxə-ni)	(pəskəxə-ni)
200(298)うつ(打)	minǰee-ni	бить	minǰee-ni	minǰee-ni
	(mindəxə-ni)		(mindəxə-ni)	(mindəxə-ni)
201(308)おす(押)	annee-ni	толкать	annee-ni	annee-ni
	(anaxa-ni)		(anaxa-ni)	(anaxa-ni)
202(308)	čirree-ni (おさえる)	давить	čirree-ni (čirəxə-ni)	čirree-ni (čirəxə-ni)
	(čirəxə-ni)			
203(310)もつ(持)	dapuččee-ni	держать	dapuččee-ni	dapuččee-ni
	(daputaxa-ni)		(daputaxa-ni)	(daputaxa-ni)
204(316)あるく(歩)	gičči-ni	ходить	gičči-ni	gičči-ni
	(gituxa-ni)		(gituxa-ni)	(gituxa-ni)
205(319)はしる(走)	tuksee-ni	бегать	tuksee-ni	tuksee-ni
	(tuksaxa-ni)		(tuksaxa-ni)	(tuksaxa-ni)
206(321)たつ(立)	illi-ni	[встать,	illi-ni	illi-ni
	(ilixa-ni)	вставать]	(ilixa-ni)	(ilixa-ni)
207(322)すわる(坐)，こしかける(腰掛)	təəri-ni	садиться	təəri-ni	təəri-ni
	(təəxə-ni)		(təəxə-ni)	(təəxə-ni)
208(324)ねる(寝)，ねている，	apaačči-ni	ложиться	apakaačči-ni	apaačči-ni

よこたわる(横)	(apaačixa-ni)		(apakaačixa-ni)	(apaačixa-ni)
209(324)	toroočči-ni(あおむけになっている)		toroočči-ni	toroočči-ni
	(toroočixa-ni)		(toroočixa-ni)	(toroočixa-ni)
210(325)ねむる(眠)	auri-ni	спатъ	akpanǰi-ni	akpanǰi-ni
	(auxa-ni)		(akpačči-ni)	(akpačči-ni)
	akpanǰi-ni(寝る〔よこになる〕)			
	(akpačči-ni)			
211(328)たべる(食)	dəpči-ni	[кушать]	dəpči-ni	dəpči-ni
	(dəptuxə-ni)		(dəptuxə-ni)	(dəptuxə-ni)
212(329)のむ(飲)	ummi-ni	пить	ummi-ni	ummi-ni
	(umixa-ni)		(umixa-ni)	(umixa-ni)
213(331)うえる(飢)，はらがへる(腹)	lalli-ni	голодать		lalli-ni
	(laluxa-ni)			(laluxa-ni)
214(337)とぶ(飛)	səgǰee-ni	летать,	səgǰee-ni	səgǰee-ni
	(səgdəxə-ni)	лететь	(səgdəxə-ni)	
215(345)やく(焼)	dəgǰi-ni	жечь		dəgǰi-ni
	(dəgǰixə-ni)			(dəgǰixə-ni)
216(349)ころす(殺)	waari-ni	убивать	waari-ni	waari-ni
	(waaxa-ni)		(waaxa-ni)	(waaxa-ni)
217(356)きる(着)	təčči-ni	надевать	təčči-ni	təčči-ni
	(tətuxə-ni)		(tətuxə-ni)	(tətuxə-ni)
218(359)よむ(読)	taunǰi-ni	читать	taunǰi-ni	taunǰi-ni (taučči-ni)
(393)かぞえる(数)	(taučči-ni)	считать		taunǰi-ni
219(361)きる(切)	miiri-ni	резать	miiri-ni	miiri-ni
	(miixə-ni)			(miixə-ni)
220(362)つくる(作)	andusi-ni	изготовлять,	andusi-ni	andusi-ni

	(anduči-ni)	делать		
221(363)あける(開), ひらく(開)	niiri-ni	открывать	niiri-ni	niiri-ni
	(niixə-ni)			(niixə-ni)
222(364)しめる(閉), とじる(閉)	sommi-ni	закрывать	sommi-ni	sommi-ni
	(somixa-ni)			(somixa-ni)
223(365)すむ(住)	bii-ni	жить	bii-ni	bii-ni
	(bičči-ni)			(bičči-ni)
224(394)うむ(産)	bakkee-ni	родить	balǰuuri-ni	balǰuuri-ni
	(baaxa-ni)		(balǰuuxa-ni)	(balǰuuxa-ni)
225(395)うまれる(生)	balǰi-ni	родиться	balǰi-ni	balǰi-ni
	(balǰixa-ni)			
226(397)しぬ(死)	buǰi-ni	умереть	buǰi-ni	buǰi-ni
	(bučči-ni)			(bučči-ni)
227(407)わすれる(忘)	oŋbee-ni	забыть	oŋbee-ni	omgee-ni
	(oŋboxo-ni)		(oŋboxo-ni)	(omgoxo-ni)
228(408)おく(置)	əksee-ni	положить	əksee-ni	əksee-ni
	(əksəxə-ni)			(əksəxə-ni)
229(410)でる(出)	nəəri-ni	выходить	nəəri-ni	nəəri-ni
	(nəəxə-ni)			(nəəxə-ni)
230(411)はいる(入)	iiri-ni	входить	iiri-ni	iiri-ni
	(iixə-ni)			(iixə-ni)
231(412)くる(来)	sinǰee-ni	приходить	sinǰee-ni	sinǰee-ni
	(sindaxa-ni)			(sindaxa-ni)
232(413)いく(行)	ŋənnee-ni	идти	ŋənnee-ni	ŋənnee-ni
	(ŋənəxə-ni)			(ŋənəxə-ni)
233(416)うごく(動)	tučči-ni	двигаться	tučči-ni	
	(tuttuxə-ni)		(tuttuxə-ni)	

234(418)あたえる(与),やる	bəəri-ni (bəəxə-ni)	давать	bəəri-ni (bəəxə-ni)	bəəri-ni (bəəxə-ni)
235(420)おもう(思)	mərəčči-ni (mərəčixə-ni)	думать	mərəčči-ni	mərəčči-ni (mərəčixə-ni)
236(421)しる，しっている(知)	saari-ni (saaxa-ni)	знать	saari-ni	saari-ni (saaxa-ni)
237(422)できる(出来)	utulli-ni (utulixa-ni)	уметь	utulli-ni	utulli-ni, saari-ni (utulixa-ni)
238(424)(が)ある(存在)	bii-ni (bičči-ni)	быть	bii-ni	
239(426)ない(無)	anaa	нет	anaa	anaa
240(427)おおきい(大),おおきな(大)	daaji, kadara	большой	kadaara, daaji	kadara, daaji
241(428)ちいさい(小)	nuuči, nučiikə	маленький	nučuukə	nuuči, nučuukə
242(429)たかい(高)	gugda	высокий	gugda	gugda
243(430)ひくい(低)	nəktə	низкий	nəktə	nəktə, nəktəukə
244(437)つよい(強)	masi, maŋga	сильный, крепкий	maŋauli, masi	masi, maŋga
245(438)よわい(弱)	ugdəə	слабый		ugdəə, əbələ
246(455)ながい(長)	ŋonimi	длинный	ŋonimi	ŋonimi
247(456)みじかい(短)	xurumi	короткий	xurumi	xurumi, xurumuukə
248(457)とおい(遠)	goro	далекий	goro	goro
249(458)ちかい(近)	laxa	близкий	laka	laka
250(461)あつい(暑),あつい(熱)	xəkkuuli(暑い) xulduu(熱い)	жаркий, горячий	xəkkəəli (горячий)	xəkkəəli(жаркий, горячий)
251(462)さむい(寒)	nuŋǰuuli	холодный	nuŋǰuuli	nuŋǰuuli
252(463)あたたかい(暖)	namauli	теплый	namauli	namauli
253(467)あたらしい(新)	sitəu	новый	sitəu	sitəu
254(468)ふるい(古)	goropči	старый	goropči	goropči

255(471)たくさん，おおい(多)	bara	многий, много	bara	bara
256(472)すくない(少)	oi, ojuuka	мало	ojiika	ojiika, ojuuka
257(474)あかるい(明)	ŋəəgdə	светлый	gəəgdə	ŋəəgdə
258(477)しろい(白)	taagda	белый	taagda	taagda
259(478)くろい(黒)	saari	черный	sagari	sagari
260(479)あかい(赤)	səəgdə	красный	səəgdə	səəgdə
261(485)いい(良，善)	aja, uliŋga	хороший	uliŋga	uliŋga
262(486)わるい(悪)	orki	плохой	orki	orki
263(488)おなじ(同)	ɵmɵttɵ	тот же, одинаковый	ɵmɵttɵ	
264(492)はい	ii	да	ii	ii
265(493)いいえ，いや	anaa	нет	anaa	anaa

注記

6　isal mɵɵni‘目の水’O の表現は南方言にもある。

60　omo M の語はŋojokko omoni‘たまごの巣’M からとり出したもの。

74　ojosko N は，移動の際に荷物にまとめて運ぶ衣類，ふとんなどの家財の意。

114 南方言（N）にも suunə の語があるが，suun‘太陽’とちがって，日の輝き，日光のような意である。北方言でも suunə が同様の意ではないか，さらに調べなければならない。

142 以下の親族名称その他の名詞，代名詞の -bi は第 1 人称単数語尾，-ni は第 3 人称語尾。187 以下の動詞 -ni も第 3 人称語尾である。

160，161　M の tari，əri，noo-ni は 160，161 のどちらにもあてることのできる語である。

173 北方言（MO）の xau, xauduma, xamačiga は，南方言と同様に，前二者はどちら（который），後一者はどんな（какой）の意だろう。

183 doo MO は，答としてえた duku doo-du-ni‘家の中に’M, duku doo-ni‘家の中’O からそれぞれとり出した語。

184 boo O は boodu ‘そとで’ O からとり出した語。

264 筆者の質問 sindu kəskə biinii. ‘あなたのところにはねこがいますか’ に対して ii biini. ‘はい，います’ O の答をえた。また čeennee purəixənii. ‘きのう小雨がふりましたか’ に対して ii. ‘はい’ O をえた。

265 筆者の（夏ワールでの）質問 sindu muri biinii. ‘あなたのところには馬がいますか’，また čeennee simanaxanii. ‘きのう雪がふりましたか’ に対してそれぞれ anaa. ‘いいえ’ O の返事をえた。

これらの調査項目の多くについては，南・北方言とも同じ語を使っているが，いくつかの項目について両方言は相異なる語根からなるそれぞれ別の語を使っている。すなわち，13（歯），15（ほお），18（くび），72（衣服），79（のみ），98（草），113（空），116（星），194（話す），224（産む）では相異なる語根からなる語が使われている。

13 については，iktə の語が南方言にもあるが，くまや犬の歯の意である。

15　dərə O は 17 の dərəl と同根語だろう。F には ‘ほお’ の意の語として pulpi とともに pulči もあるようである。

18 の koǰi O については，澗潟（1981）に kozi（首）があって，ulā kozini（となかいの首）の例があげられているが，南方言で，くびを一般に意味する語は moŋo だろう。

72　одежда に対して北方言の O はまず bagduxi をあげるが，O にも tətuwə の語はあるようである。南方言にも bagduxu ‘装身具一切’［澗潟　1981］の語があるが，衣服の意味の語としては，tətuwə の語がまずあげられよう。

79　北方言の pөččөxi は動詞 pөččө-xө-ni（跳ねた）の語幹と同じ語幹をもち，これはこの動詞の語幹から生じた語であろう。

98 においては，南・北方言が顕著な違いを示している。

113 について，南方言では boo naŋnani（天）を採録したが，空の意につかう語は普通 boo のようである。

116　星を意味する xosikta の語は，北方言ではえられなかった。

194　南方言にも ləədənǰi-ni の語があるが，不満などをくどくどとしゃべるの意である。

224については，南方言にもbalǰuuri-niの語があるが，動植物を繁殖させるの意である。

また，上記の調査項目のいくつかにおいては，南・北方言で同じ語根からなる語をつかっていても音形の一部が異なる語もある。たとえば82（魚），189(嗅ぐ)。また，同じ方言，同じ個人においても，異なる発音がある。257におけるŋəəgdəの頭音が，Mの発音ではgである。Aの発音でも，同じ語の頭音のŋがgとなることがある［池上　1993a, 97, 98］。Oにおいても，189のsiのiがuのようにも発音され，261ではlがnともきこえることがある。

なお，南・北方言間の差異とは別に，全域にわたって小方言間の差異とみられるような差異もまたみられる。たとえば，2（かみのけ）については，北方言にniruktə，nuriktəの両形があるが，南方言においても，（佐藤チヨさんより一歳年上で佐知に生まれ，1947年北海道へ移住した）故中川カヨさん（Kと略す）からは同義のnuriktəの語をえた。また北方言には，相撲をとる意の語にŋooččee-ni M，mooččee-ni Oの2形があるが，南方言にも，同義の語にŋooččee-ni NJのほかに，mooččee-niの語形が小川ウメ（Ǝəktəŋgu）さん（1919年野頃に生まれ，1歳で留久玉に移り，あと，こどものうちにオタスに移る，1958年北海道に移住した）からえられた。

5　北方言とエウェンキー語サハリン方言の類似点

ツングース・満洲諸語のなかでウイルタ語に親縁関係がもっとも近い言語は，サハリンの対岸の大陸のアムール川下流地方のウルチャ（オルチャ）語とナーナイ語である。ウイルタ語は，この二言語との間に同じ祖語から共通に保持してきた多くの一致点をもつ。

一方，サハリンの少数民族の一つとして，エウェンキー人がいる。エウェンキー族は対岸の大陸に広くエニセイ川地方まで分布し，エウェンキー語を話すが，サハリンのエウェンキー人はその一部であり，かれらはエウェンキー語サハリン方言を話す。エウェンキー語も，ツングース・満洲諸語の一つであり，話し手の数や分布地域の広さから言って，これらの言語のなかでは，優勢な言語である。ウイルタ語との親縁関係は，ウルチャ語，ナーナイ語のウイルタ語との関係よりは遠いものの，エウェンキー語とウイルタ語が同じ祖語から保持した共通点は少なくない。

ウイルタ語は，エウェンキー語に対して，隣接するサハリン方言を通して密接な関係をもつ。ウイルタ語に入った本来ヤクート語のものである単語には，エウェンキー語サハリン方言を通して入ったものもあろう。例，北方言 kipti F‘はさみ’，エウェンキー語サハリン方言 kipti‘同上’［Василевич 1958, 202］，ヤクート語　кыптый‘同上’。また，南方言の口頭文芸の英雄物語は，語りの部分とふしをつけてうたう部分から成るが，前者はウイルタ語であるが，後者はエウェンキー語であり，あきらかにエウェンキー語から入ったものである。こうしたことからみて，エウェンキー語とウイルタ語の言語接触によっておこる干渉も考えられ，エウェンキー語がウイルタ語の音韻・文法の面にも影響を与えているかどうかは，一つの問題であろう。

以下には，音韻・文法上の上述の南・北方言の相違点のいくつかについて，エウェンキー語サハリン方言からの影響の有無を，ナーナイ語・ウルチャ語との関係にも目を向けつつ，考察してみたい。

2音韻の1　唇音と軟口蓋音の子音音素連続に関して，北方言における前者がさき，後者があとの順序は，エウェンキー語のサハリン方言などの諸方言と一致する。

サハリン方言　ǰapkʊn　‘8’［池上　1993b］
ǰowgo-　‘もりを投げる’［Василевич　1948, 326］，
ただし ǰəwgə̄-‘もりで殺す’［Василевич 1958, 110］
damga　‘たばこ’［池上　1993b］
amŋa　‘口’［同上］

この点，ウルチャ語［Петрова 1936］やナーナイ語の文語［ナイヒン方言］［Петрова 1960］では，ウイルタ語南方言と同じ順序をとる。ナーナイ語のボロン方言［Улитин 1933］，サマル方言［Schmidt　1928］もそのようである。ただし，ナーナイ語のさらに南のシカチ・アリャン方言［Аврорин 1959］，ビ

キン方言［Сем 1976］，中国領ヘジェン方言，中国領キーレン方言［安 1986］，クル・ウルミ方言［Суник 1958］，また北のサマギル方言［Schmidt 1928］ではウイルタ語北方言にもみられる唇音・軟口蓋音の順をとる。

シカチ・アリャン方言の語例（1979年の筆者採録資料による）

ǰapkʊn ‘8’，damxi ‘たばこ’，amga ‘口’。

中国領ヘジェン方言の語例（1990年に筆者が黒竜江岸八岔のヘジェン（ナーナイ人）から採録した資料による）

ǰapkʊ ‘8’（ただしこの語のpkの発音はほとんど二重調音である），tupkə ‘くぎ’，subgu ‘魚皮’，simkisi-，simki- ‘せく，せきをする’，omgo- ‘忘れる’，amŋa ‘口’。

中国領キーレン方言の語例（1990年に筆者が黒竜江岸街津口で採録した資料による）

sʊbgʊ（母音はoか）魚皮’，simki- ‘せきをする’，omŋo- ‘忘れる’，amŋa- ‘口’。

ナーナイ語のナイヒン方言などやウルチャ語・ウイルタ語では音位転換がおきて各単語一律に軟口蓋音・唇音の順となったとみられるが［池上　1989b, 1072, 1073参照］，上記のシカチ・アリャン方言以下の諸方言のその順序がナーナイ語における古い段階のものなのか［Аврорин 1959, 52–54も参照］，あるいは，ナイヒン方言などと関係のないナーナイ語の一部の方言だけにかかわるある要因によることかの問題にはここではふれない。しかし，軟口蓋音・唇音の順の型は，ナーナイ語ナイヒン方言など，またウルチャ語，さらにウイルタ語北方言をとび越えてその南方言に分布する。この分布はもとは連続的なもので北方言にも分布していたとの見方をすると，南方言の順序の型は上述の音位転換によって生じた型であり，北方言の唇音・軟口蓋音の順の型はさらにのちの改新であろう。そしてこの改新がサハリン方言を通してのエウェンキー語の影響によるものであったことはありえよう。なお，エウェンキー語においてomgo- ‘忘れる’ という動詞語幹の形はトッコ方言などにあるが［Романова, Мыреева 1968, 127］，サハリン方言では採録されていない。しかし，エウェンキー語の上記の唇音・軟口蓋音の順をウイルタ語北方言がとり入れ，それがこの方言で一般的な型となると，個々の単語中のその子音音素連続がその型の順序にかえられることはありうるだろう。

3文法の2　北方言の動詞語尾-bukkiはエウェンキー語の動詞語尾-wkīと同じものとみられる。サハリン方言の用例をあげると，bəjŋəl sō kətə biwkīl.‘けものは大変たくさんいる’［Василевич 1948, 316］。この-wkīは方言によっては-pkīの形をとる［Константинова 1964, 143］。

北方言の-bukkiは，南方言にも，ウルチャ語，ナーナイ語にもみられないことから，ウイルタ語の固有の語尾でなく，エウェンキー語から借用したものともみられよう。しかし-bukkiは語幹との結びつきかたが単純でなく，接尾する異なる語幹の音形に応じて形を変えたり，語幹と融合したりするが，そのしかたは，ウイルタ語の本来のものとみられるいくつかの語尾と軌を一にしている。このことからみると，-bukkiはウイルタ語が古くから有していた語尾であるようであり，隣接のエウェンキー語の方言から借用されたとしても，比較的新しく借用されたものではなさそうである。

3文法の3　名詞述語構文のなかで連辞の役をする動詞語幹bi-の直説法過去形（形動詞［＝動名詞］過去形）に第3人称語尾も接尾する例（bičini）はナーナイ語［風間　1991, 126］，ウルチャ語［Петрова 1936, 78, 80］にもみられ，またエウェンキー語サハリン方言にも同様のことがある。例を挙げる。tar bi sārɪw bəjə bičạn.‘これはわたしの知った人であった’［Василевич 1948, 318］，bī əwənki bixim.‘わたくしはエウェンキー人です’［池上　1993b, 164］。bičạn‘だった’の-nは第3人称語尾，bixim‘だ’の-mは第1人称単数語尾である。第2の文は，bi-の直説法現在形（形動詞現在形）も連辞の役をする例である。ウイルタ語北方言で連辞の役をする動詞語幹bi-の動名詞形に第3人称語尾がつくことのあるのは，近い親縁関係にあるウルチャ語・ナーナイ語におけるように古くからウイルタ語にあったのか，あるいは地理的に近いエウェンキー語サハリン方言の影響によることなのかなどの問題については，確実なことがいまだ言えない。

3文法の4　エウェンキー語において，サハリン方言をふくめて東部の諸方言では，ウイルタ語北方言と同様に，第1・2人称単・複数人代名詞が所有者を表す所有構造のなかで，その人代名詞が主格形をとる。サハリン方言の例を挙げると，bī akinmi ‘おれの兄’，sī gərbis ‘きみの名’［池上　1993b, 170］。

ウルチャ語のそのような第1・2人称単・複数人代名詞をふくむ所有構造では，ウイルタ語南方言の人代名詞属格形に相当する形がつかわれるようである［Петрова 1936, 31, Суник1985, 42］。また，ナーナイ語のそのような所有構造では，人代名詞主格形がつかわれる［Аврорин 1959, 250, Петрова 1960, 184, 185］。しかし，ナーナイ語の南部のビギン方言では，かつてはウイルタ語南方言の人代名詞属格形に相当する形がつかわれていたようであり，ナーナイ語ではやはり古くはこのような人代名詞の形がつかわれていたとみられる［Сем 1976, 54–56］。すなわち，人代名詞属格形ないしこれに相当する形をつかう所有構造は，ウイルタ語南方言，また，その北方言を隔ててウルチャ語に分布し，さらに，その向こうのナーナイ語においてもかつて同様の所有構造が分布していたとみられる。この所有構造の分布地域がもとは連続的でウイルタ語北方言にもそれが分布していたとみると，ウイルタ語においては，南方言の所有構造が古いものであり，一方，北方言の人代名詞主格形をつかう所有構造は改新によるものであろう。そして，その改新は隣接するエウェンキー語サハリン方言の影響によっておこり，この言語の所有構造が北方言にとり入れられ，南方言におけるようなもとの所有構造に代ったのではないかと思われる。

ウイルタ語は，一方で，カラフト対岸の大陸のオロチ族の話すオロチ語（やはりツングース・満洲諸語の一つ）と歴史上言語接触があり干渉がおきたことがないかどうかもみなければならないが，以上みてきたウイルタ語南・北方言の相違点のうち**2音韻**の**1**や**3文法**の**4**でふれた点は，北方言がエウェンキー語サハリン方言の影響を受けて南方言との相違をきたした蓋然性が大きいだろう。

引用文献

池上二良，1980.『ウイルタ語基礎語彙』札幌　北海道大学文学部言語学研究室。

——— 1989a.「ウイルタ語生活語彙」『ウイルタ語生活語彙・ウイルタの刺繍』　札幌　北海道教育委員会，網走　網走市北方民俗文化保存協会。

——— 1989b.「ツングース諸語」『言語学大辞典』2　東京　三省堂。

——— 1993a.「ウイルタ語テキスト」　村崎恭子編『サハリンの少数民族』。

——— 1993b.「エウェンキー語サハリン方言小語彙」　村崎恭子編『サハリンの少数民族』。

風間伸次郎，1991.「ナーナイ語テキスト」　黒田信一郎・津曲敏郎編『ツングース言語文化論集』1　札幌　北海道大学文学部。

澗潟久治，1981.『ウイルタ語辞典』網走　網走市北方民俗文化保存協会。

村崎恭子，1993.『サハリンの少数民族』。

東京外国語大学アジア・アフリカ言語文化研究所，1966，1967.『アジア・アフリカ言語調査票』上（1966），下（1967）東京。

安俊，1986.『赫哲語簡・志』北京　民族出版社。

Ikegami, J., 1956. “The Substantive Inflection of Orok”, *Gengo Kenkyu (Journal of the Linguistic Society of Japan)* 30.

——— 1959. “The Verb Inflection of Orok”, *Kokugo Kenkyu* 9, Kokugakuin Daigaku Kokugokenkyukai, Tokyo.

——— 1985. “The Category of Person in Tungus: Its Representation in the Indicative Forms of Verbs”, *Gengo Kenkyu (Journal of the Linguistic Society of Japan)* 88.

Schmidt, P., 1928. “The Language of the Samagirs”, *Acta Universitatis Latviensis* 19. Riga.

Аврорин, В. А., 1959. Грамматика нанайского языка, 1. Москва-Ленинград.

Василевич, Г. М., 1948. Очерки диалектов эвенкийского (тунгусского) языка. Ленинград.

——— 1958. Эвенкийско-русский словарь. Москва.

Горцевская, В. А., Колесникова, В. Д., Константинова, О. А., 1958. Эвенкийскорусский словарь. Ленинград.

Константинова, О.А., 1964. Эвенкийский язык, Фонетика, Морфология. Москва-Ленинград.

Петрова, Т. И., 1936. Ульчский диалект нанайского языка. Москва-

Ленинград.

——— 1960. Нанайско-русский словарь. Ленинград.

——— 1967. Язык ороков (ульта). Ленинград.

Романова, А. В., Мыреева, А. Н., 1968. Диалектологический словарь эвенкийского языка, Материалы говоров эвенков Якутии. Ленинград.

Сем, Л. И., 1976. Очерки диалектов нанайского языка, Бикинский (уссурийский) диалект. Ленинград.

Суник, О. П., 1958. Кур-урмийский диалект, Исследования и материалы по нанайскому языку. Ленинград.

Улитин, А., 1933. "Материалы по гольдскому (нанайскому) языку". *Язык и мышление* 1. Ленинград.

Summary

1. The Uilta language is divided into two dialects: the southern dialect, which is spoken mainly in the district of Poronaisk (abbreviated to S) and the northern dialect, which is spoken mainly in Val, a village in the northern part of Sakhalin (abbreviated to N).

2. On phonological differences between the southern and northern dialects.

1 As to the order of a labial and a velar in the intervocalic consonant sequence, we find S a velar + a labial || N a velar + a labial or a labial + a velar.

In the intervocalic positions of some words, we find :

2 S *x* || N *k*. 3 S Ø (zero) || N *g*. 4 S *iga* or *ee* || N *iga*, *ee* or *aa*, and S *igə* or *ee* || N *əə*.

3. On grammatical differences between the southern and northern dialects.

1 In S a verb stem ending in a consonant (or two consonants) + a vowel and the verbal noun ending *-ri* are fused. For instance, the verb stem

ŋənə-'to go' and *-ri* are fused into *ŋənnee* 'someone going'. In N such a fused form appears, but also a form, in which the noun stem and the verbal noun ending *-ri* are joined but not fused, e. g., *ŋənə-ri* 'someone going'. According to I. Ja. Fedjaeva at Val, the former form has the definite meaning, whereas the latter form has the indefinite meaning. This form is not found in S.

2 In N the verb ending *-bukki* meaning usual action is used, while in S it is not found.

3 In the nominal predicate construction of S (such as in *bii lučabi.* 'I am a Russian', *bii saldaa biččimbi.* 'I was a soldier.') the predicate is accompanied by the predicative personal ending in both the present and past forms in cases where the subject is the first or second person singular or plural, but the predicate is not accompanied by any personal ending in cases where the subject is in the third person. In N, however, we also find instances, in which the predicate is accompanied by the personal ending in the past form in cases where the subject is in the third person.

4 In the possessive construction, in which the concept of the possessor is expressed with the first or second person singular or plural pronoun, S uses the genetive case-form, but N uses the nominative case-form, e.g., S *mini ŋaalabi* and N *bii ŋaalabi* 'my hand'.

4. On basic words in the southern and northern dialects.

The present writer questioned S and N informants about 260 basic words. The majority of these words each have a stem common to both the S and N dialects. The stems or roots of only about 10 basic words are different between S and N, e.g., S *orokto*, N *pəiktə* 'grass' and S *kəənǰini*, N *ləədənǰini* 'he speaks'.

5. On similarities between the northern dialect of Uilta and the Sakhalin dialect of Evenki.

2 1. N is identical with Sakhalin Evenki in the order of a labial + a

velar. The order of a velar + a labial in the intervocalic position is distributed in the Naikhin dialect and some other dialects of Nanai, in Ulcha and in the S dialect of Uilta. If we assume that the previous distribution of the order of a velar + a labial had continuity and included also the N dialect of Uilta situated between Ulcha and the S dialect of Uilta, it is probable that the order of a labial + a velar in N is a later innovation.

3 2. The verb ending *-bukki* in N appears to be the same as the Evenki verb ending *-wkī*.

3 3. In the Sakhalin dialect of Evenki, the Naikhin dialect of Nanai and Ulcha, as well as in N, we find instances in which the third person predicate ending is added to the copula verb in the past form.

3 4. The possessive construction using the nominative case-form of the personal pronoun prevails in the Sakhalin dialect and some other dialects of Evenki, and also in Nanai. The possessive construction using a dependent possessive pronoun is found in Ulcha, and it seems to have formerly been used in Nanai. The dependent possessive pronoun is regarded as being identical with the genetive case-form of the personal pronoun. The possessive construction using the genetive case-form of the first or second person pronoun or a dependent possessive pronoun is distributed in the S dialect of Uilta and in Ulcha, and it was also probably in Nanai formerly. Assumimg that the distribution of this possessive construction had continuity in former times, and that it also included the N dialect of Uilta (which is situated between the S dialect and Ulcha), it is probable that the possessive construction of N is a later innovation.

There seems to be a strong probability that in both the order of labial and velar consonants in the intervocalic cluster and in the possessive construction using the first or second person pronoun, the N dialect of Uilta made innovations under the influence of the neighbouring Sakhalin dialect of Evenki.

本稿は，はじめに記したサハリンの少数民族言語調査の研究成果報告書である村崎恭子編『サハリンの少数民族』（1993年）に，筆者のほかの報告とともに載せてもらうつもりであったが，この原稿は作製がおくれ，その刊行に間に合わなかった。今回，北海道立北方民族博物館の好意によりここに発表することができたことを感謝する。

初出　『北海道立北方民族博物館研究紀要』3号［網走　平成6年（1994年）3月25日］9－38ページ。

追記

1の末尾でふれたウイルタ語の方言分布については，過去における住民の広域にわたる移動も考慮に入れなければならない。

3文法の4.の条について。第1・2人称人代名詞を所有者とする所有構造には，南方言でも，上に扱ってきた1910年代生まれの世代より下の世代では，北方言におけるような人代名詞主格形を使うようである。1919年野頃生まれのƎəktəŋguさん（女子）は，なおも，mini ŋaalabi（わたしの手）と言い，もしbii ŋaalabiと言うと，変に感ぜられるようである。しかし，1943年Neva地方生まれのМинато Сирюкоさん（女子）からは，bii amimbi（わたしの父），bii ŋindabi（わたしのいぬ）のような例を得た。なおさらに，bii sundattaŋubi（わたしのさかな）と言うとともにminiŋŋi sundattaŋubi（同義）とも言うということが注意される。エウェンキー語の影響を受けたとみられるウイルタ語北方言の影響が南方言にまでも及んできているといえるだろうか。

4語彙の257（474）のgəəgdəの語形はgəəgdə（きれいな）の語との混同によることも考えられよう。

5の一部はその後削除した。

ウイルタ語研究及びウイルタ語の現状

The Study of Uilta and
the Present State of Uilta

一　はじめに

サハリン（樺太）の少数民族，ウイルタ族が話すウイルタ語は，ツングース・満洲諸語の一つである。まとめてツングース・満洲諸語とよぶ言語は約十あり，東シベリアや中国東北部などに分布するが，これらはもとは同じ一つの言語である。この言語は，モンゴル語，チュルク語（広義のトルコ語）と多くの類似点・一致点をもち，この三言語はあわせてアルタイ諸語とよばれる。ウイルタ語は以前オロッコ語とよばれたが，今日はウイルタというその民族の自称によってよばれる。なお，ウイルタのイを小字で書くのは，本来の発音からみて適当でない。

二　今日までのウイルタ語調査研究

これまでのおもなウイルタ語調査研究を略記すると，ウイルタ語分布地域の南部のポロナイスク（敷香）などの地方のウイルタ語については，すでに江戸時代末，すなわち十九世紀なかばに松浦武四郎が単語とわずかな短文を採集筆記しているが，二十世紀はじめにポーランド人B・ピウスツキが本格的に調査研究をおこなった。その後，大正のはじめに中目覺氏が，昭和３年以来50年あまりにわたって凋潟(浮)久治氏が調査研究をおこなった。ロシヤのT・I・ペトローワは1936年以来ウイルタ語の調査研究をおこなった。（J. Ikegami,

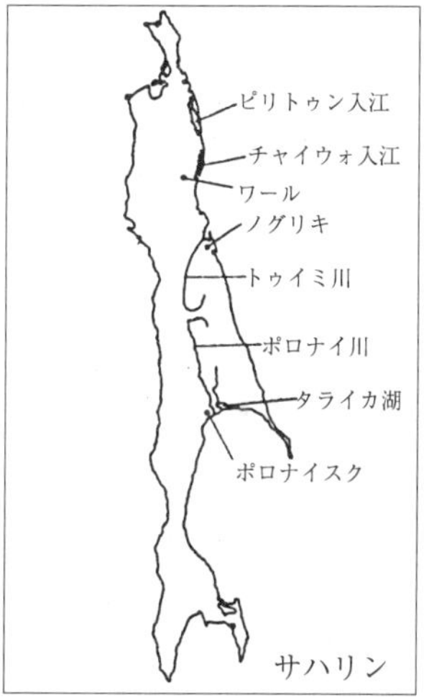

“A History of the Study of the Uilta Language”　村崎恭子編『サハリンとB・ピウスツキ』［札幌　1992年］参照。）筆者は，戦後北海道へ移住したウイルタについて昭和24年以降南の地方のウイルタ語の調査研究をしてきた。昭和52年度から3年間は文部省科学研究費補助金を受けた「オロッコ族（ウイルタ族）の言語文化の総合的実地調査研究」（代表筆者）がおこなわれ，言語調査は筆者と津曲敏郎氏が当った。

これに続いて，北海道教育委員会が，昭和53年度から8年間，さらに昭和62年度から5年間「ウイルタ民俗文化財緊急調査」を実施し，調査は多く筆者が当ったが，この調査では，これまでに得ているウイルタ資料をさらに質問の材料として北海道在住のウイルタ族出身者に尋ねる方法がとられた。この調査の報告書は，同教育委員会と網走市北方民俗文化保存協会から発行された。報告書としては，澗潟久治氏が労作『ウイルタ語辞典』を刊行し，また川村秀弥氏の樺太諸民族の覚え書『土語と土俗』が整理されて刊行され，北川源太郎氏（ウイルタ名ゲールダーヌ，俗称ゲンダーヌ）のかな書きのウイルタ語文例集『ウイルタのことば』も筆者と津曲敏郎氏による音韻表記と日本語訳を加えて刊行された。また，その他の旧資料や筆者の採集したウイルタ語の語彙・テキストも刊行された。(拙文「「ウイルタ民俗文化財緊急調査」をふりかえって」『北海道の文化』56号参照。) この調査は，北海道在住のウイルタの調査であるとともに，文化的面でのいわばわが国樺太領有の残務整理でもあると上記拙文に記したが，一方この調査の成果は，新しいウイルタ語研究への踏台でもあると言えよう。

さらに，平成２年度から３年間村崎恭子氏を代表として文部省科学研究費補助金交付を受けた「サハリンにおける少数民族の言語に関する調査研究」が，ロシヤなど海外の研究者も参加しておこなわれ，ウイルタ語調査は，初年度は筆者と村崎恭子氏，佐藤知己氏ほかが，あとは筆者と井上紘一氏が当った。われわれにとって，サハリンにおいて，南のポロナイスク地方のウイルタ語とともに，北のワール地方のウイルタ語の調査が実現したことは，つぎにふれるように，大きな意味をもつ。

三　最近のウイルタ調査研究の課題

先に記したようなウイルタ語の調査研究がこれまでおこなわれてきたが，ポロナイスクなどをふくむ南の地方とワールなどをふくむ北の地方の両ウイルタ語をくらべてその相違点をとり上げて精細に扱うことは，知るかぎり普通なかった。南北二地方のウイルタ語は同じウイルタ語といっても，音韻，語彙，文法のそれぞれの面においていくつもの点で方言差があり，ウイルタ語を大別すれば，南北二方言に分かれるとみられる。このウイルタ語の方言差異は，最近のウイルタ語研究において重要な課題であると言える。その研究では，両方言の境界の地理的位置などの問題ばかりでなく，さらにその方言差異はどんな起因によったものかなどが研究上の重要な問題となる。

語彙においては，たとえば基礎語彙の方言差異も一つの問題であるが，文法の面において方言差を示す二つの例を以下にあげる。まず，第１・２人称単・複数人代名詞をふくむ所有構造（以下では略して単に所有構造と記す）についてみると，たとえば「わたくしの手」の意味を，南の方言では mini ŋaalabi と言うのに対して，北の方言では通常 bii ŋaalabi と言う。南の方言では，元

飼育トナカイの列。ワールから北へ約50キロ
（ピリトゥン入江の南方）にて

来こうは言わないようである。mini（末尾の i はときに脱落する）は南の方言における第１人称単数人代名詞の属格（所有格）である（ロシヤの研究者はツングース語の代名詞のこのような形をロシヤ語文法式に物主代名詞とよんでいる）。bii はウイルタ語の第１人称単数人代名詞の主格であるが，北の方言では所有構造において所有者を表すのにも使われている。ŋaala は手を意味し，-bi はこの ŋaala（手）の所属を示す第１人称単数所属語尾である。両方言の所有構造では，所属人称語尾が義務的に接尾し，さらにこの語尾のまえに譲渡可能性の接尾辞が入ることがある。

ほかのツングース・満洲諸語についてみると，満洲語では名詞および代名詞全般に，属格形があり，第１人称単数人代名詞の属格形は，文語形を示すと，ウイルタ語と同様の mini である。ツングース諸語のなかでも，末尾の i のない形 min がエウェン語の文語とその基礎をなす方言，ネギダル語，オルチャ語で使用されているし，しかもオルチャ語では，ペトローワによれば，末尾に i をもつ形 mini もときにきかれるという。またナーナイ語のウスリ川岸のビキン方言も口碑で mini を使い，中国領キーレン方言には mini，min 両形があらわれる。後者方言では名詞の属格形の存在も指摘されている。

満洲語やこれらのツングース諸語の所有構造は，ウイルタ語南方言のそれと同様で，そのような人代名詞の形が使用される。ただし，満洲語には，所属人称語尾や譲渡可能性接尾辞がなく，所有構造でも使用されない。また，ナーナイ語の中国領キーレン方言も，譲渡可能性接尾辞がないとみられ，所属人称語尾はあるが，この構造で使われないこともある。一方，ツングース諸語のうち，ナーナイ語の文語とその基礎をなす方言やウデヘ語，オロチ語では，ウイルタ語北方言と同様に，所有構造に人代名詞主格が使われ，ナーナイ語ビキン方言でも今日では主格形が使われる。また，ネギダル語にも前記の所有構造とともにこのような所有構造がある。

なお，ツングース諸語のうちエウェンキー語の所有構造では，上記の他言語の人代名詞の主格形や属格形のかわりに，人代名詞の自立所有形，たとえば，エウェンキー語文語の第１人称単数形なら minŋi（わたくしのもの）が使われる。ただし，サハリン方言などでは主格形を使う。

さて，ウイルタ語の南方言と北方言の上述の二つの所有構造のどちらがウイルタ語において古いものかは一つの問題である。それを解くには，上にふれたようなツングース・満洲諸語における相異なる所有構造の分布との関係も考慮される。筆者は，説明を省くが，南方言の所有構造の方が北方言のものより古い見込みが大きいと考える。

つぎに，ウイルタ語北方言の動詞語尾の一つに -bukki という語尾がある（ペトローワは -buki と表記している）。この動詞語尾は，接尾辞 -bu^{3}- と語尾 -kki からなるとみられる。若干の例から推測すると，動詞語幹に -bu^{3}- が接尾する仕方は，-bu^{2}- とほぼ一致するようである。1.1類の動詞語幹と -bu^{3}- との間では融合がおこり，2.3類の動詞語幹には -bu- が接尾し，1,2類動詞語幹には交替形 -wu が，0.2類動詞語幹には交替形 -pu が接尾することは，-bu^{2}- と同様である。ただし，0.3類動詞語幹の場合は -ptu-kki となる。（拙文「オロッコ語動詞語幹形成接尾辞」（英文）（本書収載）の -bu^{2}- の条参照。）この語尾に，動作主体が複数であることを表す -l が接尾することもある。-bukki のついた動詞形は，多くの場合，行動が習慣的におこることを表し，また文を終結するはたらきをもつが，またあとに bičči（あった）をともなうことによって，その行動が過去におきたことを表す。この動詞語尾は南方言には普通みられないようである。

トゥイミ川下流ノグリキ付近

この動詞語尾の由来も一つの問題となるが，これはエウェンキー語の動詞語尾 -wki（文語形をあげる）と同じものかもしれず，この問題はウイルタ語以外のツングース語にも関連する。

ウイルタ語の研究は，ウイルタ語という一言語の解明であるだけでなく，ツングース・満洲諸語研究への一つの視点ともなり，また周囲の諸言語の研究にも寄与する。さらに言語一般の研究へ資料を提供することにもなろう。

四　ウイルタ語の現状

ウイルタ人の人口は，今日三百を越えるというが，正確な数は明らかでない。とにかく極少数である。ウイルタ語の話し手の数となると，一層少い。それもウイルタ語を話す人は高齢者であり，若い人は少い。ウイルタ人は今日ロシヤ語を常用し，ウイルタ語を話すことのできる人も，ロシヤ語も使う二言語使用者である。また，ウイルタ語は口語（口頭語）として使用されていても，ウイルタ語を書き表す一定の文字を有せず，ウイルタ語には文語（書写語）がいまだにない。学校ではロシヤ語で教育がおこなわれ，ウイルタ語の授業はない。このようにウイルタ語は，今日極めて劣勢の言語であると言え，現代における世界の多くの少数民族の言語と同様に，近い将来に消滅していく可能性は非常に大きいことが憂慮される。

そうしたなかにおいても，ワールのウイルタ婦人イ・ヤ・フェジャーエワさんのように，ウイルタ語の保持に強い熱意をもっている人もいる。この方は，かつて小学校で課外にウイルタ語を教えることを試みたが，ウイルタの児童はウイルタ語に興味を示さず，授業は成功しなかったという。そこで昨年あらたに幼稚園でウイルタ語を教えることを計画し，くわしい教案をつくった。できれば昨年九月からはじめたいよしであった。このほか同村のウイルタ婦人エ・ア・ビービコワさんもウイルタ語に深い関心をもっている。

五　ウイルタ語対策

サハリン州政府は少数民族対策の一環として，ウイルタ族に小学校でのウイルタ語教育の実施を計画していることを，1991年，州政府のこの計画を担当するエヌ・ア・ライグン氏（ニヴフ婦人・教育学博士候補（カンジダート））からきいた。実施には，まずウイルタ語を表記する文字を定め，その文字の用法である正書法をとりきめ，それによってウイルタ語の文語を確立しなければならない。学校教育には，教科書，学習用辞典の編集も必要である。この計画に，筆者も請われて，サンクトペテルブルグのユ・ア・セム教授，前述のフェジャーエワさんらとともにかかわることになった。同年十一月はじめて四人が州政府で打合せをしたが，各人が遠くはなれていて，なかなか事が進まない。基礎的な事項についての筆者の意見は1992年もとめられ，要点を短く記した私案（Проект письменности уйльтинского языка）を送付した。この私案がそのまま採用されなくても，少しでも役にたてばと思う。私案にはつぎのようなことを記した。

ウイルタ語文語の基礎は南方言におくが，ただし北の方言を文語で用いることも許容する。文字は，ロシヤ字よりローマ字が適当であるが，実際に実施しやすいロシヤ字を，一部の軟音字は除いて採用する。ただし，ウイルタ語の文字表記が普及した段階でローマ字に替えることが望ましい。文字表記は，異なる音素は異なる字母で表し，一つの音素はいつも同じ字母で表すことを原則とする。（拙文「北方諸言語の文字－ロシヤ字がいいか，ローマ字がいいか」

ウイルタの神像。ポロナイスク対岸のサチガリにて

[『月刊言語』21巻2号 1992年]（本書にも収載）参照。）その上でウイルタ語の音素とその表記法を，特に長母音音素の表記法にもふれて記した。付表に，ウイルタ語表記のためのローマ字・ロシヤ字両方の字母表を試案としてそえた。

しかしながら，州政府のこの対策によって，ウイルタ語教育が成功をおさめ，ウイルタ語の復興につながるかについては，楽観的ではいられない。しかし，ウイルタ語が消えていくのをくいとめる試みは，なおもできるかぎりおこなってみるべきであろう。

追記

1．ウイルタ語南北両方言の文法における第1・2人称単・複数人代名詞をふくむ所有構造の相違点をみたが，これは1910年代生まれの高齢層の話し手によって南北両方言の相違点をみた調査結果であった。それより低い年齢層については，北方言では上の年齢層とやはり同様の言い方をするが，南方言でも下の年齢層はやはり bii ŋaalabi の言い方もするようであり，この点をくわしく調べなければならない。

2．ウイルタの人口は，1989年の人口調査では200人となっている（統計に関するソ連邦国家委員会『1989年のソ連邦国民経済　統計年鑑』（露文）［モス

ウィルタ婦人　イ・ヤ・フェジャーエワさん（右）と
ア・ヴェ・セミョーノワさん（中央）。左は筆者。ワー
ルのフェジャーエワさん宅にて（写真：井上紘一氏）

クワ　1990］に拠る）が，この数は正しくない。1990年にL・キタジマさんから筆者に示された同年のポロナイスク区北方民族人口統計表では，同区のウイルタは173人であり，また1991年イ・ヤ・フェジャーエワさんからの情報では，ワールのウイルタは127人となっているが，しかし同氏自身の調査によるとそれより多く，ワールにウイルタは少なくとも144人いるという。これだけの合計でも300人を越えるが，ほかにノグリキやオハ地方などにもウイルタが居住するようである。サハリン州政府（行政庁）の資料によれば，1995年はじめサハリンのウイルタの人口は350人であるという（ロシア連邦出版委員会・ロシア図書局『サハリン少数民族諸言語による図書・情報の需要の充足』（露文）（サハリン州図書出版所　ユジノ・サハリンスク　1995）7，8ページに拠る）。

3．拙文「ウイルタ語文字案」（Проект письменности уйльтинского языка）は北大スラブ研究センターの欧文紀要 Acta Slavica Iaponica XII (1994) に載る（本書にも収載）。この文字案を検討する会が1993年モスクワのロシアアカデミー言語学研究所で筆者も出席しておこなわれ，文字はロシヤ字を採るのが妥当とされた。筆者はこの会においても年来の考えを述べた。筆者をふくめて出席者の発言等，会の模様は『母語（Родной язык）』1994

№1（連邦と民族に関するロシア連邦国家委員会　モスクワ）61，62ページの「ウイルタへの文字案」の条に載る。その後，筆者は上記の文字案についての補足「ウイルタ語における文字の実践」（Письменная практика на уйльтинском языке）およびその続きを書いたが，これは前記の文字案についての諸問題を挙げ，使い手としてのウイルタの意見を問うためのものでもある。この拙文は Acta Slavica Iaponica XIV，XVI（1996，1998）に載る（本書にも収載）。

この文は，はじめ北海道立北方民族博物館友の会季刊誌『アークティック・サークル』6号（1993年）に掲載したが，三の条に2箇所を増補し，新しくさらに追記を加えて，『第12回特別展　樺太1905−45　――日本領時代の少数民族――』（北海道立北方民族博物館　1997年）に転載した。本書に収載したこの文は，さらに三の条の動詞語尾 -bukki の箇所の前半を書き改めたものである。

A Brief History of the Study of the Uilta Language

In this paper, I will give a brief account of studies of the Uilta language (formerly known as the Orok language), which will mainly focus on descriptive studies of Uilta based on field work. Accordingly, I do not touch on researches in other linguistic fields, such as the comparative study or classification of Uilta and the other Tungus languages. Researchers whose works I have failed to notice, especially Russian researchers whose works may have escaped my notice, should be added in the future.

The history of the study of Uilta began with the collection of words in the middle of the nineteenth century. Although this is not linguistic research per se, we could say that such work is antecedent to linguistic study.

One such collection is in the form of two anonymous manuscripts entitled "Orokko-go (=the Orok language)". Presumably written in the middle of the nineteenth century, these manuscripts contain a collection of words and short sentences of Orokko (Uilta), Santan (Olcha) and Nikubun (Nivkh). The entry items number 369. They were edited and published by J. IKEGAMI in 1971.

In 1980 it was ascertained by Shôichi TANISAWA that the older of these two manuscripts was written by Takeshirô MATSUURA, who compiled the words and sentences on the basis of materials he himself collected in southern Sakhalin.

He traveled throughout Hokkaido, Shikotan, Kunashiri, Etorofu and southern Sakhalin in the middle of the nineteenth century and made detailed geographical and ethnographical records of these areas. In addition, he made a collection of Uilta words he heard from Uilta speakers in the vicinity of the mouth of the Poronai river in southern Sakhalin. Some of these words were recorded in another work of his, "Ampoku Koshô", which was annotated and published by Shin'ichirô TAKAKURA in 1978. The Uilta words were represented with kana, Japanese syllabic letters. It is difficult to transcribe Uilta word-forms accurately with kana. This work, however, is very useful, since one can presume the word-forms to a considerable extent, provided one has an intimate acquaintance with the usage of kana in the transcription of Uilta.

At the beginning of the twentieth century, the Polish researcher Bronislaw PILSUDSKI brought the study of Uilta to a much higher level. He collected Uilta words and prepared Uilta texts on the basis of field work among the Uilta inhabitants of Socihare at the mouth of the Poronai river in 1904. He made grammatical remarks on the Uilta language, and he also compiled a collection of Uilta texts of (a folk tale, riddles, songs and the like) with Polish translations and an Orok-Polish vocabulary comprising 1500~2000 words (2730 entries). At the time of his appearance, researches into Siberian native languages were flourishing in Russia, but no one other than PILSUDSKI investigated Uilta on Sakhalin. Moreover, he was an eminent investigator of languages, which therefore makes his works invaluable. His works were published posthumously by A. F. MAJEWICZ in 1985 and 1987.

PILSUDSKI's description of Uilta, however, is sometimes incorrect or inadequate. This must be considered an inevitable consequence of the early nature of his research. However, it is rather important that he made an analysis of Uilta language materials for the first time. The Uilta materials that he wrote down are still valuable today. If PILSUDSKI's works on Uilta had been placed at the disposal of following generations of researchers much earlier, it would have been highly instructive and useful to them.

In 1912, Kyôsuke KINDAICHI, a scholar of Ainu, collected Uilta words and short sentences and published them. Also, Akira NAKANOME published an Orok grammar on the basis of field studies he made in the Poronai River area in 1912 and 1913. It marked a milestone in the development of the study of Uilta.

In the second quarter of the twentieth century, the study of the Uilta language attained a higher level through the contributions of Hisaharu MAGATA and Taisiia Ivanovna PETROVA.

MAGATA, who was endowed with a linguistic talent, began collecting materials from Uilta inhabitants in southern Sakhalin in 1928 and wrote an Uilta grammar and compiled an Uilta vocabulary, both in manuscript form. After the World War II, he collected materials from some Uilta immigrants to Hokkaido while consulting the materials obtained by PETROVA and IKEGAMI. MAGATA continued to revise and enlarge his Uilta vocabulary until his death in 1981, and his dictionary of the Uilta language was published in the same year. Each item in the dictionary contains a group of cognate words (after the gnezdo method). His grammar is a valuable result of his early study of Uilta. It is far in advance of NAKANOME's grammar. His dictionary furnishes detailed lexical descriptions and a wealth of examples. On the other hand, in some places there is a lack of precision in the transcription of Uilta word-forms.

In addition to MAGATA, Hideya KAWAMURA, who taught native pupils in the school of the Otasu settlement near Sisuka (or Sikuka which is now Poronaisk), also collected materials on the Uiltas and Nivkhs and their languages. These were published by IKEGAMI in 1983. Takeshi HATTORI, a scholar in Gilyak published a short Uilta text in 1943. Among the field books of the Ainu scholar Mashiho CHIRI, there is one book in which he recorded Uilta words. However, this is still in the form of an unpublished manuscript.

Takechiyo KASAI recorded about 360 Uilta words and a smaller number of Nivkh words, which were put into mimeographed form in 1928 and 1975. In 'Giriyaku Orokko Kibutsu Kaisetsusho (=An Explanation of Gilyak and Orokko Artifacts)', an anonymous manuscript published in 1986 that seems to be a part of the catalog of the former Karafuto-chô Museum, we also find a hundred words of Uilta. These words were acquired from an informant named Wasilai at Otasu in 1928. Seitarô OZAWA prepared a work with a vocabulary containing about 190 Uilta words along with Nivkh, Evenki, Olcha and Yakut words, which was put into mimeographed form in 1931. This work was published with word indexes in 1992.

According to what is written in the work of the Russian ethnographer B. A. VASIL'EV (1929), he made a collection of about three hundred Uilta words, but it is not clear whether or not it was published.

Charles HAGUENAUER, a French scholar acquired Uilta words from native speakers at the mouth of the Poronai river in 1931.

Tetsuo INUKAI, a Japanese zoologist recorded Uilta words concerning seal-hunting and others. Keitarô MIYAMOTO participated in an ethnological expedition to South Sakhalin in 1938 and collected about a hundred Uilta words concerning food, clothing and shelter. Toshio (alias Yûkô) YAMAMOTO recorded a number of Uilta words in 1939–1946 while collecting many folktales from the aboriginal peoples on Sakhalin.

As for PETROVA, she began collecting materials from Uilta students in Leningrad in 1936. They seem to have come from northern Sakhalin. After the World War II, she also collected Uilta materials during a field trip to Sakhalin including the Poronaisk region. The Uilta words she obtained are included in a comparative dictionary of the Tungus-Manchu languages compiled by a group of Russian scholars under the direction of Vera Ivanovna CINCIUS (=SSTMIA). In 1967 PETROVA published a work entitled "The language of the Oroks" containing phonetics, morphology and texts. It gives us an outline of the Uilta grammar with an abundance of examples. She also wrote an article that gives a brief outline of the Uilta grammar in Vol. 5 of "Iazyki narodov SSSR", which was published in 1968. PETROVA brought the study of Uilta to the same level as that of the other Tungus languages. The form of her linguistic description of Uilta is on a par with descriptions of the other Tungus languages given by other Russian researchers of the Tungus languages.

I would like to discuss some problems that are found in PETROVA's works.

First, she distinguishes between short vowels and long vowels, but it is doubtful whether the distinction of vowel length is maintained consistently in her work. In the word meaning 'hand', which is transcribed as *ŋala* in her work, the first vowel is short according to her, but it is really a long vowel. This was corrected in SSTMIA . In the word meaning 'sleigh', which is transcribed as *okso* in both of her work (1967) and SSTMIA , the final vowel is short, but it is correctly a long vowel.

Secondly, she transcribes a certain vowel in the same word differently. For example, *buju(n), bojo(n)* 'a bear' and *muru, muro, moro* 'thought, mind'. Such transcription makes one suspect that in the dialect under her investigation the vowel in question represents the phoneme ɵ, which is to be distinguished from the other rounded vowel phonemes in the same way that it is distinguished in the dialect of southern Sakhalin.

Thirdly, she refers to the accusative form *narrē* of the substantive *nari* 'man', but she does not give any explanation for the repetition of the consonant *r* in this accusative form. This is an accusative form that was morpho-phonologically modified through a process we call compensatory doubling(or gemination).

Compensatory doubling is a term we use to refer to the modification that occurs in the inflection of a word-stem followed by a certain ending, such as *-ba* (the accusative ending of a substantive), *-ri* (an ending of the imperfect verbalnoun), etc. When a word-stem ends in the succession of phonemes VCV, the initial consonant phoneme of the ending *b* or *r* is usually dropped. To compensate for this, the last consonant phoneme of the stem, which is in a postvocalic position, is doubled (or geminated). (See note 1.) When the *b* or *r* is dropped, the preceding stem-final vowel phoneme and the following vowel phoneme of the ending form a succession of two vowel phonemes VV (pronounced as a long vowel or a diphthong) or a single phoneme V (pronounced as a short vowel). An example of this is *nari* plus *-ba* → *narree* (the accusative form of *nari* 'man'). Compensatory doubling also occurs in the suffixation of certain productive suffixes, such as *-bu* (a verbal suffix). This morpho-phonological modification plays an important role in the inflection of substantives and verbs in Uilta. If this is disregarded, inflection in Uilta cannot be adequately analyzed and explained.

Strictly and consistently distinguishing between a short vowel (corresponding to V) and a long vowel (corresponding to VV), distinguishing between the vowel phoneme *ɵ* and other rounded vowel phonemes, and analyzing in terms of the morpho-phonological modification mentioned above are indispensable to the linguistic description of Uilta. On the other hand, we should take note of the fact that changes are taking place in present-day Uilta. To a considerable extent, long vowels are confused with short vowels, the vowel phoneme *ɵ* is changing into the vowel phoneme *u*, and accusative forms are being simplified.

Klavdiia Aleksandrovna. NOVIKOVA participated in an expedition to Sakhalin in 1952 and collected materials on Uilta. The Uilta words she obtained are included in SSTMIA. One short text she obtained is found in her work of 1961. Kengo YAMAMOTO collected materials on Uilta in Hokkaido, some of which are found in an encyclopaedia article he wrote.

A number of Uilta immigrants to Hokkaido (from the Poronaisk area in Sakhalin), who served as linguistic informants for investigators, provided abundant materials on their language and made valuable contributions to the study of Uilta, though they themselves did not write anything. These were Chiyo SATÔ, an Uilta woman whose given name was Napka, Gorô KITAGAWA, a male shaman whose given name was Gɵrgɵlɵ, Washirô NAKAGAWA, an Uilta man whose given name was Jəuriŋənu and Ume OGAWA, an Uilta woman whose given name was Ʒəktəŋgu.

Another noteworthy Uilta who immigrated into Hokkaido was Gentarô KITAGAWA, an Uilta man whose given name was Geeldaanu. He wrote a reader of Uilta in Japanese kana entitled "*Uilta Kəsəni* (=the Uilta language)", which consists of Uilta words and short sentences used in daily life. After his death in 1984, this voluminous work was published with phonemic transcription and Japanese translation by J. IKEGAMI and Toshirô TSUMAGARI as a multi-volume work in 1986, 1988, 1990 and 1991. His work is very useful for learning Uilta. It also presents some important facts on the daily use of Uilta, such as the appearance of some future indicative forms that were modified through analogy with some other inflected forms. The original future indicative forms are also used in his work. Such analogical formations in the inflected forms of present-day Uilta suggest that analogy has been and will continue to be an important cause of linguistic change in the case of agglutinative languages, such as the Tungus languages of which Uilta is a member.

Others who have investigated the Uilta language in recent times are :

Robert AUSTERLITZ, an American researcher who collected Uilta materials from Gilyak and Uilta informants on Hokkaido in 1954 and

1956–1958, while investigating Gilyak.

L. I. SEM, a Russian researcher who collected Uilta materials during an expedition to Sakhalin in 1963. The Uilta words she obtained are included in SSTMIA.

Kan WADA, a Japanese anthropologist who obtained some Uilta shamanistic terms from Napka and Gəəgələ on Hokkaido. Shin'ichirô KURODA, a Japanese anthropologist who recorded a number of Uilta cultural terms from Napka, in addition to a short folkloric text that she dictated to him.

J. IKEGAMI, a Japanese researcher who has been working with Uilta informants on Hokkaido and Sakhalin since 1949 and 1990, respectively. He published some articles on the morphology of Uilta, a collection of Uilta texts and an Uilta dictionary. T. TSUMAGARI, a Japanese researcher who has also been working with Uilta informants on Hokkaido since 1977. He published some articles on phonological, grammatical and typological problems of Uilta.

Irina Iakovlevna FEDIAEVA and Elena Alekseevna BIBIKOVA, Uilta women who live at the village Val and are engaging in collecting materials on the northern dialects of their own language.

Larisa Viktorovna Ozolinia, a Russian researcher who compiled an Uilta dictionary.

I will not discuss the study of Uilta today, since this does not yet belong to the past history.

Note

1) The doubling of a consonant is phonetically realized as a double consonant after a short vowel, typically the short vowel of the first syllable. Also, it is realized as a single consonant preceded by the tension of the larynx (or the closure of the glottis) after a long vowel or a diphthong, or occasionally after a short vowel of a syllable other than the first syllable.

References

AUSTERLITZ, Robert. "Native seal nomenclatures in South-Sahalin", *Papers of the CIC Far Eastern Languages Institute, the University of Minnesota, 1966 and the University of Michigan, 1967.* Ann Arbor, 1968.

CHIRI, Mashiho. Field Books, No.3 (in manuscript).

CINCIUS, V. I. et al., *Sravnitel'nyi slovar' tunguso-man'čžurskikh iazykov,* 2 vol., Leningrad, 1975, 1977.

HAGUENAUER, Charles. "Note à propos de japonais *ha,* lame, tranchant", *Études choisies de Charles Haguenauer,* Volume l, Japon Études de linguistique, E. J. Brill, Leiden, 1976.

HATTORI, Takeshi. "Orokko-go 'Kita-kaze to taiyô' (=An example of transcription of 'the north wind and the sun' in the Orok language)", *Onsei-gaku Kyôkai Kaihô (the Bulletin of the Phonetic Association of Japan)* 72/73, Tokyo, 1943.

IKEGAMI, Jirô. "Tsungûsu-go Orokko hôgen no boin-onso ö ni tsuite (On the vowel phoneme ö in the Orokko dialect of Tungus)", *Gengo Kenkyu (Journal of the Linguistic Society of Japan),* 22/23, 1953.

—— " 'Tsungûsu-Manshû-sho-go Hikaku Jiten' ni tsuite (=Remarks on 'A Comparative Dictionary of the Tungus-Manchu Languages')", *Mado* 16, Nauka, Tokyo, 1976.

—— "Uiruta-go Orucha-go kenkyû ni okeru B. Piusutsuki (B. Pilsudski in Uilta and Olcha studies)", *PSHMBK KMHKH*B (*BPMNPC BNME*SI) 5, Osaka, 1987 (which is the revised version of his article, B. Pilsudski in Uilta and Olcha studies, *PISPPRAC,* Hokkaido University, Sapporo, 1985).

INUKAI, Tetsuo. "Karafuto Orokko no kaihyô-ryô (The seal hunting of Saghalien-Orochon)", *Hoppô Bunka Kenkyû Hôkoku* (= Studies from the Research Institute for Northern Culture) 4, Hokkaido Imperial

University, Sapporo, 1941.

KASAI, Takechiyo. *Karafuto Dojin Kenkyû Shiryô* (=Materials for the Study of the Natives of Karafuto), Tonnai, Karafuto, 1928 and Hokkaido, 1975.

KAWAMURA Hideya Sairoku Karafuto Sho-minzoku no Gengo to Minzoku (Hideya KAWAMURA's Materials on the Languages and Folklore of the Peoples of Sakhalin) edited by Jirô IKEGAMI, *UMBKCH (RURUCF)* 5, HBE, Sapporo and SPNRCF, Abashiri, 1983.

KINDAICHI, Kyôsuke. *Nihon Kokunai Sho-jinshu no Gengo* (=Languages of the Peoples in Japan), Tokyo, 1912.

KITAGAWA Gentarô hitsuroku 'Uiruta no Kotoba' (1) (Gentaro KITAGAWA's Written Records of Uilta (1)) in *Giriyaku Orokko Kibutsu Kaisetsu-sho, Kitagawa Gentarô Hitsuroku 'Uiruta no Kotoba'* (1) (*An Explanation of Gilyak and Orokko Artifacts and Gentaro Kitagawa's Written Records of Uilta* (1)) edited by Jiro IKEGAMI, *UMBKCH (RURUCF)* 8, HBE, Sapporo and SPNRCF, Abashiri, 1986.

KITAGAWA Gentarô Hitsuroku 'Uiruta no Kotoba' (Gentarô KITAGAWA's Written Records of Uilta) (2,3,4), translated with phonemic transcription and Japanese translation by Jirô IKEGAMI and Toshirô TSUMAGARI, *UMBKCH (RURUCF)* 9, 11, 12, HBE, Sapporo and SPNRCF, Abashiri, 1988,1990, 1991.

KURODA, Shin'ichirô. "Mingu · sekai-kan · yume (Handicrafts, world-view and dreams)", *UGBCKH (RRLCUO)* 1, Hokkaido University, Sapporo, 1980.

—— "Uiruta (Orokko) chôsa oboegaki (Some brief notes concerning research among the Orok)", *Minzokugaku-kenkyu (The Japanese Journal of Ethnology)*, Vol. 44 No. 3, 1979.

MAGATA, Hisaharu. *Uiruta-go Jiten (A Dictionary of the Uilta Language)*, SPNRCF, Abashiri, 1981.

MATSUURA, Takeshiro. "Orokko-go (=The Orok language)" in *Karafuto*

Nishi-okuchi Risû-sho (=A Record of the Survey of the Far Western District of Sakhalin), a manuscript and *Hokuchi Risû Torishirabe-sho* (=A Report of the Survey of the Northern Region) a manuscript, published by Jirô IKEGAMI in his article "Jû-kyû-seiki nakagoro no Orokko goshû — Santan-go Giriyaku-go o fukumu— (A vocabulary of mid-nineteenth century Orok —including Santan (Olcha) and Gilyak words)", *Hoppo Bunka Kenkyu (Bulletin of the Institute for the Study of North Eurasian Cultures, Hokkaido University*) 5, Sapporo, 1971.

—— *Ampoku Koshô, Matsuura Takeshirô Nikki* (=The Diary of Matsuura Takeshirô, an Attendant of the Inspection Tour in the Northern Region) in manuscript (*Takeshirô Kaiho Nikki*, annotated by Shin'ichirô TAKAMURA, Sapporo, 1978).

MIYAMOTO, Keitarô. "Orokko·Giriyâku no ishokujû (Clothing, food and housing of Oroks and Gilyaks)", *Minzokugaku-kenkyu (The Japanese Journal of Ethnology)*, Vol. 22 No. 1·2, 1958.

NAKANOME, Akira. *Karafuto no Hanashi* (=An Account of Sakhalin), Tokyo 1917.

—— *Orokko Bunten* (=An Orokko Grammar), Tokyo, 1917. (The German translation by W. OTHMER —*Grammatik der Orokko-Sprache*, Osaka Tôyôgakkai, (The Osaka Asiatic Society), Osaka, 1928.)

NOVIKOVA, K. A. *Proekt edinoi fonetičeskoi transkripcii dlia tunguso-man'-čžurskikh iazykov.* AN SSSR, Institut Iazykoznaniia, Komissiia po unificirovannoi fonetičeskoi transkripcii (UFT) dlia iazykov narodov SSSR, Moskva-Leningrad, 1961.

—— Ėkspedicionnye leksičeskie materialy K. A. Novikovoi (1952 g.) which are included in *SSTMIA*, Leningrad, 1975, 1977.

OZAWA, Seitarô. *Ainu gai Dojin Chôsa* (1) (=Investigation of the Natives other than the Ainus(1)), Karafuto, 1931. This work is included in *Materials on the Natives of Sakhalin in 1931 and Additions to 'An Uilta*

Vocabulary of Daily Living' by Jirô IKEGAMI, *UMBKCH (RURUCF)* 13, HBE, Sapporo and SPNRCF, Abashiri, 1992.

PETROVA, T. I. *Iazyk orokov (ul'ta)*, Leningrad, 1967.

—— "Orokskii iazyk", *Iazyki narodov SSSR*, V, Leningrad, 1968.

—— Materialy po orokskomu slovariu, priložennye k dissertacii na soiskanie učenoi stepeni kand. nauk T. I. Petrovoi 《Grammatičeskii ocerk iazyka orokov》 (1946 g.) which are included in *SSTMIA*, Leningrad, 1975, 1977.

PIŁSUDSKI, Bronisław. *Materials for the Study of the Orok (Uilta) Language and Folklore*, I, Fonetičeskie i grammatičeskie zamečaniia k iazyku orokov, orokskie teksty, transcribed from the manuscript and edited by Alfred F. Majewicz, *UAMPILWP* 16, Poznań, 1985.

—— *Materials for the Study of the Orok (Uilta) Language and Folklore*, II, Grammatical notes on Orok, Orok texts, Orok-Polish Dictionary, transcribed from the manuscripts by Elżbieta Majewicz, provided with English translation and equivalents by Elżbieta and Alfred F.Majewicz, introduction by Władysław Kotwicz, prefaced and edited by Alfred F. Majewicz, *UAMPILWP* fasc. 17, Poznań, 1987.

SEM, L. I. Ėkspedicionnye leksičeskie materialy L. I. Sem (1963 g.) which are included in *SSTMIA*, Leningrad, 1975, 1977.

TSUMAGARI, Toshirô. " 'Tsungûsu-Manshû-sho-go Hikaku Jiten' no Uiruta-go tango no kentô (Remarks on Uilta words in 'Comparative Dictionary of the Tungus-Manchu Languages')", *UGBCKH (RRLCUO)* 1, Hokkaido University, Sapporo, 1980.

—— "On B. Pilsudski's Orok vocabulary", *PISPPRAC*, Hokkaido University, Sapporo, 1985.

—— "B. Piusutsuki no Orokko-go bunpô-kijutsu ni tsuite (Remarks on B. Pilsudski's Orok grammatical sketch)", *PSHMBK KMHKHB* (*BPMNPC BNMESI*) 5, Osaka, 1987.

VASIL'EV, B. A. "Osnovnye čerty ėtnografii orokov, Predvaritel'nyi očepk po materialam ėkspedicii 1928 g.", *Ėtnografiia*, 1929 No. 1, Moskva-Leningrad.

WADA, Kan. "Uiruta-zoku no shamanizumu-teki gûzô (The shamanistic effigies of the Uilta)", *UGBCKH (RRLCUO)* 1, Hokkaido University, Sapporo, 1980.

YAMAMOTO, Kengo. "Tungûsu-go (=The Tungus language)", *Sekai Dai Hyakka-jiten* (=Encyclopaedia Heibonsha), Heibonsha, Tokyo, 1972.

YAMAMOTO, Yûkô. *Hoppô Shizen-minzoku Minwa Shûsei —Orokko, Giriyâku, Yakûto, Karafuto-Ainu* (= A Collection of the Folktales of the Aboriginal Peoples of the North —Orokko, Gilyak, Yakut, Sakhalin-Ainu), Sagami-shobô, Tokyo, 1968.

anonymous. "Giriyaku Orokko kibutsu kaisetsu-sho (=An Explanation of Gilyak and Orokko Artifacts)" in *Giriyaku Orokko Kibutsu Kaisetsu-sho, Kitagawa Gentarô Hitsuroku 'Uiruta no kotoba'* (1) (*An Explanation of Gilyak and Orokko Artifacts and Gentaro Kitagawa's Written Records of Uilta* (1)) edited by Jirô IKEGAMI, *UMBKCH (RURUCF)* 8, HBE, Sapporo and SPNRCF, Abashiri, 1986.

ABBREVIATION

BNME SI	*Bulletin of the National Museum of Ethnology*, Special Issue
BPMNPC	*Bronislaw Pilsudski's Materials on Northern Peoples and Cultures*, edited by Kyûzô KATÔ and Yoshinobu KOTANI
HBE	Hokkaido Board of Education
KMHKH B	*Kokuritsu Minzoku-gaku Hakubutsukan Kenkyû Hôkoku*, Bessatsu
PISPPRAC	*Proceedings of the International Symposium on B. Pilsudski's Phonographic Records and the Ainu Culture*
PSHMBK	KATÔ Kyûzô, KOTANI Yoshinobu hen, *Piusutsuki Shiryô to Hoppô Sho-minzoku-bunka no Kenkyû*
RRLCUO	*Research Reports on the Language and Culture of the Uiltas (Oroks)*
RURUCF	*Reports on Urgent Research concerning Uilta Culture and Folklore*
SPNRCF	The Society for the Preservation of Northern Region Culture and Folklore

SSTMIA	V. I. CINCIUS i dr., *Sravnitel'nyi slovar' tunguso-man'čžurskikh iazykov*, 2 toma.
UAMPILWP	*Uniwersytet im. Adama Mickiewicza w Poznaniu, Institute of Linguistics, Working Papers*
UGBCKH	*Uiruta-zoku Gengo Bunka Chôsa Kenkyû Hôkoku*
UMBKCH	*Uiruta Minzoku Bunka-zai Kinkyû Chôsa Hôkoku-sho*

This article is the second revised and enlarged version of my paper "A History of the Study of the Uilta Language," which I read at the International Conference B. O. Pilsudskiy in Yužno-Sakhalinsk in 1991. It was printed in *Saharin to B. Piusutsuki* (=Sakhalin and B.Piłsudski), which was published by Piusutsuki-o Meguru Hoppô-no Tabi Jikkô-iinkai in 1992. A Russian translation of the original article, entitled "Istorija issledovanija jazyka uilta (a translation from the English by V. G. Svalova)" appeared in *B. O. Pilsudskij —issledovatel' narodov Sakhalina (Materialy meždunarodnoj-naučnoj konferencii. 31 oktjabrja—2 nojabrja 1991 g. Yužno-Sakhalinsk)* (Sakhalinskij oblastnoj kraevedcheskij muzej, Yužno-Sakhalinsk, 1992), Vol. 2, pp. 5–10.

The first revised and enlarged version of my paper appeared in a research report entitled *Ethnic Minorities in Sakhalin* in 1993. This report is a compilation of the research results of a research project called "Research on the Languages of Minorities in Sakhalin—Ainu, Uilta, Nivkh", which was organized by Kyôko MURASAKI and supported by the grant-in-aid from the Japanese Ministry of Education.

Addenda

1. American Orientalist Berthold LAUFER did field work among the Ainus, Gilyaks, and Uiltas in Sakhalin in 1898 and 1899 and obtained materials for Uilta (according to Kôichi INOUE and Tat'jana Petrovna ROON). Cf. LAUFER, Berthold, "Ethnographical Work on the Island of Saghalin", *Science*, New Series Vol. IX No. 230, Washington, 1899.

2. Shûzô ISHIDA, a Japanese anthropologist visited Sisuka (now Poronaisk) and other places along the seacoast to the east of Sisuka in 1907, 1909, 1912 and 1917 in order to collect ethnographic and linguistic materials from the Ainu, Gilyak and Orok inhabitants. At his death he left abundant ethnographic descriptions of these peoples along with illustrations and a number of words and short sentences of Gilyak and Uilta. The linguistic materials were written in kana. Cf. KONISHI, Masanori, "Ishida

Shûzô no Minami-Karafuto Chôsa-kô ni tsuite (=On Shûzô Ishida's Field Study in Southern Sakhalin)", *Nomura Sensei Kanreki Kinen Ronshû, Hoppô no Kôkogaku (=Archaeological Researches Concerning Northern Regions)*, Sapporo, 1998.

On the Santan Vocabularies of the Eighteenth and Nineteenth Centuries

The basin of the lower reaches of the Amur was called 'Santan' or 'Sandan' by the Japanese in the Tokugawa period (1603–1867). At that time the people of the Santan region often visited Sakhalin and traded with the natives there. Ethnically what are these people? Rinzô MAMIYA, a Japanese official who visited the basin of the lower Amur River in 1809, in the account of his travels, *Tôtatsu Kikô* restricted the name 'the Satans' to a tribe on the lower Amur River. On the basis of their distribution mentioned by MAMIYA, Dr. L. VON SCHRENCK regarded the Santans in this account as the Olchas. VON SCHRENCK considered, however, that the name, 'the Satans', refers to the Goldis and the Olchas, for, in his opinion, the word 'Satan' is derived from the Gilyak name for the Goldis, *jant* or *janta*. On the other hand, in some Japanese records regarding Sakhalin, we also find Gilyaks among the visitors from the Santan region. Prof. K. SHIRATORI has already pointed out this fact in his article, *The Santan in the Tôtatsu-kikô*.

We possess some collections of the words used by the people of the Santan region, which were noted down by Japanese travellers at the end of the eighteenth century and in the nineteenth century. We call these words "Santan words" and the collections of them "Santan vocabularies". So far as we know at present, there are the following :

1. A Santan vocabulary, probably gathered by a Japanese traveller in 1786, appearing in Tokunai MOGAMI's *Ezo Zôshi*, which contains the author's essays on Yezo. One copy in the possession of the Historiographical Institute of the University of Tokyo, which was written in

the author's own hand, is cited here. The preface is dated 1790.Contains 26 words.

2. A list of trade goods, with the Santan terms, in *Karafuto-jima Zakki*, the record of the author's journey to Saghalien in 1790. We can make use of the three handwritten copies of this book here. 20 words.

3. A Santan vocabulary in *Ezo Fudoki* (Description of Yezo) by NÎYAMA (alias Inze KASAI) which was written, at the latest, by 1799. We can make use of the five handwritten copies of this book here. 52 words.

4. A Santan vocabulary dated 1792, an appendix to a handwritten copy of Tokunai MOGAMI's *Ezo Zôshi* in the possession of the Archives and Mausolea Division, Imperial Household Agency, Tokyo. 148 words.

5. A Santan vocabulary in *Ezo Fudoki* (Description of Yezo) by Sekijô SEKI. The preface is dated 1793. 49 words.

6. A Santan vocabulary in *Karafuto Zakki*, the record of the author's travel in Saghalien in 1801. The manuscript in the possession of the Hokkaidô Prefectural Government in Sapporo is cited here. 59 words.

7. Santan words included in *Ezo Goshû*, an Ainu-Japanese dictionary in the possession of the Cabinet Library, Tokyo. The compiler may have been born about 1760. 53 words.

8. A Santan vocabulary in *Einige Nachrichten über Krafto und Sandan* by Ph. Fr. VON SIEBOLD, a manuscript which was written presumably between 1826 and 1829. 73 words.

9. Santan numerals at the end of a manuscript of *Karafuto Nikki* in the possession of the Cabinet Library, Tokyo. It is an account of the author's journey in Saghalien in 1854. 10 words.

10. *Santan Goi*, a Santan vocabulary, a manuscript which we suppose to have been written between 1882 and 1886. It is in the possession of the Hokkaidô Prefectural Government in Sapporo. 43 words.

These sources, except Source No. 5, furnish the material for this paper.

We omit the detailed bibliographical notes on these sources. In addition, we have two manuscripts of a vocabulary entitled *Orokko-go* (Orok), which was compiled probably at the end of the Tokugawa period and contains not only Orok words but also Gilyak words and Santan words. Other Santan vocabularies, which seem to have been derived from the above-mentioned sources, are omitted here, e.g. a list of the trade goods of Ainus and Santans in *Hen'yôbunkaizukô* by Morishige KONDÔ, the preface of which is dated 1804.

Except for Sources Nos. 5 and 8 the Santan words are transcribed in the Japanese syllabic characters called kana. In Source No. 5 the words are transcribed in Chinese characters, and in Source No. 8 in the Roman alphabet. The Santan words are translated into Japanese except in Source No. 8, where most of the Santan words are translated into German, some of them, however, have no translation. Kana are here romanized following Hepburn's system. According to this system, the kana エ and ヱ are romanized to *e* and the kana オ and ヲ to *o*. However, in these sources where エ is found only in one word and オ not at all, it is open to question, whether エ and ヱ respectively are pronounced *e* or *ye*, ヲ *o* or *wo*. The transcription of the Santan words by VON SIEBOLD is instructive for this question, because he obtained them from Japanese sources.

It is evident that the Santan words are not accurately transcribed in these sources. For instance, the distinction between voiceless and voiced consonants is neglected very often in the kana transcription of the Santan words. This is perhaps partly due to the fact that these words were noted down after hearing the pronunciation of them by Ainus. On the other hand, the manuscripts seem to contain many errors made by copyists.

In these vocabularies we find, in all, about 220 different Santan words. What language or languages do these Santan words belong to ? This is the problem we deal with here.

On the basis of the correspondence of Manchu words to fifteen of the Santan words presented by VON SIEBOLD, J. KLAPROTH pointed out in the *Journal Asiatique* in 1829 that the language of the Santans is “un dialecte de la langue toungouse, qui se rapproche beaucoup du mandchou”. We can say that the opinion of KLAPROTH is true in respect of the Tungus words in the Santan vocabularies. However, the supposed correspondence of the Santan words *ton* ‘soleil’ and *bi* ‘lune’ to Manchu *šun* and *biya* is open to question, because Ainu *tombe* ‘the sun or moon’ (according to J. BATCHELOR'S Ainu dictionary[4]) may have been mistakenly divided into *ton* and *bi* by the Japanese compilers of the Santan vocabularies.

About fifty of these Santan words are not yet identified in any language. About twenty of them coincide with Ainu words, e.g. ,

Santan	Ainu
amama ‘kome (= rice)’ (S. No. 6)	*amam*
gû ‘yumi (= bow)’ (8. No. 10)	*ku*
ningari, ninkari ‘mimiwa (= earring)’ (S. No. 3)	*ninkari*
seta ‘inu (= dog)’ (S. No. 10)	*seta*
shiyumari ‘kitsune (= fox)’ (S. No. 6)	*sumari*

We believe that these vocabularies may contain Ainu words, rather than loan-words from Ainu to another language. The following accounts for this. Some Japanese travellers, such as the author of Source No. 6, probably collected Santan words through an Ainu interpreter or from an Ainu having some knowledge of the speech of the people in the Santan region and so may have mistaken some Ainu words for Santan words. The Santan vocabulary of Source No. 6 consists of two parts, each with the name of an Ainu, which seems to be the informant's name. Some compilers of the vocabularies, such as the author of Source No. 10, seem to have failed to distinguish Santan words from Ainu words in their sources. Furthermore, the people of the Santan region may have used some Ainu words in trading with the Ainus, so that these Ainu words were mistakenly regarded by Japanese travellers as Santan words.

The Santan vocabularies also acquaint us with what may be Gilyak words, as *funji* (S. Nos. 1, 3), *sonshi* (S. No. 4) 'yumi (= bow)', *tunzi* (S. No. 8) 'Bogen' (It seems that the ソ (= so) in *sonshi* is a miscopy of フ (= *fu*) and the *tu* in *tunzi* is derived from the pronunciation of the ツ (= *tsu*) which is a miscopy of フ (= *fu*).), cf. Gilyak *punt* 'Bogen'. Some Santan words are similar to both Tungus and Gilyak words, which are loan-words from one of them to the other or from other languages to both of them, e.g. *chiyanke* (S. Nos. 3, 4, 7, 10), *chiyante* (S. No. 4) 'tômoku (= chief), yakunin (= official) etc.', *dsjanke* (S. No. 8) 'ein Priester' (The テ (= *te*) in *chiyante* is a miscopy of ケ (= *ke*).), cf. Olcha *ʒaŋgin* 'orator, načal'nik', Gilyak *ʒ́ắṅgin* 'Herr, ein Mann aus höherem Stande'.

Some words are loan-words from Chinese, e.g. *shiyohahan* 'soroban (= abacus)' (S. No. 4), Chinese *suan*^{4} *p'an*^{2}; *antai* 'kiseru (= tobacco pipe)' (S. No. 4), Chinese *yen*^{1} *tai*^{4}.

At least half the Santan words in these vocabularies are Tungus words, e.g. *omou* (S. Nos. 3, 6, 9, 10), *omo͜u* (S. No. 1), *omô* (S. No. 4) 'ichi (= one)', *womô* (S. No. 8) 'eins'; *mou* (S. Nos. 1, 3, 4) 'maki (= firewood)', *mô* (S. No. 8) 'Brennholz'; *namo* (S. Nos. 1, 3, 4, 8) 'umi (= sea), die See'.

A number of Tungus words in the Santan vocabularies have the same peculiarities as Goldi, Olcha and Orok words have. We find the following sound correspondences :

The intial *h* in some Santan words, which represents presumably *x*, corresponds to *h* (*x*) in Goldi and Olcha, *x* in Orok, and zero in the other Tungus languages.

Santan	Olcha	Evenki
hamuta 'hara (= belly)' (S. No. 4)	*həmdə*	*əmugdə* 'vnutrennosti'
hurei 'yama (= mountain)' (S. No. 6)	*hụrən*	*urə*
huri 'tsuru, yumizuru (= bowstring)' (S. No. 7)	*hụlin*	*il*

The *o* in some Santan words, which represents presumably *u*, corresponds to *u* or *ụ* in Manchu, Goldi, Olcha and Orok, and *i* in the other Tungus languages.

Santan	Olcha	Evenki
ton 'mune (= breast)' (S. No. 4)	*tụŋgən*	*tingən*
tonta 'ame (= rain)' (S. No. 4)	*tụgdə*	*tigdə*

To which language or languages of Goldi, Olcha, Orok (or a language closely related to them) do the Tungus words in these vocabularies belong ?

Many Tungus words in the Santan vocabularies coincide with both Goldi and Olcha words. These two languages have many points of similarity, but also some differences. We find that some Santan words have the Olcha sound peculiarity. The Santan numeral 'go (= five)' is a good example :

tsuchiya (S. No. 1);

tsudeya (S. No. 3) (in one manuscript of this source *te* is found instead of *de*);

tsukeya (S. No. 4);

katsushichiya (S. No. 6) (*ka* is perhaps a redundant letter. The シ (= *shi*) is a miscopy of ン (= *n*).);

pudsja (S. No. 8) 'fünf' (The *pu* seems to have derived from a miscopy of ツ (= *tsu*).);

donshiya (S. No. 9);

donjiya (S. No. 10).

Cf. Goldi *tojŋga*, Olcha *tuŋ̹ʒa*. We can say that *tsukeya* in Source No. 4 resembles the Goldi form. However, the ケ (= *ke*) here may be a miscopy of チ (= *chi*). In the same source we find *tonshiyo* 'shitajubi (= the little finger)', which is presumably the numeral 'five'. The Santan word *hanshiya* 'ashishita' (= sole)' (S. No. 4) seems also to have the same peculiarity as the Olcha word has. Cf. Goldi *palgan* 'stupnja, podošva', Olcha *palʒan* 'the same'. These Santan words may be considered to contain the same phoneme as the Olcha *ʒ*. In the words corresponding to these Santan words, Olcha *ʒ* corresponds to Goldi *g*. We consider that in these words Common Tungus **g* remains unchanged in Goldi but was changed in Olcha to *ʒ*. Accordingly these Santan words cannot be considered as belonging to Goldi. The Santan words *eshiyaru* 'me (= eye)' (S. No. 4) is also nearer to Olcha *isali* than to Goldi *nasal*, *ŋasar* (according to P. SCHMIDT's Olcha vocabulary).

Tungus words in the Santan vocabularies, on the whole, resemble more closely Olcha and Goldi words than Orok words :

Santan	Goldi	Olcha	Orok
omou, omou͜, omô, womô 'one' (see above)	*əmun*	*omon, umun*	*geeda*
tokishiyo 'kumo (= cloud)' (S. No. 4)	*təwəksə*	*təwəksə*	*təwəskə*

Among them we find the Santan word *mekuta* 'kami' (= hair)' (S. No. 4). The メ (= *me*) here is considered to be a miscopy of ヌ (= *nu*). This word is also nearer to Goldi *nuktə* and Olcha *nu̇ktə* than to Orok *niruktə* and *nuriktə*. The *nuktə* (*nu̇ktə*) results from the loss of the **r* in **niruktə* or **nuriktə*. It seems evident that this Santan word does not belong to Orok.

From the above we draw the conclusion that, for the most part, the Tungus words in the Santan vocabularies may be considered to be Olcha words of an earlier period (or words of an old language more closely related to Olcha than to Goldi and Orok). We cannot suppose, however, that no word of any other Tungus language is included in the Santan vocabularies, for the Santan words do not all belong to one and the same language. The Santan word *hoshikiku* 'hoshi (= star)' (S. No. 4) (the ク (= *ku*) is undoubtedly a miscopy of タ (= *ta*)) is nearer to Goldi *hosekta* or Orok *xosikta* than to Olcha *hosta*. This Santan word may indeed belong to Goldi or Orok, but it is also possible that Olcha *hosta* results from the syncope of the Santan word which represents presumably *xosikta*. Through the Santan vocabularies we can turn back to the end of the eighteenth century.

Finally, as a specimen of the Santan vocabularies we give the Santan words recorded in Source No. 1.

1. *hotsutou* 'jittoku (a king of coat)'
2. *harata* 'konji-nishiki (= blue brocade)'
3. *boushi* 'momen (= cotton)'
4. *chiyoshichiyo* 'akaji-nishiki (= red brocade)'
5. *chiyuei* 'aodama (= blue gem)'
6. *haraki* 'sake (= spirits)'
   'h' at the beginning of this word may possibly represent unusual aspiration.
7. *funji* 'yumi (= bow)'
8. *chiyatsuputsu* 'ya (= arrow)'
9. *tawowo* 'hi (= fire)'
10. *san' ya* 'kemuri (= smoke)'
11. *untaa* 'fune (= ship)'
12. *namo* 'umi (= sea)'
13. *buri* 'kome (= rice)'
14. *mou* 'maki (= firewood)'
15. *wata* 'nami (= wave)'
16. *hotambe* 'wan (= bowl)'
17. *omou* 'ichi (= one)'
18. *nata* 'ni (= two)'
19. *chiyatsupo* 'san (= three)'
20. *eraa* 'shi (= four)'
21. *tsuchiya* 'go (= five)'
22. *yukuu* 'roku (= six)'
23. *tsui* 'shichi (= seven)'
24. *hari* 'hachi (= eight)'
25. *horei* 'ku (= nine)'
26. *tsuwaa* 'jû (= ten)'

The first four words are not found in many other handwritten copies of this book.

Cf. 1. Olcha *hụktụ* 'zimnij chalat na vate', *pokto* 'rubaška iz tonkoj materii', Gilyak *xukt* 'Rock aus baumwollenem Zeuge, nach Art der mandschurischen', 3. O. *ʙusu* 'materija, bumažnaja manufaktura', G. *pos* 'Leinwand, Baumwollenzeug', 4. ? O. *səgʒən* 'krasnyj', 5. Chinese?, 6. O. *araki* 'vodka', G. *árak* 'Branntwein', 7. G. *punt* 'Bogen', 8. O. *ʒaʙdun* 'strela (samostrela)', 9. O. *tawa* 'ogon'', 10. O. *saŋn̦an* 'dym', 11.? O. *ugda* 'lodka', 12. O. *nāmu* 'more', 13. O. *handu-ʙələ* 'ris', 14. O. *mō* 'derevo, drova, palka', 15. O. *wata* 'volna', 16. O. *kotan, kutan* 'tarelka, derevjannaja tarelka' + *ʙa* (accusative ending), 17. O. *omon, umun* 'odin', 18. O. *nadan* 'sem'', 19. O. *ʒakpun* 'vosem'', 20. O. *ilan* 'tri', 21. O. *tun̦ʒa* 'pjat'', 22. O. *n̦uŋgu̦n* 'šest', 23. O. *du̦in* '*četyre*', 26. O. *ʒuan* 'desjat''.

The Olcha and Goldi words are cited from T. I. PETROVA'S Nanai-Russian dictionary (1935) and Ul'čskij dialekt nanajskogo jazyka (1936), the Evenki words from G. M. VASILEVIČ'S Evenki-Russian dictionary (1958), the Gilyak words from W. GRUBE'S Gilyak vocabulary, and the Orok words from the collection of Orok words made by the writer himself. The Ainu words were acquired from an Ainu who speaks the Sakhalin dialect[1].

Note

1) The writer presents this article as an improvement of his paper read in the XXVth International Congress of Orientalists (Moscow, 1960). He wishes to thank Prof. V. I. CINCIUS and Mrs. T. I. PETROVA for the beneficial remarks made by them there. The original paper "On the Santan vocabularies of the XVIIIth and XIXth centuries" was printed in *Trudy dvadcat' pjatogo meždunarodnogo kongressa vostokovedov Moskva 9–16 avgusta 1960*, tom III (Moscow, 1963), pp. 439–442.

This article was published in *Ural-Altaische Jahrbücher*, Band 33, Heft 1–2 (1961), pp. 73–77.

ナーナイ語のシカチ・アリャン方言の無声唇摩擦音について

On the Voiceless Labial Fricative Consonant of the Sikachi-Alyan Dialect of Nanai

ツングース語祖語に推定される語頭の *p- および語中母音間の *-p- は，その後推移し，ツングース諸語において *p- はp，またはf（＝f，ɸ），またはx（またはh）（～［iのまえでは］s），またはゼロとなり，*-p- はp，または f，または w，ゼロとなっている。

ツングース語の一つ，ナーナイ語において，アムール川の支流アニュイ川河口近くのナイヒン方言に基礎をおくナーナイ語文語では，p-，-p- の音を保っている。しかし，ウスリ川下流右岸のビキン方言やウスリ川河口より本流アムール川のやや川上右岸（勤得利より川下）の八岔（バーチャ）方言では f-，-f- となっている。

19世紀なかごろウスリ川沿岸で採録したブルィルキン（1861）のホゼン語（ナーナイ語方言）語彙には，語頭に p- が立つ語が7語あり，なかには pikta（子）の語もある。しかし，語頭に f- が立つ語は40語載り，そのなかには，周囲の他方言や他のツングース語と共通する語が少なくない。また，語中母音間および子音の前後に -f- が現れる語例があり，一方，džeptā（食物）の語のように語中子音のまえに -p- の現れる例はあるが，母音間に -p- の現れる語例は載っていないようである。この方言では，当時すでに *p→ f の改新がおきていたことが知られる。

金を建国した女真（女直）族の女真語においては，今日まで残るその記録文献によると，金代（12世紀前半－13世紀前半）には語頭で p- であったが，明代（14世紀後半－17世紀）には f- になっている。また，女真語の方言に由来するとみられる満洲語でも記録にはじめてあらわれる17世紀初頭にすでに f-, -f- であったとみられる。

さて，ウスリ川河口より川下，ナイヒンより川上のアムール川右岸に位置するシカチ・アリャンの方言でも p であるが，-f- の発音もあることは注目に値する。p は語頭に，f は語中母音間に現れる例が目立つ。

ナーナイ語のシカチ・アリャン方言について，筆者は1979年９月ハバーロフスクの教育大学で同大学の T.Z. Pukšanskaja 氏のお世話で N.I. Suslova さん（ハバーロフスク区 Sikači-Aljan 出身，1957年生，当時医学生）から短時間ききとり，約100語の同方言資料を採録した。これは同方言小語彙として本文末尾に付す。語末に聞きとれた弱い鼻音または鼻母音は n の小字で表記した。語彙中の oforo（鼻）の f は両唇無声摩擦音とみられ，ā^{p}fu^{n}（帽子），dolǰixa^{p}fu（われわれは聞いていた）の ^{p}f はそのはじめに弱い p をともなう f である。なお，この発音者はこれら３語の当該子音をロシヤ字の f（ф）で書き表した。ハバーロフスクよりさらに北のこの方言に f の音が現れることは，思いがけなかったので，筆者は興奮と感動さえおぼえたのだった。

なお，この方言の資料としては，ポニアトフスキ（1923）が採録し英語で訳解した語彙がある。この資料には語中母音間および子音のまえまたはあとに f の現れる例が oforo (nose), sefa (sable), mafa (old man, bear) など15語ほど載る。語中において子音に隣接して p が現れる語例はあるが，母音間に p が現れる語例は載っていない。また，語頭に p が現れる例（14語）のほか f が現れる例（７語）が載る。このほか fatalmeni の語形が patalmeni に併記されていて，ともに falling star の意としてある。なお，pački (caudal fin of fish), pikte (child), poinia (knee), poje (forehead), posi (knife-handle) のような基礎的単語やナーナイ語諸方言や近隣ツングース諸語に共通する単語には p- が現れている。

なお，ダンヴィユ（1737）に載る18世紀初期康熙帝の命によりイエズス会士が実地に測量して作成したこの地方の地図には，シカチ・アリャンのあたり（ウクスミ村 Oucsoumi Cajan より川上）に Coufati Cajan（グファティ村）という地名が記されている。当時のこの地名はすでに語中母音間に f が現れることを示している。その後に作成された『満漢合璧清内府一統輿地秘図』ではその地名が満洲字で Gufatin gašan と記されている。また『清代中俄関係檔案史料選編』(1981) 所載の順治十年 (1653年) 三月十二日の礼部尚書郎丘等題本 (礼科史書) には「使狗地方谷発亭姓」(9ページ) とあり，漢字で谷発亭と記されている。

上に述べたように，同じナーナイ語においても，その文語の基礎となっている北のナイヒン方言ではpを保っているが，南のビキンや八岔の方言では，女真語や満洲語のように，fにかわっている。それに対し，シカチ・アリャン方言では，その中間的様相を呈し，pもあるが，fの音も現れる。(付表参照。ナーナイ語のビキン方言はセム (1976) から，八岔方言は筆者の1990，91年の調査資料から，その文語はオーネンコ (1980) から引用する。なお表中の満洲語の oktoron，hūrka はエウェンキー語かそれに近い他のツングース語からの借用語であろう。またナーナイ語の八岔方言の xakin，siktə，同じくビキン方言の肝臓の意の語も他の方言または言語からの借用語であろう。) これらの方言におきた *p～f の改新はどのようにしておきたのであろうか。ほかの言語と関係なく，その言語の一部に自然発生的変化としておきたものか，または女真語や満洲語との言語接触による干渉でおきたものであろうか。

このことをみるためには，南の満洲語と北のナーナイ語との中間地域の言語に関する状況がどうであったかを知りたい。清代前期 (17世紀) についてみると，そのような地域としては，虎爾哈(フルハ)河 (牡丹江)，松花江下流，アムール川の松花江河口からウスリ川河口までの部分とそれよりやや下流まで，ウスリ川の地方が重要と考えられる。ここでは必要があってこの地方をさすとき三江会流地方とよぶことにする。

『満文老檔』の天命三年 (1618年) 正月の条に，Hūrha gurun (虎爾哈国) をさして emu gisun i jušen gurun ([太祖の国のことばと] 同一のことばの女真国) と言っている。ここから明確な事実をつかみとることはもちろんできないが，このことは，虎爾哈地方には太祖にとって満洲語と同じと言えるような言語が当時おこなわれていたことを示すものと言えよう。

ここで上記の地方の住民の氏族名についてみたいが，『太祖実録』の崇徳六年（1641年）十二月甲寅の条に載る進貢した東方巴牙喇以下八姓（八氏族）は，1700年ごろの著述である楊賓の『柳辺紀略』巻之三においてこれらの姓は虎爾哈，松阿里（松花江）にあることが記されている。その八姓のうち努牙喇・克宜克勒はナーナイ族の氏族 Nuėr，Gėjker の名称と一致し，ナーナイ人系の氏族とみられる。一方，そのうちの脱科洛は『八旗満洲氏族通譜』巻四十九に托活洛とあり，その満文本では満洲字で tohoro と書かれている。同じ実録の崇徳二年（1637年）十二月甲子の条に載る進貢した黙爾車勒の姓は『柳辺紀略』の同じ個所にこれも虎爾哈にあることが記されており，『八旗満洲氏族通譜』巻五十二に墨爾哲勒とあり，その満文本では満洲字で meljere と書かれている。この二つの姓の名称は toho-，melje- という動詞語幹に不完了連体形（動名詞）語尾 -ro，-re がついた満洲語のような語形とみることもできよう。満洲語文語には，tohombi，meljembi の動詞があるが，ただし，族名におけるその動詞語幹の本来の意味は明らかでない。池上（1993）を参照されたい。すでにシロコゴーロフ（1924 : 23，26ページ）は，満洲族の新しい氏族の名として挙げた meld̊žere と tokoro について，前者は満洲語の動詞 meljembi（意味は to avenge, especially with the knife とあり，ほかにザハーロフの辞典に載る意味も引用している）に当てており，また満洲語アイグンの口語形 medėr を挙げている。一方，後者についてこれを音声的に満洲人は to harness などの意（ザハーロフの辞典に載る意味も引用している）の動詞と結びつけると述べ，満洲語アイグンの口語形 tokoro，tokur，toɢoro も挙げている。こうみるとこれらの姓の人々は満洲語に近い言語を使う満洲人系の種族である可能性があろう。なお上述の八姓のうちに馬爾遮頼という姓があり，これは黙爾車勒と同じ姓かもしれないが，『柳辺紀略』巻之三はこの二つを別々に挙げている。

デュ・アルド（1735）4巻13，14ページには，18世紀初期に地図作製のため上述の地方からさらに北まで踏査したイエズス会士の見聞に基づくとみられるつぎのような記事が載る。イラン・ハラとよばれる人々は，真の満洲人である。イラン・ハラが三姓の意であることは，魚皮韃子と混住していたのでこの人々の種族（nation）の残りの人々から遠く隔てられていたがこの残りの人々が征伐された（la conquête）あと再び集められ三つの部族（trois familles）に組み立てられたことを示す。寧古塔の近傍，虎爾哈河，松花江に沿って皇帝から土地が与えられて現在かれらの村のほとんど全部がそこにある。その婦女子・召使は大抵魚皮韃子のような服装をしているが，魚皮韃子と異なることは牛馬をもち，一定の収穫をあげていたことであると記されている。

魚皮韃子とは当時三江会流地方にいたナーナイ人のことであろう。清は兵員補充のため徙民政策をとり，清初からくりかえし，周辺の部族を徴発して南へ移動させた。上のデュ・アルドの記述のなかの征伐とは強制的なその徴発のことではないだろうか。(ただし，デュ・アルドの言うイラン・ハラには，ロシヤ人を避けて退去した満洲族系の人々もふくまれていたかもしれない。) それらの人々のあとには別の地からほかの人々（ナーナイ人など）が移動して来たとみられるが，一方，三江会流地方に居残った者もあり，一つ地方にそれらの人々がともに居住していたであろう（上のデュ・アルドの記述参照)。また，種族の分布はくりかえされる徙民によって年代的に随時変化していたろう。

一方，『柳辺紀略』巻之三に，現在寧古塔に入貢する者について，虎爾哈河・松花江両岸に住む者は拏耶勒・革依克勒・祜什喀里であり，この三つのハラ（氏族）は（中略）いわゆる窩稽韃子であり，また新満洲とよばれ，その地は貂を産すとある。

『柳辺紀略』にある拏耶勒と革依克勒は，上記の八姓のうちの努牙喇，克宜克勒と同じであり，満洲人系とナーナイ人系を対比させると，これらはナーナイ人系であろう。上掲のデュ・アルドが満洲人というイラン・ハラとは異なる人々と考える。上記の三江会流地方には，満洲人系・ナーナイ人系のどちらの人々だけが居住していたというものでなく，少なくとも当時はその両方の人々がともに居住していたとみられる（上のデュ・アルドの記述も参照)。かれらの言語も満洲語の特徴をもつ言語とナーナイ語の特徴をもつ言語が共存したと考えられ，そこには言語接触が生じ，それによる干渉もおきたことが想像されよう。このようにみて来ると，はじめの問題であるナーナイ語南部方言における *p→f の改新は満洲語の影響または文献に残るような女真語がもっと古い時代に及ぼした影響によるとみるのが妥当ではないだろうか。

そして，ナーナイ語の南部方言でおきた *p→f の改新が遠く北に位置するシカチ・アリャン方言においてまでもおきたのは，南の方言における f への改新が北のこの方言まで伝播したものとみることもできよう。なお，方言の話し手たちの自称についてみると，シカチ・アリャン方言から Akani という自称を得ている。この名称はビキン方言の話し手たちも使うという（セム 1976：12ページ）。八岔方言の話し手からもこの名称を筆者は聞いており，自分たちをかつてこうよんだのかもしれない。この名称を共通にもつとすると，この三方言の話し手たちは親密な関係にあったとみられ，その中での言語伝播は容易におきえたろうから，f への改新もそのうちのある方言から北のシカチ・アリャン方言への伝播はたやすく届いたことだろう。

このことについては，言語外の歴史的事情も考慮に入れてさらにみてみたい。17世紀なかばにアムール川下流に侵入して来たロシヤ人の隊長の V. ポヤルコフの報告には，当時ゼーヤ川河口からウスリ川河口までのアムール川沿岸，ウスリ川の上流を除くその沿岸，さらにウスリ川河口から下流のアムール川のある距離までの沿岸には農耕定住民のデュチェル（Djučer）人がおり，なお，上流は別として松花江沿いには農耕定住民のシュンガル（Šungal）人が住んでいたと記されている。ただしつぎの隊長 E. ハバーロフの報告には，デュチェル人は松花江河口より下流のアムール川沿岸で農耕家畜飼育をおこない，集落をなして生活していたとある。(『歴史文書補遺』 3の12号（1646），102号（1652）による。）アムール川沿岸における17世紀のデュチェル人の分布の北東限について，V.I. オゴロードニコフ（1927：23－25ページ）はポヤルコフやハバーロフのアムール川航行日数を手がかりに，それはウスリ川河口から170－175露里下流のドンドン川河口に近いところであったと推定している。その後，しかし，清国は侵入するロシヤ人からの被害を防ぐ対策をたて，ロシヤ人の新しい隊長の O. ステパーノフの1656年の報告によると，清の皇帝がアムール川と松花江下流のデュチェル人の虎爾哈河沿岸，松花江上流への移住を命じ，かれらはすでにこの地方から姿を消しており，松花江の川上のデュチェル人はマルジンスキー部落（Malzinskij ulus）とその川上までどこにも姿をみせなかったという（『歴史文書補遺』 4の31号（1656）による)。

17世紀にロシヤ人がデュチェル人とよんだこの人々はどんな種族であったか

については，シュレンク（1981：150ページ）は，ある一種の満洲族としたが，のちにはそれに対してナーナイ人（ゴルディ人）とみる説（島田　1944，パレヴォイ　1979など）がある。

上記のステパーノフの報告にある Malzinskij ulus については，ドルギフ（1960：595ページ）に載るステパーノフの1655年のヤサク帳のなかの Šingal 川（松花江）の川上のマンジンスキー部落（Manzinskij ulus）の名称もこれと同じものであろう（このことは吉田（1973：39ページ，1984：382ページ）にすでにふれられている)。しかし，また Malzinskij は上述の八姓のうちの馬爾遮頼という姓と同じものであろう。すると，17世紀のロシヤ人がデュチェル人とよび，その世紀のなかばに旧地を退去した人々のなかにはこの氏族もふくまれていたことになる。さらに，一方，上述の『太祖実録』等に載る黙爾車勒の姓については『八旗満洲氏族通譜』に，その姓は世々松花江地方に居たとあり，その姓の人物の筆頭に強図理が挙げられている。かれは『太祖実録』の天聰五年七月甲戌の条に載る黒龍江地方虎爾哈部落の頭目の一人羌図礼であるとみられている。松浦（1987）参照。ところで，1682年の高士奇の『扈従東巡日録』下巻に，寧古塔から東に行くこと六百里羌突里噶尚というところがあり，松花・黒龍二江はここで合流すると記されていること，そしてこの村（噶尚）の名の羌突里は羌図礼であるとの指摘もすでに松浦（1987）にみえる。このようにみると，かつて羌図礼が頭目であった黙爾車勒氏族は，松花江河口に居住していたことになる。

上述のポヤルコフのデュチェル人とシュンガル人の区分によれば，馬爾遮頼族はシュンガル人に入るが，黙爾車勒族がシュンガル人・デュチェル人のどちらとみられたかは明確でない。しかし，当時デュチェル人とよばれた者のなかに入っていたこともありえよう。従って17世紀なかばロシヤ人がデュチェル人とよんだ者には，満洲語に近い言語を話した可能性がある黙爾車勒族のような人々がふくまれていたかもしれないと思われる。すると，デュチェル人の分布の北限に近いもののその分布地域内にあるシカチ・アリャンあたりにもデュチェル人によって満洲語に近い言語がおこなわれた可能性はなくはないだろう。そしてこの言語との言語接触によってナーナイ語シカチ・アリャン方言にも*p

のｆへの改新がおきたこともありえよう。しかし，シカチ・アリャン方言には，母音間に ᵖf のような発音があることはすでに述べたが，pā（肝臓）の語頭のｐも破裂が弱い。この方言には，古く *p にこうした発音の傾向があって，それが *p→ f の改新の下地となっていたこともあるかもしれない。

これらの点について今後さらに事実を明らかにしたいものである。

付記

アヴローリン（1959：32ページ）は，ナイヒン方言のｐに対してサカチ・アリャン方言ではｆ（ɸ）が現れる（例 foro（黒雷鳥），ofa（穀粉））と記述している。

引用文献

Arkheografičeskaja kommissija（史料編纂委員会），1848，1851. Dopolnenija k aktam istoričeskim（歴史文書補遺）. Tom 3.，Tom 4.，Sankt-Peterburg.

アヴローリン，Avrorin，V. A.，1959. Grammatika nanajskogo jazyka. Tom 1.，Moskva-Leningrad.

ブルィルキン，Brylkin，A.，1861. "Zamečanija o svojstvakh jazyka khodzenov i Khodzenskij slovar'". Maak，R.，1861. Putešestvie po doline reki Usuri. Tom 1.，S.-Peterburg.

ダンヴィユ，D'Anville，1737. Nouvel Atlas de la Chine，de la Tartarie chinoise，et du Thibet. La Haye（ハーグ）.

ドルギフ，Dolgikh，B. O.，1960. Rodovoj i plemennoj sostav narodov Sibiri v. XVII v. Moskva.

デュ・アルド，Du Halde，J. B.，1735. Description geographique，chronologique，politique，et physique de l'Empire de la Chine et de la Tartarie chinoise. Paris.

高士奇，1682.『扈従東巡日録』（『遼海叢書』所収）。

池上二良，1993.「満洲人とツングース人－清初の東北辺境の住民について－」（報告要旨)『満族史研究通信』3号。

松浦茂, 1987.「清朝辺民制度の成立」『史林』70巻4号。

オゴロードニコフ, Ogorodnikov, V.I., 1927. Tuzemnoe i russkoe zemledelie na Amure v XVII v. Vladivostok.

オーネンコ, Onenko, S. N., 1980. Nanajsko-russkij slovar'. Moskva.

パレヴォイ, Palevoj, B. P., 1979. "Djučerskaja problema (po dannym russkikh dokumentov XVII v.)". Sovetskaja ėtnografija, 3 maj-ijun' 1979, Moskva.

ポニアトフスキ, Poniatowski, S., 1923. Materials to the Vocabulary of the Amur River Gold. Varsaviae (ワルシャワ).

シュレンク, Schrenck, L. von, 1881. Reisen und Forschungen im Amur-Lande in den Jahren 1854-1856. Band III, Erste Lieferung, St. Petersburg.

セム, Sem, L. I., 1976. Očerki dialektov nanajskogo jazyka : Bikinskij (ussurijskij) dialekt. Leningrad.

島田好, 1944.「清初薩哈連部考」『満洲学報』8・9号, 新京。

シロコゴーロフ, Shirokogoroff, S. M., 1924. Social organization of the Manchus. Shanghai. シロコゴロフ著, 大間知篤三・戸田茂喜訳, 1967.『満洲族の社会組織』東京, 刀江書院。

楊賓, 1700ごろ.『柳辺紀略』(『遼海叢書』所収)。

吉田金一, 1973.「十七世紀中ごろの黒龍江流域の原住民について」『史学雑誌』82編9号。

———, 1984.『ロシヤの東方進出とネルチンスク条約』東京, 東洋文庫。

中国第一歴史檔案館, 1981.『清代中俄関係檔案史料選編』第一編上冊, 北京。

付表

満洲語・ナーナイ語の *p に関する音韻対応

	満洲語	ナーナイ語			
	文語	八岔方言	ビキン方言	シカチ・アリャン方言	文語(ナイヒン方言)
1《窓》	fa	fā	fā		pāva[pāwa]
2《尾ひれ》	fethe	fački	fačɪ	pačxī	pačī
3《肝臓》	fahūn	xakin	χak′ɪ(n-)	pā	pā
4《唇》	femen	fəmə	fəmu(n-)	pəu^{n}	pəmun
5《ひざ》		fuǐŋgə			pəǐŋgən [pəǐŋən]
6《こども》		fixtə, siktə	f′iktə		piktə
7《道，足跡》	oktoron 《うさぎの足跡》	fukto	foqto, foχto	pokto	pokto
8《跳ねる》		fuǐkuri	fŭiku-		puǐku-
9《きず》	feye	fujə	fəi		pue[pujə]
10《赤い》	fulgiyan	fulgjā	fol′ɢ′ǣ (n-)		
11《掛けぶとん》		fulta	folta, forta		polta
12《姉妹，娘》		fundaǰu	fondaǰo		pondadē̆ [pondaǰō]
13《わな》	hūrka	fuǐka	foɪqa		poǐka
14《帽子》		afun	āfo(n-), āfʊ(n-)	āfu^{n}, āpu^{n}	āpon
15《鼻》	oforo	oforo	oforo	oforo	oporo
16《食品，焼菓子》	efen	əfən	əfu(n-)		əpən

八岔方言は，1990年に筆者が同地の董風明氏から採録した資料による。

ナーナイ語シカチ・アリャン方言小語彙

akani シカチ・アリャンのナーナイ人の自称.

amga　くち（口）－rot.

aɲa とし（年）－god.

āpu^{n}, ā^{p}fu^{n} ,āfu^{n} 帽子 －šapka.

arki　さけ（酒）－liker, vino.

bəgǰi あし（足）－noga.

bəjə　からだ －telo.

bja つき（月）－luna.

bō　ぼくら －my.

buda　めし（飯），かゆ（粥）
　－otvarnoj ris, ǰidkaja kaša.

čiktə　しらみ －voš'.

čipča あか（垢）－grjaz'.

damxi たばこ －tabak.

darma こし（腰）－pojasnica.

dausu^{n} しお（塩）－sol'.

dəuǰə　かお（顔）－lico.

dolǰivri　聞く －slušat' : dolǰu. 聞きなさい。－Slušaj.／dolǰisu. お聞き下さい。－Vy poslušajte.／mi dolǰii. ぼくは聞いている。－Ja slušaju.／mi dolǰixambi. ぼくは聞いていた，ぼくは聞いた。－Ja slušal, Ja poslušal.／bō dolǰixa^{p}fu. ぼくらは聞いていた。－My slušali.／si dolǰixasi. おまえは聞いていた。－Ty slušal.／sō dolǰixasu. あなたらは聞いた。－Vy poslušali.／ɲān dolǰixani. かれは聞いていた。－On slušal.／ɲāči dolǰixači. かれらは聞いていた。－Oni slušali.

dui^{n} (acc. duimbə) 四 －četyre.

əmu^{n} (acc. əmumbə) 一 －odin.

ənəvri 行く －idti : ənəxəni　かれが行った －šel.

ənū　病気 －bolezn'.

garmakta　か（蚊）－komar.

girmaksa　ほね －kost'.

gᴜgakta ひげ －usy.

ičeǰivri　見る －smotret' : ičəǰini かれが見ている －smotrit／ičəǰixəni かれが見ていた－smotrel.

iču 見なさい，ičəru　見ろ －smotri.
（前者ハ後者ヨリオダヤカナ表現，後者ハヤヤ粗野トイウ）

ila (acc. ilamba) 三 —tri.

inda いぬ —sobaka.

ixa うし —korova.

ǰapkU^n (acc. ǰapkumba, ǰapkuva 前者ハ古イ語形，後者ハ現代ノ語形トイウ) 八 —vosem'.

ǰaxa かね（金）—den'gi.

ǰiǰu 来なさい，ǰiǰəru 来い —pridi. （前者ハ後者ヨリオダヤカナ表現，後者ハヤヤ粗野トイウ）

ǰili あたま —golova.

ǰiloksa（1ハ暗イ1）つば（唾）—sljuna.

ǰō いえ（家）—dom.

ǰobu しごと —rabota.

ǰolU (acc. ǰoluva) いし（石）—kamen'.

ǰōr (acc. ǰōrbə) 二 —dva.

ǰua (acc. ǰuamba) 十 —desjat'.

ǰuanǰōr (acc. ǰuanǰōrbə) 十二 —dvenadcat'.

kō^n ちぶさ（乳房）—grud'.

kučə (acc. kučəmbə) ナイフ —noǰ.

kUta のど —gorlo.

maŋbu（末尾ニnガアルラシイ発音モアル）アムール川，またおそらく河 —reka Amur.

mi ぼく —ja.

mjāva (acc. mjāvamba) 心臓 —serdce.

mō き（木）—derevo.

moŋgo くび（頸）—šeja.

muiki (acc. muikivə) へび（蛇）—zmeja.

muirə かた（肩）—plečo.

mukə (acc. mukəvə) みず（水）—voda.

muri^n (acc. murimbə) うま（馬）—lošad'.

nada (acc. nadamba) 七 —sem'.

nāla て（手），うで —ruka.

nasal め（目）—glaz.

nuktə かみの毛，人間の毛 —volos, volosy.

ɲān かれ —on.

ɲāči（末尾ノiハ口語デオチルコトガアルトイウ）かれら —oni.

ɲēčka とり（鳥）—ptica.

ɲuŋgu^n (acc. ɲuŋgumbə) 六 —šest'.

oforo はな（鼻）—nos.

okto (acc. oktova) くすり —lekarstvo.

omokto たまご —jajco.

oŋgo しり（尻）—zad.

pā　肝臓 —pečen'.

pačxī　尾びれ —khvostovoj plavnik ryby.

pəijə, pōja　ひたい（額）—lob.

pəu^n くちびる —guba.

pokto みち（道）—put', doroga.

saŋga　あな（穴）—dyra.

si　おまえ —ty.

siku^n 新しい —novyj.

simsə　脂肪，あぶら —ǰir, maslo.

sinakta けだものの毛 —šerst'.

sirmu した（舌）—jazyk.

siu^n 太陽 —solnce.

sja^n みみ（耳）—ukho.

sokta さかな —ryba.

sora　のみ（蚤）—blokha.

sorgᴜ 魚皮 —ryb'ja koǰa.

sormokta　まゆげ —brov'.

sə̄ あなたたち —vy.

sə̄ksə　ち（血）—krov'.

taŋgu（acc. taŋgumba）百 —sto.

tava　ひ（火）—ogon'.

toiŋga（acc. toiŋgava）五 —pjat'.

tugdə　あめ（雨）—doǰd'.

tuŋgə　むね（胸）—grud'.

ᴜgda（acc. ᴜgdava）ふね —lodka.

ukə(acc. ukəvə), uikə ドア —dver'.

uləksə　にく（肉）—mjaso.

xāli　いつ（何時）—kogda.

xausa^n かみ（紙）—bumaga.

xəmdə　はら（腹）—ǰivot.

xori^n(acc. xorimba)二十 —dvadcat'.

xuigə　重い —tjaǰelyj.

xuju^n（acc. xujumbə）九 —devjat'.

xuktə　は（歯）—zub.

xuŋguli　むし（虫）—červjak.

xusjakta　つめ（爪）—nogot'.

初出　宮岡伯人・津曲敏郎編『環北太平洋の言語』3号［京都大学大学院文学研究科平成9年（1997年）12月］121−130ページ。

謝辞　ポニアトフスキ（1923）の著作は，そのコピーをポーランドのA. F. Majewicz氏をわずらわして入手した。同氏に謝意を表す。

Tungus Dialects in the Vicinities of Yakutsk and Okhotsk in the Eighteenth Century[1)]

One rare source of the eighteenth century Tungus language is P. S. PALLAS' comparative glossary, *Linguarum totius orbis vocabularia comparativa* (VC, for short), which was edited by him at the behest of Empress CATHERINE II. of Russia in 1786 (1787) and 1789. This glossary includes Manchu words and also words of nine Tungus dialects: Tungus dialects of Nerchinsk province (or Dauriya province, to which only numerals belong), and of Enissy and Mangazeya districts; dialects of Barguzin Tungus and of Upper-Angara Tungus; Tungus dialects from the vicinities of Yakutsk and Okhotsk; and Lamut and Chapogir.

The two dialects near Yakutsk and Okhotsk lie in the boundary zone between Evenki and Even (= Lamut). These dialects will be dealt with here from the dialectological point of view.

As already mentioned by V. A. GORTSEVSKAYA (1959, p. 8), we can identify the dialect near Okhotsk as a dialect of Even, and the dialect near Yakutsk as an Evenki dialect; and except for these two and Lamut, the other six dialects can undoubtedly be identified as Evenki.

As V. I. TSINTSIUS (1946) and others already pointed out, Even underwent peculiar sound-changes, such as 1. the loss of the first of certain two consonants in succession, 2. the loss of any first short vowel (an open vowel as well as a close vowel) after a vowel plus one consonant, and 3. the reduction of a short vowel in the second and following syllables.

The dialect near Okhotsk as well as Lamut in the VC also possess words which underwent the above-mentioned syncope, apocope and reduction, such as, for instance, the following :

The dialect near Okhotsk	Lamut		Present-day Even	Present-day Evenki
1. горгатъ	гергатъ	'boroda (beard)'	gurgat	gurgakta
нуритъ	ню̂ритъ	'volos (hair)'	ɲūrīt	ɲuriktə
оро́ть	ора́ть	'trava (grass)'	orāt 'old, withered'	orokto
гуда́нь	гу́дань	'vysoko (high)'	gūd	gugda 'high'
			gūdan	gugdan 'height'
2. делъ	дэлъ	'golova (head)'	del	dil
намь	ламь, намь	'more (sea)'	nam	lāmu, lām
нгалъ	нгалъ	'ruka (hand)'	ŋāl	ŋālə
миръ	миръ	'plecho (shoulder)'	mīr	mirə
тогъ	тоӷ	'ogon' (fire)'	tog	togo
3. ангынь	ангань,	'god' (year)'	anngan	anngan ī
оде́нь	одань, удань	'dozhd' (rain)'	udan	udun
моронь	мурань	'kon' (horse)'	muran	murin

These instances show that the dialect near Okhotsk belongs to Even. We can say that these three sound-changes had already occurred in Even in the eighteenth century or earlier. In addition, we may assume that of these elisions the loss of the first of two successive consonants had preceded the loss of a final short vowel. Otherwise, no final vowel would have been dropped after two successive cosonants. Lamut in the VC, however, also had word-forms which had not yet undergone the loss of a final short vowel, such as :

The dialect near Okhotsk	Lamut		Present-day Even	Present-day Evenki
джоль	джола́, джо́ль	'kamen' (stone)'	ǰol	ǰolo

онгóтъ	онгатá, оготъ	'nos (nose)'	oŋat	oŋokto
ботъ	ботá	'grad (hail)'	bot	bōkta (in some eastern dialects)

In instances such as онгатá and ботá, the loss of a final short vowel had not yet occurred after the loss of the first of two successive consonants.

The vocabulary of the Tungoose (or Lamut) language in *An Account of a Geographical and Astronomical Expedition to the Northern Parts of Russia, Performed by J. Billings in the Years 1785, etc. to 1794* (London, 1802), also gives some words which have undergone these sound-changes, such as *nioorit* 'hair', *del* 'head', *gal* 'hand', *mir* 'shoulder', *dzshool* 'rock', *ogot* 'nose', but also *bota* 'hail'.

Some Tungus words found in the VC, such as, for instance, the following words, also lexically confirm that the dialect near Yakutsk belongs to Evenki and the dialect near Okhotsk to Even.

The dialect near Yakutsk	
питéма	'lug (meadow)'
сигýнъ	'solntse (sun)'
умдау	'pit' (drink)'
The dialect near Okhotsk	
бýдалъ	'noga (foot)'
мóми	'sudno (sailing vessel)'
оньянгь	'pesok (sand)'

However, some words of the dialect near Okhotsk in the VC do not coincide with words of the present-day Okhotsk dialect :

	The dialect near Okhotsk		Present-day Okhotsk dialect
(1)	сенъ	'ukho (ear)'	korat
(2)	илнга	'iazyk (tongue)'	īnŋə

(3)	че́уки	‘bog (god)’	həvki
(4)	чака́ринь	‘cherno (black)’	hakarɪn
(5)	унаджу́	‘doch’ (daughter)’	hʊnāǰ
(6)	ула́тинь	‘krasno (red),	hʊlan′ā, hʊlatɪ
(7)	арбась (ending in *s*)	‘gus’ (goose)’	ə̄rbə̄č (ending in *č*)

We have a cognate of the first word above in Evenki. It is noteworthy that this word *sēn* is distributed widely in Evenki, but is absent in Even now. The second words above and Lamut илгэ ‘iazyk (tongue)’ in the VC preserve the original **l*, which is not found in the present-day Okhotsk and other dialects of Even, but exists in *ilŋi* in the Chumikan and Maya dialects of Eastern Evenki and in Manchu *iləŋgů*. The third and fourth words above possess the initial *č*; and in Lamut сə̄вкӣ ‘bog (god)’ and сахринь ‘cherno (black)’ in the VC as well as in *sə̄vki* ‘god, icon’ in the Arman dialect *s*- appears. In the cognate words of the present-day Okhotsk and many other dialects **s*- was changed to *x*-. In the fifth and sixth words the old **x*- was dropped in conformity with the Arman word-forms, such as *onāǰ* (and *ʊɲāǰ*) ‘girl, daughter (adult)’ (Rishes, 1955, p. 119), whereas the present-day Okhotsk and many other dialects preserve **x*- in their cognate words. The final *s* (probably < **č*) of the last word above is found in the Arman dialect (Rishes, 1955, p. 120), but this word ends in *č* in the present-day Okhotsk dialect. In the last three instances the dialect near Okhotsk in the VC is closer to the present-day Arman dialect than to the present-day Okhotsk dialect. However, умта ‘yaitso (egg)’, олло ‘ryba (fish)’ and ну́лтанъ ‘solntse (sun)’ of the dialect near Okhotsk in the VC are different from the present-day Arman word-forms *olŋa*, *ol′čɪ* and *jōltəŋ* respectively (Rishes, 1955, pp. 119, 121).

The above words suggest that some Even words and/or their distributions in the area around Okhotsk have changed since the eighteenth century. However, it may also be assumed that the dialect near Okhotsk did not represent a single dialect, but various dialects around Okhotsk including the Arman dialect, which might have been distributed not only in Arman but also perhaps in other places near Okhotsk at that time.

We also find the word амарь 'reka (river)' in the dialect near Okhotsk in the VC. The same word *āmār* is said to be peculiar to the Arman dialect (cf. RISHES, 1955, p. 118). We might assume that this word was distributed more widely than now. According to L. D. RISHES (1955, pp. 117, 118), the river-name *Amur* is derived from this Arman word. The assumption of the wider distribution of this word in the eighteenth century seems to be more convenient to this etymology. Lamut in the VC possesses the word амаръ meaning 'bog (god)'. This word may be regarded as a homonym of the above word meaning 'river', although there is a difference between the marks ъ and ь in the VC. We also find the word *amar* meaning 'god' in the language of the 'Tongusi-Sabatschi, alias Lamuti, who live on the Gulf of Kamtschatki' in the Polyglot Table of P. J. von STRAHLENBERG's *Das Nord- und Ostliche Theil von Europa and Asia* (Stockholm, 1730 and the English edition—London, 1738).

In the dialect near Yakutsk in the VC we find the word такь 'sol' (salt)'. It may be a loanword from Even, for this word is distributed in some Even dialects, but not in Evenki.

It is noticeable that as numeral forms for 'ten' in the dialect near Yakutsk in the VC we find джань and also мень and мань in the compound word мань-нямаль 'one thousand', of which the second member нямаль means 'hundreds'. At the present time the form such as мень or мань belongs to Even. In the VC, the vocabulary of the dialect near Yakutsk may possibly include admixtures from Even. It is possible that the form мень (мань) is a loan from Even.

As to the etymology of the Even numeral *mēn* 'ten', we may assume that it derives from **ǰʊan* (or **ǰʊān*) (> Evenki *ǰān* 'ten') through **mɪan*<**wɪan* which was caused by the change of the affricate *ǰ* to the fricative *j* and the metathesis of *j* (> *ɪ*) and *ʊ* (> *w*). In the process of **wɪan* > **mɪan*, the initial *w* is assumed to have been changed to the nasal *m* in the same way as in Even *mina* (< Russian *vino*) and *māŋgāj* given below.

The change of **w*- to the nasal *m*- is a well-known sound-change in Even. In some words it may be regarded as regressive assimilation. In the VC we find one Lamut instance, мина 'vino (wine)' (a loanword from Russian). Another instance is the present-day Even word *māŋgāj* 'sterile doe' corresponding to Evenki *waŋgaj*. We also find the form *māŋgāj* in some eastern Evenki dialects, such as those of Maya and Totta. This Evenki form might have been borrowed from Even.

The Even verb-stem *mā*- 'to kill' is derived from **wā*- (>Evenki *wā* 'to kill'), though this **w* is not accompanied by any nasal consonant in the stem. The verb-stem *mā*- 'to kill' is also found in some eastern Evenki dialects, such as those of Ayan, Totta, Aldan and Chul'man. In these Evenki dialects we find few derivatives from this verb-stem. Although Even is situated very far from the last two dialects of Evenki, could it still be possible that this verb-stem of Evenki was borrowed from Even ? This remains a problem.

There is also a possibility that the change of **w*- to *m*- and the spread of the resultant forms occurred in the Even area and some areas of Eastern Evenki, for Even and Eastern Evenki seem to have possibly once had dialectal continuity, if we take the lexical evidences to be given below into consideration. Accordingly, we refrain from concluding that *ma*- and *māŋgāj* in Eastern Evenki and мень (мань) in the dialect near Yakutsk in the VC are later loanwords from Even.

It is not a little remarkable to note that the distributions of some Even words stretch into eastern areas of Evenki but not into the other Evenki areas. As an example we give one Even word *n'ɪrɪ* 'spina (back), pozvonochnik (spine)' (Tsintsius et al., 1975, p. 640) which is the same word as *n'irī* 'spine' in eastern Evenki dialects. The same word meaning 'back' is also found in the dialect near Okhotsk (нерú) and Lamut (нирú) in the VC.

There is one more example. The distribution of the word *bot* 'hail' in Even is contiguous to that of *bōkta* 'hail' in some eastern areas of Evenki. As given above, this Even word is also found in the dialect near Okhotsk and Lamut in the VC, and is assumed to have been changed from **bōkta.* In the other areas of Evenki the word-form *bōna* 'hail' is distributed in place of *bōkta.* The former form is also found in some eastern areas.

Some words common to Even and Eastern Evenki, such as the two words above, might have originated from a time before the split into Evenki and Even, viz. before the single Evenki-Even language was divided into dialects. Presumably they belonged to eastern dialects which seem to have since developed into Even and some eastern dialects of Evenki. We believe the study of words common to Even and Eastern Evenki is helpful in considering prehistoric connections between Evenki and Even. It would be useful for this study to make maps marking the distributions or isoglosses of these words.

Note

1) This is a revised version of the paper "Tungus dialects near Yakutsk and Okhotsk in the eighteenth century" that I read at the XIV Pacific Science Congress held in Khabarovsk on the 29th August 1979. The abstract of the original paper was published in *XIV Pacific Science Congress, USSR, Khabarovsk, August 1979, Committee L. Social sciences and humanities, Section LIV Languages of the Pacific region, Abstracts of Papers,* Vol. II (Moscow, 1979), p. 257. In this paper I do not refer to G. M. Vasilevich's article "K voprosy o tungusakh i lamutakh severo-vostoka v XVII-XVIII vv.," *Uchenye zapiski Instituta iazyka, literatury i istorii Yakutskogo filiala AN SSSR* 5 (1958), because I obtained access to it in the Khabarovsk Territorial Science Library for the first time only after completion of this paper. The data on the present-day Tungus languages are, except when the source is noted, based on the following sources : Even on Tsintsius and Rishes (1952), Evenki on Vasilevich

(1958). When referring to the individual dialects of Even and Evenki, the Okhotsk and Arman dialects of Even on TSINTSIUS et al. (1975 and 1977) and the eastern dialects of Evenki on ROMANOVA and MYREEVA (1968).

REFERENCES CITED

GORTSEVSKAIA, V. A., 1959. *Ocherk istorii izucheniia tunguso-man'chzhurskikh iazykov*, Leningrad.

RISHES, L. D., 1955. "Osnovnye osobennosti armanskogo dialekta ėvenskogo iazyka," *Doklady i soobshcheniia Instituta iazykoznaniia AN SSSR* 7.

ROMANOVA, A. V. and MYREEVA, A. N., 1968. *Dialektologicheskii slovar' ėvenkiiskogo iazyka*, Leningrad.

TSINTSIUS, V. I., 1946. "Ėvenskii (lamutskii) iazyk," *Uchenye zapiski LGU* 69, *seriia filologicheskikh nauk* 10.

TSINTSIUS, V. I. and RISHES, L. D., 1952. *Russko-ėvenskii slovar'*, Moskva.

TSINTSIUS, V. I. et al., 1975 and 1977. *Sravnitel'nii slovar' tunguso-man'chzhurskikh iazykov*, Leningrad.

VASILEVICH, G. M., 1958. *Ėvenkiisko-russkii slovar'*, Moskva.

要旨

十八世紀後半のP. S.パラスの『欽定全世界言語比較語彙』は満洲語と九つのツングース語方言の単語を記載している。本稿はそのうちヤクーツクとオホーツクの付近のツングース二方言を方言学的に扱う。前者はエウェンキー語，後者はエウェン語とみられている。エウェン語は特有の音韻変化をうけた。同書のラムート方言とオホーツク付近の方言もこの音韻変化をうけた語を有し，この例証は，後者の方言もエウェン語に属することを，さらにその変化が十八世紀またはそれ以前におきたことを示している。しかし同書のオホーツク付近の方言の単語のあるものは今日のオホーツク方言と一致しない。このことは，同方言のある単語やその分布がその後変化したことを示唆するが，またその方言というのは，単一の方言でなく，アルマン方言をふくむ付近の諸方言であったとも考えられる。

同書のヤクーツク付近の方言にмень（十）の語がある。同書はこの方言にエウェン語の単語を混入しているのかもしれないし，またそれがエウェン語からの借用語であることもありうる。なお，エウェン語のmēn（十）もエウェンキー語のǰān（十）も同じ原形にさかのぼると考えられよう。またエウェン語mā-（殺す）は*wā-に由来するが，このmā-はエウェンキー語の東部の一部の方言にもあり，これはエウェン語からの借用か問題となる。しかし，後述の語例を考慮すれば，エウェン語と東部のエウェンキー語がおそらくかつて方言的に連続していたと思われるので，エウェンキー語の東部の方言にも*w- → m-がおきた可能性がある。

エウェン語のある単語の分布は，エウェンキー語の東部の地域へのびるが，その他のエウェンキー語の地域へはのびていない。たとえば，エウェン語のn'irı（背，脊柱）はエウェンキー語の東部の方言のn'iri（脊柱）に連接している。エウェン語と東部のエウェンキー語に共通する単語は，両言語に分裂する以前の時代に由来するかもしれず，そのころ単一のエウェンキー・エウェン語はまた方言にわかれていたろう。そしてかかる単語は東部方言に属し，この方言はのちにエウェン語と東部のエウェンキー語に発展したのだろう。エウェン語と東部のエウェンキー語に共通する単語の研究は，エウェンキー語とエウェン語の史前の関係を考察する上にたすけとなると思われる。

This article was published in *Hoppo Bunka Kenkyu, Bulletin of the Institute for the Study of North Eurasian Cultures Hokkaido University,* 14 (January, 1981), pp. 141–147.

Bemerkungen zu einigen sprachgeographischen und areallinguistischen Problemen in der Erforschung der tungusischen Sprachen[1)]

Das Mandschurische findet sich im südlichsten Verbreitungsgebiet der tungusisch-mandschurischen Sprachen und ist dem Mongolischen und Chinesischen benachbart. Die Kontakte des Mandschurischen mit dem Mongolischen und Chinesischen haben zahlreiche Entlehnungen von Wörtern aus diesen beiden Sprachen ins Mandschurische verursacht. Ehedem war auch das Dschurdschenische in der gleichen Lage. Außerdem ist das Mandschurische im grammatikalischen Bau in verschiedenen Punkten dem Mongolischen ähnlicher als dem Tungusischen. Diese Tatsache läßt uns fragen, ob das Mongolische das Mandschurische auch in seinem grammatikalischen Bau beeinflußt hat—eine Frage, die man in der Areallinguistik behandelt.

Die Imperativformen der tungusischen Verben sind mit einer Imperativendung versehen. Im Mandschurischen haben mit Ausnahme von einigen unregelmäßigen Verben, die erstarrte Imperativendungen besitzen, die Imperativformen der Verben keine Imperativendung, sondern dieselben Formen wie die Verbstämme. Das Mandschurische ist in dieser Hinsicht viel mehr dem Mongolischen ähnlich als dem Tungusischen.

In der tungusischen Negativkonstruktion werden das Negationsverb *ə-* und das zu verneinende Verb mit der Endumg *-ra* oder ihrer Variante zusammengestellt. Dieser Konstruktion gleicht die mandschurische

Prohibitivkonstruktion: *umə* plus dem zu verneinenden Verb mit der Endung *-ra*. Die Form *umə* scheint eigentlich vom Negationsverbstamm plus der Verbendung *-mə* herzukommen. In dieser Form stellt sich der Negationsverbstamm als *u-* dar. Obwohl dieser Stamm *u-* anders als der tungusische Negationsverbstamm *ə-* ist, findet man im mandschurischen Sprachführer Man-han-tzŭ Ch'ing-wên ch'i-mêng, der mit einem Vorwort von 1730 versehen ist, außer der Form *umə* auch eine andere Form mit dem Anlaut *ə* statt *u*. Aber die gewöhnliche Negativkonstruktion im Mandschurischen besteht aus dem zu verneinenden Verb und der negativen Partikel *aků*, die auch ein Nomen ist. Diese Konstruktion gleicht der mongolischen Negativkonstruktion.

Ein Unterschied zwischen der Dativ- und Lokativendung findet sich im Tungusischen, aber nicht im Mandschurischen und auch nicht im Chalcha-Mongolischen. Im Mandschurischen findet man die Dativendung *-də* und keine besondere Lokativendung, aber eine geringe Anzahl der Ortsadverbien mit dem Suffix *-la*, das der tungusischen Lokativendung *-la* entspricht.

Aus dem Vorhergehenden folgt, daß sich eine Anzahl von Ähulichkei-ten im grammatikalischen Bau zwischen dem Mandschurischen und seiner Nachbarsprache, dem Mongolischen, finden läßt, die in den tungusischen Sprachen fehlen, und daß die oben erwähnten unregelmäßigen eingeschränkten oder erstarrten Fälle im Mandschurischen den tungusischen Formen oder Konstruktionen entsprechen. Auf Grund dieser Tatsachen glaube ich, wie bereits in meinem Aufsatz von 1979 erwähnt, annehmen zu können, daß das Mandschurische ehemals wie die tungusischen Sprachen Imperativformen mit der Imperativendung, eine Negativkonstruktion, die aus dem Negativverb und einem zu verneinenden Verb besteht, und Dativ- und Lokativendungen besaß und daß das Mandschurische, außer in einigen nachgebliebenen Formen, Umbildungen durchgemacht hat, die dem Einfluß des Mongolischen zuzuschreiben sind.

Nebenbei sei bemerkt, daß Prof. M. B. EMENEAU in seinem Werk aus dem Jahre 1980 (p. 3) sein methodologisches Prinzip für die areallinguistischen Forschungen über die Sprachen des indischen Subkontinents, besonders die indoarischen und drawidischen Sprachen, folgendermaßen beschreibt: "These (= the languages of the area) include a language or languages that belong to a family (F_1) whose languages outside the area do not have the feature, the feature in question not being reconstructable as belonging to the proto-language of that family. If the feature is found in languages of a second family (F_2) in the area and is to be considered a part of the reconstructable proto-language of that family F_2, the assumption can then, it seems, be safely made that there has been diffusion from the family F_2 into the language or languages of family F_1 within the area." Doch kann man diese Methode nicht auf die Beziehungen zwischen den altaischen Sprachen anwenden, weil alle diese Sprachen von derselben Ursprache hergekommen sein dürften.

*

Aus dem Mandschurischen (und wahrscheinlich schon aus dem Dschurdschenischen) sind viele Kulturlehnwöter einerseits in das Solonische, Dahurische und wahrscheinlich in die ewenkischen Mundarten der Chingan-Gebirge wie auch die mongolischen Mundarten der Inneren Mongolei eingedrungen und anderseits in die Sprachen des Sichota-Alin-Gebiets und des unteren Amur-Beckens, das heißt in tungusische Sprachen wie das Nanaische (Goldische), Oltschaische, Udiheische, Orotschische und das Negidalische, besonders in dessen Dialekt am Unterlauf des Flusses Amgun, und auch in eine andere, nicht-tungusische Sprache, das Niwchische (Giljakische) eingeströmt. (Vgl. SCHMIDT 1923.) Eine Anzahl von diesen Wörtern hat auch das Uiltaische (Orokische) auf der Insel Sachalin entlehnt. Zum Beispiel:

ma. *fa*, nan., oltsch, orotsch. *pāwa*, neg. *pāγā*, niwch. *p'aχ*, uilt. *paawa* 'Fenster'.

ma., nan., oltsch. *turi*, ud. *tuli*, orotsch., neg. *turi*, niwch. *tur*, uilt. *turi* 'Bohne'.

ma. *ufa*, nan. *opa*, oltsch. *ʊpan*, neg. *opa*, niwch. *ova*, uilt. *upa*(*n*) 'Mehl'.

ma. *johan*, nan. *joxan*, oltsch. *jʊha*, *joha*, orotsch. *juxa*(*n*), neg. *jōxan*, niwch. *joγo*, uilt. *juxa*(*n*) 'Watte'.

ma. *joosə* (< chin. *yao*^{4} 'Schlüssel, Schloß'), nan., oltsch. *joso*, ud. *jausu*, orotsch. *joso*, neg. *jāsa*, uilt. *jooso* 'Vorhängeschloß'.

Unter diesen Lehnwörtern findet man viele Wörter chinesischen Ursprungs.

Einige dieser Wörter scheinen vom Mongolischen oder Türkischen oder durch Zentralasien von noch entfernteren Sprachen hergekommen zu sein. In dieser Hinsicht kann man sagen, daß in Zentral- und Nordostasien Kulturwörter sich nicht unr vom Westen nach dem Osten, sondern auch vom Süden nach dem Norden verbreitet haben. Aber es ist bemerkenswert, daß diese mandschurischen Kulturlehnwörter im allgemeinen nicht in das Ewenkische und das Ewenische durch das untere Amur-Gebiet eingedrungen sind. Die Verbreitung der mandschurischen Kulturlehnwörter ist in diesen Richtungen nur auf diese Gegenden beschränkt.

Außerdem findet man eine Anzahl Wörter, die allen oder einigen tungusischen Sprachen im Sichota-Alin-Gebiet und unteren Amur-Gebiet und auf der Insel Sachalin gemeinsam sind. Im Negidalischen sind sie besonders im Dialekt am Unterlauf des Flusses Amgun (vgl. SCHMIDT 1923) anzutreffen. Aber diese Wörter finden sich nicht in den anderen benachbarten tungusischen Sprachen, das heißt, dem Ewenkischen und Ewenischen außer den ewenkischen Mundarten am Urmi-Fluß und auf der Insel Sachalin, obwohl alle tungusischen Sprachen viele Wörter einschließlich der Grundwörter gemeinsam besitzen. Einige von jenen Wörtern findet man auch im Niwchischen. Zum Beispiel:

nan. *ilxin*, oltsch. *irhi*, uilt. *irki*, orotsch. *ixi*, niwch. *irxi* 'Zahnfleisch'.

nan. *ixərə*, oltsch. *ihərə*, uilt., orotsch., neg. *ixərə* 'Lampe'.

nan. *kaorī*, oltsch. *kaʊri*, uilt. *kaurii*, orotsch. *kaʊri*, neg. *kawrixī*, *kaʊrixī*, ew. (Sach.) *kawrikī*, niwch. *q'aur*, Ainu (Sachalin) *kawre* 'Bremsstange beim Schlitten'.

nan. *oksaran*, oltsch. *ʊksaran*, uilt. *uksara*, orotsch. *ʊksara(n)*, neg. (am Unterlauf) *oksarı* 'Eule'.

nan. *tagdaori*, oltsch., uilt., ud., orotsch., neg. *tagda-* 'sich ärgern'.

nan. *tugbuwuri*, oltsch. *tugwu-*, uilt. *tugbu-*, ud. *tugwu-*, orotsch. *tugbu-*, *tubbu-*, neg. *tibgu-* 'fallen lassen'.

Das Bündel der Isoglossen einiger dieser betreffenden Wörter umgrenzt die oben erwähnten Gegenden. Folglich stimmt der geographische Verbreitungsbereich dieser Wörter auch mit dem der mandschurischen Kulturlehnwörter überein. Ferner wurden einige von diesen Wörtern von der Ainu-Sprache auf der Insel Sachalin entlehnt.

Das Mandschurische besitzt Kulturwörter, die von diesen Sprachen entlehnt wurden, und auch einige nicht im Ewenkischen und Ewenischen vorkommenden Wörter mit diesen Sprachen gemeinsam. Zum Beispiel:

ma. *hoto*, nan., uilt., orotsch., neg. *xoto* 'Glatze, Kahlkopf, kahl'.

Aber einige dieser mandschurischen Wörter weichen von den entsprechenden tungusischen Wörtern lautlich oder bedeutungsmäßig ab. Zum Beispiel:

ma. *səlbi* 'Ruder', nan. *səul*, oltsch. *səuli*, uilt. *səul*, ud. *səu*, orotsch. *səu(g)*, neg. *səwul*, *səul* 'Steuerruder'.

ma. *gəsə* 'gleich wie, gleichwie' — nan., oltsch, uilt. *gəsə*, ud *gəhiə*, orotsch., neg. *gəsə* 'zusammen'.

Das zeigt einen Unterschied zwischen dem Mandschurischen und diesen tungusischen Sprachen.

Einige dieser gemeinsamen Wörter scheinen aus einer dieser Sprachen von den anderen Sprachen entlehnt worden zu sein. Aber es kann auch sein, daß diese Sprachen in alten Zeiten einige Wörter von irgendwelchen heute unbekannten Sprachen übernommen haben.

Es ist bemerkenswert, daß man unter diesen gemeinsamen Wörtern einige Namen von Fischen und Seetieren und auch einige zum Schiffswortschatz oder zum Wortschatz der Fischerei und Seetierjagd gehörenden Wörter findet. Zum Beispiel:

oltsch. *arko*, uilt. *arku*, orotsch. *ākʊ*, neg. *arkaj*, niwch. *arqe* 'Stint'.

nan. *gioksa*, oltsch. *gēuksa* 'Seehund', uilt. *geuksa* 'Name für einen einjährigen Seehund einer besonderen Art: Phoca richardii pribilofensis J. A. Allen', neg. *gɪwʊ*, *gɪwʊksa*, *gɪoksa*, *gɪʊksa*, niwch. (in Tschaiwo auf der Insel Sachalin nach Krejnovič 1955) *keoxta* 'Seehund'.

nan. *ǰogbo* 'Harpune', oltsch. *ǰogbo* 'Fischspieß', uilt *ǰogbo* 'Harpume', ud. *ǰow'o* 'Fischspieß', orotsch. *ǰobbo* 'Harpune', neg. *ǰobgo* 'Harpune, Fischspieß', ew. (Urm., Sakh.) *ǰəwgə* 'Harpune'.

oltsch. *makori*, *makʊri*, uilt. *mauri*, orotsch. *makʊi*, *makʊri*, neg. *maxoj*, niwch. *maqr ma* 'Lachsfilet'.

nan. *ogda*, oltsch. *ʊgda*, uilt. *ugda*, orotsch. *ʊgda* 'Boot'.

Diese beiden Beschäftigungen gehören zu den Hauptgewerben der die betreffenden Sprachen sprechenden Völker, die am Unterlauf des Amur-Flusses und seinen Nebenflüssen und an den Küstenstrichen wohnen.

Das Negidalische ist, nach der Klassifikation der tungusischen Sprachen, die der Verzweigung des Urtungusischen gemäß ist, sowohl vom Nanaischen, Oltschaischen und Uiltaischen, die eine Gruppe bilden, als auch vom Udiheischen und Orotschischen, die eine andere Gruppe bilden, getrennt und steht in der Nähe des Ewenkischen und Ewenischen (s. Ikegami 1974). Deshalb verdient es Beachtung, daß einige Wörter dem Negidalischen und den oben erwähnten tungusischen Sprachen außer dem Ewenkischen und Ewenischen gemeimsam eigen sind.

Das Niwchische unterscheidet sich von den anderen oben erwähnten Sprachen dadurch, daß es nicht zu den tungusischen gehört. Trotzdem sind auch einige niwchische grammatikalischen Elemente denen der tungusischen Sprachen in diesen Gegenden ähnlich. Dr. E. K. KREJNOVIČ weist in seinem Aufsatz aus dem Jahre 1955 auf die morphologischen Übereinstimmungen zwischen dem Niwchischen und den tungusisch-mandschurischen Sprachen in 26 Punkten hin. Diese Übereinstimmungen behandle ich hier nicht. Aber es ist zu erwähnen, daß eine uiltaische Imperativendung *-ja*, die als sanfter oder höflicher Ausdruck gebraucht wird, dem niwchischen Imperativsuffix der zweiten Person Singularis *-ja* ähnlich ist. Diese uiltaische Endung nimmt immer dieselbe Form und keine Varianten an, die nach den verschiedenen Verbstammauslauten vorkommen. Diese Evidenz scheint die Ansicht zu begünstigen, daß diese Imperativendung aus dem Niwchischen ins Uiltaische entlehnt wurde. KREJNOVIČ hat schon auf die Üdereinstimmung zwischen dem niwchischen Imperativsuffix *-ja* und der udiheischen Imperativendung der zweiten Person *-ja* hingewiesen. Es mag sein, daß das *k*-Element in der oltschaischen Imperativendung der zweiten Person Pluralis *-ruksu* mit dem udiheischen Pluralsuffix *-gətu* oder dem niwchischen Pluralsuffix *-ku* identisch ist. KREJNOVIČ scheint die udiheische Endung der zweiten Person Pluralis *-hu*, die der Imperativendung *-ja* angehängt ist, mit dem niwchischen Pluralsuffix *-guta* gleichzusetzen. Aber man kann dieses *-hu* von der tungusischen Pluralendung *-*su* herleiten. Zwischen den tungusisch-mandschurischen Sprachen in den betreffenden Gegenden und dem Niwchischen bestehen vielleicht auch Lehnbeziehungen der grammatikalischen Elemente.

Aus dem Vorhergehenden ergibt sich die Möglichkeit, daß das untere Amur-Becken, das Sichota-Alin-Gebiet und die Insel Sachalin ein sogenanntes linguistisches Areal bilden und daß dort das Nanaische, Oltschaische, Uiltaische, Udiheische, Orotschische, Negidalische und das Niwchische in einer Art Sprachbund stehen. Auf dieses linguistische Areal hat übrigens bereits im Jahre 1978 Herr Juha JANHUNEN, Helsinki, in einem Vortrag hingewiesen, den er an der Hokkaido Universität gehalten hat (s. seinen Aufsatz von 1983).

Eine derartige Begrenzung dieser Gegenden wird auch durch den Gemeinbesitz der mandschurischen Kulturlehnwörter und der eigentümlichen Fisch- und Seetiernamen, Schiffsbezeichnungen und Wörter aus der Fischerei und Seetierjagd charakterisiert, die sich in den tungusischen Sprachen in den anderen Gegenden nicht finden.

Ich führe noch ein Beispiel an, das die Begrenzung der betreffenden Gegenden deutlich macht. Das Wort *xoton*, das 'Stadt' bedeutet, wurde vom Mandschurischen (<Mongolisch) ins Nanaische, Oltschaische, Uiltaische, Udiheische. Orotschische, Negidalische und in das Solonische entlehnt. Andererseits wurde das Wort *koton*, das 'Viehstall' bedeutet, aus dem Burjat-Mongolischen oder vielleicht aus dem Jakutischen ins Ewenkische und Ewenische entlehnt. Diese beiden Wörter gehen eigentlich auf dasselbe Wort zurück.

In diesem Beispiel weist das gleiche Wort auf die zwei wichtigen Typen der Einführung der Lehnwörter aus den südlichen Sprachen ins Tungusische hin, das heißt, die eine ist eine Entlehnung aus dem Mandschurischen in die tungusischen Sprachen des unteren Amur-Beckens usw. und die andere ist eine Entlehnung aus dem Mongolischen ins Ewenkische und Ewenische.

*

Nördlich und westlich vom unteren Amur-Gebiet findet man das Ewenische und Ewenkische. Man sieht heutzutage jede von diesen Sprachen als eine eigene tungusische Sprache an. Wie in meinem Aufsatz von 1981 erwähnt, ist es bemerkenswert, daß sich einige Wörter in den ewenischen Mundarten und auch in den östlichen ewenkischen Mundarten, aber nicht in den westlichen Dialekten des Ewenkischen verbreitet haben. Ihre Isoglossen erstrecken sich aus dem ewenischen Gebiet bis ins Gebiet der östlichen ewenkischen Mundarten.

Ich gebe die folgenden Beispiele:

Erstens die ewenischen Wörter *bajikar* 'Morgen, am Morgen', und *baǰ, baǰič* 'früh'. Die entsprechenden ewenkischen Wörter *baǰikir* und *baǰigir*, die 'früh am Morgen' bedeuten, finden sich nur in den östlichen Mundarten (wie in Tungir, Zeja, Totta, Čumikan, Aja, Sachalin und Urmi).

Das nächste Beispiel ist der Verbstamm *kōl-*, der 'trinken' bedeutet. Diesen Verbstamm findet man im Ewenischen und in den östlichen ewenkischen Mundarten (wie in Maja, Totta, Čumikan, Aja, Sachalin und Urmi) wie auch im Negidalischen.

Drittens das ewenische Wort *bōt* und das ewenkische Wort *bōkta*, die 'Hagel' bedeuten. Dieses Wort findet sich nur in den östlichen ewenkischen Mundarten (wie in Čul'man, Učur, Maja, Čumikan, Aja, Sachalin und Urmi) im Gegensatz zum Wort *bōna*, das sich von den westlichen Dialekten bis zu einigen östlichen Mundarten (wie in Tungir, Tokko, Tommot, Čul'man, Ober-aldan-Zeja, Ajan, Chingan) verbreitet hat. Die ewenische Wortform *bōt* hat sich wahrscheinlich aus der Urform **bōkta* entwickelt, während die alte Form *bōkta* in den östlichen ewenkischen Mundarten erhalten ist. Die fortlaufende Verbreitung dieses Wortes in dem Ewenischen und in den östlichen ewenkischen Mundarten scheint auf die Zeit vor der Entwicklung der ewenischen Form *bōt* aus der Urform **bōkta* zurückzugehen.

Es mag wohl sein, daß die Verbreitung einiger dieser Wörter eine Folge der Entlehnungen zwischen dem Ewenischen und den östlichen ewenkischen Mundarten ist. Aber diese Verbreitung geht vielleicht auf die Zeit vor der Spaltung ins Ewenkische und Ewenische zurück. Die Verbreitung der Wörter im Ewenischen und im östlichen Teil des ewenkischen Gebietes außer den anderen Teilen scheint auf die enge Beziehung zwischen dem Ewenischen und den östlichen ewenkischen Mundarten hinzudeuten. Man müßte allerdings noch nähere sprachgeographische Untersuchungen hierfür anstellen.

Ferner führe ich noch die Wörter mit der Bedeutung 'Gold' als

Beispiel an. Als Ausdruck für Silber werden das Wort *məŋun* und seine Varianten in den tungusisch-mandschurischen Sprachen allgemein gebraucht. Das Wort *məŋun* wurde aus dem Mongolischen—teilweise wahrscheinlich über das Mandschurische—entlehnt. Im Gegensatz zu 'Sillber' wird 'Gold' je nach Gegend anders ausgedrückt. In den oben erwähnten Sprachen im unteren Amur-Becken und Sichota-Alin-Gebiet und auf der Insel Sachalin ist das Wort *ajsin* verbreitet, das wahrscheinlich aus dem Mandschurischen entlehnt wurde. Im Ewenkischen findet sich das Wort *altan*, das aus dem Mongolischen entlehnt worden ist, außer in den östlichen Mundarten, wo das zusammengesetzte Wort (*h*)*ularīn məŋun* 'rotes Silber' gebraucht wird. Die Variante *hulaɲā məŋən* (od. *mɵŋɵn*) erstreckt sich auf einige westliche Mundarten des Ewenischen, in dem man sonst das russische Lehnwort *zoloto* findet. Im Jakutischen trifft man auf eine Parallele zu diesem tungusischen zusammengesetzten Wort, nämlich das Wort *kɪhɪl kömüs* 'Gold', das sich aus *kɪhɪl* 'rot' und *kömüs* 'Silber, Gold' zusammensetzt.

Nebenbei bemerkt finden sich das Wort *altan* und seine Varianten auch anderswo. In den östlichen Mundarten des Ewenkischen und im Negidalischen bedeuten sie aber 'Kupfer', ebenso wie das jakutische Wort *altan*. Im Udiheischen. Orotschischen, Nanaischen, Oltschaischen und Uiltaischen bedeutet *altan* 'Blech'.

Die Wörter mit der Bedeutung 'Gold' zeigen verschiedene Verbreitungstypen der tungusischen Wörter, das heißt, das Wort *ajsi*(*n*) zeigt die Verbreitung, die auf das untere Amur-Gebiet und das Sichota-Alin-Gebiet und auf die Insel Sachalin beschränkt ist, und das zusammengesetzte Wort *hulaɲā məŋən* oder (*h*)*ularīn məŋun* zeigt die Verbreitung, die sich aus dem Gebiet des Ewenischen bis in die östlichen ewenkischen Mundarten erstreckt. Anderseits zeigt das Wort *altan* mit der Bedeutung 'Gold' die Verbreitung im Ewenkischen außerhalb der östlichen Mundarten.

*

Die sprachgeographischen und die areallinguistischen Forschungen, ebenso wie die vergleichende Forschung, sind für die Aufklärung der Vorgeschichte der einzelnen tungusisch-mandschurischen Sprachen unentbehrlich. Auch auf dem Gebiet der anderen altaischen und zentralasiatischen Sprachen findet man sprachgeographische und areallinguistische Probleme, obwohl diese durch Faktoren wie Nomadisieren oder Stammeswanderungen viel komplizierter werden. Derartige Forschungen sind für die Aufklärung der Sprachverhältnisse im alten Zentralasien, der früheren Beziehungen zwischen den einzelnen altaischen Sprachen und der Entwicklung der mongolischen und türkischen Sprachen wie auch der anderen zentralasiatischen Sprachen in der Vergangenheit sehr nützlich und notwendig. Auch die tungusisch-mandschurischen Sprachen hängen mit diesen Fragen zusammen.

In diesem Zusammenhang wird das Erscheinen der Sprachatlanten für die altaischen und zentralasiatischen Sprachen die betreffenden Forschungen sicherlich fördern. Für den Bereich des Mongolischen wurde ein Sprachatlas der Äußeren Mongolei schon im Jahr 1979 von der Akademie der Wissenschaften der Mongolischen Volksrepublik in Ulan Bator veröffentlicht.

Anmerkung

1) Überarbeitete Fassung meines Vortrages „Bemerkungen zu einigen Problemen der tungusischen Sprachen im Rahmen der sprachgeographischen und areallinguistischen Forschungen der altaischen und zentralasiatischen Sprachen" bei dem Symposion „Neue Ergebnisse der Zentralasienforschung", das anläßlich des 80. Geburtstages von Frau Professor Dr. Annemarie v. Gabain im Jahre 1981 in Hamburg stattfand.

Die nanaischen, oltschaischen, udiheischen, orotschischen, ewenischen und niwchishen Wörter sind resp. aus den Wortschätzen von PETROVA (1960), PETROVA (1936), ŠNEJDER (1936), AVRORIN-LEBEDEVA (1978) CINCIUS-RIŠES (1952) und SAVEL'EVA-TAKSAMI (1970) angeführt und die negidalischen Wörter nach CINCIUS et al. (1975 und 1977), die ewenkischen Wörter nach VASILEVIČ (1958) und ROMANOVA-MYREEVA (1968) und die uiltaischen Wörter nach IKEGAMI (1980) und dem anderen von ihm gesammelten Material.

Literatur

AVRORIN, V. A., LEBEDEVA, E. P., 1978. *Oročskie teksty i slovar'*, Leningrad.

CINCIUS, V. I., RIŠES, L. D., 1952. *Russko-ėvenskij slovar'*, Moskva.

CINCIUS, V. L. et al., 1975 und 1977. *Sravnitel'nyj slovar' tunguso-man'čžurskich jazykov*, Leningrad.

EMENEAU, M. B., 1980. *Language and Linguistic Area. Essays by M. B. EMENEAU*, selected and introduced by A. S. DIL, Stanford, California.

IKEGAMI, J., 1974. Versuch einer Klassifikation der tungusischen Sprachen. In: HAZAI, G. und ZIEME, P. (Hrsg.), *Sprache, Geschichte und Kultur der altaischen Völker*, Berlin.

—— 1979. Manshū-go to Tsungūsu-go—Sono Kōzō-jō no sōiten to Mōko-go no eikyō (= Manchu nad Tungus—Differences in Their Construction and the Mongolian Influence), *Tōhōgaku* (*Eastern Studies*) 58, Tokyo.

—— 1980. *Uiruta-go Kiso Goi* (= An Uilta Basic Vocabulary), Sapporo.

—— 1981. Tungus Dialects in the Vicinities of Jakutsk and Okhotsk in the Eighteenth Century, *Hoppo Bunka Kenkyu* (*Bulletin of the Institute for the Study of North Eurasian Cultures Hokkaido University*) 14.

JANHUNEN, J., 1983. Kita Azia no minzoku to gengo no bunrui (= A classification of the peoples and languages of North Asia), *Gekkan Gengo*, 142, Tokyo.

KREJNOVIČ, E. A., 1955. Giljacko-tunguso-man'čžurskie jazykovye paralleli, *Doklady i soobščenija Instituta jazykoznanija AN SSSR*, 8.

PETROVA, T. I., 1936. *Ul'čskij dialekt nanajskogo jazyka*, Moskva-Leningrad.

PETROVA, T. I., 1960. *Nanajsko-russkij slovar'*, Leningrad.

ROMANOVA, A. V., MYREEVA, A. N., 1968. *Dialektologičeskij slovar' ėvenkijskogo jazyka*, Leningrad.

SAVEL'EVA, V. N., TAKSAMI, Č. M., 1965. *Russko-nivchskij slovar'*, Moskva.

—— 1970. *Nivchsko-russkij slovar'*, Moskva.

SCHMIDT, P., 1923. The Language of the Negidals, *Acta Universitatis Latviensis*, 5.

ŠNEJDER, E. P., 1936. *Kratkij udėjsko-russkij slovar'*, Moskva-Leningrad.

VASILEVIČ, G. M., 1958. *Ėvenkijsko-russkij slovar'*, Moskva.

Dieser Aufsatz ist in : *Ural-Altaische Jahrbücher*, Neue Folge Band 3 (1983), S. 170–178 erschienen.

ツングース語祖語の一つの動詞語尾について
——*-si に関して——

On the Proto-Tungus Verb Ending *-*si*

ツングース諸言語には動詞の連体形，終止形をつくる -ra という語尾があるが，動詞によってはこれが -ra という形とは異なる形すなわち別の交替形としてあらわれる。ツングース語の一つラムート語では，この語尾が母音音素におわる動詞語幹につくときは -ra の形をとり，種々の子音音素におわる動詞語幹には -ra のほかにまた -da, -ta, -a のような交替形がつくが，さらにその交替形の一つとして -sa という形が一群の動詞にみられる。またほかのツングース語にもこの -sa に対応する形があらわれる(1)。

この動詞語尾はツングース語動詞の基本的な語尾であるゆえ，ラムート語の -sa という形および他のツングース語のこれに対応する形がどんな動詞にあらわれる交替形か，またこの形がどんな起源をもつかはツングース語ではかなり重要な問題であると思われる。このことについては，J. Benzing がすでにとりあげており，同氏はツングース諸言語を比較してラムート語の -ra は *-ra という祖形にさかのぼり，その -sa およびこれに対応する他のツングース語の形は *-sa という祖形にさかのぼるとしている(2)。同氏はツングース語におけるこの重要な点を見落とさずよくとらえて扱っているが，くわしい点にわたると，筆者は異論もあるので，本稿はそれに関して要点について簡略にふれるものである。

この問題の解明には，Benzing が扱ったラムート語その他のツングース語の資料とともに，やはりツングース語の一つであるオロッコ語の資料も重要であり，ここではそれも用いる(3)。

オロッコ語においてはこの動詞語尾として -ra が母音音素二つの連続におわる動詞語幹につき，その交替形の -da，-ta が子音音素におわる動詞語幹につくが，ほかに -si という形が一群の動詞にみられる。したがってこの動詞語尾は -ra〜-da〜-ta〜-si と交替するが，さらにほかに母音音素におわる動詞語幹とこの語尾との融合形もある。(4)

まずラムート語の上述の動詞語尾の -sa に，ほかのツングース語の動詞語尾としてどんな形が対応するかを示す。

ラムート語文語（子音音素のあとで）-ca，-cэ，（母音音素のあとで）-c ‖ ネギダル語 -si(5) ‖ ウデヘ語 -hi(6) ‖ オロッコ語 -si

ラムート語の文語 -ca，-cэ の母音のそれぞれは К．А．Новиковаによれば，そのオラ方言では第2音節以下にあらわれるいわゆる弱化した（中舌の）a，ə である。(7)ラムート語の文語の第2音節以下の a，э は多くオラ方言のこれらの母音に対応するとみられ，そしてその a，э はツングース語祖語の *a，*ə にさかのぼることがあるばかりでなく，そのほかの母音音素たとえば *i（または *ɪ）にもさかのぼることがあると考えられる。(8)またオロッコ語の第2音節以下の i は祖語の*i（または*ɪ）あるいは*ii（または*ɪɪ）にさかのぼるだろう。なおウデヘ語の -h- はラムート語，ネギダル語，オロッコ語の -s- とともに*-s- に由来するとみられる。したがってこの語尾においては，祖形の*-si（または*-sɪ）にさかのぼるものであろう。筆者には，この動詞語尾が*-sa にさかのぼるとはみられない。(9)

なおゴリド語文語の -си（例　пулси-‘ходить, бродить, путешествовать’），オルチャ語の -si（例　pụlsi-‘ходить, бродить’）は上述の*-si あるいはこの*-si をふくむ融合形に由来するものであろうが，両言語においてそれは動詞語幹形成接尾辞である。ただしオルチャ語には，たとえば上例の動詞の現在形 pụlsini に対して，過去形として pụlsihəni のほかに pụlcini という形がある。なおのちにふれるように同言語では母音音素におわる過去形の語尾は -han，子音音素におわる過去形のそれは -cin である。pụlcini のような形があることは，Т．И．Петрова が述べているように，ゴリド語文語の -си，オルチャ語の -si も以前はオロッコ語のように動詞語尾であったことを物語るものであろう[10]。

さて一方，ツングース諸言語のこの語尾において母音音素におわる動詞語幹につく -ra の方は，祖形 *-ra にさかのぼると考えられる。なお子音音素におわる動詞語幹につくほかの -da，-ta，-a のような形がどんな祖形にさかのぼり，祖語においてこの語尾が全体的にどんな動詞変化をしていたかの問題についてはここにはふれないが，この*-ra に対して上の*-si は一体どんな関係にあるのであろうか。共時論的にみて祖語で両者は単なる音韻的環境による交替形か，文法的交替形か。あるいはまた通時論的には*-si は*-ra と同源のものか，補充法によっていて起源を異にするものか。このことを扱うためには，*-si に対応するツングース諸言語の形の用例におけるそのあらわす意味内容の面を注意しなければならない。それぞれの言語の若干の語例を以下にあげる。ラムート語文語の -н または -ни，ウデヘ語の -ni は第３人称単数語尾。ネギダル語の -m，オロチ語の -м は第１人称単数語尾。

ラムート語文語

(1) дэгсэн ‘лететь, улететь, вылететь, прилететь’
нгāлсан ‘держать, нести в руках’
туксэн ‘нести, носить, таскать, тащить, и т. п.’
уйсэн ‘кипеть’
хулсэн ‘идти, скитаться и т. п.’
бисни ‘быть и т. п.’
эсни ‘не делать чего-нибудь’ (отрицательный вспомогательный глагол)

(2) ичимсэн ‘стремиться увидеть’
едарсан ‘быть горьким’
нямсан ‘быть теплым’
утунсан ‘чесаться, зудиться’

ネギダル語

(1) bisim ‘(я) есмь’
ösim ‘(я) не есмь’

(2) wāmusim ‘мне хочется убить’

ウデヘ語（下にあげる動詞形の -ni のまえの -hi は*-si とほかの語尾とが融合していることも考えられる。）

(1) əhini ‘рычать, ворчать (о животных)’

ilihini ‘стоять’

tәhini ‘сидеть (о человеке)’

tōhini ‘лежать (о животных)’

xuihini ‘кипеть’

xulihini ‘ходить, ездить, путешествовать, скитаться, разъезжать, расхаживать по разным местам’

вuktaganahini ‘раскалываться, разламываться (поперек) на много кусков’

вihini ‘быть, жить, существовать, находиться, иметься’

əhini (отриц. глагол, 3-ье л. ед. ч. наст. вр.)

(2) wāmuhini ‘желать (иметь потребность, жаждать) убить’

səвʒəŋkəhini ‘интересоваться’

əgdəŋgəhini ‘удивляться’

なお ilihini, tәhini, tōhini, xuihini はやはり同語幹の直説法現在の別の動詞形 ilīni, tәini, tōini, xuīni と意味上の差異を示し，これらの動詞はそれぞれ‘вставать’,‘садиться’‘ложиться (о животных)’, ‘кипятить’をあらわす。[11]

オロチ語（下にあげる動詞形の -м のまえの -си は*-si とほかの語尾とが融合していることも考えられる。）

(1) бисим ～ биhим ‘есмь’

эсим ～ эгим ‘не…делаю’

хулисим ‘хожу’

オロッコ語

(1) ilisi ‘立っている’

ŋaalisi ‘手にさげてあるく’

puisi ‘にえたっている’
pulisi ‘あるいている’
təəsi ‘すわっている’
miinəsi ‘切りつづける’
əsi ‘…しない’（否定動詞）
andusi ‘つくる’
panusi ‘問う’

(2) ŋənəmusi ‘行きたい’
munalisi ‘おしむ’
namasi ‘あたたかい’
xuturisi ‘かゆい’

なお ilisi，təəsi は同じ語幹に語尾*-ra がついた(または両者が融合した）動詞 illee（*ilira に由来する)，təərə と意味上差異を示し，これらの動詞はそれぞれ‘立つ’，‘すわる’をあらわす。

動詞の不完了の連体形，終止形をつくる当該語尾は，上例についてみるとさらにある意味をもち，その意味の範囲はこれら五言語でほぼ重り合うようにみられる（ただしそのうちネギダル語，オロチ語の資料は十分でない)。この意味の範囲は大体においておそらくこの語尾の祖形にまでそのままさかのぼるものであろう。したがって祖語でも*-si は動詞の不完了の連体形，終止形を形成する上に，さらにある意味内容をもち，それは上述のツングース諸言語の語例にもとづいてつぎのようにまとめて記すことができよう。(1) 語幹が意味する運動，状態を継続するか，くりかえす（一回だけでない）こと，すなわちその運動，状態が時間的に長引くことをあらわし，あるいはまた (2) 語幹が意味する感情，欲求が存在することをあらわし，また語幹が意味するある感覚を，ものごとの属性としてでなく，また知覚の単なる表象としてでなく知覚作用としてあらわしていたようにおもわれる。

ツングース諸言語の語例からみて，この語尾が語幹にむすびつくとき(1)と(2)の意味内容をあらわす動詞のあいだには一般にはちがいがあり，前者では動詞語幹にその語尾がつき，後者では形容詞語幹にそれがついていたとみられる。

したがって(1)の動詞におけるその語尾と(2)の動詞におけるその語尾は一括して扱っても正確には同音意義である二つの語尾ということができよう。

しかしある語例における当該語尾は上記の意味の説明からはみ出るかもしれず[12]，当該語尾の意味内容はさらに拡大することもありうる。なおオロッコ語の o-o 'する' に対立する o-si 'なる' のような意味は，上に述べたところからだけでは説明することがむずかしい。

上の例におけるように，各言語間には同一語幹に当該語尾がついた動詞も見出される[13]。これはその語幹のあらわす意味がこの*-si のあらわす意味とむすびつきやすいためでそれぞれの言語でのちにあらたに別々に形成されたとも考えられるが，あるいは祖語からそれぞれの言語が伝えているのかもしれない。

ゴリド語文語，オルチャ語の動詞語幹形成接尾辞 -си と -si も，上記のツングース諸言語とは語尾と接尾辞のちがいがあるが，上記の(1)，(2)の意味内容をあらわしているようである[14]。例，ゴリド語文語 пулси- 'ходить, бродить, путешествовать', тэ̄си- 'сидеть', эрдэнгэси- 'удивляться, интересоваться и т. п.', демуси- 'хотеть есть, быть голодным, недоедать', オルチャ語 pụlsi- 'ходить, бродить', tə̄si- 'сидеть', əldəŋgəsi- 'интересоваться', ʒəmsi- 'хотеть есть'. なお(2)の意味内容をあらわしていたとみられる動詞が，ゴリド語文語，オルチャ語では -си，-si におわる形で，またウデヘ語でも -hi におわる形で，あとに語尾をともなわず，形容詞，名詞，または副詞の機能をもっているいくつかの語例がみられる。例，ゴリド語文語 гичиси 'холодно', холодный', хуйгэси 'тяжелый, тяжесть', オルチャ語 gitisi 'холодный', ウデヘ語 ṇamahi 'теплый (о всем, кроме жидкостей), тепло'.

さてそれでは上述の*-si は*-ra とどんな関係にあったかの問題にかえると，以上みてきたように*-si は動詞の不完了の連体形，終止形をつくる点では*-ra と文法的機能をひとしくする動詞語尾であったが，*-si は特に上記の意味内容をあらわしていたと考える。したがって*-si は*-ra に対して一つの文法的交替形であって，単に音韻的条件によってある一定の語幹につく交替形ではないようである。また*-si は*-ra に対して補充法による形ではないかとも思われる。

しかし筆者には，*-si に関して以下に述べるようなもう一つの仮説をたてることも可能なように考えられる。

動詞語尾*-ra と*-si においてはまず a と i という母音音素が異なるが，ツングース語においてはおなじ接尾辞ないし語尾の母音音素が，一般には語幹末音素が母音音素であるか，子音音素であるかと関連して，a であったり，i であったりするつぎのような例がある。

オロッコ語における‘なになにするために行く’という動詞語幹形成接尾辞は，その接尾する語幹の末尾の音素の如何によって -nda～-ŋda～-ni～-i と交替する。-nda は CV におわる語幹のあとに，-ŋda は VV におわる語幹のあとに，-ni は l または ŋ におわる語幹のあとに，-i は n におわる語幹のあとについている。(15)

またオロッコ語で -xan～-čin という完了の動詞語尾は，語幹末尾が母音音素か，子音音素かによって交替し，前者の場合は -xan，後者の場合は -čin があらわれる。ただし p におわる動詞語幹には -tu という音節が介入して -xan がつく。なお不規則動詞 bi-‘ある’，ə-‘…しない’（否定動詞），ga-‘買う’ o-‘する’，o-‘なる’には -čin がつくが，語幹末尾にもう一つ č があらわれる。bul-‘死ぬ’は buč-čin となる。また上述の語尾 -si をとるような動詞には -čin があらわれる。

オルチャ語の -han～-cin という直説法過去および過去能動形動詞(16)の語尾の交替形は，母音音素における語幹には前者が，また子音音素 n または l におわる語幹には後者があらわれる。若干の動詞 bi-‘быть，существовать，иметься’，ga-‘покупать’，ʒi-‘приходить’，o-‘делаться，становиться’には -cin がつく。なお子音音素 p におわる語幹においては，その p と語尾の頭音が転倒して kpin となる。

ゴリド語文語の -хан～-кин～-чин という直説法過去および過去能動形動詞の語尾の交替形は，母音音素におわる語幹には -хан が，子音音素 н，л におわる語幹には -кин があらわれ，若干の動詞 би-‘быть，существовать’，га-‘покупать’，ди-‘приходить’，о-‘делаться，становиться’，には -чин

がつく。なお子音音素пにおわる語幹においては，そのпと語尾の頭音が転換してкпинとなる。

ウデへ語の直説法過去および過去能動形動詞の語尾は，-ha ～ -ki～-si と交替するが，動詞語幹の末尾が母音音素の場合には，-ha，子音音素n，gの場合には -ki があらわれる。否定動詞 ə- においてはこの語尾は -si となる。なお子音音素 p，m におわる語幹にこの語尾がつくときは，その p，m と語尾の頭音が転換してそれぞれ kpi，ŋpi となる。

オロチ語の直説法過去の動詞語尾は，-xa ～ - ки ～- пи ～- чи と交替するが，動詞語幹の末尾が母音音素または w の場合には -xa，пの場合には - пи，その他の子音音素の場合には - ки があらわれる。ただし - ки のまえでнはнгと，дはкとなる。ある動詞 би- ‘быть’, э- ‘не’（делать чего- либо）などには - чи があらわれる。すなわち хулчим ‘ходил’. これらはいずれも直説法現在で - си をとる動詞である。[(17)]

これらの諸言語における上述の接尾辞や語尾の交替形の母音音素のちがいは，すでにふれたように，通例それらの接尾辞，語尾が母音音素におわる語幹につくか，子音音素におわる語幹につくかによるが，その形が補充法によるものかどうかは今後十分にあきらかにせねばならない。ここで扱う動詞語尾*-ra と*-si の関係も同様のことが問題となる。しかしこの動詞語尾および上述の接尾辞，語尾においてそれらの母音音素は，形態音素として交替しているのではないかとも考えられよう。ただしたとえばオロッコ語におけるように，g，n，l，p の子音音素におわる語幹につく動詞語尾 -ra の交替形 -da，-ta の母音音素がaである点，その語尾 -ra は上述の接尾辞，語尾と異なることを注意せねばならない。しかしその*-si は以下に述べるようにある種の子音音素におわる語幹につくその動詞語尾の形ではなかったかと考えられるのである。

さてつぎに動詞語尾*-ra と*-si の子音音素のちがいについてであるが，祖語のこの語尾においては母音音素におわる語幹につく形のかしらに r があらわれるのに対して，ある種の無声子音音素におわる語幹につく形ではその点が異なっていたのではないだろうか。

オロッコ語においては，すでにふれたように完了の動詞語尾の -xan～-čin

は，おおよそ前者は母音音素におわる語幹に，後者は子音音素におわる語幹につき，語尾 -si をとるような動詞においては後者の -čin があらわれる。このことはかかる動詞の語幹が母音音素におわっているが，かつては子音音素におわっていたことをおもわせる。

またオロッコ語において動詞語尾 -bi-la-xam は，話し手のある動作が過去においておころうとしたことまたはそれがおこればよかったと話し手がおもうことをあらわすが，この語尾が語尾 -si をとるような動詞の語幹に対しては -ppi-la-xam という形となって，語幹と語尾のさかいにこのように pp があらわれるのは，語尾 -si をとる動詞の語幹が古くある無声子音音素におわっていたことを考えさせるのである。

またおなじオロッコ語において，動詞語幹に接尾して，運動の主体が明示されないことをあらわす接尾辞 -bu は，普通にはあとに -ri という動詞語尾をともなって -buri としてあらわれるが，この -bu がどんな語幹につくかによって別の交替形もあらわれ，また語幹と融合した形もあらわれる。語尾 -si をとるような動詞の語幹に対してはこの -bu が -pu という交替形としてあらわれるが[18]，このことは古くその動詞の語幹がある無声子音音素におわっていたことを示す証拠となろうか。

やはりオロッコ語において，動詞語幹に接尾してある運動がおこなわれつつもとの状態にもどることをあらわす接尾辞 -du が，語尾 -si をとるような動詞の語幹につくとき，-tu という交替形としてあらわれることも[19]，古くこの動詞の語幹がある無声子音音素におわっていたことをおもわせる。ただし -tu は上述の接尾辞への類推によって生じたことも考えられる[20]。

では語幹末のその無声子音音素とはどんな子音音素であったか，またそれにつく例の語尾はどんな形をしていたかということが問題となるが，それについては筆者は二つの見方を示したい。その一つにおいては，一つの語尾とみなされた*-si は，実は*-s が語幹の末尾音で，*-i がこれにつく動詞語尾*-ra の交替形であったとみる。すでに К. М. Мыльникова と В. И. Цинциус はネギダル語について，たとえば上掲単語を bis-i-m，wā-mus-i-m のように区切っている。事実 за-mus-ча-n ‘ему захотелось есть’ という(2)の意味内容の動詞の例があげられており，この語形では未完了の動詞語尾 -чa のまえで mu のあとの語幹末尾に現に s がある。[21]

もう一つの見方は，*-si が一つの語尾としてなんらかの無声子音音素におわる語幹に接尾していたとみる。この場合はその語幹末の子音音素が*s であったとみるのが自然ではないだろうか。そして語幹末の*s とむすびついた*-si のどちらか一方の*s がのちに消失したのであろう。しかしこの*-si がつく語幹には他の無声子音音素，たとえば*t（のちに消失）におわるものもあったかもしれない。

なおまた*-si をどう区切るか，すなわち語幹末の*s プラス語尾*-i か，または語幹末のある無声子音音素プラス語尾*-si かのちがいは，動詞語幹末尾にどんな無声子音音素がたつかにより，二つの区切り方が両立することも考えられる。とにかくこれらの見方によれば，祖語においては共時論的にみて*-i または*-si は動詞語尾*-ra の交替形であり，これは*s またはある無声子音音素におわる語幹のあとという音韻的条件によってあらわれる交替形であったとみられよう。

さて語幹末尾にたつ*s かまたはある無声子音音素は，あるいは少数の語では語根の末尾をなすこともあったかもしれないが，多くの場合おそらく一つの動詞語幹形成接尾辞であったろう。そしてはじめに述べた仮説では語尾*-si があらわすとみた上述の意味内容を，この仮説ではこの接尾辞がもっていたとみたい。しかし上述の(1)と(2)の意味内容をあらわす動詞ではその子音音素がちがっていてそれぞれ形を異にする別の接尾辞であったことも考えられる。そして上に記したようにネギダル語で зamusчan ‘ему захотелось есть’ のような語例において語幹末尾に s があるのであれば、少なくとも(2)の意味内容をあらわす動詞には古く語幹末尾に*s があってそれが保たれているとみられ，その*s が (2)の意味内容をあらわす接尾辞であったと考えられよう。なお二番めの見方においては，接尾辞は消失したが，そのあらわす意味内容はその動詞形によって保たれたとみられよう。[補注]

またなお二番めの見方は上述の意味内容をもつとみることのむずかしい動詞を説明する可能性ももつ。たとえば上述のオロッコ語の o-o ‘する’（おそらく

*o-ro に由来する）に対立する o-si ‘なる’ は，子音音素（たとえば t ）一つからなり自動詞語幹を派生する接尾辞が少なくとも前オロッコ語で後者の語幹についていたがその子音音素が消失したものかもしれない。(22)

以上二つの仮説を見返してみると，はじめのにくらべてあとの方が多くの事実を説明できるようである。上述の問題についてツングース語内で今日なお十分に解明することはむずかしい。しかしツングース語と親族関係をもつ見込みのある他言語にそれに対応する事実が見出され，それとの比較研究がすすむこともこの問題を解くことをたすけるだろうし，また同時にそれによってその親族関係の確実さがつよまるであろう。(23)

注

(1) ツングース諸言語において，通例，a をふくむ接尾辞，語尾は，その a が母音調和によって ə またさらに o（さらに ɵ）と交替する形をほかにもつが，これらの形を一一掲げて扱うことは特別の場合を除き省略したい。

(2) Benzing，1956，123ページ以下。

(3) 特に記さぬかぎり，ラムート語（エウェン語）は Цинциус и Ришес, 1952, 1957。エウェンキ語は Василевич, 1958。ネギダル語は Мыльникова и Цинциус, 1931。ウデヘ語は Шнейдер, 1936。オロチ語は Цинциус, 1949。ゴリド語（ナーナイ語）は Петрова, 1960。オルチャ語は Петрова, 1936。オロッコ語は Ikegami，1959 および池上の採集資料による。

(4) なおオロッコ語において -ri ～ -ǰi ～-či ～-si と交替する動詞語尾の -si は以下で問題とする*-si と他のおそらく*i をふくむ語尾とが合した別の語尾であると考えられる。

(5) たとえば ommosin ‘ему хочется курить, пить.’

(6) たとえば tə̄himi ‘сижу’, isənəhimi ‘многократно хожу смотреть.’

(7) Новикова, 1960，36 ページなど。

(8) たとえばラムート語文語のつぎの語の第 2 音節の a，э は，上述の -ca，-cэ と同様に二つの子音音素のあとにあらわれるものであるが，他のツングース語の語形と下記の対応を示し，はじめの 2 語ではそれぞれ*a，*ə にさかのぼり，あとの

3語では*i にさかのぼるとみられる。

L амнга ‘рот’ ‖ E амнга ‘同上’ ‖ U aŋma ‘同上’ ‖ Ok aŋma ‘口’

L уркэ ‘дверь’ ‖ E уркэ ‘同上’ ‖ U ukə ‘同上’ ‖ Ok utə ‘戸口’

L хилтэс ‘трут’ ‖ E（エルボゴチョン方言の廃語）силтыкса ‘同上’ ‖ U siktihə ‘同上’ ‖ Ok silčiskə ‘ほくち’

L нэлкэ ‘весной’ ‖ E нэлки ‘同上’ ‖ U nəki ‘同上’

L хӣмкэ- ‘кашлять’ ‖ E симки- ‘同上’ ‖ Ok siikpi- ‘せきをする’

L＝ラムート語文語，E＝エウェンキ語，N＝ネギダル語，U＝ウデヘ語，Oc＝オロチ語，Ok ＝オロッコ語。以下同様。

(9) ウデヘ語の動詞 вi- ‘быть’の現在能動形動詞 вiə は*bisə でなく*birə に由来するものであろう。

(10) Петрова, 1936，49ページ。また満洲語の bisire の si もその*-si に対応するかまたはその*-si と他の語尾（*i をふくむ）との融合形に対応するものであろう。なおこのことは Benzing，1956，124ページ以下にも述べられている。さらにまた満洲語の bisu の -su や oso の -so，さらにあるいはひょっとすると baisu, gaisu の -su が，*-si をとる動詞の命令形語尾*-su に由来するものであろうこと（Ikegami，1960，125ページ）は，オロッコ語で上記動詞語尾 -si をとる動詞の命令形が語尾に -su をとることから考えられる。

(11) ただし引用した Шнейлер, 1936 では，ilihini と対立する ilīni のように tōmohini ‘греться у огня’, ulihini ‘шить’ と対立する tōmoini，ulīni にはその意味として同じくそれぞれ ‘греться у огня’，‘шить’ と記されている。

(12) たとえば，諸言語の否定動詞（ə-）やオロッコ語の andusi ‘つくる’，panusi ‘問う’。

(13) L нгāлсан ‖ Ok ŋaalisi. L уйсэн ‖ U xuihini ‖ Ok puisi. L хулсэн ‖ U xulihini ‖ Oc хулисим ‖ Ok pulisi. L нямсан ‖ Ok namasi. L утунсан ‖ Ok xuturisi. U ilihini ‖ Ok ilisi. U təhini ‖ Ok təəsi. L ичимсэн の -м，N wāmusim の -mu，U wāmuhini の -mu，Ok ŋənəmusi の -mu はたがいに対応するおなじ接尾辞。欲求を意味する。U вuktaganahini の -na,

Ok miinəsi の -nə もたがいに対応するおなじ接尾辞。反復などを意味する。

⑭　Аврорин, 1961, 18, 19, 46ページにもその記述がある。

⑮　Cは子音音素, Vは母音音素をあらわす。

⑯　ソ連の研究者の用語による。以下同様。

⑰　ツングース諸言語の上述の不規則的な動詞あるいはここで問題とする語尾 -si (-си) をとるような動詞は語幹が母音音素におわるが, これに接尾する上記のオロッコ語の‘…しに行く’の接尾辞や諸言語の完了または過去の語尾は母音音素としてiをふくむ。このことは, 一般にはこの語尾が母音音素におわる語幹につく形には a, 子音音素におわる語幹につく形には i があらわれる点から推して, これらの動詞の語幹の末尾音が古くは子音音素でなかったかということをおもわせるが, 少なくとも語尾 -si をとる動詞はその語幹がかつておそらく子音音素におわっていただろうと思われることは以下にあらためてふれる。

⑱　この接尾辞がどんな語幹に対してどんな形をとるかを Ikegami, 1959 にあげた各動詞類とその語例について以下に示す。なおこの接尾辞がつく語幹はⅣ組の語幹（ただし 2.3 類の語幹の末音は n でなく m ）である。1.1 類と 0.1 類には語幹とこの接尾辞の融合形があらわれる。1.2 類, 0.2 類（これが問題の語尾*-si をとるような動詞の類), 0.3 類, 2.類にはそれぞれ -gu-ri, -pu-ri, -u-ri, -bu-ri の交替形があらわれる。語例,1.1 類 ŋənnəuri, moollouri, ŋənnuri, sommuri, aundauri, tokpouri, silturi, barguri ; 0.1 類 bakkauri, palukkauri, sapčikkauri, xəəkkəuri, lokkouri, gajakkuri, bəlikkuri, gəjjuri ; 1.2 類 uuwuri, bɵɵwuri ; 0.2 類 gatapuri, ələpuri, andupuri, moolipuri, allaupuri ; 0.3 類 dəpuri ; 2 類 bujalburi, xɵɵlburi, xaagburi, orogburi, umburi, kɵjɵɵmburi ; 不規則動詞 biwwuri, owwuri‘すること’, opuri‘なること’, bulburi, gawwuri。

⑲　例, andu-tu-‘修繕する’。

⑳　オロッコ語の -du は他のツングース語の動詞語幹形成接尾辞, すなわち L -pra ～ -prэ, N -ygi-, U -gi に対応し, それゆえ祖形*-rgu にさかのぼるとみられる。-tu は, 無声子音の語幹末につく交替形*rku [r̥ku] があるいはあってこれにさかのぼるか, すでに*-du となった形が語尾*-si をとるような動詞とその

後はじめてむすびついたとき*d が*t に変化したか，または上記の -bu～-pu のような接尾辞への類推形成による。

オロッコ語の n や l におわる語幹につくときの -du，あるいはウデヘ語の上記の -gi が n におわる語幹につくときの交替形 -ŋi については，祖語における語幹末子音音素プラス*-rgu（またはウデヘ語への過程における*-rgi）としてあったものに由来するものか（子音音素プラス rg という連続があったことになるが，たとえばオロッコ語にもまれに bujalpčini ‘かれがこわすことができる’ のような例がある），またはすでにそれぞれ*-du，*-gi となった形がそれらの語幹にその後はじめてつき，ウデヘ語の -ŋi ではさらに*g が*ŋ に変化したものであろう。

(21) Мыльникова и Цинциус, 1931，177，178ページ。未完了の用語はもとの論文の用語 Imperfectum によるもの。

(22) これに対応する動詞が L ōдни，U odoini（いずれも ‘делаться’ を意味する直説法現在第3人称単数形）においてとっている語尾が d（д）をもっているが、これらの言語でこの語尾がある子音音素におわる動詞語幹につくときかしらに d（д）があらわれる点が，古くこの動詞形の語幹末尾にやはりある子音音素があったことをおもわせる。

(23) たとえばツングース語と日本語との比較はツングース諸言語間の比較にくらべれば，その確実さははなはだしく減ずるが，日本語の動詞の語尾のなかの r をふくむ要素とシク活用形容詞の語尾のシならびにその両者の関係が，ツングース語の上述の語尾 *-ra と*-si（または少なくとも(2)の意味内容の動詞の接尾辞として推定した場合の *-s）およびその両者の関係と対応することがもしもたしかになれば，その比較はツングース語のこの点の解明をたすけるであろうし，またこれら二言語の親族関係に対する一つのつよい証左になろう。

（補注） オロッコ語の -ppi-la-xam のはじめの音素は語幹末音に由来し，二つめの音素は*-bi の頭音に由来するものであろうが，特に両者間に相互同化があった場合を考えると，語幹末音は古くは s のほかに無声閉鎖音の音素であった見込みも強いだろう。一方，-ppi-la-xam は，-si をとる動詞語幹でしかも(1)の意味内容をあらわすものにつくのが普通とみられるが，このことと考えあわせると，これらの動詞語幹の方は末音が無声閉鎖音であったかもしれない。

引用文献

Benzing, J., 1956. Die tungusischen Sprachen—Versuch einer vergleichenden Grammatik. Wiesbaden.

Ikegami, J., 1959. The verb inflection of Orok. 国語研究（国学院大学国語研究会）9.

——, 1960. Versuch einer vergleichenden Grammatik der tungusischen Sprachen. Ural-Altaische Jahrbücher, Band 32. Benzing, 1956 の書評。

Аврорин, В. А., 1961. Грамматика нанайского языка, II. Москва-Ленинград.

Василевич, Г. М., 1958. Эвенкийско-русский словарь. Москва.

Мыльникова, К. М. и Цинциус, В И., 1931. Материалы по исследованию негидальского языка. Тунгусский Сборник, I. Ленинград.

Новикова, К. А., 1960. Очерки диалектов эвенского языка, Часть I. Москва-Ленинград.

Петрова, Т. И., 1936. Ульчский диалект нанайского языка. Москва-Ленинград.

——, 1960. Нанайско-русский словарь. Ленинград.

Цинциус, В И., 1949. Очерк морфологии орочского языка. Ученые Записки ЛГУ, 98, Серия востоковедческих наук, вып. 1.

Цинциус, В. И. и Ришес, Л. Д., 1952. Русско-эвенский словарь. Москва.

——, 1957. Эвенско-русский словарь. Ленинград.

Шнейдер, Е. Р., 1936. Краткий удэйско-русский словарь. Москва-Ленинград.

初出　『現代言語学』［東京　三省堂　昭和47年（1972年）3月15日］651−663ページ。

An English translation of this article appeared in *Acta Asiatica*, *Bulletin of the Institute of Eastern Culture*, 24 (The Tōhō Gakkai, Tokyo, 1973), pp. 45−56. This translation was entitled "On One Verb Ending in Proto-Tungus ——About *-si——". The Japanese version in the present volume is a revision of the original article (published in 1972).

追記

下記の接尾辞は，359ページ以下に述べる語幹末音素が母音であるか，子音であるかによって接尾辞の母音音素がaとなり，iとなる好箇の例である。すなわち，動作の繰返しを意味する動詞語幹形成接尾辞 -na ～ -i は，末尾が母音音素である語幹には -na が，末尾が n である語幹には -i が接尾する。なお，この接尾辞がついて形成された動詞語幹は，動詞語尾 -si が接尾してその動詞の未完了の動名詞が形成される。

361ページおよび補注でウイルタ語の -ppi-la-xam のはじめの p について述べたことは，同じウイルタ語の əpulə anduppoo '作らなかった（作られなかった）もの' のような動詞否定構造のなかの動詞語幹 andu- '作る' についている -ppoo のはじめの p についても同様に言えよう。

注（18）にある1.2類の動詞 uuwuri，bəəwuri，不規則動詞 biwwuri, owwuri, gawwuri の語形は，旧稿ではそれぞれ uuguri，bəəguri, biguri, oguri, gaguri とあったのを改めたものである。

The Category of Person in Tungus: Its Representation in the Indicative Forms of Verbs

In the Tungus languages (not including Manchu), the category of person finds its grammatical representation not only in personal pronouns and the personal possessive endings of substantives (and of adjectives in some Evenki and Even dialects), but also in the personal endings of verbs which indicate the person of the subject. Indicative (affirmative) forms of a Tungus verb ordinarily take an indicative ending and a personal ending which appears after the indicative ending. However, some indicative verb forms take only either an indicative ending or a personal ending. In this paper the writer will deal with the personal inflection of the indicative forms of Tungus verbs.

We find two sets, 1 and 2, of the personal endings which are added to indicative endings in the Tungus languages. However, Orochi has only one set, Set 1 given below. Solon, another special case in this respect, will be dealt with later separately.

Set 1 is found in all the Tungus languages and contains personal endings for the first, second and third person in the singular and plural. The personal endings of Set 1 are also added to substantives and function as the possessive endings of substantives. As for Nanai, Olcha, Uilta and Udehe, Set 2 contains personal endings only for the first and second person in the singular and plural, but no personal endings for the third person, excepting the plural element *-l* which appears in the third person plural forms in Nanai, Olcha and Uilta. However, Set 2 forms of Negidal, Evenki and Even have personal endings for the first and second person in the singular and plural and for the third person singular, but no personal ending for the third person plural. Except for Solon, the fundamental difference between Sets 1 and 2 is the presence or absence of a personal ending for the third person plural.

The indicative endings may be grouped into two classes, I or II according to whether an indicative ending is accompanied by a personal ending of either Set 1 or 2. Orochi has only one class, Class I. An indicative ending of Class I is accompanied by a personal ending of Set 1, whereas an indicative ending of Class II is followed by a personal ending of Set 2. In the case of the third person in the singular and plural in Nanai, Olcha, Uilta and Udehe, an indicative ending of Class II is not followed by a personal ending. In the third person plural forms of Negidal, Evenki and Even, an indicative ending of Class II is not followed by a personal ending. Class I verb endings also serve in the formation of verbal nouns.

The classes of indicative endings and the sets of personal endings of each Tungus language will be given in the following :

Nanai (PETROVA, 1960)

Class I: present I -(*r*) *i* and past I -*xa*(*n*).

Class II: present II -*ra* or zero, past II -*ka*, future I -*ǰā*(*n*) plus (-*ra*), and future II -*ŋā*.

Set 1: -*i*∼-*mbi* (1. sing.), -*pu* (1. pl.), -*si* (2. sing.), -*su* (2 pl.), -*ni* (3. sing.), and -*či* (3. pl.).

Set 2 : -*i*∼-*mbi* (1. sing.), -*pu* (1. pl.), -*si*∼-*či* (2. sing.), and -*su* (2. pl.).

Olcha (PETROVA, 1936)

Class I : present I -(*r*) *i* and past -*xa*(*n*).

Class II : present II -*ra* or zero, future I -(*r*) *ila*, and future II -*ŋa*.

Set 1 : -*i*∼-*mbi* (1. sing.), -*mu* (1. pl.), -*si* (2. sing.), -*su* (2. pl.), -*ni* (3.

sing.), and *-ti* (3. pl.).

Set 2 : *-i*~*-mbi* (1. sing.), *-mu*~*-m* (1. pl.), *-si*~*-s*~*-ti* (2. sing.), and *-su* (2. pl.).

Uilta (= Orok) (IKEGAMI, 1959)

Class I: imperfect *-ri* and perfect *-xa(n-)*.

Class II: present *-ra*, past *-ta*, future I *-rila*, and future II *-raŋa*.

Set 1: *-wi*~*-bi* (1. sing.). *-pu* (1. pl.), *-si* (2. sing.), *-su* (2. pl.), *-ni* (3. sing.), and *-či* (3. pl.).

Set 2: *-mi* (1. sing.), *-pu* (1. pl.), *-si* (2. sing.), and *-su* (2. pl.).

Udehe (SHNEIDER, 1936)

Class I: present I (3. sing. and pl.) *-(da) i*, past I *-ha*, and future II *-ǰaŋa*.

Class II: present II (1. and 2., sing. and pl.) *-da* or zero, past II *-ka*, future I *-ǰa*, and future III *-(da) ta*.

Set 1: *-i*~*-mi* (1. sing.), *-u*~*-mu* (1. pl. excl.), *-fi* (1. pl. incl.), *-hi* (2. sing.), *-hu* (2. pl.), *-ni* (3. sing.), and *-ti* (3. pl.).

Set 2: *-i*~*-m (i)* (1. sing.), *-u* (1. pl. excl.), *-ti*~*-f(i)* (1. pl. incl.), *-hi* (2. sing.), and *-hu* (2. pl.).

Orochi (TSINTSIUS, 1949)

Class I: present *-(da)j*, past *-xa(n-)*, future I *-ǰa*, and future II *-ǰaŋa*.

Set 1: *-wi*~*-j*~*-m(i)* (1. sing.), *-mu* (1. pl. excl.), *-pi* (1. pl. incl.), *-si* (2. sing.), *-su* (2. pl.), *-n(i)* (3. sing.), and *-ti* (3. pl.).

Negidal (TSINTSIUS, 1982)

Class I: past *-ča* and future *-ǰa(ŋā)*.

Class II: present *-ja* or zero.

Set 1: *-w*(1. sing.), *-wun* (1. pl. excl.), *-t* (1. pl. incl.), *-s* (2. sing.), *-sun*

(2. pl.), *-n* (3. sing.), and *-tin* (3. pl.).

Set 2: *-m* (1. sing.), *-wun* (1. pl. excl.), *-p* (1. pl. incl.), *-s* (2. sing.), *-sun* (2. pl.), and *-n* (3. sing.).

Evenki (GORTSEVSKAYA, KOLESNIKOVA and KONSTANTINOVA, 1958)

Class I: past I *-čā*, past II *-ŋki*, and future III *-ǰaŋā*.

Class II: present *-ra* or zero, future I *-ǰa(ra)*, and future II *-ǰal (la)*.

Set 1: *-w* (1. sing.), *-wun* (1. pl. excl.), *-t* (1. pl. incl.), *-s* (2. sing.), *-sun* ~ *-s* (2. pl.), *-n* (3. sing.), and *-tin* (3. pl.).

Set 2: *-m* (1. sing.), *-w* (1. pl. excl.), *-p* (1. pl. incl.), *-nni* (2. sing.), *-s* (2. pl.), and *-n* (3. sing.).

Even (TSINTSIUS and RISHES, 1952)

Class I: past *-rī*.

Class II: present *-r(a)* or zero and future *-ǰi(r)*.

Set 1: *-w* (1. sing.), *-wun* (1. pl. excl.), *-t* (1. pl. incl.), *-s* (2 sing), *-san* (2. pl.), *-n* (3. sing.), and *-tan* (3. pl.).

Set 2: *-m* (1. sing.), *-u* (1. pl. excl.), *-p* (1. pl. incl.), *-nri* (2. sing.), *-s* (2. pl.), and *-n(i)* (3. sing.).

Solon (Poppe, 1931)

Class I: *-ri* (nomen praesentis), *-ǰigā* (nomen futuri), *-sā* ~ *-čā* (nomen perfecti), and *-ŋki* (nomen necessitatis).

Class II: *-ra* or zero (praesens imperfecti).

Set 1: *-ū* (1. sing.), *-mun* (1. pl. excl.), *-ti* (1. pl. incl.), *-š* (2. sing.), and *-sun* (2. pl.).

Set 2: *-mi* (1. sing.), *-mun* (1. pl. excl.), *-tti* (1. pl. incl.), *-ndi* (2. sing.), *-sun* ~ *-čun* (2. pl.), and *-n* (3. sing. and pl.).

Of the six indicative endings of Nanai, the -(*r*)*i* of the present I and the -*xa*(*n*)of the past I are included in the Class I while the -*ra* (or zero) of the present II, the -*ka* of the past II, the -*ǰā*(*n*) plus (-*ra*) of the future I, and the -*ŋa* of the future II are included in Class II.

Of the five indicative endings of Olcha, the -(*r*)*i* of the present I and the -*xa*(*n*) of the past are included in Class I and the -*ra* (or zero) of the present II, the -(*r*)*ila* of the future I and the -*ŋa* of the future II in Class II. According to SUNIK (1968a, 154), the first person plural ending of Set 1 appears as -*pu*.

Of the indicative endings of Uilta, the -*ri* of the imperfect and the -*xa*(*n*-) of the perfect are included in Class I and the -*ra* of the present, the -*ta* of the past, the -*rila* of the future I and the -*raŋa* of the future II in Class II.

Of the indicative endings of Udehe, the -(*da*)*i* of the present I, the -*ha* of the past I and the -*ǰaŋa* of the future II are included in Class I and the -*da* (or zero) of the present II, the -*ka* of the past II, the -*ǰa* of the future I and the -(*da*)*ta* of the future III in Class II.

In Orochi there are four indicative endings, the -(*da*)*j* of the present, the -*xa*(*n*-) of the past, the -*ǰa* of the future I and the -*ǰaŋa* of the future II, which are all included in Class I. To all of them, the personal endings of Set 1 are added. These indicative endings all serve to form verbal nouns. We do not find any of the indicative endings of Class II or any personal endings of Set 2. According to AVRORIN and LEBEDEVA (1968), the present ending is -(*da*)*i*, the past ending is -*xa*(*n*), and the future I ending is -*ǰā*(*n*).

Of the three Negidal indicative endings, the -*čā* of the past and the -*ǰa*(*ŋā*) of the future belong to Class I and the -*ja* (or zero) of the present to Class II. Accoding to KOLESNIKOVA and KONSTANTINOVA (1968), the future ending appears as -*ǰa*, which is accompanied by the personal endings of Set 1, but the first person pl. incl. ending added to *-ǰa* is *-p*.

Of the six Evenki indicative endings, the *-čā* of the past I, the *-ŋki* of the past II and the *-ǰaŋā* of the future III belong to Class I, and the *-ra* (or zero) of the present, the *-ǰa(ra)* of the future I and the *-ǰil(la)* of the future II to Class II.

Of the three Even indicative endings, the *-rī* of the past is included in Class I and the *-r(a)* (or zero) of the present and the *-ǰi(r)* of the future in Class II.

In Solon we find that Sets 1 and 2 of the personal endings are added to indicative forms. However, these two sets of Solon personal endings are very different from the two sets stated above in the other Tungus languages. Set 1 contains personal endings for the first and second person in the singular and plural, but no personal endings for the third person. Set 2 contains personal endings for the first and second person in the singular and plural and also the ending *-n* for the third person in both the singular and plural.

Indicative endings in Solon are also grouped into Classes I and II. A personal ending of Set 1 follows an indicative ending of Class I, whereas a personal ending of Set 2 follows an indicative ending of Class II. All the Solon indicative endings serve to form verbal nouns. The ending *-ri* of nomen praesentis, the *-ǰigā* of nomen futuri, the *-sā* ~ *-čā* of nomen perfecti and the *-ŋki* of nomen necessitatis are included in Class I, whereas the ending *-ra* (or zero) of praesens imperfecti stands alone in Class II.

Next, the personal endings of the indicative forms will be considered from the diachronical point of view. (Cf. IKEGAMI, 1981.)

It seems that in Orochi indicative endings of Class II and personal endings of Set 2 disappeared or moved to Class I or Set 1.

The Nanai present II, the Olcha present II, the Uilta present, the Udehe present, the Negidal present, the Evenki present, the Solon present imperfect and the Even present are formed by means of the verb ending *-ra*, a variant of it (*-r*, *-ja* or *-da*) or zero. These endings belong to Class II. These endings go back to **-ra* in Common Tungus. The first *n* of the Evenki *-nni*, Solon *-ndi* and Even-*nri* for the second person singular and the *m* of the Nanai and Olcha *-mbi* for the first person singular may be assumed to be one and the same element which was originally **-n* functioning as a verb ending or forming the final part of a verb ending. This element precedes a personal ending. Nanai and Olcha indicative forms, such as *būrəmbi* 'I give', show that this element appears after the *-ra*. The element **-n* referred to above and the first person singular ending **-bi* were amalgamated in the ending *-mi* of Uilta and Solon, the ending *-m*(*i*) of Udehe and Orochi and the ending *-m* of Negidal, Evenki and Even, all of which represent the first person in the singular. A similar amalgamation is found also in the first person plural endings of some other Tungus languages. Some first person endings of Set 2 seem to have been also included in Set 1 in some Tungus languages. The Evenki future II is formed by combining the endings *-ǰa-l* with a variant of *-ra* or zero.

The verb endings of the Nanai future I, the Evenki future I and the Even future, all of which belong to Class II, and one verb ending of the Solon nomen praesentis (Poppe, 1931, 128–130) originate from the suffix **-ǰa* plus **-ra* mentioned above. It is possible that the verb endings of the Udehe future I and the Orochi future I go back to the same combination, for the intervocalic **r* disappeared in Udehe and disappeared or became *j* in Orochi. The Negidal *-ǰa* of the future remains to be investigated.

The indicative endings of the Nanai past II, the Uilta past and the Udehe past II, all of which are included in Class II, seem to be originally the same.

The Nanai *-ŋā* of the future II and the Olcha *-ŋa* of the future II, both of which are included in Class II, go back to **-ŋā*. The Udehe *-ǰaŋa* of the future II, the Orochi *-ǰaŋa* of the future II, the Negidal *-ǰa(ŋā)* of the future, the Evenki *-ǰaŋā* of the future III and the Solon *-ǰiŋā* of nomen futuri, all five of which belong to Class I, may be traced back to the suffix **-ǰa* plus **-ŋā* mentioned above. The Even future verbal noun formative *-ǰiŋā* (~*-dŋā*) (Tsintsius and Rishes, 1952, 746) also originates from this combination. According to Sunik (1968 b, 224–225), the Udehe form belongs to Class II as well as Class I. Whether the **-ŋā* belonged to Class I or Class II at earlier stages is yet uncertain.

The Olcha *-(r)ila* of the future I and the Uilta *-rila* of the future I included in Class II were originally the same.

The Nanai *-(r)i* of the present I, the Olcha *-(r)i* of the present I, the Uilta *-ri* of the imperfect, the Udehe *-(da)i* of the present in the third person, the Orochi *-(da)j* of the present, the Negidal verbal noun formative *-ǰī* of the present (Tsintsius, 1982, 37), the Evenki verbal noun formative *-rī* (Gortsevskaya, Kolesnikova and Konstantinova, 1958, 266), the Even *-rī* of the past and the Solon *-ri* of nomen praesentis, all of which belong to Class I, originate from the combination of **-ra* plus some element used to form a verbal noun in Common Tungus.

The Nanai *-xa(n)* of the past I, the Olcha *-xa(n)* of the past, the Uilta *-xa(n-)* of the perfect, the Orochi *-xa(n-)* of the past, and probably also the Udehe *-ha* of the past I, all of which are included in Class I, were originally the verbal noun formative **-xan*. According to Sunik (1968 b, 224), the Udehe form belongs to Class II as well as Class I.

The Negidal past *-čā*, the Evenki *-čā* of the past I and the Solon *-sā* ~*-čā* of nomen perfecti, all of which belong to Class I, go back to the verbal noun formative **-čā*. The Even verbal noun formative *-čā* of the past (Tsintsius and Rishes, 1952, 745, 746) is also originally the same.

The Evenki *-ŋki* of the past II and the Solon *-ŋki* of nomen necessitatis, both of which are included in Class I, were originally **-ŋki*.

Judging from the above, there is a possibility that some indicative forms, such as the indicatives formed by the set of *-ra* etc. (Class II) and the indicatives formed by the Nanai *-ka* and its cognates in some other Tungus languages (Class II) were originally accompanied by the first or second person ending, singular or plural, but no personal ending was used for the third person. On the other hand, some indicative forms, such as the indicative forms formed by the Nanai *-ri* and its cognates in many other Tungus languages (Class I) may be assumed to have been followed by the first, second or third person ending, singular and plural, as are substantives and verbal nouns.

We assume that the third person plural forms of the Negidal, Evenki and Even indicatives formed by *-ra* etc. were in use without any personal endings at earlier stages in the same way as they are used now. On the other hand, the element *-n*, which was hitherto regarded as the third person ending, is used in the third person singular forms of the same indicatives of these languages and in the third person singular and plural forms of the Solon present imperfect. These forms might have been formed on the analogy of the personal inflection of verbal nouns. However, it is possible that the *-n* may not be the third person ending but the same as the element **-n* mentioned, which is assumed to have been a verb ending or a part of it. If this is so, then we can assume that these third person singular forms of Negidal, Evenki and Even and the third person singular and plural forms of Solon stated above were not accompanied by a personal ending. The Even ending *-ǰir* of the future in the third person plural form might have lost the final vowel *a*, or the *r* might perhaps have resulted from the amalgamation of the same element **-n* plus the plural element *-*l*. For instance, *xā-ǰi-r* 'they will know'. A similar amalgamation is found ordinarily in the plural forms of the Evenki and Even substantives ending in -*n*.

In the Uilta third person forms of the present, such as *uurakka* (sing.) 'he is riding (on a boat or sledge)', and *uurakkal* (pl.) 'they are riding', the former *k* might go back to **n*, since **nk* became *kk* in Uilta. It is possible that the *k* was the element -*n* stated above, and not the third person ending, for the plural element -*l* does not appear after a personal ending.

Some Solon indicatives which are not followed by a third person ending may have resulted from the influence of Manchu or a Mongolian dialect, in which no personal ending is added to verbs.

In conclusion, it is possible that in order to represent the category of person, the original indicative forms of Tungus had a system in which only the first and second persons were expressed by personal endings or enclitic pronouns. The use of the third person ending in addition to the use of the first and second person endings in indicative forms seems to have resulted from the use of a verbal noun as a predicate.

The third person endings might have been formerly used only with substantives and verbal nouns. Aside from a third person plural ending, such as -*tin* or -*či*, it is possible that the origin of the third person ending -*ni* may be different from that of the first and second person endings in the singular and plural. In fact, the third person ending -*ni* may not have originally been a personal ending, but rather a substantive ending expressing definiteness.

References Cited

Avrorin, V. A., Lebedeva, E. P., 1968. "Orochskii iazyk", *Iazyki narodov SSSR*, V, Leningrad.

GORTSEVSKAYA, V. A., KOLESNIKOVA, V. D., KONSTANTINOVA, O. A., 1958. *Ėvenkiisko-russkii slovar'*, Leningrad.

IKEGAMI, J., 1959. "The Verb Inflection of Orok", *Kokugo Kenkyu* (Kokugakuin Daigaku, Tokyo) 9.

—— 1981. "Indicative Forms of Manchu Verbs—In Comparison with Those of Tungus Verbs", *The Bulletin of the International Institute for Linguistic Sciences Kyoto Sangyo University*, Vol. 11. No. 4.

KOLESNIKOVA, V. D., KONSTANTINOVA, O. A., 1968. "Negidal'skii iazyk", *Iazyki narodov SSSR* V, Leningrad.

PETROVA, T. I., 1936. *Ul'chskii dialekt nanaiskogo iazyka*, Moskva-Leningrad.

—— 1960. *Nanaisko-russkii slovar'*, Leningrad.

POPPE, N., 1931. *Materialy po solonskomu iazyku*, Leningrad.

SHNEIDER, E. R., 1936. *Kratkii udėisko-russkii slovar'*, Moskva-Leningrad.

SUNIK, O. P., 1968a. "Ul'chskii iazyk", *Iazyki narodov SSSR* V, Leningrad.

—— 1968b. "Udėgeiskii iazyk", *Iazyki narodov SSSR* V, Leningrad.

TSINTSIUS, V. I., 1949. "Ocherk morfologii orochskogo iazyka", *Uchenye zapiski Leningradskogo gosudarstvennogo universiteta, seriia vostokovedcheskikh nauk*, t. 98, vyp. 1.

—— 1982. *Negidal'skii iazyk*, Leningrad.

TSINTSIUS, V. I., RISHES, L. D., 1952. *Russko-ėvenskii slovar'*, Moskva.

This article is the second revised version of the paper with the same title that I read at the XXXI International Congress of Human Sciences in Asia and North Africa in Tokyo on September 2 1983. The summary of the original paper appeared in the *Proceedings of the Thirty-First International Congress of Human Sciences in Asia and North Africa, Tokyo-Kyoto 1983* (The Tōhō Gakkai, Tokyo, 1984), pp. 332–333.

The first revised version was published in *Gengo Kenkyu, Journal of the Linguistic Society of Japan*, No. 88 (December, 1985), pp. 86–96. After it was published, the author divided the indicative present verb forms of Udehe into the present I and the present II. This division was introduced into this article.

The Element -*n* in the Indicative Forms of Verbs in Tungus Languages

INTRODUCTION

In my previous article "The Category of Person in Tungus: Its Representation in the Indicative Forms of Verbs", *Gengo Kenkyu*, 88, 1985, I temporarily regarded the element *-*n* in some indicative forms of Tungus verbs as a verb ending or a part of one. In the present article I will deal with this element *-*n* more elaborately.

From a diachronical point of view, the Tungus-Manchu languages can be classified into the following four groups: 1. Negidal, Solon, Evenki and Even, 2. Udehe and Orochi, 3. Nanai, Olcha and Uilta, and 4. Manchu, Sibe and Juchen (a historical language).

The verb forms of Nanai (Written Nanai), Olcha, Uilta, Udehe, Orochi, Negidal, Solon, Evenki (Written Evenki) and Even (Written Even) are cited from T. I. PETROVA (1960), id. (1936), J. IKEGAMI (1959) and his unpublished materials, E. R. SHNEIDER (1936); V. I. TSINTSIUS (1949), id. (1982), N. POPPE (1931), V. A. GORTSEVSKAYA, V. D. KOLESNIKOVA, O. A. KONSTANTINOVA (1958), and V. I. TSINTSIUS, L. D. RISHES (1952) respectively. The indicative present forms of Nanai and Olcha mentioned in this article refer to those of the present tense II in PETROVA (1960 and 1936).

In Nanai, Olcha and Uilta, the verb stems are grouped into the three main classes, Class 1.1, Class 1.2 and Class 2. and others. The verb stems of Class 1.1 end in a short vowel, the verb stems of Class 1.2 end in a long vowel and the verb stems of Class 2. end in a consonant.

In Udehe, Solon, Evenki and Even, the verb stems are classified into the two main classes, Class 1. and Class 2. and others. The verb stems of Class

1. end in a vowel. The verb stems of Class 2. end in a consonant. The Class 2. of Evenki and Even includes the verb stems ending originally in a consonant but also the verb stems which lost the final vowel and now end in the penultimate consonant. In the paradigms of the indicative present inflection of Orochi and Negidal in Tsintsius (1949 and 1982) we find only forms made from the verb stem ending in a vowel. I tentatively regard this verb stem as a stem of Class 1.

In Orochi the indicative present forms are derived from the verbal nouns which do not include the element **-n* as their component.

In the indicative forms of Evenki and other Tungus language dialectal differences are found, but in this article I do not make mention of the details of these differences.

The indicative present forms of Manchu and the other language of the fourth group, which seem not to be derived from the verb stem + the aorist ending **-ra* + the element **-n*, are not dealt with in this article.

1.

In Nanai and Olcha the indicative present (II) first person singular forms made from the verb stem of Class 1.2 or Class 2. can be analysed into the stem + the aorist ending *-ra* + the element *-m* + the first person singular ending *-bi.* E.g., Nanai and Olcha *bū-rə-m-bi* 'I give', Nanai *un-də-m-bi* 'I say' and Olcha *wən-də-m-bi* 'ditto'. The nasal element found here forms the subject of this article.

The aorist (or imperfect) ending appears as *-ra*~*-rə*~*-da*~*-də*, etc. in most Tungus languages, but as *-ja* in Negidal, and as *-a*, etc. in Udehe and Orochi. It is believed the basic form of this verb ending was originally **-ra.*

This aorist ending is used without any following verb ending in the negative construction of Tungus verbs. However, it is also accompanied by various formatives of verb forms or amalgamated with these formatives, as follows:

The endings Evenki *-raki*, Solon *-rki* and Uilta *-rai*, which form a conditional converb, are composed of the aorist ending *-r(a)* + the formative *-(k)i*.

In Nanai, Olcha and Uilta, the verb ending *-ru* forms an imperative form. This probably resulted from the amalgamation (fusion) of the aorist ending **-ra* and an imperative ending which ends in the vowel *u*.

The endings of Even *-rī*, Olcha and Uilta *-ri*, Negidal *-ji* and others, which form a verbal noun, resulted from the amalgamation of the aorist ending **-ra* + the formative **-gī*, as J. BENZING (1955: 123, etc.) assumes. A variety of the Olcha indicative present third person singular and plural forms, such as *bū-ri* 'he (she, it) gives' and *bū-ri-l* 'they give', are composed of a verb stem + the verbal noun ending (+ *-l* in the plural number). The verb ending *-dai* in the Udehe indicative present third person singular and plural forms, such as *nag-dai-ni* 'he hits the mark' and *nag-dai-ti* 'they hit the mark', is believed also to go back to **-ra* + **-gī* here. In the Orochi indicative present forms such as *anaᵊ-j-wi* 'I push', etc. the verb stem ending in a vowel seems to have been amalgamated with **-ra*, which is followed by **-gī*.

Besides these, in the Nanai and Olcha indicative present forms given above, we have the aorist ending *-ra* accompanied by the element *-m* in question. This element *-m* appearing before the labial consonant is probably a combinatory variant of the formative *-n*. This formative is considered to go back to the **-n* in earlier stages.

2.

Further, in the Nanai and Olcha indicative present (II) second person singular forms formed from the verb stem of Class 1.2 or Class 2., the stem is accompanied by the aorist ending *-ra* + the second person singular ending -*či* or -*ti*. E.g., Nanai *bū-rə-či* 'you [sing.] give' and *un-də-či* 'you [sing.] say', Olcha *bū-rə-ti* 'you [sing.] give' and *wən-də-ti* 'you [sing.] say'. These -*či* and -*ti* are considered to go back to the second person singular ending *-*si* assimilated to the preceding element *-*n* which was also used in these forms at earlier stages. The *-*n*, in its turn, dropped out, probably after it was assimilated to the initial consonant of the following *-*či* or *-*ti* and bacame *-*t*.

The Olcha indicative present (II) first person plural form formed from the verb stem of Class 1.2 or Class 2. can be divided into the stem + the aorist ending -*ra* + the first person plural ending -*mu*. E.g., *bū-rə-mu* 'we give' and *wən-də-mu* 'we say'. It is believed the -*mu* results from the assimilation of the initial **p* of the first person plural ending *-*pu*(*n*) to the preceding element *-*n* which dropped out thereafter.

What is the function of the *-*n* ? This element seems to have served to form an indicative form (a finite form) of a verb rather than a verbal noun. It is believed that this is an element different from the verbal noun formative -*n*.

3.

Traces of the formative *-*n* are also found after -*ra* in some indicative present verb-forms of other Tungus languages. These forms are as follows: In the indicative present first person singular forms made from the verb stem of Class 1.2 or Class 2. in Uilta, made from the verb stem of Class 1. or Class 2. in Even, or made from the verb stem of Class 2. in Udehe and Solon, the stem is accompanied by the aorist ending + the first person singular ending -*mi* in Udehe and Solon, -*mi* followed by the additional ending -*ga* (~-*gə*) (←**ka*) or -*mee* (amalgamation of -*mi* and -*ga*) in Uilta or -*m* in Even. E.g., Uilta *təə-rə-mee* 'I sit down', *un-də-mee* 'I am saying', Udehe *digan-a-mi* 'I speak', Solon *āsin-a-mi* 'I fall asleep or will fall asleep',

Even *xā-ra-m* 'I know' and *gūn-ə-m* 'I say'. These endings *-mi* and *-m* seem to result from assimilation of the initial *b* of the first person singular ending **-bi* to the preceeding element **-n* which dropped out thereafter.

As to the indicative present third person forms, the Solon third person singular and plural forms, the third person singular forms and some third person plural forms of Evenki, the Even third person singular forms made from the verb stem of Class 2. (except such forms as *gūn-ni* 'he says') and the Negidal third person singular forms made from the verb stem of Class 1. are composed of the verb stem + the aorist ending *-ra* + *n* in the final position. E.g., Solon *ǰawa-ra-n* 'he seizes or will seize, they seize or will seize' and *āsin-a-n* 'he falls asleep or will fall asleep, they fall asleep or will fall asleep', Evenki *ī-rə-n* 'he enters, they enter' and *gūn-ə-n* 'he says', Even *bokn-a-n* 'he overtakes' and Negidal *wā-ja-n* 'he kills'. I consider the final *n* to be derived from the **-n* stated above, and not as a personal ending of the third person. It is probable that in the Uilta indicative present third person singular and plural forms the **-n* was assimilated to the **k* of the following additional ending **-ka* (~**-kə*). E.g., *un-də-k-kə* 'he is saying' and *un-də-k-kə-l* 'they are saying'. Cf. J. IKEGAMI (1985: 94–5).

4.

On the other hand, in some indicative present forms of Tungus languages, the aorist ending is not found. These forms are as followes :

The first person singular forms of Nanai and Olcha (II) formed from the verb stem of Class 1.1 are composed of the stem + the element *-m* + the first person singular ending *-bi.* E.g., Nanai *xola-m-bi* 'I read' and Olcha *ŋənə-m-bi* 'I go'. The *-m* goes back to the **-n.*

The second person singular forms made from the verb stem of Class 1. in Solon and made from the verb stem of Class 1. or Class 2. in Evenki and Even are composed of the stem (+ the connective vowel *-i-* in Evenki or *-a-*

in Even which appears between the stem-final consonant and the initial consonant of the following ending) + the -*n* + the second person singular ending -*di* in Solon, -*ni* in Evenki or -*ri* in Even. E.g., Solon *ǰawa-n-di* 'you [sing.] seize or will seize', Evenki *ī-n-ni* 'you [sing.] enter' and *gūn-i-n-ni* 'you [sing.] say', Even *xā-n-ri* 'you [sing.] know' and *gūn-ə-n-ri* 'you [sing.] say'. N. Poppe (1931: 134–5) assumes the -*n* in Solon to be the formative praesentis imperfecti. K. Menges (1943: 241) regards the -*n* in Evenki as a temporal element. However, these -*n*'s are considered to have been derived from the *-*n* stated above.

The Nanai and Olcha second person singular forms made from the verb stem of Class 1.1 are composed of the stem + the second person singular ending -*či* in Nanai or -*ti* in Olcha. E.g., Nanai *xola-či* 'you [sing.] read' and Olcha *ŋənə-ti* 'you [sing.] go'. The Olcha first person plural form made from the verb stem of Class 1.1 is composed of the stem + the first person plural ending -*mu*. E.g., *ŋənə-mu* 'we go'. For these three personal endings of Nanai and Olcha see above.

The first person singular forms made from the verb stem of Class 1. in Udehe, Negidal and Solon and made from the verb stem of Class 1. or Class 2. in Evenki are composed of the stem (+ the connective vowel -*i*- appearing between the stem-final consonant and the initial consonant of the personal ending in Evenki) + the first person singular ending -*mi* in Udehe and Solon or -*m* in Negidal and Evenki. E.g., Udehe *umi-mi* 'I drink', Negidal *wā-m* 'I kill', Solon *ǰawa-mi* 'I seize or will seize', Evenki *ī-m* 'I enter' and *gūn-i-m* 'I say'. The initial consonant *m* of these personal endings is considered to result from the assimilation to the preceding *-*n* which dropped out thereafter.

The Solon indicative present first person plural exclusive form made from the verb stem of Class 1. is composed of the stem + the first person plural exclusive ending -*mun*. E.g., *ǰawa-mun* 'we [excl.] seize or will seize'.

This personal ending is used in verbal nouns as well as in indicative forms, but it is probable that it was originally used in indicative forms. Poppe (1931: 135) assumes the personal ending *-mun* to go back to **-bun* ← **-rbun* ← **-rawun*. However, there also seems to be a possibility that it came from the first person plural ending **-pun* assimilated to the preceding **-n* which dropped out thereafter.

5.

In some indicative present forms of Tungus languages, the verb stem is accompanied by the aorist ending *-ra* (~*-rə*) + the personal ending. There we find no traces of **-n*. These forms are as follows:

In the first person plural forms of Nanai (in the present II) and Uilta formed from the verb stem of Class 1.2 or Class 2., the stem is accompanied by the aorist ending + the first person plural ending *-pu* in Nanai or *-pu* followed by the additional ending *-wa* (~*-wə*) (← **ka*) or *-poo* (amalgamation of *-pu* and *-wa*) in Uilta. E.g., Nanai *bū-rə-pu* 'we give', *un-də-pu* 'we say' and Uilta *təə-rə-pɵɵ* 'we sit down' and *un-də-pɵɵ* 'we are saying'.

In the first person plural exclusive forms made from the verb stem of Class 2. in Udehe, made from the verb stem of Class 1. in Negidal and made from the verb stem of Class 1. or Class 2. in Evenki and Even, the stem is accompanied by the aorist ending + the first person plural exclusive ending *-wun* in Negidal, *-w* in Evenki or *-u* in Udehe and Even. E.g., Negidal *wā-ja-wun* 'we [excl.]kill', Evenki *ī-rə-w* 'we [excl.] enter', *gūn-ə-w* 'we [excl.] say', Udehe *nag-da-u* 'we [excl.] hit the mark', Even *xā-r-u* 'we [excl.] know' and *ŋən-r-u* 'we [excl.] go'. The first person plural exclusive endings *-wun* in Negidal, *-w* in Evenki and *-u* in Udehe and Even diachronically correspond to the Nanai and Uilta first person plural ending *-pu* given above. All these endings are considered to go back to the earlier first person plural ending **-pun*.

In the first person plural inclusive forms made from the verb stem of Class 2. in Udehe, made from the verb stem of Class 1. in Negidal and made from the verb stem of Class 1. or Class 2. in Evenki and Even, the stem is accompanied by the aorist ending + the first person plural inclusive ending *-fi* in Udehe, or *-p* in Negidal, Evenki and Even. E.g., Udehe *nag-da-fi* 'we [incl.] hit the mark', Negidal *wā-ja-p* 'we [incl.] kill', Evenki *ī-rə-p* 'we [incl.] enter' and *gūn-ə-p* 'we [incl.] say', Even *xā-ra-p* 'we [incl.] know' and *gūn-ə-p* 'we [incl.] say'.

In the second person singular forms made from the verb stem of Class 1.2 or Class 2. in Uilta and made from the verb stem of Class 2. in Udehe, the stem is accompanied by the aorist ending + the second person singular ending *-si* followed by the additional ending *-ga* or *-see* (amalgamation of *-si* and *-ga*) in Uilta or *-hi* in Udehe. E.g., Uilta *təə-rə-see* 'you [sing.] sit down', *un-də-see* 'you [sing.] are saying' and Udehe *nag-da-hi* 'you [sing.] hit the mark'.

In the second person plural forms made from the verb stem of Class 1.2 or Class 2. in Nanai, Olcha and Uilta, made from the verb stem of Class 2. in Udehe and Solon and made from the verb stem of Class 1. or Class 2. in Evenki, the stem is accompanied by the aorist ending + the second person plural ending *-su* in Nanai and Olcha, *-su* followed by the additional ending *-wa* or *-soo* (amalgamation of *-su* and *-wa*) in Uilta, *-hu* in Udehe or *-s* in Evenki. E.g., Nanai and Olcha *bū-rə-su* 'you [pl.] give', Nanai *un-də-su* 'you [pl.] say', Olcha *wən-də-su* 'you [pl.]say', Uilta *təə-rə-sөө* 'you [pl.] sit down', *un-də-sөө* 'you [pl.] are saying', Udehe *nag-da-hu* 'you [pl.] hit the mark', Solon *āsin-a-sun* 'you [pl.] fall asleep or will fall asleep', Evenki *ī-rə-s* 'you [pl.] enter' and *gūn-ə-s* 'you [pl.] say'.

6.

Further, in some indicative present forms of Tungus languages neither the aorist ending nor the element *-n* (nor any traces of it) is found. These forms are as follows:

In the first person plural forms made from the verb stem of Class 1.1 in Nanai and the first person plural exclusive and inclusive forms made from the verb stem of Class 1. in Udehe, the stem is accompanied by the first person plural ending *-pu* in Nanai or the first person plural exclusive or inclusive ending *-u* or *-fi* in Udehe. E.g., Nanai *xola-pu* 'we read' and Udehe *umi-u* 'we [excl.] drink' and *umi-fi* 'we [incl.] drink'.

In the second person singular forms made from the verb stem of Class 1. in Udehe and Negidal, the stem is accompanied by the second person singular ending *-hi* in Udehe or *-s* in Negidal. E.g., Udehe *umi-hi* 'you [sing.] go' and Negidal *wā-s* 'you [sing.] kill'.

In the second person plural forms made from the verb stem of Class 1.1 in Nanai and Olcha, made from the verb stem of Class 1. in Udehe, Negidal and Solon and made from the verb stem of Class 1. in Even, the stem is accompanied by the second person plural ending *-su* in Nanai and Olcha, *-hu* in Udehe, *-sun* in Negidal and Solon or *-s* in Even. E.g., Nanai *xola-su* 'you [pl.] read', Olcha *ŋənə-su* 'you [pl.] go', Udehe *umi-hu* 'you [pl.] drink', Negidal *wā-sun* 'you [pl.] kill', Solon *ǰawa-sun* 'you [pl.] seize or will seize' and Even *xā-s* 'you [pl.] know'.

In the Solon indicative present first person plural inclusive form made from the verb stem of Class 1., the stem is accompanied by the element *-tti*. According to Poppe (1931:135), this *-tti* came from **-rti* (←**-ra-ti*). However, it is possible that the *-tti* may go back to the original form of the first person plural inclusive ending.

7.

Menges (1943: 239, 241–3) and Benzing (1955: 132) assume the intermixture of two originally different paradigms in the aorist forms of Tungus languages. The one paradigm uses the aorist suffix *-*ra* and a pronominal element, whereas the other uses *-*n* and a pronominal element. The inflection systems which these two paradigms belong to may be called the -*ra* inflection system and the -*n* inflection system. Although the possibility of the existence of these two inflection systems in earlier stages cannot be eliminated, I would posit a single system of the indicative verb inflection for the early stage of Tungus. In this system the indicative present forms were composed of the verb stem and the aorist ending *-*ra* + the formative of the indicative form (finite form) *-*n* accompanied by the personal endings for the first and second persons, but not accompanied by any personal ending for the third person. This system can be called the -*ra-n* inflection system.

8.

In the indicative present forms made from the verb stem of Class 1.2 or Class 2. in Nanai, Olcha and Uilta and made from the verb stem of Class 2. in Udehe and Solon and a number of the indicative present forms made from the verb stem of Class 1. in Negidal and Solon and made from the verb stem of Class 1. or Class 2. in Evenki and Even, we find the aorist ending -*ra*. On the other hand, in the indicative present forms made from the verb stem of Class 1.1 in Nanai and Olcha and made from the verb stem of Class 1. in Udehe and the other indicative present forms made from the verb stem of Class 1. in Negidal and Solon and made from the verb stem of Class 1. or Class 2. in Evenki and Even, the aorist ending -*ra* is not found. The indicative present forms accompanied by the -*n* or traces of *-*n* but not by the aorist ending perhaps belonged to the -*n* system. However, they may have belonged to the -*ra-n* system originally.

In the Uilta indicative present forms made from the verb stem of Class 1.1 the stem and the aorist ending -*ra* are fused to a single form. They are composed of the stem amalgamated with the aorist ending **-ra* + the personal ending and the additional ending *-ga*~*-wa* or the personal ending amalgamated with the *-ga*~*-wa* in the first and second persons or *-k* (← **-n*) and the additional ending *-ka* (with *-l* for the plural number but without any personal ending) in the third person. E.g., *dappaa-mi-ga, dappaa-mee* 'I am seizing', *dappaa-pu-wa, dappaa-poo* 'we are seizing', *dappaa-see* 'you [sing.] are seizing', *dappaa-soo* 'you [pl.] are seizing', *dappaa-k-ka* 'he is seizing' and *dappaa-k-ka-l* 'they are seizing' formed from the verb stem *dapa-* 'to seize'. As stated in 1. above, the fusion of the verb stem and the aorist ending **-ra* seems to have occurred also in the Orochi indicative present forms. It seems that in the indicative present forms of the first and second persons formed from the verb stem of Class 1.1 in Nanai and Olcha as well as in Uilta, the aorist ending *-ra* was amalgamated with the stem into a single form and lost. Further, also in a number of the indicative present forms made from the verb stem of Class 1. in Udehe, Negidal and Solon and made from the verb stem of Class 1. or Class 2. in Evenki and Even, the aorist ending *-ra* is assumued to have disappeared probably after it was amalgamated with the stem. Although in these indicative present forms the aorist ending is not now found, it seems possible that it was originally present.

9.

The indicative present forms which are not accompanied by the element *-n* or any traces of the **-n* perhaps belong to the *-ra* inflection system. However, we see also a possibility that they originally belonged to the *-ra-n* inflection system. The absence of the **-n* in these forms is found before the first person plural exclusive and inclusive endings **-pun* and **-pti* and the second person singular and plural endings **-si* and **-sun.* This fact suggests that the **-n* disappeared in these phonetic and phonological environments. It disappeared perhaps after the assimilation to the following voiceless consonants **p* and **s*. And after it disappeared, the initial **p* of the first person plural exclusive ending was changed to *w* or zero in Udehe, Negidal, Evenki and Even. Further, in Even the aorist ending *-ra* and this personal ending were contracted to *-ru*. In Udehe, after the *-*n* disappeared, the initial **s* of the second person plural ending changed to *h*, an instance of the regular change **s* → *h* in the intervocalic position, whereas the *f* (ϕ) appears to be a variant of *p* in the same position. In these indicative present forms which are not accompanied by the element -*n* or any traces of the element *-*n*, it is probable that this element was also originally present.

It seems that the indicative present third person singular and plural forms of Nanai and Olcha were composed of the verb stem + the aorist ending + the element *-*n*, but lost the word-final **n* (viz., the element *-*n*) at the same stage that the indicative present first person and second person plural forms of these languages lost the **n* of the personal ending *-*pun* or *-*sun* in the word-final position.

As to the two indicative present third person plural forms of Even, *xā-r* 'they know' and *gūn* 'they say', the *-r* in the former form seems to be derived from the aorist ending *-*ra* or from the element *-*n* in question + the plural formative *-*l*. The latter form *gūn* apparently consists of only a verb stem. This is an isolated instance.

10.

In some Olcha and Uilta indicative future and preterite forms as well, we find some traces of the element *-*n* in question.

In the Olcha indicative future (I) first person singular form which is formed from the verb stem of Class 1.2 or Class 2., the stem is accompanied by the verbal noun formative *-ri* + the future formative *-la* (~*-lə*) +

-m a positional variant of the element *-n* + the first person singular ending *-bi*. E.g., *bū-ri-lə-m-bi* 'I will give' and *wən-di-lə-m-bi* 'I will say'.

In the Olcha indicative future (I) first person plural or second person singular form and the Uilta indicative future (near future) first person singular form made from the verb stem of Class 1.2 or Class 2., the stem is accompanied by the verbal noun formative *-ri* + the future formative *-la* (~*-lə*) + the first person plural ending *-mu* or the second person singular ending *-ti* (in the Olcha form) or the first person singular ending *-mi* (in the Uilta form). E.g., Olcha *bū-ri-lə-mu* 'we will give', *wən-di-lə-mu* 'we will say', *bū-ri-lə-ti* 'you [sing.] will give' and *wən-di-lə-ti* 'you [sing.] will say', Uilta *təə-ri-lə-mi* 'I will sit down' and *un-ǰi-lə-mi* 'I will say'. Also, in the Uilta indicative preterite first person singular form made from the verb stem of Class 1.2 or Class 2., the stem is accompanied by the preterite ending *-ta* (~*-tə*~*-to*~*-tɵ*) + the first person singular ending *-mi* followed by the additional element *-ga* (~*-gə*) or *-mee* (amalgamation of *-mi* and *-ga*). E.g., *ŋənə-tə-mi-gə*, *ŋənə-tə-mee* 'I went' and *ut-tə-mee* 'I said'. These indicative forms of Olcha and Uilta may also originally have had the element **-n* stated above between the future or preterite ending and the personal ending.

REFERENCES CITED

BENZING, J., 1955. *Die tungusischen Sprachen*, Mainz.

GORTSEVSKAYA, V. A., KOLESNIKOVA, V. D., KONSTANTINOVA, O. A., 1958. *Ėvenkiisko-russkii slovar'*, Leningrad.

IKEGAMI, J., 1959. "The Verb Inflection of Orok", *Kokugo Kenkyu* (Kokugakuin Daigaku, Tokyo) 9.

IKEGAMI, J., 1985. "The Category of Person in Tungus : Its Representation in the Indicative Forms of Verbs", *Gengo Kenkyu*, 88.

MENGES, K. H., 1943. "The Function and Origin of the Tungus Tense in *-ra* and Some Related Questions of Tungus Grammar", *Language*, 19.

PETROVA, T. I., 1936. *Ul'chskii dialekt nanaiskogo iazyka*, Moskva-Leningrad.

—— 1960. *Nanaisko-russkii slovar'*, Leningrad.

POPPE, N., 1931. *Materialy po solonskomu iazyku*, Leningrad.

SHNEIDER, E. R., 1936. *Kratkii udėisko-russkii slover'*, Moskva-Leningrad.

TSINTSIUS, V. I., 1949. "Ocherk morfologii orochskogo iazyka", *Uchenye zapiski Leningradskogo gosudarstvennogo universiteta, seriia vostokovedcheskikh nauk*, t. 98, vyp. 1.

—— 1982. *Negidal'skii iazyk*, Leningrad.

TSINTSIUS, V. I., RISHES, L. D., 1952. *Russko-ėvenskii slovar'*, Moskva.

要旨

ツングース諸語中，ナーナイ語現在直説形 bū-rə-m-bi《ぼくが与える》は動詞語幹＋アオリスト語尾（不完了語尾）＋ -m ＋人称語尾からなる。-m は，かつてあったろう直説形（定動詞）形成要素 *-n と考える。N. Poppe はソロン語現在直説形 ǰawa-n-di《きみがつかむ》中の-n を不完了現在形形成要素とし，K. Menges はエウェンキー語のこの要素 -n を時制的要素とする。これらの -n も筆者は上記の *-n とみる。しかし，上のソロン語例やエウェンキー語 ī-rə-s《きみらが入る》のように，ツングース諸語の現在直説形のあるものにアオリスト語尾や -n がないのは，消失したのだろう。Menges や J. Benzing は，現在直説形のパラダイムには，アオリスト語尾がつく式のものと，-n がつく式のものが混在するとするが，筆者は現在直説形は本来 *-ra-n が接尾したもので，これに人称語尾が第1，2人称でつき，第3人称ではこれを欠くとみる。未来・過去直説形にもその *-n がついていたかもしれない。

This article is the second revised version of my paper "The Element 'n' in Some Indicative Forms of Tungus Verbs" that I read at the XXXII International Congress for Asian and North African Studies (Hamburg, 1986). The summary

of the original paper appeared in the *Proceedings of the XXXII International Congress for Asian and North African Studies, Zeitschrift der Deutschen Morgenländischen Gesellschaft*, Supplement IX, 1992: 195.
The first revised version was published in *Gengo Kenkyu, Journal of the Linguistic Society of Japan*, No. 107 (March, 1995), pp. 1–15.

Addenda

Note to Section **4**. In Solon, Evenki and Even, it seems that the second person sing. ending **-si* changed to Solon *-di*, Evenki *-ni* and Even *-ri* after **-n* in question, and that this **-n* was then dropped before the initial consonant *s* or *p* of the personal endings **-si*, **-sun* and **-pun*.

Note to Section **5**. The disappearance of *n* before *p* or *s* is also found in Uilta. The stem-final *n* in some verbs disappeared before the verb-stem-forming suffixes *-pila* ('to be moved by a natural phenomenon') and *-si* ('to regard …as …'). E.g.: *xədu-pilə-* 'to be carried away by the wind' (*xədun-* '(of a wind) to blow'), *orki-si-* 'to think ill of [somebody]' (*orkin-* 'bad'). Cf. pp. 84, 85 in this book.

Versuch einer Klassifikation der tungusischen Sprachen

Dieses Referat beabsichtigt, kurz eine Klassifikation der tungusischen Sprachen zu geben.

Der Referent teilt die tungusischen Sprachen wie folgt ein:

I. das Ewenkische, das Solonische, das Negidalische, das Lamutische (d. h. Ewenische) ;

II. das Udiheische, das Orotschische ;

III. das Goldische (d. h. das Nanaische), das Oltschaische, das Orokische;

IV. das Mandschurische.

Diese Klassifikation beruht hauptsächlich auf den Lautentsprechungen: 1. ew. sol. neg. lam. udh. orotsch. *i*, go. oltsch. orok. ma. *u* ; 2. ew. sol. neg. lam. udh. orotsch. *x*- od. Null, go. oltsch. orok. *p*-, ma. *f*-; 3. ew. sol. neg. lam. udh. orotsch. ma. Null, go. oltsch. orok. *x*- ; 4. ew. sol. neg. lam. gol. oltsch. orok. *l* vor *t* od. *d* (im Goldischen und Orokischen auch vor *či* und *ǰi*), udh. orotsch. *k* vor *t* od. *g* vor *d*, ma. *n* (dieses *n* ist jetzt nur vor *t* und *ǰi* belegt), und auf einem grammatikalischen Unterschied, nämlich ob es Personal- und Reflexivendungen, fossile Formen ausgenommen, gibt oder nicht.

Der Referent nimmt an, daß diese Klassifikation die Verzweigung des Urtungusischen widerspiegelt.

Schon bisher sind von manchen Forschern verschiedene Klassifikationen der tungusischen Sprachen vorgelegt worden. V. I. Cincius hat die traditionelle Klassifikation in eine nördliche und eine südliche Gruppe widerlegt.[1)] Ihre kritischen Bemerkungen darüber bestehen zu Recht. G. M. Vasilevič, V. A. Avrorin und O. P. Sunik trennen in ihren Klassifikationen das Mandschurische und das Dschurdschenische von den anderen tungusischen Sprachen, was zutreffend ist. Andererseits gruppieren die letzten drei Forscher das Udiheische, das Orotschische, das Goldische, das Oltschaische und das Orokische in ein und dieselbe Gruppe.[2)]

Auch der Referent folgt nicht der traditionellen Klassifikation in eine nördliche und eine südliche Gruppe und nimmt an, daß das Mandschurische und vielleicht das Dschurdschenische von den anderen Sprachen getrennt werden kann. Aber er zieht sowohl den Unterschied zwischen der zweiten und der dritten Gruppe als auch den Unterschied zwischen diesen Gruppen und den anderen Gruppen in Erwägung.

Anmerkungen

1) Siehe V. I. Cincius, *Sravnitel'naja fonetika tunguso-man'čžurskich jazykov*, Leningrad 1949.

2) Ihre Klassifikationen finden sich in : G. M. Vasilevič, K voprosu o klassifikacii tunguso-man'čžurskich jazykov, *Voprosy Jazykoznanija*, 1960, Nr. 2; V. A. Avrorin, O klassifikacii tunguso-man'čžurskich jazykov, *Trudy Dvadcat'pjatogo Meždunarodnogo Kongressa Vostokovedov* III, Moskau 1963; O. P. Sunik, Tunguso-man'čžurskie jazyki, *Mladopis'mennye jazyki narodov SSSR*, Moskau-Leningrad 1959.

Dies ist ein Referat anläßlich der XII. Tagung der Permanent International Altaistic Conference in Berlin 1969. Dieses Referat ist mit demselben Titel in *Sprache, Geschichte und Kultur der Altaischen Völker, Protokollband der XII. Tagung der Permanent International Altaistic Conference 1969 in Berlin* (Akademie-Verlag, Berlin, 1974), S. 271–272 erschienen.

ツングース語の変遷

Tungus in the Past

I 歴 史

歴史上，明らかにツングース語である言語として，はじめて現われてくるのは女真語である。そしてこれに次いで満洲語が現われる。この両言語の歴史の大要については拙著『満洲語研究』(1999) 中の「満洲語史概略」を参照されたい。

エウェンキー語とエウェン語（ラムート語）については，17世紀後半にモスクワにいたオランダ人ウィツェン（N. Witzen）の著書『北および東韃靼』(*Noord en Oost Tartarye*, Amsterdam, 1692) に掲載されているものが，これらの言語の最古の資料とみられている。1692年の第１版（Amsterdam および Utrecht の大学図書館蔵）にはラムート語のものという数詞が載り，1705年の第２版には，ラムート語の数詞のほか，ツングース語に訳した祈禱文「主の祈り」が加えられている。その数詞「９」と「10」は，今日のエウェン語よりエウェンキー語の語形に類する。なお，シベリア経略に関するロシアの17世紀の文書には，主に固有名詞が記されて残っているようである。

その後，1709年にポルタワの戦いで捕虜となり，1722年に帰国するまで長くシベリアにいたスウェーデンの士官ストラーレンベルク（Ph. J. von Strahlenberg）が，その著書『ヨーロッパ・アジアの北部と東部』(*Das Nord- und Ostliche Theil von Europa und Asia*, Stockholm, 1730) の付表「博言表（Tabula Polyglotta)」に，ダウリア（Dauria）地方およびネルチンスク町付近（bey der Stadt Nerschinskoi）の馬ツングース人，アンガラ

(Angara) 川およびツングース (Tungus) 川沿岸のとなかいツングース人，カムチャツカ湾の犬ツングース（別名ラムート）人の，3種のツングース語の総計約90の単語を記している。馬ツングース人の単語として記されているものは，満洲語に類似する。また，メセルシュミット（D. G. Messerschmidt）は，1720年代に，シベリアのエニセイ川地方などを調査旅行し，その旅行日誌（*Forschungsreise durch Sibirien 1720-1727*, Berlin, 1962−77）に，ニジニャヤ・ツングースカ川などのツングース人から採集したエウェンキー語の単語を記録している。

18世紀の30〜40年代か，あるいは，もっと前にできたとみられているフィシェル（J. E. Fischer）の『シベリアを主とする三十四民族の三百語収録語彙』（*Vocabularium continens trecenta vocabula triginta quatuor gentium, maxima ex parte Sibiricarum*）（G. Doerfer, *Ältere westeuropäische Quellen zur kalmückischen Sprachgeschichte*, Wiesbaden, 1965所収）には，満洲語とともに，ツングースカ川の（ad Tunguscam fl.）ツングース人と，セレンガ州およびネルチャ州の（in provinciis Selengiensi et Nertschiensi）ツングース人との，2種のツングース語が記されている。

なお，シレーツェル（A. L. Schlözer）著『近代全世界史続編』(*Fortsetzung der Algemeinen Welthistorie der Neuern Zeiten durch eine Geselschaft von Gelehrten in Teutschland und Engeland ausgefertiget*, Dreyzehnter Theil, Halle 1771）の第4章アジア北部の全概要の§17ツングース人の条には，ツングースカ川沿いのツングース人，(Tungusen an der Tunguska)，ペンジナ湾地方のツングース人（Penschinische Tungusen），ネルチャ川地方のツングース人（Nertschinische Tungusen），満洲人（Mandschu）の4言語のそれぞれの神（Gott）と数詞1-10，100，1000の13語を挙げ，ツングース語と満洲語の類似を示している。ペンジナ湾地方のツングース人の言語はその ujun（8），menn（9）の語からみてもエウェン語，残りの二つのツングース人の言語はエウェンキー語であろう。

パラス（P. S. Pallas）の編集したロシア女帝エカテリーナ2世の『欽定全世界言語比較語彙』(*Linguarum totius orbis vocabularia comparativa*,

Petropoli, Pars prior 1786 (1787), Pars secunda (1789) にも，満洲語のほかに，ネルチャ（ネルチンスク）州（ダウリア州），エニセイ管区，マンガゼヤ管区（Мангазейский округ）のツングース語，バルグジンのツングース人と上アンガラのツングース人（Верхне-Ангарские）のツングース語，ヤクーツク付近とオホーツク付近のツングース語，ラムート語，チャポギル（Чапогир）語の，合わせて9種のツングース語の単語が掲載されている。そのうち，ラムート語とともにオホーツク付近のツングース語はエウェン語で，ほかの7つはエウェンキー語である（J. Ikegami, "Tungus Dialects in the Vicinities of Yakutsk and Okhotsk in the Eighteenth Century",『北方文化研究』14，札幌，1981）。

ビリングズ（J. Billings）によって1785年から1794年にわたりおこなわれたシベリア東北部の沿岸と島々の探検に関するザウエル（M. Sauer）の記録（M. Sauer, *An Account of a Geographical and Astronomical Expedition to the Northern Parts of Russia, performed by J. Billings in the year 1785, etc. to 1794*, London, 1802）にも，その付録の二つの語彙のうち「ユカギル・ヤクート・トゥングース（ラムート）語語彙」に，ラムート語の184語が載っている。また，1787－1788年カムチャツカを旅行したレセプスの日誌（J. B.-B. de Lesseps, *Journal historique du voyage de M. de Lesseps*, Première Partie・Seconde Partie, Paris, 1790）［英訳本『1787年と1788年のカムチャツカ旅行』（*Travels in Kamtschatka, during the years 1787 and 1788*. London, 1790）もある］の末尾の「カムチャダル・コリヤク・チュクチ・ラムート語彙」のなかに，ラムート語の253語が載る。

さらに，アーデルング（J. Ch. Adelung）の『ミトリダーテス』（*Mithridates oder allgemeine Sprachkunde mit dem Vater Unser als Sprachprobe in bey nahe fünfhundert Sprachen und Mundarten*, Erster Theil, Berlin, 1806; Vierter Theil, Berlin, 1817）にも，満洲語とともにツングース語（エウェンキー語）の「主の祈り」が載る。クラプロート（J. Klaproth）の『アジア博言集』（*Asia Polyglotta*, Paris, 1823）にも，満洲語とともに，エウェンキー語，エウェン語の単語があげられている。なお，ここには，メセル

シュミット，パラスの上掲書の資料が転載されている。

このような歴史的資料によってうかがえる音韻変化の例をあげると，デルフェルは，次の点を指摘している。上記のフィシェルの18世紀のネルチンスク方言資料などでは，エウェンキー語の *i，*ɪ，*u（*ʊ の例は載っていない）に由来する語末や動詞語幹末の i がまだ保たれているが，その後，カストレン（A. Castrén）が記す19世紀中ごろの同地方方言では，その i が少なくとも語末では消失している（G. Doerfer, “Urtungusisch *-ï，*-i，*-u，*-ü im Evenkischen”, *Zeitschrift der Deutschen Morgenländischen Gesellschaft*, Band 117, 1967）。

ソロン語については，18世紀に漢字とさらに満洲字で記された索倫語の単語が残っている。『金史』の「欽定金国語解」に 9 語，『欽定遼金元三史国語解（遼史語解，金史語解，元史語解）』に20数語が載る（たとえば，taraga「田」；「遼史語解」巻4，5葉後）。ただし，この索倫語が，今日いうソロン語のものか，あるいは，中国東北の別のエウェンキー語のものかは，なお検討の余地があろう。

そのほかのツングース語，すなわち，ネギダル語，ウデヘ語，オロチ語，ナーナイ語，オルチャ語，ウイルタ語の言語資料は，大体において，19世紀までしかさかのぼれない。これらの言語は，当時，たいてい，欧人によってはじめて採録された。

しかし，オルチャ語については，18世紀末に日本人が書きとめた資料にまでさかのぼる。それは，江戸時代末期に，黒龍江下流地方からカラフトへ交易に来たサンタン（山丹，山靼）人のことばを，主としてかなで記録したものである。サンタン人とは，一部にギリヤーク（Gilyak）人を含むが，主としてオルチャ人とみなされ，また，それから採集した単語は，一部はアイヌ語，ギリヤーク語とみられるが，主としてオルチャ語の単語とみられる。すなわち，サンタンことばは，オルチャ語の古い資料であるとみられる。一番古いとみられるものは，1786年（天明 6 年）にカラフトへ渡った大石逸平が採取したもので，最上徳内の『蝦夷草紙』に載る（例：ナモ「海」，モウ「薪」）。なお，この書物の普通みられる写本では，数詞の順序に誤りがある。その後に採集されたサンタンことばは種々の文献に載り，近藤重蔵の『辺要分界図考』にも引用されている。池上二良「サンタンことば集」[『北方文化研究』2，1967] 参照。

ウイルタ語（オロッコ語）については，江戸時代末のものとみられる写本『カラフト西奥地里数書』（北海道庁蔵）のなかの「ヲロッコ語」の条に，ウイルタ語の単語が，ギリヤーク語，サンタン語の単語をまぜてかなで記されている。これは，松浦武四郎（竹四郎）の筆になり，おそらく，1856年（安政3年）のカラフト踏査の際に採集した資料とみられる。また，松浦竹四郎の『北蝦夷余誌』（1860年［万延元年］刊）にも，わずかなウイルタ語単語が載る。これらは，ウイルタ語のもっとも古い資料とみられる。（池上二良「十九世紀なかごろのオロッコ語集」[『北方文化研究』5，1971]，谷澤尚一「安政三年採録のニクブン語彙を繞って」[『北方文化研究』13，1980] 参照。

なお，エウェンキー語，エウェン語，ナーナイ語，ウデヘ語は，1930年代はじめから文字を使用し，文語をもった。はじめローマ字で書いたが，1930年代後半からは，ロシア字を使うようになった。ただし，ウデヘ語は，その後，文字で書かれることがなく，文語は失われた。

ツングース諸語の話し手の数は，過去において，人口の減少や他言語使用者の増加によって，次第に減少してきたとみられる。今日，ソ連においては，各ツングース語をになうツングース諸民族の人口は，最近20年間増加の傾向にあるが，しかし，ロシア語を母語とする者が，漸次増加しつつあり，ツングース諸語が将来存続するか否かの重大な問題がある。

ツングース諸語のうち，特に，エウェンキー語，エウェン語についてその研究史を概観すると，19世紀はじめまでは，ツングース語にふれる著述も，主として単語だけを扱い，ツングース語研究史においても，トムセン（V. Thomsen）の『言語学史』にいう旧言語学の時代に当たるといえる。ツングース語研究において，新言語学は，19世紀なかばのフィンランド人カストレンの研究（M. A. Castrén, *Grundzüge einer tungusischen Sprachlehre*, St. Petersburg, 1856）にはじまる。カストレンは，シベリアのほかの諸言語とともに，エウェンキー語の外バイカルのウルルガ・マニコヴァ（Urulga-Mankova）方言について，言語学的に非常に進んだ文法記述を行ない，これがツングース語研究の土台となったといえよう。しかし，19世紀中ごろから20世紀はじめは，18世紀より進んだ自然科学者の言語調査研究や，人類学・民族学研究家のその幅広い研究のなかに位置をしめる言語調査研究が主流をなし，後者の研究は，その広い視野が評価されよう。このあと，1920年代からソ連の研究者によるツングース語の言語学的調査研究がさかんになっていく。

エウェンキー語，エウェン語の研究は，古くは，ほとんど欧人によるものであったが，満洲語，女真語の研究史には，欧人の研究のほか，清代の中国の研究が大きくかかわり，また，朝鮮，日本における学習や研究があって，事情が異なる。また，ソロン語の研究史は18世紀の記録に，オルチャ語の研究史は18世紀末の記録にさかのぼるが，一方，その他のツングース語の研究史は，19世紀の資料採録とともにはじまる。

ツングース語全体の古い過去の変遷を知るためには，その歴史的研究の資料は十分とはいえないが，ツングース諸語の比較研究によって，われわれは，これらの言語の過去を遠くたどることができる。かくして，それらツングース諸語がツングース祖語（共通基語）にさかのぼることが明らかになり，また逆に，それからどのように変化してきたかを，種々の点について知ることができる。ただし，なお将来の研究にまつべき多くの不明の点がある。

II　比較研究によってみた過去

各ツングース語については，下記の資料に基づく，これらは，記述の方法も同一でなく，精粗一様でないが，音の区別や解釈はもとのままとし，その記述に従った。ただし，表記記号を統一的にするため，基礎資料のロシア字はローマ字にし，一部の表記記号のローマ字をかえた。また，ロシア字の文語形をローマ字に書きかえた際に，相異なる音素を表す同じ母音字を区別して表したものがある。

エウェン語は，ツィンツィウス・リーシェス（Цинциус и Ришес, 1952）によるとともに，音韻については特にノーウィコワ（Новикова, 1960）により，対応例の文語形を前者から，オラ方言形を／／に入れて後者から引用する。

なお，ノーウィコワにおける第2音節以下の a，o，ᴜ，ɪ，ə，ɵ，u，i（a，ə の弱化変種の場合を除く）は，ツィンツィウス・リーシェス（1952）では，長母音音素として記されていることが多いようである。エウェンキー語は，ゴルツェフスカヤ・コレスニコワ・コンスタンチーノワ（Горцевская, Колесникова и Константинова, 1958）により，対応例の文語形のそれに載っていないものは，ワシレーヴィチ（Василевич, 1958；略号 в.）から引用する。ソロン語は，ポッペ（Поппе, 1931）による。д. は，ソロン化したダグール人の方言。ネギダル語は，ツィンツィウス（1982）による。ウデヘ語は，シュネイデル（Шнейдер, 1936）による。オロチ語は，ツィンツィウス（1949b），アヴローリン・レーベデワ（Аврорин и Лебедева, 1978）により，語例は後者から，語尾および接尾辞の例は前者から引用する。ナーナイ語は，ペトローワ（Петрова, 1960），オーネンコ（Оненко, 1980）により，語などの例は後者から引用する。オルチャ語は，ペトローワ（1936），スーニク（Суник, 1985）により，語などの例は後者から引用する。ウイルタ語は，Ikegami［池上］（1956，1959，1980，1985），満洲語は，文語については，羽田（1937），服部（1937），山本（1955）による。満洲語文語の転写朝鮮字に関する第1・2類の w を，それぞれ w_1，w_2 で表す（池上 1950，1963を参照）。満洲語口語については，服部・山本（1955，1956），山本（1960，1962，1963，1969）を参照されたい。以下において，単に満洲語という用語は，その文語をさす。

ツングース語の比較研究には，すでにツィンツィウス（1949b），ベンツィング（Benzing, 1955）が大きな寄与をしている。本項の記述も，それに負うところが大きい。しかし，これは，あらためて基礎資料に立って変遷のあとをたしかめたものであり，細部については必ずしもツィンツィウスやベンツィングと一致しないので，その異同については，同書も参照されたい。

以下，V は母音音素，C は子音音素，［　］内は該当音声を表わす。VV は，長母音または二重母音，ないし，連続する2つの短か母音に該当する。

A）音　韻

1）現代のツングース諸語の音韻　それぞれのツングース語の子音音素には，

特に記さぬかぎり，p，b，t，d，č，ǰ，k，g，m，n，ɲ，ŋ，l，r，s，x，w，j がある。

a）エウェン語　いくつかの方言に分かれるが，そのうち，エウェン語文語の主たる基礎をなすオラ方言の音韻。

母音音素：Ⅰ類 a，o，ʊ，ɪ，ā，ō，ʊ̄，ɪ̄，æ;

Ⅱ類 ə，ɵ（後舌），u，i，ə̄，ɵ̄，ū，ī，ie.

第2音節以下においては，a,ə に，それぞれ，いわゆる弱化した変種が現われることがある。なお，以下の文語形の表記においては，文語の書写法によって，u が ʊ や ɵ を，i が ɪ を表すことがある。

子音音素：č は［c］，ǰ は［ɟ］，k は［k，q］，g は［g，ɣ］．なお，č，ǰ は，それぞれ［t′，d′］のようにも聞こえるという。

b）エウェンキー語　その方言のうち，エウェンキー語文語の主たる基礎をなすポリグス方言の音韻。

母音音素：Ⅰ類 a，o，ā，ō，ē；Ⅱ類 ə，ə̄；Ⅲ類 u，i，ū，ī.

いくつかの下位方言では，u，i，ū，ī のそれぞれに2種の区別がある。

c）ソロン語

母音音素：Ⅰ類 a，o，u，ā，ō，ū；Ⅱ類 ə，ɵ，ʉ，ə̄，ɵ̄，ʉ̄；

Ⅲ類 i，ė（i の変種），ī，ē.

ほかに，鼻母音 Ṽ，VṼ；V̄Ṽ（Vn；V̄n と解釈されよう）がある。第2音節以下の短か母音は，あいまいに発音される。

子音音素には，前記のほかに，ɸ，š［ʃ］（s の変種か），c［ts］（č か s の変種），ć（c のシュー音，č の変種か，なお，č と s は1つの音素の位置的変種か），z（ǰ の変種），ç（s か x の変種であろう），h（x の変種），k（x の変種か），ɣ（g の変種）がある。

d）ネギダル語

母音音素：Ⅰ類 a，o，e(ɪ)，ā，ō，ē；Ⅱ類 ə，ə̄；Ⅲ類 u，i，ū，ī.

ə には，（円唇化した）$ə_0$ や e の位置的変種がある。ə̄ には，ạ̄，ọ̄ の変種がある。o の変種には，a のような o もあるようである。カレスニコワ・コンスタンチーノワ（1968）は，i，ī をⅡ類に入れ，ほかに，ɵ，ɵ̄ の音素も認めており，また，Ⅰ類に o，ō のほかに ɔ，ɔ̄ を区別して挙げている。

子音音素のうち，k には q，x には χ，g には ɣ，$ɣ^{w}$ の位置的変種がある。ŋ には，母音間で ŋɣ の発音がある。

e）ウデヘ語　その方言のうち，ホル方言の音韻。

母音音素：Ⅰ類 a, æ, e ; o, œ, y; Ⅱ類 ə ; Ⅲ類 u, i.

短か母音の音素として，a，ə，o，u，i，e，œ，iə; 長母音の音素として，ā，ə̄，ō，ū，ī，ē，yi，yœ，iə，eæ.（短い iə も，長い iə も，表記は同じ。）ほかに，中断母音音素 ‘V（‘は中間に喉頭閉鎖があることを表す。例：‘a），有気母音音素VhV（例：aha），中断有気母音音素‘VhV, Vh‘V（例：‘aha，ah‘a）がある。

f）オロチ語

母音音素：a，ə，o，u，i，e（i の変種か）；ā，ə̄，ō，ū，ī，ie, ǣ.

子音音素には，前記のほかに，ɸ，pf ; ɣ，$ɣ^{w}$ の表記があるが，それぞれ，p ; g の変種であろう。また，h は，語頭で x の，母音間で s の変種のようである。語末の n は，ツィンツィウスが，鼻母音として ^{n} で表記するものである。

アヴローリン・レーベデワ（1978）は，短か母音音素 a，ə，o，ʊ，u，i，長母音音素 ā，ə̄，ō，ʊ̄，ū，ī，æ を認めている。ほかに，a͜i，i͜a，a͜ʊ，その他の二重母音がある。

子音には，ɣ の表記もある。

g）ナーナイ語　その方言のうち，ナーナイ語文語の主たる基礎をなすナイヒン方言の音韻。

母音音素：a，ə，o，ʊ，u，ɪ，i ; ā，ə̄，ō，ʊ̄，ū，ɪ̄，ī.

なお，以下に引用する文語形は，文語の書写法によって，ɪ も i で，ʊ も o で書き表わす。

アヴローリン（1959）は，ʊ は音素 o の位置的変種であるとし，ʊ，ʊ̄ の音素を認めない。

h）オルチャ語　ペトローワによれば，

母音音素：a，ə，o，ʊ, u, i（2種あり，その1種は e と同種か），e（?）;
ā，ə̄，ō，ʊ̄，ū，ī，ē.

子音音素には，前記のほか，ǩ [kx]（k の変種か）がある。

スーニクによれば，母音音素 a，ə，ʊ（～o），u，i，ɪ（～e）；ā，ə̄，ʊ̄（～ō），ū，ī，ɪ̄（～ē）が区別される。この記述では，ʊ と o の音韻的区別がなされていない（辞書の部では書き分けられている）。

子音音素の，k には q，x には χ，g には ɣ の変種がある。w の音素には，v の発音のほかに w の発音もある。池上（1976）は，オルチャ語の母音音素に，さらに，ɵ の音素もあるのではないかとみる。

i）ウイルタ語

母音音素：Ⅰ類 a，o [ɔ]；Ⅱ類 ə，ɵ [ɵ，o]；Ⅲ類 u，i，e.

これらはまた，VV（長母音・二重母音）という連続としてある。

子音音素の č は [tʃ]，ǰ は [dʒ]。

j）満洲語文語

母音字：a，ə，o，ů，u，i.

子音字：p，b，t，d，č（破擦音），ǰ（同），k [k，q]，g [g，ɢ]，m，n，ng [ŋ]，l，r，f，s，š，h [x，h]，w，j.

なお，f，s，š，h の表す摩擦音は，母音間で有声のことがある。語中の ngg は，通常は ŋ を表すとみられる。

なお，これら各ツングース語には母音調和が行われ，Ⅰ類とⅡ類の母音音素は1語中に普通そのどちらかの類のものだけが現われる。言い換えれば，Ⅰ類とⅡ類の母音音素は，普通1語中に共存しない。Ⅲ類をもつツングース語では，これは，どの母音音素とも共存できる。オロチ語では a，o と ə とが（あるいは，さらに ʊ と u が），ナーナイ語では a，o，ʊ，ɪ と ə，u，i が，オルチャ語では a, o, ʊ, i（の1種）と ə，u，i（の別の1種）が，1語中に共存しない。満洲語では，a，o，（k，g，h のあとの）ů [ʊ] と ə，（語頭の）ů [ɵ]（あるいは前舌か）とは，普通，1語中に共存しないが，u，i はどれとも共存できる。əo, io の母音調和については，池上（1954，1963）を参照されたい。

ツングース語の母音調和の基礎にあるⅠ，Ⅱ類の母音音素の示差的特徴についてみると，上記のエウェン語のⅠ，Ⅱ類の各母音音素は a と ə，o と ɵ，ʊ と u，ɪ と i の間でそれぞれその母音の調音における舌の高さが平行的に異なり，

Ⅰ類のa，o，ʊ，ɪ，は低く，Ⅱ類のə，ɵ，u，iは高く，舌の高低の違いで対立する。Ⅰ類とⅡ類の母音音素が舌の高低による違いを示す例は，他のツングース語にも広くみられ，たとえば，ウイルタ語は，Ⅲ類を別にして，Ⅰ，Ⅱ類の母音音素のaとə，oとɵが舌の高低の違いを示す。しかし，エウェン語では，Ⅰ類とⅡ類を区別するさらに別の示差的特徴があり，Ⅰ類の母音音素は，その調音において，舌根を後方へ引き，喉頭をもち上げ，緊張収縮した咽頭が呼気の通路をせばめて生じた噪音が付加される咽頭音化があるが，Ⅱ類の母音音素はこれがないことが，ノーウィコワ（1960）によって指摘されている。すなわち，両類の母音音素は咽頭音化をともなう調音の有無によっても区別される。なお，エウェン語の母音音素についての上記の咽頭音化という母音特徴の有無は，Ⅰ，Ⅱ類の各母音音素の特徴であるとともに，それをふくむ各単語の音韻特徴であるとも言えよう。

また，少なくともウイルタ語では，oやɵに関して，1語中の母音音素配列に制限があり，a，ə，uのあとに，短か母音のo，ɵは続かない。

2）**ツングース諸語間の音韻対応**　各ツングース語は，あとに挙げる語例におけるように，下記の音韻対応を示す。ただし，それと異なる対応を示す種々の語例もあり，条件的音韻変化，その他の原因によるものであろう。

a）母音音素　表1の第1音節における母音対応から，ツングース諸語の母音音素は，同表に示すような祖語の母音音素にさかのぼるとみられる。

エウェン語のツィンツィウス・リーシェス（1952）のeは，以下にɪと表記する。ネギダル語のツィンツィウス（1982）において，同一語にe，иの両表記のあるものは，ɪと表記する。

祖語の母音音素がどんなものであったかは，なお断言できないが，今日のウイルタ語，エウェン語の母音体系も考慮して，ベンツィング（1955）がすでに指摘するように，対応*4*，*6*については，それぞれ *ɵ，*u であったとみておくことにする（Ⅱ章末に付した表1参照）。なお，対応*4*において，唇音のあとのような位置では，祖語の *u が対応することがある。一方，今日でも，ウイルタ語，エウェン語などに，ɵという音素を含む語例がある。これらのɵは，ある位置においては，のちに他の母音音素から変化したとみられよう。たとえば，語例 8（後述，3）「音韻対応の語例」を参照）のウイルタ語 bɵdɵ は，おそらく *bərgə に由来するものであろう（エウェン語には／bārgə／の語形があるが，誤記ではないかとみられ，取り上げないことにする）。しかし，語例56のような例を含めて，すべてのちに他の母音音素から変化したものであろうか。祖語の *ɵ が，ある一定の条件では保存されたこともありえよう。この音素については，他のツングース語の諸資料の記述が十分に正確かどうか疑問の点もあり，それについて明確にするには，正確で豊富な語例がえられなければならない。なお，満洲語の ů が表す［ɵ］については，池上（1946, 1950, 1963）を参照されたい。

第 1 音節以外の母音対応も，大体それと変わりないが，ただしエウェン語では，一般には，祖語の *a のほか，*o，*ᴜ，*ɪ が a に対応し，祖語の *ə のほか，*ɵ，*u，*i が ə に対応している。また，同じエウェン語で，語末ないし語幹末において，すぐ前に C が 1 つしかないとき，祖語の短か母音の *V は消失した。エウェンキー語では，同じ位置で *i，*ɪ が消失した。また，たとえば，語例 2 で，ナーナイ語の o，オルチャ語の ᴜ，ウイルタ語の u が，エウェンキー語とウデヘ語の i，ネギダル語の ɪ に対応している。祖語の *ᴜ は，第 2 音節以下で唇音が前に立たないとき，一般には，かかる対応を生んだとみられる。

また，エウェン語，エウェンキー語，ソロン語，ナーナイ語などの長母音音素と，ウイルタ語の VV（長母音）の対応がみられる語例がある（35, 43, 61; 37, 15; 64; 26; 42 の語例を参照）。これによって，祖語に *VV（長母音）があったと考えられる。語例 42 の第 1 音節母音は，*uu にさかのぼるものであろう。ただし，いくつかのツングース語の ē（ee）や，エウェン語の æ，ⁱe，オロチ語の ǣ，ie，ウデヘ語の eæ，iə は，新しい音韻変化によって生じたものであろう（たとえば，語例90）。なお，満洲字では，長母音を表すともみられる moo「木」（語例37）のような例以外，母音の長短は区別されていない。ツングース諸語のある資料は，長母音をすべての場合に区別して表記しているか疑問であり，この点についての有力な資料となりえない。ウイルタ語では，祖語の第 2 音節以下の *VV（長母音）が，一般には V（短か母音）になったとみられる。これは，母音間の *k の消滅前におきた。

また，たとえば，語例21，44，89における，それらの母音音素は，その対応から，くだり二重母音に該当する *oɪ，*ui（あるいは *ɵi か）へさかのぼるとみられる。これらが，さらに別の音素連続にさかのぼる痕跡は見いだせず，祖語には二重母音に該当するVVがあったと一応考えられよう。満洲語のそれらの単語では，*oɪ が ůw$_1$a(ua)，wa に，*ui（*ɵi？）が wə になったとみる。63の語例も，くだり二重母音の*aɪ にさかのぼるものであろうか。

また，ツングース諸語のある単語では，祖語からの過程において，第1音節の *i，*ɪ が第2音節の母音に同化したいわゆる「i の折れ」がおきた（語例75を参照）。語例7では，語頭の鼻音が多くのツングース語で消失し，また，オロチ語，オルチャ語，ウイルタ語を除くツングース諸語では *ɪ から折れによって *ja が生じ，さらに一部の方言で æ や ē となった。なおさらにソロン語では，ī となったのであろうか。

第1音節に *o または *ɵ があるとき，第2音節以下の母音の円唇化がおきたとすれば，どんな範囲におきたかの問題は今後にゆずりたい。エウェン語にみられるような第2音節以下の弱化母音は，祖語からの過程において現れたものとみられる。ウイルタ語では，いまだに，第2音節以下でも，母音がかなり明瞭に発音される。

b）子音音素　章末の表2・3の子音対応から，ツングース諸語の子音音素は，同表に示すような，祖語の17または18の子音音素に由来するとみられる。

なお，表2において，対応 *10* ロの語例19ソロン語には，əʼū̠- の形もある。*11* については，他のツングース語の t- に対して，語例74満洲語では s が対応する。語例50満洲語ではゼロが対応する。*13* イの語例10満洲語 čalfa は，借用語かもしれない。*13* ロの語例27エウェン語 it- は，語尾 -tə̄j がつくときの語幹の形。語例27ソロン語には s とともに ᶜs，ss が現れる。*14* については，語例77のウイルタ語 ǰakpu は，他のツングース語の ǰ に対してやはり ǰ をもつ。*18* ハでゼロが対応するウデヘ語，ウイルタ語の語は，語尾がついた語形の語幹末では n を保つ。n が対応するウイルタ語の語は1音節語。*19* イの語例44ナーナイ語には，wajla の語形もある。*20* ハについては，ウデヘ語，オロチ語，満洲語には *-l に対応する複数接尾辞がないという方がむしろ正しいであろう。*24* イの語例35ウデヘ語には，u の表記もみられる。*25* ロの語例 3 ソロン語 aj の j は，二重母音の副音［ĭ］である。

なお，表3のウデヘ語，ウイルタ語の各2形の分化については，Ikegami（1960）を参照されたい。対応 *46* は，あるいは *ŋ にさかのぼるものかもしれない。しかし，また，語例85，86の対応も *ŋ にさかのぼるものであろうか。

対応 *11*，*12* に関して，女真語では，まだそれぞれ i のまえで t，d が対応している（長田 1949，李 1958を参照）。対応 *13*，*14* のウイルタ語 t，d は，*č，*ǰ から，エウェン語の č，ǰ に該当する［t′］［d′］のような音を通して変化してきたものかもしれない。対応 *32*〜*36* は，それぞれが平行して，エウェン語，エウェンキー語，ネギダル語では，唇音＋軟口蓋音，ウデヘ語，ナーナイ語，オルチャ語，ウイルタ語では，逆に，軟口蓋音＋唇音である。ただし，ナーナイ語の一部方言は，反対の順序をとる（アヴローリン，1961，Ⅱ参照）。その子音音素の順序の違いは，音位転換によって生じたであろうことは明らかであるが，それがどこにおきたかについては，

ウデヘ語 bakpi「わかった」（bap-「わかる」）

ナーナイ語 ǰalokpin「一杯になった」（ǰalop-「一杯になる」）（アヴローリン，1959，Ⅰ参照）

オルチャ語 ǰəkpin「食べた」（ǰəp-「食べる」）

のような，語幹末と語尾の頭の間の音位転換があることから，これらの語群に転換がおきたことが考えられる。しかし，祖語において，語により，これら子音連続に二様の順序があったものが，両言語群で転換がおきて，それぞれ一様化したことも考えられようが，その二様の順序が音韻的対立をなしたかは問題だろう。ソロン語では，唇音＋軟口蓋音の連続に逆行同化がおき，オロチ語では，軟口蓋音＋唇音の連続に逆行同化または消失がおきたものであろう。対応 *41*〜*44*，*51*，*52*，*55*，*56* の語例においては，オルチャ語で，*k，*g，*ŋ の調音点が，先行する *r，*l，*n の調音点に引かれて前へ移り，č，ǰ，ɲ となった。満洲語でも，その一部に同様の変化がおきた。ウイルタ語では t，d，n となった。なお，その後，*r および *42*，*44* の *ŋ のまえの子音は脱落した。

このほかにも，別の *CC に由来する部分をもつ語がある。なお，対応 *43*，*44* の語例の母音間の子音連続は，*jng，*jnŋ か，または *ɲg，*ɲŋ にさかのぼると思われ，もし後者であるならば，祖語にも *ɲ があったことになる。

3）**音韻対応の語例**　E はエウェン語（／／は，オラ方言形），Ek はエウェンキー語（в. はワシレーヴィチ，1958 からの引用），S はソロン語（д. はソロン化したダグール人の方言形），N はネギダル語，U はウデヘ語，Oc はオロチ語，Nn はナーナイ語，Ol はオルチャ語，Ut はウイルタ語，M は満洲語を示す。

1　E abgar ‖ Ek awgarā ‖ S awgar，aggar「丈夫な」

2　E adal ‖ Ek adil ‖ N adɪl ‖ U adili ‖ Oc adʊli ‖ Nn adoli ‖ Ol adʊlɪ ‖ Ut aduli「あみ」

3　E aj「よい」‖ Ek aja「同」‖ S aja，aj「同」‖ N，U，Oc aja「同」‖ Nn aja「健康な」‖ Ol，Ut aja「よい」

4　E，Ek amaskī ‖ S amašxī ‖ N amaskī ‖ U amaixi ‖ Oc amāsi ‖ Nn xamasi ‖ Ol xamasɪ ‖ Ut xamasai ‖ M amasi「あとへ」

5　E，Ek amŋa ‖ S amma ‖ N amŋa ‖ U aŋma ‖ Oc amma ‖ Nn，Ol，Ut aŋma ‖ M angga「口」

6　E an- ‖ Ek，N，U，Oc，Nn，Ol，Ut，M ana-「押す」

6⁺　E anŋan ‖ Ek anŋanī ‖ S aɲē ‖ N aɲŋanī ‖ U aŋa-ni ‖ Oc aŋŋanɲi ‖ Nn ajŋani ‖ Ol aɲa(n) ‖ Ut anani ‖ M aniya「年」

6‡　Nn aŋgo- ‖ Ol anǰu- ‖ Ut andu-si-「つくる」

7　E æsal ‖ Ek ēsa ‖ S īsal ‖ N ēsa ‖ U jehæ ‖ Oc isa(g) ‖ Nn nasal ‖ Ol ɪsal(ɪ) ‖ Ut isal ‖ M jasa「目」

8　E bərgə ‖ Ek burgu ‖ S bʉrgʉ ‖ N bəjgə ‖ U bogo ‖ Oc boggo，bugu ‖ Nn bujgu ‖ Ol buǰu(n) ‖ Ut bɵdɵ「脂肪の多い，ふとった」

9　E bi- /bi-/ ‖ Ek，S bi- ‖ N bi-，bī- ‖ U，Oc，Nn，Ol，Ut，M bi-「ある，いる」

9⁺　E bɪlga ‖ Ek bilga ‖ N bɪlga ‖ Oc bigga ‖ Nn bilga ‖ Ol bɪlǰa ‖ Ut bilda ‖ M bilha「のど」

10 E čālban「かば（木)」‖ Ek čalban「同」‖ S cālbāã, sālbāã「同」‖ N čālban「同」‖ Oc čabba, čāba「同」‖ M čalfa「かばの皮」

11 U čaligi ‖ Oc čāgǰa(n) ‖ Nn čāgǰan ‖ Ol čāgǰa(n) ‖ Ut taagda ‖ M šanggijan, šanjan「白い」

12 E čīrit「銅」‖ N čijiktə「同」‖ Oc čīktə「真ちゅう」‖ Nn Ol čīriktə「青銅」‖ Ut čiiriktə「真ちゅう」‖ M sirin「同」

12+ E dabda- ‖ Ek dawda- ‖ N, Oc, Ol, Ut dabda-「負ける」

13 E dɪl「あたま」‖ Ek, S dil「同」‖ N dɪl「同」‖ U, Oc dili「同」‖ Nn ǰili「同」‖ Ol dɪlɪ「同」‖ Ut ǰili「同」‖ M ǰili「しかなどの角の根」

13+ E dɪram ‖ Ek diram ‖ S dirami ‖ N dɪjam ‖ U deæmi ‖ Oc dijami ‖ Nn dirami ‖ Ol dɪramɪ ‖ Ut ǰirami ‖ M ǰiramin「厚い」

14 E, Ek, S, N dolbo ‖ U dogbo ‖ Oc dobbo ‖ Nn, Ol, Ut dolbo ‖ M dobori「夜」

15 E dolda- ‖ Ek dōldī- ‖ S, N dōldi- ‖ U dogdi- ‖ Oc dōgdi- ‖ Nn dōlǰi- ‖ Ol dōldɪ- ‖ Ut doolǰi- ‖ M donǰi-「聞く」

16 Ek dugə̄ ‖ N duwə ‖ U duə ‖ Oc duwə(n) ‖ Nn duwə ‖ Ol duwə(duə) ‖ Ut duwə ‖ M dubə「端」

17 E ədən ‖ Ek ədin ‖ S ədĩ ‖ N ədin ‖ U ədi ‖ Oc ədi(n) ‖ Nn xədun ‖ Ol xədu(n) ‖ Ut xədu(n-) ‖ M ədun「風」

18 Ek əjə̄-「水に沈む」‖ S əji-「流れる」‖ N əjə̄-「同」‖ U, Oc əjə-「同」‖ Nn, Ol, Ut xəjə-「同」‖ M əjə-「同」

19 E, Ek əw- ‖ S əgʉ- , əwʉ-, ə̉ʉ̄- ‖ N əw- ‖ U əu- ‖ Oc ə͜u- ‖ Nn əu- ‖ Ol əwu- ‖ Ut əu- ‖ M əbu-「おりる」

20 E garpu- ‖ Ek, S garpa- ‖ N gappa- ‖ U gakpa- ‖ Oc gappa- ‖ Nn, Ol, Ut garpa- ‖ M gabta-「射る」

21 E gæ ‖ Ek gē ‖ S gēĕ ‖ N gē ‖ U geæ ‖ Nn goj ‖ Ol goj(ɪ) ‖ Ut goi ‖ M gůwɪa「ほかの」

22 E gərbə ‖ Ek, S gərbī ‖ N gəlbi ‖ U gəgbi ‖ Oc gəbbi ‖ Nn gərbu ‖

Ol, Ut gəlbu ‖ M gəbu「名」

23 E gɪramra「墓」‖ Ek giramna「骨」‖ S giranda「同」‖ N gɪjamna「骨格」‖ U geæmaha「骨」‖ Oc gi͜amsa「同」‖ Nn girmaksa「同」‖ Ol gɪramsa「同」‖ Ut girapsa「同」‖ M giranggi「同」

24 E gor「遠い」‖ Ek, S goro「同」‖ N gojo「同」‖ U, Oc gō「同」‖ Nn goro「同」‖ Ol goro「遠く」‖ Ut, M goro「遠い」

25 E gūd「高い」‖ Ek, S gugda「同」‖ N gogda「同」‖ U gugda「同」‖ Oc gʊgda「同」‖ Nn gogda「同」‖ Ol gʊgda「同」‖ Ut gugda「同」‖ M gukduhun「高いところ」

26 E ī- / ī-/ ‖ Ek, S, N, U, Oc, Ol ī- ‖ Ut ii-「はいる」

27 E ičinri「おまえが見る」, it-「見る」‖ Ek ičə-「同」‖ S i^{c}sə-, isə-, issə-「同」‖ N ičə-「同」‖ U isə-「同」‖ Oc, Nn, Ol ičə-「同」‖ Ut itə-「同」

28 E ɪdūn ‖ Ek igdiwūn ‖ S iddūũ, irdūũ ‖ N ɪgdiwun ‖ Oc igdʊ(n) ‖ Nn sigǰipun ‖ Ol sigdupu(n) ‖ Ut sigǰipu(n-) ‖ M iǰifun「くし」

29 E ɪnŋat「毛」‖ Ek inŋakta「同」‖ S iŋakta, iŋatta「同」‖ Nɪɲakta, ɪnɲakta, ɪɲɲakta, ɪɲŋakta, ɪŋɲakta「同」‖ U iŋakta「同」‖ Oc iŋakta「同」‖ Nn siŋakta「同」‖ Ol sɪɲakta「同」‖ Ut sinakta「けだもの,（頭，顔以外の）人間の毛」‖ M inggaha「鳥の綿毛」

30 E ǰalsa「つば（つばき）」‖ Ek ǰaliksa「同」‖ S ǰalikči「同」‖ N ǰalsa「同」‖ U ǰalehæ「同」‖ Oc dilʊksa「同」‖ Nn ǰiloksa「同」‖ Ol ǰēlčʊksa「同」‖ Ut ǰeluska「よだれ」

31 E ǰaw-「つかむ，取る」‖ Ek, S ǰawa-「つかむ」‖ N, U, Oc ǰawa-「つかむ，取る」‖ Nn, Ol ǰapa-「同」‖ Ut dapa-「同」‖ M ǰafa-「つかむ」

32 E ǰuganī /ǰʊwʊnɪ, ǰʊʊnɪ/ ‖ Ek, S ǰuga ‖ N ǰoga ‖ U ǰua ‖ Oc ǰʊwa ‖ Nn ǰoa ‖ Ol ǰʊwa（ǰʊa）‖ Ut duwa ‖ M ǰuw$_2$ari「夏」

33 E ǰuk /ǰuk/「厚い氷」‖ Ek ǰukə「氷」‖ N ǰuxə, ǰukə「同」‖ U ǰugə「同」‖ Oc, Nn ǰukə「同」‖ Ol ǰuwə「同」‖ Ut duwə「同」‖ M ǰuhə

「同」

34 E kaltak「半分」‖Ek kaltaka「同」‖S xaltaxa「一対のものの１つ」‖N kaltaxa, kaltaka「半分」‖U kakt‘a「同」‖Oc kakta-「割る」‖Nn kaltā「半分」‖Ol kalta「同」‖Ut kaltaa「同」‖M hontoho「同」

34⁺ Ek, N kamnun‖U kamnu ‖Oc kamnᴜ‖Nn kamdon ‖Ol kamdᴜ‖Ut kamdu(n-)‖M amdun「にかわ」

35 E mā- ‖Ek, S, N wā- ‖U wā-, ua- ‖Oc, Nn, Ol wā- ‖Ut waa-‖M wa-「殺す」

36 E man-「なくなす」‖Ek mana-「なくなす，終える」‖S mana-「終わる」‖N, Oc, Nn mana-「なくなす」‖Ol mana-「なくなす，終わる」‖Ut mana-「なくなす」‖M mana-「やぶれる」

36⁺ E monŋa-「揉んでやわらかくする」‖Ek mənŋī-「同」‖N monŋi-, moŋni-「揉む」‖Oc moŋiči-「同」‖Nn moŋgiči-「同」‖Ol monǰɪčᴜ-「同」‖Ut, M monǰ-「同」

37 E, Ek, S, N, U, Oc, Nn, Ol mō‖Ut, M moo「木」

38 E nanra「皮」‖Ek nanna「同」‖S nanda「同」‖N nana「同」‖U nehæ「同」‖Oc nasa「同」‖Nn, Ol nanta「同」‖Ut natta「けだものの皮」

39 E nəgnənī, nəgni ‖Ek, N, Oc, Nn, Ol ɲəŋɲə‖Ut nəŋnə‖M nijəngnijəri「春」

40 E nok-‖Ek loko-‖S loxo-, loko- ‖N loxo- ‖U l‘o-‖Oc loko-‖Nn lō-‖Ol loko-‖Ut loo- ‖M lakija-「掛ける」

41 E ɲājā-「シャマン教の儀式を行う」‖N jaja-「歌う（シャマンが）」‖U jeæ-「シャマン教の儀式を行う」‖Oc jaja-「同」‖Nn jāja-「同」‖Ol jaja(n)「歌」‖Ut jaaja-「歌う」

42 E ɲūt ‖Ek ɲutə‖N nūtə‖U ɲutə‖Oc ɲūtə‖Nn, Ol nūtə‖Ut nuutə「やに」

43 E ŋāl ‖Ek ŋālə‖S nāla, nāli‖N ŋāla, ŋala ‖U ŋala ‖Oc, Nn,

Ol ŋāla ‖ Ut ŋaala ‖ M gala「手」

44 E ŋæla「下に」‖ Ek в. ŋēlā「同」‖ N ŋēlā, nēlā「同」‖ U ŋeæla「岸に」‖ Oc ŋæla「同」‖ Nn ŋojla, wajla「同」‖ Ol ŋojsɪ「前へ」‖ Ut ŋoila「前に」‖ M wala「下に」

45 E od- ‖ U wadi- ‖ Oc odi- ‖ Nn xoǰi- ‖ Ol xodᴜ- ‖ Ut xoǰi- ‖ M waǰi-「完了する」

46 E oldan ‖ Ek oldon ‖ S oldōõ ‖ N oldōn ‖ U ogdo ‖ Oc ogdo(n) ‖ Nn xoldon ‖ Ol xoldo(n) ‖ Ut xoldo(n-)「側」

47 E omŋa- ‖ Ek omŋo- ‖ S ommo- ‖ N ommo-, omŋo- ‖ U oŋmo- ‖ Oc ommo- ‖ Nn, Ol, Ut oŋbo- ‖ M onggo-「わすれる」

47+ E oŋka-「放牧されている」‖ Ek ōŋko-［同」‖ N oŋko-「同」‖ U oŋkos-「同」‖ Oc oŋko-「同」‖ Nn ōŋko-「同」‖ Ol oŋko-「同」‖ Ut okko-「となかいがこけを食う」‖ M ongko「放牧地」

47‡ Ek silki- ‖ N sɪlki- ‖ U siki- ‖ Oc sikki- ‖ Nn silko- ‖ Ol silču- ‖ Ut siltu- ‖ M silgija-「洗う」

48 Ek suwgu ‖ N sobgu ‖ U sugbu ‖ Oc sᴜbbᴜ ‖ Nn sogbo ‖ Ol sᴜgbᴜ ‖ Ut sugbu「さかなの皮」

48+ E təg-「すわる」‖ Ek, S, N təgə-「同」‖ U tə̄-hi-「すわっている」‖ Oc, Nn, Ol, tə̄-「すわる」‖ Ut təə-「同」‖ M tə-「すわっている」

49 E, Ek təǰə̄-「信ずる」‖ S təǰə̄-「証明する」‖ N təǰə̄- 「信ずる」‖ U čəǰə-「同」‖ Nn təǰə-「同」‖ Ol təǰə「真実」‖ Ut tədə-「信ずる」

50 E, Ek tət- ‖ S tətə-, təti- ‖ N tət- ‖ U təti- ‖ Oc tətu-, təti- ‖ Nn, Ol, Ut, tətu- ‖ M ətu-「着用する」

51 N tibgu- ‖ U tugbu- ‖ Oc tugbu-, tubbu- ‖ Nn, Ol, Ut tugbu-「おとす」

52 E, Ek tiŋən ‖ S tiŋə̃ ‖ N tiŋən ‖ U tiŋə ‖ Oc tiŋə(n) ‖ Nn tuŋgən ‖ Ol tuŋgə(n) ‖ Ut tuŋə(n-) ‖ M tunggən「胸」

53 E tɪmɪnak, tɪmɪn, tɪmɪna, ‖ Ek timātnə ‖ S timāšī ‖ N tɪmana, tɪmanan, tɪmanna, tɪmatna ‖ U timana ‖ Nn čimana ‖ Ol tɪmana

‖ Ut čimanaa ‖ M čimari「あす」

54 E tipkir「くぎ」‖ Ek tipkən「小さい棒くい」‖ S tikkəsʉ̃「くぎ」‖ N tipkən「同」‖ U tikpə「くぎ，小さい棒くい」‖ Oc tippə(n)「くぎ」‖ Nn tukpən「同」‖ Ol tukpə(n)「同」‖ Ut tukpə(n-)「同」

54⁺ Ek tolkin「ゆめ」‖ S tolkiši̅-「ゆめをみる」‖ N tolkin「ゆめ」‖ U t'osi-「ゆめをみる」‖ Oc tokki(n)「ゆめ」‖ Nn tolkin「同」‖ Ol tolčin「同」‖ Ut tolči(n-)「同」‖ M tolgin「同」

54‡ Ek toŋno「正しい」‖ S tondōxõ「まっすぐな」‖ N toŋno「同」‖ U tōŋdo「同」‖ Oc toŋno「同」‖ Nn, Ol, Ut toŋdo「同」‖ M tondo「同」

55 E tūs- ‖ Ek tuksa- ‖ N toksa- ‖ U tukeæ-, tukeæn- ‖ Ut tuksa-「走る」

56 E uliki̅ /əliki̅/「りす」‖ Ek uluki̅「同」‖ S ʉlʉxi「同」‖ N oloxi̅, uluki̅, oloki̅, oluki̅「同」‖ U oloxi「同」‖ Oc oloki「同」‖ Nn xulu「同」‖ Ol xʊlʊ「同」‖ Ut xələ「同」‖ M ulhu「銀鼠灰鼠の類」

57 E ulrə /ulrə/ ‖ Ek ullə ‖ S ʉldə ‖ N ulə ‖ U uləhə ‖ Oc uktə ‖ Nn uliksə ‖ Ol ulsə ‖ Ut ulisə「肉」

58 E, Ek urgə ‖ S ʉggərdi ‖ N ujgəgdi ‖ U ugəhi ‖ Oc uggə, uggəsi ‖ Nn xujgə ‖ Ol xuǰə, xuǰəuli ‖ Ut xudə, xudəuli ‖ M uǰən「重い」

59 E, Ek urkə「戸，入口」‖ S ʉrkə, ʉkkə「戸」‖ N ujkə, uśkə, ut'kə「同」‖ U ukə「戸口」‖ Oc ukkə「戸」‖ Nn ujkə「同」‖ Ol učə「同」‖ Ut utə「戸口」‖ M učə「家の門」

59⁺ E xabda- ‖ N, U, Nn, Ol, Ut, M sabda-「したたる」

60 E xagdi̅「老いた」‖ Ek sagdi「同」‖ S sagdi̅, saddi̅, saddē「同」‖ N sagdi̅「同」‖ U, Oc sāgdi「大きい，老いた」‖ Nn sagǰi「老いた」‖ Ol sagdɪ「同」‖ Ut sagǰi「同」‖ M sakda「同」

61 E xākan ‖ Ek в. xakin ‖ S āxi̅ ‖ N xāxin, xākin ‖ Oc xaki(n) ‖ Nn, Ol pā ‖ Ut paaxa ‖ M fahůn「肝臓」

62 E xaŋār ‖ Ek, S saŋār ‖ N saŋā ‖ U, Oc saŋa ‖ Nn saŋgar ‖ Ol

saŋgal(ɪ) ‖ Ut saŋa ‖ M sangga「あな」

63 E xæ-「かむ（歯で）」‖ Ek, N sē-「同」‖ U sa-「同」‖ Oc sæa-, sæ-「同」‖ Nn sia-「食べる」‖ Ol sē-「かむ（歯で）」‖ Ut see-「同」‖ M sai-「同」

63+ E, Ek xənŋən ‖ S əŋə̃ ‖ N xəɲŋən ‖ Oc xəŋŋə(n) ‖ Nn pəjŋən ‖ Ol pəɲə ‖ Ut pənə(n-)「ひざ」

64 E xəs ‖ Ek səksə ‖ S səkčə, sətčə ‖ N səksə ‖ U sakeæ ‖ Oc, Nn, Ol səksə ‖ Ut səəksə ‖ M sənggi「血」

65 E, Ek, N xig- ‖ U sī- ‖ Nn pui- ‖ Ol puju- ‖ Ut pui- ‖ M fujə-「皮をはぐ」

66 E xil ‖ Ek silə ‖ S šil ‖ N, U, Oc, Nn, Ol, Ut, M silə「煮出し汁」

67 E xiltəs「ほくち」‖ Ek в. siltiksa「同」‖ N siltik「ほくち袋」‖ U siktihə「ほくち」‖ Oc siktiksə「同」‖ Nn silčiksə「同」‖ Ol siltə-ku(n)「同」‖ Ut silčiskə「同」

68 E xīmkə-「せきをする」‖ Ek в. simki-「同」‖ S д. šīŋkīī「せき」‖ N simki-「せきをする」‖ Oc simpisi-「同」‖ Nn siŋbisi-「同」‖ Ol siŋbu「せき」‖ Ut siikpi-si-「せきをしている」

68+ E xot ‖ Ek, N, U, Oc xokto ‖ Nn, Ol, Ut pokto「みち」

69 E xulra ‖ Ek xulla ‖ N xola ‖ U xulaha ‖ Oc xʊkta ‖ Nn polta ‖ Ol xʊlta ‖ Ut pulta「掛けぶとん」

69+ E xunāǰ「おとめ」‖ Ek xunāt「同」‖ S unāǰi「同」‖ N xonāt「おとめ，（拡大意味の）姉妹」‖ U xunaǰi「（拡大意味の）姉妹」‖ Oc xʊnaǰi「同」‖ Nn pondaǰō「同」‖ Ol pʊndaǰʊ「姉妹」‖ Ut pundadu「（拡大意味の）姉妹」

69‡ E xūnta ‖ Ek suŋta ‖ S sūnta ‖ N soŋta ‖ U suŋta ‖ Oc sʊŋta ‖ Nn soŋta ‖ Ol sʊŋta ‖ Ut sukta「深い」

語例70～91は，表6，7を参照されたい。

4）**音韻構造**　祖語の単語（該当する発音において，音の長い休止を前後におくことはあるが，中間に普通おくことがない単位）は，現代ツングース諸語も参照してみて，次のような構造をもっていたのではないかと考える（ただし，音象徴は除く）。1つの単語は，r 以外の C または V で始まり，V または n, l あるいは r で終わる。g で終わる単語もあったかもしれないが，なお明らかでない。語頭または語末には C が2つ立たない。語全体は VV だけからなるか，V または VV と C または CC との交互の連続からなる。

また，祖語には本来の8母音音素の存在と関連して母音調和がおそらくすでにおこなわれたとみたい。その母音調和は，上記のエウェン語におけるような咽頭音化があるⅠ類とそれがないⅡ類の2類の母音音素による母音調和であったろう。その母音調和において，一つの単語はⅠ類の *a，*ɔ，*ʊ，*ɪ か，Ⅱ類の *ə *ɵ，*u，*i かのどちらかの母音音素だけをふくむものであったろう。その後，多くのツングース語では上記の咽頭化調音が弱まって消失したとおもわれる。それにともない，狭い母音音素の *i と*ɪ の区別，*u と *ʊ の区別は，広い母音音素にくらべて舌の高さの差が小さいのであいまいとなって失われて行き，*i と*ɪ は合一して i となり，*u と *ʊ は合一して u となり，Ⅲ類をなしたのであろう。

B）**文　法**

今日のツングース諸語において，名詞，数詞，代名詞，（エウェン語や一部のエウェンキー語では，さらに形容詞）および動詞は，語幹に語尾が接尾して語変化を行う。ただし，動詞以外の語幹は単独でも使われる。すなわち，満洲語を除く各言語の名詞，数詞，代名詞は，語幹に種々の格語尾が接尾して格変化を行い，名詞，数詞，一部の代名詞は，さらに人称語尾または反照語尾が接尾して人称変化，反照変化を行う。満洲語の名詞，数詞，代名詞では，格語尾が接尾するか，ないし，格助詞が後置されるといいうる。なお，エウェン語，エウェンキー語では，形容詞も名詞のように格変化を行う。次に，動詞は，ツングース各言語で，語幹に種々の動詞語尾が接尾し，満洲語以外では，ある動詞語尾のあとに，さらに，人称語尾または反照語尾が接尾する。ただし，満洲語にも，動詞語尾 -ki「～しよう」とともに，第3人称語尾 *-ni が化石化している動詞語尾 -kini「～させよ」がある（ポッペ 1931，125ページ；服部 1948を参照)。ツングース語全般において，以上の品詞以外の語には，上述の語尾は付かない。なお，ウイルタ語では，語幹と語尾が融合した形をとることもある。

祖語においても，名詞，数詞，代名詞は，語尾（ないし助詞）をとってできた種々の格形が格体系をつくり，動詞は，動詞語尾が接尾してできた種々の動詞形が動詞変化の体系をなしていたと考えられよう。人称語尾については，本書369ページ以下も参照されたい。

語幹は，ツングース各言語において，通常，語幹だけからなるか，または，語幹にさらに接尾辞がついて形成されている。祖語においても，語幹はこのように形成されていたであろう。

以下にあげる語尾，接尾辞については，いくつかの交替形（位置的変種）があるものは，基本的なもの，または代表的なものだけを挙げる。祖語においても，語尾，接尾辞には交替形があったことが考えられよう。

1）　**名　詞**　ツングース各言語の格語尾の数は，エウェン語，エウェンキー語，ソロン語は少なくとも12，ネギダル語，ウデヘ語，オロチ語，ナーナイ語，オルチャ語，ウイルタ語も7ないし9はあり，満洲語の格語尾（ないし格助詞）の数は，限られた語だけに残るものを除いて，4ないし5である。そのうち，少なくとも表4の語尾は，多くのツングース語にみられ，おそらく，祖語にまでさかのぼるものであろう。

満洲語においては，dəri のほか，ǰuləri「前を通って」なども同じ -ri を含む。手段格の *-ǰi は，満洲語では，所属格語尾（ないし助詞）*-i～*-ni と合一して i となっているとみられる。満洲語動詞語尾 -hai「～したまま」は，完了の動詞語尾 *-ha プラスこの手段格にさかのぼるものかもしれない。満洲語の位置格の də は，蒙古語の格語尾 -da の借用かもしれない。また，満洲語の amasi（語例4）などの -si は，正確には，*-tikii の交替形 *-sikii に対応するものであろう。

名詞語幹を形成する接尾辞には，たとえば，表5の複数の接尾辞がある。オロチ語，満洲語の -sa が，*-l の脱落した形かどうかは問題である。元来，-sa であったかもしれず，他のツングース語の -sal の方が，*-sa へのちに *-l が接尾した形かもしれないことも考えねばならないであろう。また，語例28は，

*-pun「道具」にさかのぼる接尾辞を含んでいる。エウェン語，ソロン語，オロチ語の語形では，語幹と接尾辞が融合している。一方，語例56，61において，他のツングース語にみられる *-kii，*-kin という接尾辞が，ナーナイ語，オルチャ語，ウイルタ語にはみられない。語例64において，他のすべてのツングース語の形がさかのぼるとみられる *-ksa という接尾辞に対して，満洲語の -nggi は，おそらく別の接尾辞であろう。

2）**数　詞**　「1」から「10」までの数詞は，表6の対応を示す。ウイルタ語の ɵmɵ は，ɵmɵ niŋi「ゆび1本のはば」に現われる。しかし，これは，他のツングース語からの借用語かもしれない。

エウェン語 tuŋŋan の末音 -n は，他の数詞の -n への類推によって生じたものではないであろうか。なお，オロチ語の「6」の数詞を，ツィンツィウス（1949b）は ɲuŋᵞun と記している。サンタン語（「歴史」を参照）のユクウ「6」の頭音は，＊n（または ɲ）から変化した j であろう（池上，1967を参照）。「9」のエウェン語，オロチ語，ナーナイ語，オルチャ語，ウイルタ語，満洲語の形と，エウェンキー語，ソロン語，ネギダル語，ウデヘ語の形は，それぞれ別の祖形にさかのぼることが考えられ，同じ語に由来するとは必ずしもいえない。エウェンキー語の一部の方言の ǰəgin「9」（ワシレーヴィチ，1958を参照）の ǰ は，＊j から生じたものであろう。「9」の語が，祖語でどんな形であったかは，まだ明らかに言えないが，「1」から「10」までの他の上記の語は，祖語にさかのぼるものであろう。ウイルタ語の geeda「1」は，このツングース語が分化したのちに数詞となったものであろう。

3）**代 名 詞**　人代名詞，指示代名詞，疑問代名詞には，表7の対応がある。

1・2人称複数代名詞のナーナイ語，オルチャ語，満洲語の形は，*buu，*suu に，ナーナイ語，オルチャ語で *-gə，満洲語で *-gəə のような，ある接尾辞がついた形から変化したものではないであろうか。エウェン語，エウェンキー語，ソロン語，ネギダル語，ウデヘ語，オロチ語，満洲語では，表7の語例81が1人称複数代名詞の除外形，語例82がその包括形として区別される。（満洲語口語については，服部・山本，1955を参照）。ただし，ナーナイ語，オルチャ語，ウイルタ語とエウェン語内のアルマニ（Армань）方言には，1人称複数代名詞として，語例82に対応する形がなく，その区別がない。また，エウェン語の西部方言には，語例82に対応する形だけがあって，その区別がない。

語例85，86は，3人称人代名詞である。満洲語以外のツングース語のその形は，*nuŋan（または *ɲuŋan）に由来する語幹（または，その複数形）に3人称接尾辞（または，3人称複数接尾辞），あるいは，さらに複数接尾辞 -lがついてつくられたものである。ウイルタ語では，それは，ほかの第三者と対照された第三者に対する代名詞である（Ikegami, 1968を参照）。*nuŋan は，あるいは〈ほかの第三者に対する彼の方〉の〈方〉の意味に関連があるような名詞に由来するものかもしれない。3人称代名詞として，満洲語には，単数の i，複数の čə がある。

語例88のウデヘ語，オロチ語，ナーナイ語，オルチャ語の語形では，*a が，次に狭い *i があるため ə となり，オルチャ語の tɪjɪ，tɪ は *əi が ɪjɪ，さらに ɪ となったものであろう。満洲語の tərə は，このような *ə が次の * i をさらに同化させたものか，あるいはまた，蒙古語の tere「それ」を借用したものかもしれない。また，語例90のエウェン語，エウェンキー語，ネギダル語，ウデヘ語，オロチ語の語形は，接尾辞を含むものであろうが，この語はまた，蒙古語の jaɣun「なに」と同じ語かもしれない。

語例82の語は，祖語までさかのぼるかどうか，3人称人代名詞は祖語にあったかどうか，あればどんな語があったか。また，語例90，91の語は，どちらかが，または，どちらもが祖語までさかのぼるものか，あるいは，どちらも否かは，なお明らかでない。

4）**動　詞**　連体形（動名詞）や終止形（定動詞）を形成する表8の2つの語尾（「～ている」または「～た」）についてだけみる。

これらの語尾は，ウイルタ語では，それぞれ，-ra ～-da ～-si，-ri～-ǰi ～-si と交替し，ほかにも，この種の交替をするツングース語がある。この交替は，ツングース語比較文法上重要である（ベンツィング 1955を参照）。

-10 の語尾は，ナーナイ語，オルチャ語で，動詞否定形の語尾（前者の -rāsi，後者の -rasi）に含まれ，他のツングース語では，動詞の否定の句構造において，否定動詞（語幹は -ə）のあとに立つ否定される動詞の語尾として現れる。

満洲語では，動詞の否定形 -raků に含まれ，否定命令の句構造にも現れるほか，ひろく連体形語尾としてある。-11は連体形（動名詞）語尾である。また，この -10 と -11 の 2 つの語尾は，多くのツングース語で終止形語尾としても現れる。ただし，オロチ語の -j, -aj は，定動詞の語尾としてだけ記録されている。

-10 の語尾は，祖語の動詞語尾 *-ra へさかのぼるとみられる。-11 の語尾は，上の *-ra に *-i（あるいは，なんらかの C プラス i）という語尾がついてできているものであろう。ウデヘ語，オロチ語の -ai, -aj の形は，あるいは，まだ融合しない形かもしれない。もしそうならば，祖語では，まだ融合しない 2 つの語尾の連結としてあったであろう。

また，エウェン語，エウェンキー語，ソロン語，ネギダル語，ウイルタ語には，上の *-ra に *-ki という語尾が連結してなる条件形語尾があり，満洲語には，これがさらに変化してなった条件形語尾 -či，および逆接条件形語尾 -čibə（さらに -bə「も」がついている）がある（池上，1953を参照）。ナーナイ語，オルチャ語，ウイルタ語の命令形語尾 -ru は，上の *-ra に *-u（あるいは，なんらかの C プラス u）という語尾がついて生じたとみられる。満洲語のある不規則命令形は，この *-u（または*-ru）を含むとみられる（Ikegami, 1957を参照）。

動詞語幹形成接尾辞の，たとえば次のものは，動詞語幹に接尾するもので，表 9 の対応を示す。

-12 は他動詞形成の接尾辞，-13 は受身形形成の接尾辞，-14 は使役形形成接尾辞とよんでおく。ただし，ウイルタ語では，-13 の -bu^2 は，むしろ主語（動作主体）に触れずに動詞意味内容を伝える非人称接尾辞であり，-14 の -boon は使役・受身形形成接尾辞である。

-12 の接尾辞は-13 の接尾辞とおそらく本来は同じものかもしれない。-14 のエウェンキー語，エウェン語，ソロン語，ネギダル語，ナーナイ語の接尾辞は -w と -kān，または -ū と -xān，-bo と -wan の二つの接尾辞に分離でき，その前部は-13 の接尾辞と元来は同じものであろう。またその-14 のウイルタ語の -boon は，-14 の上記の -w と -kān に相当する二つの接尾辞が融合した形であろう。なお，満洲語には，動詞使役・受身形形成接尾辞 -bu があり，これは，満洲語文語の字面の上ではウイルタ語の -bu に一致し，意味は -boon に似ており，その -bu²，-boon のいずれかに対応するものだろう。

-15 は，各ツングース語で，開始（～しはじめる）の意味をもつ。

C）　Ⅱの概要

語彙については，借用語の比較的入りにくい基本的語彙において各方言が対応する多くの語を有することが上の語例からうかがえよう。以上から各方言がツングース祖語という一つの祖語にさかのぼることはまず問題なかろう。ただしその祖語についてくわしいことはさらに考察すべき問題である。

さて，いま特に音韻対応*6*，*9*，*23*，*48*，*49*，また文法において人称語尾，反照語尾がその方言に生きて行われているか否か，また語例56，61，64におけるようなある接尾辞の有無に注目すると，各方言はそれらの点に関する相互の異同によりⅠ．L，E，S，N，　Ⅱ．U，Oc，Ⅲ．G，Ol，Ok，　Ⅳ．M の4群に分類されうる。その異同に関する各群の相互の関係によって，Ⅱ群はⅠ，Ⅲ群の中間的位置を占めると言えよう。Ⅳの満洲語は著しく異なるが，Ⅲ群に近い点がある。しかしまたある点ではむしろ他の群に近い。今日の方言におけるそれらの点の異同は，変遷の過程においてそれぞれの群ごとに著しい違いがあったことを示すもののようにみえる。その各群はツングース祖語からの変遷の過程においてそれぞれ一つの中間祖語をもつことが考えられよう。なお満洲語は他方言と特に著しく異なる変遷をとげたとみられる。また各方言には他方言からの借用とともに，近隣言語，たとえば蒙古語などからの借用があったであろう。あるいは今日すでに死滅してしまった言語からの借用があったことも考えられよう。満洲語においては他言語からの借用が特に著しかったかもしれない。なおまたある方言が他方言または他言語を素地としていないかということも考えねばならない。

〈表 1〉　第 1 音節における母音対応

	E	Ek	S	N	U	Oc	Nn	Ol	Ut	M	祖語	語例
1	a	a	a	a	a	a	a	a	a	a	*a	31
2	ə	ə	ə	ə	ə	ə	ə	ə	ə	ə	*ə	17
3	o	o	o	o	o	o	o	o	o	o	*o	47
4	u	u	ʉ	u	u	u	u	u	u	u	*ɵ	33,57
5	ʊ	u	u	o	u	ʊ	o	ʊ	u	u	*ʊ	32
6	i	i	i	i	i	i	u	u	u	u	*u	52
7	ɪ	i	i	ɪ	i	i	i	ɪ	i	i	*ɪ	13,53
8	i	i	i	i	i	i	i	i	i	i	*i	9

注：E はエウェン語，Ek はエウェンキー語，S はソロン語，N はネギダル語，U はウデヘ語，Oc はオロチ語，Nn はナーナイ語，Ol はオルチャ語，Ut はウイルタ語，Mは満洲語を示す．

〈表 2〉　子音対応 I ―祖語の子音音素 1 つの対応

		E	Ek	S	N	U	Oc	Nn	Ol	Ut	M	祖語	語例
9	イ	x	x	ø	x	x～s〔i〕	x	p	p	p	f	*p	61,68⁺,
	ロ	w～ø	w	w～ø	w	w	w～ø						65,31
10	イ	b	b	b	b	b	b	b	b	b	b	*b	9,16,
	ロ	w	g～w	g～w	w	ø	w～ø	w～ø	w～ø	w～ø			19

11	イ，ロ	t	t	t	t	t	t	t~č〔i〕	t	t~č〔i〕	t~č〔i〕	*t	53,52,50
12	イ，ロ	d	d	d	d	d	d	d~ǰ〔i〕	d	d~ǰ〔i〕	d~ǰ〔i〕	*d	14,17,45
13	イ ロ	č	č	s~c	č	č s	č	č	č	t~č〔i〕	š~s （~č？）	*č	10,11,12, 27
14	イ，ロ	ǰ	ǰ	ǰ	ǰ	ǰ	ǰ	ǰ	ǰ	d~ǰ〔i〕	ǰ	*ǰ	31,30,49
15	イ ロ	k	k	x k~x	k k~x	k ‘~g	k k	k k~Ø	k k~Ø	k w~Ø	h~k	*k	34,40, 33
16	イ ロ	g g~w~Ø	g	g	g	g Ø	g w~Ø	g Ø	g w~Ø	g w~Ø	g w~Ø	*g	24, $32,48^+$
17	イ，ロ	m	m	m	m	m	m	m	m	m	m	*m	37,4
18	イ，ロ ハ	n	n	n Ṽ	n	n Ø	n n（~Ø）	n	n	n n~Ø	n	*n	76,6,36 17,73
19	イ	ŋ	ŋ	n	ŋ~n	ŋ	ŋ	ŋ	ŋ	ŋ	g~Ø	*ŋ	43,44
20	イ ロ ハ	n l	l	l	l	l l Ø	l l Ø	l	l l l(i,ɪ)	l	l l Ø	*l	40, 43,66, -8,-9
21	ロ ハ	r	r	r	j Ø	Ø Ø	Ø~j Ø	r	r l(ɪ)	r Ø	r Ø	*r	13^+,23,24, 62
22	イ ロ	x s	s	s（~š）	s	s h	s	s	s	s	s	*s	63,66, 7

		E	Ek	S	N	U	Oc	Nn	Ol	Ut	M	祖語	語例
23	イ	Ø	Ø	Ø	Ø	Ø	Ø	x〜s〔i〕	x〜s〔i,I〕	x〜s〔i〕	Ø	*x	17,28,29
24	イ	m	w	w	w	w	w	w	w	w	w	*w	35
25	イ	ɲ	j	j	j	j	j	j	j	j	j	*j	41,
	ロ	j											3,18

注：イは語頭，ロは語中〔母音間〕，ハは語末に現れる場合。Øはゼロを示す。表2，3において〔　〕を後にともなう音素は，〔　〕内の音素の前に現れる。

〈表3〉子音対応Ⅱ—祖語における子音音素2つの連続の対応〔語中に現れる場合〕

	E	Ek	S	N	U	Oc	Nn	Ol	Ut	M	祖語	語例
26	s	ks	kč〜tč	ks〜s	k〜h	ks	ks	ks	ks〜sk		*ks	30, 64, 55
27	t	kt	kt〜tt	kt	kt	kt	kt	kt	kt		*kt	29
28	gd〜d	gd	gd〜dd	gd	gd	gd	gd〜gǰ〔i〕	gd	gd〜gǰ〔i〕	kd	*gd	25, 60
29	nt	ŋt	nt	ŋt	ŋt	ŋt	ŋt	ŋt	kt		*ŋt	$69^{\ddagger}$
30		ŋn	nd	ŋn	ŋd	ŋn	ŋd	ŋd	ŋd	nd	*ŋd	$54^{\ddagger}$
31	bd	wd		bd	bd	bd	bd	bd	bd	bd	*bd	12^{+}, 59^{+}

32	pk	pk	kk	pk	kp	pp	kp	kp	kp	k	*pk (*kp?)	54, 77
33	bg	wg	wg～gg	bg	gb	gb～bb	gb	gb	gb		*bg (*gb?)	48, 1, 51
34	mk	mk	ŋk	mk		mp	ŋb	ŋb	kp		*mk (*ŋp?)	68
35	mŋ	mŋ	mm	mŋ～mm	ŋm	mm	ŋb	ŋb	ŋb	ngg	*mg (*ŋb?)	47
36	mŋ	mŋ	mm	mŋ	ŋm	mm	ŋm	ŋm	ŋm	ngg	*mŋ (*ŋm?)	5
37		mn		mn	mn	mn	md	md	md	md	*md	34^{+}
38	mr	mn	nd	mn	mVh	ms		ms	ps		*ms	23
39	n	n	n	n	n	n	nd	nd	nd		*nd	69^{+}
40	nr	nn	nd	n	h	s	nt	nt	tt		*ns	38
41	nŋ	nŋ		nŋ～ŋn		ŋ	ŋg	nǰ	nd～nǰ〔i〕	nǰ	*ng	36^{+}, $6^{\ddagger}$
42	nŋ	nŋ	ŋ	ɲŋ～ŋɲ～nɲ～ɲɲ～ɲ	ŋ	ŋ	ŋ	ɲ	n	ngg	*nŋ	29
43	nŋ	nŋ	ŋ	ŋɲ～ɲŋ	ŋ	ŋ	jŋg	ɲǰ	nd	nǰ	*jng (*ɲg?)	74
44	nŋ	nŋ	ŋ～ɲ	ɲŋ	ŋ	ŋŋ	jŋ	ɲ	n	niy	*jnŋ (*ɲŋ?)	6^{+}, 63^{+}

	E	Ek	S	N	U	Oc	Nn	Ol	Ut	M	祖語	語例
45	ŋk	ŋk		ŋk	ŋk	ŋk	ŋk	ŋk	kk	ngk	*ŋk	47^{+}
46	ŋ	ŋ	ŋ	ŋ	ŋ	ŋ	ŋg	ŋg	ŋ	ngg	*ŋg	52
47	lb	lb	lb	lb	gb	bb	lb	lb	lb	b	*lb	14
48	lt	lt	lt	lt	kt	kt～xt	lt～lč〔i〕	lt	lt～lč〔i〕	nt	*lt	34, 67
49	ld	ld	ld	ld	gd	gd	ld～lǰ〔i〕	ld	ld～lǰ〔i〕	nǰ〔i〕	*ld	46, 15
50	lr	ll		l	lVh	kt	lt	lt	lt		*ls	69
51		lk	lk	lk	‘～k	kk	lk	lč	lt～lč〔i〕	lg	*lk	47^{+}, 54^{+}
52	lg	lg		lg		gg	lg	lǰ	ld	lh	*lg	9^{+}
53	rp	rp	rp	pp	kp	pp	rp	rp	rp	bt	*rp	20
54	rb	rb	rb	lb	gb	bb	rb	lb	lb	b	*rb	22
55	rk	rk	rk～kk	jk～s′k ～t′k	k	kk	jk	č	t	č	*rk	59
56	rg	rg	rg～gg	jg～gg	g	gg	jg	ǰ	d	ǰ	*rg	8, 58

〈表４〉名詞の格語尾の対応

	E	Ek	S	N	U	Oc	Nn	Ol	Ut	M	祖語	
-1	-w ～-bu etc.	-wa etc.	-wə ～-bə	-wa ～-ba etc.	-wə	-wa ～-ba etc.	-wa ～-ba etc.	-wa ～-ba etc.	-wa ～-ba etc.	bə	*-ba 「～を」	対格
-2	-lā～ -dulā etc.	-lā～ -dulā etc.	-lā～ -dulā etc.	-lā～ -dolā etc.	-la～ -dula etc.	-la～ -dula etc.	-la～ -dula etc.	-la～ -dʊla etc.	-la～ -dula etc.	語例44 walaなどの-la	*-laa 「～において」	場所格
-3	-lī～ -dulī etc.	-lī～ -dulī	-lī～ -dulī etc.	-lī～ -dulī	-li～ -duli etc.	-li～ -duli				dəri 「～を通って」	*-lii 「～を通して」	縦走格
-4	-dū etc.	-dū etc.	-du etc.	-dū etc.	-du	-du	-du etc.	-du etc.	-du	də	*-duu 「～に」	位置格
-5	-duk etc.	-duk etc.	-duxi etc.	-dukkoj etc.	-digi	-duj(i)			-duu		*-duku 「～から」	起点格
-6	-č～ -ǰi etc.	-t～ -ǰi etc.	-ǰi	-ǰi etc.	-ǰi	-ǰi	-ǰi	-ǰi etc.	-ǰi	i	*-ǰi 「～で」	手段格

	E	Ek	S	N	U	Oc	Nn	Ol	Ut	M	祖語	
-7	-tkī～ -takī etc.	-tkī～ -tikī	-txī～ -tixī	-tkī～ -tixī etc.	-tigi	-ti	-či	-ti etc.	-tai etc.	語例 4 amasi など の-si	*-tikii （*-takɪɪ？）	指向格

〈表 5〉 名詞語幹を形成する複数接尾辞の対応

	E	Ek	S	N	U	Oc	Nn	Ol	Ut	M	祖語	
-8	-l	-l		-l				-l(ɪ) ～-l(i)	-l		*-l	（複数）
-9	-sal ～-səl	-sal etc.	-sal ～-sul etc.	-sal etc.		-sa ～-sə	-sal ～səl	-sal(ɪ) ～-səl(i)	-sal ～səl	-sa etc.	*-sal または *-sa(＋*-l)	（複数）

〈表 6〉 数詞の対応

語例	E	Ek	S	N	U	Oc	Nn	Ol	Ut	M	祖語
70	umən /əmən/	umūn	əmʉ̃	omon	omo	omo(n)	əmun	ʊmʊ(n) (omo(n))	ɵmɵ	əmu	*əmun 「1」
71	ǰūr /ǰər/	ǰūr	ǰʉ̄r	ǰūl	ǰū,ǰu	ǰū(g)	ǰuər, ǰuə	ǰuəl(i)	dɵɵ	ǰuw₂ə, ǰuru	*ǰugər 「2」
72	ɪlan	ilan	ilã	ɪlan	ila	ila(n)	ilān	ɪla(n)	ilaa(n-)	ilan	*ilaan または*ilanか 「3」

73	digən	digin	digī̃	digin, dijin	dī	dī(n)	duin	dui(n)	ǰiin	duin	*dugin 「4」
74	tunŋan	tunŋa	toŋa	toɲŋa, tuŋɲa	tuŋa	tʊŋa(n)	tojŋga	tʊɲǰa	tunda	sunǰa	*tʊjnga 「5」
75	ɲuŋən	ɲuŋun	ɲʉŋʉ̃	ɲuŋun	ɲuŋu	ɲuŋu(n)	ɲuŋgun	ɲuŋgu(n)	nuŋu(n-)	ninggun	*niŋgən 「6」
76	nadan	nadan	nadã	nadan	nada	nada(n)	nadān	nada(n)	nada(n-)	nadan	*nadan 「7」
77	ǰapkan	ǰapkun	ǰakkũ	ǰapkun	ǰakpu	ǰappʊ(n)	ǰakpon, ǰakpun	ǰakpʊ(n)	ǰakpu(n-)	ǰakůn	*ǰapkun (*ǰakpʊn?) 「8」
78	ujūn	jəgin	jəgī̃	ijəgin, (i)jegin	jəji, jəi	xuju(n)	xujun	xuju(n)	xuju(n-)	ujun	「9」
79	mæn	ǰān	ǰāā̃	ǰān	ǰā	ǰā(n)	ǰoan	ǰʊa(n)	ǰoon	ǰuwɪan	*ǰʊgaan 「10」

注：E欄の／／内は，オラ方言形。

〈表7〉人代名詞，指示代名詞，疑問代名詞の対応

語例	E	Ek	S	N	U	Oc	Nn	Ol	Ut	M	祖語	
80	bi	bi	bi	bi	bi	bī	mī	bi	bii	bi	*bii	「おれ」
81	bu	bu	bʉ̄	bu	bu	bū	buə	bū, buə	buu	bə	*buu	「おれたち」

82	mut	mit	miti	bittə, buttə, bit	minti	biti				musə		「おれたち」
83	xi	si	ši	sī	si	sī	sī	si	sii	si	*sii	「おまえ」
84	xu	su	sʉ̄	sū	su	sū	suə	sū, suə	suu	suwıə	*suu	「おまえたち」
85	noŋan	nuŋan		noŋan, nugan	nua	nʊŋaɲi	ɲoani	nānɪ, nān	nooni (noon-)	(i)		「かれ」
86	noŋar-tan	nuŋar-tin		noŋatil, noŋaltin	nuati	nʊŋanti	ɲoanči	nātɪ, nāt	nooči (noon-)	(čə)		「かれら」
87	ər	ər	əri	ə₀j	əji	ə̰j	əj	əj	əri	ərə	*əri	「これ」
88	tar	tar	tari	taj	təji, təi	təu̯	təj	tɪ, tɪjɪ	tari	tərə	*tari	「それ」
89	ŋī	ŋī	nīxẽ	nī, ŋī	nī	ɲi	uj	ŋuj, uj	ŋui	wə	*ŋui (あるいは*ŋəi)	「だれ」
90	æk	ēkun	ī	ēxun, ēkun	j'əu	jā				ja		「なに」
91							xaj	xaj	xai	ai		「なに」

〈表 8〉 連体形，終止形を形成する動詞語尾の対応

	E	Ek	S	N	U	Oc	Nn	Ol	Ut	M	祖語
-10	-ra etc.	-ra etc.	-ra etc.	-ja etc.	-a etc.	-a etc.	-ra etc.	-ra etc.	-ra etc.	-ra etc.	*-ra
-11	-rī etc.	-rī etc.	-ri	-jī	-i~-ai etc.	-j~-aj etc.	-j~-ri etc.	-j~-ri etc.	-ri etc.		*-rai

〈表 9〉 動詞語幹形成接尾辞の対応

	E	Ek	S	N	U	Oc	Nn	Ol	Ut	M	祖語
-12	-w etc.	B.-w(u)	-wū~ -gū etc.				-wo~ -bo etc.	-wu~ -bu etc.	-bu[1] etc.		*-bu
-13	-w etc.	-w etc.	-wū~ -gū~ -w etc.	-w etc.	-u		-wo~ -bo etc.	-wu~ -bu etc.	-bu[2] etc.	-bu	*-bu
-14	-wkān etc.	-wkān etc.	-ūxān etc.	-wkān etc.			-wan~ -bowan etc.	-wan etc.	-boon etc.		*-bUkān
-15	-l	-l		-l	-li		-lu~-lo	-lu~lU	-lu		*-lu

注：B. はワシレーヴィチ（1958）からの引用。

「比較研究によってみた過去」の引用文献

羽田亨，1937.『満和辞典』（京都帝国大学満蒙調査会，京都）。

服部四郎，1937.「満洲語音韻史の為めの一資料」『音声の研究』6（文学社，東京）。

———，1959.『日本語の系統』（岩波書店，東京）。

服部四郎，山本謙吾，1955.「満洲語の一人称複数代名詞」『言語研究』28。

———，1956.「満洲語口語の音韻の体系と構造」『言語研究』30。

池上二良，1946.「満洲語の若干の文語形中の ū の表す母音に就いて」『Tôyôgo Kenkyû』1（東京帝国大学文学部言語学研究室会，東京）——『満洲語研究』（汲古書院，東京，1999）収載。

———，1953.「満洲語の動詞語尾 -ci 及び -cibe について」『金田一博士古稀記念言語民俗論叢』（三省堂，東京）——『満洲語研究』収載。

———，1950，1954.「満洲語の諺文文献に関する一報告」『東洋学報』33巻2号，36巻4号（東洋学術協会，東京）——『満洲語研究』収載。

———，1963.「ふたたび満洲語の諺文文献について」『朝鮮学報』26（朝鮮学会，天理）——『満洲語研究』収載。

———，1967.「サンタンことば集」『北方文化研究』2（北海道大学，札幌）。

———，1980.『ウイルタ語基礎語彙』（北海道大学文学部言語学研究室，札幌）——『ウイルタ語辞典』（北海道大学図書刊行会，札幌，1997）収録。

———，1985.『ウイルタ民俗語彙』（北海道教育委員会，札幌；網走市北方民俗文化保存協会，網走）——上記『ウイルタ語辞典』収録。

李基文，1958.「中世女真語音韻論研究」『서울大学校論文集（人文科学）』7（서울）。

長田夏樹，1949.「満洲語と女真語」『神戸言語学会報』1号（神戸言語学会，神戸）。

山本謙吾，1955.「満洲語文語形態論」『世界言語概説』下巻（市河三喜,服部四郎編，研究社，東京）。

———，1960，1962，1963.「満洲語基礎語彙」Ⅰ，Ⅱ，Ⅸ『言語研究』37，『跡見学園短期大学紀要』1，『言語研究』43。

———，1969.『満洲語口語基礎語彙集』（東京外国語大学アジア・アフリカ言語文化研究所，東京）。

Benzing, J., 1953. ──「参考文献」を参照。

──, 1955. ──「参考文献」を参照。

Hattori, S.〔服部四郎〕, 1948. "Gensi-Altai-go no dôsi-gokan ni setsubi sita *-ki(～*-gi)", *Tôyôgo Kenkyû* 4.

Ikegami, J.〔池上二良〕, 1956. "The substantive inflection of Orok",『言語研究』30──本書収載。

──, 1957. "Über die Herkunft einiger unregelmäßiger Imperativformen der mandschurischen Verben", *Studia Altaica*. Otto Harrassowitz, Wiesbaden.──『満洲語研究』収載。

──, 1959. "The verb inflection of Orok",『国語研究』9（国学院大学国語研究会，東京）──本書収載。

──, 1960. "Versuch einer vergleichenden Grammatik der tungusischen Sprachen", *Ural-Altaische Jahrbücher*, Band 32, Heft 1-2. Otto Harrassowitz, Wiesbaden. ──Benzing（1955）の書評 ──本書収載。

──, 1968. "The Orok third person pronoun *nooni*", *Ural-Altaische Jahrbücher*, Band 40, Heft 1-2. Otto Harrassowitz, Wiesbaden. ──本書収載。

Аврорин, В. А., 1959, 1961. Грамматика. нанайского языка I, II. Изд. АН СССР, Москва/Ленинград.

Аврорин, В. А. и Лебедева, Е. П., 1978. Орочские тексты и словарь. НАУКА, Ленинград.

Василевич, Г. М., 1958. Эвенкийско-русский словарь. Гос. изд. иностр. и нац. словарей, Москва.

Горцевская, В. А., Колесникова, В. Д. и Константинова, О. А., 1958. Эвенкийско-русский словарь. Учпедгиз, Ленинград.

Колесникова, В. Д. и Константинова, О. А., 1968. "Негидальский язык", Языки народов СССР, том 5. НАУКА, Ленинград.

Новикова, К. А., 1960, 1980. Очерки диалектов эвенского языка, часть 1(Изд. АН СССР, Москва/Ленинград), Глагол, служебные слова, тексты, глоссарий (НАУКА, Ленинград).

Оненко, С. Н., 1980. Нанайско-русский словарь. Изд. Русский язык, Москва.

Петрова, Т. И., 1936. Ульчский диалект нанайского языка. Учпедгиз, Москва/Ленинград.

——, 1960. Нанайско-русский словарь. Учпедгиз, Ленинград.

Поппе, Н. Н., 1931. Материалы по солонскому языку. Изд. АН СССР, Ленинград.

Суник, О. П., 1985. Ульчский язык. НАУКА, Ленинград.

Цинциус, В. И., 1949 a. ——「参考文献」を参照。

——, 1949 b. "Очерк морфологии орочского языка", Ученые записки ЛГУ 98, Серия востоковедческих наук, вып. 1. Ленинград.

——, 1982. Негидальский язык. НАУКА, Ленинград.

Цинциус, В. И. и Ришес, Л. Д., 1952. Русско-эвенский словарь. Гос.изд. иностр. и нац. словарей, Москва.

Шнейдер, Е. Р., 1936. Краткий удэйско-русский словарь. Учпедгиз, Москва/Ленинград.

Ⅲ　ツングース・満洲諸語の分類

ツングース・満洲諸語の相互の関係を適切に示そうとして，従来，研究者がこれらの言語の相異なるさまざまな分類をしてきた。

1854年から1856年までアムール川流域を調査したシュレンクは，言語の点から，アムール川流域のツングース諸種族に４つの群があることを認め，次のように分類している（L. v. Schrenck, *Reisen und Forschungen im Amur-Lande in den Jahren 1854−1856*, St. Petersburg, 1858−1900, Band Ⅲ）。

1）ダウル（Daur; ダグール Dagur）族およびソロン族——蒙古人と強度の混淆をなしたツングース種族

2）　満洲族，ゴルディ族，オロチ族

3）　オロチョン族，マネギル族，ビラル族，クル川沿岸のキレ（Kile；キリ Kili）族

4）　アムール川沿岸のオルチャ族，および，カラフトのオルチャ族（オロッコ族），ネギダル族，サマギル族

これに付言して，「先の2群はツングース民族の南方派すなわち満洲派をなし，後の2群はその北方派，すなわち，エニセイ川，北氷洋およびカムチャツカまで広がるシベリア派の諸分派を含む」と述べている。ツングース民族を大別して，南北2派としている点が注目されるが，ダグール人の言語は蒙古語の一方言であるから，ダグール人をここに含めたのは正しくない。

次に，シロコゴーロフは，ツングース・満洲語について，以下のように方言分類をしている（S. M. Shirokogoroff, "Study of the Tungus languages", *Journal of the North-China Branch of the Royal Asiatic Society* LV, 1924）。

北方派――エニセイ川，ヤクーツク（Yakutsk）州およびアムール州の諸方言，外バイカルの諸方言，興安嶺ツングース方言，ソロン方言，ビラル方言（クマル方言もともに），オロッコ方言，オロチ方言，ネギダル方言，カラフトのとなかいツングース方言，その他

南方派――おそらく，ある南満洲方言に起源した，満洲語文語，松花江，ウスリ川およびアムール川のゴルディ方言，さらにまた，オルチャ方言，ウデヘ方言，おそらく，他のある未調査の諸方言

この分類はシュレンクの分類と比べると，やはり南北2派に大別しているが，ソロン方言をその北方派に入れているのは進んでおり，妥当である。しかし，ウデヘ方言とオロチ方言とを，また，ゴルディ方言，オルチャ方言とオロッコ方言とをそれぞれ別々の派に属させているのは，妥当とはいえないであろう。なお，シロコゴーロフは，オロッコ族がオロチ族とおそらく同起源であると述べているが，オロッコ方言はオロチ方言よりオルチャ方言に近いとみられる（池上二良「ツングース語オロッコ方言のその近隣方言間における位置」[『民族学研究』14巻2号，1949] ―本書收載）。

一方，ラムステッド（G. J. Ramstedt）は，古い時代に存したと考えられる語頭の p の変化の結果に基準を求めるという方法で，簡単ではあるが，現代および歴史上のツングース・満洲諸言語を分類している。なお，ラムステッドは，古い時代の語中の r のそれにも基準を求めうると記している。（ジー・ジェー・ラムステッド，長谷川理衛訳「アルタイ諸民族とその言語」『民族』I巻4号，東京，1926。）

1） p方言　ゴルディ人およびオルチャ人の言語

2） f方言　満洲語，女真語，そしてたぶん，契丹語もこれに属する

3） h方言　オロチ人およびネギダル人などの言語

4） 古代語における語頭の p の最後の形跡をすでに失った方言

ただし，今日，契丹語は，蒙古語であるとみられている。

ソ連では，ツングース諸言語のそれぞれの研究が進むにつれ，それに基づいて，まず，次のような分類がなされた。

《アリコルの分類》（Я. П. Алькор（Кошкин），Проект алфавита эвенкийского（тунгусского）языка，Ленинград，1930）カッコ内は，話し手である。

ツングース諸言語

1） 本来のツングース語（ツングース人，オロチョン人，マネギル人，ビラル人，ソロン人）

2） ラムート語（ラムート人，オホーツク・カムチャツカのオロチョン人）

3） ネギダル語（ネギダル・アムグニ人）

満洲諸言語

1） 本来の満洲語（満洲人）

2） ゴルディ語（アムール川，ウスリ川，松花江のゴルディ人，オルチャ人，オロッコ人，サマギル人，キリ人）

3） オロチ語（オロチ人，キャカラ人 кякары，ウデヘ人）

《チェルニャコーフの分類》　この分類では，いくつかの言語，方言はさらに細分されているが，引用を略す。（З. Е. Черняков，“Карта распространения языков народов Севера СССР", Г. Н. Прокофьев (ред.), Языки и письменность народов Севера, часть I, Языки и письменность самоедских и финноугорских народов, Москва / Ленинград, 1937)

ツングース群
　エウェンキー語
　　1）北部方言
　　2）南部方言
　　3）東部方言
　　4）アムグン方言（ネギダル方言）
　エウェン語
　　1）東部方言
　　2）アルマニ方言
　　3）西部諸方言（未研究）
満洲群
　ナーナイ語
　　1）本来のナーナイ方言
　　2）オルチャ方言
　　3）オロッコ方言
　ウデヘ語
　　1）本来のウデヘ方言
　　2）オロチ方言
　満洲語

以上の2つの分類は，基本的には等しいものである。

しかし，上掲のシュレンク以来の諸分類のように，南北2派に大別することは問題であり，ツィンツィウスがこのような南北2派に大別する分類が妥当でないことを論じているのは正しい。しかし，ツィンツィウスは，研究上は各方言を個々のものとして扱うとしているが，一応この伝統的な分類をとり，次のように分類している。

《ツィンツィウスの分類》（В. И. Цинциус, Сравнительная фонетика тунгусо-маньчжурских языков, Ленинград, 1949）

北方群

エウェンキー語，エウェン（ラムート）語，ネギダル語，ソロン語

南方群

満洲語，ナーナイ（ゴルディ）語，オルチャ語，オロッコ語，ウデヘ語，オロチ語

その後，さらにソ連の3人の研究者によって，それぞれ次のような分類がなされた。後の2つの分類は，まず，2群に大別するという分け方をあえておこなっているが，3つとも結局，同じ3群に分類しているといえる。なお，後の2つの分類は，分け方が同じものとなっている。

《アヴローリンの分類》（В. А. Аврорин, "О классификации тунгусо-маньчжурских языков", Труды XXV Международного конгресса востоковедов, том III, Москва, 1963）

南方派

ナーナイ語，オルチャ語，オロッコ語，オロチ語，ウデヘ語

北方派

エウェンキー語，ネギダル語，ソロン語，エウェン語

西方派

満洲語，錫伯方言，女真語

《スーニクの分類》（О. П. Суник, "Тунгусо-маньчжурские языки", Младописьменные языки народов СССР, Москва / Ленинград, 1959）

第1群　満洲諸言語

満洲語文語，その方言（特に錫伯方言，おそらくまた，その他の方言），女真語，おそらく，ダグール人，一部のソロン人の以前の言語，おそらくまた，古代のツングース・満洲族の若干の他の言語

第2群　ツングース諸言語

エウェンキー語小群――エウェンキー語，エウェン語，ソロン語（ハイラ

ル方言)，ネギダル語

ナーナイ語小群——ナーナイ語，オルチャ語，オロッコ語，オロチ語，ウデヘ語

《ワシレーヴィチの分類》（Г. М. Василевич, “К вопросу о классификации тунгусо-маньчжурских языков”, Вопросы языкознания, 1960）

満洲派

満洲語（錫伯方言とともに)，女真語

ツングース派

シベリア小群——エウェンキー語（ソロン方言とともに)，ネギダル語，エウェン語

アムール川下流小群——ナーナイ語，オルチャ語，オロッコ語，オロチ語，ウデヘ語

次に，池上の分類をあげる。

《池上の分類》　（J. Ikegami, “Versuch einer Klassifikation der tungusischen Sprachen”, *Sprache, Geschichte und Kultur der altaischen Völker, Protokollband der XII. Tagung der Permanent International Altaistic Conference 1969 in Berlin,* Akademie-Verlag, Berlin, 1974）

第Ⅰ群

エウェン語（ラムート語)，エウェンキー語，ソロン語，ネギダル語

第Ⅱ群

ウデヘ語，オロチ語

第Ⅲ群

ナーナイ語（ゴルディ語)，オルチャ語，ウイルタ語（オロッコ語)

第Ⅳ群

満洲語，女真語

この分類は，すでに述べたように，ツングース諸語の間の音韻対応 *6*，*9*，*23*，*48*，*49*（表１，２，３を参照）と，文法上の人称語尾，反照語尾の有無をおもな根拠としている。この分類の主たる点は，ウデヘ語とオロチ語が１群を

なし，他の３群と区別されていることである。

その後，デルフェルは，注目すべき方法によって，次の分類をおこなった。

《デルフェルの分類》　（G．Doerfer，“Classification Problems of Tungus”, *Beiträge zur Nordasiatischen Kulturgeschichte, Tungusica*, Band I，Otto Harrassowitz，Wiesbaden，1978）

北方派

北東群——ラムート語，アルマン語

北西群——エウェンキー語，ネギダル語，ソロン語

中央派

中東群——オロチ語，ウデヘ語

中西群——キリ語，ナーナイ語，アムール下流方言（オルチャ語，ウイルタ語［オロッコ語］）

南方派

満洲群——女真語，満洲語

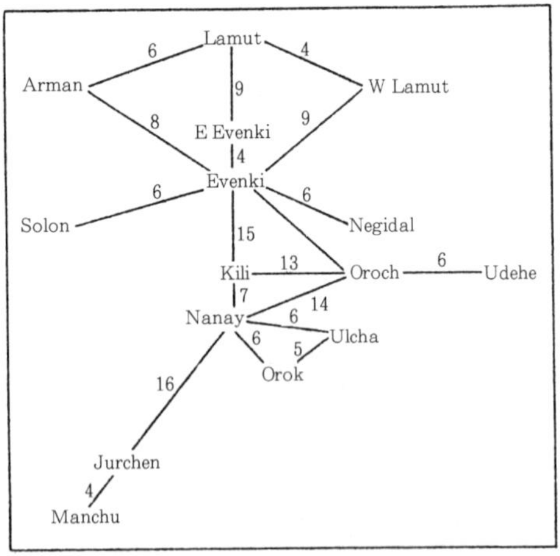

〈図１〉　ツングース諸語間の差異

（G．Doerfer）

デルフェルは，ツングース語の非常に多くの特徴をとりあげ，そのそれぞれの特徴について，ツングース諸語の各2言語を比べ，ある特徴が一致するか否かを調べた。そして，各2言語の間の一致しない特徴の和をとり，そのようなそれぞれの和を小から大へ等級づけ，その等級を1から21までの数で示し，この数により2言語間の類同，相違の度合いを表した。1はわずかな下位方言的差異（Mundart，говор），（2，3は略），4はわずかな方言的差異（Dialekt，диалект），5は中位の方言的差異，6は強い方言的差異，7，8は小さい言語的差異，9，10は中位の言語的差異，10（11の誤りか）～12は強い言語的差異，13～15はわずかな語派的差異，16～20は中位の語派的差異，≧21は強い語派的差異を意味する。デルフェルは，この方法によって，ツングース諸語のそれぞれの間の差異を図示した（図1参照）。

デルフェルの分類は，ツングース諸語間におけるこの差異に基づいたものである。なお，このキリ語は，ナーナイ語のクル・ウルミ方言，松花江下流方言などを合わせてさしている。

ウデヘ語，オロチ語とナーナイ語などとの間の差異は，デルフェルの分類法でも，13，14の程度にはあり，これはわずかな語派的差異である。アヴローリン，スーニク，ワシレーヴィチの分類は，この差異を認めていない点が適切でないといえよう。池上の分類は，その分類法に照らせば，語派的差異の最低段階である13およびそれ以上の度合いの差異によって，語派に分ける分類といえる。デルフェルの分類は，わずかな語派的差異という13，14，15のうち，15を16以上とともに派のレベルの差異とし，13，14を，はるかに低位の8，9の度合いとともに，等しく群のレベルの差異とした点が妥当を欠くように思われる。

Ⅳ　系　統

ツングース語は，蒙古語，チュルク語，フィン・ウゴル諸語，サモエード諸語とともに，1つの語族をなすとかつてはみられ，それはウラル・アルタイ語族とよばれた。その後，この語族は2分して考えられるようになった。フィン・ウゴル諸語とサモエード諸語は互いに親縁関係をもち，1つの語族をなすとみられ，これをウラル語族とよぶが，ツングース語，蒙古語，チュルク語は，それらの言語と親縁関係にあると認めるのはむずかしいとされ，ウラル語族とは切り離して，別の１つの語族をなすと考えるようになった。そして，これをアルタイ語族とよぶ。しかし，ツングース語と蒙古語，チュルク語の親縁関係もまだ証明されたとはいえない。この点からは，これら３言語をアルタイ諸言語とよんでいる。この３言語が親縁関係をもつか否かについては，３言語の間には，音韻，文法の構造に類似があり，代名詞を含めて，多くの共通する単語があるが，数詞も含めた基礎語彙に共通する語が少なく，また，３言語の共通単語の多くは，それら３言語間の借用によるものともみられるので，これら３言語が親縁関係をもつとするのを疑問としたり，ないしは，否定する見方も有力である。また，朝鮮語や，さらに日本語の系統論において，これらの言語は，ツングース語やこれを含めた上述のアルタイ語族と親縁関係にあるとの説もあるが，その親縁関係も証明されたわけではなく，今後の問題である。（池上二良「アルタイ語系統論」(『岩波講座　日本語12（日本語の系統と歴史)』，1978）を参照。）

参考文献

Benzing, J., 1953. *Einführung in das Studium der altaischen Philologie und der Turkologie*. Otto Harrassowitz, Wiesbaden.

———, 1955. *Die tungusischen Sprachen — Versuch einer vergleichenden Grammatik, Abhandlungen der Akademie der Wissenschaften und der Literatur, Geistes- und Sozialwissenschaftliche Klasse*, Jahrgang 1955, Nr. 11. Verlag der Akademie der Wissenschaften und der Literatur in Mainz, Mainz.

Fuchs, W., Lopatin, I. A., Menges, K. H. und D. Sinor, 1968. “Tunguso-logie”, *Handbuch der Orientalistik*, 1. Abteilung, 5. Band, 3. Abschnitt. E. J. Brill, Leiden/Köln.

Poppe, N., 1960. *Vergleichende Grammatik der altaischen Sprachen*, Teil 1, Vergleichende Lautlehre, *Porta Linguarum Orientalium*,

Neue Serie 4. Otto Harrassowitz, Wiesbaden.

———, 1965. *Introduction to Altaic Linguistics, Ural-Altaische Bibliothek* 14. Otto Harrassowitz, Wiesbaden.

Ramstedt, G. J., 1952, 1957, 1966. *Einführung in die altaische Sprachwissenschaft*, *Mémoires de la Société finno-ougrienne* 104. Suomalais-ugrilainen Seura, Helsinki.

Скорик, П. Я. и др., 1968. Монгольские, тунгусо-маньчжурские и палеоазиатские языки, Языки наролов СССР, том 5. НАУКА, Ленинград.

Цинциус, В. И., 1949a. Сравнительная фонетика тунгусо-маньчжурских языков. Учпедгиз, Ленинград.

Цинциус, В. И. и др., 1975, 1977. Сравнительный словарь тунгусо-маньчжурских языков, Материалы к этимологическому словарю, том 1, том2. НАУКА, Ленинград.

この記述は，拙文「ツングース語の変遷」(『言語の系統と歴史』［岩波書店　昭和46年（1971)］所収）と「ツングース諸語」(『言語学大辞典』第２巻［三省堂　平成元年（1989)］所載）を合わせ，一部を除き，補訂したものである。

Versuch einer vergleichenden Grammatik der tungusischen Sprachen[1)]

In den letzten zehn Jahren sind, abgesehen von dem nachgelassenen Werke RAMSTEDTS, Einführung in die Altaische Sprachwissenschaft, zwei ausgezeichnete Werke auf dem Gebiete der vergleichenden Forschung der tungusischen Sprachen erschienen. Das eine ist das umfassende Werk von Prof. V. CINCIUS, Vergleichende Phonetik der tungusisch-mandschurischen Sprachen. Das andere ist das hier zu besprechende Werk von Dr. J. BENZING, Die tungusischen Sprachen, Versuch einer vergleichenden Grammatik. Dieses Buch ist im Vergleich zum Werk von CINCIUS zwar klein, aber es behandelt die Hauptfragen der Phonetik, Morphologie und Syntax. Der Verf. nimmt zu Einzelfragen scharfsinnig und vorsichtig Stellung. Er kommt in vielen Punkten zu eigenen, beachtenswerten Ansichten, in vielen Fällen aber stimmen seine Ergebnisse auch mit den bisherigen Arbeiten anderer Forscher überein. Im Folgenden will der Besprecher kurz den Inhalt des vorliegenden Buches geben und einige der behandelten Fragen anführen.

Das vorliegende Werk besteht aus vier Kapiteln: I. Allgemeines über die tungusischen Sprachen (S. 7–16), II. Phonetik (S. 17–52), III. Morphologie (S. 53–147) und IV. Bemerkungen zur Syntax (S. 148–151). Kapitel II u. III bilden die Hauptteile dieses Werkes.

Im ersten Kapitel behauptet der Verf., daß, um die Frage zu klären, ob wirklich eine Verwandtschaft des Tungusischen, Mongolischen und Türkischen besteht, zunächst vergleichende Forschungen innerhalb der einzelnen Sprachen erforderlich sind. Näheres dazu findet sich schon in seinem früheren Werk Einführung in das Studium der Altaischen Philologie und der Turkologie. Weiter gibt der Verf. eine Klassifikation der tungusischen Sprachen nebst einem kurzen Überblick über die einzelnen tungusischen Sprachen. Der Verf. folgt der traditionellen Einteilung der tungusischen Sprachen in die nord- und südtungusische Gruppe und führt die Unterschiede einiger wichtiger Lautentsprechungen, grammatischer Formen, syntaktischer Regeln und einiger Beispiele des Wortschatzes zwischen den beiden Gruppen an. Jedoch bilden, wie der Verf. auch erwähnt, einige tungusische Sprachen, wie das Udiheische, den Übergang zwischen den sogenannten nord- und südtungusischen Sprachen. Diese Tatsache zeigt, daß die Einteilung in zwei Hauptgruppen: die nord- und südtungusische Gruppe in sprachlicher Hinsicht nicht zu Recht besteht, was Prof. V. CINCIUS schon im oben erwähnten Werk behauptet. Solche Klassifikation der tungusischen Sprachen kann nur in geographischer Hinsicht für die einzelnen tungusischen Sprachen Gültigkeit haben.

Das zweite Kapitel ist in A. die Aufstellung der Lautgesetze, Entlehnungen, B. die Vokale, C. die Konsonanten und D. die Betonung eingeteilt. Im Abschnitt B. setzt der Verf. als die kurzen Vokale der tungusischen Grundsprache **a, *ä, *ı, *i, *o, *ö, *u, *ü* an. Es ist von Bedeutung in der vergleichenden Erforschung der tungusischen Sprachen, daß der Verf. neben den anderen Vokalen auch den Vokal **ö* ansetzt, der nicht in der Vergleichenden Phonetik von CINCIUS behandelt ist. In bezug auf die gerundeten Vokale stellt der Verf. die folgende bemerkenswerte Hypothese auf :

Das *o/ō* ist im allgemeinen gut erhalten (S. 22).

ö/ȫ sind fast überall als *u* (*u̇*) vertreten (S. 23).

Das *u/ū* der ersten Silbe ist als *u* oder als *o* fast allgemein erhalten, während *u* der nichtersten Silben im Ntg. und im Oroč. Udh. durch *ı* (*i*) vertreten ist, wenn kein labialer Konsonant vorausgeht. Ebenso sind im Ntg. und im Oroč. Udh. sämtliche *ü*/*ǖ*, mit Ausnahme der auf *ö*-haltige Silben folgenden oder nach labialen Konsonanten stehenden, durch *i*/*ī* vertreten (S. 24).

Diese Annahme von BENZING erklärt die Vokalentsprechung, die CINCIUS mit **y*ᴵᴵ bezeichnet, sehr klar. Bei der Frage über das **ö* aber muß das heute in einigen tungusischen Sprachen erkennbare Phonem *ö* eingehender berücksichtigt werden. Vgl. J. IKEGAMI, *Tsungûsu-go Orokko hôgen no boin-onso ö ni tsuite* (Über das Vokalphonem *ö* im orokischen Dialekt der tungusischen Sprache) (Gengo Kenkyû 22, 23, [1953], 75–78). Das Orokische z. B. besitzt das Phonem *ö*. Das orok. *ö* entspricht dem udh. *o* im folgenden Wort: orok. *xölö* 'Eichhörnchen', udh. *oloxi* 'ds.'. Das * *ö* bei BENZING entspricht im Orokischen dem *ö* im oben erwähnten Worte, aber auch dem *u* in anderen Wörtern: tg. **xölü-kī* 'Eichhörnchen' (S. 23), orok. *xölö*, udh. *oloxi*; tg. **xörgä* 'schwer' (S. 42), orok. *xudə*, udh. *ugəhi*; tg. **sömü* 'Sehne' (S. 75), orok. *sumu*, udh. *sumu*. Eine Erklärung der Verschiedenheit dieser Entsprechungen ist nicht gegeben. Die Frage über die gerundeten Vokale in den tungusischen Sprachen scheint noch nicht vollständig gelöst zu sein.

Im Abschnitt C. sind die Konsonanten **k*, **t*, **p*, **č*, **g*, **d*,**b*, **ǯ* **ŋ*, **n*, **m*, **x*, **s*, **l*, **r*, **j*, **w*(?) als die der tungusischen Grundsprache angesetzt und die Entsprechungen der einfachen Konsonanten und Konsonantenverbindungen klar behandelt. Es scheint unbestreitbar zu sein, daß das anlautende und intervokalische tg. **t* im Orok. vor dem *i* dem *č* entspricht. Die Lautentsprechungstabelle auf S. 31 (und auch die Tabellen auf S. 250, 251 im oben erwähnten Werk von CINCIUS) wird ausführlicher und genauer, wenn diese Lautentsprechung hinzugefügt wird. Das anlautende und intervokalische tg. **d* entspricht nach der

Meinung des Besprechers im Orok. vor dem *i* dem *ǯ*. Was Einzelheiten anbelangt, so können wir die Bedingungen, unter denen das ewenkische (u. a.) *ks* im Udh. *k* und *h* entspricht (S. 29), näher bestimmen: das ew. (u. a.) *ks* entspricht im Udh. nach dem Vokal der ersten Silbe dem *k* (wobei nach *ks* das ew. *a* dem udh. *eæ*, das ew. *ə* dem udh *iə* entspricht) und nach dem Vokal der nichtersten Silbe dem *h* (wobei nach *ks* das ew. *a* dem udh. *æ*, das ew. *ə* dem udh. *ə* entspricht). Ebenso dem ew. (u. a.) *ks* entspricht in den orok. Wörtern nach dem ersten Vokal bzw. Vokalverbindung das *ks*, wie aus dem vorliegenden Werk (S. 29) hervorgeht, aber nach dem nichtersten Vokal das *sk*. Demnach ist es unrichtig, daß der Verf. den udh. Verbstamm *ahæ-* 'verfolgen' für den dem ew. *aksa-* 'zornig werden' u. a. entsprechenden hält (S. 29). An einer anderen Stelle (S. 124–125) aber führt der Verf. denselben udh. Verbstamm *ahœ-* auf die dem ew. *asa-* 'jagen' u. a. entsprechenden udh. *aha-*, *ā-* 'verfolgen' zurück. Im vorliegenden Buch ist das udh. *æ* mit 'æ' od. 'œ' (Druckfehler?) bezeichnet. Das dem ew. *ūksə* 'Ärmel' u. a. entsprechende udh. *ukihə* 'ds.', wobei der Verf. die Frage aufwirft, warum *k* und *h* in diesem udh. Wort vorkommen (S. 29), könnte eventuell aus dem Stamm *uki-* + dem Suffix *-hə*, das dem ew. *-ksə* entspricht, bestehen.

Im hier besprochenen Werk sind die zu vergleichenden Wörter im allgemeinen richtig zusammengestellt. Einige Zusammenstellungen jedoch sind fraglich. Zum Beispiel mit dem ew. *arpu-* 'fegen, wedeln' u. dgl. ist das orok. *axiriku* 'Besen' (*axeerikku* nach der Aufzeichnung des Besprechers) zusammengestellt (S. 48), damit ist jedoch das orok. *xalpu* 'Besen, Fächer' zu vergleichen. Das goldische *uʒi-* 'ernähren' vergleicht der Verf. ohne Vorbehalt einerseits mit dem ew. *udı-* (S. 32) und anderseits mit dem ew. *irgi-* (S. 122). Manche vom Verf. rekonstruierten Formen können in Frage gestellt werden. Um ein Beispiel anzuführen, rekonstruiert er tg. **pölti* 'Wange' aus dem ma. *fulcin* u. a. (S. 46), aber man muß wohl eher

**pultın* rekonstruieren, denn das Orokische besitzt das Wort *pulči* 'Wange', dessen Akkusativform *pulčimba* ist.

Das dritte Kapitel enthält die folgenden Abschnitte:

Wortstamm, Wortbildungselemente (§§63–69);

Nomina, Substantiva: Wortbildung (§§70–85), Formenbildung (Plural, Deklination) (§§86–102);

Adjektiva: Wortbildung (§§103–105), Formenbildung (Steigerung) (§§106–108);

Adverbien (§§109–112);

Postpositionen (§113);

Zahlwörter(§§114–120);

Pronomina (§§121–127);

Verba: Wortbildung (§§128–130), Formenbildung (§§131–150), Hilfszeitwörter (§151);

Partikeln, Onomatopöetika und dergleichen (§§152–153).

Die Abschnitte über die Nomina behandeln die einzelnen nominalen Suffixe (bzw. Endungen) ausführlich. Die Wörter „Suffix“ und „Endung“ scheinen im vorliegenden Werk ohne deutlichen Unterschied gebraucht zu sein. Über das nominale Suffix, das im Ew. z. B. als -*ŋ*(*i*) vorkommt, vertritt der Verf. gegen die üblichen Ansichten (vgl. O. P. Sunik, O kategorii otčuždaemoj i neotčuždaemoj prinadležnosti v tunguso-man'čžurskich jazykach (IAN 6 [1947], 437–451) eine interessante Auffassung, daß es nämlich angewendet wird, um zu kennzeichnen, daß man es mit einem Element aus mehr als zwei Gegenständen derselben Art oder derselben Gruppe zu tun hat (vgl. auch seine Lamutische Grammatik, S. 53).

Im Abschnitt über die Formenbildung der Verben weist der Verf. darauf hin, daß die primären und abgeleiteten Verbstämme sich nach der Bildung ihrer Aoristformen (nach Benzings Benennung) auf drei Klassen verteilen. Nach dem Verf. werden an die Verbstämme der 1. Klasse als

Aoristsuffix *-*ra* angefügt, an die der 2. Klasse *-*sa* und an die der 3. Klasse *-*da*. Der Hinweis auf die Existenz der drei Klassen, insbesondere auf die der 2. Klasse ist wichtig und wertvoll, obwohl Gründe für diese Verteilung noch nicht ersichtlich sind. Betreffs der 3. Klasse ist es bemerkenswert, daß bei zwei von den sechs Verbstämmen, die der Verf. als sichere Beispiele für diese Klasse anführt (S. 126–127), einige der heutigen tungusischen Sprachen den auslautenden Konsonanten beibehalten haben, wie in udh. *nag-* 'treffen' (aber nach BENZING *na-g-*) und auch gol. *BUR-* ~ *BUJ-* ~ *BU-* 'sterben', orok. *bul-* ~ *bu-* 'ds.'. Die Frage über das Aoristsuffix bedarf eingehender Untersuchung. Der Verf. hält *-su*, *-so* in einigen ma. Imperativformen *bisu* 'sei', *baisu* 'suche', *oso* 'werde' für einen Rest der enklitischen Personalpronomina (S. 110). Es scheint dem Besprecher, daß *-su* bzw. *-so* in ma. *bisu*, *oso* und etwa *baisu* auf die Imperativendung *-*su* für die mit *-*si* als Aoristformen zu verbindenden Verbstämme zurückgeht.

Im vierten Kapitel gibt der Verf. eine kurze Darstellung der Syntax. Hinsichtlich der Kongruenz in Kasus und Numerus zwischen dem Substantiv und dem Adjektiv lehnt er die Auffassung ab, sie auf eine Beeinflussung durch das Russische zurückzuführen. An der betreffenden Stelle gibt der Verf. an, daß K. BOUDA an eine solche Beeinflussung zu denken scheint. Aber diese Angabe scheint dem Besprecher, nach dem von BENZING erwähnten Aufsatz BOUDAS, Die Kongruenz im Tungusischen (IdgF 60 [1952], 14–20), nicht zuzutreffen.

Im ganzen betrachtet, ist diese Arbeit von BENZING ein wichtiger und nützlicher Beitrag zur vergleichenden Sprachwissenschaft der tungusischen Sprachen. Aber noch liegen sehr viele ungelöste Fragen in der vergleichenden Sprachforschung auf dem Gebiete der tungusischen Sprachen vor, was auch aus dem oben Erwähnten hervorgeht. Die Lösung solcher Fragen ist eine Sache der Zukunft. Das hier besprochene Werk wird zweifellos den Forschern der tungusischen Sprachen die weiteren vergleichenden Forschungen sehr erleichtern.

Anmerkung

1) Johannes BENZING: Die tungusischen Sprachen. Versuch einer vergleichenden Grammatik (Akademie der Wissenschaften und der Literatur [in Mainz]. Abhadlungen der Geistes- und Sozialwissenschaftlichen Klasse, Jahrgang 1955, Nr. 11), Wiesbaden 1956, 151 S.

Diese Besprechung ist in : *Ural-Altaische Jahrbücher*, Band 32, Heft 1–2 (1960), S. 123–125 erschienen.

Notes on K. A. Novikova's Tentative Scheme for the Unified Phonetic Transcription[1] of Tungus-Manchu

We highly esteem the Soviet Russian scholars' idea to establish a unified phonetic transcription of the languages of the peoples in the Soviet Union. It is convenient for us foreigners engaged in this research that the system of this transcription in Roman letters insofar as possible is coordinated with that of the IPA transcription. We believe that NOVIKOVA'S present work is a valuable contribution to the phonetic transcription of these languages. However, we hope for a few further improvements.

Each prelingual affricate is represented by a single sign, while each midlingual affricate is represented by the combination of two signs, cf. pp. 66, 67 and Tables 1 and 2. In this regard, however, it is desirable that both of these affricates be uniformly denoted either by a single sign or by the combination of two signs for a plosive and a fricative.

To us who are accustomed to the phonetic signs of IPA it seems strange that the sign ħ (p. 64 and Table 2) is used to represent a midlingual voiceless plosive in the Roman letter transcription.

The distinction between ʿ' and 'ʿ, such as between пʿ' (pʿ'), кʿ' (kʿ'), қʿ' (qʿ') and т'ʿ (t'ʿ) attracts our notice (pp. 62, 63, 65, 66 and Tables 1 and 2).

It is preferable to adopt ы rather than ꙑ (p. 56 and Table 2) as the sign of the highest mixed vowel in the Roman letter transcription as well as in the Russian letter transcription.

We find it advantageous to adopt the sign ə instead of э (p. 56) in the Roman letter transcription, because it is technically easy to invert the letter e in typesetting.

It seems necessary to refer to signs which denote mixed round vowels, such as that found in some Evenki dialects according to G. M. VASILEVIČ, Očerk grammatiki ėvenkijskogo (tungusskogo) jazyka, Leningrad 1940, P. 14.

Finally we touch on the following point, which, however, does not concern the phonetic transcription in question. The contents of the sentences 'Vstrečaetsja vo vsech tunguso-man'čžurskich jazykach, osuščestvljajas' . . .' in pp. 61 (p), 62 (b), 64 (k), 65 (g) are phonological and consequently inconsistent with the phonetic description there.

We find the following misprints :

In p. 16, 1. 16, u must be ụ (?)

In p. 17, 1. 18, a must be ạ (?)

In p. 60, 1. 12, the first ç̌' must be ç̌.

In p. 67, 1. 19, в must be b.

In Table 2, the second tʿ must be t'.

Note

1) K. A. NOVIKOVA: *Proekt edinoj fonetičeskoj transkripcii dlja tunguso-man'čžurskich jazykov.* (Akademija Nauk SSSR, Institut Jazykoznanija, Komissija po unificirovannoj fonetičeskoj transkripcii dlja jazykov narodov SSSR.) Moscow–Leningrad 1961, 83 pages + 5 tables.

This review is a revised version of the review published in *Ural-Altaische Jahrbücher*, Band 39, Heft 1–2 (1967), pp. 138–139.

『ツングース・満洲諸語比較辞典』について

V. I. Cincius et al., A Comparative Dictionary
of the Tungus-Manchu Languages

ツングース語研究に対してソ連科学学士院言語学研究所レニングラード支部アルタイ語部門の研究者はこれまですでに大きな寄与をして来たが，今度さらに同研究機関のB・И・ツィンツィウス（編集責任者）らの編集になる「ツングース・満洲諸語比較辞典――語原辞典への資料」第1巻が刊行された。その価値ははなはだ大きいと思う。

はしがきによれば2巻本であるが，第1巻は，はしがき（О・П・スーニク執筆），序言，本辞典項目の構成の説明（表記記号の目録も付いている）（はしがきによれば，以上ツィンツィウス執筆），さらに略号表，編集に利用した原資料の表（以上全部で30ページ）と本文672ページ（AからНгまで）からなっている。

本書の編集については，編集者のひとりК・А・ノーヴィコヴァさんからのときどきの私信で伺っていたが，はしがきによると，すでに1950年代末に発案され，1961年から65年の間にその主な作業が行われた。すべてのツングース・満洲諸語の単語，あるいは言語によってはその種々の方言の単語をおさめ，その材料としては，ソ連研究者による既刊ツングース語辞典の主なもの，および多くの原稿のままの調査資料を使っていて，この点でソ連のツングース語研究者によるこれまでの語彙研究の集大成でもあるが，さらにまた満洲語，女真語をふくめてロシヤ内外の研究者のこれまでの重要な文献にもよっている。このように広汎にわたる資料に典拠することは，本書に非常に大きい価値を与えていると言えよう。

辞典の構成は，ツングース・満洲諸語にある同原の単語をまとめて一つの辞典項目に挙げている。各項目を代表する見出語は，その項目のはじめに来た言語からとったものであるが，ただし，項目内に挙げられる各言語は一定の順序によっているものの，項目によって順序のはじめの方の言語を欠くことがあるので，見出語が所属する言語はまちまちで一定しない。なお項目全体に対する祖形は挙げていない。

項目の末尾の参考欄には，借用語に対するもとの言語の単語をあげたり，また蒙古語やチュルク語あるいは朝鮮語と「おそらく系統論的に共通起原を有する」(XVページ，ツィンツィウスによる) 単語 (スーニクははしがきでこれを‘совпадения’とよんでいる) について，これらの言語の単語を (その関係を特に記さずに) 挙げている。

本書の実質的内容に少々ふれたい。ツングース語は母音の長短を区別するため，長母音の表記は重要であるが，従来のソ連の研究者の表記にはまま疑問とみられるものがあった (拙文「ツングース語の辞書」[学鐙68巻7号，1971年] 参照)。本辞典が，語により従来の辞典の母音の長短の表記を改変しているのは，進歩である。上掲拙文で疑問としたエウェンキー語の мирэ (плечо) の語も мӣрэ と改められている。さらにエウェンキー語について，Г・М・ワシレーヴィチの辞書 (1958年)，В・А・ゴルツェフスカヤらの辞書 (1958年) の表記とくらべると，たとえば，この二書がともに нюриктэ (волос)，ириктэ (муравей) としているのに対し，本辞典では н'ӯриктэ，ӣриктэ となっているが，А・В・ロマーノヴァらの辞書 (1968年) (これは今度の辞典のはしがきによれば1965年後の刊行であるが特に利用されたという) ではその母音を長く表記しており，なおまたわたくしが採集した (北の Тура，南の Баунт，東の Зея の三方言の) 資料 (北方文化研究9号所載) のなかの ɲūriktə ТБЗ，īriktə ТЗ と照し合せても，その改変は正しいと考えられる。しかし疑問のあるものがなおあり，例をあげると，ワシレーヴィチやゴルツェフスカヤらの両辞典と同様に本書でも булта-(охотиться)，кумкэ (вошь) とあるのは，ロマーノヴァらの辞書で第2音節母音が長く，わたくしの採集資料でも bultā- Т；kumkọ̄ Т，kumkạ̄ БЗ であり，本辞典記載の語形が誤りであるか，もしくはかかる語形だけを挙げることが妥当でないのではないかと思われる。

各言語の記述のうち，オロッコ語についてみると，ɵ の母音を表記していないが，これは一つの欠点であり，残念である。たとえば，mɵrɵ(n-)（思い）は муро(н-)～муру(н-)（558ページ）とある。なおまた動詞（またはときに名詞）語幹として，語尾が融合した（そのため末尾母音のまえの子音が重複したり，末尾母音が交替した）語幹とみられるものが，基本的な語幹と区別なく挙げられていることがある。たとえば，иллэ-～илэ-（лизать）（311ページ），jāта-～jатче-～jaчче-（родить）（345ページ）。しかし資料をもっと分析して，もし挙げるとしてもその区別をあきらかにすべきであったろう。

ソ連のこれまでのツングース語辞典のいくつかは，日本へほとんど入っていないようであるから，これらも材料としてふくむ本書が日本にかなり入ることは，日本の研究者に大きな便宜を与えることになる。第2巻の刊行が待望される。

В. И. Цинциус, В. А. Горцевская, В. Д. Колесникова, О. А. Константинова, К. А. Новикова, Т. И. Петрова, Т. Г. Бугаева. Сравнительный словарь тунгусо-маньчжурских языков, Материалы к этимологическому словарю. Том I, А-НГ. Академия наук СССР, Институт языкознания, Изд.《НАУКА》, Ленинград, 1975.

初出　『窓』16号［ナウカ　東京，昭和51年（1976年）4月1日］54－55ページ。

池上　二良（いけがみ　じろう）
1920年　長野県松本市に生まれる
東京帝国大学文学部言語学科卒業
東京大学大学院特別研究生，群馬大学学芸学部助教授，北海道大学文学部教授（言語学講座・大学院文学研究科担当，北方文化研究施設長併任），札幌大学女子短期大学部（文化学科）教授を経る。
北海道大学名誉教授

ツングース語研究

2001年2月28日　初版発行

著　者　池上二良
発行者　石坂叡志
版下作成　富士リプロ
　　　　　東京プレス
　　　　　中西印刷
印　刷　モリモト印刷

発行所　汲古書院
東京都千代田区飯田橋2-5-4
電話(3265)9764　FAX(3222)1845

 ISBN4-7629-2657-4　C3087